3D Studio MAX® R3
Bible

3D Studio MAX® R3 Bible

Kelly L. Murdock

IDG Books Worldwide, Inc.
An International Data Group Company

Foster City, CA ✦ Chicago, IL ✦ Indianapolis, IN ✦ New York, NY

3D Studio MAX® R3 Bible

Published by

IDG Books Worldwide, Inc.
An International Data Group Company
919 E. Hillsdale Blvd., Suite 400
Foster City, CA 94404
www.idgbooks.com (IDG Books Worldwide Web site)

Copyright © 2000 IDG Books Worldwide, Inc. All rights reserved. No part of this book, including interior design, cover design, and icons, may be reproduced or transmitted in any form, by any means (electronic, photocopying, recording, or otherwise) without the prior written permission of the publisher.

ISBN: 0-7645-4621-X

Printed in the United States of America

10 9 8 7 6 5 4 3

1B/SR/RS/ZZ/FC

Distributed in the United States by IDG Books Worldwide, Inc.

Distributed by CDG Books Canada Inc. for Canada; by Transworld Publishers Limited in the United Kingdom; by IDG Norge Books for Norway; by IDG Sweden Books for Sweden; by IDG Books Australia Publishing Corporation Pty. Ltd. for Australia and New Zealand; by TransQuest Publishers Pte Ltd. for Singapore, Malaysia, Thailand, Indonesia, and Hong Kong; by Gotop Information Inc. for Taiwan; by ICG Muse, Inc. for Japan; by Intersoft for South Africa; by Eyrolles for France; by International Thomson Publishing for Germany, Austria and Switzerland; by Distribuidora Cuspide for Argentina; by LR International for Brazil; by Galileo Libros for Chile; by Ediciones ZETA S.C.R. Ltda. for Peru; by WS Computer Publishing Corporation, Inc., for the Philippines; by Contemporanea de Ediciones for Venezuela; by Express Computer Distributors for the Caribbean and West Indies; by Micronesia Media Distributor, Inc. for Micronesia; by Chips Computadoras S.A. de C.V. for Mexico; by Editorial Norma de Panama S.A. for Panama; by American Bookshops for Finland.

For general information on IDG Books Worldwide's books in the U.S., please call our Consumer Customer Service department at 800-762-2974. For reseller information, including discounts and premium sales, please call our Reseller Customer Service department at 800-434-3422.

For information on where to purchase IDG Books Worldwide's books outside the U.S., please contact our International Sales department at 317-596-5530 or fax 317-596-5692.

For consumer information on foreign language translations, please contact our Customer Service department at 800-434-3422, fax 317-596-5692, or e-mail rights@idgbooks.com.

For information on licensing foreign or domestic rights, please phone +1-650-655-3109.

For sales inquiries and special prices for bulk quantities, please contact our Sales department at 650-655-3200 or write to the address above.

For information on using IDG Books Worldwide's books in the classroom or for ordering examination copies, please contact our Educational Sales department at 800-434-2086 or fax 317-596-5499.

For press review copies, author interviews, or other publicity information, please contact our Public Relations department at 650-655-3000 or fax 650-655-3299.

For authorization to photocopy items for corporate, personal, or educational use, please contact Copyright Clearance Center, 222 Rosewood Drive, Danvers, MA 01923, or fax 978-750-4470.

Library of Congress Cataloging-in-Publication Data

Murdock, Kelly
    3D Studio Max R3 Bible /
Kelly L. Murdock.
        p.   cm.
    ISBN 0-7645-4621-X (alk. paper)
    1. Computer animation 2. 3D Studio
I. Title.
TR897.7.M87   1999
006.6'96'02855369—dc21

                                                                99-033676
                                                                CIP

Trademarks: All brand names and product names used in this book are trade names, service marks, trademarks, or registered trademarks of their respective owners. IDG Books Worldwide is not associated with any product or vendor mentioned in this book.

 is a registered trademark or trademark under exclusive license to IDG Books Worldwide, Inc. from International Data Group, Inc. in the United States and/or other countries.

ABOUT IDG BOOKS WORLDWIDE

Welcome to the world of IDG Books Worldwide.

IDG Books Worldwide, Inc., is a subsidiary of International Data Group, the world's largest publisher of computer-related information and the leading global provider of information services on information technology. IDG was founded more than 30 years ago by Patrick J. McGovern and now employs more than 9,000 people worldwide. IDG publishes more than 290 computer publications in over 75 countries. More than 90 million people read one or more IDG publications each month.

Launched in 1990, IDG Books Worldwide is today the #1 publisher of best-selling computer books in the United States. We are proud to have received eight awards from the Computer Press Association in recognition of editorial excellence and three from Computer Currents' First Annual Readers' Choice Awards. Our best-selling *...For Dummies®* series has more than 50 million copies in print with translations in 31 languages. IDG Books Worldwide, through a joint venture with IDG's Hi-Tech Beijing, became the first U.S. publisher to publish a computer book in the People's Republic of China. In record time, IDG Books Worldwide has become the first choice for millions of readers around the world who want to learn how to better manage their businesses.

Our mission is simple: Every one of our books is designed to bring extra value and skill-building instructions to the reader. Our books are written by experts who understand and care about our readers. The knowledge base of our editorial staff comes from years of experience in publishing, education, and journalism — experience we use to produce books to carry us into the new millennium. In short, we care about books, so we attract the best people. We devote special attention to details such as audience, interior design, use of icons, and illustrations. And because we use an efficient process of authoring, editing, and desktop publishing our books electronically, we can spend more time ensuring superior content and less time on the technicalities of making books.

You can count on our commitment to deliver high-quality books at competitive prices on topics you want to read about. At IDG Books Worldwide, we continue in the IDG tradition of delivering quality for more than 30 years. You'll find no better book on a subject than one from IDG Books Worldwide.

John Kilcullen
Chairman and CEO
IDG Books Worldwide, Inc.

Steven Berkowitz
President and Publisher
IDG Books Worldwide, Inc.

Eighth Annual
Computer Press
Awards ≥1992

Ninth Annual
Computer Press
Awards ≥1993

Tenth Annual
Computer Press
Awards ≥1994

Eleventh Annual
Computer Press
Awards ≥1995

IDG is the world's leading IT media, research and exposition company. Founded in 1964, IDG had 1997 revenues of $2.05 billion and has more than 9,000 employees worldwide. IDG offers the widest range of media options that reach IT buyers in 75 countries representing 95% of worldwide IT spending. IDG's diverse product and services portfolio spans six key areas including print publishing, online publishing, expositions and conferences, market research, education and training, and global marketing services. More than 90 million people read one or more of IDG's 290 magazines and newspapers, including IDG's leading global brands — Computerworld, PC World, Network World, Macworld and the Channel World family of publications. IDG Books Worldwide is one of the fastest-growing computer book publishers in the world, with more than 700 titles in 36 languages. The "...For Dummies®" series alone has more than 50 million copies in print. IDG offers online users the largest network of technology-specific Web sites around the world through IDG.net (http://www.idg.net), which comprises more than 225 targeted Web sites in 55 countries worldwide. International Data Corporation (IDC) is the world's largest provider of information technology data, analysis and consulting, with research centers in over 41 countries and more than 400 research analysts worldwide. IDG World Expo is a leading producer of more than 168 globally branded conferences and expositions in 35 countries including E3 (Electronic Entertainment Expo), Macworld Expo, ComNet, Windows World Expo, ICE (Internet Commerce Expo), Agenda, DEMO, and Spotlight. IDG's training subsidiary, ExecuTrain, is the world's largest computer training company, with more than 230 locations worldwide and 785 training courses. IDG Marketing Services helps industry-leading IT companies build international brand recognition by developing global integrated marketing programs via IDG's print, online and exposition products worldwide. Further information about the company can be found at www.idg.com.   1/24/99

Credits

About the Author

Kelly Murdock has been involved with more computer books than he cares to count—to the point that he avoids the computer book section of the bookstore, except for the graphics section, which still remains an obsession. His book credits include various Web and multimedia titles, including contributions of various editions of *HTML Unleashed* and *Laura Lemay's Web Workshop: 3D Graphics and VRML 2*.

With a background in Engineering and Computer Graphics, Kelly has been all over the 3D industry. He's used high-level CAD workstations for product design and analysis; completed several large-scale visualization projects; created 3D models for feature films, worked as a freelance 3D artist, and even done some 3D programming.

Kelly's been using 3D Studio on and off since version 3 for DOS. He is also the creative force behind the children's Web site, Animabets.com at www.animabets. com, which is soon to be sporting several new 3D characters.

When I sleep, I see the illusion of my dreams.
When I awake, I see reality in place of my dreams.
But, when I create, I see the reality of my dreams.

To Angie, 1999

Preface

Whenever I withdrew to the computer room, my wife would say that I was off to my "fun and games." I would flatly deny this, saying that it was serious work that I was involved in, but later, when I emerged with a twinkle in my eye and excitedly asked her to take a look at my latest rendering, I knew that she was right. This is pure "fun and games."

My goal in writing this book was to take all my fun years of playing in 3D and boil them down into something that's worthwhile for you — the reader. This goal was compounded by the fact that all you MAX-heads out there are at different levels. Luckily, I was given enough leeway that I could include a little something for everyone.

The audience level for the book ranges from beginning to intermediate, with a smattering of advanced topics for the seasoned user. If you're new to MAX, then you'll want to start at the beginning and move methodically through the book. If you're relatively comfortable making your way around MAX, then review the table of contents for sections that can enhance your fundamental base. If you're a seasoned pro, then you'll want to watch for coverage of the features new to Release 3.

Another goal of this book is to make it a complete reference to MAX. To achieve this, I've gone into painstaking detail on almost every feature in the basic core package, including coverage of every primitive, material and map type, Modifier, and Controller.

As this book has come together, I've tried to write the type of book that I'd like to read. There are some topics that are dry, but I've tried to infuse the book with some creativity. After all, that's what turns 3D graphics from work into "fun and games."

What Is MAX?

MAX is coming of age. Now with the number 3 attached to its name, it is starting to show some maturity.

One way we humans develop our personalities is to incorporate desirable personality traits of those around us. MAX's personality is developing as well — every new release has incorporated a plethora of desirable new features. Many of these features come from the many additional plug-ins being developed to enhance

MAX. With Release 3, this feature adoption process has occurred again. There are several new features that have been magically assimilated into the core product, including the Schematic View and the Surface Tools. These additions make MAX's personality much more likable.

Other personality traits are gained by stretching our beings in new directions. MAX and its developers have accomplished this feat as well, with such things as Render Effects and enhanced MAXScript capabilities.

As MAX grows up, it will continue to mature by adopting new features and inventing others.

About This Book

Let me paint a picture of the writing process. It starts with years of experience, which is followed by months of painstaking research. There were system crashes and personal catastrophes and the always present, ever looming deadlines. I wrote into the early hours of the morning and during the late hours of the night — burning the candle at both ends and in the middle all at the same time. It was grueling and difficult, and spending all this time staring at the MAX interface made me feel like . . . well . . . like an animator.

Sound familiar? This process actually isn't much different from what you probably go through, and, like you, I find satisfaction in the finished product.

Tutorials Aplenty

I've always been a very visual learner — the easiest way for me to gain knowledge is by doing things for myself while exploring at the same time. Other people learn by reading and comprehending ideas. In this book, I've tried to present information in a number of ways to make the information useable for all types of learners. That is why you'll see detailed discussions on the various features along with tutorials that show these concepts in action.

The tutorials appear throughout the book and are clearly marked with the "Tutorial" label in front of the section title. They always include a series of logical steps, typically ending with a figure for you to study and compare. These tutorial examples are provided to give you a hands-on experience.

I've attempted to "laser focus" all the tutorials down to one or two key concepts. This means that you probably will not want to place the results in your portfolio. For example, many of the early tutorials don't have any materials applied because I felt that using materials before they've been explained would only confuse you, the reader.

I've attempted to think of and use examples that are diverse, unique, and interesting, while striving to make them simple, light, and easy to follow. I'm happy to report that every example in the book is included on the CD-ROM along with the models and textures required to complete the tutorial from scratch.

How this book is organized

There are many different aspects of 3D graphics and, in some larger production houses, you might be focused on only one specific area, but, for smaller organizations or the general hobbyist, we wear all the hats—from modeler and lighting director to animator and post-production compositor. This book is organized to cover all the various aspects of 3D graphics.

The book is divided into the following parts:

◆ **Part I: Getting Started with 3D Studio MAX R3**—Whether it's learning about the new features in R3, understanding the interface, or discovering how to configure and customize MAX, the chapters in this part will get you up and going.

◆ **Part II: Working with Objects**—MAX objects include models, cameras, lights, Space Warps, and anything that can be viewed in a viewport. This part includes chapters on how to reference, select, transform, and modify these various objects.

◆ **Part III: Modeling**—MAX includes several different ways to model objects. This part includes chapters on working with primitives, spline shapes, meshes, patches, NURBS, and a variety of specialized compound objects like Lofts and Morphs.

◆ **Part IV: Materials and Maps**—With all the various material and map types and parameters, it can be difficult to understand how to create just what you want. These chapters explain all the various types and how to use them.

◆ **Part V: Lights and Cameras**—This part describes how to control lights and cameras as well as several lighting special effects and the camera utilities.

◆ **Part VI: Particle Systems and Space Warps**—Particle systems can be used to create groups of thousands of particles, and Space Warps can add forces to a MAX scene. Chapters in this part explain and provide examples of working with these two unique object types.

◆ **Part VII: Model Systems**—Linked systems and Inverse Kinematics are covered in this part along with a chapter on the new Schematic View feature.

◆ **Part VIII: Animation**—To animate your scenes, you'll want to learn about keyframing, the Track View, and Controllers. All of these topics are covered here. Expressions and dynamic simulations are also covered in this part.

✦ **Part IX: Rendering and Post-Production** — To produce the final output, you can render the scene or composite it in the Video Post dialog box, as described in this part. In addition, this part discusses environments, Render Effects, and network rendering.

✦ **Part X: Extending MAX** — Plug-ins provide a way to add to and extend the features of MAX. The chapters in this part explain plug-ins and MAXScript.

At the very end you'll also find three appendixes, covering system configuration, plug-ins exclusive to this book, and the contents of the book's CD-ROM. Finally, if you ever find yourself unsure about some of the terminology used in these pages, check the glossary I also include.

Using the book's icons

The following margin icons are used to help you get the most out of this book:

Note boxes are used to highlight information that is useful and should be taken into consideration.

Tips are included to provide an additional bit of advice that will make a particular feature quicker or easier to use.

Cautions are meant to warn you of a potential problem before a mistake is made.

Features that are new to Release 3 are highlighted with this icon.

Watch for this icon to learn where in another chapter you can go to find more information on a particular feature.

This icon is used to point you toward related materials that are included on the book's CD-ROM.

The book's CD-ROM and exclusive plug-ins

Computer book CD-ROMs are sometimes just an afterthought that includes a handful of examples and product demos. This book's CD-ROM, however, is much more than that — its content was carefully selected to provide you with an additional resource that can supplement the book. Appendix C, "What's On the CD-ROM?" supplies the details of the files on the CD-ROM.

The CD-ROM includes a large selection of 3D models that you can use in your projects if you choose. Many of these models are used in the tutorials. The CD-ROM also includes the MAX files for every tutorial.

If you haven't noticed yet, most of this book is printed in black and white. This can make it difficult to see the details (and colors) of the figures. The CD-ROM includes a complete searchable version of the book along with all the figures in color.

The CD-ROM also includes the complete 3D Studio MAX R3 demo produced by Kinetix. This demo includes detailed system information, examples, and tutorials for MAX and Character Studio.

As a special bonus, the CD-ROM also includes several custom-built, exclusive plug-ins developed by Furious Research and Dave Brueck, one of this book's contributing authors. To find out more about these plug-ins, see Appendix B, "Exclusive Bible Plug-Ins."

Feedback

I've put a lot of effort into this book, and I hope it helps you in your efforts. I present this book as a starting point. In each tutorial, I've purposely left all the creative spice out, leaving room for you to put it in — you're the one with the vision. However, I'd be interested to see and hear where this vision takes you, so if you feel like sharing it with me, drop me a line at murdocks@itsnet.com.

Acknowledgments

I have a host of people to thank for their involvement in this major work. The order in which they are mentioned doesn't necessarily represent the amount of work they did.

Thanks to my sweet wife Angela for her patience and love: Love is a dreamy reality, eh?

To my eldest son, Eric: Okay, Dad's done. How about a game of chess or two?

To my youngest son, Thomas: The CD-ROM drive really isn't broken; I hope you understand.

A big thanks to my two talented and dedicated coauthors, Dave Brueck and Sanford Kennedy, for joining me in the pressure cooker.

Dave Brueck spends his days developing business-related software for TenFold Corporation, but he keeps his love of computer graphics alive by working on graphics-related projects in his free time. His work in the past has included writing 3D graphics engines, ray tracers, and modeling programs, so he fully appreciates the power and flexibility of 3D Studio MAX. Besides spending time with his family, Dave uses what little spare time he has to design and build games, research distributed computing, and help out with Animabets.com. Dave currently lives in Eagle Mountain, Utah, with his wife, Jennie, and their daughter, Rachael. Dave wrote Chapter 38, "Network Rendering," and Chapter 41, "Using MAXScript," as well as Appendixes A, "Configuring a System for 3D Studio MAX," and B, " Exclusive Bible Plug-Ins."

Dave deserves a second huge thanks for pouring his brilliance and creativity into plug-ins that, just in themselves, make this book worth having. Thanks for your friendship and efforts.

Sanford Kennedy is the force behind Sanford Kennedy Design. He has written about 3D Graphics for many years, and his articles have appeared in a plethora of magazines, including *Computer Graphics World*, *3D Artist*, and *3D Design*. Sanford has also contributed to *3D Studio MAX: Tutorials From the Masters*, published by Autodesk Press, and *Inside 3D Studio MAX, Vol. 3, Advanced Animation*, published by New Riders Press. Sanford wrote Chapter 16, "Working with NURBS."

Major thanks and choruses of gratitude go out to the editors at IDG Books Worldwide. To Kathy Yankton, who started the whole ball rolling and for holding my virtual hand; to Kathi Duggan, who carefully pointed out many of the book's misconstructions before they were published, and to John Duggan for his insightful questions. Additional thanks go out to the entire staff at IDG Books who helped me on this journey, including Stefan Grünwedel, Colleen Dowling, Michael Welch, Lenora Chin Sell, and many other unknown helpers.

The various people who work in the graphics industry are amazing in their willingness to help and support. I'd like to thank first of all Jo-Ann Panchek and the entire Kinetix beta team for getting me the product when I needed it. Thanks also to Alexandra Maier and all her helpers in the Autodesk PR department.

I'd also like to thank the following individuals and companies for supplying software:

- ✦ Bernadette Macedo at Adobe
- ✦ Dorthy Eckels at MetaCreations
- ✦ Robert Landsdale at Okino Computer Graphics
- ✦ Robert McNeel at Robert McNeel and Associates
- ✦ Lee Dickholtz and Brent McMiking at ID8 Media
- ✦ Lavina Larkey at Digimation
- ✦ Elena Tsoupko-Sitnikova at Animatek
- ✦ Dolores Santos at REM Infografica

Thanks to the following contacts for supplying models and images used in the tutorials included on the CD-ROM:

- ✦ John Mellor at Viewpoint Datalabs
- ✦ Dan Farr at Zygote Media
- ✦ Hou Soon Ming at 3D Toon Shop
- ✦ William Capozzi at Dedicated Digital
- ✦ Marvin A. Lee II at 3D Paralex
- ✦ Chip Maxwell at Corel

Finally, a special thanks to those individuals and groups who gave you a good reason to pick up this book in the first place by providing images for the color insert pages:

- ✦ "Suburbs 2100" by Dawid Michalczyk
- ✦ "Memories of Alexander Green" by Victoria Brace
- ✦ "Chateau Brumal" by Molly Barr
- ✦ "'Phint (A gift to my wife, Angela)" by Joe Poppa
- ✦ "Schmetterling über Rose" (Butterfly over Rose) by Takara Ookami
- ✦ "Luna" by Victor Garrido
- ✦ "Forestgirl" by Lars Müller for Virgin Lands, Germany
- ✦ "Energy Rifle" by Arild Wiro
- ✦ "School of Fish II" by Ian Dale
- ✦ "Woman World" by Szymon Masiak
- ✦ "Lost World" by Paul Rance
- ✦ "The Number Forest" by Van Spragins, Christopher Sherrill, Cynthia Levine, Steven Marshall, Arnaldo Laboy, and Joey Elardy for Zenimation
- ✦ "The Traveler" by Tim Wallace
- ✦ "Telescope" by Gary Butcher
- ✦ "Einstein's Legacy" by Michael Lawson
- ✦ "Soccer Ball" by Thomas Suurland

Contents at a Glance

Contents

· ·

Part II: Working with Objects

Part V: Lights and Cameras   585

Getting Started with 3D Studio MAX R3

What's New in Release 3

Ah, a new release of MAX with all the new features, a new interface, new tools, and plenty of new headaches. If you're accustomed to a certain software package and you know it like the back of your hand, then a new version isn't always welcome news. One of your first questions will be, "What's changed?" This chapter covers all the new features of MAX R3 right up front, so you'll know what to expect and what to watch out for with the new version.

New User Interface

The interface is the same in many ways but radically different in others. Figure 1-1 shows the improved interface with many of its new elements. Notice that the button icons are larger. Buttons can also be set to use icons or text.

Note You can set the interface to use the older, smaller buttons or the newer, larger buttons in the Preferences dialog box.

The biggest news for the interface is that it is now completely customizable. Once you've tweaked the interface to your liking, you can save your settings and have MAX start up with your personalized interface. So, for example, if you're left-handed and always wanted to move the Command Panel to the left side of the screen, you'll now get your chance.

Cross-Reference Chapter 3, "Customizing the MAX Interface," explains how to create a customized interface with 3D Studio MAX.

Tab Panel   Command Panel   Rollout Titles

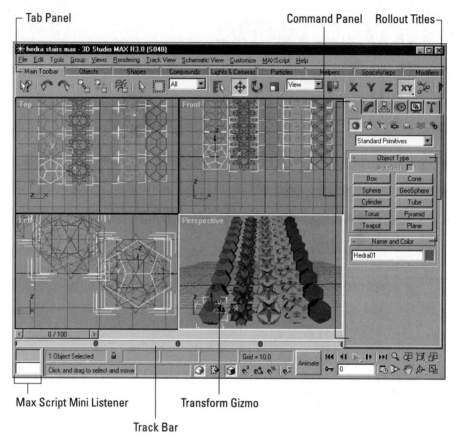

Max Script Mini Listener   Transform Gizmo

Track Bar

Figure 1-1: The new and improved MAX interface

Floating and docking toolbars

All toolbars, menus, and even the Command Panel are now floatable and dockable. You can pull them away and float them wherever you want, or you can "dock" them along the window edge of your choice. Floating toolbars will always appear on top of the standard window, so you never need to worry about losing them. Figure 1-2 shows toolbars docked at the edges of the viewport with the Objects toolbar floating in the middle.

Docked toolbars

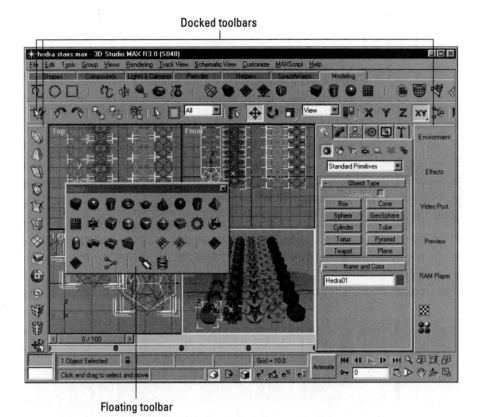

Floating toolbar

Figure 1-2: This figure shows docked and floating toolbars.

Customizable toolbars

Did it ever bother you that the first icon on the main toolbar was the Help Mode button? With the new customizable toolbars, you can remove, replace, or add buttons, creating your own personalized toolbars that contain only the commands you need, including buttons for custom macros and scripts.

Cross-Reference   Chapter 3, "Customizing the MAX Interface," explains how to create a custom setup.

Right-click menus

Right-click menus have been added to objects and buttons throughout the interface. These menus provide quick access to common features and commands. For example, right-clicking an object opens a menu with Transform options, access to the Properties dialog box, Select or Modify mode, the ability to convert the object to an Editable Mesh or an Editable Spline, and access to the object track in the Track View, as shown in Figure 1-3.

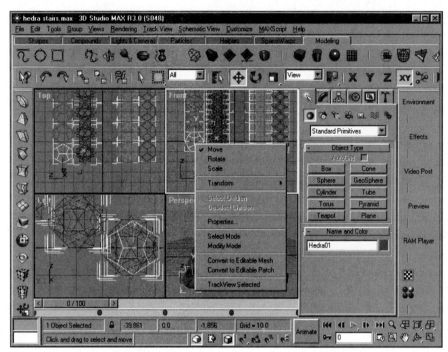

Figure 1-3: Right-clicking an object reveals this pop-up menu.

Tab panel

With complete control over toolbar position, you may be tempted to cover all of the viewports with toolbars. There's no need to do that, however, thanks to the Tab Panel.

The Tab Panel is a new interface element that declutters the screen and enables you to switch between toolbars by clicking the labeled tabs that rest above the panel.

Track bar

Between the Time Slider and the Status Bar is a new interface element called the Track Bar. The Track Bar displays the animation keys for the selected object, as you'd normally see in the Track View. Keys in the Track Bar can be moved, copied (by holding down the Shift key while moving), or deleted. Right-clicking the Track Bar keys opens the parameter dialog box.

For more information on using the Track Bar and its parameter dialog box, see Chapter 30, "Animation Basics."

Transform gizmo

The Transform Gizmo is an improved version of the object axes, letting you control object movements reliably even in Perspective mode. When enabled in the Views menu, the Transform Gizmo displays coordinate axes and corner marks for transforming the selected object. The corner marks let you transform within a plane. These axes and marks change to yellow when the mouse moves over them. Then when you drag with the mouse, the object is transformed only along the yellow-highlighted axes or plane. This feature gives you much greater control over moving, rotating, and scaling objects.

For additional information on using the Transform Gizmo, see Chapter 8, "Transforming Objects."

Viewport improvements

Each viewport displays color-coded coordinate axes in the lower left corner to help remind you of your orientation as the view is changed. Viewports can also hold windows like the Asset Manager, Track View, or Schematic View. A new display property called See-Through enables objects in the viewport to be partially transparent. The default arrow cursor can be changed to an AutoCAD-style crosshair cursor with lines that extend horizontally and vertically.

Panel scroll bar

When the Command Panel expands to fill its allotted area, a small scroll bar appears to the right of the panel. This scroll bar gives you an idea of how many rollouts are available and open. Rollouts are panels that hold parameters and settings. They can be collapsed and expanded by clicking the rollout's title. This same scroll bar appears in all dialog boxes where the rollouts exceed the vertical screen space, including the Render Scene and Material Editor dialog boxes.

Vertex numbers

Each vertex in an object or spline can be set to display a number based on its order. This can help to eliminate redundant vertices and is useful in cases where the order of vertices is important, such as for Loft objects and Surface Tools.

For more information on viewing Vertex Numbers, check out Chapter 11, "Working with Spline Shapes."

Schematic view

The Schematic View is a new option that displays all relationships between objects in a visual manner, as opposed to the Track View, which provides all the gory details of a scene but doesn't provide a visual look at the hierarchy. From within the Schematic View, you can cut, copy, and paste nodes and branches; link and unlink objects; and name and recall views. Schematic View can even be used to copy materials and Modifiers between objects. Figure 1-4 shows the Schematic View.

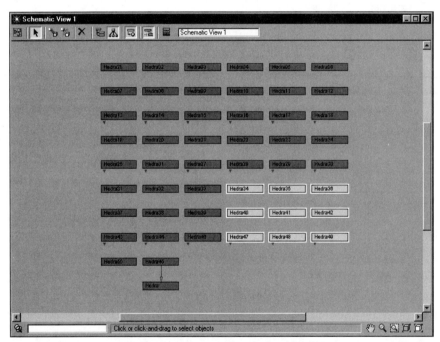

Figure 1-4: The new Schematic View provides a visual look at the scene elements.

Chapter 28, "Using Schematic View," explains more about how to use the Schematic View.

MAXScript Mini Listener

To the left of the Status Bar are two MAXScript Mini Listener fields. Right-clicking either field lets you open a Listener Window that is used to record all the actions in MAX. These recorded actions, or macros, can be turned into scripts for automating repetitive functions.

Cross-Reference

For all the details on using MAXScript and the new Listener functions, check out Chapter 43, "Using MAXScript."

External References

With Release 3, Kinetix has finally realized how production studios and animation houses put together projects — using a team. External References (XRefs) enable several users to collaborate on a single project without getting in each other's way. This is accomplished through two new features — XRef Scenes and XRef Objects.

Cross-Reference

XRef Scenes and XRef Objects are both covered in Chapter 4, "Referencing External Objects."

XRef Scenes

An externally referenced (XRef) scene is one that will appear in the current MAX session but will not be accessible for editing or changing. Using these, an individual artist can start a MAX session and reference all the work that the team is currently working on. The artist's session can be set to be automatically updated any time a change is made to any of the referenced scenes. The artist also doesn't need to worry about altering the work of others on the team. Figure 1-5 shows what the XRef Scenes dialog box looks like.

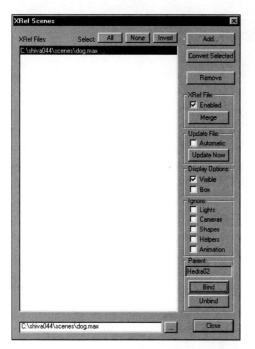

Figure 1-5: The XRef Scenes dialog box lets you specify which scenes to load as external references.

XRef Objects

XRef Objects are similar to their XRef Scenes counterparts, except that XRef Objects can be moved and positioned within the scene. They cannot, however, be modified. This feature provides a mechanism for creating a library of common objects that can be loaded and replaced at any time. XRef Objects can also be replaced with a proxy to keep scene complexity to a minimum.

Figure 1-6 shows the XRef Objects dialog box. The right side of this dialog box is divided into two sections. The top section displays the externally referenced files, and the lower section displays the objects selected from that file.

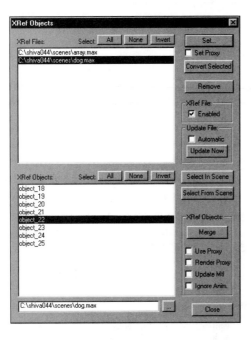

Figure 1-6: The XRef Objects dialog box lets you choose which objects' files to include as external references.

Updated Modeling Tools

There are many different things that you can model and many different techniques you can use to do the modeling. In fact, new modeling methods are being invented and implemented all the time.

Release 3 includes some new features and some improved features intended to make the modeling job easier. This section introduces you to some of these features. More information on these improvements can be found in the various modeling chapters in this book.

New primitives

A quick scan of the list of primitives reveals two new ones: Plane and Ringwave. The Plane primitive creates a simple flat polygon mesh that can be infinitely expanded when rendered. This is perfect for creating a ground plane.

The Ringwave is a flat ring made of two circles. The edges of these circles can be animated and roughed up. This primitive can be used to simulate the rapidly expanding and chaotic gas resulting from an explosion, such as a shockwave.

 Both of these primitives are explained in Chapter 10, "Creating Primitive Objects."

AutoGrid

The AutoGrid feature creates a temporary construction grid based on the normal version of a selected face. This lets you build a new object and be assured that it connects precisely with the selected face.

 Chapter 8, "Transforming Objects," explains the new AutoGrid feature and includes an example.

Terrain Compound Object

The Terrain Compound Object enables you to develop terrain objects by creating splines for each elevation contour. Terrains can be smooth or terraced, and you can assign different colors to different elevations.

 The Terrain Compound Object is discussed in Chapter 15, "Building Compound Objects."

Dynamic Objects

The Create panel now includes a new subcategory of objects called Dynamic Objects. The two available objects are a Spring and a Damper. These objects can be used in a Dynamic Simulation.

 Dynamic Objects are covered in Chapter 34, "Creating a Dynamic Simulation."

Subobject icons

New icon buttons for each subobject appear at the top of the Select Parameters rollout for the various editable objects. These buttons provide another way to enter Sub-Object mode and are available for all modeling types. These buttons provide an alternative to clicking the Sub-Object button and selecting the subobject from the drop-down list.

Editable mesh

When mesh subobjects are selected, the new Soft Selection feature enables subobjects surrounding the selected subobjects to be modified to a lesser extent. This makes for smoother transitions across the object surface.

Objects of any type can now be attached to a mesh, including splines, patches, and NURBS objects. Attaching to a mesh converts the object to a mesh.

Finally, the Extrude and Bevel rollouts now include a Chamfer function.

To learn about these and other mesh features, check out Chapter 12, "Working with Meshes."

Editable splines

Selected spline sections can be broken up with the Explode feature. Splines can now be assigned material IDs, and with the new Vertex Numbers feature, you can see the order of vertices in a spline. New vertices are inserted automatically when two splines cross paths.

Numerous other improvements and additions have been added to all subobject modes.

Editable Splines are covered in Chapter 11, "Working with Spline Shapes."

Editable Patches

An object can now be converted to an Editable Patch object. Editable Patches no longer include a patch lattice. Patches can now be edited by working directly with the patch surface. Editable Patches also require less memory than the Edit Patch Modifier.

Patches are covered in Chapter 13, "Using Patches."

NURBS improvements

The big modeling improvement in Release 3 is with NURBS. Previous versions of MAX NURBS left something to be desired, but they are starting to mature with this release. A new surface subobject called Fillet Surface has been added. This subobject rounds the corners where two edges meet.

Curves are now automatically attached when you create loft or sweep surfaces, and the curves no longer need to be part of the NURBS object before being selected. While working with a NURBS object, you can set a surface to be rigid so it cannot be edited. Almost any object can be converted to a NURBS model.

These and many more NURBS improvements are covered in Chapter 16, "Working with NURBS."

Loft improvements

The Loft object has been relocated under the Compound Objects subcategory. Other improvements include the Quad Sides, Flip Normals, and Transform Degrade options. Loft can be set to output NURBS or patches.

 Check out Chapter 14, "Creating Loft Objects," for more information on Loft objects.

Boolean improvements

A new Boolean operation—Cut—has been included in Release 3. Cut can use one object to split another.

 Booleans and the other Compound objects are covered in Chapter 15, "Building Compound Objects."

New Modifiers

You can never be too rich or too thin or have too many Modifiers. Modifiers enable modeling miracles. With this release of MAX, several new Modifiers have been added to the list:

✦ **Flex**—Causes surfaces to lag when in motion and then to overshoot after the motion stops, like the surface of a trampoline.

✦ **Volume Select**—Lets you select subobjects by enclosing them in another object or map.

✦ **Skin Modifier**—Uses one object to deform another object, like bones deforming a skin surface.

✦ **CrossSection**—One of the new Surface Tools Modifiers. This Modifier can link together several splines into a network over which the Surface Modifier can apply a patch skin.

✦ **Surface**—The other Surface Tools component. This Modifier is used to build complex organic models by stretching a skin across a network of splines created with the CrossSection Modifier.

✦ **MaterialByElement**—Assigns material IDs randomly for some great material effects.

✦ **Unwrap UVW**—Provides more control over the texture vertices than previous versions, includes new nonuniform scale and mirroring features, and enables locking, hiding, and freezing of selections.

✦ **Disp Approx Modifier** — A Modifier that enables displacement-mapping settings via the Stack.

✦ **Displace Mesh (WSM)** — A World-Space Modifier that lets you see the effect of displacement mapping.

✦ **Surface Mapper** — A World-Space Modifier that takes a map from a NURBS surface and projects it onto another object.

✦ **VertexPaint** — Enables different colors and opacity to be painted directly on geometry objects.

✦ **Morpher** — Supports up to 100 Morph channels. This Modifier can deform one object into another over time. It works with the new Morph material to change the material colors as the surface morphs.

✦ **Melt** — Does just what you'd expect. Try it on your favorite snowman.

✦ **Push** — Causes all internal vertices to move outward, like a pump filling the object with air.

✦ **Squeeze** — Causes objects to become narrow at the middle and bulge at either end, like a balloon.

Chapter 9, "Modifying Objects," explains these new Modifiers in more detail and with examples.

Material Editor Changes

Several new features have been added to the Material Editor. Key among these is the addition of Shaders, a SuperSampling feature, and several new map types.

For more information on the new Material Editor features introduced here, see Chapter 17, "Exploring the Material Editor."

Shaders

Shaders have long been the power behind popular renderers such as Renderman. The Material Editor now includes several standard Shaders, including

✦ **Oren-Nayar-Blinn** — Used for soft materials like cloth.

✦ **Anisotropic** — Used to create realistic metals and glass by setting nonsymmetrical highlights.

✦ **Multi-Layer** — Consists of two anisotropic layers.

✦ **Strauss** — Another alternative for creating metals, only faster than anisotropic.

Figure 1-7 shows the Material Editor with the Shader drop-down list selected.

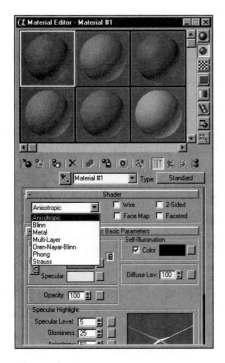

Figure 1-7: The Material Editor includes several new Shaders.

SuperSampling

SuperSampling reduces artifacts even further than standard anti-aliasing. The Material Editor includes four different SuperSampling methods, including Adaptive Halton, Adaptive Uniform, Hammersley, and MAX 2.5 Star.

New compound materials

Release 3 includes several new compound materials, including Composite, Shellac, and Morpher. The Composite material can layer up to nine different materials. The Shellac material layers two materials and offers transparency control between them. The Morpher material can transition to a different material as an object morphs.

Gradient Ramp map

This new map can create gradients using any number of colors and several different gradient types, including Diagonal, Pong, Radial, Sweep, Spiral, Tartan, and more. The map also includes controls for specifying the amount of noise.

Improved Falloff map

The Falloff map has been enhanced with three new falloff types, including Fresnel, Shadow/Light, and Distance Blend.

Multi-Texture mapping channels

MAX Release 3 now includes 99 different texture-mapping channels. These new channels enable you to create complex textures with multiple layers.

New Rendering Engine

3D Studio MAX R3 sports a new Scanline rendering engine. This new engine is faster and produces better-quality images. It also supports new anti-aliasing filters and interactive Render Effects.

 More information on the improved Scanline renderer and other improvements can be found in Chapter 36, "Setting Rendering Parameters."

Anti-aliasing filters

Instead of using a single anti-aliasing algorithm for all images, Release 3 lets you specify which filter to use. Options include Area, Blackman, Blend, Catmull-Rom, Cook Variable, Cubic, Mitchell-Netravali, Quadratic, Sharp Quadratic, Soften, and Video. Each of these filters will produce different results. Figure 1-8 shows these new filters, which can be found in the MAX Default Scanline A-Buffer rollout of the Render Scene dialog box.

Render effects

Formerly available only through the Video Post interface, post-process Render Effects can now be added as part of the rendering cycle. These Render Effects can be adjusted interactively to produce the perfect effect. Render Effects include Lens Effects, Blur, Brightness and Contrast, Color Balance, Depth of Field, File Output, and Film Grain. Figure 1-9 shows the new Render Effects dialog box.

 Render Effects are covered in Chapter 37, "Using Render Effects."

New Render types

The Render dialog box includes two new ways to render: Render Crop and Render Box Selected. The first renders to a cropped section of the scene specified in the Region section of the viewport. The second renders only the currently selected box.

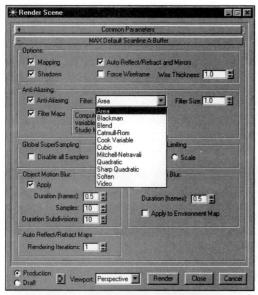

Figure 1-8: The Render Scene dialog box includes several new anti-aliasing filters.

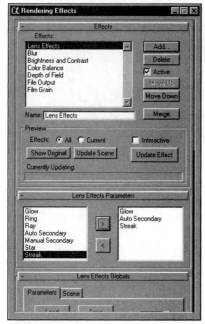

Figure 1-9: The Render Effects dialog box lets you select effects to apply during the rendering process.

RAM Player

The new RAM Player lets you load an animation into RAM, where it can be played back at any frame rate. There are two channels in the RAM player, enabling you to compare different animations side by side.

Figure 1-10 shows the two images loaded into the two channels available in the RAM Player. The image in channel A, on top, is clear, and the image in channel B is blurred.

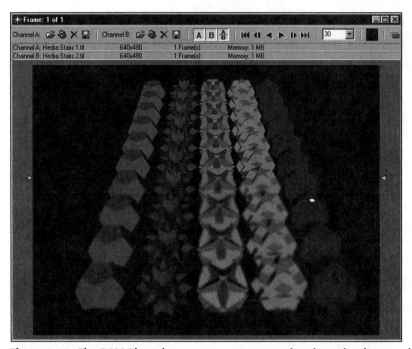

Figure 1-10: The RAM Player lets you compare two animations simultaneously.

Lighting Updates

MAX R3 has made subtle changes to the standard lighting features. It has also added a Shadow Color feature.

Cross-Reference   Chapter 20, "Controlling Lights," explains these improvements in more detail.

Shadow Color

When a light is created, a new color swatch appears in the Shadow Parameters rollout that lets you alter the Shadow Color. You can specify the Color Amount and Opacity of the shadow.

Switching light types

After creating a light, you can switch it to a different type. For instance, an Omni light can be easily converted to a Target Spot light.

Using Default Lights

The new Views ⇨ Add Default Lights to Scene command converts the default lights into actual objects. You can also convert one or both of the default lights.

Vertex lighting

You can pre-light all vertices in a scene with attenuation and color. This effect can be used to simulate radiosity.

New Controllers

Animation Controllers provide automatic animation intelligence to objects. Release 3 includes several new Controllers.

 Cross-Reference The new Controllers are covered along with the rest of the Controllers in Chapter 32, "Animating with Controllers."

Block Controller

The Block Controller can group several tracks together into one easy-to-manage group. Any changes made to the animation keys are applied to all the tracks in the group.

Local Euler XYZ Rotation Controller

This new Controller works the same way as the Euler XYZ Rotation Controller except that rotations are applied to the local coordinate system.

Scale XYZ Controller

The Scale XYZ Controller can independently control the scale of each axis of an object. This feature can be used to scale animation keys for a specific axis.

Reactor Controller

The Reactor Controller can be used to change parameters based on changes produced by any other Controller. For example, this Controller can be used to turn on a light when another object moves. The Reactor Controller includes five different forms: Position, Rotation, Point3 for colors, Scale, and Float for parameter values.

Particle Systems

Although there aren't any new particle types, several features have been added that make it easier to work with particle systems.

Particle systems are covered in Chapter 24, "Creating and Controlling Particle Systems."

Inter-particle collisions

Particles can be set to collide with one another. In previous versions of 3D Studio MAX, they would just pass on through. Be warned, however, that with a large number of particles, this effect requires a lot of memory.

MetaParticles

MetaParticles can now spawn additional MetaParticles. You can also set MetaParticles to render only one connected blob.

Space Warps

Release 3 includes several new Space Warps for adding forces to the scene. These can be used to control objects. The new Space Warps are specifically used in conjunction with Dynamic Simulations.

These Space Warps and many others are covered in Chapter 25,"Using Space Warps."

PDynaFlect, SDynaFlect, UdynaFlect

These three new Space Warps enable particle objects to affect other objects. They are intended to be used in dynamic simulations. The difference between these Space Warps is their shapes, which can be Planar, Spherical, and the shape of any other object.

POmniFlect, SOmniFlect, UOmniFlect

These Space Warps replace the older Deflector Space Warps. They add several new features and controls and come in three different shapes: Planar, Spherical, and the shape of any other object.

Efficient Scripting and Macros

MAXScript has been re-implemented to be more accessible to all MAX users. In addition, the new Listener function enables you to record macros and play them back immediately. This can save you from the drudgery of performing boring, repetitive tasks.

Chapter 41, "Using MAXScript," covers scripting in detail.

The MAXScript menu

The menu now includes a MAXScript option that holds commands for managing scripts. It also enables the MAXScript Listener and the Macro Recorder.

Macro Recording

The Macro Recording option in the MAXScript menu keeps track of every command that MAX is executing when enabled. These commands can be selected and pasted into a script within the Listener window. Figure 1-11 shows the MAXScript Listener window. The top half of the window records all available actions. These actions can be copied and pasted into the script in the bottom half of the window.

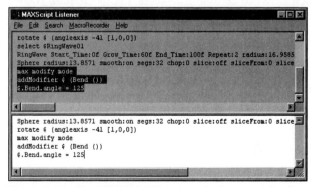

Figure 1-11: The MAXScript Listener window records all actions in the top half and enables you to build a script in the bottom half.

MAXScript Mini Listener on the status bar

At the right end of the Status Bar is a two-line version of the MAXScript Listener. This Listener displays any MAX actions along with the current script. You can also use the Listener to immediately replay any actions.

Hardware Support

Updated drivers and built-in support enable MAX users a faster working environment with fewer crashes.

Pentium III support

MAX R3 supports the OpenGL, Direct 3D, and Heidi display drivers that have been optimized for Streaming SIMD, a new technology included in the Pentium III Xeon processors. These new drivers have produced a 30% increase in viewport refresh rates.

Improved video card support

Many video cards built for playing games have made OpenGL and Direct3D drivers available. These new drivers enable you to build game graphics on the same machine that you use to play the games.

Summary

The new features in MAX R3 span the product. Almost every area of MAX has been improved, and certain new features such as Schematic View and the MAXScript Listener will make it much easier to complete projects. In this chapter, you learned about the following:

✦ 3D Studio MAX R3's new interface and capabilities

✦ How the updated modeling tools work

✦ The new object modifiers and what they do

✦ Material Editor changes, including the addition of Shaders and a Super Sampling feature

✦ Changes and additions to lighting tools and controllers

✦ New hardware support

Now that you've had a chance to see what's new, let's take a look at the most visible change to Release 3: the user interface. The next chapter covers all aspects of the interface.

✦   ✦   ✦

Exploring the MAX Interface

How important is a software interface? Well, consider this. The interface is the set of controls that enables you to access the program's features. Without a good interface, you may never use many of the best features of the software. A piece of software can have all the greatest features, but if the user can't find or access them, then the software isn't going to be used to its full potential. MAX is a powerful piece of software with some amazing features and, luckily, the interface makes these amazing features easy to find and use.

Prior to MAX, 3D Studio had a loyal following of users in the DOS realm. These experienced users were comfortable with the interface and knew how to quickly access any feature they needed. Redesigning any interface is tough, but to mess with an interface used for years by devoted users is often unforgivable. The loyal 3D Studio users eventually came to understand that DOS-based systems were going away and that MAX had been created to fill the void.

Has the MAX interface succeeded? Yes, to a degree, but like most interfaces, there is always room for improvement. In the evolutionary progression of the MAX interface, we're ready for the next major step. MAX R3's interface has some great improvements, but they, like any kind of change, will take some getting used to.

This chapter examines the latest incarnation of the MAX interface and presents some tips that will make the interface feel comfortable, not cumbersome.

Understanding 3D Space

It seems silly to be talking about 3D space because we live and move in 3D space. 3D space is natural to us, if we stop and think about it. For example, consider a filing cabinet with four drawers. Within each drawer you can stuff papers in the front, back, or sides, as well as in the drawers above or below. These positions represent three unique directions.

When I ask my wife where our passports are and she says, "They're in the top drawer toward the back on the left side," I know exactly where they are and can find them immediately (unless of course my kids have been in the cabinet). The concept of three dimensions is comfortable and familiar.

Now consider the computer screen, which is inherently 2D. If I have many windows open, including a scanned image of my passport, and I ask my wife where the scanned image is, she'd reply, "It's somewhere behind the large window where you're writing that book." And I'd look and search before locating it. In 2D space, I understand top and bottom and left and right and a little notion of above and below, but it isn't as natural.

This is the conundrum that 3D computer artists face — how do you represent 3D objects on a 2D device? The answer that 3D Studio MAX provides is to present several views, called *viewports*, of the scene. A *viewport* is a small window that displays the scene from one perspective. These viewports are the windows into MAX's 3D world. Each viewport has numerous settings and viewing options.

Cross-Reference This section introduces the MAX viewports. For information on configuring these viewports, see Chapter 3, "Customizing the MAX Interface."

Orthographic views

Orthographic views are displayed from the perspective of looking straight down an axis at an object. This reveals a view in only one plane. Because orthographic viewports are constrained to one plane, they show the actual height and width of the object. Available orthographic viewports in MAX include Front, Back, Top, Bottom, Left, and Right. MAX starts up with the Top, Front, and Left orthographic viewports visible, as shown in Figure 2-1. The Top left corner of the viewport displays the viewport name.

Perspective view

The fourth viewport is a Perspective view (shown in Figure 2-1). Although not as precise when manipulating objects, this view is the closest to what we see in reality and gives a more intuitive definition of the relationship between objects.

Top View   Front View

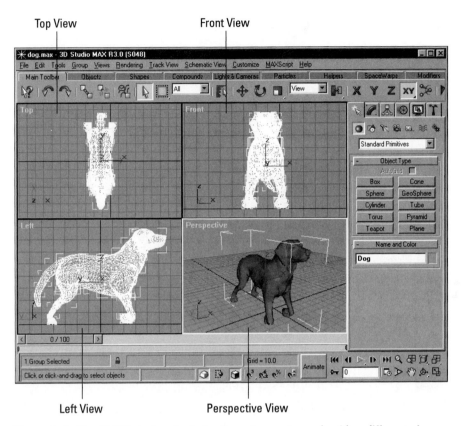

Left View   Perspective View

Figure 2-1: The MAX interface includes four viewports, each with a different view.

Using the Pull-Down Menus

The pull-down menus at the top of the screen contain many of the features available in MAX. Several of the menu commands have corresponding toolbar buttons. To execute a menu command, you can choose it from the menu where it resides, or you can just click its toolbar button if it has one.

This section describes the MAX menus and their commands.

The File menu

The File menu includes commands for managing MAX files. These commands enable you to open, save, and view files in various ways.

Opening and saving files

The File menu includes the standard New, Open, Save, and Save As commands for handling scene files. All file dialog boxes that work with MAX scenes include a thumbnail image of the active viewport, as shown in Figure 2-2. This is helpful in preventing you from opening the wrong scene by mistake. If MAX cannot locate resources used within a scene (such as maps) when you open a MAX file, then a dialog box appears enabling you to locate or skip the missing files.

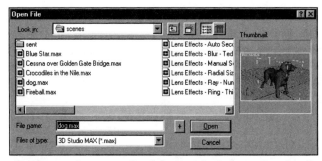

Figure 2-2: The Open File dialog box includes a thumbnail of the scene.

The Save command saves the current scene to its given name, but the Save As command lets you rename the current scene. All MAX scene files are saved with the .max extension. The Save Selected command saves only the selected objects to a MAX file.

Tip   MAX includes an AutoSave feature. This feature is configured in the Preference Settings dialog box covered in Chapter 3, "Customizing the MAX Interface."

The Archive command enables you to save your scene along with all referenced bitmaps in a space-saving, compressed file format such as Zip. The external archiving program used to compress files is specified in the File panel of the Preference Settings dialog box. By archiving a MAX scene along with its reference bitmaps, you can ensure that it will include all the necessary files. The File Type drop-down list also includes an option to create a List of Files. This option lists all relevant files and their paths in a text file.

Combining MAX scenes and objects

The File menu also includes several commands that are used to combine elements from different MAX files. The XRef Objects and XRef Scenes commands open dialog boxes for using referenced objects or scenes in the current scene. These commands are key to enabling powerful collaboration features.

New Feature

The XRef Objects and XRef Scenes commands provide an easier environment for collaborative projects. See Chapter 4, "Referencing External Objects" for information on how to use these commands.

The Merge and Merge Animation commands let you merge MAX scenes or specific tracks into the current scene. The Replace command replaces objects with the same name from another scene.

Resetting the interface

The Reset command returns the environment to the same state as when you started MAX. This produces the same effect as exiting the program without saving any changes you have made during that session and starting it again. When reset, all interface settings are returned to their default states. Use of this command also eliminates any customization that you've done to the interface.

Note

The Reset command is different from the New command. The File ⇨ New command doesn't reset all the settings.

Importing and exporting files

The Import and Export commands can load objects or scenes from or save to different formats. Most of the supported formats are 3D formats, but selected objects can be saved to other formats such as the Illustrator AI format. Export Selected will export just the selected objects.

Cross-Reference

See Chapter 5, "Importing and Exporting," for more information on using these commands.

Displaying scene fnformation

The Summary Info command displays all the relevant details about the current scene, such as the number of objects, lights, and cameras; total number of vertices and faces; and various model settings, as well as a Description field where you can describe the scene. Figure 2-3 shows the Summary Info dialog box.

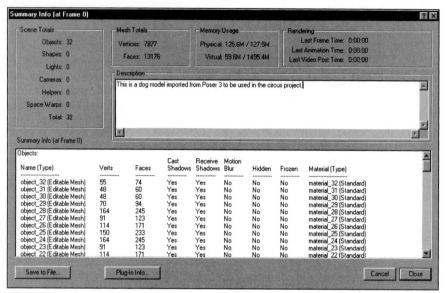

Figure 2-3: The Summary Info dialog box shows all the basic information about the current scene.

The Plug-In Info button on the Summary Info dialog box displays a list of all the plug-ins currently installed on your system. Even without any external plug-ins installed, the list will be fairly long because many of the core features in MAX are implemented as plug-ins. The Summary Info dialog box also includes a Save to File button for saving the scene summary information as a text file.

The Properties command opens the File Properties dialog box. This dialog box, shown in Figure 2-4, includes three tabs: Summary, Contents, and Custom. These tabs hold information such as the Title, Subject, and Author of the MAX file and can be useful for managing a collaborative project. For example, the Custom tab can be used to enter revision dates for the scene.

Tip

You can also view the Properties dialog box information while working in Windows Explorer by right-clicking the file and selecting Properties. Two unique tabs are visible—Summary and Statistics. The Summary tab holds the file identification information, including the Author, Keywords, Comments, Title, Subject, and Template. The Statistics tab displays the creation and modification dates, the name of the user who last saved the file, a revision number, and any descriptive information.

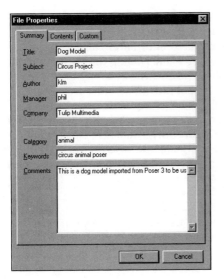

Figure 2-4: The File Properties dialog box contains workflow information such as the scene author, comments, and revision dates.

Viewing Files

The View File command opens the View File dialog box shown in Figure 2-5. This dialog box lets you view graphic and animation files using the Virtual Frame Buffer or the default Media Player for your system.

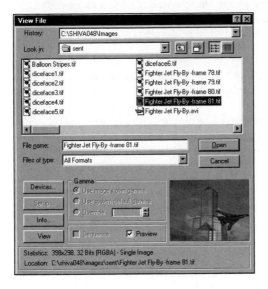

Figure 2-5: The View File dialog box can open an assortment of image and animation formats.

Cross-Reference

The Virtual Frame Buffer window is discussed in more detail in Chapter 36, "Setting Rendering Parameters."

The View File dialog box includes several controls for viewing files. The Devices and Setup buttons let you set up and view a file using external devices such as Video Recorders. The Info button lets you view detailed information about the selected file. The View button opens the file for viewing while leaving the View File dialog box open. The Open button closes the dialog box. At the bottom of the View File dialog box, the statistics and path of the current file are displayed.

Note   The View File dialog box can open many types of files, including Microsoft videos (AVI), Bitmap images (BMP), Kodak Cineon (CIN), Autodesk Flic images (CEL), Graphics Image Format (GIF), IFL images, Paint* by Discreet Logic (IPP), JPEG images (JPG), PNG images, Adobe Photoshop images (PSD), QuickTime movies (MOV), SGI images (RGB), RLA images, RPF images, Targa images (VST), Tagged image file format images (TIF), and YUV images.

The Gamma area on the View File dialog box is used to specify whether an image uses its own gamma settings or the system's default setting, or if an override value should be used.

The Edit menu

The Edit menu includes commands for recovering from mistakes, cloning and selecting objects, and displaying the object Properties dialog box.

Recovering from mistakes

The first commands on the Edit menu are Undo and Redo. You can set the levels of undo in the Preference Settings dialog box. The Undo command lets you reverse an operation. Many operations such as applying or deleting Modifiers and changing parameters cannot be undone.

Tip   By right-clicking the Undo and Redo buttons, you can see a list of recent operations and select specific commands to undo or redo.

The Hold command saves the scene into a temporary buffer for easy recovery. Once a scene is set with the Hold command, it can be brought back instantly with the Fetch command. These commands provide a quick way to backtrack on modifications to a scene or project without having to save and reload the project. These are the commands to use before applying or deleting Modifiers.

Tip   It is a good idea, along with saving your file often, to use the Hold command before applying any complex Modifier to an object.

Deleting and Cloning objects

The Delete command removes the selected object from the scene. (You can also use the Delete key on the keyboard.)

The Edit menu doesn't include the common cut, copy, and paste commands. This is because there are many objects and subobjects that cannot be easily cut and pasted into a different place. There is however, a Clone command, which duplicates a selected object.

Note The duplicate object appears directly on top of the selected object. To see the cloned object you'll need to move the cloned object or its original.

A Clone Options dialog box appears when you execute the Clone command. This simple dialog box lets you choose whether the cloned objects are to be Copies, Instances, or References. Copies become unique objects, but instances and references retain links to the original object. These links modify the instanced or referenced copy when the original is modified.

Cross-Reference Check out Chapter 6, "Cloning Objects and Using Arrays," for more information on the Clone feature.

Selecting objects

The Edit menu also includes several commands for selecting objects. Select All selects all the selectable objects in the scene. Select None deselects any objects already selected. Select Invert deselects any currently selected objects and conversely selects any unselected objects. Select By opens a submenu that enables you to select objects by Name or Color.

Cross-Reference Selecting objects is covered in Chapter 7, "Selecting and Grouping Objects."

The Region command lets you select objects using one of two different selection methods — Crossing or Window. The Crossing method selects objects if they intersect the area dragged by the mouse. In the Window method, the entire object must be included in the dragged area in order for it to be selected.

The Edit Named Selections command opens a dialog box that lists all the named selections. A *Named Selection* is a selection of objects that are identified with a name. You create a name by entering it in the Named Selection field on the main toolbar. Named Selections can then be recalled quickly at any time. The Edit Named Selections dialog box, shown in Figure 2-6, will let you Delete, Combine, Subtract, or Intersect selections. You can also select objects and Remove them from the selection set.

Cross-Reference See Chapter 7, "Selecting and Grouping Objects," for more information on Named Selections.

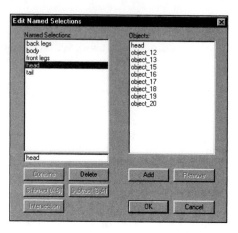

Figure 2-6: The Edit Named Selections dialog box helps manage selections of objects.

Viewing Object Properties

Properties, the final command in the Edit menu, opens the Object Properties dialog box for the current selection, as shown in Figure 2-7. The Object Properties dialog box includes information about the object and settings for Rendering Control, Display Properties, and Motion Blur. The Object Properties dialog box can also be used with multiple objects selected, but only the common properties are displayed. Right-clicking an object and selecting Properties from the pop-up menu can also open the Object Properties dialog box.

Cross-Reference

Each of the Object Properties settings is explained in more detail in Chapter 7, "Selecting and Grouping Objects."

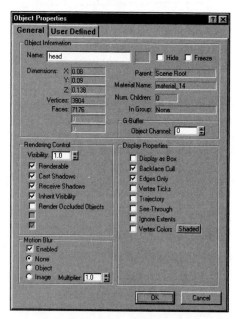

Figure 2-7: The Object Properties dialog box includes settings for controlling how an object is displayed.

The Tools menu

The Tools menu provides access to most of the main dialog boxes in MAX. These dialog boxes along with the Command Panel hold many of the main functions of MAX. They are briefly described here and will be covered throughout the remaining chapters in more detail.

Object dialog boxes

The Tools menu includes several commands for controlling individual objects. The Transform Type-In lets you input precise values for moving, rotating, and scaling objects. This provides more exact control over the placement of objects than dragging with the mouse.

The Transform Type-In is covered in more detail in Chapter 8, "Transforming Objects."

The Display Floater command opens a dialog box with the same name that lets you hide, freeze, and control display properties. The Selection Floater command also opens a dialog box with the same name that lists all the objects in a scene sorted alphabetically, or by type, color, or size. From the list you can select several objects, groups, or sets.

The floater dialog boxes are discussed in Chapter 7, "Selecting and Grouping Objects."

Additional Cloning commands

The Edit menu has several methods for cloning objects — in addition to the Clone command. The Mirror command uses the Mirror dialog box to create a symmetrical copy of an object across a designated axis. The Array command opens an Array dialog box where you can create multiple instances of an object with each instance offset from the others. The Snapshot command clones objects over time using the Snapshot dialog box.

The Mirror, Array, and Snapshot commands are covered in Chapter 6, "Cloning Objects and Using Arrays."

Aligning objects

The Tools menu includes several ways to align objects. The Align command opens an Align dialog box where you can line up objects by axis, edges, or centers. The Align Normals command enables you to align the face normals of two objects.

The Place Highlight moves the selected light in order to reproduce a highlight in the location you specify. The Align Camera moves the selected camera in order to be directly in front of the point you select. The Align to View command aligns the object to one of the axes.

The alignment commands are discussed in Chapter 8, "Transforming Objects."

Other dialog boxes

The Material Editor and Material/Map Browser commands open their respective dialog boxes for creating, defining, and applying materials.

Chapter 17, "Exploring the Material Editor," covers the Material Editor, and Chapter 18, "Using Material Maps," covers the Material/Map Browser.

The Spacing Tool command opens the Spacing Tool dialog box, which creates and spaces objects along a path. This is perhaps the easiest way to hang laundry out to dry.

The Spacing Tool is covered in Chapter 11, "Working with Spline Shapes."

The Group menu

The Group menu commands let you control how objects are grouped together. Selecting several objects and using the Group command opens a simple dialog box where you can type a name for the group. The Ungroup command disassembles the group and is only active if a group is selected. Groups can be nested one inside another. Groups can also be opened, which enables individual group objects to be transformed or deleted. Objects can be attached or detached from a group; the Explode command ungroups all nested group objects.

For a more complete examination of groups and grouping, check out Chapter 7, "Selecting and Grouping Objects."

The Views menu

The Views menu controls all aspects of the viewports. Separately from manipulating an object, you can manipulate a view with the Viewport Navigation Controls in the lower right corner of the interface. These controls will be covered in a later section ("Using the Additional Interface Controls").

Undo and Redo give you control over viewport changes, enabling you to undo and redo any changes made with the Viewport Navigation Controls.

You can also save and restore each viewport's active view with the Save Active View and Restore Active View commands.

Saving an active view uses a buffer, so it only remembers one view for each viewport.

Controlling the Viewport display

Grids are helpful in establishing your bearings in 3D space. The Grids command opens a submenu with the following options: Show Home Grid, Activate Home Grid, Activate Grid Object, and Align to View.

 Chapter 8, "Transforming Objects," covers grids in more detail.

The Viewport Background command opens a dialog box, shown in Figure 2-8, where you can select an image or animation to appear behind a viewport. The displayed background image is helpful for aligning objects in a scene, but it is for display purposes only and will not be rendered. To create a background image to be rendered, use the Environment command in the Rendering menu.

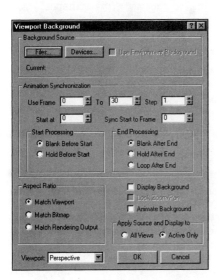

Figure 2-8: The Viewport Background dialog box can load background images or animations.

 Viewport Background can come in handy when you want to load as a reference an image or sketch of an object you're modeling.

If the background image changes, you can update the viewport using the Update Background Image command. The Reset Background Transform command automatically rescales and recenters the background image to fit the viewport.

Next on the Views menu are several commands that control what is displayed in the viewport. If these commands are enabled, a check mark will appear to the left of the command. The Show Transform Gizmo command displays axes and special handles to move, rotate, and scale the object in different directions.

The Show Ghosting command displays the position of the selected object in the previous several frames, the next several frames, or both. This lets you see the path and motion of objects as they are animated. The Ghosting settings are set in the Viewport tab of the Preference Settings dialog box. The Show Key Times command displays frame numbers along the trajectory where every animation key is located. Figure 2-9 shows Ghosting and Key Times.

Frame 50 Key Time

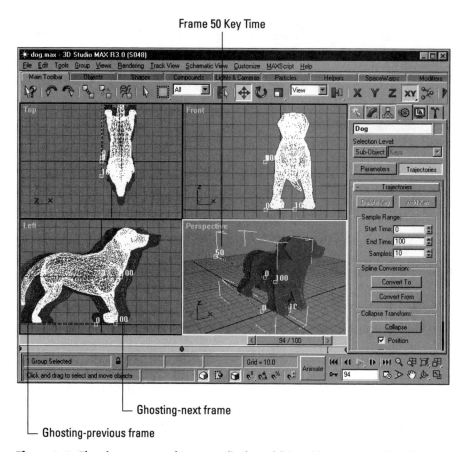

Ghosting-next frame

Ghosting-previous frame

Figure 2-9: The viewports can be set to display additional information like Ghosting and Key Times.

The Shade Selected command turns shading on for the selected object in all viewports and the Show Dependencies command shows any objects that are linked or instanced from a parent object.

Miscellaneous Viewport settings

There are several miscellaneous commands in the Views menu that control the viewport. The Match Camera to View command repositions a selected camera to match the current scene (you first need to have a camera in the scene and selected). It is often easier to use the Viewport Navigation Controls to interactively line up a perspective view. Once the view is correct, the Match Camera to View command can position and point a camera at exactly what you want to see.

More details on the Match Camera to Scene command can be found in Chapter 22, "Controlling Cameras."

The Add Default Lights to Scene command will convert the default lights to actual light objects in the scene. This will let you start with the default lights and modify them as needed.

More details on controlling lights can be found in Chapter 20, "Controlling Lights."

The Redraw All Views command will refresh each viewport and make everything visible again (as objects get moved around, they will often mask one another and lines will disappear). You can also access this command by pressing the 1 key.

Deactivate All Maps will turn off all maps. Material maps can take up a lot of memory and can slow a machine down. If you're positioning or animating items, then turning all maps off makes sense.

Update During Spinner Drag will cause a viewport to interactively show the results of a parameter value change set with spinner controls. *Spinners* are fields with up and down arrows to their right.

Running in Expert Mode

The Expert Mode command maximizes viewport space by removing the menus, main toolbar, Command Panel, Viewport Navigation buttons, status bar, and prompt line from the interface.

You use features in Expert Mode by accessing the keyboard shortcuts. To re-enable the default interface, click the Cancel Expert Mode button. Figure 2-10 shows the interface in Expert Mode.

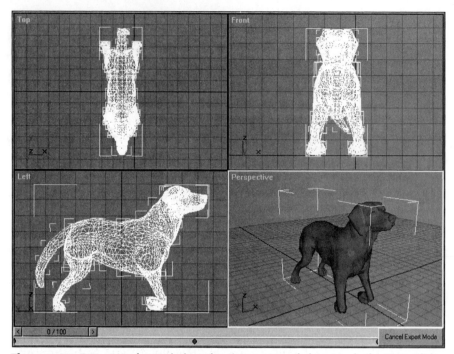

Figure 2-10: Expert Mode maximizes the viewports and shows only the Time Slider control and Cancel Expert Mode button.

The Rendering menu

The Rendering Menu is the doorway to the final output. The Render command opens the Render Scene dialog box where you can set output options such as which frames to render and final image size. You can also choose to render to a file or to a device such as a Digital Recorder.

Cross-Reference The Render command and its parameters are covered in depth in Chapter 36, "Setting Rendering Parameters."

The Video Post command opens a dialog box for scheduling and controlling any video post work. The dialog box manages events for compositing images and including special effects such as glows and blurs.

Cross-Reference Chapter 39, "Using the Video Post Interface," tells you all you need to know about Video Post.

The next command on the Rendering menu is Show Last Rendering. This command will immediately recall the last rendered image produced by the Render command.

The Environment command opens the Environment dialog box where you can specify the environment settings such as a background color or image, global lighting settings, and atmospheric effects such as Combustion, Fog, and Volume Lights.

To learn how to work with the Environment effects, see Chapter 35, "Working with Backgrounds, Environments, and Atmospheric Effects."

The Effects command opens a dialog box new to Release 3 — Rendering Effects. The Rendering Effects dialog box adds rendered effects to an image without using the Video Post dialog box. The Effects categories include options such as Lens Effects, Blur, and Color Balance.

The Rendering Effects dialog box adds post-rendered effects to an image without using the Video Post dialog box. Chapter 37, "Using Render Effects," covers all these effects.

Previews give you a chance to see your animation before spending the time to render it. Preview commands include Make Preview, View Preview, and Rename Preview.

Chapter 36, "Setting Rendering Parameters," covers Previews and the RAM Player, as well as final renderings.

The RAM Player is a new utility in Release 3. It can display images and animations in memory and includes two channels for overlaying images.

The RAM Player interface enables you to work with animation segments in RAM and view your animation at different frame rates. The RAM Player has two channels for comparing animations side by side.

The Track View menu

The Track View presents all the aspects of a project in a hierarchical form, letting you control the objects, transformations, and materials. The Track View menu commands let you open the current Track View, create a new Track View, or delete an existing Track View.

More information on this menu and its commands can be found in Chapter 31, "Working with Track View."

The Schematic View menu

The Schematic View is very similar to the Track View. It includes the same commands, but works with a different type of view that is new to Release 3.

Schematic View presents a visual scene graph of all the objects in a scene and their relationships. See Chapter 28, "Using Schematic View," for more information on this new tool.

The Customize menu

The Customize menu is also new to Release 3. It provides commands for controlling and customizing the new Release 3 interface. The Load Custom UI and Save Custom UI As commands let you load and save different custom interfaces. The Lock UI Layout prevents an interface from being changed. This is helpful if you accidentally keep dragging toolbars out of place. If your customization gets confusing, you can reset the layout with the Revert to Startup UI Layout command.

The Customize Menu enables you to create custom interfaces. Custom interfaces can be loaded and saved. Chapter 3, "Customizing the MAX Interface," explains how to do this.

The Customize UI command opens the Customize User Interface dialog box where you can customize the toolbars. The Configure Paths command opens the Configure Paths dialog box where you can define all the default paths. The Preferences command opens the Preference Settings dialog box for controlling many aspects of MAX.

The Viewport Configuration command lets you configure the viewport using the Viewport Configuration dialog box. The Units Setup command opens the Units Setup dialog box for establishing system units. The Grid and Snap Settings command opens the Grid and Snap Settings dialog box for controlling grid objects and determining which points to snap to.

The MAXScript menu

MAXScript is another new Release 3 menu. From this menu, you can create, Open, and Run Scripts. You can also open the MAXScript Listener and enable the Macro Recorder.

The MAXScript menu includes commands for creating, accessing, and running new scripts. There is also a new MAXScript Listener command for recording macros. Chapter 43, "Using MAXScript," covers the basics of MAXScript.

The Help menu

The Help menu is a valuable resource that provides access to reference materials and tutorials. The Online Reference and the MAXScript Reference are comprehensive help systems. The Learning 3D Studio MAX command loads the tutorials. Additional Help presents help systems for any external plug-ins that are loaded. The Connect to Support and Information automatically opens a web browser and loads the Kinetix Support pages at www.ktx.com/support/html/3dsmaxr3.html. The About 3D Studio MAX command opens the About dialog box shown in Figure 2-11. This dialog box displays the serial number and current display driver.

Figure 2-11: The About 3D Studio MAX R3 dialog box shows the serial number, current driver, and release number.

Using the Tab Panel

The Tab Panel is like a super toolbar with tabs across the top that let you switch between many different toolbars. This is an efficient use of space if you want toolbar access to all commands. The standard setup includes the default Tab Panel at the top of the window. (If the Tab Panel does not appear, you can open it by right-clicking the menu bar or on any toolbar and selecting Tab Panel from the pop-up menu.)

The toolbars included in the default Tab Panel include the following: Main Toolbar, Objects, Shapes, Compounds, Lights & Cameras, Particles, Helpers, SpaceWarps, Modifiers, Modeling, and Rendering. Any of these individual toolbars can be removed from the Tab Panel and repositioned by dragging its tab away from the Tab Panel. Figure 2-12 shows a portion of the Tab Panel.

Chapter 3, "Customizing the MAX Interface," provides more information on customizing the Tab Panel.

Figure 2-12: The Tab Panel can hold multiple toolbars.

Learning the Main Toolbar

The Main Toolbar is the first tab in the Tab panel. MAX includes many toolbars, but the Main Toolbar is perhaps most useful for managing the major functions of MAX. For this reason, the Main Toolbar and its buttons will be described here, while the other toolbars will be covered in various chapters throughout this book. Figure 2-13 shows the Main Toolbar as a floating panel.

Figure 2-13: The Main Toolbar includes buttons for controlling many of the most popular MAX functions.

On smaller resolution screens, the entire toolbar will not be visible. To view the entire toolbar, position the cursor over an empty space on the toolbar, such as in between buttons (you'll know you're in the right place when the cursor changes to a hand). Then click and drag the toolbar in either direction. Using the hand cursor to scroll also works in the Command Panel, Material Editor, and any other place where the panel exceeds the given space.

Tip   The General tab in the Preference Settings dialog box includes an option for using Large Toolbar Buttons or the small buttons from the previous versions. Once you select a different button size you will need to restart MAX in order to use it.

All buttons include *tooltips*, which are identifying text labels. Hold the cursor over the icon to display the tooltip label.

The toolbar buttons with a small triangle in the lower right-hand corner are flyouts. A *flyout* is a button that holds additional buttons. Click and hold on the flyout to reveal the additional icons and drag to select one.

The icons on the Main Toolbar are described in the following table. Buttons with flyouts are separated with commas.

	Table 2-1 Main Toolbar Buttons	
Toolbar Button	**Name**	**Description**
	Help Mode	Provides context-sensitive help by opening the Online Reference with information on the item you clicked on.

Toolbar Button	Name	Description
	Undo	Removes the last performed command. The levels of Undo can be set in the Preferences dialog box.
	Redo	Brings back the last command that was undone.
	Select and Link	Establishes links between objects.
	Unlink Selection	Breaks links between objects.
	Bind to Space Warp	Assigns objects to be modified by a space warp.
	Select Object	Chooses an object.
	Rectangular Selection Region, Circular Selection Region, Fence Selection Region	Determines the method for selecting objects.
All	Selection Filter drop-down list	Limits the type of objects that can be selected.
	Select by Name	Opens a dialog box for selecting objects by name.
	Select and Move	Selects an object and enables positional transformations.
	Select and Rotate	Selects an object and enables rotational transformations.
	Select and Uniform Scale, Select and Non-Uniform Scale, Select and Squash	Selects an object and enables scaling transformations.
View	Reference Coordinate System drop-down list	Specifies the coordinate system used for transformations.
	Use Pivot Point Center, Use Selection Center, Use Transform Coordinate Center	Specifies the center about which rotations are completed.
X	Restrict to X	Allows objects to transform only along the X axis.

Continued

Table 2-1 *(continued)*

Toolbar Button	Name	Description
Y	Restrict to Y	Allows objects to transform only along the Y axis.
Z	Restrict to Z	Allows objects to transform only along the Z axis.
XY YZ ZX	Restrict to XY Plane, Restrict to YZ Plane, Restrict to ZX Plane	Allows objects to transform only along a specified plane.
	Inverse Kinematics Toggle	Turns Inverse Kinematics mode on or off.
	Mirror Selected Objects	Creates a mirrored copy of the selected object.
	Array, Snapshot, Spacing Tool	Creates an array of the selected objects, or copies, over time.
	Align, Normal Align, Place Highlight, Align Camera, Align to View	Opens the alignment dialog box for positioning objects, enables objects to be aligned by their normals, determines the location of highlights, or aligns objects to a camera or view.
My Selection	Named Selection Sets drop-down list	Selects a set of named objects.
	Open Track View	Opens the Track View.
	Open Schematic View	Opens the Schematic View.
	Material Editor	Opens the Material Editor window.
	Render Scene	Opens the Render Scene dialog box for setting rendering options.
	Quick Render (Production), Quick Render (Draft)	Produces a quick test rendering of the current viewport without opening the Render Scene dialog box.
View	Render Type drop-down list	Selects the area to render.
	Render Last	Renders once again the last viewport to be rendered.

Using the Command Panel

If there is a heart to the MAX interface, it would be the Command Panel. This is where most of the functions and parameters are located. The Command Panel dynamically updates the parameters associated with each function in rollouts. Each rollout includes a title bar with a plus or minus sign. Clicking the rollout title will display or retract the rollout.

Displaying all the rollouts for a given function will often exceed the screen space allotted to the Command Panel. To access the rollouts at the bottom of the Command Panel, move the cursor around the Command Panel until a hand cursor appears. With the hand cursor, left-click and drag in either direction to scroll the Command Panel. Right-clicking within the rollout sections will enable a pop-up menu that enables you to open or close any or all rollouts.

The Command Panel has six tabs across the top, each displaying a separate icon. These icons open different function panels, including Create, Modify, Hierarchy, Motion, Display, and Utilities. Figure 2-14 shows the Command Panel.

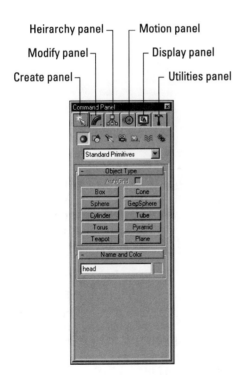

Heirarchy panel ┐ ┌ Motion panel

Modify panel ┐ ┌ Display panel

Create panel ┐ ┌ Utilities panel

Figure 2-14: The Command Panel includes several tabs.

Create panel

The Create panel is used to create a variety of scene objects. The panel includes several categories and subcategories of objects. The categories, shown in Figure 2-15, are displayed as icons directly under the Command Panel tabs and include Geometry, Shapes, Lights, Cameras, Helpers, Space Warps, and Systems. Subcategories are displayed in the drop-down list under the category icons. These subcategories will be presented in their respective chapters.

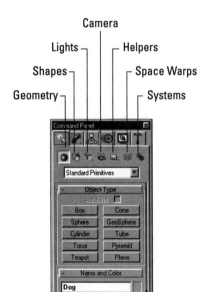

Camera
Lights ─── ┌─ Helpers
Shapes ┐   ┌─ Space Warps
Geometry ┐   ┌─ Systems

Figure 2-15: The Create panel includes several different categories.

The parameters for newly created objects are presented in rollouts. Every object created with the Create panel is given a Name and a Color. The Name can be used to select objects from the Select by Name dialog box and to identify objects. The Color specifies the color used to display the object in the viewports if no material is applied. Both of these parameters can be altered using the Name and Color rollout.

Modify panel

The Modify panel, shown if Figure 2-16, displays Modifiers that can be used to alter objects. To apply a modifier, simply select an object and click the Modifier name button. You can access additional Modifiers by clicking the More button. Any Modifier parameters are displayed in rollouts at the bottom of the panel. The Configure Button Sets button is used to change the buttons that are displayed in the panel.

Configure Button Sets

Figure 2-16: The Modify panel includes buttons for applying Modifiers to an object.

Cross-Reference

More information on the Modify panel can be found in Chapter 9, "Modifying Objects."

The Modify panel also includes the Modifier Stack rollout for managing the Modifiers applied to an object. The *Modifier Stack* is a list, displayed as a drop-down list, of all the Modifiers that have been applied to an object. This Stack lets you revisit any Modifier and change its parameters.

Hierarchy panel

The Hierarchy panel, shown in Figure 2-17, includes three buttons for accessing settings for Pivots, Inverse Kinematics, and Link Information. The Pivots button lets you move and reorient an object's Pivot point. A *Pivot point* is the point about which transformations are applied. *Inverse Kinematics* is a method of defining the connections between parts for easier animation.

Cross-Reference

The details on Pivots, links, and hierarchies are included in Chapter 27, "Building Linked Hierarchies," and details on Inverse Kinematics can be found in Chapter 29, "Creating an Inverse Kinematics System."

Figure 2-17: The Hierarchy panel offers controls for adjusting Pivot Points.

Motion panel

The Motion panel, shown in Figure 2-18, includes two buttons: Parameters and Trajectories. One common way of modifying object motion is to apply *Controllers*. The Parameters button opens the controls that enable you to access animation Controllers. Controllers affect the position, rotation, and scaling of objects in preset ways. You can access a list of Controllers by clicking the Assign Controller button.

The Trajectories button displays the motion path of an object as a spline and opens a rollout for controlling its parameters.

Cross-Reference   Trajectories and Controllers are the subject of Chapter 32, "Animating with Controllers."

Display panel

The Display panel, shown in Figure 2-19, controls how objects are seen within the viewports. Display parameters can be set for individual objects. Using this panel, you can hide or freeze objects and modify all display parameters.

Cross-Reference   Many aspects of the Display panel are covered in Chapter 7, "Selecting and Grouping Objects."

Assign Controller

Figure 2-18: The Motion panel lets you assign animation Controllers.

Figure 2-19: The Display panel includes Display Properties options for the viewport.

Utilities panel

The Utilities panel, shown in Figure 2-20, includes an assortment of miscellaneous tools such as Asset Manager, Camera Match, Measure, Dynamics, Motion Capture, and MAXScript. Clicking the More button can access additional utilities. Many plug-ins are added to this panel when installed. To execute a utility, simply click its button. The functions of these utilities are diverse and are covered in various chapters throughout the book. This panel also includes the Configure Button Sets button.

Figure 2-20: Click the More button to access a list of additional utilities.

Using the Additional Interface Controls

At the bottom of the MAX R3 window are several elements that help you control what's displayed while you're working with the program. These elements are the Viewport Navigation Controls, the Time Controls, the Track Bar, the Status Bar, the Prompt Line, and the MAXScript Listener, as shown in Figure 2-21. This section describes how to use each of these control elements.

Using the Viewport Navigation controls

The standard viewports will show you several different views of your current project, but to alter these basic views you'll need to use the Viewport Navigation buttons. These eight buttons are located at the bottom right corner of the window. With these buttons you can Zoom, Pan, and Rotate views.

Tip   Right-clicking any of these buttons will open the Viewport Configuration dialog box.

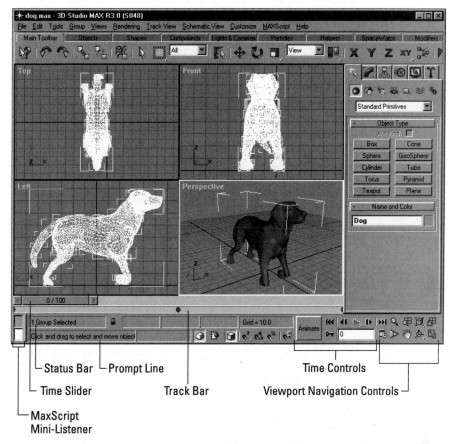

Figure 2-21: Several additional interface controls are located at the bottom of the window.

Table 2-2
Viewport Navigation Controls

Toolbar Button	Name	Description
	Zoom	Simulates moving closer or farther from the objects in the active viewport.
	Zoom All	Zooms in or out of all the viewports simultaneously.
	Zoom Extents, Zoom Extents Selected	Zooms in on the objects or the selected object until it fills the current viewport.

Continued

Table 2-2 (continued)

Toolbar Button	Name	Description
	Zoom Extents All, Zoom Extents All Selected	Zooms in on the objects or the selected object until it fills all the viewports.
	Region Zoom	Zooms into the region selected by dragging the mouse.
	Pan	Moves the view to the left, right, up, or down.
	Arc Rotate, Arc Rotate Selected, Arc Rotate SubObject	Rotates the view around the global axis or selected object. You can spin the base plane by dragging on the viewport or rotate along the perpendicular planes by dragging the green handles shown in the viewport.
	Min/Max Toggle	Makes the current viewport fill the screen. Clicking this button a second time shows all four viewports again.

Tip   The flyout buttons are different only in that they have a different color. All buttons that include solid white apply only to the selected objects. Icons without any white apply to all objects. Yellow applies to subobjects.

Any viewport can be set to be a camera view or a light view. When either of these views is active, the Viewport Navigation buttons change. In camera view, controls for dolly, roll, truck, pan, orbit, and field of view become active. A light view includes controls for falloff and hotspots.

Cross-Reference   Chapter 22, "Controlling Cameras," and Chapter 20, "Controlling Lights," cover these changes in more detail.

Using the Time Controls

Although the Time Controls sound like an interface to a time machine, they are used in MAX to control animation sequences. The buttons that make up the Time Controls are positioned to the left of the Viewport Navigation Controls.

Table 2-3
Time Controls

Toolbar Button	Name	Description
	Toggle Animation Mode	Turns animation mode on and off. This is the largest button in the whole interface and changes to red when active.
	Go to Start	Sets the time to frame 1.
	Previous Frame	Decreases the time by one frame.
	Play Animation, Play Selected	Cycles through the frames. This button becomes a Stop button when an animation is playing.
	Next Frame	Advances the time by one frame.
	Go to End	Sets the time to the final frame.
	Key Mode Toggle	Alters the controls to move between keys. With Key Mode on, the icon turns light blue and the Previous Frame and Next Frame buttons change to Previous Key and Next Key.
	Current Frame field	Indicates the current frame. A frame number can be typed in this field for more exact control than the Time Slider.
	Time Configuration	Opens the Time Configuration dialog box where settings like frame rate, time display, and animation length can be set.

Time Slider

The Time Slider is actually part of the Time Controls. It is the scrollable bar along the bottom of the window that identifies the current frame. The arrows surrounding the slider function the same as the Previous Frame and Next Frame buttons. The slider can be dragged to quickly locate a frame.

Track Bar

Directly underneath the Time Slide is the Track Bar. This bar displays the animation keys. These keys can be selected, moved, and deleted using the Track Bar.

The Track Bar controls are covered in Chapter 30, "Animation Basics."

Learning from the Status Bar and the Prompt Line

As you work, the Status Bar provides valuable information such as the number and type of objects selected, coordinates, and grid size. There is also a Lock Selection Set button. Clicking this button will prevent the selection of any additional objects. The button is yellow when selected.

The spacebar is a keyboard shortcut for toggling the Lock Selection Set button.

The Coordinate fields display the world coordinates or the cursor, unless an object is being transformed. For transformation, these fields show the offset dimensions of the transformation (units for moves, degrees for rotation, percentages for scaling).

The Prompt Line is directly below the Status Bar. If you're stuck as to what to do next, look at the Prompt Line for information on what MAX is expecting. To the right of the Prompt Line are seven buttons:

	Table 2-4 Prompt Line Buttons	
Toolbar Button	**Name**	**Description**
	Plug-In Keyboard Shortcut Toggle	Enables keyboard shortcuts specified by plug-ins instead of MAX's defaults.
	Crossing/Window Selection	Determines how multiple objects are selected. For an object to be selected using Crossing Selection, it must intersect the dragged window. Window Selection requires that the entire object be included. The button default setting is Crossing Selection; depressing the button enables Window Selection.
	Degradation Override	Tells MAX to ignore the degradation settings when rendering an animation in a viewport.

Toolbar Button	Name	Description
	3D Snap Toggle, 2.5D Snap Toggle, 2D Snap Toggle	Specifies the snap mode. 2D snaps only to the active construction grid, 2.5 snaps to the construction grid or to geometry projected from the grid, and 3D snaps to anywhere in 3D space.
	Angle Snap Toggle	Causes rotations to snap to specified angles.
	Percent Snap	Causes scaling to snap to specified percentages.
	Spinner Snap Toggle	Determines the amount a spinner value changes with each click.

Tip   Right-clicking the Degradation Override button opens the Viewpoint Configuration dialog box and displays the Adaptive Degradation settings. Right-clicking the snap toggles opens the Grid and Snap Settings dialog box, except for the Spinner Snap Toggle, which opens the Preference Settings dialog box.

MAXScript Listener

At the right end of the Status Bar is the MAXScript Listener control. By right-clicking in this control, you can view all the current commands recorded by the Listener.

New Feature   The ability to record macros with the MAXScript Listener is new in Release 3. See Chapter 41, "Using MAXScript," for information on how to use this valuable tool.

Interacting with the Interface

Knowing where all the interface elements are located is only the start. MAX includes several interactive features that make the interface work. Learning these features will make a difference between an interface that works for you and one that doesn't.

Right-click menus

Right-click menus have always been a part of the MAX interface, but in Release 3, their function has been greatly expanded. Almost every button, feature, and area has right-click menus associated with it.

Floating and docking panels

All the toolbars, the Tab Panel, the Command Panel, and even the menu bar can be floated and docked around the window. To float a toolbar, drag its title bar into the center of the window. Floating toolbars can be resized and positioned anywhere on the screen. They will always appear on top of the default MAX window.

 New Feature The ability to float and dock toolbars and panels is new to Release 3.

To dock a floating toolbar, move it close to the edge of MAX's window and release the mouse. Or you could right-click the title and select Dock and the location where it should be located. Once a toolbar has been docked and then floated again, double-clicking the title bar will return it to its former docked location.

Understanding the color cues

MAX's interface uses color cues to help remind you of the current mode. For example, when the Animate button is depressed, it turns red. The edge of the current viewport being animated also turns red. This reminds you that any modifications will be saved as keys.

Working in Inverse Kinematics mode is denoted by the color blue. Green indicates normal transform functions and yellow warns of nondefault settings such as working with a subobject. Watching for these color cues can remind you of the current mode.

All these color cues can be altered using the Preference Settings dialog box.

Drag-and-drop features

Dialog boxes that work with files benefit greatly from MAX's drag-and-drop features. The Material Editor, Background Image, View File, and Environmental Settings dialog boxes all use drag-and-drop. One of the best places to use drag-and-drop is with the Asset Manager utility.

Controlling spinners

Spinners are those little controls throughout the Command Panel with a value field and two arrows to the right. As you'd expect, clicking the up arrow increases the value and the down arrow decreases the value. The amount of the increase or decrease depends on the setting in the General tab of the Preference Settings dialog box. Another way to control the spinner value is to click the arrows and drag with the mouse. Dragging up increases the value and down decreases it.

Keyboard shortcuts

Many features include keyboard shortcuts. These shortcuts can give you direct access to a command without moving the mouse. The default shortcuts for the menu commands are listed to the right of the command. You can use the Keyboard panel of the Preference Settings dialog box to view and change the keyboard shortcuts for any feature.

Modeless and persistent dialog boxes

Many dialog boxes in MAX are *modeless*. This means that the dialog box doesn't need to be closed before you can work with objects in the background. The Material Editor is an example of this. With the Material Editor open, you can create, select, and transform objects in the background. Other modeless dialog boxes include the Material/Map Browser, the Render Scene dialog box, the Video Post dialog box, the Transform Type-In dialog box, the Display and Selection Floaters, and the Track and Schematic Views.

Another feature of many, but not all, dialog boxes is *persistence*. This means that values added to a dialog box remain set when the dialog box is reopened. This only applies within a given MAX session. The Reset button and exiting and restarting MAX reset all the dialog boxes.

Using the Asset Manager utility

The Asset Manager utility is opened via the Utilities panel. The Asset Manager, shown in Figure 2-22, resembles Windows Explorer, except that it displays thumbnail images of all the supported formats contained within the current directory. With the Asset Manager open, files can be dragged and dropped directly into locations that accept files, such as the Material Editor map buttons.

The supported file types include AVI, BMP, CIN, CEL, GIF, IFL, IPP, JPEG, PNG, PSD, MOV, RGB, RLA, RPF, VST, TIF, and YUV. These are the same types that the File ⇨ View File command can open.

Once the Asset Manager is opened, it can also be displayed within a viewport by right-clicking the viewport title and selecting Views ⇨ Extended ⇨ Asset Manager from the pop-up menu.

Across the top of the Asset Manager window are several buttons. These buttons will let you open the selected thumbnail in the Virtual Frame Buffer; view the image properties; sort by name, extension, size, or date; display three different thumbnail sizes; filter image types to display; and take advantage of other useful features such as working with cached images.

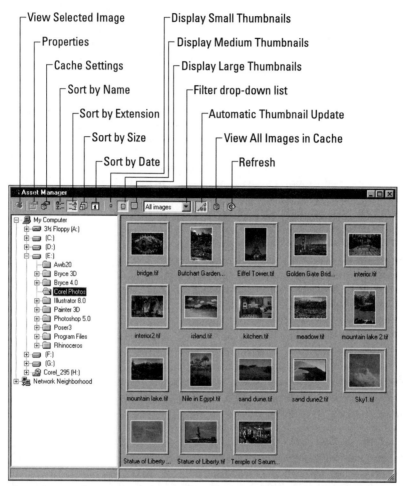

Figure 2-22: The Asset Manager utility displays thumbnails of all the images in the local directory.

Getting Help

The first icon on the main toolbar has an arrow and a question mark. This tool is the context-sensitive help. To get help on any item in the interface, simply click this tool and click again on the item in question. This will cause the online help window to open with the needed information.

MAX's comprehensive online reference is also available by selecting Help ⇨ Online Reference. This opens the Online Reference window, shown in Figure 2-23, that enables searches by index and keyword. The Help menu also includes a Learning 3D Studio MAX option that launches tutorials. Both of these help systems are based on Microsoft's HTML Help engine that enables them to update their content via the Web and keeps the reference materials and tutorials current and accurate.

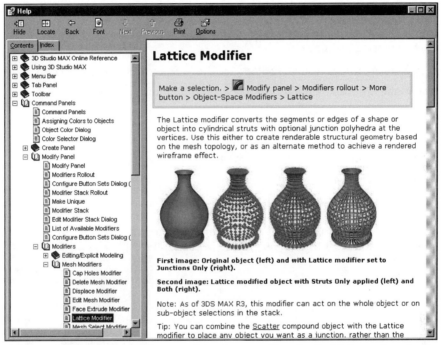

Figure 2-23: The Online Reference dialog box provides detailed information about all of MAX's features.

The Additional Help option offers additional reference guides — the MAXScript Reference and Product Support Help. Help files for any installed plug-ins are accessible from the Additional Help command.

The Kinetix Web site has several tutorials on a variety of topics and new ones are being added all the time. You can locate these resources by going to www.ktx.com.

Summary

You should now be familiar with the interface for MAX, including many of the new features added with this release. Understanding the interface is one of the keys to success in using 3D Studio MAX. MAX includes a variety of different interface elements. Among the menus, toolbars, and keyboard shortcuts, there are several ways to perform the same command. Discover the method that works best for you.

This chapter covered the following topics:

✦ Exploring 3D space

✦ Viewing the pull-down menus

✦ Using the Tab Panel, Main Toolbar, and Command Panel

✦ Navigating the viewport

✦ Controlling animation sequences with Time Controls

✦ Getting information from the Status Bar and Prompt Line

✦ Interfacing with the MAX interface

✦ Obtaining and updating online help

Now that you've learned about all the various elements that make up the interface, you can customize it to your liking. The next chapter explains how to customize the interface.

✦   ✦   ✦

Customizing the MAX Interface

◆ ◆ ◆ ◆

In This Chapter

Using the Customize menu

Customizing toolbars, the Tab Panel, and Command Panel buttons

Configuring paths and viewports

Setting preferences

Selecting system unit, grid, and snap settings

◆ ◆ ◆ ◆

When you get into a new car, one of the first things you do is to rearrange the seat and mirrors. You do this to make yourself comfortable. The same principle can apply to software packages — arranging or customizing an interface makes it more comfortable to work with.

Previous versions of MAX allowed only minimal changes to the interface, but Release 3 enables significant customization. This chapter covers various ways to make the MAX interface more comfortable.

The Customize Menu

You can tell that Kinetix was serious about enabling users to customize the interface with the inclusion of the new Customize menu. This menu lets you not only customize the interface settings, set preferences, and configure the viewports, but also load and save customized interface setups. This is especially helpful for users who share a copy of MAX. (Now if we could only get cars that could save a custom setup.)

New Feature The Customize menu is new to Release 3, as are many of the commands contained therein.

Loading a custom interface

Custom interface setups are saved with the .CUI extension. The default MAX install includes several predefined interface setups that are located in the UI subdirectory. Select Customize ➪ Load Custom UI. The standard available interfaces include

✦ **DefaultUI** — Default interface that opens when first installed. Opens with only the Tab Panel.

✦ **DefaultUI_Option2** — Adds the main toolbar underneath the Tab Panel.

✦ **GamesModeling** — Includes easy access to several modeling and custom toolbars including a button to Hide the Command Panel.

✦ **GamesModeling_Option2** — Same as the GamesModeling layout, except there is only one toolbar to the left of the viewports and the Tab Panel is used to organize the available toolbars.

✦ **MAXCustom** — Includes the Tab Panel, the main toolbar, and select modeling tools around the viewports.

✦ **MAXStart** — Same as the DefaultUI. This is the interface that MAX loads when it first starts.

✦ **TextUI** — Includes text-labeled Primitives and Modifiers toolbars on either side of the viewports.

 Tip   Any custom .cui file can be loaded as the default interface from the command line by adding a **–c** and the .cui file name after the 3dsmax.exe file (for example, **3dsmax.exe –c my_interface.cui**).

Tutorial: Saving a custom interface

Personalized interfaces can be saved for later recall in the UI subdirectory. Select Customize ➪ Save Custom UI.

To have MAX start with your custom interface, follow these steps:

1. Customize your interface by making any desired changes.

2. Select Customize ➪ Save Custom UI As. The Save UI File As dialog box opens.

3. Open the UI subdirectory (if you are not already there), select the MAXStart.cui file, and click OK.

4. Click OK to replace the existing file.

 Tip   MAX can be set to automatically save your interface changes when exiting. Select the Save UI Configuration on Exit option in the General tab of the Preference Settings dialog box.

Locking the interface

Once you're comfortable with your interface changes, it is a good idea to lock the interface to prevent accidental changes. To lock the current interface, choose Customize ➪ Lock UI Layout.

Reverting to the startup interface

When you're first playing around with MAX's customization features, it can be easy to really mess things up. If you get in a bind, you can reload the default startup interface with the Customize ➪ Revert to Startup UI Layout command.

 Tip   If your MAXStart.cui file gets messed up, you can reinstate the original default interface setup by deleting the MAXStart.cui file before starting MAX.

Customizing Toolbars

The key to customizing the interface is the Customize ➪ Custom UI command. This will open the Customize User Interface dialog box where you can control all toolbars, tooltips, and icons. Figure 3-1 shows this dialog box.

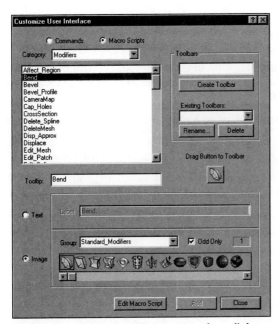

Figure 3-1: The Customize User Interface dialog box enables you to create new toolbars.

 Tip   Right-clicking any button and choosing Customize from the pop-up menu can also open the Customize User Interface dialog box.

Tutorial: Creating a custom toolbar

If you've been using MAX for a while, you probably have several favorite commands that you use extensively.

To create a custom toolbar with your favorite commands, follow these steps:

1. Open the Customize User Interface dialog box by choosing Customize ➪ Custom UI.

2. Under Toolbars, enter the name of your new toolbar and click Create Toolbar. The new toolbar appears behind the dialog box.

3. View all the MAX commands by clicking the Commands radio button at the top of the dialog box. Select the first command you wish to include as a button on a toolbar.

4. Type a Tooltip for the selected command in the Tooltip field below the list of commands.

5. Select a Text label or an Image icon by clicking the Text or Image radio button.

6. Do one of the following:

   • If you selected the Image option in Step 5, choose a Group and an icon from the scroll box below it. The selected icon will be displayed in a button to the right of the Tooltip.

   • If you selected the Text option in Step 5, change the text label as desired. The text will appear inside a button to the right of the Tooltip.

6. To add the command to your toolbar, drag the button to the toolbar.

7. Repeat these steps for each new command to add to the toolbar. When you've completed the toolbar, click the Close button to exit the dialog box.

With the new toolbar created, you can float, dock, or add this toolbar to the Tab Panel just like the other toolbars.

Changing a button's appearance

You can easily change the buttons on any toolbar by right-clicking the button. This will open a pop-up menu where you can select the Edit Button Appearance command. This command opens the Edit Macro Button dialog box, shown in Figure 3-2. This dialog box is a subset of the Customize User Interface face dialog box and enables quick changes to an icon, tooltip, or text label.

Tip   If a text label doesn't fit within the toolbar button, you can increase the button width using the Fixed Width Text Buttons spinner in the General tab of the Preference Settings dialog box.

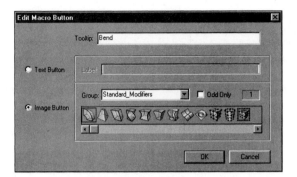

Figure 3-2: The Edit Macro Button dialog box provides a quick way to change an icon, tooltip, or text label.

Removing toolbars and buttons

Custom toolbars can be removed by opening the Customize User Interface dialog box with the Customize ➪ Custom UI command. Next, select the toolbar name from the Existing Toolbars drop-down list and click the Delete button. Alternatively, the toolbar can be renamed using the Rename button.

You can remove toolbar icons or text labels by right-clicking the button and selecting Delete Button from the pop-up menu.

Using the Delete Button function, you can even delete the buttons on the main toolbar. If you accidentally delete a required toolbar, simply load the Startup interface with the Customize ➪ Revert to Startup UI Layout command.

Adding scripts to a toolbar

You can display a list of Macro Scripts, divided by category in the Customize User Interface dialog box, by selecting the Macro Scripts radio button at the top of the dialog box. Following the same steps described earlier in the "Creating Custom Toolbars" section, scripts can be added to the toolbars.

Many of the standard functions such as creating primitive objects are implemented as Macro Scripts.

The Customize User Interface dialog box also includes a button that enables scripts to be edited. Clicking the Edit Macro Script button opens the currently selected script in a text editor. Edit Macro Script is also accessible by right-clicking any macro script button.

Tutorial: Adding custom icons

The MAX interface uses two different sizes of icons. Large icons are 24×24 pixels and small icons are 16×15 pixels. Large icons can be 24-bit color and small ones must be only 16-bit. All icons are loaded from the UI subdirectory. The easiest way to create some custom toolbars is to copy an existing set of icons into an image-editing program, make the modifications, and save them under a different name.

To create a new group of icons, follow these steps:

1. Select a group of current icons to edit from the UI directory and open them in Photoshop. I've selected the Cameras group. This group includes only two icons. To edit icons used for both large and small icon settings and both active and inactive states, open the following four files: Cameras_16a.bmp, Cameras_16i.bmp, Cameras_24a.bmp, and Cameras_24i.bmp.

2. In each file, the icons are all included side by side in the same file, so the first two files are 32×15 and the second two are 48×24. Edit the files, being sure to keep each icon within its required dimensions.

3. When you've finished editing or creating the icons, save each file with the name of the icon group in front of the underscore character. My files were saved as Kels_16a.bmp, Kels_16i.bmp, Kels_24a.bmp, and Kels_24i.bmp. Make sure the files are placed in the UI directory.

4. Once the files are saved, you'll need to restart MAX. The icon group will then be available within the Customize User Interface dialog box.

Figure 3-3 shows the Edit Macro Button dialog box with my custom icon group named "Kels" open.

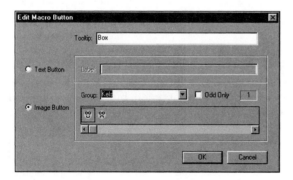

Figure 3-3: This figure shows the Edit Macro Button dialog box with a custom icon group selected.

Customizing the Tab Panel

The Tab Panel makes all possible toolbars available. When you click a tab, its toolbar appears. The default toolbars include the following: Main Toolbar, Objects, Shapes, Compounds, Lights & Cameras, Particles, Helpers, SpaceWarps, Modifiers, Modeling, and Rendering.

New Feature   The Tab Panel is a new, efficient way to work with toolbars.

By right-clicking any tab, you can modify the Tab Panel. From the pop-up menu you can choose to add a tab, delete a tab, or rename a tab. There are also options to move tabs to the left or the right.

Tabs on the Tab Panel can be converted to floating toolbars by selecting Convert to Toolbar from the tab's right-click menu, or simply by dragging the tab away from the Tab Panel.

A toolbar can be added to the Tab Panel by right-clicking its title bar and selecting Move to Tab Panel. It will be added to the right end of the Tab Panel.

Configuring Paths

When strolling through a park, you can be assured that any paths you encounter lead somewhere. One might take you to the lake and another to the playground. Knowing where the various paths lead can help you as you navigate around the park. Paths in MAX lead, or point to, various resources, either locally or across the network.

All paths can be configured using the Configure Paths dialog box, shown in Figure 3-4. This dialog box is opened using the Customize ➪ Configure Paths command. The dialog box includes four tabs: General, Plug Ins, Bitmaps, and XRefs.

New Feature

The XRefs tab is new to Release 3. It specifies where to look for external resources and can include several paths.

When MAX Release 3 is installed, all the paths are set to point to the default subdirectories where MAX was installed. To modify a path, select the path and click the Modify button. A file dialog box will let you locate the new directory.

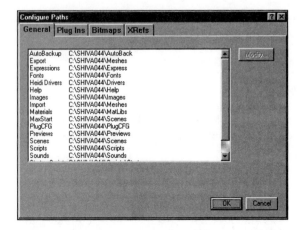

Figure 3-4: The Configure Paths dialog box specifies where to look for various resources.

The General tab includes paths for the following:

✦ **AutoBackup** — Directory where backups are saved

✦ **Export** — Directory where exported files are saved

✦ **Expressions** — Directory containing expression files

✦ **Fonts** — Directory containing fonts

✦ **Heidi Drivers** — Directory containing the Heidi Drivers

✦ **Help** — Directory containing help files

✦ **Images** — Directory to open when loading images

✦ **Import** — Directory to open when importing geometry

✦ **Materials** — Directory containing material files

✦ **MAXStart** — Directory containing programs to execute when MAX is started

✦ **PlugCFG** — Directory containing plug-in configuration files

✦ **Previews** — Directory where previews are saved

✦ **Scenes** — Directory where saved scene files are stored

✦ **Scripts** — Directory where scripts are stored

✦ **Sounds** — Directory to open when sound files are loaded

✦ **Startup Scripts** — Directory containing scripts that load when MAX is started

✦ **VideoPost** — Directory where Video Post output is saved

Under the Plug Ins, Bitmaps, and XRefs tabs, you can add and delete additional paths. All paths will be searched when looking for resources such as plug-ins, but file dialog boxes will open only to the first path. Use the Move Up and Move Down buttons to realign path entries.

Note   Using the Customize ➪ Revert to Startup UI Layout command will not reset path configuration changes.

Setting Preferences

The Preference Settings let you configure MAX so it works in a way that is most comfortable for you. This dialog box is opened by selecting Customize ➪ Preferences.

General preferences

The first tab in the Preference Settings dialog box is for General settings. Figure 3-5 shows the dialog box with the General tab selected.

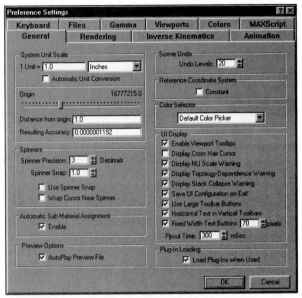

Figure 3-5: The General panel enables you to change the unit scale, among other options.

The General panel includes many global settings that affect several features.

Setting the System Unit Scale

The System Unit Scale option enables you to define the measurement system used by MAX. Options include Inches, Feet, Miles, Millimeters, Centimeters, Meters, and Kilometers. Units directly relate to parameters entered with the keyboard. For example, with the units set to meters, a sphere created with the radius parameter of 2 would be 4 meters across.

There is also a multiplier field that can be used to alter the value of each unit. The Automatic Unit Conversion toggle will convert all existing objects to a new unit system, so you could change all objects in a scene from feet to meters.

Origin and Spinner settings

The Origin control helps you determine the accuracy of an object as it is moved away from the scene origin. If you know how far objects will be located from the origin, then entering that value will tell you the Resulting Accuracy. This can be used to determine the accuracy of your parameters. Objects farther from the origin will have a lower accuracy.

Spinners are interface controls that enable you to enter values or interactively increase or decrease the value by clicking the arrows on the right. The Preferences Settings dialog box includes settings for changing the number of decimals displayed in spinners and the increment or decrement value for clicking an arrow. The Use Spinner Snap option enables the snap mode. The snap mode can also be enabled using the Spinner Snap button on the Status Bar.

You can also change the values in the spinner by clicking the arrows and dragging up to increase the value or down to decrease it. The Wrap Cursor Near Spinner option keeps the cursor close to the spinner when you change values by dragging with the mouse, so you can drag the mouse continuously without worrying about hitting the top or bottom of the screen.

Tip   A quick way to access these spinner settings is to right-click the Spinner Snap Toggle button at the bottom of the screen.

Sub-Material and Preview settings

The Automatic Sub-Material Assignment option, when enabled, enables materials to be dragged and dropped directly onto a subobject selection.

The AutoPlay Preview File setting will automatically play Preview Files in the default media player when they are finished rendering.

Undo, Constant Coordinate System, and Color Selector settings

The Scene Undo spinner sets the number of commands that can be kept in a buffer for undoing. A smaller number will free up memory, but will not let you backtrack through your work.

The Reference Coordinate System, when set to Constant, causes all transforms to use the defined coordinate system. When the Reference Coordinate System is not set to Constant, each transform will use the coordinate system last selected.

The Color Selector section lets you pick which type of color selector to use.

Interface Display settings

Finally, toggle switches in the UI Display section control additional aspects of the interface. Enable Viewport Tooltips can toggle tooltips on or off. Display Cross Hair Cursor will change the cursor from the Windows default arrow to a crosshair cursor similar to the one used in AutoCAD.

For some actions, such as nonuniform scaling, MAX will display a warning dialog box asking if you are sure of the action. To disable these warnings uncheck the corresponding settings. Actions with warnings include nonuniform scaling, topology-dependence, and collapsing the Modifier Stack.

The Save UI Configuration on Exit switch will automatically save any interface configuration changes.

Use Large Toolbar Buttons can be deselected, enabling the use of smaller toolbar buttons and icons that will reclaim valuable screen real estate.

The Horizontal Text in Vertical Toolbars options will fix the problem of text buttons that take up too much space, especially when printed horizontally on a vertical toolbar. You can also specify a width for text buttons. Any text larger than this value will be clipped off at the edges of the button.

The Flyout Time spinner will adjust the time the system waits before displaying flyout buttons.

Loading Plug-Ins

The Load Plug-Ins When Used option keeps plug-ins out of memory until they are accessed. This saves valuable memory and still makes the plug-ins accessible.

Rendering preferences

Figure 3-6 shows the Preference Settings dialog box with the Rendering tab selected. Many of these settings will be discussed in greater detail in the Rendering sections, but a few are mentioned here.

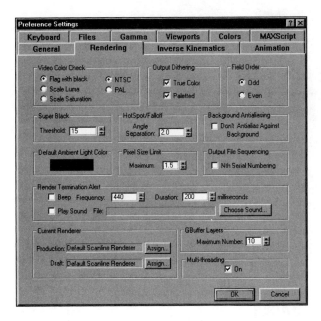

Figure 3-6: The Rendering panel includes settings such as the ambient light color and the current renderer.

Cross-Reference The Rendering Preferences are discussed in detail in Chapter 36, "Setting Rendering Parameters."

The Rendering panel includes controls for setting the Video Color Check, Output Dithering, and Field Order. In addition, you can set the Super Black Threshold, Hotspot Falloff, Background Anti-Aliasing, Default Ambient Light Color, and Output

File Sequencing in this panel. There are also controls for playing an alert sound when a rendering is finished, and you can select different renderers to use for production and draft output. There are also settings to determine the number of Gbuffers and for enabling multi-threading.

Inverse Kinematics preferences

The Inverse Kinematics panel, shown in Figure 3-7, includes Positional, Rotational, and Iteration Thresholds for both Applied IK and Interactive IK.

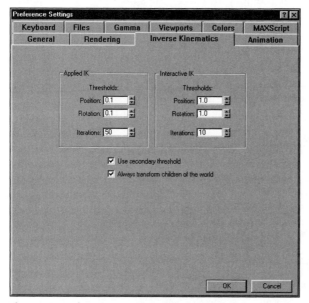

Figure 3-7: The Inverse Kinematics panel of the Preference Settings dialog box includes threshold values for Inverse Kinematics systems.

Cross-Reference   These will be discussed in greater detail in Chapter 29, "Creating an Inverse Kinematics System."

Animation preferences

The Animation panel, shown in Figure 3-8, contains options dealing with animations. When a specific frame is selected, all objects with keys for that frame are surrounded with white brackets. The Animation panel offers options that specify which objects get these brackets. Options include All Objects, Selected Objects, and None. You can also limit the brackets to only those objects with certain transform keys.

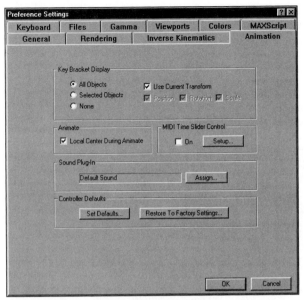

Figure 3-8: The Animation panel includes settings for displaying Key Brackets.

The Local Center During Animate option causes all objects to be animated about their local centers. Turning this option off enables animations about other centers (such as screen and world).

The MIDI Time Slider Controls include an On option and a Setup button. The Setup button opens the MIDI Time Slider Control Setup dialog box shown in Figure 3-9. When this control is set up, you can control an animation using a MIDI device.

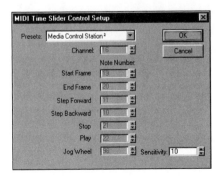

Figure 3-9: The MIDI Time Slider Control Setup dialog box lets you set up specific notes to start, stop, and step through an animation.

The Animation panel can be used to assign a new Sound Plug-In to use. This panel can also be used to set the default values of all animation Controllers. Clicking the Set Defaults button opens the Set Controller Defaults dialog box. This dialog box includes a list of all the Controllers and a Set button. When you select a Controller and click the Set button, another dialog box appears with all the values for that Controller.

Keyboard preferences

If used properly, keyboard shortcuts can increase your efficiency dramatically. Figure 3-10 shows the Keyboard panel of the Preferences Settings dialog box. In this panel you can assign shortcuts to any command, and define sets of shortcuts. Keyboard shortcuts can be assigned for the Main interface, Track View, Schematic View, Material Editor, Video Post, and any installed plug-ins.

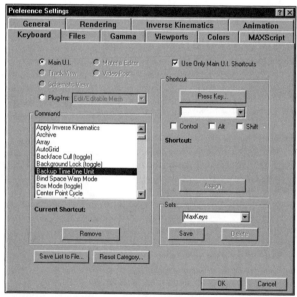

Figure 3-10: The Keyboard panel enables you to create keyboard shortcuts for any command.

Tutorial: Assigning keyboard shortcuts

Do you use both hands to control the mouse? If not, then you have one hand that is idle most of the time. If you can train this hand to control features using the keyboard, then you will be much more efficient.

To assign a keyboard shortcut, follow these steps:

1. Open the Preferences Settings dialog box by selecting Customize ➪ Preferences.

2. Click the Keyboard tab. This will display a list of available commands for the Main UI, Track View, Schematic View, Plug-Ins, Material Editor, and Video Post.

Note

If only the Main UI feature is available, deselect the Use Only Main UI Shortcuts box to view all options.

3. From the list of commands, select the one to which you want to assign a keyboard shortcut; then from the Shortcut section on the right, choose a keystroke to use for the shortcut. You can use the drop-down list of special keys or click the Press Key button to have MAX intercept the keyboard keys as you press them.

4. When the correct shortcut is displayed, click the Assign button to add this shortcut to the current set. If you've made a mistake, click the Remove button to eliminate the shortcut.

5. Click the Save button to save any changes to the current keyboard set.

File preferences

The Files panel holds the controls for backing up, archiving, and logging MAX files. Files can be set to be backed-up, saved incrementally, or compressed when saved. Figure 3-11 shows this panel.

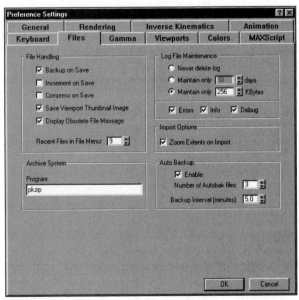

Figure 3-11: The Files panel includes an Auto Backup feature.

Handling files and archives

The Files panel includes several options that define how to handle files. You can enable an option to Backup on Save. This causes the existing copy of a file to be saved as a backup (with the .bak extension) before saving the new file. This always retains two copies of the file.

The Increment on Save option adds an incremented number onto the end of the existing file every time it is saved. This retains multiple copies of the file.

The Compress on Save option compresses the file automatically when it is saved. Compressed files require less file space, but take longer to load.

The Save Viewport Thumbnail Image option saves a 64×64 pixel thumbnail of the active viewport along with the file. This thumbnail is displayed in the Open dialog box.

When a MAX file created in a previous version of MAX is opened, a warning dialog box appears that says, "Obsolete data format found – Please resave file." To eliminate this warning, disable the Display Obsolete File Message option.

The Recent Files in File Menu option determines the number of recently opened files that appear at the bottom of the File menu.

The Archive System lets you specify which archive program MAX will use to archive your files.

Maintaining log files

You can also use the Files panel to control log files. Logs keep track of any Errors, general command Info, and any debugging information. You can set log files to never be deleted, expire after so many days, or keep a specified file size with the latest information. If your system is having trouble, checking the error log will give you some idea as to what the problem is. Logs are essential if you plan on developing any custom scripts or plug-ins.

The name of the log file is MAX.log. It is saved in the "network" subdirectory. Figure 3-12 shows a portion of the log file.

Import Options

The Import Options group has only a single option: Zoom Extents on Import. When this option is enabled, it automatically zooms all viewports to their extents. Imported objects can often be scaled so small that they aren't even visible. This option helps you to locate an object when imported.

Caution   If you are importing an object into a scene with several objects, then this option will not necessarily make the imported object visible.

```
Max.log - Notepad                                                    _ □ ×
File  Edit  Search  Help
1999/05/12 19:29:50 DBG: Starting network
1999/05/12 19:57:31 INF: Loaded C:\shiva048\scenes\Lens Effects - Size and Intensity.max
1999/05/12 19:57:48 DBG: Starting network
1999/05/12 19:58:15 INF: Loaded C:\shiva048\scenes\Lens Effects - Size and Intensity.max
1999/05/12 19:58:17 WRN: Can't open file or file has no audio streams.
1999/05/12 19:58:18 INF:    Job: C:\shiva048\scenes\Lens Effects - Size and Intensity.max

1999/05/12 20:32:07 INF: Loaded C:\shiva048\scenes\Lens Effects - Ray - Num and Sharp.max
1999/05/12 20:32:07 INF:    Job: C:\shiva048\scenes\Lens Effects - Ray - Num and Sharp.max

1999/05/12 21:17:44 INF: Loaded C:\shiva048\scenes\Lens Effects - Auto Secondary.max
1999/05/12 21:17:45 INF:    Job: C:\shiva048\scenes\Lens Effects - Auto Secondary.max

1999/05/12 23:40:32 DBG: Stop network
1999/05/13 06:05:13 DBG: Starting network
1999/05/13 06:06:28 INF: Loaded C:\shiva048\scenes\sent\hedra stairs.max
1999/05/13 06:06:29 INF:    Job: C:\shiva048\scenes\sent\hedra stairs.max

1999/05/13 07:49:18 DBG: Stop network
1999/05/13 21:26:12 DBG: Starting network
1999/05/13 21:26:32 INF: Loaded C:\shiva048\scenes\sent\dog.max
1999/05/13 21:26:34 INF:    Job: C:\shiva048\scenes\sent\dog.max

1999/05/13 22:04:40 WRN: WSD - Configuration not found. Using defaults.
1999/05/13 22:04:44 ERR: TCP/IP - Error resolving accon.
Invalid name or TCP/IP subsystem not installed correctly.1999/05/13 22:04:47 ERR: WSD - Cann
1999/05/13 23:13:59 DBG: Stop network
1999/05/14 06:31:03 DBG: Starting network
1999/05/14 06:31:39 INF: Loaded C:\shiva048\scenes\dog.max
1999/05/14 06:31:42 INF:    Job: C:\shiva048\scenes\dog.max
```

Figure 3-12: The log file keeps track of all files that are opened in MAX.

Tutorial: Setting Auto Backup

The Auto Backup feature in MAX can save you from the nightmare of losing all your work due to a system crash. With Auto Backup enabled, you can select the number of Autobak Files and how often the files are backed-up.

To set up this feature, follow these steps:

1. Open the Preferences Settings dialog box by selecting Customize ⇨ Preferences and click the Files tab.

2. Turn on Auto Backup by selecting the Enable option.

3. Set the number of Autobak files to **3**.

Tip   To maintain version control of your MAX scenes, use the Increment on Save feature instead of increasing the Number of Autobak Files.

4. Set the Backup Interval to the amount of time to wait between backups. The Backup Interval should be set the maximum amount of work that you are willing to redo. (I keep my settings at 15 minutes.)

5. Auto Backup will save the files in the directory specified by the Auto Backup path. To view where this path is located, select Customize ⇨ Configure Paths.

Gamma preferences

The Gamma panel, shown in Figure 3-13, controls the gamma correction for the display and for bitmap files.

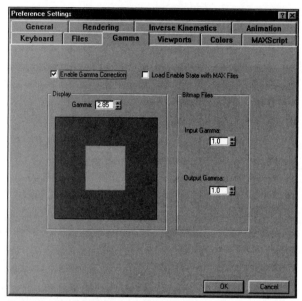

Figure 3-13: Enabling gamma correction makes colors consistent regardless of the monitor.

Setting screen gamma

Have you ever noticed in an electronics store that television screen displays vary in color? Colors on monitor screens may be fairly consistent for related models, but may vary across brands. *Gamma settings* are a means by which colors can be consistently represented regardless of the monitor that is being used.

Gamma value is a numerical offset required by an individual monitor in order to be consistent with a standard. To enable gamma correction for MAX, open the Gamma panel in the Preferences Settings dialog box, and click the Enable Gamma Correction option. To determine the gamma value, use the spinner or adjust the value until the gray square blends in unnoticeably with the background.

Setting bitmap gamma

Many bitmap formats, such as TGA, contain their own gamma settings. The Input Gamma setting for Bitmap files sets the gamma for bitmaps that don't have a gamma setting. The Output Gamma setting is the value set for bitmaps being output from MAX.

Tip   Match the Input Gamma value to the Display Gamma value so that bitmaps loaded for textures will be displayed correctly.

Viewport preferences

The viewports are your window into the scene. The Viewports panel, shown in Figure 3-14, contains many options for controlling these viewports.

Figure 3-14: The Viewports panel contains several viewport parameter settings.

Viewport Parameter options

In the Viewport Parameters group are several options specific to viewports. The Use Dual Planes option enables a method designed to speed up viewport redraws. Objects close to the scene are included in a front plane and objects farther back are included in a back plane. When this option is enabled only the objects on the front plane are redrawn.

In subobject mode, the default is to display vertices as small plus signs. The Show Vertices as Dots option lets you display vertices as either Small or Large dots.

The Draw Links as Lines option shows all displayed links as lines that connect the two linked objects.

The Backface Cull on Object Creation option shows the backfaces of objects when viewed in wireframe mode.

Note   There is also a Backface Cull option in the Object Properties dialog box.

The Attenuate Lights option causes objects farther back in a viewport to appear darker. *Attenuation* is the property that causes lights to diminish over distance.

In the Viewport Configuration dialog box, you can set Safe Regions, which are borders that the renderer will include. The Mask Viewport to Safe Region causes the objects beyond the Safe Region border to be invisible.

The Update Background While Playing option causes viewport background bitmaps to be updated while an animation sequence plays. Viewport backgrounds can be filtered if the Filter Environment Background option is enabled, but this slows the update time. If this option is disabled, the background image appears aliased and pixelated. For quicker refresh times, enable the Low-Res Environment Background option. This reduces the resolution of the background image by half and resizes it to fill the viewport. Enabling this option results in a blocky appearance, but the viewport updates much more quickly.

The Display World Axis option displays the axes in the lower left corner of each viewport.

The arrow keys can be used to nudge objects into position. The Grid Nudge Distance is the distance that an object moves when the arrow keys are pressed.

Objects without scale, such as lights and cameras, appear in the scene according to the Non-Scaling Object Size value.

Transform options

The Viewports panel includes several options for controlling viewport transforms. There are two options for moving objects in a Perspective view: Intersection and Projection. Intersection moves the object a greater distance into the scene as the cursor approaches the horizon. It can move the object a great distance quickly. The Projection option moves the object slowly and consistently, but it will require mouse movement. The sensitivity of the movements in Projection mode is controlled by the Perspective Sensitivity value. The Rotation Increment value controls the sensitivity of the mouse for rotations. The Viewport Arc Rotate Snap Angle is the angle that is used by the Angle Snap button in the Status Bar.

Transform Gizmo is an apparatus that enables you to visually constrain the transform motion of an object. The On option enables the gizmo in all viewports, and the Size value determines how big it appears. The Use Labels option labels each axis with a letter. The Use Center Box displays a box in the center of the gizmo. Dragging the box moves the object along the axis that is active in the main toolbar. The Use Planes option corner markers are displayed for transforming an object in a plane.

Enabling Ghosting

Ghosting is similar to the use of "onion-skins" in traditional animation, enabling an object's prior position and next position to be displayed. When producing animation, it is helpful to know where you're going and where you've come from. Enabling Ghosting will enable you to produce better animations.

There are several Ghosting options. You can set whether a ghost appears before the current frame, after the current frame, or both before and after the current frame. You can set the total number of ghosting frames and how often they should appear. You can also set an option to show the frame numbers. Figure 3-15 shows some objects with ghosting enabled.

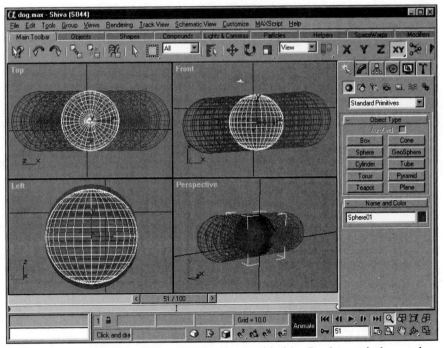

Figure 3-15: Viewing an object with ghosting enabled for five frames before and after the current frame.

Tutorial: Changing display drivers

When MAX was first launched, a simple dialog box asked you which display driver to use (see Figure 3-16). If you were like me, you were anxious to get a look at MAX and didn't pay much attention to this dialog box. However, weeks later when you happen to be looking through your video card information, you realize that your card supports other drivers like OpenGL and Direct 3D. The Viewports panel includes an interface for changing and configuring this driver.

Figure 3-16: The 3D Studio MAX Driver Setup dialog box is used to select the display drivers.

To change display drivers, follow these steps:

1. Open the Preferences Settings dialog box by choosing Customize ➪ Preferences and click the Viewports tab.

2. In the Display Drivers section, the current driver is displayed. Click the Choose Driver button. This opens the 3D Studio MAX Driver Setup dialog box.

3. Select a new driver to use by clicking the appropriate radio button and clicking OK to close the dialog box. The new display drivers will be used the next time you start MAX.

4. Each driver will have unique configuration settings. To access these settings, click the Configure Driver button to the right of the Choose Driver button. In the configuration dialog box that appears, make your changes and click OK.

Note   The driver you use really depends on the video card that you have in your system. Check with the documentation that came with your video card to see what drivers it supports. If you're unsure, use the default Heidi drivers.

Color preferences

Colors are used throughout the MAX interface to indicate various objects, views, and modes. All these colors can be configured through the Colors panel, shown in Figure 3-17. The main sections for colors include the Main UI, Gizmo and Apparatuses, Other Views, Objects, and Grids.

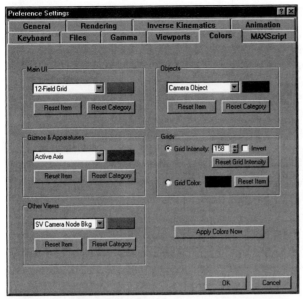

Figure 3-17: The Colors panel lets you set the default colors for the entire interface.

To change a color, select the item from the drop-down list and click the color swatch to the right. This will open the Color Selector. Select the color to use and click OK. When the Apply Colors Now button is clicked, all items are updated. Colors can be set for the elements in the following general categories: Main UI, Objects, Gizmos and Apparatuses, Grids, and Other Views.

MAXScript preferences

Settings for working with MAXScript are included in MAXScript panel, shown in Figure 3-18. These commands include options for loading Startup scripts, controlling the Macro Recorder, the font used in the MAXScript window, and the amount of Memory to use.

New Feature   The MAXScript panel and all of its settings are new to Release 3. The MAXScript commands are covered in detail in Chapter 43, "Using MAXScript."

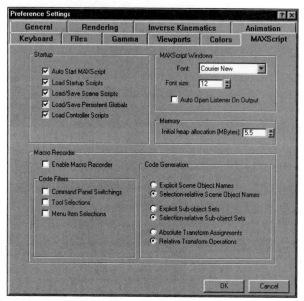

Figure 3-18: The MAXScript panel includes options for controlling MAXScript.

Configuring the Viewports

You can configure each viewport independently by right-clicking the viewport title and selecting Configure from the pop-up menu. The pop-up menu itself includes many of the commands found in the Viewport Configuration dialog box, but the dialog box will let you alter several settings at once.

Note   The Views ⇨ Save Active Viewport command saves the viewport navigation settings for recall, but it does not save the viewport configuration settings.

Setting the Viewport rendering level

Complex scenes take longer to display and render. If every viewport is set to display the highest quality view, then updating each viewport can slow the program to a crawl even on a fast machine. The Viewport Configuration dialog box's Rendering Method panel, shown in Figure 3-19, lets you set the rendering for the Active Viewport, All Viewports, or All But Active viewport as well as the rendering level. The Rendering Level options, from slowest to fastest include the following:

✦ **Smooth + Highlights** — Shows smooth surfaces with lighting highlights. This is the slowest rendering type.

✦ **Smooth** — Shows smooth surfaces without any lighting effects.

✦ **Facets + Highlights** — Shows individual polygon faces and lighting highlights.

✦ **Facets** — Shows individual polygon faces with any lighting effects.

✦ **Lit Wireframes** — Shows polygon edges with lighting effects.

✦ **Wireframe** — Shows polygon edges.

✦ **Bounding Box** — Shows a box that encloses the object. This is the quickest rendering type.

✦ **Edged Faces** — Shows the edges for each face when a shaded rendering method is selected.

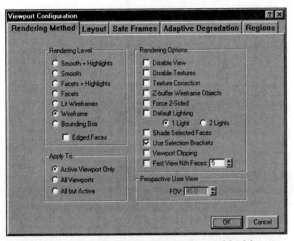

Figure 3-19: The Rendering Method panel holds controls for specifying the Rendering Level and several other Rendering Options.

The most common rendering setting is Wireframe. Faceted rendering displays every face as a flat plane, but it shows the object as a solid model and is good for checking whether objects overlap. The Smooth rendering level shows a rough approximation of the final rendering. Setting the rendering level to include highlights shows the effect of the lights in the scene. Figure 3-20 shows an example of each of the rendering types.

Note   Several effects cannot be seen in the viewport and only show up in the final render. These effects include bump maps, transparent maps, and shadows.

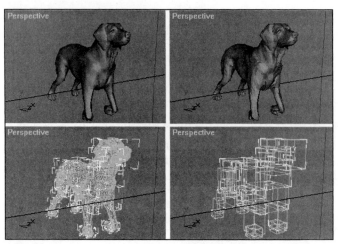

Figure 3-20: Examples of various viewport-rendering types:
Smooth, Faceted, Wireframe, and Bounding Box.

In addition to these shading types, the Rendering Method panel includes several
other options such as Disable View, Disable Textures, Texture Correction, Z-Buffer
wires, Force 2-Sided, and Default Lighting. These options help speed up viewport
updates.

Tip   At any time during a viewport update, you can click the mouse or press a key to
       cancel the redraw. MAX doesn't make you wait for a screen redraw to be able to
       execute commands with the mouse or keyboard shortcuts.

The Disable View option causes a viewport not to be updated when changes are
made. This will increase the speed with which the other viewports update. To
reactivate the viewport, simply select Disable View again. Disable Textures turns off
texture rendering for quick viewport updates. Texture Correction speeds rendering
updates by interpolating the current texture rather than re-rendering. A Z-Buffer is
used to keep track of each object's distance from the camera. Enabling Z-Buffer
Wireframe Objects takes advantage of this buffer for quicker updates.

Force 2-Sided makes both sides of a face visible. For example, suppose you have a
sphere with a hole in it. This setting would enable you to see the interior surface of
the sphere through the hole.

The Default Lighting toggle deactivates your current lights and uses the default
lights. This can be helpful when you're trying to view objects in a dark setting. You
can also specify whether default lighting uses one light or two. Scenes with one
light update quicker than scenes with two.

The Shade Selected Faces is used to shade selected faces in a red, semitransparent look. This enables you to see the faces shaded, but still see what is behind them.

The Use Selection Brackets option displays white corners around the current selection. Selection brackets are useful for helping to see the entire size of a grouped object, but can be annoying if left on with many objects selected, as our previously shown dog in Figure 3-20. Uncheck this option to make these brackets disappear.

Clipping planes defines an invisible barrier beyond which all objects are invisible. For example, if you have a scene with many detailed mountain objects in the background, it can be difficult to work with an object in the front of the scene. By setting the clipping plane between the two, you can work on the front objects without having to update the mountain objects every time you update the scene.

Viewport Clipping places a red line with two arrows on the right side of the viewport, as shown in Figure 3-21. The top arrow represents the back clipping plane and the bottom arrow is the front clipping plane. Drag the arrows to set the clipping planes.

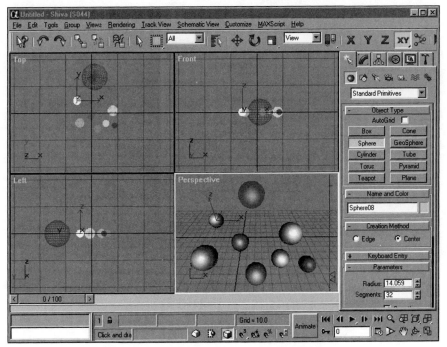

Figure 3-21: Hiding the back half of the viewport with a Clipping Plane

Fast View speeds viewport updates by only drawing a limited number of faces. The spinner value determines how often faces are drawn. For example, a setting of 5 would only draw every fifth face. Fast View will render viewport updates much quicker and give you an idea of the objects without displaying the entire object. Figure 3-22 shows a sphere rendered using the Fast View option. Because each viewport can be configured differently, the Top view is set to display every second polygon. The Front view is set to 3, the Left view to 4, and the Perspective view to 5.

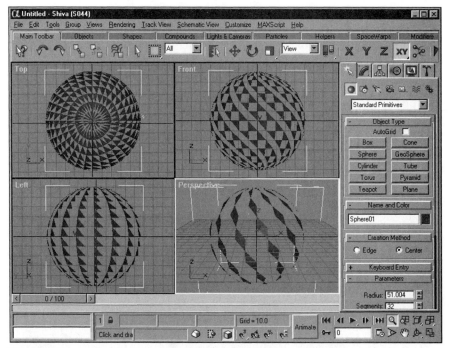

Figure 3-22: Cool patterns created with the Fast View setting in the Viewport Configuration dialog box

Note   If any of these spheres were rendered, the entire sphere would be visible. The Fast View option only affects the viewport display.

You can also alter the Field of View for the Perspective view. To create a fish-eye view, increase the FOV setting to 10 or less. Figure 3-23 shows three views with different FOV settings. The scene on the left has an FOV setting of 80, the middle scene has a normal FOV setting at 50, and the scene on the right has an FOV setting of 10.

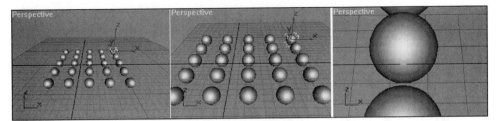

Figure 3-23: Views with different Field of View settings

Altering the Viewport layout

The Layout panel in the Viewpoint Configuration dialog box offers layouts as alternatives to the default layout with its four equally sized viewports. These viewports of differing sizes and positions are shown in Figure 3-24.

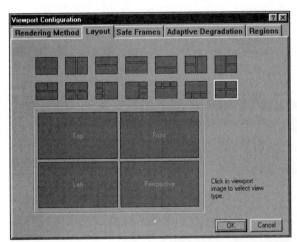

Figure 3-24: The Layout panel offers many layout options.

After selecting a layout from the options at the top of the panel, each individual viewport can be assigned a different view by clicking the viewport and selecting a view from the pop-up menu. The view options include Perspective, User, Front, Back, Top, Bottom, Left, Right, Track, Schematic, Grid, Extended, and Shape.

Views can also be set to Camera and Spotlight if they exist in the scene. Each camera and light that exists will be listed by name.

Tip   MAX includes several keyboard shortcuts for quickly changing the view in the active viewport. The *W* key will expand the active viewport to fill the screen. Pressing *W* a second time will return the viewport to its normal size. Other keyboard shortcuts include *T* (Top View), *B* (Bottom View), *F* (Front View), *K* (Back View), *L* (Left View), *R* (Right View), *C* (Camera View), *S* (Spotlight View), *P* (Perspective View), *U* (User View), *G* (Grid View), and *E* (Track View).

Using Safe Frames

It can be discouraging to complete an animation and convert it to some broadcast medium, only to see that the whole left side of the animation is being cut off in the final screening. Using the Safe Frames feature, you can display some guides within the viewport that will show where these clipping edges are. You can define several different safe frame options, as shown in Figure 3-25, including

✦ **Live Area**—Renders the full screen

✦ **Action Safe**—The area ensured to be visible in the final rendered file

✦ **Title Safe**—The area where the title can safely appear without distortion

✦ **User Safe**—The output area defined by the user

✦ **12-Field Grid**—Displays a grid in the viewport

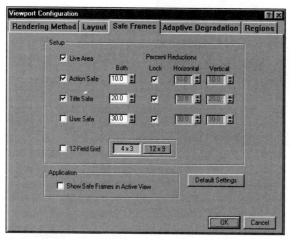

Figure 3-25: The Safe Frames panel lets you specify areas to render.

For each type of safe frame, you can set the percent reduction by entering values in the Horizontal, Vertical, or Both fields. The 12-Field Grid option offers 4×3 and 12×9 aspect ratios.

Understanding Adaptive Degradation

When you are previewing a complex animation sequence in a viewport, slow updates can affect the timing of the animation. This can make it difficult to proof your work and would require many additional, fully rendered tasks. The feature in MAX that addresses this issue is called Adaptive Degradation. It enables you to force a viewport to display at a pre-specified number of frames per second. If the display update takes too long to maintain this rate, then it automatically degrades the rendering level in order to maintain the frame rate. This is very helpful because when you're testing an animation, you are not as concerned about the model details or textures.

The Adaptive Degradation panel is available on the Viewport Configuration dialog box as shown in Figure 3-26.

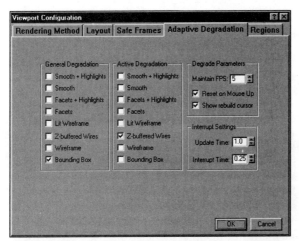

Figure 3-26: The Adaptive Degradation panel maintains a defined frame rate by degrading the rendering level.

Defining regions

Regions, the final panel in the Viewport Configuration dialog box, enables you to define regions and focus your rendering energies on a smaller area. Complex scenes can take considerable time and machine power to render. Sometimes you'll want to test render only a portion of a viewport to check material assignment, texture map placement, or lighting. You can define a Blowup Region, a Sub Region, or a Virtual Viewport. Figure 3-27 shows the Regions panel.

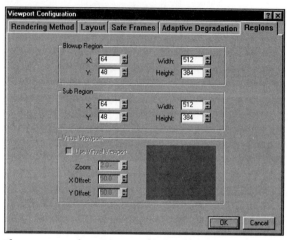

Figure 3-27: The Regions panel enables you to work with smaller regions within your scene.

Selecting System Units

MAX supports several different measurement systems, including Metric and U.S. standard units. You can also define a custom units system. Working with a units system enables you to work with precision and accuracy.

To specify a unit system, use the Customize ➪ Units Setup command. This will display the Units Setup dialog box, shown in Figure 3-28. For the Metric system, options include Millimeters, Centimeters, Meters, and Kilometers. The U.S. standard units system can be set to default units of Feet or Inches. You can also select to work with fractional inches or decimal inches from the drop-down list.

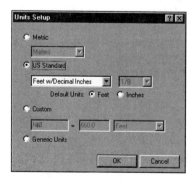

Figure 3-28: The Units Setup dialog box lets you choose which units system to use. Options include Metric, U.S. Standard, Custom, and Generic.

To define a custom units system, modify the fields under the Custom option, including a units label and its equivalence to known units. The final option is to use the default Generic units. Generic units relate distances to each other, but the numbers themselves are irrelevant.

Selecting Grid and Snap Settings

The final Customize menu option is for Grid and Snap Settings. The associated dialog box lets you define which points to snap to and general grid settings. Figure 3-29 shows the four panels in the Grid and Snaps Settings dialog box. This dialog box includes four tab panels, including Snaps, Options, Home Grid, and User Grids.

Figure 3-29: The Grid and Snap Settings dialog box includes four different panels.

The Snaps panel offers several options for snapping objects. Possible snap points include Grid Points and Lines, Pivots, Bounding Box, Perpendicular, Tangent, Vertex, Endpoint, Edge, Midpoint, Face, and Center Face. The drop-down list offers Standard snap points and NURBS snap points as options.

The Options panel will let you set markers in order to see the various specified snap points. You can set the size and color of the markers. The Options panel also contains settings for the Snap Strength (which determines how close an object must be to a snap point in order to be snapped) as well as toggles for Snap to frozen objects and using Axis constraints when translating.

The Home Grid and User Grids panels define the values, such as Grid Spacing and the alignment of the AutoGrid. Once snap settings are defined, they can be easily turned on and off using the four snap toggle buttons located to the right of the Prompt Line at the bottom of the window.

Tutorial: Customizing the command panel buttons

The Configure Button Sets button is a feature that enables you to configure which buttons are displayed at the top of the Modify and Utilities panels. This feature is accessed by a small button located at the top right of the Modify and Utility Command panel, to the right of the More and Sets buttons.

Clicking this button opens the Configure Buttons Sets dialog box, shown in Figure 3-30. This dialog box includes a list of all the possible Modifiers or Utilities that are available. To the left of the dialog box are the current default buttons. You can edit the total number of buttons by changing the value in the Total Buttons field. Several buttons sets can be created, saved, and managed using this dialog box.

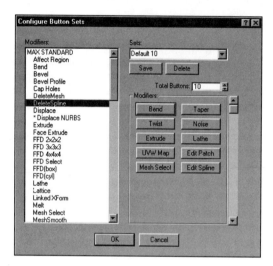

Figure 3-30: The Configure Button Sets dialog box enables you to create custom button sets for the Modify and Utility panels.

Tip   Buttons sets can include anywhere from 1 to 32 buttons.

To configure a new button set, follow these steps:

1. Click the Configure Button Sets button to open its dialog box in either the Modify or Utility Command Panel.

2. Select the button set you want to configure from the drop-down list labeled Sets at the top right of the panel. To create a new set, simply type a new name into the Sets field.

3. Choose the total number of buttons you want to appear in this set by adjusting the Total Buttons spinner.

4. To clear a current button location, drag the button to the list on the left.

5. To add buttons to the set, select a modifier or utility from the Modifiers or Utilities list on the left and drag it to an available button on the right.

6. When your button set is configured the way you want it, click the Save button.

Summary

There are many ways to customize the MAX interface. Most of these customization options are included under the Customize menu. In this chapter, you learned how to use this menu and its commands to customize many aspects of the MAX interface. Customizing the MAX interface will make the interface more efficient and make you more comfortable working with it.

Specifically, this chapter covered the following topics:

✦ Using the Customize menu

✦ Customizing toolbars, the Tab Panel, and Command Panel buttons

✦ Configuring paths and viewports

✦ Setting preferences

✦ Selecting system unit, grid, and snap settings

This is the end of the Getting Started part of the book. The next chapter begins a new part on Working with Objects and will teach you how you can use XRef commands to collaborate with your production team members.

✦   ✦   ✦

Working with Objects

Referencing External Objects

In This Chapter

Using externally
referenced scenes

Using externally
referenced objects

Configuring XRef
paths

No man is an island, and if Kinetix has their way, no MAX user will be an island either. Release 3 features XRefs, which make it easy for workgroups to collaborate on a project without having to wait for one or the other group member to finish his or her respective production tasks. The XRef term is short for *External Reference*. External references are objects and scenes contained in separate MAX files and made available for reference during a MAX session. This arrangement enables several artists on a team to work on separate sections of a project without interfering with one another or altering each other's work.

This chapter explains the two different types of XRefs — XRef Scenes and XRef Objects — and how to use them.

Using XRef Scenes

An externally referenced scene is one that will appear in the current MAX session, but that will not be accessible for editing or changing. The scene can be positioned and transformed when linked to a parent object and can be set to update automatically as changes are made to the source file.

New Feature XRef Scenes and Objects and all their functions are new to Release 3.

As an example of how XRef Scenes facilitate a project, let's say a design team is in the midst of creating an environment for a project while the animator is animating a character model. The animator can access the in-production environment as an XRef Scene in order to help him move the character correctly about the environment. The design team will be happy because the animator didn't modify any of their lights, terrain models, maps, and props. The animator will be happy because he won't have to wait for the design team to finish all their tweaking before he can get started. The end result is one large happy production team (if they can meet their deadlines).

XRef Scenes are loaded into a file using the XRef Scenes dialog box. This dialog box can be opened using the File ➪ XRef Scenes command. Figure 4-1 shows this dialog box.

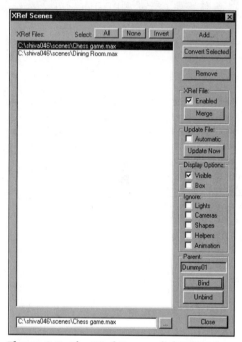

Figure 4-1: The XRef Scenes dialog box lets you specify which scenes to load as external references.

XRef Scene options

In the XRef Scenes dialog box are several options for controlling the appearance of the scene objects, how often the scene is updated, and which object the scene is bound to. This dialog box is modeless and the options in this dialog box can be opened and changed at any time.

The pane on the left lists all XRef Scenes in the current scene. To the right are the settings, which can be different for each XRef Scene in the list. To view or apply a setting, you first need to select the scene from the list. You can remove any scene by selecting it from the list and clicking the Remove button.

Caution   If an XRef Scene in the list is displayed in red, then the scene could not be loaded. If the path or name is incorrect, you can change it in the Path field at the bottom of the list.

The Convert Selected button converts any selected objects in the current scene to XRef Objects by saving them out as a separate file. This button opens a dialog box to let you name and save the new file. If no objects are selected in the current scene, then this option is disabled.

All XRef Scenes can be enabled or disabled using the Enabled option. Disabled scenes are displayed in gray. The Merge button lets you insert the current XRef Scene into the current scene. This button removes the scene from the list and acts the same way as the File ⇨ Merge command.

Updating an external scene

Automatic is a key option that can set any XRef Scene to be automatically updated. Enable this by selecting a scene from the list and checking the Automatic option box; thereafter, the scene is updated any time the source file is updated. This option can slow the system down if the external scene is updated frequently, but the benefit is that you can work with the latest update.

There is also an Update Now button for manually updating the XRef Scene. Clicking this button updates the external scene to the latest saved version.

External scene appearance

Other options let you decide how the scene is displayed in the viewports. You can choose to make the external scene invisible or to display it as a box. Making an external scene invisible only removes it from the viewports, but the scene will still be included in the rendered output. To remove a scene from the rendered output, deselect the Enabled option.

The Ignore section lists objects such as lights, cameras, shapes, helpers, and animation; selecting them causes them to be ignored and to have no effect in the scene. If an external scene's animation is ignored, then the scene will appear as it does in frame 0.

Positioning an external scene

Positioning an external scene is accomplished by binding the scene to an object in the current scene (a dummy object, for example). The XRef Scenes dialog box is modeless, so you can select the object to bind to without closing the dialog box. Once a binding object is selected, the external scene transforms to the binding object's pivot point. The name of the parent object is also displayed in the XRef Scene dialog box.

Transforming the object that the scene is bound to can control how the external scene is repositioned. To unbind an object, click the Unbind button in the XRef Scenes dialog box. Unbound scenes are positioned at the World origin for the current scene.

Working with XRef Scenes

XRef Scenes cannot be edited in the current scene. Their objects are not visible in the Select by Name dialog box or the Track and Schematic Views. You also cannot access the Modifier Stack of external scenes' objects. However, you can make use of external scene objects in other ways. For example, you can change a viewport to show the view from any camera or light in the external scene. External scene objects are included in the Summary Info dialog box.

Tip

Another way to use XRef Scenes is to create a scene with lights and/or cameras positioned at regular intervals around the scene. You can then use the XRef Scenes dialog box to turn these lights on and off or to select from a number of different views without creating new cameras.

XRef Scenes can also be nested within each other, so you can have one XRef Scene for the distant mountains that includes another XRef for a castle.

Note

If a MAX file is loaded with XRef files that cannot be located, a warning dialog box will open enabling you to browse to the file's new location. If you click OK or Cancel, the scene will still load, but the external scenes will be missing.

Tutorial: Adding an XRef Scene

As an example of a project that would benefit from XRefs, I've created a maze environment. I will open a new MAX file and animate a diamond moving through this maze that will be opened as an XRef Scene.

To set up an XRef Scene, follow these steps:

1. Create and save the maze environment. For this tutorial, save it as **maze.max**. Make sure to deselect the Backface Cull option in the Object Properties dialog box in order to see the back sides of the walls.

2. Create a new MAX file by selecting File ➪ New. Then select the File ➪ XRef Scenes command to open the XRef Scenes dialog box. Click the Add button, locate the maze.max file, and click Open to add it to the XRef Scene dialog box list.

Tip

You can add several XRef Scenes by clicking the Add button again. You can also add a scene to the XRef Scene dialog box by dragging a .max file from Windows Explorer or from the Asset Manager window.

3. In the new scene, open the Create panel, select the Helpers category, and click the Dummy Object button. Then create a simple dummy object in the scene.

4. In the XRef Scenes dialog box, click the Bind button and select the dummy object. This will enable you to reposition the XRef Scene as needed. Also select the Automatic update option and then click the Close button to exit the dialog box.

5. Now animate objects moving through the maze.

Figure 4-2 shows the maze.max scene included in the current MAX file as an XRef.

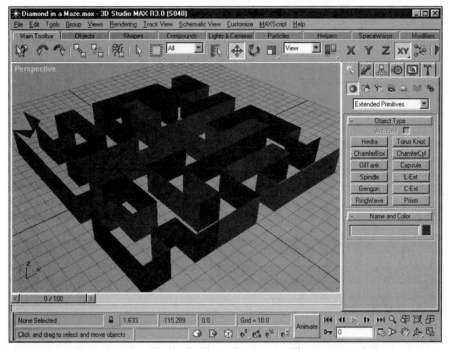

Figure 4-2: The maze.max file loaded into the current file as an XRef Scene

Using XRef Objects

XRef Objects are slightly different from XRef Scenes. They are objects that appear in a scene and that can be transformed and animated; but the original object's structure and Modifier Stack cannot be changed.

An innovative way to use this feature would be to create a library of objects that could be loaded on the fly as needed. For example, if you had a furniture library, you could load several different styles until you got just the look you want.

You can also use XRef Objects to load low-resolution proxies of complex models in order to lighten the system load during a MAX session. This will increase the viewport refresh rate.

Many of the options in the XRef Objects dialog box, shown in Figure 4-3, are the same as in the XRef Scenes dialog box.

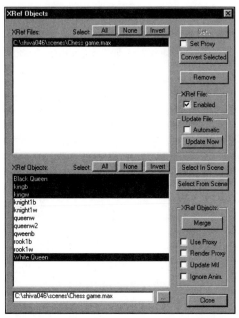

Figure 4-3: The XRef Objects dialog box lets you choose which files to look in for external objects.

XRef Objects options

The left side of the XRef Objects dialog box is divided into two sections. The top section displays the externally referenced files, and the lower section displays the objects selected from that file. A file needs to be selected in order for you to see its objects.

The Convert Selected button works the same as in the XRef Scenes dialog box. It enables you to save the selected objects in the current scene to a separate file just like the File ➪ Save Selected command. Many other controls work in the same manner.

In the XRef Objects dialog box, you can choose to automatically update the external referenced objects or use the Update Now button. You can also Enable and Disable all objects in a file.

The Select In Scene and Select From Scene buttons are useful for seeing which objects in the scene are related to which items in the XRef Objects dialog box list.

Using Proxies

The Add as Proxy button opens a low-resolution proxy object in place of a more complex object. This saves memory by not requiring the more complex object to be kept in memory. You can also select to render the proxy, update its materials, or ignore its animation.

If an object in the lower list is selected, then the Add button changes to a Set button. The Set button will let you choose a file and object to use as a proxy. The proxy will be displayed in place of the actual referenced object.

 Tip   The real benefit of using proxies is to replace complex referenced objects with simpler objects that update quickly. When creating a complex object, remember to also create a low-resolution version to be used as a proxy.

Controlling the Appearance of XRef objects

There are several options for controlling how the XRef Objects are displayed. The Use Proxy option lets you choose between displaying the proxy and displaying the actual object. The Render Proxy option forces the proxy object to be rendered instead of the actual referenced object. If this option is not selected, then the referenced object will be rendered regardless of the object displayed in the viewports.

The Update Materials option enables the object's materials to update as the source gets updated.

The Ignore Animation option turns off any Modifier Stack animations associated with the object.

Working with XRef Objects

XRef Objects will appear and act like any other object in the scene. About the only difference you'll see will be if you open the Modifier Stack. The Stack displays "XRef Object" as its only entry.

When the XRef Object item is selected in the Modifier Stack, a rollout, shown in Figure 4-4, appears. The rollout includes many of the same controls displayed in the XRef Objects dialog box discussed previously. These controls include the XRef File Name, Object Name, Proxy File Name, and Proxy Object Name.

Figure 4-4: The XRef Object rollout in the Modify panel lets you choose which objects from which files to include as external references.

Tutorial: Using an XRef Proxy

To set up an XRef Proxy, follow these steps:

1. Create a file that uses the Old Tree and Park Bench models created by Zygote Media and save the file. Open the Create panel and click the Cylinder button. Then create a cylinder that is roughly the same diameter as the tree. With the cylinder still selected, choose File ➪ Save Selected and name the file **Tree Lo-Res**.

2. Open a new scene and import the Post Box model, also created by Zygote Media. Then open the XRef Objects dialog box by selecting the File ➪ XRef Objects command. Click the Add button and locate the first scene file with the tree and the park bench. Select the desired file and click Open to add the file. The XRef Merge dialog box, shown in Figure 4-5, will automatically open and display a list of all the objects in the file just added. Select the objects to add to the current scene and click OK. (Holding down the Ctrl key will let you select several objects.) Use the Filter and Sort options to locate specific objects.

Note   If an object you've selected has the same name as an object that is currently in the scene, the Duplicate Name dialog box will appear to let you rename the object, merge it anyway, skip the new object, or delete the old version.

3. Select the Tree object in the lower pane and click the Set button with the Set Proxy option selected. In the Open File dialog box that appears, select the Tree Lo-Res file, select the cylinder object, and click OK.

4. Select the Use Proxy option to see the proxy object and deselect it to see the actual object.

Figure 4-5: The XRef Merge dialog box lets you choose specific objects from a scene.

XRef Objects that you add to a scene instantly appear in the current scene as you add them. Figure 4-6 shows the Post Box with the actual tree object. The XRef Objects dialog box will let you switch to the proxy object at any time.

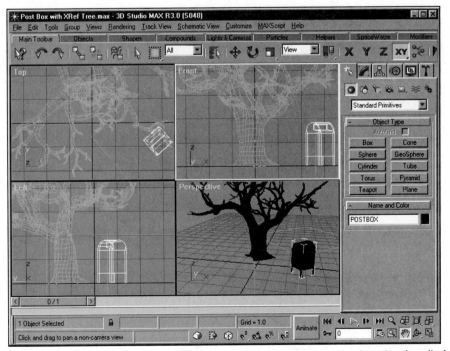

Figure 4-6: The tree object is an XRef from another scene. Its proxy is a simple cylinder.

Configuring XRef Paths

The Configure Paths dialog box includes an XRefs tab for setting the paths for XRef Scenes and objects, shown in Figure 4-7. Select Customize ⇨ Configure Paths to open the XRefs panel.

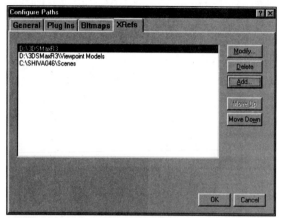

Figure 4-7: The XRefs panel in the Configure Paths dialog box lets you specify paths to be searched when an XRef cannot be located.

MAX keeps track of the path of any XRefs used in a scene, but if it cannot find them, it will look at the paths designated in the XRefs panel of the Configure Paths dialog box. For projects that use a lot of XRefs, it is a good idea to populate this list with potential paths. Paths will be scanned in the order they are listed, so place the most likely paths at the top of the list.

To add a new path to the panel, click the Add button. You can also modify or delete paths in this panel with the Modify and Delete buttons.

Summary

This chapter covered the basics of using MAX's new XRef features, including how to

✦ Use externally referenced scenes and objects to work on the same project at the same time as your fellow team members without interfering with their work (or they with yours)

✦ Configure XRef paths to help MAX track your XRef Scenes and objects

In the next chapter, you'll learn about importing and exporting objects as a way to pass formats between MAX and other, external tools.

✦   ✦   ✦

Importing and Exporting

Modeling is a complex process and good modelers will use an assortment of tools. Just as a wood shop doesn't just use a saw and hammer, modelers will often use various software packages as part of the model production process. As larger teams work together on projects, incorporating different formats will become more important.

This chapter focuses on moving objects and scenes into and out of MAX. The process of importing and exporting can be tricky, and the tips in this chapter can prove invaluable.

The Quickest Way to Model Objects

Suppose you've just gotten a job delivering pizza, but you don't have a car. A hot pizza lands in your lap, a thirty-minute delivery deadline looms. Given a choice, you could build a car from the asphalt up or you could buy one that's already made. I don't know how expert you are in car mechanics, but it would take me a very long time to build a car. The easier (and perhaps cheaper) method would be to buy the one that is already made.

This example is preposterous, but, when applied to production modeling, it isn't so far-fetched. Modeling the details of a car can be very time consuming if you're striving for realism, especially with deadlines looming —a very real problem for many 3D artists and animators. Companies such as Viewpoint Datalabs, Zygote Media, and others have been formed to give you a hand (literally).

These companies have huge catalogs of pre-built models for every budget. Their models can be seen in every aspect of 3D animation from commercials and films to product design and architectural renderings. For more information on these companies, check out their Web sites:

✦ Viewpoint DataLabs: www.viewpoint.com

✦ Zygote Media: www.zygote.com

Viewpoint Datalabs, Zygote Media, and others have provided many of the models used in this book. Examples of some of their models are included on the CD-ROM.

Modeling Types

There are many ways to skin a cat, and there are many ways to model one. You could make a cat model out of primitive objects like blocks, cubes, and spheres, or you could create one as a polygon mesh. As your experience grows, you'll discover that some objects are easier to model using one method and some are easier using another. MAX offers several different modeling types to handle various modeling situations.

3D Studio MAX R3 includes the following modeling types:

✦ **Primitives**—Basic parametric shapes such as cubes, spheres, and pyramids.

✦ **Polygon Meshes**—Complex models created from many polygon faces that are smoothed together when the object is rendered.

✦ **Patches**—Based on spline curves; patches can be modified using control points.

✦ **Loft Objects**—Named after the traditional manner of building ships by draping a skin over several cross sections.

✦ **NURBS**—Stands for Non-Uniform Rational B-Splines. NURBS are similar to loft objects in that they also have control points that can control a surface's spread over curves.

✦ **Booleans**—Created by adding, subtracting, or intersecting overlapping shapes.

In addition to these basic modeling types there are several distinct types that are good at modeling one specialized type of object such as Terrain or Morph objects.

For more information on each of these modeling types, check out the chapters in Part III, "Modeling."

Modeling Formats

Just as there are several different modeling types, there are many formats
that support these types. 3D Studio MAX saves its scenes and objects in a unique
proprietary format denoted by the extension MAX. This format is different from
the 3D Studio for DOS product that is denoted by the extension 3DS.

 Note   There are some differences between the MAX formats for early MAX versions.
Files from early MAX versions need to be converted to the Release 3 format.
This conversion is done automatically.

Some formats, such as IGES, support NURBS, and others, such as Adobe Illustrator
(AI), only support 2D shapes.

Outside of 3D Studio, the DXF format is probably the most commonly supported
format for polygon meshes. For NURBS models, use IGES. The AI and SHP formats
are vector formats mainly used to load and export 2D drawings such as logos and
animation paths.

These formats are only a fraction of all the possible formats. To import from
formats not supported by MAX, you'll need to make the format conversion in
several steps by first converting from the other package to a format that MAX
supports and then importing the converted file. Exporting can work in a similar
way. This method is used later in the chapter to work with files from Rhino, Poser,
and Bryce.

An alternative to converting non-MAX formats by hand is to use one of the many file
conversion plug-ins that are available. You'll learn how to use one of these plug-ins,
PolyTrans, later in this chapter.

Importing Geometric Objects

In the "Quick Start" at the beginning of the book, we imported several models, but
there were a lot of settings that we just accepted. In this section, we'll examine
these imported settings in closer detail.

The Import dialog box looks like a typical Windows file dialog box. The real power
comes with the various Import Settings dialog boxes that are available for each
format. For example, let's say that you want to import an old 3DS file into a current
MAX session. After you select the file to import, a small dialog box titled 3DS Import
appears asking if you want to merge the imported objects with the current scene or
completely replace the current scene (you'll also have the option to convert units
on the imported file). If the selected file happens to be a .WRL file, a dialog box
entitled VRML Import gives you the Input Options of Reset Scene, Turn to 3DS
Coordinates, and Create Primitives.

MAX can import several different formats. Files that MAX can import include:

✦ 3D Studio Mesh, Projects and Shapes (3DS, PRJ, SHP)

✦ Adobe Illustrator (AI)

✦ AutoCAD (DWG, DXF)

✦ IGES

✦ StereoLithography (STL)

✦ VRML (WRL, WRZ)

Note   You can set MAX to reorient all the viewports by automatically zooming to the extents of the imported object by setting the Zoom Extents on Import option in the Files panel of the Preference Settings dialog box.

Importing 3D Studio files (3DS, PRJ, SHP)

It shouldn't be a surprise that MAX can import 3D Studio (3DS) files without much headache—after all, 3DStudio was the predecessor to MAX.

Everything in a 3DS file is imported into MAX except for Morph Keys, Keyframer Instances, .CUB cubic maps, and decal transparency defined by the upper-left pixel. Imported SHP files convert 2D polygons created with 3D Studio's Shaper tool into Bezier splines. The shapes can be imported as a single object or as multiple objects. PRJ files are simply 3DS files that include shapes. Or, you can select to not import shapes.

Importing a 3D Studio file opens a simple dialog box, shown in Figure 5-1. The dialog box offers options to merge or replace the current scene. It also includes an option to Convert Units. With the Convert0 Units option selected, MAX assumes that the 3DS file is based in inches and converts it to the currently defined units.

Figure 5-1: The 3DS Import dialog box enables you to merge objects into or completely replace the current scene.

Importing Illustrator files (AI)

Files created using Adobe Illustrator can be imported into MAX. Once you have selected an Illustrator file, the AI Import dialog box will offer the options of merging the objects into the current scene or replacing the current scene. This dialog box looks just like the one displayed in the previous figure. Following the AI Import dialog box, the Shape Import dialog box, shown in Figure 5-2, will ask whether the objects should be imported as a single objects or as multiple objects. During the import process, the 2D polygons are all converted to Bezier curves. MAX can only import curves and paths from Illustrator. All effects such as fills, gradients, and filter effects will be lost in the translation.

Figure 5-2: The Shape Import dialog box enables you to import shapes as a single object or as multiple objects.

Caution   MAX cannot import text created in Illustrator unless it has been converted to outlines. In Illustrator, this is done by selecting the text and then the Type ⇨ Outlines command.

There are many different Illustrator versions. When saving a file in Illustrator, you can specify to use version 3.0, 4.0, 5.0/5.5, 6.0, 7.0, and now 8.0. The AI88 refers to the format used prior to version 3.0. MAX can import all these different formats.

Importing AutoCAD files (DWG, DXF)

AutoCAD is a sister product to MAX, aimed at the Computer-Aided Design market. It is produced by the same parent company and for that reason interacts very well with MAX. AutoCAD uses two main formats — DWG (which stands for Drawing files) and the older DXF (which stands for Drawing Exchange Format).

Importing DWG files

Objects in AutoCAD are named differently from MAX objects. For example, AutoCAD includes a 3D Face object, a Polyline Mesh object, a Polyface Mesh object, and an ACIS Object. During the import process, all these objects are converted to corresponding mesh objects in MAX, because MAX doesn't distinguish among these types.

Note AutoSurf and AutoCAD Designer use the 3DSOUT command to export models to MAX.

The Import AutoCAD DWG File dialog box, shown in Figure 5-3, includes many options that help define the translation process. Distinct objects in an AutoCAD file can be identified by layer, color, or type. The Import AutoCAD DWG dialog box can specify how to interpret these separate objects through the Layer, Color, and Entity options in the Derive Objects By section.

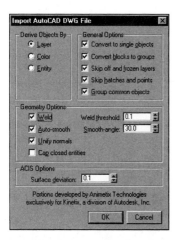

Figure 5-3: The Import AutoCAD DWG File dialog box determines how the file is imported.

In AutoCAD, objects are grouped together as blocks. In the Import AutoCAD DWG File dialog box, these blocks can be converted to single objects or to groups. You can also select to skip layers that are turned off or frozen, and to ignore hatch patterns and point objects.

When DWG files are saved, extra vertices are often saved with the model. The Weld option will automatically combine vertices that are closer than the Threshold value. This can quickly reduce the complexity of the model.

The Smooth-angle setting defines whether adjacent polygons are rendered smoothly or with a sharp edge. The angle is calculated by comparing the normals of the adjacent polygons (a *normal* is a vector that is perpendicular to the polygon face). Polygons that are coplanar (existing in the same plane) have normals that point in the same direction, so their angle would be zero. On the other hand, two polygons that are at right angles would have an angle of 90 degrees and would appear as a sharp edge if the smooth angle were less than 90.

The single ACIS option lets you specify a Surface deviation value. Small values produce more faces for greater detail, and larger values do the opposite.

Importing DXF files

After the initial merge/replace dialog box, the Import DXF File dialog box, shown in Figure 5-4, opens. This dialog box includes settings for extracting different objects within the DXF file. DXF models can also be separated into different parts with the Layers, Colors, and Entities options. The most common way of separating various parts is by Layer. If your object appears as one solid mass, try importing again and changing this setting.

Figure 5-4: The Import DXF File dialog box offers settings for making the file import correctly.

The Arc Subdivision section specifies degree values between successive vertices required to begin a new mesh or spline on imported polygon meshes and splines. A setting of 90 for splines means that if the difference between this node and the next node is less than 90 degrees, then the node will be part of the existing spline.

The Miscellaneous options can fix common problems with DXF files such as duplicate faces, noncapped meshes being mistaken for splines, and normals that point toward the center of the object, producing a hole when rendered.

Other options include a Weld Threshold, Auto Smoothing of angles, and Unify Normals.

Importing IGES files (IGES)

IGES stands for Initial Graphics Exchange Standard. The IGES format supports NURBS and provides a standard way to import and export NURBS objects.

With IGES import and export features, MAX files can share objects with packages such as Mechanical Desktop 3.0, Maya, Pro/ENGINEER, SoftImage, CATIA, among others.

New Feature   The ability to import IGES files is new to Release 3.

When you import an IGES file, the only dialog box to appear is the Merge/Replace dialog box seen in earlier sections.

In the IGES format, all entities have an entity number and name. The MAX Online Reference includes a table that correlates the conversion of the various IGES entities to MAX objects. For example, an IGES element labeled 100 is a Circular Arc that will be converted to a MAX Arc Shape.

IGES conversion can be tricky, so a log file of the process is saved with the .XLI extension. An IGES file with several meshes is converted to a single NURBS surface in MAX with each original mesh being a separate sub-object surface. To work with these sub-object surfaces, you'll need to make them independent from the NURBS object. Chapter 16, "Working with NURBS," explains this process.

Importing StereoLithography files (STL)

StereoLithography is a file format used by various manufacturing machines for rapid prototyping of products. Importing an STL file opens the Import STL File dialog box, shown in Figure 5-5. Available options include Weld Vertices, (including a Quick Weld feature) which is used to combine vertices closer than the Weld Threshold value; Auto-Smooth, which defines whether adjacent polygon faces should be smoothed; Unify Normals, which causes all normals to point the same direction, and Remove Double Faces, which simplifies the geometry.

Figure 5-5: The Import STL File dialog box enables you to name the STL file and set other options.

Importing VRML files (WRL, WRZ)

VRML stands for Virtual Reality Modeling Language and like HTML, it defines scenes that can be interpreted by VRML browsers imbedded within a Web browser.

Two different versions of VRML exist. VRML 1.0, also known to Kinetix users as VRBL, is the earlier standard. It is not compatible with the current standard, VRML 2.0, also called VRML 97.

The VRML Import dialog box, shown in Figure 5-6, includes options to Reset Scene, Turn to 3DS Coordinates, and Create Primitives. The Reset Scene option deletes the existing scene. Once deselected, the imported file is merged into the current scene. The Turn to 3DS Coordinates option switches the Y and Z coordinates. In VRML scenes the Y-axis points up, but in MAX the Z-axis points up. The Create Primitives option converts VRML primitives to their MAX equivalents.

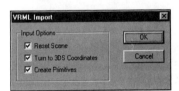

Figure 5-6: The VRML Import dialog box lets you import VRML scenes.

Importing Additional Formats

Even if MAX could import several times the current number of import formats, new formats are being created for new products all the time, many of which MAX wouldn't support. This does not mean that MAX cannot use objects created in these new products. The trick is to find a common format that both products support.

Importing human figures from Poser 3

Many animation projects require human figures. Modeling a human figure from scratch can require the same patience and artistic skill that Michelangelo exercised when painting the ceiling of the Sistine Chapel. Luckily (for those of us facing deadlines), this level of commitment isn't necessary. MetaCreations has developed a tool devoted to modeling the human body. It is named Poser 3. Its features include posing and animating lifelike characters; importing Poser 3 models into MAX can save some major modeling headaches.

With Poser 3, you can choose from a variety of male and female human figures, both unclothed and clothed in all sorts of attire. There are even animal models available. These figures can be easily positioned to any pose. Figure 5-7 shows the Business Man model posed as if hailing a taxi.

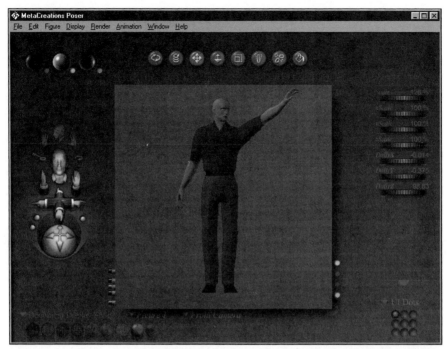

Figure 5-7: Poser 3 by MetaCreations is an excellent tool for modeling human figures.

Poser can animate characters. To change the pose, simply click and drag a body part to its desired location. Poser 3 also includes modules for controlling basic facial expressions and hand gestures.

Tutorial: Using Poser 3 models in MAX

Poser 3 makes modeling and positioning human figures easy, but the tricky part is importing these models into MAX and ending up with a useable model. Poser can export several formats, but only two that coincide with MAX — 3DS and DXF.

To use Poser 3 models in MAX, follow these steps:

1. Position your figure in Poser and export it by selecting Poser's File ➪ Export command.

2. In the Export dialog box, select the 3DS file type and save the file.

3. In MAX, import the file by selecting File ➪ Import.

4. Select the Completely Replace Current Scene and Convert Units options and click OK.

5. When the model is imported, several sections appear to be missing, including the hip section. This is caused by normals that are pointing the wrong way. You can fix these with the Normal Modifier. Select the Edit ⇨ Select All command. Then open the Modify panel and click the More button. Select the Normal Modifier from the list and click OK. In the Parameters rollout, select both Unify Normals and Flip Normals until the model looks correct.

The model will appear in the four viewports, as shown in Figure 5-8. You may need to use the Zoom Extents command to see it or even to scale the model. To select individual objects, click the Select by Name button in the main toolbar.

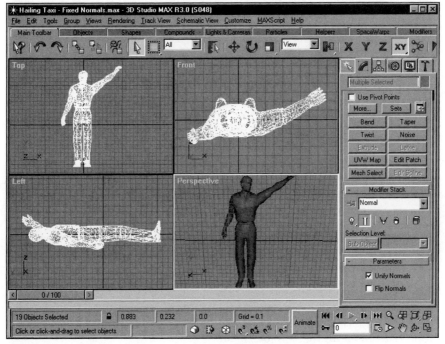

Figure 5-8: A Poser model imported into MAX using the 3DS format

If you repeat the previous steps using the DXF format, you can see the results in Figure 5-9. Notice how the details of the face have been oversimplified.

You can fix the face problems by turning off the Weld Vertices option in the Import DXF File dialog box. Turning off this option results in the model in Figure 5-10. Although you have the face details, there are still several sub-object areas with incorrect normals that the Normal Modifier hasn't fixed. These areas are shown in black in the figure.

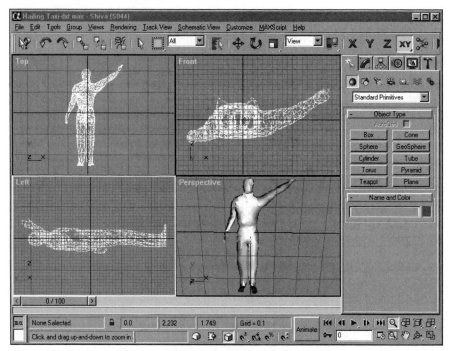

Figure 5-9: A Poser model imported into MAX using the DXF format with Weld Vertices set to 0.01

Note   The black sections are actually the back face of these polygons. These are visible because the Backface Cull option in the Object Properties dialog box is disabled. If the Backface Cull display option were enabled, then these areas would be invisible.

Although it will take some work, you can correct these sub-objects with the incorrect normals using the Flip Normal Mode button under the Surface Properties rollout for the Editable Mesh.

Neither format will import the model perfectly, but both types of import will give you a jumpstart on modeling a human figure. To see all the problems that your imported model has, apply the STL Check Modifier. This will help identify abnormal geometry.

Importing Bryce 4 landscapes

Similar to what Poser 3 enables for human figure models, Bryce 4, shown in Figure 5-11, does for landscapes. Bryce 3D is an excellent tool for creating landscapes and terrains. It also offers a range of atmospheric effects and many preset textures and materials.

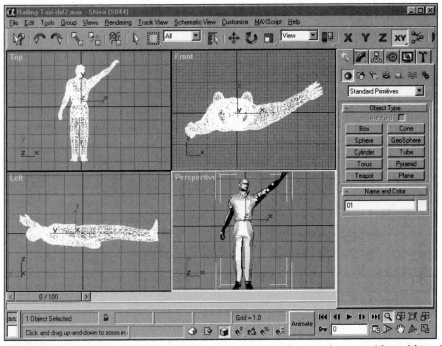

Figure 5-10: A Poser model imported into MAX using the DXF format with Weld Vertices turned off.

Bryce 4 includes a Terrain Editor for creating advanced landscapes. The landscapes are all based on the grayscale image shown in the upper right corner of Figure 5-12. Bryce 4 interprets the lighter pixels in the image as higher elevations and the darker pixels as lower elevations. Controls include Fractal, Spikes, Mounds, Erode, and Equalize. You can also load in your own images to use for landscapes.

With a landscape model completed, Bryce enables you to select textures, backgrounds, and objects to include in the scene. You can also export the terrain object in many different formats, including DXF. The Export Terrain dialog box in Bryce includes an interactive slider and display for controlling and viewing the model details. Figure 5-13 shows the landscape set to 5,000 polygons, and Figure 5-14 shows the same landscape set to over 32,000 polygons. Bryce also lets you export maps for the landscape.

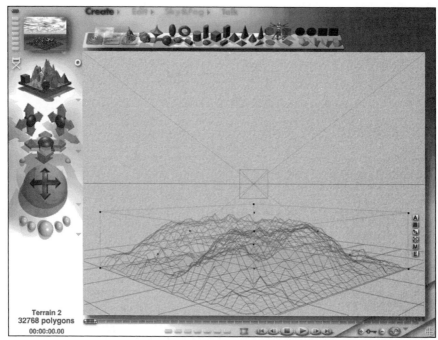

Figure 5-11: Bryce 4 by MetaCreations is an excellent tool for creating landscapes.

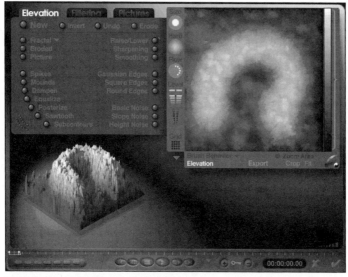

Figure 5-12: The Terrain Editor in Bryce 4 was used to create my original Horseshoe Mountain.

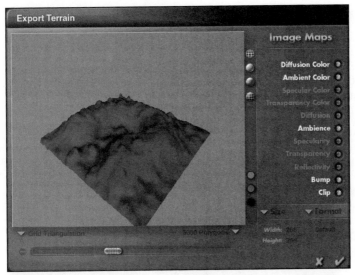

Figure 5-13: A Bryce landscape exported to DXF at a medium resolution

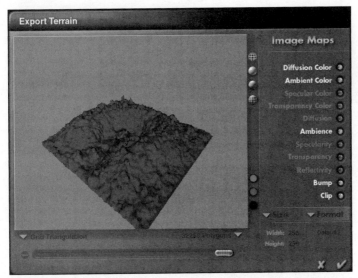

Figure 5-14: A Bryce landscape exported to DXF at the highest resolution

Tutorial: Importing a Bryce 4 terrain

To import a Bryce 4 terrain, follow these steps:

1. Import the terrain object into MAX using the File ⇨ Import command. The object will be imported without any layer or group information, because it is all contained in one object. Make sure the Unify Normals option is selected in the Import DXF Files dialog box.

2. When the terrain is imported, all the normals are together, but they need to be flipped. Open the Modify panel, click the More button, select the Normal Modifier, and click OK. In the Parameters rollout, enable the Flip Normals option.

Figure 5-15 shows the landscape after being imported into MAX.

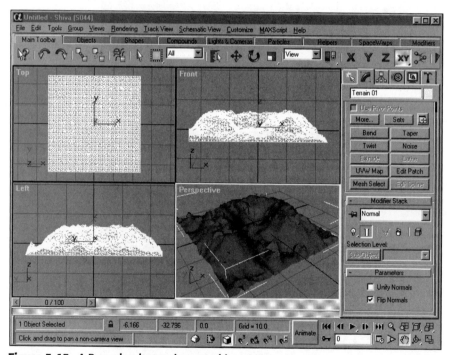

Figure 5-15: A Bryce landscape imported into MAX

Tip   If the model displays as a solid white mass when selected, right-click the object and from the Properties dialog box deselect the Backface Cull option.

Tip

An alternative method for creating a Bryce landscape is to save the gradient image from Bryce and apply it to a surface in MAX using the Displacement Modifier.

In addition to landscapes, Bryce can be used to create some great sky backgrounds with the Sky Lab utility.

Importing Rhino models

The Rhinoceros is an animal that lives in Africa, and it is also the name of powerful piece of software made by Robert McNeel and Associates. Rhinoceros (or Rhino for short) is a NURBS modeling system. Its main purpose is to model objects — it doesn't have any animation features, and its rendering engine is fairly basic.

You may be asking why Rhino is even used now that MAX has implemented some serious NURBS improvements. MAX's NURBS, prior to R3, had some shortcomings that frustrated many modelers. Rhino was the well-accepted alternative — easy to use with an interface focused on modeling with NURBS. My assertion is that, even with all the NURBS improvements in R3, Rhino is still an excellent tool for modeling. If you're frustrated by constant scrolling in the Command Panel when working with NURBS, then maybe you should look at Rhino. Figure 5-16 shows the Rhino interface.

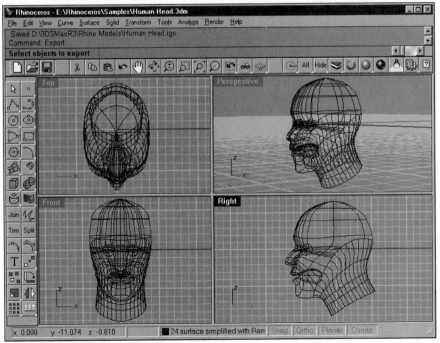

Figure 5-16: Rhinoceros, a NURBS modeler produced by Robert McNeel and Associates

When you are working with MAX, an external modeling tool is only as good as its export abilities. Rhino can export objects in the following formats: IGES, Wavefront (OBJ), AutoCAD (DWG, DXF), 3D Studio (3DS), LightWave (LWO), Raw Triangles (RAW), POV-Ray Mesh (POV), Moray UDO, STL, VRML (WRL), Adobe Illustrator (AI), Windows Metafile (WMF), Renderman (RIB), and AG—quite an impressive list including several formats that MAX can import.

Tutorial: Importing models created with Rhino

To import a model created in Rhino, follow these steps:

1. Open Rhino and create a model. I've opened the Human Head model from Rhino's Sample directory. This is the model that was shown in Figure 5-16.

2. Select all the objects in the model and choose File ➪ Export Selected. A File dialog box opens, enabling you to choose a location and file name.

3. There are many export options under the Save as Type drop-down list. You are going to try two of them. First, select the 3D Studio type and click Save.

4. The 3DS format is a polygon format, so Rhino displays a dialog box with a slider, shown in Figure 5-17, that lets you specify the number of polygons to use. You can also preview the mesh by clicking the Preview button. The Detailed Controls button sets the smooth angle and other settings. Click OK when ready.

Figure 5-17: This Rhino slider control lets you specify the detail of the export model.

5. To save the model in a different format, repeat Step 3, but this time select the IGES format. The IGES Export dialog box, shown in Figure 5-18, includes a drop-down list for selecting the IGES Type. These types contain settings for different 3D and CAD packages. The dialog box lets you enter notes about the model, such as the Author and Organization. You can also specify the Units to use. You can specify a new type by clicking the Edit Types button and then clicking New.

Tip   If you know the unit system for the MAX scene that will include this model, then enter the matching units in the IGES units field.

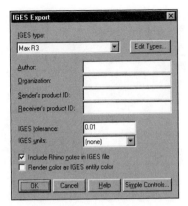

Figure 5-18: When exporting IGES formats from Rhino, you can select from many preset export types.

6. Clicking the New button opens the settings dialog box, shown in Figure 5-19. Type the name **MAX R3** in the Name field; then select IGES version 5.3, the CRLF text file type, and a scale value of 1. You can accept the default settings for the Points and Curves and Surfaces tabs. Click OK when you're ready to proceed.

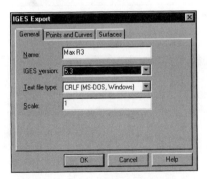

Figure 5-19: This Rhino dialog box can be used to configure how Rhino models export IGES files for MAX.

7. In MAX, use the File ⇨ Import command to import the saved files Figures 5-20 and 5-21 show the results of importing the mesh (3DS) object and the NURBS (IGES) object.

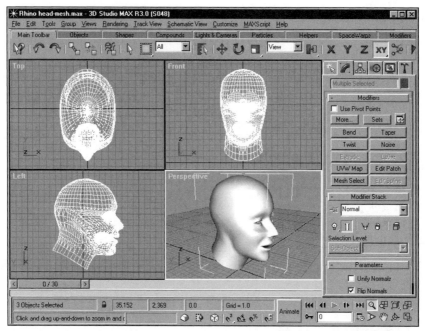

Figure 5-20: A human head model imported from Rhino as a mesh using the 3DS format

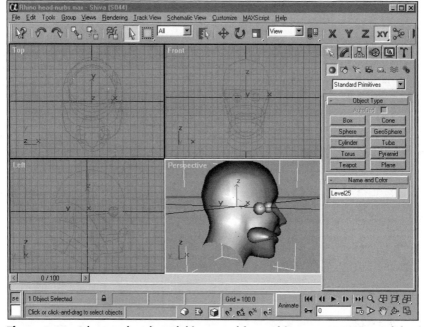

Figure 5-21: A human head model imported from Rhino as a NURBS model using the IGES format

Exporting Geometric Objects

There will be times when you'll want to export MAX objects for use in other systems. The Export command is accessible by choosing File ➪ Export. There is also a command to Export Selected (available only if an object is selected). Selected objects can only be exported to 3DS, AI, ASE, and DXF formats.

Note   The AutoCAD (DWG), StereoLithography (STL), and VRML (WRL) formats are scene formats that cannot save individual objects.

MAX can export the following formats:

✦ 3D Studio Mesh, Projects, and Shapes (3DS)

✦ Adobe Illustrator (AI)

✦ ASCII Scene Export (ASE)

✦ AutoCAD (DWG, DXF)

✦ StereoLithography (STL)

✦ VRML 1.0/VRBL (WRL)

✦ VRML 97 (WRL)

Exporting 3D Studio files

MAX can only export to the 3DS format and not the PRJ and SHP formats. After selecting Export, the Export Scene to .3DS File dialog box appears with only one option — to Preserve MAX's Texture Coordinates. When you are exporting to the 3DS format, all mesh characteristics are exported except for any composite or procedural maps, UV mapping coordinates, any transformations applied to a group, and global shadow parameters.

Any objects that aren't represented by meshes, such as NURBS and procedural primitives, are converted to meshes.

Exporting Illustrator files (AI)

Only shapes and splines can be exported to the AI format. If you try to export a MAX file containing any objects except for shapes to the AI format, you'll receive an AIEXP error message. You can export shapes from within a scene using the Export Selected command.

Exporting ASCII scene files (ASE)

To see all the gritty detail of a MAX file, try exporting the file as an ASCII Scene file. The ASCII Export dialog box, shown in Figure 5-22, includes Output Options and Mesh Options. With this dialog box you can also select which object types to export as well as specify an individual frame to export and a precision value.

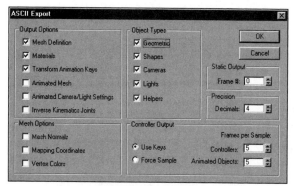

Figure 5-22: The ASCII Export dialog box exports the MAX scene to a file that can be read by a text editor.

Exporting AutoCAD files (DWG, DXF)

Exporting to the DXF format opens the Export DXF File dialog box with the Save To Layers options of By Objects, By Materials, and 1 Layer. The Export AutoCAD DWG File dialog box is more complicated than other export options, as shown in Figure 5-23. The Convert Groups To option enables you to choose Groups or Layers. The General Options enable you to save the file in the AutoCAD R14 format. The default is to save it as an AutoCAD 2000 file. Additional General Options include Convert Instances to Blocks, Skip Hidden Objects, Ignore Extrude Capping, and Export Selected Objects Only.

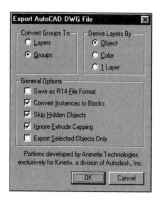

Figure 5-23: The Export AutoCAD DWG File dialog box can export groups as well as layers.

Exporting StereoLithography files (STL)

The Export STL File dialog box offers options for choosing whether to export the STL file as a Binary or ASCII file. Be aware that StereoLithography objects must be closed surfaces. MAX includes the STL-Check Modifier that verifies this. Using this Modifier can save some headaches while exporting.

Cross-Reference   Modifiers such as the STL-Check Modifier are discussed in Chapter 9, "Modifying Objects."

Exporting VRML files (WRL)

You can export MAX scenes in two different VRML formats — VRML 1.0/VRBL and VRML97 (which is also called VRML 2.0).

VRML 1.0/VRBL

The VRML 1.0/VRBL format is the older VRML format. Figure 5-24 shows the Export VRML 1.0/VRBL File dialog box. The VRBL language is used by Kinetix's Hyperwire program and enables additional animation features. If you don't intend to use a browser that takes advantage of the VRBL features, then select VRML 1.0 as the Output Language.

Figure 5-24: The Export VRML 1.0/VRBL File dialog box can specify VRML 1.0 or VRBL files.

The Initial View drop-down lets you select a camera to display when the file is first loaded into a browser. Many VRML browsers support multiple viewpoints. Each camera in the scene will become a different viewpoint when the VRML file is viewed in a browser. You can select Export Hidden Objects, but by default they are not exported. The Show Progress Bar is only visible while the file is being exported.

The Normals option aids the browser in rendering smooth objects. The Indentation option aligns the actual code to make it more readable in a text editor.

Primitives supported by the VRML browser are much more efficient than polygonal meshes. This Primitives option converts objects to primitive objects when possible.

VRBL browsers use the Morph Forms option to animate vertices. The spinner at the bottom of the dialog box sets the number of Morph Forms per Second. Larger settings result in smoother transitions, but also larger files.

The Color per Vertex option exports any vertex colors that are defined in the scene. You can also select Use MAX's Settings or Calculate on Export , which will calculate vertex colors based on scene lighting. The Digits of Precision and Morph Forms per Second can also be defined.

By default all texture maps must reside in the same directory as the WRL file. The Use Prefix option will let you define a sub-directory for holding any texture maps.

VRML 97

VRML97 is the latest VRML format. Many of the settings in the VRML97 Exporter dialog box are the same as in the dialog box for VRML1.0. This dialog box, shown in Figure 5-25, includes several additional options, including Generate ⇨ Coordinate Interpolators and Flip-Book.

Figure 5-25: The VRML97 Exporter dialog box ncludes options set by the VRML97 Helper.

The Coordinate Interpolators option exports animation effects caused by Modifiers and Space Warps. The Flip-Book option exports VRML scenes as multiple files. Clicking the Sample Rates button opens the Animation Sample Rates dialog box shown in Figure 5-26 and enables you to specify frame rates for the Flip-Book, Transform Controllers, and Coordinate Interpolators.

Figure 5-26: The Animation Sample Rates dialog box lets you define the frames per second for exporting a VRML97 file.

Caution   Exporting animation effects using the Coordinate Interpolators can produce huge VRML files.

The Polygons Type section of the VRML97 Exporter dialog box lets you specify how individual faces are exported — options include Ngons, Quads, Triangles, and Visible Edges. The Initial View drop-down is still available, and below it are drop-downs for Initial Navigation Info, Initial Background, and Initial Fog. All three are set by the VRML97 helper and are found as subcategories under the Helpers category in the Create panel.

The World Info button opens the World Info dialog box where the VRML file can be given a Title and file description.

The VRML Export Bonus Tools

To aid in the creation of VRML worlds, MAX includes two additional Bonus Tools that you can install. The VRML 1.0/VRBL Export and VRML97 Export tools provide a way to add anchors and sensors to scene objects in preparation for exporting to VRML. Both tools, once installed, can be found as subcategories under the Helpers category in the Create panel.

The VRML 1.0/VRBL export tool

Opening the VRML 1.0/VRBL subcategory under the Helpers category of the Create panel reveals three buttons—LOD, Inline, and VRML/VRBL.

LOD stands for *Level of Detail*. This button opens a rollout containing a Pick Object button, a Distance value, and a list of objects. To add an object to the list, click the Pick Object button and then specify a Distance value for that object. When the VRML Browser gets closer than the specified distance, the object will appear. This procedure can be used to display a scaled-down version of an object when far away and a more detailed version up close.

The Inline button opens a rollout where you can add a Web URL link to the selected object. VRML Browsers will recognize this link when the object is clicked on.

The VRML/VRBL button opens a rollout where Actions, Triggers, and Hyperlinks can be defined. For more information on these features, refer to a VRML reference.

The VRML97 export tool

Of the two VRML Export tools, you'll be more likely to use this version. The VRML97 standard is widely accepted and includes many features not available in the VRML 1.0 version.

You can open the VRML97 Export tool by selecting the VRML97 subcategory from the Helper category in the Create panel. It includes buttons for the following VRML97 features: Anchor, TouchSensor, ProxSensor, TimeSensor, NavInfo, Background, Fog, AudioClip, Sound, Billboard, LOD, and Inline. Each of these buttons opens a rollout containing its parameters. Many of these features are beyond the scope of this book, but are covered in detail in the many VRML references that are available.

The Anchor rollout lets you pick a Trigger object that will hyperlink the user to a separate URL. The TouchSensor rollout lets you select objects to animate when a Trigger object is touched. The ProxSensor rollout lets you set a trigger when a user gets within a certain defined proximity to an object. The TimeSensor rollout sets regular time intervals.

The NavInfo rollout tells the VRML Browser how the user can navigate about the VRML Scene. The Background rollout specifies the sky and ground colors and any images to use for the background. The Fog rollout lets you define how fog appears in the scene.

The AudioClip rollout is used in conjunction with the Sound rollout. The Sound rollout defines the sound characteristics, and the AudioClip rollout specifies where the sound clips are located.

The Billboard rollout creates images that always face the user. The LOD and Inline rollouts work as described earlier in the "The VRML 1.0/VRBL Export Tool" section.

The Polygon Counter utility

For VRML worlds, the polygon count is important in figuring out how quickly a scene will load over the Web. To accurately determine the number of polygons in a scene, use the Polygon Counter utility. This simple utility, displayed in Figure 5-27, enables you to set a Budget value for the Selected Objects and for All Objects. It also displays the number of polygons and a graph for each. This utility is located in the Utilities panel and can be opened by clicking the More button and selecting the Polygon Counter utility.

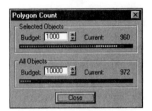

Figure 5-27: The Polygon Counter utility helps you understand how complex an object or scene is.

Plug-In Translators

Although there are many formats not included in MAX, the plug-in nature of the program makes it possible to add functionality via plug-ins. This includes file format translators, such as PolyTrans.

Tip   In many cases, plug-in translators do a better job at translating formats than the default MAX options.

Converting Between Formats with PolyTrans by Okino Computer Graphics is a stand-alone software product for converting 3D file formats. It can also work as a plug-in within MAX. After installation, it will show up as an option under the Utilities tab in the Command Panel. PolyTrans can import the following formats: 3D Studio (3DS), Alias Triangle (TRI), CAD 3D (3D2), DXF Files (DXF), Detailer (VDU), Haines (NFF), Imagine (IOB), LightWave (LWO), Minolta 3D Scanner (CAM), Okino Files (BDF), Pro/E (SLP), Quickdraw 3D (3DM), Stereo Lithography (STL), Strata StudioPro 1.75 (VIS), TrueSpace (COB), USGS Topographical (DEM), VistaPro, and Wavefront (OBJ). It can export to several additional formats.

Note   For more information on PolyTrans, visit Okino's Web site at www.okino.com.

Tutorial: Using the PolyTrans plug-in

In this simple example, I'll use the PolyTrans plug-in to convert some files that aren't supported by MAX.

To convert MAX files to other formats, follow these steps:

1. After installing the plug-in version of PolyTrans, click the Utilities panel in the Command Panel and select the More button. This will open a list of all the currently installed plug-ins.

2. Select PolyTrans I/O Converters from the list and click OK. The PolyTrans rollout appears in the Command Panel, as shown in Figure 5-28.

Figure 5-28: The PolyTrans utility is used to extend MAX's I/O capabilities.

3. From within the PolyTrans utility interface, select the Import tab to see the list of Import types.

4. Select the Lightwave Files option from the list. A File dialog box opens where you can locate the Lightwave file to import.

5. Before you import the file, an options dialog box is displayed to enable you to set import options. This dialog box will be different for every format.

Summary

So many formats, so little time. In this chapter, you have learned about the different format types that MAX supports in order to extend its reach. Specifically, this chapter covered the following:

✦ Some modeling jumpstarts

✦ Each of the import and export types

✦ Models that can be imported from other programs like Poser, Bryce, and Rhino to make all your modeling tasks easier

✦ The VRML export options, including the VRML Export tools

✦ How plug-ins, such as PolyTrans, can make many additional formats accessible

Once you've figured out how to get objects into MAX, you can start to clone them and use them to create arrays of objects. These topics are covered in the next chapter.

✦   ✦   ✦

Cloning Objects and Using Arrays

Now that you are familiar with MAX's new features and the interface, you're ready to begin creating objects. The Create Command Panel includes categories for creating all objects. Once an object is created, you'll be able to clone it, and use it to create arrays of similar objects.

Using the Create Panel

Not only can the Create panel create geometric objects such as spheres and NURBS; it can also create scene objects such as lights and cameras. Coverage of all of the objects that can be created using the Create panel is spread over the remainder of this book, but in this section we take a quick look at creating some simple objects to aid us as the Cloning and Array features are discussed.

Of all the panels in the Command Panel, only the Create panel includes both categories and subcategories. After you click the Create tab in the Command Panel, seven category icons are displayed: Geometry, Shapes, Lights, Cameras, Helpers, Space Warps, and Systems. The button on the left end is the Geometry category button. Clicking it displays a drop-down list with several subcategories. The first available subcategory is Standard Primitives. When this subcategory is selected, several buttons appear that enable you to create some simple objects.

As an example, click the Sphere button. Several rollouts appear at the bottom of the Command Panel—these rollouts contain the sphere parameters. At this point, there are two ways to build our sphere. You could enter values in the Keyboard Entry rollout and click the Create button to create a sphere. This method enables the sphere to be constructed with precise parameters. An easier and more visual way to create a sphere is to click and drag the cursor in one of the viewport windows. When you release the mouse button, the sphere will appear. This method is, of course, less precise, but much quicker. Figure 6-1 shows the new sphere and its parameters.

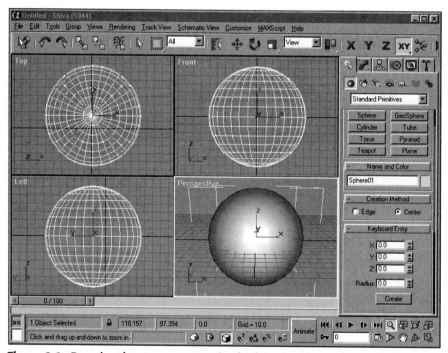

Figure 6-1: Dragging the mouse or entering keyboard values in the Keyboard Entry rollout can create a simple sphere.

When an object button, such as the Sphere button, is selected it turns light green. This is to remind you that you are now in creation mode. Clicking within any viewport window will create an additional sphere. To get out of creation mode, click the Select Object button or one of the transform buttons on the main toolbar.

Naming Objects and Assigning Colors

Every object in the scene can have both a name and color assigned to it. Names and colors are useful for locating and selecting objects, as you will see in Chapter 7, "Selecting and Grouping Objects."

Each object is given a default name and random color when first created. The default name is the type of object followed by a number. You can change the object's name at any time by modifying the Name field in the Name and Color rollout of the Command Panel. Likewise, clicking the color swatch next to the Name field will enable you to alter the object's assigned color.

Tip   When an object is cloned, the Clone Options dialog box includes a Name field where the object can be named.

Clicking the color swatch in a Name and Color rollout opens the Object Color dialog box, shown in Figure 6-2. Within this dialog box you can select from the standard 3D Studio MAX palette or the AutoCAD ACI palette. The AutoCAD palette has many more colors than the MAX palette, but the MAX palette allows a row of custom colors. These custom colors are defined by clicking the Add Custom Colors button. This button opens a Color Selector dialog box, shown in Figure 6-3.

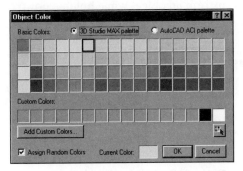

Figure 6-2: The Object Color dialog box is used to define the color of objects displayed in the viewports.

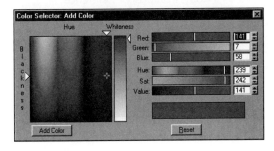

Figure 6-3: The Color Selector: Add Color dialog box lets you choose new custom colors.

The Color Selector: Add Color dialog box defines colors using the RGB (red, green, and blue) and HSV (hue, saturation, and value) color systems. Another way to select colors is to drag the cursor around the rainbow palette to the left. When you've found the perfect custom color to add to the Object Color dialog box, click the Add Color button.

Back in the Object Color dialog box, if the Assign Random Colors option is selected, then a random color from the palette is chosen every time a new object is created. If this option is not selected, the color of all new objects is the same until a different object color is chosen. Making objects different colors makes it easier to distinguish between the two objects for selection and transformation.

The Select by Color button opens the Select Objects dialog box and selects all objects of the current color.

Note
Objects can be set to display an object's default color or its Material Color. These options are in the Display Color rollout under the Display panel. You can set them differently for Wireframe and Shaded views.

Cloning Objects

There are a couple of ways to clone objects. One method is to use the Edit ⇨ Clone command and another method is to transform an object while holding down the Shift key.

Using the Clone command

Creating a duplicate object is accomplished using the Edit ⇨ Clone command. An object must be selected before the Clone command becomes active. Selecting this command opens the Clone Options dialog box, shown in Figure 6-4, where the clone can be given a name and specified as a Copy, Instance, or Reference.

Figure 6-4: The Clone Options dialog box defines the new object as a Copy, Instance, or Reference.

A Copy has the same geometry as the original, but all links to the original are cut. An Instance maintains a link to the original and changes as the original is modified. A Reference lies somewhere between a Copy and an Instance, in that only some of the modifications applied to the original affect the Reference.

Cross-Reference

For more information on which modifications apply, see Chapter 9, "Modifying Objects."

When a clone is created, its position is on top of the original, making it difficult to distinguish. To verify that it has been created, open the Select by Name dialog box from the main toolbar and look for the cloned object (it will have the same name but an incremented number). To see both objects, click the Select and Move button on the main toolbar and move one of the objects away from the other.

Using shift-clone

An easier way to create clones is with the Shift key. The Shift key can be used when objects are transformed using the Select and Move, Select and Rotate, and Select and Scale commands. Holding the Shift key down while you use any of these commands on an object will clone the object and open the Clone Options dialog box. This Clone Options dialog box is identical to the dialog box previously shown in Figure 6-4, except it includes a spinner to specify the Number of Copies.

Performing a transformation with the Shift key held down defines an offset that is applied repeatedly to each copy. For example, holding the Shift key down while moving an object 5 units to the left (with the Number of Copies set to 5) will place the first cloned object 5 units away from the original, the second cloned object 10 units away from the original object, and so on.

Tutorial: Cloning cows

The scientific world has been in an uproar lately with the successful cloning of a sheep. With MAX, we can perform similar experiments on our own, but we'll be using a cow named "Rolly." Viewpoint Datalabs created this cow model.

To investigate cloning objects, follow these steps:

1. Import the cow model using the File ⇨ Import command.
2. Select the entire cow using the Edit ⇨ Select All command. With all parts of the cow selected, select Group ⇨ Group to group the cow parts as one entity. The

Group dialog box will open. In the Group name field, give the newly grouped cow the name **Rolly**.

Note
You can verify the name assignment in the Command Panel by checking the Create panel. In the Name and Color rollout, the name will be displayed.

3. With the cow model selected, select the Edit ⇨ Clone command. The Clone Options dialog box will be displayed. Name the clone **Rolly's Clone**, select the Copy option, and click OK.

4. Click the Select and Move button (the black cross with four arrows) in the main toolbar. Then in the Left viewport, click and drag the cow model to the right. As the model is moved, it reveals the original model beneath it. Select each model in turn and notice the name change in the Create panel's Name field. Figure 6-5 shows both cows. Notice that it is even the same color as the original.

5. With the Select and Move button still active, hold down the Shift key, click the cloned cow in the Left viewport and move it to the right again. In the Clone Options dialog box that appears, select the Copy option, set the Number of Copies to **3** and click OK.

6. Click the Zoom Extents All button in the lower right-hand corner to view all the new cows. Three additional cows have appeared, equally spaced from each other. The spacing was determined by the distance that you moved the second clone before releasing the mouse.

Figure 6-6 shows the results of our cow cloning experiment. (It's starting to feel like a dairy.)

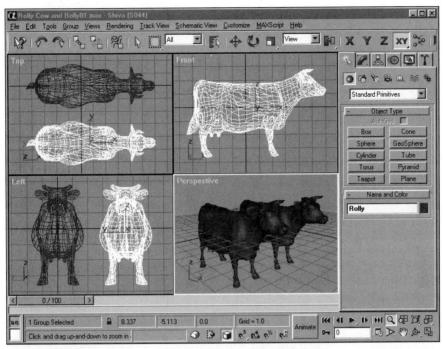

Figure 6-5: The cloned cow positioned next to its original.

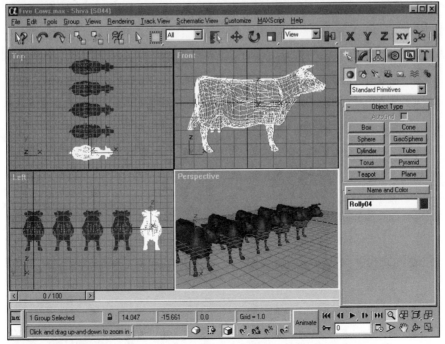

Figure 6-6: Cloning multiple objects is easy with the Shift-Clone feature.

Understanding Copies, Instances, and References

When creating copies in MAX, you'll be offered the option to create the copy as a Copy, an Instance, or a Reference. This is true not only for objects, but for materials and Modifiers as well.

Working with copies, instances, and references

When an object is cloned, the Clone Options dialog box appears. This dialog box enables you to select to make a copy, an instance, or a reference of the original object. Each of these clone types is unique and offers different capabilities.

A copy is just what it sounds like—an exact replica of the original object. The new copy maintains no links to the original object and will be a unique object in its own right. Any changes to the copy will not affect the original object or vice-versa.

Instances are different from copies in that they maintain strong links to the original object. All instances of an object are interconnected, so that changes to any single instance changes all other instances. For example, if you create several instances of a sphere and then change the color of one of the spheres, all instances with be updated with the same color.

References are objects that inherit any changes from their parent objects, but do not affect the parent when modified.

Note   At any time, you can break the link between objects with the Make Unique button in the Modifier Stack rollout.

Tutorial: Copied, instanced, and referenced cows

Learning how the different Clone options work will save you lots of future modifications. To investigate these options, let's revisit our growing herd of cows. Follow these steps:

1. Import the cow model using the File ⇨ Import command.

2. Select the entire cow using the Edit ⇨ Select All command. Then select Group ⇨ Group, and in the Group dialog box give the newly grouped cow the name **Polly**.

3. With the cow model still selected, click the Select and Move button. Hold the Shift key down and in the Left viewport, move the cow to the right. In the Clone Options dialog box select the Copy option, set the Number of Copies to **1**, name the new cow **Polly's Copy**, and click OK. Click the Zoom Extents All button to widen your view.

4. Select the original cow again and repeat Step 3, but this time select the Instance option from the Clone Options dialog box and name the newly cloned cow **Polly's Instance**.

5. Select the original cow again and repeat Step 3 again, but this time select the Reference option from the Clone Options dialog box and name the new cloned cow **Polly's Reference**.

Caution

Be sure to select the original cow each time you make a clone or you'll accidentally make a Reference of an Instance.

6. Click the Zoom Extents All button. You should now see four cows.

7. Select the original cow again.

Tip

If you have trouble locating the original cow, click the Select by Name button on the main toolbar to open the Select Objects dialog box, select Polly from the objects listed, and click the Select button.

8. In the Command Panel, click the Modify tab and then click the Bend button. Under the Parameters rollout in the Bend section, enter **45** in the Angle field, and then press the Enter key on the keyboard to apply the value. Notice how the instanced and referenced objects were modified along with the original, as shown in Figure 6-7.

9. Select the Instanced copy and open the Modify panel. Change the Direction value for the Bend Modifier to **125**. This will change the Instanced copy as well as the original and Referenced objects. Then select the Referenced copy and change the Direction value to **−125**. Notice that the original and instanced objects don't change.

Understanding how these various copy types work will enable you to create duplicates of objects and modify them without taking the time to change each one individually.

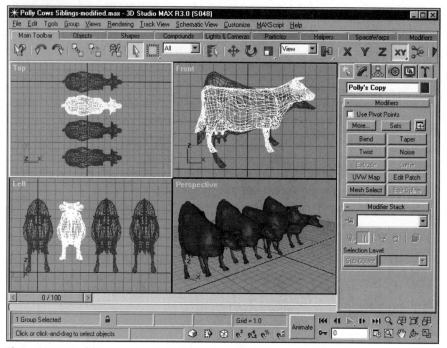

Figure 6-7: Modifying an original object also modifies any instanced or referenced clones.

Creating Arrays of Objects

Once you've figured out how to create objects, the Array command multiplies the fun by making it easy to create many copies instantaneously. The Array dialog box lets you specify the array dimensions, offsets, type of object, and transformation values. These parameters enable you to create many objects easily.

The Array dialog box is accessed by selecting an object and using the Tools ➪ Array command, or by clicking the Array button in the main toolbar. Figure 6-8 shows the Array dialog box. The title of the Array dialog box displays the center about which the transformations are performed.

The Array dialog box is *persistent*, meaning that, after being applied, the settings remain until they are changed. You can reset all the values at once by clicking the Reset All Parameters button.

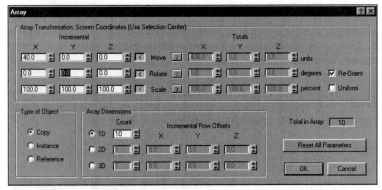

Figure 6-8: The Array dialog box defines the number of elements and transformation offsets in an array.

Linear arrays

Linear arrays are arrays where the objects form straight lines. Using the Array dialog box, you can specify an offset along the X, Y, and Z-axes, and define this offset as an incremental amount or as a total amount. To change between incremental values and total values, click the arrows to the left and right of the Move, Rotate, and Scale labels. For example, an array with 10 elements and an incremental value of 5 would position each successive object a distance of 5 units from the previous one. An array with 5 elements and a total value of 100 would position each element a distance of 20 units from the previous one.

The Type of Object section lets you define whether the new objects are copies, instances, or references. In the Array Dimensions section, you can specify the number of objects to copy along three different dimensions. You can also define incremental offsets for each individual row.

Tutorial: Building a white picket fence

To start with a simple example, we'll create a white picket fence. Because a fence repeats, we only need to create a single slat and use the Array command to duplicate it consistently.

To create a picket fence, follow these steps:

1. Click the Create tab in the Command Panel and select the Shapes category.

2. Click the Line button and, in the Front viewport, draw the outline of the single picket. To finish the outline, click the first point (where you started). At this point, a Spline dialog box will ask if you want to close the spline. Click OK.

Tip It is helpful if you set the Snap settings to Snap to Grid Points. To do this, open the Grid and Snap Settings dialog box by right-clicking any of the Snap buttons at the bottom of the window and select Grid Points from the Snaps panel. Then activate the Snap to Grid feature by clicking the 3D Snap Toggle.

3. With the outline finished, click the Select button in the main toolbar and select the outline. (If you forget to do this step, a new shape will be created the next time you click in a viewport.) Then select the Use Pivot Point Center flyout (to the right of the Reference Coordinate System drop-down).

4. Click the Modify tab in the Command Panel and click the Extrude button. The Extrude button is only available once you've selected a shape object.

5. In the Parameters rollout, enter **40** for the Amount and make sure that Cap Start and Cap End are selected. The picket now has depth as well as a top and bottom.

6. With the picket still selected, select Tools ➪ Array to open the Array dialog box (previously shown in Figure 6-8).

7. In the Array dialog box, enter a value of **150** in the X column's Move row under the Incremental section. (This is the incremental value for spacing each successive picket.) Next, enter **20** in the Array Dimensions section next to the 1D radio button. (This is the number of objects to include in the array.) Click OK to create the objects.

Figure 6-9 shows the completed fence.

Tutorial: Filling the survivalist's pantry

In order to gain more experience with using the Array command, let's help our favorite survivalist get ready for the Y2K crisis by stockpiling cans of food.

To create a 2D linear array of objects, follow these steps:

1. Create or import an object to duplicate. I've elected to create a can using a simple cylinder primitive. If you want to use a material map to label the cans, do this before opening the Array dialog box.

2. Select the can object and open the Array dialog box by choosing Tools ➪ Array or by clicking the Array button in the main toolbar.

3. In the Array Dimensions section, click the 2D-radio button and enter a value of **10** in the 2D Count field. Enter a value of **5** in the 1D Count field. This will create a two-dimensional array of 50 cans.

4. Notice the Radius value in the Parameters rollout in the Command Panel. This value tells you what the incremental value should be to keep the objects from overlapping. In the Array dialog box, enter an offset number greater than twice the radius value in the X column's Move row. For my example, the Radius is almost 15, so I set the Move offset to **35**.

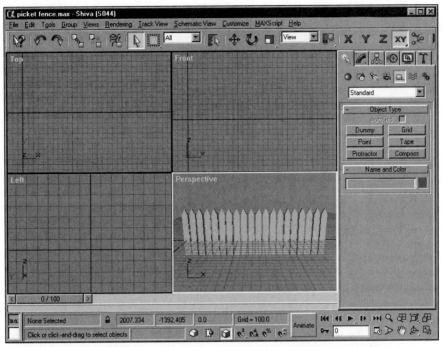

Figure 6-9: A picket fence created with ease using the Array command

Note   Don't worry if you don't get the values right the first time. The most recent values you entered into the Array dialog box will stay around until you exit MAX.

5. Set the Incremental Row Offset value (to the right of the 2D radio button) for the Y column to a value that is greater than twice the radius value.

6. If you plan on modifying the original object, select Instance as the Type of Object.

7. Click the OK button to apply the Array command.

Figure 6-10 shows the completed array. Our survivalist is now set. (Too bad that these are only virtual boxes of food.)

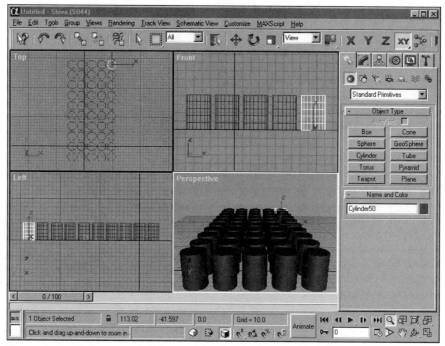

Figure 6-10: A 2D array of objects created with the Array command

Ring arrays

The Array dialog box can be used for creating more than just linear arrays. For the last example, all transformations were done around the Pivot Point Center. Notice that in Figure 6-8 (shown previously) the Screen Coordinates (Use Selection Center) are listed in the title at the top of the Array dialog box. In the next tutorial, you'll see how changing the transform center can create ring arrays.

All transformations are done relative to a center point. You can change the center point about which transformations are performed using the Use Center button on the main toolbar located immediately to the right of the Coordinate System drop-down list. There are three flyout options — Use Pivot Point Center, Use Selection Center, and Use Transform Coordinate Center.

Cross-Reference

For more about how these settings affect transformations, see Chapter 8, "Transforming Objects."

Tutorial: Building a Ferris wheel

Ferris wheels, like most of the rides at the fair, entertain by going around and around, with the riders seated in chairs spaced around the Ferris wheel's central point. The Array dialog box can also create objects around a central point. In this example, we'll use the Rotate transformation along with the Use Transform Coordinate Center to create a ring array.

To create a ring array, follow these steps:

1. In the front viewport, create the Ferris wheel chair object by drawing an outline (see Figure 6-11 for an example of the finished shape) using the Line tool under the Shape tab in the Command Panel.

2. To make the outline corners smooth, select the Modify tab and click the Edit Spline button.

3. In the Selection rollout, click the Vertex button (the four red dots icon). This will put the spline into Edit mode, and the Sub-Object label and Vertex buttons will turn yellow.

4. Right-click the vertices that you wish to smooth, and select Smooth from the pop-up menu. Click the Sub-Object button again to get out of Edit mode.

5. Click the Extrude button and enter a value of around **250** in the Amount field. This completes a single Ferris wheel chair.

6. From the Use Center button on the main toolbar, select the Use Transform Coordinate Center flyout.

7. From the Viewport Navigation buttons at the bottom of the screen, click the Zoom button and, in the Front View, zoom out (clicking and dragging up zooms in; clicking and dragging down zooms out). Click the Select and Move button on the main toolbar and then click the Ferris wheel chair. The cursor will change to the transform cursor (a black cross with four arrows). Position the Ferris wheel chair where the right-most chair would be located if the center of the viewport were the center of the wheel. Create a simple box that extends from the center to the chair and select it with the chair.

8. Open the Array dialog box by selecting Tools ➪ Array or by clicking the Array button in the main toolbar.

9. In between the Incremental and Totals sections, you see the labels Move, Rotate, and Scale. Click the arrow button to the right of the Rotate label. Set the Z column value to **360** degrees and make sure the Re-Orient option is disabled. A value of 360 degrees defines one complete revolution. Disabling the Re-Orient option will keep each chair object from rotating individually.

10. Set the 1D spinner Count value to **8**.

11. Click the OK button to create the array.

12. Add a Tube primitive to the outside of the struts to complete the Ferris wheel.

Figure 6-11 shows the resulting array.

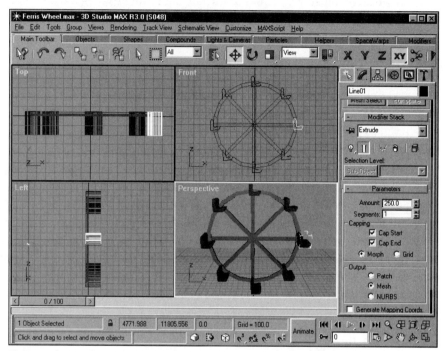

Figure 6-11: A ring array created by rotating objects about the Transform Coordinate Center

Spiral arrays

Before leaving arrays, there is one more special case to examine: spiral arrays. A spiral array results from moving and rotating objects along the same axis. Combinations of transforms in the Array dialog box can produce many interesting modeling possibilities.

Tutorial: Building a spiral staircase

To create a spiral staircase, we will first need to create a simple rectangular box that can be used for the steps. Because a spiral staircase winds about a center pole, we will need our transform's center to be located at one end of the stair object.

To create a spiral staircase, follow these steps:

1. Create an object to be used for the steps by clicking the Create tab in the Command Panel and selecting the Shape tab.

2. Create a wedge-shaped step by selecting the Line button. In the Front view, click where the vertices are located. (Turning on the Snap to Grid feature will help.) See Figure 6-12 for an example of the shape.

3. To smooth the wide end of the step, select the Modify tab and click the Edit Spline button. In the Selection rollout, click the Vertex button. Then right-click the vertex to be smoothed and select Smooth from the pop-up menu. You should have one wedge-shaped stair now.

4. To give the stair some depth, click the Extrude button and enter a value of **20** in the Amount field. Make sure the Cap Start and Cap End options are selected.

5. Click the Move and Select button in the main toolbar, then click and drag the stair object until the narrow end touches the center of the viewport in the Front view.

6. Select the Use Transform Coordinate Center flyout from the Use Center button on the main toolbar. This will transform the selected object about the center of the active viewport. You should notice the axes will be relocated to the center of the viewport.

7. Open the Array dialog box by choosing Tools ⇨ Array, or by clicking the Array button in the main toolbar.

8. In the Incremental section, enter the value of **50** in the Z column of the Move row, and **45** in the Z column of the Rotate row.

9. Set the 1D Count spinner to **20** or the number of steps you want.

10. Click the OK button to create the array.

11. Open the Create panel, click the Cylinder button, and create a cylinder that runs along the center axis.

Figure 6-12 shows the results of the spiral array.

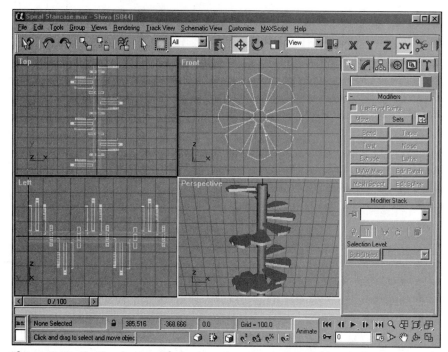

Figure 6-12: Getting fancy with the Array feature produced this spiral staircase.

Cloning over Time

Another way to create clones is to have them appear at different times in an animation. This cloning over time is accomplished with the Snapshot feature.

Using Snapshot

Another useful way to create multiple copies of an object is with the Snapshot command. This command creates copies, instances, references, or even meshes of a selected object as it is transformed over time. For example, you could create a series of stairs by positioning the bottom stair at frame 1 and the top stair at frame 100, and then select Tools ⇨ Snapshot and enter the number of steps to appear between these two in the Snapshot dialog box. Be aware that the Snapshot command will only work with objects that have an animation path defined.

You can open the Snapshot dialog box by selecting Tools ⇨ Snapshot or through the Array button flyout on the main toolbar. In the Snapshot dialog box, shown in Figure 6-13, you can choose to produce a single clone or a range of clones over a given number of frames. Selecting Single creates a single clone at the current frame.

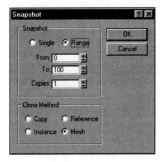

Figure 6-13: The Snapshot dialog box lets you clone a Copy, Instance, Reference, or Mesh.

Tip   Use the Snapshot command with the Snow Particle System to make snow pile up.

Tutorial: Following dancing footsteps

A fine example of the Snapshot tool would be to display the footsteps required for a tricky dance step, much like a dance school would use. (Not being a proficient dancer, I'm afraid my ignorance will show.)

First, we'll need to create some footsteps that can be accomplished easily enough by extruding a simple spline. Then, we'll animate these footsteps moving through the dance step and use the Snapshot tool to create clones at individual frames of interest.

To use the Snapshot tool to create clones at individual frames, follow these steps:

1. Create some footstep outlines using the Shape tool or import them from Illustrator as I have done. (See Figure 6-13 for an example of a footstep.) Click the Select Object button on the main toolbar and select all the footstep shapes.

2. Before we can extrude these outlines, we need to make sure that the splines are closed. Click the Modify tab in the Command Panel and click the Edit Spline button.

3. In the Selection rollout, click the Spline button to enter Sub-Object mode.

4. Select one of the footsteps (the spline should turn red to indicate that it is selected). Near the bottom of the Command Panel in the Geometry rollout, click the Close button to ensure that the spline is a closed path. Check the prompt line at the bottom of the screen—it may say, "No valid splines selected." This means that the spline is already a closed path. Repeat this for each footstep. When you're done, be sure to click the Sub-Object button to leave edit mode.

Note If you're unable to select one of the footsteps, then you didn't select them all before entering Edit Spline mode and you'll have to leave edit mode, select the footstep, then re-enter edit mode again.

5. You're now ready to extrude the spline. Select all the footsteps and click the Extrude button at the top of the Command Panel. Enter a value of **0.5** and make sure the Cap Start and Cap End options are checked.

6. Now for a quick animation lesson. Click the Animate button at the bottom of the window, and then click the Select and Move button. Move the Time Slider (located right below the bottom viewports) to Frame 20 and then position the footsteps in the Top View in their first position (you may need to Zoom and Pan). Repeat by moving the Time Slider to its next position and repositioning the footsteps. When you're finished, click the Play Animation button to check the steps. When you're finished animating, be sure to turn the Animate button off.

7. To take a Snapshot of each footstep, select a footstep and then select the Key Mode Toggle button (with a key icon) from the Playback controls. This changes the playback controls to Key mode. Click the Next Key button—your footsteps will move to their next position.

8. At each key, select the Tools ➪ Snapshot command to create a Snapshot clone.

Figure 6-14 shows a frame of the dance step animation with several footstep snapshots created.

Mirroring Objects

Have you ever positioned your face at the edge of a mirror? Many objects have a natural symmetry that you can exploit to require that only half an object be modeled. The human face is a good example. Symmetrical parts can be cloned using the Mirror command.

Using Mirror

The Mirror command creates a clone (or No Clone if you so choose) of the selected object about the current coordinate system. To open the Mirror dialog box, shown in Figure 6-15, choose Tools ➪ Mirror, or click the Mirror button located in the Array flyout. The Mirror dialog box can only be accessed if an object is selected.

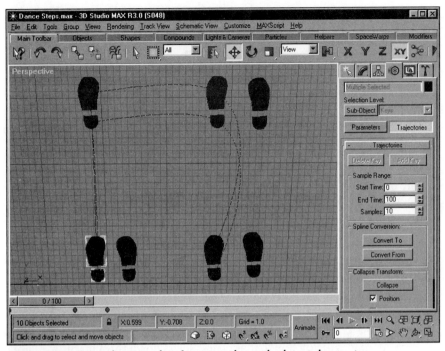

Figure 6-14: Using the Snapshot feature to learn the latest dance step

Figure 6-15: The Mirror dialog box can create an inverted clone of an object.

Within the Mirror dialog box, you can specify an axis or plane about which to mirror the selected object. You can also define an offset value. As with the other clone commands, you can specify whether the clone is to be a copy, an instance, or a reference, or you can choose No Clone, which will flip the object around the axis you specify. The dialog box also lets you mirror Inverse Kinematics limits, which reduces the number of IK parameters that need to be set.

Inverse Kinematics are covered in Chapter 29, "Creating an Inverse Kinematics System."

Tutorial: Mirroring a human figure

Creating a decent human figure is one of the tougher, more time-consuming modeling tasks that confront today's modelers. Luckily, the human body is one of the best examples of symmetry (as long as you're looking at only the external parts). Using the Mirror command, you can save time and effort by having to create only one half of a human figure.

After you model or import a human figure, work on details like eyes, ears, and arms on only one half of the figure. You can then cut off the unneeded half with the Slice modifier, and mirror the remaining half to create a perfectly symmetrical human figure.

To mirror a human figure, follow these steps:

1. Create or import a human figure. I've imported a man model from Poser.

2. Use the Slice Modifier to cut the human figure in half along the Y-axis. To do this, select Remove Top from the Slice Parameters rollout and rotate the Slice Plane subobject.

3. Select the Modify tab on the Command Panel and click the More button. On the Modifiers dialog box that appears, scroll down through the available modifiers and select Slice. Click OK. The Slice plane will appear in the viewports.

4. Make sure your figure is in the same position as shown in Figure 6-14 by using the Select and Rotate tool from the main toolbar. (You may want to constrain your rotations by using the X, Y, or Z Transform Axis Constraints buttons.)

5. Select the Sub-Object button to enable the Slice Modifier; then use the Slice Modifier to cut the human figure in half along the Y-axis. To do this, click the Remove Top radio button in the Slice Parameters rollout and rotate the Slice Plane subobject until only the half you wish to retain remains. (You may find it helpful to restrict the Slice Plane subobjects rotation by clicking the Restrict to Y button before beginning.)

6. With the half figure selected, choose Tools ➪ Mirror to open the Mirror Screen Coordinates dialog box or click the Mirror button in the main toolbar.

7. In the Mirror Screen Coordinates dialog box, select X as the Mirror Axis and Copy as the Clone Selection. If you've established any IK parameters, be sure to check the Mirror IK Limits option. Click OK to close the dialog box. If necessary, use the Select and Move tool to adjust the cloned half's position.

Tip   By making the Clone Selection an Instance, you can ensure that any future modifications to the right half of the figure will be automatically applied to the left half.

Figure 6-16 shows the resulting figure.

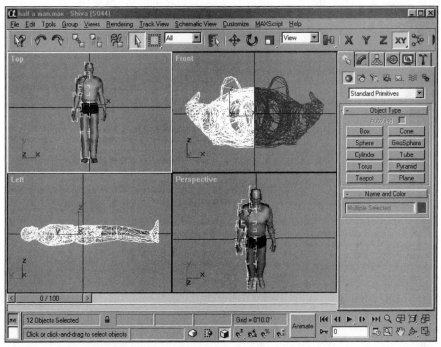

Figure 6-16: A perfectly symmetrical human figure, complements of the Mirror tool

Spacing Cloned Objects

Although the Array dialog box offers a lot of different options for positioning clones about regular dimensions, there are still other ways to regularly space cloned objects. The Spacing tool, for example, can position clones at regular intervals along a path, and the Ring Array System can position clones in a circular oscillating pattern.

Using the Spacing tool

The Spacing tool can only be accessed as a flyout under the Array button. When clicked, it opens the Spacing Tool dialog box, shown in Figure 6-17. This dialog box has buttons to Pick a Path or Pick Points. You can also specify Count, Spacing, and Offset values. The drop-down list offers several preset options including Divide Evenly, Centered, End Offset, and more.

Figure 6-17: The Spacing Tool dialog box lets you select how to position clones along a path.

There are two options for determining the spacing width: Edges and Centers. The Edges option spaces objects from the edge of its bounding box to the edge of the adjacent bounding box. The Follow option aligns the object with the path if the path is selected. Each object can be a Copy, Instance, or Reference of the original.

Tutorial: Building a roller coaster

To create a roller coaster, we'll need a path and a single cart. Then we can use the Spacing tool to clone this cart along the path.

To create a line of roller coaster carts by using the Spacing tool, follow these steps:

1. Open the Create panel and select the Shapes category. Then click the Line button and create a wavy roller coaster path.

2. Use the Line button again to create a simple outline of a roller coaster cart. Open the Modify panel and click the Extrude button; enter an Amount of **75**, and select both the Cap Start and Cap End options. You now have a cart to clone.

3. Open the Spacing Tool by selecting the flyout under the Array button. In the Spacing Tool dialog box, click the Pick Path button and select the wavy roller coaster path. The path name will appear on the button.

4. From the drop-down list, select the Start Offset ⇨ Divide Evenly option. Enter a Count value of **9** and a Start Offset of **100**.

5. Select the Edges Context option and make all clones Instances. Click Apply when the result looks right and close the Spacing Tool dialog box.

Figure 6-18 shows the simple results.

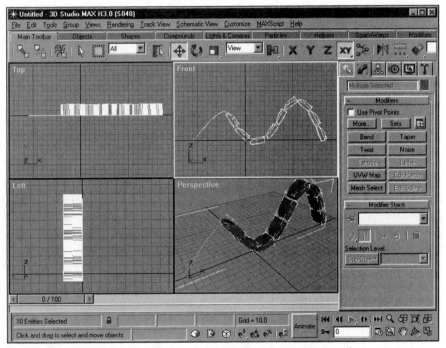

Figure 6-18: This roller coaster was created using the Spacing Tool.

Working with a Ring array

The Ring Array System can be found by opening the Create panel and selecting the Systems category. Clicking the Ring Array button opens a Parameters rollout, shown in Figure 6-19. In this rollout are parameters for the ring's Radius, Amplitude, Cycles, Phase, and the Number of elements to include.

Figure 6-19: The Parameters rollout of the Ring Array system can create an oscillating circular array of objects.

The actual array is created by clicking and dragging the Radius value for the array. Initially, all elements are simple box objects.

These boxes can be changed to another object. To change the object, open the Track View and locate the object that you would like to have appear in the array. Select the object and click the Copy Object button. Then locate the Box object for the Ring Array (this can be found under a Dummy object). Select the Box object and click the Paste Object button. If you select the Replace All Instances option, all Ring Array elements will be replaced.

Tip   If you are having trouble locating the Ring Array, give the array object a name and look for the name in the Track View.

The Amplitude, Cycles, and Phase values define the sinusoidal nature of the circle. The Amplitude is the maximum distance the objects can be positioned from the center axis. If the Amplitude is set to 0, then all objects lie in the same plane. The Cycles value is the number of waves that occur around the entire circle. The Phase determines which position along the circle starts in the up position.

For example, Figure 6-20 shows a Ring Array with 20 elements, a Radius of 100, an Amplitude of 25, a Cycles value of 2, and a Phase of 0. The Dummy object in the middle lets you control the entire ring's position and orientation.

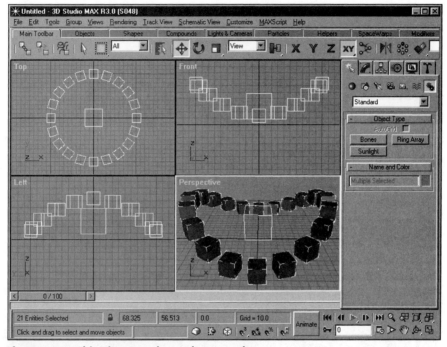

Figure 6-20: This Ring Array has only two cycles.

Tutorial: Creating a carousel

Continuing with the theme park attractions motif, this example will create a carousel. The horse model comes from Poser.

To use a Ring Array system to create a carousel, follow these steps:

1. Import a horse model. Then create and position a cylinder object in the middle. Select the horse and open the Modify panel. In the Edit Geometry rollout, click the Attach button and select the cylinder.

2. Open the Create panel, select the Systems category, and click the Ring Array button. Drag in the Top viewport to create a Ring Array. Then enter a Radius value of **2**, an Amplitude of **0.2**, a Cycles value of **3**, and a Number value of **8**. (The Phase value doesn't really matter.)

3. Select the Track View ⇨ Open Track View command. Click the plus sign to the left of the Object track. Click the plus sign next to the Horse object and then locate the "Object (Editable Mesh)" object and select it. Click the Copy Object button at the top of the Track View.

4. Right-click the plus sign next to the Dummy01 object and again on the Box01 track. Select the "Object (Box)" track and click the Paste Object button. This will open the Paste dialog box shown in Figure 6-21. Select Instance and the Replace all Instances option and click OK. Close the Track View.

Figure 6-21: This Paste dialog box lets you replace all instances.

5. Select the Dummy object and scale it until the horses become visible. Right-click the Dummy object and select Properties from the pop-up menu. Then select the Ignore Extent option. Now you can use the Zoom Extents All button to see all the horses.

6. To complete the carousel, add two more cylinders and a cone.

   Figure 6-22 shows the finished carousel. Notice how each horse is at a different height.

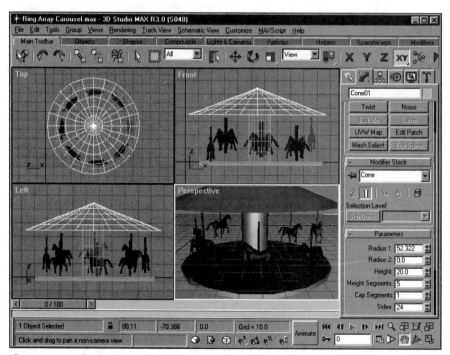

Figure 6-22: The horses in the carousel were created using a Ring Array system.

Summary

There are many ways to clone an object. You could use the Clone command under the Edit menu or the Shift Clone feature for quickly creating numerous clones. Clones can be copies, instances, or references. Each differs in how it retains links to the original object.

This chapter covered the following object creation and cloning topics:

✦ Using the Create panel

✦ Using object names and colors

✦ Cloning copies, instances, and references

✦ Building Linear, Ring, and Spiral arrays of objects

✦ Using the Snapshot and Mirror features

✦ Using the Spacing Tool and the Ring Array System

Arrays are another means of cloning. You can use the Array dialog box to produce clones in three different dimensions, and you can specify the offset transformations. In the next chapter you will learn to select and group objects, and to change their properties.

✦   ✦   ✦

Selecting and Grouping Objects

One of the drawbacks of using the Array command is that it generates many objects. With all these objects onscreen, it can become very tricky to locate the one object you wish to work with. This chapter covers selecting and grouping objects.

MAX offers many different ways to select objects. You can select by name, color, type, and even material. Along with the need to select objects, it is natural to want to group objects together in an easily accessible form, especially as a scene becomes more complex. MAX's grouping features enable you to organize all of the objects that you're dealing with, thereby making your workflow more efficient.

Selecting Objects

Now that you've learned to create objects, you've probably gone on a crazy creation spree and have created a scene with so many objects that you can't keep them straight. Once an object is created, it can be edited, manipulated, and controlled, but only if it can be selected.

MAX includes several methods for selecting objects — the easiest being simply clicking it in one of the viewports. Selected objects turn white and are enclosed in brackets. With many objects in a scene, clicking directly on a single object, free from the others, can be difficult. In complicated scenes, selecting an object by referring to its name is often much easier.

There are many different ways to select objects. These will be discussed in the sections to follow.

Selection filters

Before examining the selection commands in the Edit menu, Selection Filters need to be explained. With a complex scene that includes geometry, lights, cameras, shapes, and so on, it can be difficult to select the exact object that you want. Selection Filters can simplify this task.

A Selection Filter specifies which types of objects can be selected. The Selection Filter drop-down list is located on the main toolbar. Selecting Shapes, for example, makes only shape objects available for selection. Clicking a geometry object with the Shape Selection Filter enabled, does nothing.

The available filters include All, Geometry, Shapes, Lights, Cameras, Helpers, and Warps. There is also a Combos option that opens the Filter Combinations dialog box. From this dialog box, you can select combinations of objects to filter. Figure 7-1 shows the Filter Combinations dialog box for selecting a custom filter of several object types.

Figure 7-1: The Filter Combinations dialog box enables you to create a custom selection filter.

Select buttons

On the main toolbar are four buttons used to select objects. The Select Object button looks like the arrow cursor. The other three buttons select and transform objects. They are Select and Move, Select and Rotate, and Select and Scale. (These transformations will be discussed in Chapter 8, "Transforming Objects.") Any of these tools can be used to select objects.

Tip

At any time, you can return to the Select Object button by right-clicking an object and choosing Select Mode from the pop-up menu.

Selecting with the Edit menu

The Edit menu includes several convenient selection commands.

Select All

The Edit ⇨ Select All command does just what you would think. It selects all objects in the current scene of the type defined by the Selection Filter.

Select None

The Edit ⇨ Select None command deselects all objects. You can also simulate this command by clicking in any viewport away from all objects.

Select Invert

The Edit ⇨ Select Invert command selects all objects defined by the Selection Filter that are currently not selected and deselects all currently selected objects.

Select by Color

Selecting the Edit ⇨ Select by ⇨ Color command lets you click a single object in any of the viewports. All objects with the same color as the one you selected will be selected.

Note Even if you already have an object of that color selected, you still must select an object of the desired color.

This command, of course, will not work on any objects without an associated color such as cameras and Space Warps. Geometry, Shapes, Lights, and Grid Helper Objects all have object colors.

Select by Name

The Edit ⇨ Select by ⇨ Name command opens the Select Objects dialog box. Clicking the Select by Name button on the main toolbar, positioned to the right of the Selection Filter drop-down list, can also open this dialog box. Figure 7-2 shows the dialog box.

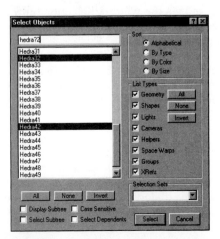

Figure 7-2: The Select Objects dialog box displays all objects in the current scene by name.

Tip   The Select Objects dialog box can be opened at any time by pressing the H keyboard shortcut.

You select objects by clicking their names in the list and then clicking the Select button. To pick and choose several objects, hold down the Ctrl key while selecting. Holding down the Shift key selects a range of objects.

Tip   There is an identical version of the Select Objects dialog box that works in a modeless state and enables you to interact with the viewports behind the dialog box. This dialog box is called the Selection Floater, and it can be accessed by selecting Tools ➪ Selection Floater.

You can also type an object name in the field above the name list. All objects that match the typed characters will be selected. The Sort options affect how the list is displayed. Selecting the Sort by Size option sorts the objects by the number of faces.

The Display Subtree option will include all child objects in the list. By enabling the Select Subtree option, you select all child objects along with their parent objects. The Select Dependents option automatically selects all instances and references.

The Select Object dialog box isn't subject to the Selection Filter because the object types can be selected in the dialog box. Selection Sets are also accessible from the Select Objects dialog box. They will be discussed shortly.

Select by Region

The Edit ➪ Select by Region command lets you select from one of two different methods for selecting objects in the viewport using the mouse. To select objects, make sure you're in select mode and click away from any of the objects and drag over the objects to select. The first method for selecting objects is Window Selection. This method selects all objects that are contained completely within the dragged outline. The Crossing Selection method selects any objects that are inside or overlapping the dragged outline.

These two selection methods can be accessed via the Window Selection button on the Prompt Line at the bottom of the screen (the second button to the right of the Prompt Line).

You can also change the shape of the selection outline. The Selection Region button on the main toolbar to the left of the Selection Filter drop-down list includes flyout buttons for Rectangular, Circular, and Fence Selection Regions.

Selecting multiple objects

As you work with objects in MAX, there will be times when you'll want to apply a modification or transform to several objects at once. There are several ways to select multiple objects. With the Select by Name dialog box open, you can choose several objects using the standard Ctrl and Shift keys. Holding the Ctrl key down selects or deselects multiple items, but holding the Shift key down selects all consecutive items between the first selected and the second selected items.

The Ctrl key also works when selecting objects in the viewport if one of the Select buttons is enabled. You can tell if you're in select mode by looking for a button that's highlighted green. If you hold down the Ctrl key and click an object, then the object is added to the selection set. If you click an item that is already selected, then it is deselected. If you drag over multiple objects while holding down the Ctrl key, then all items in the dragged selection are added to the selection set.

The Alt key deselects objects from the current selection set, opposite of what the Ctrl key does.

If you drag over several objects while holding down the Shift key, then the selection set will be inverted. Each item that is selected will be deselected and vice versa.

Object hierarchies can be selected by double clicking an object. If you double-click, any children of those objects will be selected. You can also right-click the object and select the Select Children or Deselect Children commands. When an object with a hierarchy is selected, the Page Up and Page Down keys select the next object up or down the hierarchy.

Another way to select multiple objects is by dragging within the viewport using the Window and Crossing Selection methods discussed previously in the "Selecting by Region" section.

Tutorial: Selecting objects

Every Saturday morning, a regular activity for most children is deciding which cartoons to watch on TV. Now that you've learned all about selecting objects, you can try this activity also (and it doesn't need to be on Saturday morning). Hou Soon Ming is a modeler based in Singapore who creates some fun cartoon-like characters. We'll use these characters to practice our selection skills.

On the CD-ROM

The models used in this example have been included on the CD-ROM, complements of Hou Soon Ming. You can find more of Ming's work at the 3D Toon Shop Web site at www.its-ming.com.

To select objects, follow these steps:

1. Import the 3D Toon Shop models.

2. Click the Select Object button in the main toolbar and click the yellow Crescent Moon character in one of the viewports. (This object consists of only one part, so the entire object is selected.)

3. Open the Modify panel and look at the Name for this object in the Name and Color rollout, which is "Moon."

4. Click the Select and Move button, and then click the Deer's body and drag with the cursor toward the right. As you can see, the body is an object independent of the other parts of the Deer object.

5. Select Edit ➪ Undo Move to piece the Deer back together again.

6. Still using the Select and Move tool, drag an outline around the entire Deer in the Top view to select all the Deer parts and then try moving the Deer again. This time the entire Deer moves as one entity.

Note   Grouping all these parts together will enable the objects to move together. Later in the chapter, grouping functions will be covered.

7. Select Group ➪ Group to form a group with all the Deer parts. (This will organize all the Deer objects into one easily selectable object.) The Group dialog box will open and you can name your new group. Name it **Deer**. (You can verify this in the Create panel under the Name and Color rollout.)

8. Open the Select Object dialog box by clicking the Select by Name button in the main toolbar. Notice that the Deer group is at the top of the list and all the other objects are scattered in individual parts throughout the list.

9. Complete this exercise by grouping the Fish and Ant models.

Figure 7-3 shows our cartoon friends used in this tutorial. Grouping the Deer parts together will make it easier to work with the entire character. Another way to organize the model is to link all the various body parts to the body object. Then the parts will move along with the body.

Cross-Reference   Linking objects is covered in Chapter 27, "Building Linked Hierarchies."

Locking selection sets

If you've finally selected the exact objects that you wish to work with, the Lock Selection Set button contained on the Status Bar disables the selection of any additional objects. The keyboard shortcut toggle for this command is the Spacebar.

Selecting by Material

The Material Editor includes a button that selects all objects in a scene with the same material applied. This button is found at the bottom of the toolbar to the right of the Material slots. It is only active if the current material is applied to more than one object in the scene.

When the Select by Material button is clicked, the Select Object dialog box, shown previously in Figure 7-2, opens with all objects that use the selected material.

Another way to view objects with similar materials is to open the Material/Map Browser. When you select the Scene options, all materials and the objects that they are applied to are listed.

Figure 7-3: Several cartoon friends provided by Hou Soon Ming and grouped by you.

Cross-Reference   The Material Editor and the Material/Map Browser are discussed in detail in Chapter 17, "Exploring the Material Editor."

Selecting objects in the Track view

The Track View includes a hierarchy of all aspects of the scene, including all the objects. To view the tracks for the objects, click the + that precedes the Objects entry. A hierarchy of all the objects in a scene will be displayed.

Cross-Reference   Using Track View is covered in Chapter 31, "Working with Track View."

At the bottom left of the Track View window is the Select by Name text field. Typing an object name in this field will automatically select the object's track in the Track View window, but not in the viewport. Figure 7-4 shows the Track View with the Object tracks displayed. In this figure, the word "moon" has been typed to help locate the moon object.

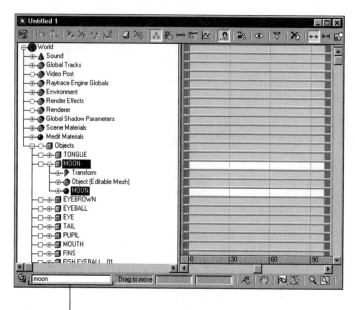

Select by Name text field

Figure 7-4: The Track View can be used to select objects.

Tip   Within the Select by Name text field, you can use wildcards to locate objects. Acceptable wildcards include an asterisk (*) for multiple characters in a row and a question mark (?) for single characters. For example, an entry of **hedra*** will select all objects beginning with "hedra" regardless of the ending.

Selecting objects in the Schematic views

The Schematic View offers another hierarchical look at your scene. It displays all links and relationships between objects and can be used to select objects. Each object in the Schematic View is displayed as a rectangular node.

Cross-Reference   More information on the Schematic View is presented in Chapter 28, "Using Schematic View."

To select an object in the viewport, find its rectangular representation in the Schematic View and simply double-click it. To select multiple objects in the Schematic View, drag an outline over all the rectangular nodes that you wish to select and enable the Synchronize Selection button. The Synchronize Selection button automatically selects any objects in the viewport that is selected in the Schematic View, and vice versa.

The Schematic View also includes the Select by Name text field just like the Track View for selecting an object by typing its name. Figure 7-5 shows the Schematic View with two objects selected.

Synchronize Selection

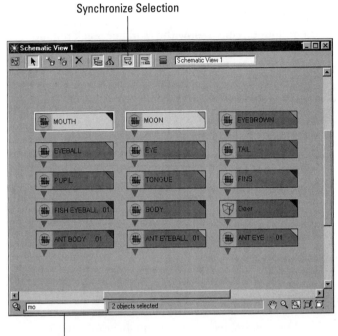

Select by Name text field

Figure 7-5: The Schematic View provides another easy way to select objects.

Selecting Subobjects

Most objects include *subobjects*. These are the geometric parts that make up the objects; examples of such parts are vertices, edges, faces, polygons, and elements. As you begin to explore the modeling features of MAX, these subobjects are the means of modeling many of the details.

Cross-Reference   For more details on working with subobjects, see Chapter 9, "Modifying Objects."

Using the Sub-Object button

When the Modify tab of the Command Panel is selected, the first rollout available is the Modifier Stack. Under this rollout is a Sub-Object button. This button is enabled when the selected object includes subobject elements. Clicking this button enables you to select the subobject type to work with. These types are displayed in the drop-down list to the right of the Sub-Object button. These types are also displayed as icons in the rollout directly below the Modifier Stack rollout.

New Feature

The Sub-Object element icons are new to Release 3.

Once a specific subobject type is selected, the selection process will be restricted to the specific subobject type. The selection process still works in the same way as when selecting entire objects, including the use of the Select All, None, and Invert commands in the Edit menu, dragging an outline over subobjects in the viewport, and using the Ctrl, Shift, and Alt keys.

Tip

When you click the Sub-Object button, you enter a Sub-Object specific mode that displays objects differently. The Sub-Object button turns yellow to remind you of this mode. To exit this mode, you'll need to click the Sub-Object button again.

Tutorial: Melting a snowball

As an example of using subobject selection, we're going to take a perfect sphere and melt it with help from the Noise Modifier.

To select and modify a sphere's subobject elements, follow these steps:

1. Create a sphere object by opening the Create panel and clicking the Sphere button. Drag in the top viewport to create a sphere.

2. Click the Select Object button (on the toolbar) to exit Create mode, then select the sphere. Open the Modify panel and click the Mesh Select button to enter a mode where you can select subobjects. This will make the Sub-Object button become accessible along with the Vertex, Edge, Face, Polygon, and Element buttons below it in the Mesh Select Parameters rollout. Click the Sub-Object button to activate it.

Note

Before you clicked the Mesh Select button, the sphere was a Parametric Primitive defined by mathematical formulas. You cannot select subobjects on a Primitive object. The Mesh Select Modifier changes the sphere to a mesh object.

3. Click the Face button, or select Face from the Sub-Object drop-down list. You are now in subobject mode, as indicated by the yellow buttons.

4. Make sure that the Ignore Backfaces option is selected in the Mesh Select Parameters rollout, then drag over a large section of the sphere in the Front view. The Ignore Backfaces option enables the front faces to be selected

without selecting any faces behind them on the other side of the sphere. The selected faces will turn red. (I guess they are embarrassed by the selection.)

5. With the faces selected, click the Noise button at the top of the Modify panel to apply the Noise Modifier. Then enter values of **5** for X, **5** for Y, and **100** for Z in the Strength section. This will cause the selected faces to be distorted mainly in the Z direction as if melting.

Figure 7-6 shows the effect of selecting several faces and applying the Noise Modifier.

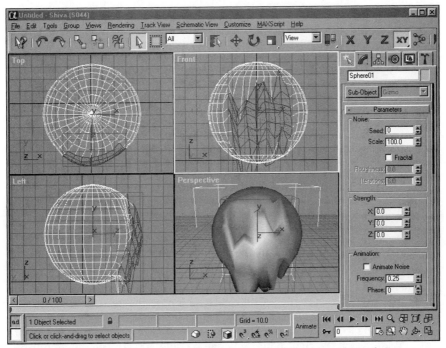

Figure 7-6: A simple sphere after selecting several faces and applying the Noise Modifier.

Using Named Selection Sets

With a group of selected objects you can establish a Selection set. Once established as a Selection Set, this group of selected objects can be recalled at any time by selecting the set name from the Named Selection Set drop-down list (or by selecting it from the Select Objects dialog box). To establish a Selection set, type a name in the Named Selection Set drop-down list toward the right end of the main toolbar.

Named Selection Sets can also be set for subobject selections. Be aware that these subobject selection sets are only available when you're in subobject edit mode and only for the currently selected object.

Editing named selections

Once several Named Selection Sets have been created, you can use the Edit Named Selections dialog box, shown in Figure 7-7, to view the objects contained in each set, delete sets, add new objects to a set, and combine the sets in several ways. Selecting the Edit ⇨ Edit Named Selections command opens this dialog box.

Figure 7-7: The Edit Named Selections dialog box lets you view and manage selection sets.

The current Named Selection Sets are viewed in the pane on the left. Selecting a set displays all the objects in the set on the right. If multiple sets are selected, then only objects similar to both sets are displayed on the right. You can add and remove objects from a set by selecting the object and clicking the appropriate button underneath the right pane. Sets can be deleted with the Delete button.

If more than one set is selected, the Combine, Subtract (A-B), Subtract (B-A), and Intersection buttons become active. Clicking any of these buttons opens a dialog box where a new set can be named.

Tutorial: Combining selection sets

When working with multiple object sets, you will often want to scale or apply a Modifier to both objects at the same time. To do this, a Selection Set that includes all the parts can make the selection process much easier. If each individual object has a selection set defined, then the Edit Named Selection dialog box can be used to combine these two sets.

To combine two selection sets, follow these steps:

1. Open the Edit Named Selection dialog box by selecting the Edit ➪ Edit Named Selection command.

2. In the dialog box, hold down the Ctrl key and click the two sets to combine them. For this tutorial, select the "Fish parts" and the "Deer parts" sets.

3. With two or more sets selected, the buttons below the Named Selections list become enabled. Click the Combine button. A simple Merge Named Selections dialog box appears where you can type in a new name for the combined sets. Type **Fish and Deer** and click OK. The new set will appear in the Edit Named Selections list.

Setting Object Properties

Once an object or multiple objects are selected, you can view their Object Properties by selecting Edit ➪ Properties. Alternatively, you could right-click the object and select Properties from the pop-up menu. Figure 7-8 shows the Object Properties dialog box.

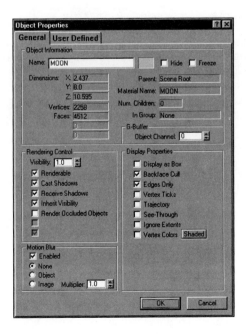

Figure 7-8: The Object Properties dialog box displays valuable information about a selected object and enables you to alter Rendering, Motion Blur, and Display settings.

The Object Properties dialog box contains valuable information about the current selection. For a single object, the dialog box lists details about the object in the Object Information section. These details include the object's name, color, XYZ dimensions, and number of vertices and faces, as well as who the object's parent is, its Material Name, the number of children, and whether it's in a group or not. The name and color can be altered using the Object Properties dialog box, but the rest of this information is for display only.

Note The two fields underneath the Vertices and Faces are used only when the properties for a Shape are being displayed. These fields show the number of Shape Vertices and Shape Curves.

If the properties for multiple objects are to be displayed, the Object Properties dialog box places the text, "Multiple Selected," in the Name field. The properties that are in common between all these objects are displayed.

The Object Properties dialog box can be displayed for all geometric objects and shapes, as well as for lights, cameras, helpers, and Space Warps.

New Feature Displaying Object Properties for lights, cameras, helpers, and Space Warps is new to Release 3.

The Object Properties dialog box also includes several settings for controlling how an object or set is rendered and displayed.

Hiding and freezing objects

You can hide or freeze objects in a scene by selecting the Hide or Freeze option at the top of the Object Properties dialog box. The Hide option makes the selected object in the scene invisible, and the Freeze option turns the selected object dark gray and doesn't enable it to be transformed or selected. To unhide or unfreeze an object open the Display Floater by selecting Tools ➪ Display Floater. Figure 7-9 shows the dialog box that includes buttons for controlling which objects are hidden and frozen.

Figure 7-9: The Display Floater dialog box controls the hiding and freezing of objects.

The Display Floater dialog box includes two tabs: Hide/Freeze and Object Level. The Hide/Freeze tab splits the dialog box into two columns, one for Hide and one for Freeze. Both columns have similar buttons that will let you let you hide or freeze Selected or Unselected objects, By Name or By Hit. Each column also has additional buttons to unhide or unfreeze All objects, By Name, or in the case of Freeze, by Hit.

The Object Level tab lets you hide objects by Category (lights, cameras, and so on) as well as set Display Properties for the current selection.

Tutorial: Playing hide and seek

Children often learn by playing games, so I've got a game for you to try. It's the classic game of Hide and Seek with a new twist. The twist is that I've hidden two objects in this scene and you need to find them.

To play Hide and Seek, follow these steps:

1. Open the Hide and Seek.max file from the CD-ROM.

2. Locate the two hidden objects in the scene by opening the Display Floater. To do this, select Tools ➪ Display Floater.

3. In the Display Floater, select the Hide/Freeze tab and in the Unhide section, click the Name button. This will open the Unhide Objects dialog box that lists all the hidden objects in the scene.

4. Select any or all objects from the list and click the Unhide button. This will close the Unhide Objects dialog box and make the hidden objects visible once again.

Note   Notice that the Display Floater is still open. That's because it's modeless. It doesn't need to be closed in order for you to keep working.

5. The Deer and Moon objects are grayed out. This means that they are frozen and you cannot Select and Move them. To unfreeze these objects, you use the Freeze column in the Display Floater. In the Unfreeze section, click the By Hit button, then unfreeze the Deer and Moon by clicking each.

Figure 7-10 shows the Hide and Seek scene before starting the game. Notice how hidden objects aren't visible and frozen objects are grayed out.

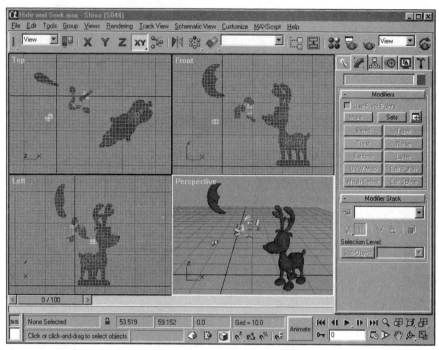

Figure 7-10: Our cartoon friends, frozen and hidden

Setting Rendering Controls

In the Object Properties dialog box, the Rendering Controls do just what you'd expect: they control how an object is rendered. The Visibility spinner defines a value for how opaque (nontransparent) an object is. The Inherit Visibility option causes an object to adopt the same visibility setting as its parent. The Renderable option causes an object to be ignored by the render engine.

Note   The Inherit Visibility option can also be animated for making objects slowly disappear.

The Cast Shadows and Receive Shadows options control how shadows are rendered for the selected object. The Render Occluded Objects option causes the rendering engine to render any objects hidden by the selected object. The hidden or occluded objects can have glows or other effects applied to them, effects which would show up if rendered.

New Feature   The Visibility spinner and the Render Occluded Objects option are both new in Release 3.

Enabling Motion Blur

Motion Blur can also be set from within the Object Properties dialog box. The Motion Blur effect causes objects that move fast, such as the Road Runner, to be blurred (which is useful in portraying speed). The render engine accomplishes this effect by rendering multiple copies of the object or image.

 More information on these blur options is in Chapter 36, "Setting Rendering Parameters."

The Object Properties dialog box can set two different types of Motion Blur: Object and Image. Object motion blur only affects the object and is not affected by the camera movement. Image motion blur applies the effect to the entire image and is applied after rendering.

 A third type of Motion Blur is called Scene Motion Blur and is available in the Video Post interface. See Chapter 39, "Using the Video Post Interface," for information on using Scene Motion Blur.

Setting Display properties

Display properties don't affect how an object is rendered, only how it is displayed in the viewport window. These options can speed up or slow down the viewport refresh rates. For example, the first option, Display as Box, will increase the viewport update rate dramatically for complex scenes, but at the expense of any detail.

The Backface Cull option will cause the faces on the backside of the object to not be displayed when turned on. MAX considers the direction that each normal is pointing and doesn't display a face whose normal is pointing away from the view.

The Edges Only option displays only the edges of each face in wireframe mode. When Edges Only is not selected, a dashed line indicates polygon faces. The Vertex Ticks option displays all object vertices as blue plus signs.

The Trajectory option displays any animated motions as paths.

 Using animated motion paths is described in more detail in Chapter 30, "Animation Basics."

The See-Through option causes shaded objects to appear transparent. This option is similar to the Visibility setting in the Rendering Control section, except it doesn't affect the rendered image. It is only for displaying objects in the viewports. This option really doesn't help in wireframe mode.

The Ignore Extents option causes an object to be ignored when you are using the Zoom Extents button in the Viewport Navigation controls. For example, if you have a camera or light that is positioned at a distance from the objects in the scene, then any time you use the Zoom Extents All button, the objects would be so small that you would not be able to see them. If you set the Ignore Extent option for the camera or light, and then the Zoom Extents All button would zoom in on just the objects.

New Feature The See-Through and Ignore Extents display options are new to Release 3.

The Vertex Color option will display the colors of any Editable Mesh vertices that have been assigned colors. The Shaded button causes the meshes to be shaded by the vertex colors.

Cross-Reference Assigning Vertex Colors is discussed in Chapter 19, "Working with Materials and Maps."

Working with Groups

Grouping objects together organizes your objects. Groups are different from Selection Sets in that groups exist like one object. Selecting any object in the group selects the entire group, whereas selecting an object in a Selection Set will only select that object and not the Selection Set. Groups can be opened to add, delete, or reposition objects within the group. Groups can also contain other groups. This is called *nesting groups*.

Creating groups

The Group command enables you to create a group. To do so, simply select the desired objects and choose the Group ⇨ Group command. A simple Name Group dialog box will open and enable you to give the group a name. The newly created group will display a new bounding box that encompasses all the objects in the group. Groups can also be created or nested within groups.

Tip You can always identify groups in the Select by Name dialog box because they are surrounded by square brackets.

Dissolving groups

The Ungroup command enables you to break up a group. To do so, simply select the desired group and choose the Group ⇨ Ungroup command. This dissolves the group, and all the objects within the group revert to separate objects. The Ungroup command only breaks up the currently selected group. All nested groups within a group stay intact.

The easiest way to dissolve an entire group, including any nested groups, is with the Explode command. This command eliminates the group and makes each object separate.

Opening and closing groups

The Open command enables you access to the objects within a group. Grouped objects will move, scale, and rotate as a unit when transformed, but individual objects within a group can be transformed independently once a group is opened with the Open command.

To move an individual object in a group, select the group and use the Group ⇨ Open command. The white bounding box will change to pink. Then select an object within the group and move it with the Select and Move button. Select the Group ⇨ Close command to reinstate the group.

Attaching and detaching objects

The Attach and Detach commands enable you to insert or remove objects from an opened group without dissolving the group. To do this, use the Group ⇨ Attach or Detach command. Remember to close the group when finished.

Summary

Selecting objects enables you to work with them, and MAX includes many different ways to select objects. In this chapter you've done the following:

✦ Selected objects with the Edit menu by Name, Color, and Region

✦ Selected objects with similar materials and used the Track and Schematic Views

✦ Learned about several different selection features such as the Selection Filter and Named Selection Sets

✦ Accessed the Object Properties dialog box to set Rendering and Display settings for an object

✦ Discovered how to work with groups

In the next chapter, you'll learn how to transform objects using the move, rotate, and scale features.

✦   ✦   ✦

Transforming Objects

Transforming an object is the fundamental process of "repositioning" or changing an object's position, rotation, and scale. Transformations occur when you select an object or objects, click one of the transformation buttons located on the main toolbar, and then drag in the viewport to apply the transformation. MAX includes various tools to help in the transformation of objects, including the Transform Gizmo, the Transform Type-In dialog box, and the Transform Managers.

This chapter will cover each of these tools and several others that make transformations more automatic. Examples are the Alignment dialog box and the Snap features.

Viewing Coordinates on the Status Bar

The Status Bar includes three fields for displaying transformation coordinates. Moving an object will display the XYZ offsets of the move in these fields. Rotating an object will display the angle offsets of the rotation. For scaling, the fields will show the scale as a percentage of the original size. When no objects are being transformed, these fields show the absolute position of the cursor in world coordinates based on the active viewport.

Figure 8-1 shows the coordinates for the cursor at –7.996, 5.518, and 0.

◆ ◆ ◆ ◆

In This Chapter

Viewing coordinate values

Using the transform buttons and gizmo

Transforming accurately with the Transform Type-In

Moving, rotating, and scaling objects

Aligning objects to one another

Using the various Helpers

Transforming objects using the Snap functions

◆ ◆ ◆ ◆

Transform Gizmo

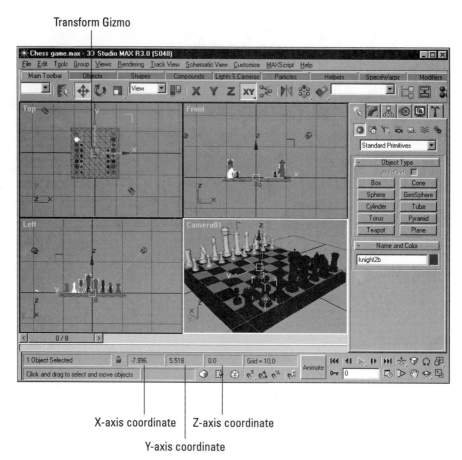

X-axis coordinate   Z-axis coordinate

Y-axis coordinate

Figure 8-1: The coordinate fields give you precise coordinate information.

Using the Transform Buttons

There are three transform buttons located on the main toolbar: Select and Move, Select and Rotate, and Select and Uniform Scale, as displayed in Table 8-1. Using these buttons, you can select objects and transform them by dragging with the mouse.

Table 8-1
Transform Buttons

Toolbar Button	Name	Description
✛	Select and Move	Enters move mode where clicking and dragging an object moves it.
↻	Select and Rotate	Enters rotate mode where clicking and dragging an object rotates it.
◰ ◳ ◱	Select and Uniform Scale, Select and Non-Uniform Scale, Select and Squash	Enters scale mode where clicking and dragging an object scales it.

Only the Select and Uniform Scale button is a flyout, consisting of two additional buttons: Select and Non-Uniform Scale, and Select and Squash. When either of these buttons is selected, a warning dialog box appears. This warning dialog box states that using either the Non-Uniform Scale or Squash commands can cause difficulty for other Modifiers that might be applied. You can disable this warning by selecting the "Do not show this message again" option on the dialog box, or by opening the Preference Settings dialog box and turning off the warning.

Working with the Transform Gizmo

The Transform Gizmo (shown previously in Figure 8-1) is displayed at the center of the selected object when one of the transform buttons is selected. Its orientation is determined by the current coordinate system. It includes three color-coded arrows representing the X, Y, and Z-axes. The X-axis is colored red, the Y-axis is colored green, and the Z-axis is colored blue.

 New Feature The Transform Gizmo is new to Release 3.

If the Transform Gizmo is not visible, you can enable it in the Viewport panel of the Preference Settings dialog box. You can also set its size and whether it uses Labels, a Center Box, and Planes. The Transform Gizmo can be hidden by selecting the View ➪ Show Transform Gizmo command.

 Tip The keyboard shortcut for displaying and hiding the Transform Gizmo is the X key. The = and - keys can be used to increase and decrease the Transform Gizmo's scale.

When the cursor is moved over the top of one of these axes' arrows in the active viewport, the axis is selected and changes to yellow. Dragging the selected axis restricts the transformation to that axis only.

At each corner of the Transform Gizmo are two perpendicular lines for each plane. These lines let you transform along two axes. The colors of these lines match the various colors used for the axes. For example, in the Perspective view, dragging on a red and blue corner would constrain the movement to the XZ plane.

At the center of the Transform Gizmo is a Center Box that can be used to transform the object along all three axes.

Using the Transform Type-In

The Transform Type-In dialog box allows you to enter numerical coordinates or offsets that can be used for precise transformations. This dialog box can be opened by selecting Tools ⇨ Transform Type-In, or by right-clicking the Select and Move, Select and Rotate, or Select and Scale button. The Transform Type-In dialog box is different for each transform type.

Note   Right-clicking any of the transform buttons will open the Transform Type-In dialog box, but the dialog box will open for whichever button is enabled, regardless of which button you right-click.

The Transform Type-In dialog box is modeless and allows you to select new objects as needed, or switch between the various transforms.

Tip   You can also open the Transform Type-In dialog box by pressing the F12 key.

Within the Transform Type-In dialog box are two columns. The first column displays the Absolute World coordinates and the second displays the Offset Screen values. Figure 8-2 shows the Transform Type-In dialog box for the Move Transform.

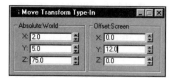

Figure 8-2: The Transform Type-In dialog box displays the current Absolute World coordinates and Offset Screen values.

Understanding Transform Managers

The Transform Managers are three different types of controls that help you define the system about which objects are transformed. These controls are all positioned to the right of the transform buttons and are shown and described in Table 8-2.

Table 8-2
Transform Managers

Toolbar Button	Name	Description
View ▼	Reference Coordinate System drop-down list	Defines the coordinate system used to transform the object.
	Use Pivot Point Center, Use Selection Center, Use Transform Coordinate Center	Defines the center point about which the object transformations take place
X	Constrain to X-axis	Restrict transformations to the X-axis.
Y	Constrain to Y-axis	Restrict transformations to the Y-axis.
Z	Constrain to Z-axis	Restrict transformations to the Z-axis.
XY YZ ZX	Constrain to XY Plane, Constrain to YZ Plane, Constrain to ZX Plane	Restrict transformations to a specific plane.

Understanding coordinate systems

MAX supports several different coordinate systems, and it is important to know which coordinate system you are working with as you transform an object. Using the wrong coordinate system can produce unexpected transformations.

To understand the concept of coordinate systems, imagine you're visiting the Grand Canyon and are standing precariously on the edge of a lookout. To nervous onlookers calling the park rangers, the description of your position would vary from viewpoint to viewpoint. A person standing by you would say you are next to him. A person on the other side of the canyon would say that you're across from her. A person at the floor of the canyon would say you're above him. And a person in an airplane would describe you as being on the east side of the canyon. Each person would have a different viewpoint of you (the object), even though you have not moved.

The coordinate systems that MAX recognizes include the following:

✦ **View Coordinate System** — A coordinate system based on the viewports; X points right, Y points up, and Z points out of the screen (toward you). The views are fixed, making this perhaps the most intuitive coordinate system to work with.

✦ **Screen Coordinate System** — Identical to the View Coordinate System, except the active viewport determines the coordinate system axes while the inactive viewports will show the axes as defined by the active viewport. Once again, the views are fixed, except in this case, the view has been defined by the active viewport.

✦ **World Coordinate System** — Specifies X pointing to the right, Z pointing up, and Y pointing into the screen (away from you). The coordinate axes remain fixed regardless of any transformations applied to an object.

✦ **Parent Coordinate System** — Uses the coordinate system applied to a linked object's parent and maintains consistency between hierarchical transformations. If an object doesn't have a parent, then the world is its parent and the system is set to the World Coordinate System.

✦ **Local Coordinate System** — Sets the coordinate system based on the selected object. The axes are located at the Pivot Point for the object. The Pivot Point can be reoriented and moved using the Pivot button in the Hierarchy panel.

✦ **Grid Coordinate System** — Uses the coordinate system for the active grid.

✦ **Pick Coordinate System** — Lets you select an object about which to transform. The Coordinate System list keeps the last four picked objects as coordinate system options.

All transforms occur relative to the current coordinate system as selected in the Referenced Coordinate System drop-down list found on the main toolbar.

Each of the three basic transforms can have a different coordinate system specified, or you can set it to change uniformly when a new coordinate system is selected. To do this, open the General panel in the Preference Settings dialog box and select the Constant option in the Reference Coordinate System section.

Tutorial: Exploring the coordinate systems

It can be confusing to work with the various coordinate systems, so I've put together a simple example to help you understand them better. In this example, I'll be using two Fourth of July icons — an ice cream cone and a firecracker. Both of these models were created by Zygote Media.

To explore the various coordinate systems, follow these steps:

1. Import both models using the File ⇨ Import command and position them side-by-side in the Front view.

2. Select Tools ⇨ Transform Type-In to open the Transform Type-In. Move it off to the side so you can still see the viewports.

3. The default coordinate system is View. Select the ice cream cone in the Front view and notice that the Transform Gizmo has the Y-axis pointing up. If you drag the arrows next to the Y-axis Offset in the Transform Type-In, the ice cream cone moves up.

4. Now with the View coordinate system still selected, click the ice cream cone in the Top view and drag the Y-axis Offset value in the Transform Type-In. This time the cone again moves upward in the Top view, but this is a different direction in the other views. The View and Screen coordinate system always moves the selected object up, down, left, or right in the active viewport.

5. Select the World coordinate system and notice that the Transform Gizmo for the selected object always matches the world coordinate axes in the lower left corner of every viewport. Dragging the Y-axis value in the Transform Type-In will always move the object in the same direction, regardless of which viewport is active.

6. If the Parent coordinate system is selected, then the object moves according to its parent's system, but since neither object has a linked parent, the world is the parent and this coordinate system behaves just like the World option.

7. When the Local coordinate system is selected, the objects move according to the World coordinate system until its Pivot is changed. Open the Hierarchy panel, click the Pivot button, and click Affect Pivot Only. Then use the Select and Rotate button to reorient the Pivot. Click the Affect Pivot Only button again to deactivate it. Once you have realigned the pivot, dragging on the Y-axis value in the Transform Type-In moves the object in the direction that the Y-axis is pointing.

Figure 8-3 shows the ice cream cone moving off toward the reoriented local Y-axis.

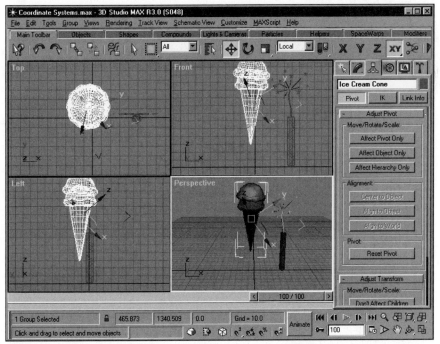

Figure 8-3: The local coordinate system transforms an object according to its Pivot axes.

Using a transform center

All transforms are done about a center point. When transforming an object, it is important to understand what the object's current center point is, as well as the coordinate system that you're working in.

The Transform Center flyout consists of three buttons: Use Pivot Point Center, Use Selection Center, and Use Transform Coordinate Center. Each of these buttons, previously shown in Table 8-2, will alter how the transformations are done. The origin of the Transform Gizmo is always positioned at the center point specified by these buttons.

Adjusting Pivot Points

Pivot Points are typically set to the center of an object when the object is first created, but they can be relocated anywhere within the scene including outside of the object. Relocating the Pivot Point allows you to change the point about which objects are rotated. For example, if you have a car model that you want to position along an incline, moving the Pivot Point to the bottom of one of the tires will allow you to easily line up the car with the incline.

 Cross-Reference   Working with Pivot Points is discussed in Chapter 27, "Building Linked Hierarchies."

Using Selection Center

The Use Selection Center button sets the transform center to the center of the selected object or objects regardless of the individual object's Pivot Point. If multiple objects are selected, then the center will be computed to be in the middle of a bounding box that surrounds all the objects.

Using Transform Coordinate Center

The Transform Coordinate Center uses the center of the local coordinate system. If the View Coordinate System is selected, then all objects are transformed about the center of the viewport. If an object is selected as the coordinate system using the Pick option, then all transformations will be done about that object's center.

When the Local Coordinate System is selected, the Use Transform Center flyout is ignored and objects are transformed about their local axes. If multiple objects are selected, then they all transform individually about their local axes. Grouped objects transform about the group axes.

Tutorial: Exploring the Transform Centers

Using the Transform Centers can transform objects in many different ways. This example will use the ice cream cone and the firecracker models again.

To explore the Transform Center features, follow these steps:

1. Import both models using the File ⇨ Import command and position them side-by-side in the Front view.

2. Select the ice cream cone model and click the Select and Rotate button. Then drag on the ice cream cone and notice how it spins about the Pivot Point.

3. Open the Hierarchy panel, click the Pivot button, and click Affect Pivot Only. Then use the Select and Move button to move the Pivot Point to the base of the ice cream cone. Click the Affect Pivot Only button again to deactivate it. Click the Select and Rotate button and drag on the ice cream cone again. Notice how it rotates about the newly positioned Pivot Point.

4. Select the Use Selection Center flyout button and the View coordinate system. Then select both the ice cream cone and the firecracker and rotate them using the Select and Rotate transform button. The two objects will spin about a center selection point in between them.

5. Select the Use Transform Coordinate Center flyout button. Then select the View coordinate system, select both objects, and rotate them. This will spin both about the center of the active viewport. Switch to the World coordinate system and both will spin about the World's origin. If Local is selected, then both will spin about their local coordinate system.

Figure 8-4 shows the ice cream cone moving off toward the reoriented local Y-axis.

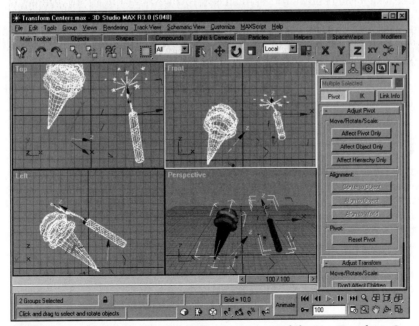

Figure 8-4: Selecting the Local coordinate system and the Use Transform Coordinate Center flyout button will rotate multiple objects about their own Pivot Point.

Selecting axis constraints

3D space consists of three basic directions defined by three axes: X, Y, and Z. If you were to stand on each axis and look at a scene, you would see three separate planes: the XY plane, the YZ plane, and the ZX plane. These planes show only two dimensions at a time and restrict any transformations to the two axes.

By default, the Top, Side, and Front viewports show only a single plane and thereby restrict transformations to that single plane—the Top view constrains movement to the XY plane, the Left or Right side view constrains movement to the YZ plane, and the Front view constrains movement to the ZX plane. This is adequate for most modeling purposes, but sometimes you might need to limit the transformations in all the viewports to a single plane. In MAX, you can restrict movement to specific transform axes using the Restrict axes buttons on the main toolbar.

The four Restrict axes buttons, previously shown in Table 8-2, are located to the right of the Transform Center buttons on the main toolbar and consist of Restrict to X, Restrict to Y, Restrict to Z, and the flyout buttons Restrict to XY, YZ, and ZX Plane. The effect of selecting one of the Restrict axes buttons will be based on the coordinate system selected. For example, if the Restrict to X button is selected and the coordinate system is set to View, then the object will always be transformed to the right because, in the View coordinate system, the X-axis is always to the right. If the Restrict to X button is selected and the coordinate system is set to Local, the axes will be attached to the object, so transformations along the X-axis will be consistent in all viewports (with this setting, the object will not move in the Left view because it only shows the YZ plane).

Additionally, you can restrict movement to a single plane with the Restrict to Plane flyouts consisting of Restrict to XY, Restrict to YZ, and Restrict to ZX. (Use the F8 key to quickly cycle through the various planes.)

Tip   All these restricted transformation options can be selected by right-clicking the object and selecting Transform and the axis or plane to restrict.

Locking axes

To lock an object's transformation axes on a more permanent basis, go to the Command Panel and select the Hierarchy tab. Click the Link Info button to open the Locks rollout, shown in Figure 8-5. The rollout displays each axis for the three types of transformations: Move, Rotate, and Scale. Make sure the object is selected, then click the transformation axes you wish to lock. Be aware that if all Move axes are selected, you won't be able to move the object until the axes are deselected.

Locking axes is helpful if you want to prevent accidental scaling of an object or restrict a vehicle's movement to a plane that makes up a road.

Figure 8-5: The Locks rollout can prevent any transforms along an axis.

Moving, Rotating, and Scaling Objects

Now that you know all about controlling the transformation settings, it's time to learn about how to actually transform an object by moving it, rotating it, and scaling it.

Moving objects

The first transformation type is Move. To move objects, click the Select and Move button on the main toolbar, then select the object to move, and drag the object in the viewport to the desired location. In the following tutorial, you'll use this transformation type to re-create a chess game.

Tutorial: Re-creating a chess game

Chess is a great game, and every time I get a book to help me become a better player, I am presented with example after example of the great matches throughout history that have been re-created using this strange notation that is completely foreign and difficult to follow — obviously a case where 3D graphics, which is all about visualization, would help.

To re-create a chess game for this tutorial, I could model a chess set and a board, or I could borrow a model from my friends at Viewpoint Datalabs. The tutorial deals with transforming objects and not with modeling, so I chose the latter option.

On the CD-ROM

The chess set is included on the CD-ROM, compliments of Viewpoint Datalabs.

With the pieces in place, I can re-create the game by moving the pieces. (Now all I need is help to understand chess game notation.)

To re-create a chess game, follow these steps:

1. Import the chess set. To prevent any extraneous movements, let's restrict any movement of the board itself by locking the transformation axes. Select the board by clicking it (be sure to get the border also). Open the Hierarchy panel and click the Link Info button. Then in the Locks rollout, select all nine boxes to restrict all transformations.

2. Back in the Top viewport, click the Select and Move button and try to drag the board in the viewport. It won't move because all its transformations are now locked.

Tip

Another way to keep the chessboard from moving would be to use the Freeze option. To freeze an object, open the Display panel and in the Freeze rollout, select Freeze Selected. Another way to do this is to use the Edit ➪ Properties command to open the Object Properties dialog box. In the Object Information section, click the Freeze option.

3. The next step is to restrict all pieces to move only in the XY plane. For this to happen, the coordinate system needs to change. Select the World coordinate system from the Reference Coordinate System drop-down list.

4. Click the Restrict to XY Plane button in the main toolbar. Select and move an object in the scene and notice how its movements stay within the XY plane.

5. Select and Move a chess piece, repositioning the object in the Top view.

6. You've made your first move. Click the Animate button to record it. Then go to the next animation frame by clicking the Next Frame button in the Time Controls.

7. Repeat these final two steps until the game is finished.

8. When the game is finished, click the Time Configuration button under the playback controls to open the Time Configuration dialog box, and set the Speed to 1/4X and the End Time to the last frame.

Figure 8-6 shows the chess game in progress.

Rotating objects

Rotation is the process of spinning the object about its axes. To rotate objects, click the Select and Rotate button in the main toolbar, select an object to rotate, and drag it in a viewport. In the next tutorial, you'll rotate objects to set a table.

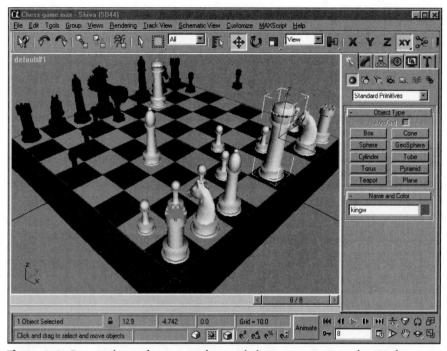

Figure 8-6: Re-creating a chess game by restricting movements to the XY plane

Tutorial: Setting the dining room table

Using MAX, the age-old chore of setting the table for dinner becomes easy (still not fun, but easy). Now, you could just move the dishes into place, but learning to rotate them will make it easier for the diners. In this tutorial, you'll start with a dining room table model provided by Zygote Media from their Sampler CD-ROM.

To set the table, follow these steps:

1. Import the dining room table and place setting models.

2. Clone the set of dishes by selecting the Dishes group and selecting Edit ➪ Clone.

3. Select the World coordinate system and Restrict to XY Plane to ensure that the dishes stay on the table plane.

4. Select and Move the cloned dishes across the table.

5. With the cloned dishes still selected, click the Select and Rotate button. Then right-click the Select and Rotate button to open the Rotate Transform Type-In dialog box.

6. In the Rotate Transform Type-In dialog box, enter **180** degrees for the Z-axis and press the Enter key; then close the dialog box. This will reorient the dishes correctly.

7. Hold down the Ctrl key while selecting both sets of dishes. Select the Use Selection Center flyout. Then select Edit ➪ Clone to create the last two sets of dishes.

8. With the second set of cloned dishes still selected, right-click the Select and Rotate button to open the Rotate Transform Type-In dialog box again. This time enter **90** in the Z offset field and press the Enter key; then close the dialog box.

9. Select and Move each individual place setting to its final place.

Figure 8-7 shows the table all set and ready for dinner.

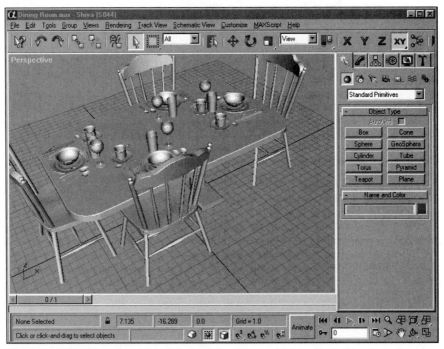

Figure 8-7: Setting the table is accomplished by moving and rotating cloned copies of the dishes.

Scaling objects

Scaling increases or decreases the overall size of an object. Most scaling operations are uniform, or equal in all directions. All Scaling is done about the Transform Center point. Scaling dimensions are referred to in percentages of the original. For example, a cube that is scaled to a value of 200 percent will be twice as big as the original. In the next example, you'll scale some sphere objects to build a snowman.

Non-Uniform Scaling

The Select and Scale button includes two flyout buttons for scaling objects nonuniformly, allowing objects to be scaled unequally in different dimensions. The two additional tools are Select and Non-Uniform Scale, and Select and Squash. With Select and Non-Uniform Scale, resizing a basketball using this tool could result in a ball that is taller than it is wide. Scaling is done about the axis or axes that have been constrained using the Restrict axes buttons.

Squashing objects

The Squash option is a specialized type of nonuniform scaling. This scaling causes the axis constrained by the Restrict axes button to be scaled at the same time the opposite axes are scaled in the opposite direction. For example, if you push down on the basketball by scaling the Z-axis, the sides or the X and Y-axes will bulge outward.

When you use the Non-Uniform Scaling or Squash command, a warning dialog box appears, shown in Figure 8-8, asking you if this is what you want to do. The reason for this warning is that nonuniform scaling would be placed at the bottom of the Modifier Stack, which could cause problems later on when you try to modify the object. To disable or enable these warnings, open the Preferences Settings dialog box by selecting Customize ⇨ Preferences and go to the General tab.

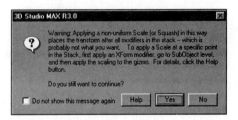

Figure 8-8: This warning dialog box appears whenever you access the Select and Non-Uniform Scale, or Select and Squash flyouts.

Cross-Reference The Modifier Stack is covered in Chapter 9, "Modifying Objects."

Tutorial: Building a snowman

A snowman is a fine example of symmetrical body parts. First, you start with a base, then duplicate the base, only smaller, and finally create the head, which is even smaller. This sounds like a good place to use the Scale transformation.

To build a snowman, follow these steps:

1. Open the Create panel in the Command Panel and click the Sphere button.

2. Create a sphere object by dragging in the Top viewport. This will be the base of your snowman.

3. Snowman parts are never perfectly round, so let's squash the sphere by clicking the Select and Squash flyout button under the Select and Scale button. When the warning dialog box appears, click OK.

4. Set the coordinate system to Local and click the Restrict to Z-Axis button. Now, drag on the sphere.

5. Select the Select and Uniform Scale flyout, and clone the sphere by holding down the Shift key while dragging on the sphere. Enter **2** in the Clone Options dialog box to create two clones at the same time (one for the upper torso and one for the head). Each successive clone will be scaled by the same offset between the original and first cloned spheres.

6. Click the Select and Move button and position the new cloned spheres on top of the original sphere.

Note   If you have any problems moving the spheres, check your coordinate system set-ting. It should be set to Local.

7. To complete the snowman, add some coal eyes, a mouth, a carrot nose, and a top hat.

Figure 8-9 shows the finished snowman produced by scaling spheres.

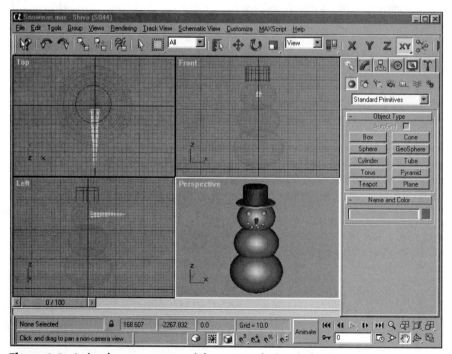

Figure 8-9: A simple snowman model composed of scaled spheres

Using the Align Commands

The Align commands are another way to automatically transform objects. These commands can be used to line up object centers or edges, Align Normals and highlights, Align to Views and grids, and line up cameras.

Aligning objects

Any object that can be transformed can be aligned, including lights, cameras, and Space Warps. After selecting the object to be aligned, click the Align flyout button on the toolbar or select the Tools ⇨ Align command. The cursor will change to the Align icon and you will then need to click a target object to align with the selected one. Clicking the target object opens the Align Selection dialog box with the target object's name displayed in the dialog box's title, as shown in Figure 8-10.

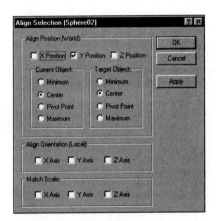

Figure 8-10: The Align Selection dialog box can align objects along any axes by their Minimum, Center, Pivot Point, or Maximum points.

The Align Selection dialog box includes settings for the X, Y, and Z positions to line up the Minimum, Center, Pivot Point, or Maximum dimensions for the selected or target object's Bounding Box. As you change the settings in the dialog box, the objects reposition themselves, but the actual transformations don't take place until the Apply button is clicked.

Aligning Normals

The Normal Align command can be used to line up points of the surface of two objects. To do this, you need to first select the object to move (this is the source object). Then select Tools ⇨ Normal Align or click the Normal Align flyout button in the main toolbar. The cursor will change to the Normal Align icon. Drag the cursor across the surface of the source object, and a blue arrow pointing out from the face center will appear. Release the mouse when you've correctly pinpointed the position to align.

Next click the target object and drag the mouse to locate the target object's align point. This will be displayed as a green arrow. When you release the mouse, the source object will move to align the two points and the Normal Align dialog box will appear as shown in Figure 8-11.

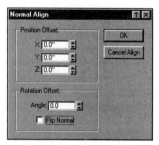

Figure 8-11: The Normal Align dialog box allows you to define offset values when aligning normals.

When the objects are aligned, the two points will match up exactly. The Normal Align dialog box lets you specify offset values that can be used to keep a distance between the two objects. You can also specify an Angle Offset, which is used to deviate the parallelism of the normals. The Flip Normal option aligns the objects so that their selected normals point in the same direction.

Objects without any faces, like Point Helper objects and Space Warps, use a vector between the origin and the Z-axis for normal alignment.

Tutorial: Creating a string of pearls

In this tutorial, you'll practice aligning normals with the Normal Align command by creating a string of pearls. Actually, the pearls will only be spheres, but once you learn to apply materials in Chapter 17, "Exploring the Material Editor," then you can make them into whatever you want.

To connect several spheres using the Normal Align command, follow these steps:

1. Create a GeoSphere using the Create panel. I've selected to use the GeoSphere primitive because it is more efficient than the normal sphere and with many spheres; these savings would result in a simpler model. I've set the number of Segments to **10** to ensure a smooth sphere.

2. Clone the GeoSphere by clicking the Select and Move button and moving it while holding down the Shift key. In the Clone Options dialog box, enter a count of **25**.

3. Select the second GeoSphere and select the Tools ⇨ Normal Align command, or click the Normal Align flyout button on the toolbar. Drag on the surface of

the GeoSphere to a point that is near the first GeoSphere and release the mouse. Then drag on the surface of the first GeoSphere to a point that is slightly deviated from the second GeoSphere and release the mouse. The second GeoSphere will be realigned to the first.

4. Repeat Step 3 for all the GeoSpheres.

Figure 8-12 shows the resulting string of pearls.

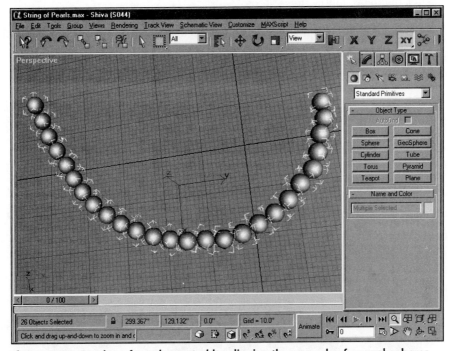

Figure 8-12: A string of pearls created by aligning the normals of several spheres

Note Another way to create a string of pearls would be to use the Spacing Tool to position spheres along a spline path. Chapter 6, "Cloning Objects and Using Arrays," covers this tool.

Placing Highlights

The Place Highlight feature enables you to control the position and orientation of a light in order to achieve a highlight in a precise location. To use this feature, you must select a light object in the scene and then select Tools ➪ Place Highlight or click the Place Highlight flyout button on the toolbar. The cursor will change to the

Place Highlight icon. Click a point on the object in the scene where you want the highlight to be positioned, and the selected light will re-position itself to create a specular highlight at the exact location where you clicked. The light's position will be determined by the Angle of Incidence between the highlight point and the light.

Tutorial: Lighting the snowman's face

The Place Highlight feature can be used to position a light for our snowman. To place a highlight, follow these steps:

1. Open the Create panel and select the Lights category; then click the Omni button and position it below and to the left of the Snowman model. Figure 8-13 shows the results.

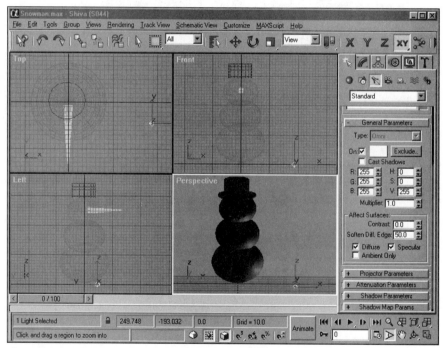

Figure 8-13: This snowman could use some additional light. A highlight on the face would help.

2. To place the highlight so it shows the Snowman's face, select the Omni light and then select Tools ➪ Place Highlight. Then click the Snowman's face where the highlight should be located, right above his right eye. Figure 8-14 shows the results.

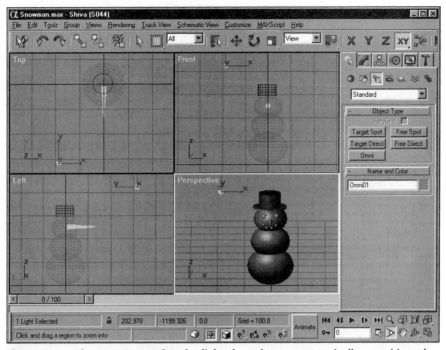

Figure 8-14: The snowman, after the lights have been automatically repositioned using the Place Highlights command.

Aligning Cameras

The Align Camera command does the same thing for cameras that the Place Highlight command does for lights. To use the Align Camera command, select a camera to realign and select the Tools ⇨ Align Camera command, or click the Align Camera flyout button on the toolbar. Drag on the surface of the object where you want to point the camera. A blue normal arrow will appear. Release the mouse to automatically reposition the camera.

Tip   The Align Camera command only points a camera at an object for the current frame. It will not follow an object if it moves during an animation. To have a camera follow an object, you'll need to use the Look At Controller. This is discussed in Chapter 22, "Controlling Cameras."

Tutorial: Seeing the snowman's good side

Returning to our snowman again, we can place a camera in the scene and realign it to coincide with the highlight.

To align a camera with an object point, follow these steps:

1. Open the Create panel, select the Cameras category, and then click the Free button. Click in any viewport to create a new Free camera in the scene.

2. With the camera selected, select the Tools ⇨ Align Camera command, or click the Align Camera flyout button. The cursor will change to a small camera icon.

3. Click the cursor at the exact point on the object where you want the camera to point.

4. To see the new camera view, right-click the viewport title and select Views ⇨ Camera01. Although the camera is pointing at the selected point, you may need to change the Field-Of-View to correct the zoom ratios.

Figure 8-15 shows our snowman from the newly aligned camera.

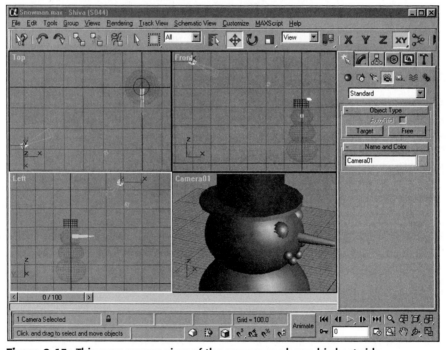

Figure 8-15: This new camera view of the snowman shows his best side.

Aligning to a View

The Align to View command provides an easy and quick way to reposition objects to one of the axes. To use this command, select an object and then select Tools ⇨ Align to View. This opens the Align to View dialog box shown in Figure 8-16.

Changing the settings in this dialog box displays the results in the viewports. There is also a Flip command for altering the direction of the object points. If no object is selected, then the Align to View command cannot be used.

Figure 8-16: The Align to View dialog box is a quick way to line objects up with the axes.

The Align to View command is especially useful for fixing the orientation of objects when you create them in the wrong view. All alignments are completed relative to the object's local coordinate system. If several objects are selected, each object is reoriented according to its local coordinate system.

Note   Using the Align to View command on symmetrical objects like spheres doesn't produce any noticeable difference in the viewports.

Tutorial: Building with pipes

Many simple structures can be created using pipes made from the Tube primitive. With a few basic shapes, the Snap to Grid feature, and the Align to View command, you can easily create complex frameworks.

To build a framework, follow these steps:

1. Set your coordinate system to View. Then create a simple pipe object by selecting the Tube primitive from the Create panel. In the Keyboard Entry rollout, enter the values of **15** for the Inner Radius, **20** for Outer Radius, and **200** for the Height. Click the Create button.

2. Clone the pipe object by selecting Edit ⇨ Clone.

3. Modify the cloned pipe to create a corner pipe object. Open the Modify panel and click the Bend button. In the Parameters rollout, enter a value of **90** for the Angle field.

4. Right-click the 3D Snap Toggle button (at the bottom of the screen) to bring up the Grid and Snap Settings dialog box and select Grid Points. Close the dialog box, then turn on the snap options by clicking the 3D Snap Toggle button. (The Snap feature is covered in more detail in the "Using Snap Options" section later in the chapter.)

5. Clone and reorient all the pieces using the Align to View command to create a structure.

Figure 8-17 shows a simple structure created from pipe objects. The positioning of all these pieces was accomplished with the Align to View command. This was possible because all the pieces lie parallel to the axes.

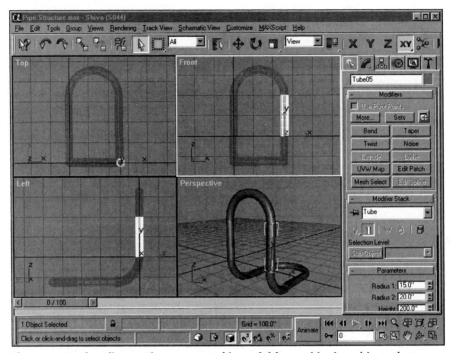

Figure 8-17: The Align to View command is useful for positioning objects that are parallel to the axes.

Using Helpers

In the Create panel is a category of miscellaneous objects called Helpers. These objects are useful in positioning objects and measuring dimensions. The buttons in the Helper category include Dummy, Point, Protractor, Grid, Tape, and Compass.

Using grids

When MAX is started, the one element that is visible is the Home Grid. This grid is there to give you a reference point for creating objects in 3D space. At the center of each grid are two darker lines. These lines meet at the origin point for the World Coordinate System, and all objects are placed there by default.

The Home grid

The default MAX setup displays a Home Grid that is used as a reference for the scene. The Home Grid can be turned on or off using the Views ➪ Grid ➪ Show Home Grid command. If the Home Grid is the only grid in the scene, then by default it is also the construction grid where new objects are positioned when created.

Tip   The keyboard shortcut for toggling the Home Grid is the G key.

You can access the parameters for the Home Grid (shown in Figure 10-18) by right-clicking the Snap, Angle Snap, or Percent Snap Toggle button to open the Grid and Snap Settings dialog box, and then selecting the Home Grid Panel. In this panel, you can set how often Major Lines appear, as well as Grid Spacing. (The Spacing value for the active grid is displayed on the Status Bar.) You can also specify to dynamically update the grid view in all viewports or just in the active one.

Figure 8-18: The Home Grid panel of the Grid and Snap Settings dialog box lets you define the grid spacing.

Creating and activating new grids

In addition to the Home Grid, new grids can be created. To create a new Grid object, open the Create panel, select the Helpers category, and click the Grid button. In the Parameters rollout are settings for specifying the new grid object's dimensions, spacing, and color, as well as which plane to display.

Any newly created Grid can be designated as the default active grid. To activate a grid, make sure it is selected and select Views ⇨ Grids ⇨ Activate Grid Object. Keep in mind that only one Grid may be active at a time. You can also activate a Grid by right-clicking the grid object and selecting Activate Grid from the pop-up menu. To deactivate the new Grid and reactivate the Home Grid, select Views ⇨ Grids ⇨ Activate Home Grid, or right-click the grid object and select Activate Grid ⇨ Home Grid from the pop-up menu.

Further grid settings for new grids can be found in the Grid and Snap Settings dialog box on the User Grids panel. The settings include automatically activating the grid when created, and an option for aligning an AutoGrid using World space or Object space coordinates.

Using AutoGrid

AutoGrid is used to create a new construction plane perpendicular to a face normal. This provides an easy way to create and align objects directly next to one another without manually lining them up.

New Feature   AutoGrid is a new feature in Release 3.

The AutoGrid feature shows up as a checkbox at the top of the Object Type rollout for every category in the Create panel. It only becomes active when you're in create object mode.

To use AutoGrid, click the AutoGrid option after selecting an object type to create. If no objects are in the scene, then the object is created as usual. If an object is in the scene, then the cursor will move around on the surface of the object as you move the mouse in the viewport. Clicking and dragging will create the new object based on the precise location of the object under the mouse.

The AutoGrid stays active until you turn off the AutoGrid option by unchecking the box or holding down the Alt key before creating the object.

Tutorial: Building a multicolored caterpillar

In an earlier tutorial, we created a string of pearls with the Normal Align command. Although the procedure worked well, it was fairly tedious. In this tutorial, we'll use spheres again to create the body of a caterpillar. The AutoGrid feature is going to make this easy.

To create the body of a caterpillar, follow these steps:

1. Open the Create panel and click the Sphere button. Select the Edge Creation Method.

2. Turn the AutoGrid on by clicking the checkbox at the top of the Create panel.

3. Drag in the Top view to create a sphere. Then position the cursor near the right-most point in the Top view, and drag again. Repeat this step until you have enough body segments.

Figure 8-19 shows the finished string of gems. Because the gems were created by dragging, the sizes differ from gem to gem.

Using Dummy and Point objects

The Dummy object is another useful object contained in the Helpers category. This object is a simple cube with a Pivot Point at its center that doesn't render and has no parameters. It is only used as an object about which to transform objects. For example, you could create a Dummy object that the camera could follow through an animation sequence. Another example would be centering a dummy object and using the Array dialog box to create a ring array like the one in Chapter 6, "Cloning Objects and Using Arrays." Dummy objects will be used in many examples throughout the remainder of the book.

Figure 8-19: The body of a caterpillar created easily with the AutoGrid feature

The Point object is very similar to the Dummy object in that it is not rendered either and has only two modifiable parameters. A point object defines a point in space and is identified by an axis tripod. This tripod and its length are the only parameters that can be altered under the Parameters rollout in the Command Panel. The main purpose for the Point object is to position other objects within the scene.

Measuring coordinate distances

The Helpers category also includes several handy utilities for measuring dimensions and directions. These are the Tape, Protractor, and Compass objects.

Using the Tape helper

The Tape object is used to measure distances. To use it, simply drag the distance that you'd like to measure and view to the resultant dimension in the Parameters rollout. You can also set the length of the Tape object using the Specify Length option. The endpoints of the Tape object can be moved and repositioned with the Select and Move button, but the Rotate and Scale buttons have no effect.

Using the Protractor helper

The Protractor object works in a manner similar to the Tape object, but it measures the angle between two objects. To use the Protractor object, click in a viewport to position the Protractor object. (The Protractor object will look like two pyramids aligned point to point and represents the origin of the angle.) Then click the Pick Object 1 button and select an object in the scene. A line will be drawn from the Protractor object to the selected object. Next, click the Pick Object 2 button. The angle-formed objects and the Protractor object will be displayed in the Parameters rollout. The value will change as either of the selected objects or the Protractor is moved.

Note   All measurement values are presented in gray fields within the Parameters rollout. This gray field indicates that the value cannot be modified.

Using the Compass helper

The Compass object identifies North, East, West, and South positions on a planar star-shaped object. This object is mainly used in conjunction with the Sunlight System, which is covered in Chapter 20, "Controlling Lights."

Tutorial: Testing the Pythagorean theorem

I always trusted my teachers in school to tell me the truth, but maybe they were just making it all up, especially my math teacher. (He did have shifty eyes, after all.) For my peace of mind, I'd like to test one of the mathematical principles he taught us, the Pythagorean theorem. (What kind of name is that anyway?)

If I remember the theorem correctly, it says that the sum of squares of the sides of a right triangle equals the sum of the hypotenuse squared. So, according to my calculations, a right triangle with a side of 3 and a side of 4 would have a hypotenuse of 5. Since MAX is proficient at drawing shapes such as this, we'll test the theorem by creating a box with a width of 40 and a height of 30 and then measuring the diagonal.

To test the Pythagorean theorem, follow these steps:

1. Open the Create panel and click the Box button.
2. Click and drag to create a box in the viewpoint.
3. In the Parameters rollout, enter a value of **40** for the Width, **30** for the Height, and **10** for the Depth.
4. Open the Snap and Grid Settings dialog box and set the Snap feature to snap to vertices by selecting the Vertex option. Close the Grid and Snap Settings dialog box and enable the Snap feature.

5. Click the Helper category in the Create panel and select the Tape object.

6. In the Top viewport, move the cursor over the upper left corner of the object and click the blue vertex that appears. Then drag down to the lower right corner and click the next blue vertex that appears. Note the measurement in the Parameters rollout.

Well, I guess my math teacher didn't lie about this theorem, but I wonder if he was correct about all those multiplication tables. . . .

Figure 8-20 shows the resulting box and measurement value.

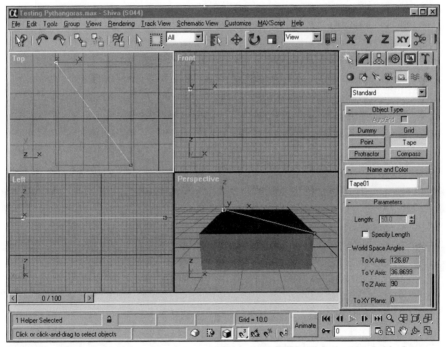

Figure 8-20: I guess old Pythagoras was right. (Good thing I have MAX to help me check.)

Using Snap Options

Often when an object is being transformed, you know exactly where you want to put it. The Snap feature can be the means whereby objects get to the precise place they should be. The Snap feature has been used in many examples already.

Snap points are defined in the Grid and Snap Settings dialog box that can be opened by selecting Customize ➪ Grid and Snap Settings or by right-clicking any of the first three Snap buttons at the bottom of the window. Figure 8-21 shows the Snaps panel of the Grid and Snap Settings dialog box.

Figure 8-21: The Snaps panel includes many different points to snap to.

Once snap points have been defined, the Snap buttons at the bottom of the screen activate the Snaps feature. The first Snaps button consists of a flyout with three buttons: 3D Snap Toggle, 2.5D Snap Toggle, and 2D Snap Toggle. The 2D Snap Toggle button limits all snaps to the active construction grid. The 2.5D Snap Toggle button snaps to points on the construction grid as well as projected points from objects in the scene. The 3D Snap Toggle button can snap to any points in 3D space.

This Snaps button controls the snapping for movement translations. To the right are two other buttons: Angle Snap Toggle and Percent Snap. These buttons control the snapping of rotations and scalings.

Tip   The keyboard shortcut for turning the Snaps feature on and off is the S key.

With the Snaps feature enabled, the cursor will become blue crosshairs wherever a Snap point is located.

Setting Snap points

The Snap tab in the Grid and Snap Settings dialog box has many different points that can be snapped to in two different categories: Standard and NURBS. The Standard snap points (previously shown in Figure 8-21) include the following:

✦ **Grid Points** — Snaps to the Grid intersection points

✦ **Grid Lines** — Snaps only to positions located on the Grid lines

✦ **Pivot** — Snaps to an object's Pivot Point

✦ **Bounding Box** — Snaps to one of the corners of a Bounding Box

✦ **Perpendicular**—Snaps to a spline's next perpendicular point

✦ **Tangent**—Snaps to a spline's next tangent point

✦ **Vertex**—Snaps to polygon vertices

✦ **Endpoint**—Snaps to a spline's end point or the end of a polygon edge

✦ **Edge**—Snaps to positions only on an edge

✦ **Midpoint**—Snaps to a spline's midpoint or the middle of a polygon edge

✦ **Face**—Snaps to any point on the surface of a face

✦ **Center Face**—Snaps to the center of a face

There are also several snap points that are specific to NURBS objects, shown in Figure 8-22. These points include

✦ **CV**—Snaps to any CV subobject

✦ **Point**—Snaps to a NURBS point

✦ **Curve Center**—Snaps to the center of the NURBS curve

✦ **Curve Normal**—Snaps to a point that is normal to a NURBS curve

✦ **Curve Tangent**—Snaps to a point that is tangent to a NURBS curve

✦ **Curve Edge**—Snaps to the edge of a NURBS curve

✦ **Curve End**—Snaps to end of a NURBS curve

✦ **Surf Center**—Snaps to the center of a NURBS surface

✦ **Surf Normal**—Snaps to a point that is normal to a NURBS surface

✦ **Surf Edge**—Snaps to the edge of a NURBS surface

Figure 8-22: The NURBS Snap points

Cross-Reference

For more information on NURBS, see Chapter 16, "Working with NURBS."

Setting Snap options

The Grid and Snap Settings dialog box holds a panel of Options, shown in Figure 8-23, in which you can set whether markers display or not, the size of the markers, and their color. The Snap Strength setting determines how close the cursor must be to a Snap point before it snaps to it. The Angle and Percent values are the strengths for any rotate and scale transformations respectively. You can also cause translations to be affected by the designated Axis Constraints with the Use Axis Constraints option.

Figure 8-23: The Options panel includes settings for marker size and color and the Snap Strength value.

Within any viewpoint, holding down the Shift key and right-clicking in the viewport can access a pop-up menu of grid points and options. This pop-up menu lets you quickly add or reset all of the current Snap points and change Snap options such as Transformed Constraints and Snap to Frozen.

Tutorial: Creating a lattice for a methane molecule

You've already seen many examples that demonstrated the various Snap features, but, just to be sure, here's another one. Many molecules are represented by a lattice of spheres. Trying to line up the exact positions of the spheres by hand could be extremely frustrating, but using the Snap feature makes this challenge, well . . . a snap.

One of the simpler molecules is methane, which is composed of one carbon atom surrounded by four smaller hydrogen atoms. To reproduce this as a lattice, we will first create a tetrahedron primitive and snap spheres to each of its corners.

To create a lattice of the methane molecule, follow these steps:

1. First create a tetrahedron primitive. In the Create panel, click the Geometry button, then select Extended Primitives from the Create panel drop-down list.

Click the Hedra button to open its Parameters rollout. In the Family section, click the Tetra radio button; then in the Family Parameters section, set the P value to **1.0**. In the Top viewport, click and drag to create the tetrahedron primitive.

2. Open the Grid and Snap Settings dialog box by right-clicking the 3D Snap Toggle button (at the bottom of the screen). In the Snaps panel, click the Clear All button to deselect any previous selections, then select the Pivot and Vertex options. Close the dialog box.

3. Enable the Snap feature by clicking the 3D Snap Toggle button.

4. In the Create panel drop-down list, select the Standard Primitives category, and then click the Sphere button.

5. Now create our four hydrogen atoms. In the Top viewport, move the cursor over the tetrahedron (note the blue bounding box). Now move the cursor over each of the four corners of the tetrahedron until a blue vertex appears. Click and drag to create a sphere; then in the Parameters rollout, enter a Radius value of **30**. Do this for each of the spheres placed at a vertex.

Tip   Entering values in the Parameters rollout can alter the size and position of an object even with Snap options turned on.

6. Open the Grid and Snap Settings dialog box and, in the Snaps panel, deselect the Vertex option while retaining the Pivot setting. Close the dialog box, and enable Snap (click the 3D Snap Toggle button). Create another sphere by clicking in the center of the tetrahedron and dragging outwards until the sphere becomes visible. In the Parameters rollout, enter a Radius value of **75**. This sphere will represent the carbon atom.

Caution   The pivot point for the tetrahedron isn't exactly in the center, so you'll need to make some adjustments. If you need to disable the Snap features while adjusting the sphere, press the S key to temporarily disable the Snap settings.

7. When you've completed the molecule, you can delete the tetrahedron by selecting it from the Select by Name dialog box (the name will probably be Hedra01).

Figure 8-24 shows the finished methane molecule.

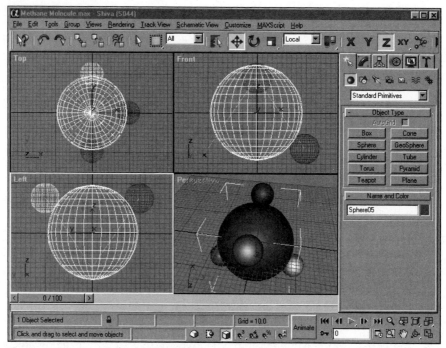

Figure 8-24: A methane molecule lattice drawn with the help of the Snap feature.

Summary

Transforming Objects in MAX is one of the fundamental actions, with three basics ways to transform objects: moving, rotating, and scaling. MAX includes many helpful features to enable these transformations to take place quickly and easily. In this chapter we covered many of these features, including:

✦ Using the Move, Rotate, and Scale buttons and the Transform Gizmo

✦ Transforming objects precisely with the Transform Type-In

✦ Aligning objects with the Align dialog box, aligning normals; and aligning lights, cameras, and views

✦ Using Helper objects like Dummy, Point, and Tape

✦ Snapping objects to snap points

We've also looked at several examples.

In the next chapter, we'll investigate the features in the Modify panel that enable you to modify objects with Modifiers.

✦   ✦   ✦

Modifying Objects

Modifying objects is the essence of modeling in MAX. These modifications are accomplished using the Modify panel. The Modify panel includes object parameters and special functions called *Modifiers* that are used to change various aspects of an object. This chapter will cover all the various Modifiers included in MAX and teach you how to use them.

Using the Modify Panel

The Modify panel includes buttons and rollouts for changing various object parameters. The buttons in the Modify panel let you access Modifiers, which will be covered later in the chapter. The rollouts will change depending on which object or Modifier is selected.

Modifying object parameters

All objects have parameters. These parameters help define how the object looks. For example, consider the primitive objects. The primitive objects contained in MAX are parametric. *Parametric objects* are mathematically defined and can be changed by modifying their parameters. The easiest object modifications to make are simply changing these parameters. For example, a sphere with a radius of 4 can be made into a sphere with a radius of 10 by simply typing a **10** in the Radius field. The viewports will display these changes automatically when the Enter key is pressed. More about primitive objects is covered in Chapter 10, "Creating Primitive Objects."

Note When an object is first created, its parameters are displayed in the Parameters roll-out of the Create panel. As long as the object remains the current object, you can modify its parameters using this rollout. Once you select a different tool or object, the Parameters rollout is no longer accessible from the Create panel. It can be found from then on under the Modify panel.

Tutorial: Filling a treasure chest with gems

I haven't found too many treasure chests lately, but if I remember right, they are normally filled with bright, sparkling gems. In this tutorial, we'll fill the chest with a number of Hedra primitives and alter the object properties in the Modify panel to create a diverse offering of gems.

To create a treasure chest with many unique gems, follow these steps:

1. Create or import a treasure chest model.
2. Click the Create panel and select the Extended Primitives subcategory. Then click the Hedra button.
3. Create several Hedra objects. The size of the objects won't matter at this time. Move all the Hedra objects to the top of the chest.
4. Open the Modify panel and select one of the Hedra objects.
5. Alter the values in the Parameters rollout to produce a nice gem.
6. Repeat Step 5 for all Hedra objects in the chest.

Figure 9-1 shows the resulting chest with a variety of gems.

Exploring Modifier Types

Modifiers are used to reshape objects, apply material mappings, deform an object's surface, and perform many other actions. Several Modifiers can be accessed via buttons at the top of the Modify panel in the Modifiers rollout, and these are but a sampling of the complete set of Modifiers available. To view and select additional Modifiers, click the More button. Figure 9-2 shows the Modifiers dialog box with its long list of additional Modifiers.

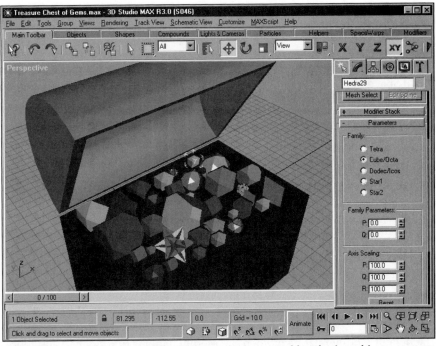

Figure 9-1: A treasure chest full of gems quickly created by altering object parameters

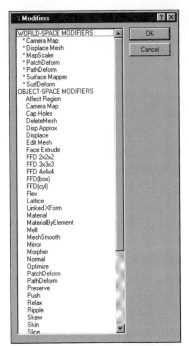

Figure 9-2: The Modifiers dialog box lists additional Modifiers.

Note   Some Modifiers aren't available for some types of objects. For example, the Extrude and Lathe Modifiers are only enabled when a spline shape is selected.

MAX's large list of Modifiers includes two basic types: Object-Space Modifiers and World-Space Modifiers. The former are applied to individual objects or subobjects and the latter can be applied to multiple objects using the scene's World Coordinates.

Many Modifiers create *gizmo objects*. These are wireframe control objects that are displayed in the viewport and that provide an actual structure for working with the Modifier. Gizmos have a center and can be transformed and controlled like regular objects. Gizmos will often show up in the Sub-Object drop-down list and must be selected before they can be transformed.

The remainder of this section takes a brief look at every Modifier included in the default installation of MAX. Because there are so many Modifiers, they will be presented in categories that define their functions. More information on specific Modifiers can be found throughout this book.

Default modifiers

The default Modifiers appear when the Modify panel is first opened and represent some of the more common Modifiers available: Bend, Taper, Twist, Noise, Extrude, Lathe, UVW Map, Edit Patch, Mesh Select, and Edit Spline.

Note   You can configure which buttons appear in the Modify panel and even define custom sets of buttons using the Configure Button Sets button at the top of the panel. Chapter 3, "Customizing the MAX Interface," explains this feature in more detail.

Object-Space modifiers

Object-Space Modifiers are Modifiers that are applied to individual objects and that use the object's local coordinate system. Object-Space Modifiers are more numerous than World-Space Modifiers. Therefore, I've selected a few (on a completely arbitrary basis) to describe in the following subsections to give you an idea of how these Modifers work.

Basic geometry modifiers

These Modifiers affect the geometry of objects by pulling, pushing, and stretching them. Modifiers in this category include Bend, Taper, Twist, Noise, Skew, Stretch, Melt, Squeeze, Spherify, and Push.

New Feature   The Melt, Squeeze, and Push Modifiers are all new to Release 3. These Modifiers are discussed in the proceeding sections.

Now we all know that destroying or vandalizing a mailbox is a Federal offense and we wouldn't dream of such an act, but in the virtual world, the worst that could happen is we could be charged a virtual fine. As the various Modifiers are presented, our friendly post box, created by Zygote Media, has volunteered to demonstrate these modifications for us where it can.

On the CD-ROM   These examples can all be found on the book's CD-ROM.

Bend modifier

This Modifier causes an object to bend along any axis. Bend parameters include the Bend Angle and Direction, the Bend Axis, and the Limits. The first post box in Figure 9-3 shows a bend of 75 degrees around the Z-axis. This Modifier is one of the default Modifiers available as a button at the top of the Modify panel. Limit settings are the boundaries beyond which the Modifier has no effect. You can set Upper and Lower Limits.

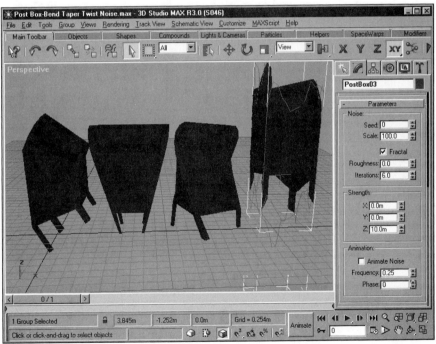

Figure 9-3: The post box with the Bend, Taper, Twist, and Noise Modifiers applied

Taper modifier

This Modifier scales only one end of an object. Taper parameters include the Amount and Curve, Primary and Effect Axes, and Limits. The second post box in Figure 9-3 shows a taper of 1.0 about the Z-axis. This Modifier is also one of the default Modifiers available as a button at the top of the Modify panel.

Twist modifier

This Modifier deforms an object by rotating one end of an axis in one direction and the other end in the opposite direction. Twist parameters include Angle and Bias values, a Twist Axis, and Limits. The third post box in Figure 9-3 has a twist angle of 75 about the Z-axis. This Modifier is also one of the default Modifiers available as a button at the top of the Modify panel.

Noise modifier

This Modifier randomly varies the position of vertices. Noise parameters include Seed and Scale values, a Fractal option with Roughness and Iterations settings, Strength about each axis, and Animation settings. The last post box in Figure 9-3 has a Noise Strength value of 10 for the Z-axis and the Fractal option selected. This Modifier is also one of the default Modifiers available as a button at the top of the Modify panel.

Skew modifier

This Modifier changes the tilt of an object by moving its top portion while keeping the bottom half fixed. This Modifier is located in the Modifier list, which can be opened with the More button. Skew parameters include Amount and Direction values, a Skew Axis, and Limits. The post box on the left in Figure 9-4 has a Skew value of 1.0 about the Z-axis.

Stretch modifier

This Modifier pulls one axis while pushing the other axes in the opposite direction. This Modifier is also located in the Modifier list that can be opened with the More button. Stretch parameters include Stretch and Amplify values, a Stretch Axis, and Limits. The post box on the right in Figure 9-4 has a Stretch value of 0.3 about the Z-axis.

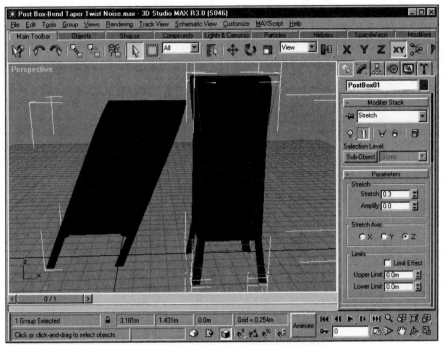

Figure 9-4: The post box with the Skew and Stretch Modifiers applied

Melt modifier

This Modifier simulates an object melting by sagging and spreading edges over time. Melt parameters include Amount and Spread values, Solidity (which can be Ice, Glass, Jelly, or Plastic), and a Melt Axis. Figure 9-5 shows the post box on the left melting with an Amount setting of 30, a Spread setting of 20, and the Solidity set to Jelly.

Squeeze modifier

This Modifier takes the points close to one axis and moves them away from the center of the object while it moves other points toward the center to create a bulging effect. Squeeze parameters include Amount and Curve values for Axial and Radial directions, and Limits and Balance settings. The post box on the right in Figure 9-5 shows the Squeeze Modifier with an Axial Bulge of 0.3 and a Radial Squeeze of 1.0.

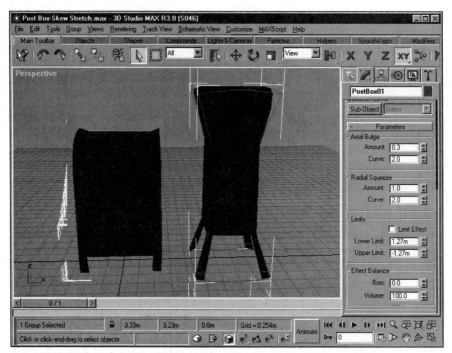

Figure 9-5: The post box with the Melt and Squeeze Modifiers applied

Spherify modifier

This Modifier distorts an object into a spherical shape. The single Spherify parameter is the Percent of the effect to apply. Figure 9-6 shows a post box with a Percent value of 40 on the left.

Push modifier

This Modifier pushes an object's vertices inward or outward as if it were being filled with air. The Push Modifier also has one parameter: the Push Value. This value is the distance to move with respect to the object's center. The post box on the right in Figure 9-6 shows the Push Modifier with a setting of 0.2.

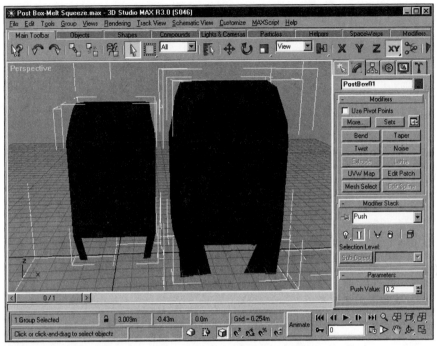

Figure 9-6: The post box with the Spherify and Push Modifiers applied

Spline modifiers

These Modifiers work with spline objects. Many of these Modifiers produce the same results as the settings in the Editable Spline rollouts. Modifiers in this category include Extrude, Lathe, Edit Spline, Spline Select, Delete Spline, Trim/Extend, Fillet/Chamfer, Bevel, Bevel Profile, and PathDeform.

Cross-Reference A more detailed explanation of splines and several of these Modifiers can be found in Chapter 11, "Working with Spline Shapes."

Extrude modifier

This Modifier copies the spline, moves it a given distance, and connects the two splines to form a 3D shape. Parameters for this Modifier include an Amount value, which is the distance to extrude, and the number of Segments to use to define the height. The Capping options let you specify a Start Cap and/or an End Cap. The Cap fills the spline area and can be made as a Patch, Mesh, or NURBS object. Only closed splines that are extruded can be capped.

You can also have Mapping Coordinates and Material IDs be generated automatically. This Modifier is also one of the default Modifiers available as a button at the top of the Modify panel. It is only available for spline shapes.

Lathe modifier

This Modifier creates an object with circular symmetry by rotating a spline about an axis. Lathe parameters include a Degrees value that determines how far to rotate the spline. You can automatically Weld Core or Flip Normals as the object is created. Lathe objects can have caps just like extruded objects. Another parameter is the axis about which the lathe takes place. You can also align the revolution axis to the object's Minimum, Center, or Maximum point. This Modifier is one of the default Modifiers and is enabled when a spline shape is selected.

Edit Spline modifier

This Modifier includes tools for editing spline objects and is also one of the default Modifiers. The Edit Spline Modifier isn't really a Modifier, but an Object type and will show up in the bottom section of the Modifier Stack. This Modifier is available as a button at the top of the Modify panel.

Spline Select modifier

This Modifier enables you to select spline subobjects including Vertex, Segment, and Spline. Named Selection Sets can be copied and pasted. The selection can then be passed up the Stack to the next Modifier.

Delete Spline modifier

This Modifier can be used to delete spline subobjects. Subobjects that can be deleted include Vertices, Segments, and Splines.

Trim/Extend modifier

This Modifier lets you trim the extending end of a spline or extend a spline until it meets another spline at a vertex. The Pick Locations button turns on Pick mode, where the cursor changes when it is over a valid point. Operations include Auto, Trim Only, and Extend Only with an option to compute Infinite Boundaries. You can also set the Intersection Projection to View, Construction Plane, or None.

Fillet/Chamfer modifier

This Modifier can be used to Fillet or Chamfer the corners of shapes. Fillets create a smooth corner and a Chamfer adds another segment where two edges meet. Parameters include the Fillet Radius and the Chamfer Distance. Both include an Apply button.

Bevel modifier

This Modifier extrudes a shape and bevels its edges. Like the Extrude Modifier, the Bevel Modifier has Capping options. You can also select Linear or Curved Sides and whether to Smooth Across Levels. The Keep Lines from Crossing option includes a Separation value to maintain line independence. The Bevel Values are defined in Levels using Height and Outline values. You must have at least one level.

Figure 9-7 shows a shape after the Bevel Modifier has been applied. This object has three Bevel levels with Height and Offset values of 10,10; 30, 0; and 10, –10.

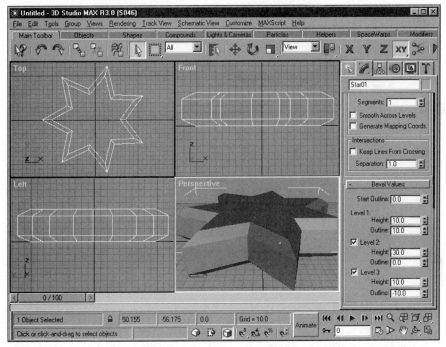

Figure 9-7: The Bevel modifier can be used to extrude and bevel shapes at the same time.

Bevel Profile modifier

This Modifier extrudes a shape and bevels its edges using another path as its profile. This is a variation of the Bevel Modifier that enables you to customize the Bevel Profile with another spline. The Pick Profile button lets you select a spline to use as this profile. Other options include Capping and Keep Lines from Crossing.

Figure 9-8 shows the same shape as in the previous figure, except this time it's extruded with a Bevel Profile. The spline to the right is the one used for the profile.

Figure 9-8: The shape has a unique beveled profile thanks to the Bevel Profile Modifier.

PathDeform modifier

This Modifier uses a spline path to deform an object. Variations of this Modifier include the PatchDeform Modifier that uses splines and the SurfDeform Modifier that uses NURBS. The Pick Path button lets you select a spline to use in the deformation process. You can select either an open or closed spline. The Parameters rollout also includes spinners for controlling the Percent, Stretch, Rotation, and Twist of the object. The Percent value is the distance the object moves along the path.

Figure 9-9 shows some text wrapped around a spline path.

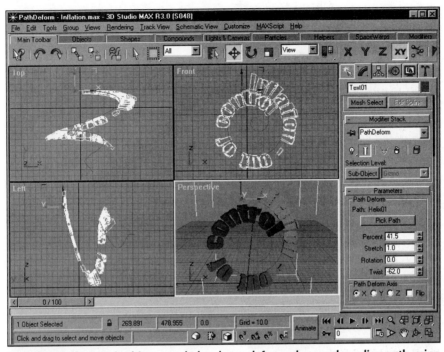

Figure 9-9: The text in this example has been deformed around a spline path using the PathDeform Modifier.

Patch modifiers

These Modifiers work with patch objects. Many of these Modifiers produce the same results as the settings in the Editable Patch rollouts. Modifiers in this category include Edit Patch and PatchDeform.

Cross-Reference A more detailed explanation of splines and these Modifiers can be found in Chapter 13, "Using Patches."

Edit Patch modifier

This Modifier includes tools for editing patch objects similar to the Edit Spline and Edit Mesh Modifiers. The Edit Patch Modifier isn't really a Modifier, but an Object type, and will show up in the bottom section of the Modifier Stack. This is another one of the default Modifiers.

PatchDeform modifier

This Modifier uses a patch to deform an object. Variations of this Modifier include the PathDeform Modifier that uses splines and the SurfDeform Modifier that uses

NURBS. The Pick Patch button lets you select a patch to use in the deformation process. Once a patch has been selected using the Pick Patch button, you can enter the Percent and Stretch values for the U and V directions, along with a Rotation value and a Deform Plane.

Mesh modifiers

These Modifiers work with mesh objects. These Mesh Modifiers enhance the features available for Editable Mesh objects. Modifiers in this category include Edit Mesh, Mesh Select, Delete Mesh, Affect Region, Face Extrude, MeshSmooth, Lattice, Slice, and Cap Holes.

A more detailed explanation of mesh objects and several of these Modifiers can be found in Chapter 12, "Working with Meshes."

Edit Mesh modifier

All mesh objects are by default Editable Mesh objects. This Modifier enables objects to be modified using the Editable Mesh feature while maintaining its basic creation parameters.

Modifying an object's parameters after applying the Edit Mesh Modifier or any Modifier that alters the geometric topology of an object can cause erratic results.

Mesh Select modifier

This Modifier lets you make a subobject selection for modification. The selection can then be passed up the Stack to the next Modifier. The Mesh Select Modifier isn't really a Modifier, but an Object type and will show up in the bottom section of the Modifier Stack. This Modifier is one of the default Modifiers.

Delete Mesh modifier

This Modifier can be used to delete mesh subobjects. Subobjects that can be deleted include Vertices, Edges, Faces, and Objects.

Affect Region modifier

This Modifier can cause a selected subobject surface region to bubble up or be indented. Affect Region parameters include Falloff, Pinch, and Bubble values. You can also select the Ignore Back Facing option.

Figure 9-10 shows the post box with a dent and bubble applied. Before applying this Modifier, I needed to use the Tessellate Modifier to add some new polygons to the post box and then the Mesh Select Modifier to select a subobject region to apply the Affect Region Modifier to. The Affect Modifier is set to Pinch with a value of 5 in the direction of the attached Gizmo.

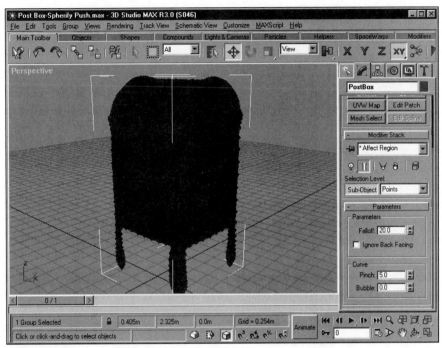

Figure 9-10: The Affect Region Modifier can be used to indent or bubble a selection on the surface.

Face Extrude modifier

This Modifier extrudes the selected faces in the same direction as their normals. Face Extrude parameters include Amount and Scale values and an option to Extrude From Center. Figure 9-11 shows a mesh object with several extruded faces. The Mesh Select Modifier was used to select the faces, and the extrude Amount was set to 30.

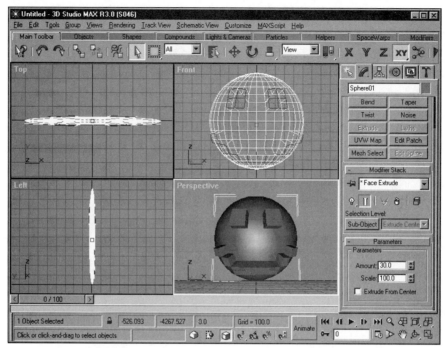

Figure 9-11: Extruded faces are moved in the direction of the face normal.

MeshSmooth modifier

This Modifier can be used to smooth a mesh object. This is accomplished by adding a face to every vertex and edge. This Modifier can be used to create a NURMS object. NURMS stands for Non-Uniform Rational MeshSmooth. NURMS can weight each control point. The Parameters rollout includes three MeshSmooth types: Classic, NURMS, and Quad Output. You can set it to operate on triangular or polygonal faces. Smoothing parameters include Strength and Relax values.

There are also settings for the number of Subdivision Iterations to run and controls for weighting selected control points. Update Options can be set to Always, When Rendering, and Manually using the Update button.

Figure 9-12 shows the post box converted to a NURMS object. Notice how the mail slot is now elliptical.

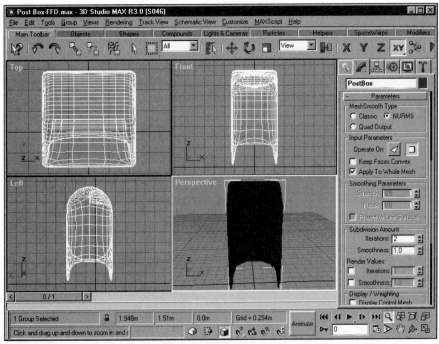

Figure 9-12: A NURMS post box created with the MeshSmooth Modifier

Lattice modifier

This Modifier changes an object into a lattice by creating struts where all the edges are located or by replacing each joint with an object. The Lattice Modifier considers all edges as struts and all vertices as Joints.

The parameters for this Modifier include several options to determine how to apply the effect. These options include the Entire Object, to Joint Only, to Struts Only, or Both (Struts and Joints). If the Apply to Entire Object option isn't selected, then the Modifier is applied to the current subobject.

For Struts you can specify Radius, Segments, Sides, and Material ID values. You can also specify to Ignore Hidden Edges, to create End Caps, and to Smooth the Struts.

For Joints, you can select Tetra, Octa, or Icosa types with Radius, Segments, and Material ID values. There are also controls for Mapping Coordinates.

Tip   Although the Joints settings enable you to select only one of three different types, you can use the Scatter compound object to place any type of object instead of the three defaults. To do this, apply Lattice Modifier and then select the Distribute Using All Vertices option in the Scatter Objects rollout.

Figure 9-13 shows the effect of the Lattice Modifier. The left-most object is the unmodified post box object. The next post box has only joints applied, the third post box object has only struts applied, and the last post box has both applied.

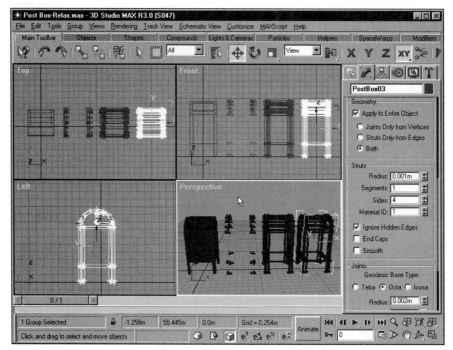

Figure 9-13: The Lattice Modifier divides an object into struts, joints, or both.

Slice modifier

This Modifier can be used to divide an object into two separate objects. Applying the Slice Modifier creates a Slice gizmo. This gizmo looks like a simple plane and can be transformed and positioned to define the slice location. To transform the gizmo, you need to select it from the Sub-Object drop-down list.

Tip

The Slice modifier can be used to make objects slowly disappear a layer at a time.

The Slice parameters include four slice type options. Refine Mesh simply adds new vertices and edges where the gizmo intersects the object. The Split Mesh option creates two separate objects. The Remove Top and Remove Bottom options delete all faces and vertices above or below the gizmo intersection plane.

Using Triangular or Polygonal faces, you can also specify whether the faces are divided. Figure 9-14 shows two post box objects that have been cut using the Slice

Modifier. The first one has had its top removed and the second one has had its bottom removed.

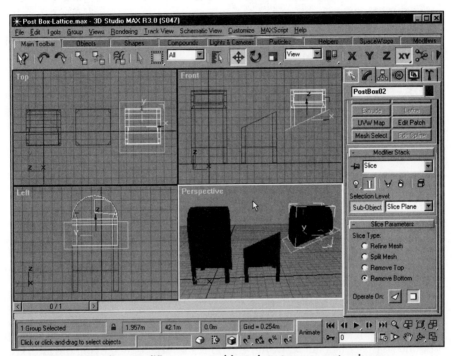

Figure 9-14: The Slice Modifier can cut objects into two separate pieces.

Note   Editable Meshes also have a Slice tool that can produce similar results. The difference is that the Slice Modifier can work on any type of object, not only on meshes.

Cap Holes modifier

This Modifier patches any holes found in a geometry object. Sometimes when objects are imported, they are missing faces. This Modifier can detect and eliminate these holes by creating a face along open edges.

For example, if a spline is extruded and you don't specify Caps, the Cap Holes Modifier will detect these holes and create a Cap. Cap Holes parameters include Smooth New Faces, Smooth with Old Faces, and All New Edges Visible. Smooth with Old Faces applies the same smoothing group used on the bordering faces.

NURBS modifiers

There are several Modifiers that work exclusively with NURBS objects, including the NCurve Sel and the NSurf Sel Modifiers for selecting NURBS subobjects and the SurfDeform Modifier.

Cross-Reference

More detailed coverage of NURBS and some of these Modifiers can be found in Chapter 16, "Working with NURBS."

NCurve Sel modifier

This Modifier lets you select a NURBS curve for passing up the Stack.

NSurf Sel modifier

This Modifier lets you select a NURBS Surface for passing up the Stack.

SurfDeform modifier

This Modifier deforms an object according to a NURBS surface. Variations of this Modifier include the PathDeform Modifier for splines and the PatchDeform Modifier that uses patches. The Pick Surface button lets you select a NURBS surface to use in the deformation process. Once a NURBS surface is selected using the Pick Surface button, you can enter the Percent and Stretch values for the U and V directions, along with a Rotation value.

Free-Form Deformation (FFD) modifiers

This category of Modifiers causes a lattice to appear around an object. This lattice is bound to the object and can alter the object's surface by moving the lattice control points. Modifiers include FFD (Free From Deformation), FFD (Box.Cyl), and FFD Select.

FFD (Free Form Deformation) modifier

This Modifier creates a lattice of control points around the object. The object's surface can deform the object by moving the control points. There are three different resolutions of FFDs: 2x2, 3x3, and 4x4. FFD parameters include options to display the Lattice and the Source Volume, to Deform Only in Volume, and All Vertices. The Reset button can be used to return the volume to its original shape if you make a mistake. The Animate All button lets you create keys for each vertex. The Conform to Shape button sets the offset of the Control Points with Inside Points, Outside Points, and Offset options.

Figure 9-15 shows how the FFD Modifier can be used to change the post box by selecting the Control Points subobjects.

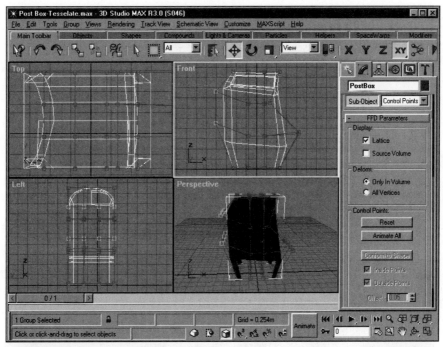

Figure 9-15: The FFD Modifier changes the shape of an object by moving the lattice of Control Points that surround it.

FFD (Box/Cyl) modifier

This Modifier can create a box- or cylinder-shaped lattice of control points for deforming objects. The Set Number of Points button enables you to specify the number of Control Points in the lattice. The Selection buttons let you choose the points along any axes.

FFD Select modifier

This Modifier enables you to select a subobject group of control points and apply additional Modifiers to the selection.

General modifiers

These Modifiers alter the entire geometry of an object, such as smoothing or optimizing an object. Modifiers in this category include Smooth, Tessellate, Optimize, Relax, Normal, Preserve, STL-Check, and Volume Select.

Smooth modifier

This Modifier can be used to auto-smooth an object. Smooth parameters include options for Auto Smooth and Prevent Indirect Smoothing along with a Threshold value. The Parameters rollout also includes a set of 32 Smoothing Groups buttons labeled 1 through 32.

Tessellate modifier

This Modifier subdivides the selected faces for higher resolution models. Tessellation can be applied to either Triangle or Polygonal Faces. The Edge option creates new faces by dividing the face from the face center to the middle of the edges. The Face-Center option divides each face from the face center to the corners of the face. The Tension setting determines whether the faces are convex or concave. The Iterations setting is the number of times the Modifier is applied.

Caution   Applying the Tessellate Modifier to an object with a high Iterations value will produce objects with many times the original number of faces.

Figure 9-16 shows the post box with the Tessellation Modifier applied. The left post box is the original, the middle post box has had only one tessellation iteration applied, and the right post box has had three iterations applied.

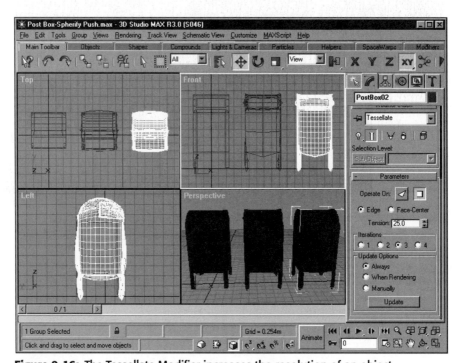

Figure 9-16: The Tessellate Modifier increases the resolution of an object.

Optimize modifier

This Modifier does the opposite of the Tessellation Modifier. It simplifies models by reducing the number of faces, edges, and vertices. The Level of Detail can be set differently for the Renderer and the Viewports. Face and Edge Thresholds determine if elements should be collapsed. Other options include Bias and Maximum Edge Length. Parameters can also be set to Preserve Material and Smoothing Boundaries. The Update button enables manual updating of the object, and the text field at the bottom of the rollout displays the number of Vertices and Faces for the current optimization.

Figure 9-17 shows a cow model that has been optimized. Notice the dramatic reduction in the number of faces from the left to the right. Viewpoint Datalabs, known for producing high-resolution models, created this model. As you can see at the bottom of the Modify panel in figure 9-17, the number of faces has been reduced from 4326 to 670 faces by setting the Face Threshold to 20. (I guess that would be considered "lean beef.")

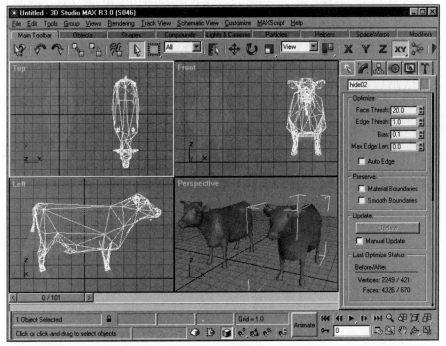

Figure 9-17: The Optimize modifier can be used to reduce the complexity of the cow model.

Caution   Applying the Optimize modifier reduces the overall number of polygons, but it also reduces the detail of the model. Be careful when using this Modifier repeatedly.

Relax modifier

This Modifier tends to smooth the overall geometry by separating vertices that lie closer than an average distance. Parameters include a Relax Value that is the percentage of the distance that the vertices move. Values can range between 1.0 and –1.0. A value of 0 has no effect on the object. Negative values have the opposite effect, causing an object to become tighter and more distorted.

The Iterations value determines how many times this calculation is computed. The Keep Boundary Points Fixed option removes any points that are next to an open hole. The Save Outer Corners maintains the vertex position of corners of an object.

Figure 9-18 shows the post box before and after the Relax Modifier is applied.

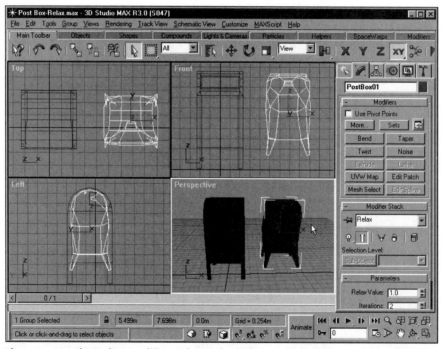

Figure 9-18: The Relax modifier reduces the tight areas of objects by averaging the distance between vertices

Normal modifier

This Modifier enables object normals to be flipped or unified. When some objects are imported, their normals can become erratic, producing holes in the geometry. By unifying and flipping the normals you can restore an object's consistency. This Modifier includes two options: Unify Normals and Flip Normals.

Preserve modifier

This Modifier works to maintain Edge Lengths, Face Angles, and Volume as an object is deformed and edited. Before an object is modified, make an additional copy. Then, edit one of the copies. To apply the Preserve Modifier, click the Pick Original button, then click the unmodified object, and finally, click the modified object. The object will be modified to preserve the Edge Lengths, Face Angles, and Volume as defined in the Weight values.

The Iterations option determines the number of times the process is applied. You can also specify to apply to the Whole Mesh, to Selected Vertices Only, or to an Inverted Selection.

STL-Check modifier

This Modifier checks a model in preparation for exporting it to the StereoLithography (STL) format. StereoLithography files require a closed surface — geometry with holes or gaps can cause problems. Any problems are reported in the Status Area of the Parameters rollout.

This Modifier can check for several common errors including Open Edge, Double Face, Spike, or Multiple Edge. Spikes are island faces with only one connected edge. You can select any or all of these options. If found, you can have the Modifier select the problem Edges or Faces or neither, or you can change the Material ID of the problem area.

Volume Select modifier

This Modifier lets you select a subobject region based on a Volume defined by a gizmo object.

 New Feature   The Volume Select modifier is new to Release 3.

In the Parameters rollout for this Modifier, you can specify whether the subobject selections should use Object, Vertex, or Face. Any new selection can Replace, be Added to, or be Subtracted from the current selection. You can also choose either a Window or Crossing Selection Type.

The actual Volume can be a Box, a Sphere, or a Cylinder of a Mesh Object. To use a Mesh Object, click the button to the right and then click the object to use in a viewport. In addition to selecting by volume, you can select by Material IDs, Smoothing Groups, or Texture Maps.

The Alignment options can Fit or Center the volume on the current subobject selection. The Reset button moves the gizmo to its original position and orientation.

Material and Maps modifiers

Material Modifiers affect the materials and maps applied to an object. These Modifiers help control how materials and/or maps are used. Modifiers in this category include Material, MaterialByElement, UVW Map, Camera Map, UVW XForm, Unwrap UVW, and Vertex Paint.

Many of these modifiers are covered in Chapter 19, "Working with Materials and Maps."

Material modifier

This Modifier lets you change the material ID of an object. The only parameter for this Modifier is the Material ID. When you select a subobject and apply this Modifier, the Material ID will be applied to only the subobject selection. This Modifier is used in conjunction with the Multi/Sub-Object Material type to create a single object with multiple materials, like the umbrella in Figure 9-19.

The Umbrella model was provided by Zygote Media from their Sampler CD-ROM.

MaterialByElement modifier

This Modifier enables you to change material IDs randomly. This Modifier can be applied to an object with several elements, such as a group of spheres attached as a single mesh object. The object needs to have the Multi/Sub-Object material applied to it.

The MaterialByElement modifier is new to Release 3.

The parameters for this Modifier can be set to assign material IDs randomly with the Random Distribution option, or according to a desired Frequency. The ID Count is the minimum number of material IDs to use. The percentage of each ID to use can be specified in the fields under the List Frequency option. The Seed option alters the randomness of the materials.

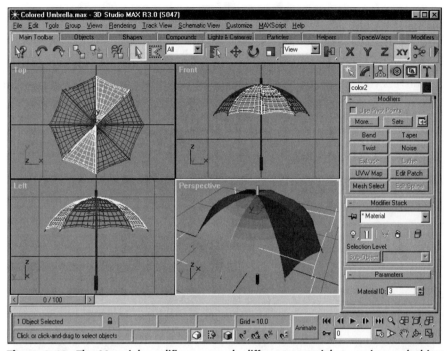

Figure 9-19: The Material modifier can apply different materials to various subobjects.

UVW Map modifier

This Modifier lets you specify the mapping coordinates for an object. It is one of the default Modifiers. Primitives, Loft Objects, and NURBS can generate their own mapping coordinates, but you need to use this Modifier to apply mapping coordinates to mesh objects and patches.

Note   Objects that create their own mapping coordinates apply them to Map Channel 1. If you apply the UVW Map Modifier to Map Channel 1 of an object that already has mapping coordinates, then the applied coordinates overwrite the existing ones.

The UVW Map Modifier can be applied to different map channels. Applying this Modifier places a map gizmo on the object. This gizmo can be moved, scaled, or rotated. To transform a UVW Map gizmo, you must select it from the subobject list. Gizmos that are scaled smaller than the object can be tiled.

There are many different types of mappings, and the parameter rollout for this Modifier lets you select which one to use. The Length, Width, and Height values are the dimensions for the UVW Map gizmo. You can also set tiling values in all directions.

The Alignment section offers eight buttons for controlling the alignment of the gizmo. The Fit button fits the gizmo to the edges of the object. The Center button aligns the gizmo center with the object's center. The Bitmap Fit button opens a File dialog box where you can align the gizmo to the resolution of the selected bitmaps. The Normal Align button lets you drag on the surface of the object, and when you release the mouse button, the gizmo origin will be aligned with the normal. The View Align button aligns the gizmo to match the current viewport. The Region Fit button lets you drag a region in the viewport and match the gizmo to this region. The Reset button moves the gizmo to its original location. The Acquire button aligns the gizmo with the same coordinates as another object.

Figure 9-20 displays a brick map applied to an umbrella using Spherical Mapping.

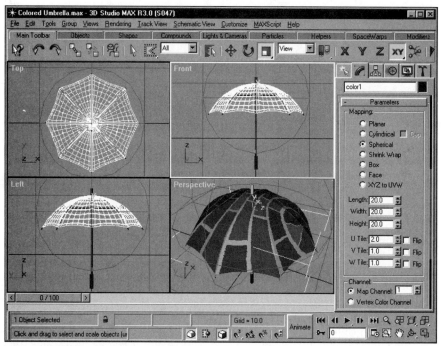

Figure 9-20: The UVW Map modifier lets you specify various mapping coordinates for material maps.

Camera Map modifier

This Modifier creates planar mapping coordinates based on the camera's position. The single parameter for this Modifier is Pick Camera. To use this Modifier, click the Pick Camera button and select a camera. The mapping coordinates will be applied to the selected object.

UVW XForm modifier

This Modifier enables you to adjust mapping coordinates. It can be applied to mapping coordinates that are automatically created or to mapping coordinates created with the UVW Map Modifier. The parameter rollout includes values for the UVW Tile and UVW Offsets. You can also select the Map Channel to use.

Unwrap UVW modifier

This Modifier, which has been improved in Release 3, lets you control how a map is applied to a subobject selection. It can also be used to unwrap the existing mapping coordinates of an object. You can then edit these coordinates as needed. The Unwrap UVW Modifier can be used to apply multiple planar maps to an object.

Vertex Paint modifier

This Modifier lets you specify a color and paint directly on the surface of an object by painting the vertices. The color is applied with a paintbrush–shaped cursor. If several vertices of one face have different colors, then the color is applied as a gradient across the face.

 New Feature The Vertex Paint modifier is new to Release 3.

The parameters for this Modifier include a Paint button, an Opacity toggle, and a color swatch for selecting the color to paint with. There are also VertCol and Shaded toggles for turning Vertex Shading and normal Shading on and off, and a 16-color palette for quick color selection.

Note There is also an Assign Vertex Color utility that can be accessed under the Utilities panel.

Figure 9-21 shows an umbrella with the Vertex Paint modifier applied.

Space Warp modifiers

Space Warp Modifiers produce the same results as Space Warps, except in Modifier form. The Modifiers' positions in the Stack affect the results. For instance, if you apply a Smooth Modifier on top of the Ripple Modifier, the ripple effect will be diminished. Modifiers in this category include Ripple and Wave.

Cross-Reference For more information on Space Warps, see Chapter 25, "Using Space Warps."

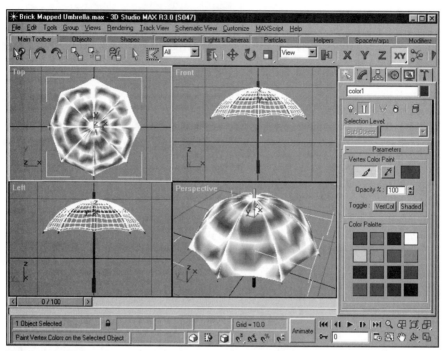

Figure 9-21: The Vertex Paint modifier lets you paint on object surfaces by coloring vertices.

Ripple modifier

This Modifier creates ripples across the surface of an object. This Modifier is best used on a single object; if several objects need a ripple effect, use the Ripple Space Warp. The ripple is applied via a gizmo that you can control. Parameters for this Modifier include two Amplitude values, and values for the Wave Length, Phase, and Decay of the ripple.

Figure 9-22 shows the Ripple Modifier applied to a simple Quad Patch on the left.

Wave modifier

This Modifier produces a wave-like effect across the surface of the object. All the parameters of the Wave Parameter are identical to the Ripple Modifier parameters. The difference is that the waves produced by the Wave Modifier are parallel, and they propagate in a straight line.

Figure 9-22 shows the Wave Modifier applied to a simple Quad Patch on the right.

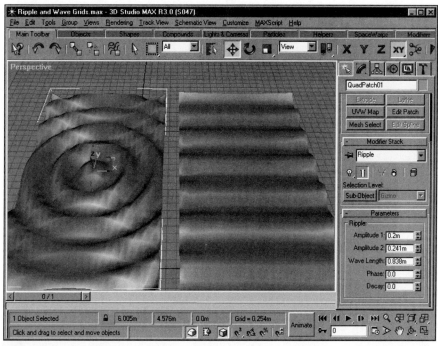

Figure 9-22: The Ripple and Wave modifiers produce concentric and parallel waves across the surface of an object.

Surface Tool modifiers

The Surface Tools are a special group of Modifiers that enable you to create a spline network of cross sections with the CrossSection Modifier and apply a surface to this network with the Surface Modifier.

New Feature The CrossSection and Surface modifiers are both new to Release 3.

CrossSection modifier

This modifier is one of the Surface Tools. It connects the vertices of several cross-sectional splines together with additional splines in preparation for the Surface Modifier. These cross-sectional splines can have different numbers of vertices. Parameters include different spline types such as Linear, Smooth, Bézier, and Bézier corner.

Figure 9-23 shows a spline network that has been created with the CrossSection Modifier.

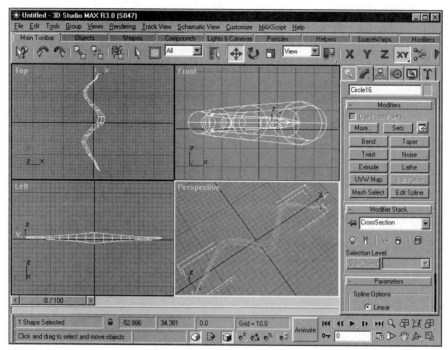

Figure 9-23: The CrossSection modifier joins several cross section splines into a network of splines ready for a surface.

Surface modifier

This Modifier is the other part of the Surface Tools. It creates a surface from several combined splines. It can use any spline network, but works best with structures created with the CrossSection Modifier. The surface created with this Modifier is a patch surface.

Parameters for this Modifier include a Spline Threshold value and options to Flip Normals, Remove Interior Patches, and to Use Only Selected Segments. You can also specify the Steps used to create the patch topology.

Figure 9-24 shows the spline structure illustrated in the previous figure with the Surface Modifier applied.

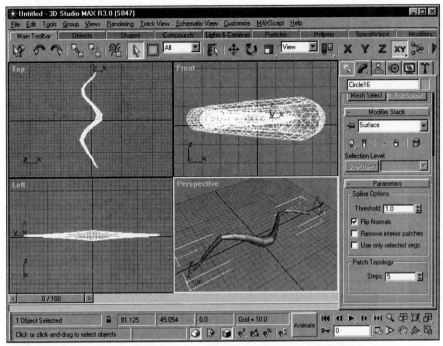

Figure 9-24: The Surface modifier applies a surface of the cross section spline network.

Surface modifiers

These Modifiers modify an object's surface. Modifiers in this category include Morpher, Disp Approx, Displace, and Skin.

Morpher modifier

This Modifier lets you change a shape from one form into another. This can only be applied to objects with the same number of vertices.

New Feature   The Morpher modifier is new to Release 3.

The Morpher modifier can be very useful for creating facial expressions and character lip-synching. It can also be used to morph materials. There are 100 separate channels available for morph targets, and channels can be mixed. The Morpher Modifier can be used in conjunction with the Morpher material.

Disp Approx modifier

This modifier is short for Displacement Approximation. It alters the surface of an object based on Displacement mapping. This Modifier can work with any object that can be converted to an Editable Mesh including primitives, NURBS, Editable Meshes, and Patches.

New Feature   The Disp Approx modifier is new to Release 3.

Parameters for this modifier include Subdivision Preset settings of Low, Medium, and High.

Displace modifier

This modifier can alter an object's geometry by displacing elements using a Displace gizmo or a grayscale bitmap image (to create terrains, for example). The Displace gizmo can have one of four different shapes: Planar, Cylindrical, Spherical, or Shrink Wrap. Gizmos can be placed exterior to an object or inside an object to push it from the inside.

The Displace Modifier parameters include Strength and Decay values. The Luminance Center value defines the center point for a grayscale bitmap. There are also buttons for Loading and Removing bitmaps and maps, and you can blur these objects with the Blur value. If a map is loaded, you can select and control its mapping coordinates. The final set of parameters lets you control the alignment of the bitmap or map.

Figure 9-25 shows the effect of the Displace Modifier on one side of a die.

Skin modifier

This modifier is useful for creating skin to surround a bones system. Each object with the Skin modifier applied gets a capsule-shaped envelope attached to it. When two of these envelopes overlap, their surfaces blend together like skin around a bone joint. These envelopes can be attached to NURBS, Meshes, Patches, Bones, or even splines.

New Feature   The Skin modifier is new to Release 3.

Parameters for this Modifier let you Add and Remove Bones, Add and Remove Bone Cross Sections, and control the position and size of the Envelopes. There are also settings to weight the various vertices. Figure 9-26 shows a simple use of the Skin modifier to bend a tube.

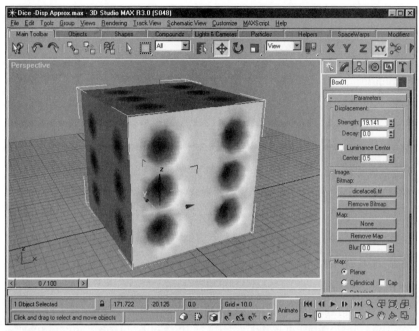

Figure 9-25: The Displace modifier can be used as a modeling tool to change the surface of an object.

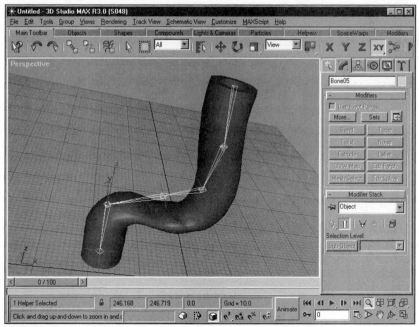

Figure 9-26: The Skin modifier simulates stretching skin over a rigid object like a tube.

Transform modifiers

Transform Modifiers can be used to transform objects. Modifiers in this category include Mirror, XForm, Linked XForm, and Flex.

Mirror modifier

This Modifier can be used to create a mirrored copy of an object or subobject. The Parameters rollout lets you pick a mirror axis or plane and an Offset value. The Copy option creates a copy of the mirrored object and retains the original selection.

XForm modifier

This Modifier enables you to apply transforms such as Move, Rotate, and Scale to objects and/or subobjects. This modifier is applied by means of a gizmo that can be transformed using the transform buttons on the main toolbar. The XForm modifier has no parameters.

Note   XForm is short for the word Transform.

Linked XForm modifier

This modifier passes all transformations of one object onto another. The object that controls the transformation is designated as the Control Object and is selected via the Pick Control Object button. Once the Control object is selected, the Control Object controls the selected object's transforms.

Flex modifier

This modifier causes an object to move like a spring flexing in response to motion. An object with the Flex modifier applied simulates the type of motion of an antenna on a car that moves back and forth as the car speeds up or slows down.

New Feature   The Flex Modifier is new to Release 3.

Parameters for this modifier include Flex, Strength, and Sway values. You can also control the Weights of vertices and work with Advanced Parameters like Ripple, Wind, and Wave Space Warps.

World-Space modifiers

World-Space Modifiers are based on world space coordinates instead of on an object's local coordinate system. Most of these Modifiers have a similar Object-Space Modifier. Modifiers in this category include Camera Map WSM, Displace Mesh WSM, Displace NURBS WSM, MapScaler WSM, PathDeform WSM, PatchDeform WSM, SurfDeform WSM, and Surface Mapper WSM.

Camera Map WSM

This Modifier creates planar mapping coordinates based on the camera's position in world coordinates. It works much like the Object-Space Camera Map Modifier, except that the mapping coordinates are based on world-space coordinates instead of on object-space coordinates.

Displace Mesh WSM

This Modifier displays in a viewport the deformed mesh that results from a displacement mapping and the Disp Approx Modifier. To create a permanent copy of the deformed mesh, use the Edit ➪ Clone function.

 New Feature The Displace Mesh World-Space modifier is new to Release 3.

Displace NURBS WSM

This Modifier converts a NURBS object into a mesh object. It can also be used to show the effect of a displacement map on a NURBS object. Parameters include an Update Mesh button, controls for the Tessellation options, and an Auto Weld threshold.

MapScaler WSM

This Modifier maintains a map scale regardless of the object's size. For example, if you have a wallpaper texture applied to a wall, you can apply this Modifier so you can scale the wall without disturbing the wallpaper texture. Parameters include a Scale value and a Wrap Texture option that wraps the texture evenly around the object. You can also specify the Up Direction according to the World Z-axis or the Local Z-axis.

PathDeform WSM

This Modifier modifies objects based on a spline path. It works much like the Object-Space PathDeform Modifier, except the World-Space Modifier moves the object to the path instead of moving the path to the object like the Object-Space Modifier.

PatchDeform WSM

This Modifier modifies objects based on a patch. It works much like the Object-Space PatchDeform Modifier, except the World-Space Modifier moves the object to the patch instead of moving the patch to the object like the Object-Space Modifier.

SurfDeform WSM

This Modifier deforms an object based on a NURBS surface. It works much like the Object-Space SurfDeform Modifier, except the World-Space Modifier moves the object to the NURBS surface instead of moving the NURBS surface to the object like the Object-Space Modifier.

Surface Mapper WSM

This Modifier projects a map from a NURBS object onto a modified object. The Parameters rollout includes a Pick NURBS Surface button for select the NURBS surface to use. You can also select Input and Output Channels and specify how the object gets updated.

 New Feature The Surface Mapper World-Space Modifier is new to Release 3.

Applying Modifiers

To apply a Modifier to an object, you simply need to select the object and click the Modifier button or select it from the Modifier list. After a Modifier is applied, the object parameter rollout is replaced with new rollouts for controlling the Modifier.

 Caution Applying a Modifier destroys the parametric nature of primitive objects.

In the Modifier rollout is an option to Use Pivot Points (available when multiple objects are selected). If this option is checked, the Modifier is applied to each object about its local pivot point. If it is not checked, the Modifier is applied about a single centralized pivot point for all the selected objects.

Tutorial: Twisting a bridge

Do you remember back in science class seeing the short little film on the collapse of the Tacoma-Narrows bridge? The Twist modifier can be used to re-create this scenario.

To use the Twist modifier on a bridge model, follow these steps:

1. Start by creating the canyon walls. In the Create panel, click the Shapes button and then select Line. In the Top viewport, draw two parallel jagged lines with the Line tool. Make each of these closed splines by dragging the last vertex on top of the first.

2. Select one of the closed spline objects, open the Modify panel, and click the Extrude button. Enter an Amount of **100** in the Parameters rollout. Repeat this for the other spline as well.

3. Click the Geometry button and select Box. Create a simple box for the bridge model that spans the two canyon walls.

4. Click the Animate button and drag the Time Slider to frame 30. Select the bridge, open the Modify panel, and click the Twist button. Enter an Angle value of **–15**. Drag the Time Slider to frame 60 and enter an Angle value of **0**. Drag the slider to frame 90 and enter **15**. At frame 100 enter a value of **0** again.

5. Click the Play Animation button to see the brief animation.

This example shows how all modifiers can be animated. Figure 9-27 includes a frame from this simple animation.

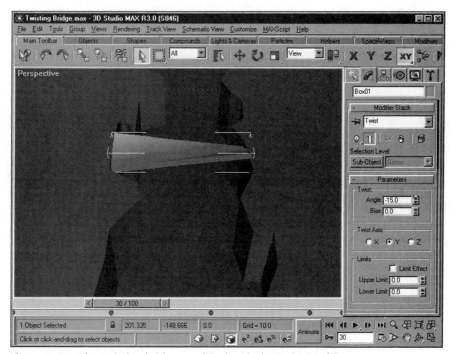

Figure 9-27: The twisting bridge modified with the Twist Modifier

Tutorial: Modeling hyperspace deformation

Why is it that whenever a person or object travels through a hyperspace portal, they deform before disappearing? It must have something to do with compressing the molecules. (Anyway, it looks like it hurts. I prefer the Star Trek method where you just twinkle and you're gone.) In this tutorial, we'll recreate this hyperspace deformation using an FFD Modifier. The object I'm transporting is a television created by Zygote Media. (Maybe the Enterprise crew wants to watch some old episodes.)

To simulate the hyperspace deformation effect, follow these steps:

1. Start by creating six Tube objects to represent the transport tubes. Right-click these tubes and select the See Through option in the Object Properties dialog box so you can see the objects within the tubes.

2. Import the television model and position it within the tubes.

3. With the television selected, click the Modify panel and click the More button. From the Modifier list, select the FFD 3×3×3 Modifier. This will place a lattice gizmo around the television.

4. Click the Sub-Object button in the Modify panel and select Control Points from the drop-down list. Then select the corner Control Points individually and move them up and outward.

Figure 9-28 shows our television being deformed as it travels through the hyperspace transporter.

Working with the Modifier Stack

All Modifiers that are applied to an object are recorded in the Modifier Stack. This Stack is the manager for all modifiers applied to an object.

An object can have several modifiers applied to it. The Modifier Stack rollout, shown in Figure 9-29, keeps track of all the various modifiers applied to an object. It provides a way to look up any existing modifiers and change their parameters. You can also use the Stack to delete modifiers as well as cut, copy, and paste Modifiers between objects.

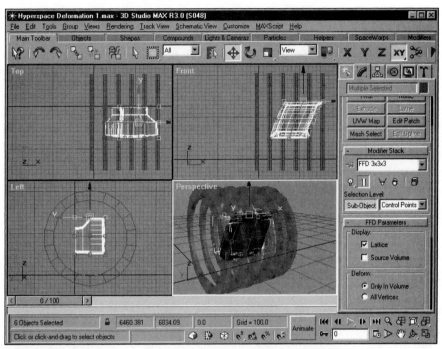

Figure 9-28: This television is being deformed via an FFD Modifier.

Figure 9-29: The Modifier Stack rollout displays all modifiers applied to an object.

Tip You can also Cut, Copy, and Paste modifiers using the Schematic View. See Chapter 28, "Using Schematic View," for more details.

Any new Modifiers applied to an object are stacked on top of the existing modifiers in the list. There can be three different divisions in the Stack list separated by lines. The bottom section lists the object type. This can be the name of a primitive or type of object. The middle section contains all the Object-Space modifiers applied, and the top section is all the World-Space modifiers and Space Warps. There will always be an object section, but the other sections will be missing if no modifiers have been applied.

Note   If an asterisk is placed before the modifier name, it indicates that the modifier has been applied to a subobject.

The Stack order is important and can change the appearance of the object. MAX applies all object definitions first, then the Object-Space modifiers, followed by any transformations, and finally, the World-Space modifiers and Space Warps.

The Modifier Stack controls

There are several controls for dealing with the Modifier Stack, as described in Table 9-1. Modifiers can be selected from a drop-down list at the top of the rollout.

Table 9-1
Main Toolbar Buttons

Toolbar Button	Name	Description
	Pin Stack	Makes a particular object's Stack available for editing even if another object is selected (like taking a physical pin and sticking it into the screen so it won't move).
	Activate/Inactivate Modifier Toggle, Activate/Inactivate in Viewport	Lets you remove the effect of a certain Modifier without deleting it and includes a flyout for removing the Modifier's visibility in a viewport.
	Show End Result	Shows the results of the entire Stack when enabled and only the Modifiers up to the current selection if disabled.
	Make Unique	Identifies the current Modifier as unique to the current object. (This control is discussed in more detail later in the chapter.)
	Remove Modifier	Used to delete a Modifier from the Stack or unbind a Space Warp if one is selected.

Toolbar Button	Name	Description
(icon)	Edit Stack	Opens the Modifier Stack dialog box, which enables you to Cut, Copy, and Paste Modifiers, among other things. (This dialog box is discussed and illustrated in the next section.) If this button is clicked when a parametric primitive is selected and no Modifiers have been applied, a pop-up menu appears that lets you convert the selection into an editable object.
Sub-Object	Sub-Object	Enables you to enter one of several subobject modes to work with Vertices, Edges, Faces, and so on. The available subobject depends on the Modifier and object type.

Copying Modifiers

If you've set a particular modifier (or modifiers) just right, there is no reason to re-create it if you want to use it again. The Edit Modifier Stack dialog box, shown in Figure 9-30, will let you reuse modifiers.

Figure 9-30: You can use the Edit Modifier Stack dialog box to select Modifiers and copy them to another object.

To copy a modifier onto another object, follow these steps:

1. Open the Edit Stack dialog box by clicking the Edit Stack button in the Modifier Stack rollout.

2. Select the Modifiers to copy and click the Copy button.

3. Exit the dialog box by clicking OK.

4. Select a new object and click the Edit Stack button again.

5. In the Edit Modifier Stack, select the modifier just above where you want the copied Modifier to be located and click the Paste button.

Caution   Modifiers can only be pasted into similar sections in the Stack. For example, Object-Space Modifiers must be pasted in the Object-Space section.

Collapsing the Stack

The Edit Modifier Stack dialog box also includes a button for collapsing the Stack. Collapsing the Stack removes its history and resets the modification history back to a baseline. All the individual Modifiers in the Stack are combined into one single modification. This eliminates the ability to change any Modifier parameters, but it also simplifies the object and conserves memory.

Modifying subobjects

In addition to being applied to complete objects, Modifiers can also be applied and used to modify *subobjects*. Subobjects are defined as portions of an object. Subobjects can be vertices, edges, faces, or combinations of object parts.

To work in subobject selection mode, click the Subobject button at the top of the Parameter section in the Control Panel. To the right of the Sub-Object button is a drop-down list where you can select the different types of subobjects available in the current object.

Several Modifiers, including Mesh Select, Spline Select, and Volume Select, can select subobject areas for passing these selections up to the next Modifier in the Stack. For example, you can use the Mesh Select Modifier to select several faces on the front of a sphere and then apply the Face Extrude Modifier to extrude just those faces.

You can identify any Modifiers that have been applied to a subobject selection by the asterisk that appears in front of the Modifier name in the Stack.

Using Instanced Modifiers

When a single Modifier is applied to several objects at the same time, the Modifier will show up in the Modifier Stack for each object. These are *Instanced Modifiers* that maintain a link to each other. If any of these Instanced Modifiers are changed, the change is propagated to all other instances. This is very helpful for modifying large groups of objects.

When a Modifier is copied between different objects, you can select to make the copy an instance.

To see all the objects that are linked to a particular Modifier, select Views ➪ Show Dependencies. All objects with Instanced Modifiers that link to the current selection will appear bright green.

At any time, you can break the link between a particular Instanced Modifier and the rest of the objects using the Make Unique button in the Modifier Stack rollout. After clicking this button, a dialog box asks if you are sure about this action. Click Yes to complete the action.

Summary

With the Modifiers contained in the Modify panel, you can alter objects in a vast number of ways. Modifiers work with every aspect of an object, including geometric deformations, materials, and general object maintenance. In this chapter, we've taken a fairly close look at the available Modifiers and learned about how to apply and control them using the Modifier Stack.

The topics covered in this chapter included

 ✦ Changing object properties
 ✦ Exploring Modifier types, including Object-Space and World-Space Modifiers
 ✦ Applying Modifiers
 ✦ Working with the Modifier Stack
 ✦ Using Instanced Modifiers

This chapter concludes Part II, "Working with Objects." You're now ready to learn about the individual modeling object types. In the next chapter, we'll cover the simplest object type, primitives.

✦   ✦   ✦

Modeling

Creating Primitive Objects

This chapter covers the basics about primitive object
types, including how to accurately create and control
them. We will also explore all of the primitive types that are
available, along with some examples of how to use them.

Working with Primitive Objects

In the modeling world, the simplest building blocks are known
as *primitives*. MAX knows how to draw these primitives without
any help other than your selecting a primitive object type and
then dragging in one of the viewports to define the primitive
object's dimensions.

Fundamentally, primitives are created by clicking in one of the
viewports to set the object's initial position, dragging the mouse
to define the object's dimensions, and then clicking again to set
each additional dimension if needed. Each primitive object type
has different dimensions and will require a different number of
clicks and drags.

For example, a sphere is one of the simplest objects to create.
To create a sphere, click in a viewport to set the location of
the sphere's center, then drag the mouse to the desired radius
and release the mouse button to complete. A Box object, on
the other hand, requires a click and drag move to define the
base (width and depth), then a drag and click again to set the
height. If you ever get lost when defining these dimensions,
check the Prompt Line to see what dimension the interface is
expecting next.

Every primitive created is assigned a name and a color automatically. These can be changed at any time, as discussed in earlier chapters.

When a primitive object button is selected, the Creation Method rollout appears and offers different methods for creating the primitives. For example, select the Sphere button and the Creation Method rollout will display two options: Edge and Center. The Edge method will define the sphere's dimensions by selecting the distance between edges. The Center method will define a dimension from the center of the sphere to the outer edge.

Using keyboard entry for precise dimensions

When creating a primitive object, you can define its location and dimensions by clicking in a viewport and dragging, or you can enter precise values in the Keyboard Entry rollout, located in the Create panel. Within this rollout you can enter the offset XYZ values for positioning the origin of the primitive, and the dimensions of the object. The offset values are defined relative to the active construction plane that is usually the Home Grid.

When all the dimension fields are set, click the Create button to create the actual primitive. Once a primitive is created, altering the fields in the Keyboard Entry rollout has no effect.

Altering object parameters

When a primitive object button is selected and a primitive is created, the Parameters rollout also appears. Compared to the Keyboard Entry rollout, which can only be used when creating the primitive, the Parameters rollout can be used to alter the primitive's parameters at any time. For example, increasing the Radius value will make an existing sphere larger. Other options, like the Generate Mapping Coordinates option, can be altered at any time. (This option automatically creates material mapping coordinates that are used to position maps.)

Note   Once an object is deselected, the Parameters rollout disappears from the Create tab and moves to the Modify tab. Future parameter adjustments can be made by selecting an object and clicking the Modify tab.

Tutorial: Guessing the number of gumballs in a jar

Have you ever entered a contest where you needed to guess the number of gumballs in a jar? (Did you ever try to cheat by filling a similar jar?) Well, this exercise won't be any easier, but it will show you how to create objects with precise dimensions (to increase your chance of a correct guess). Now, suppose that the jar is cylindrical and approximately 12 inches tall and 8 inches in diameter. The gumballs appear to be about 1 inch in diameter.

To create objects with precise dimensions, follow these steps:

1. Set your units by selecting Customize ➪ Units Setup. In the Units Setup dialog box, click the US Standard option and select Decimal Inches from the drop-down list.

2. Open the Create panel, click the Geometry category button, and select Standard Primitives from the subcategory drop-down list.

3. Click the Cylinder button and access the Keyboard Entry rollout by clicking its title. (Just a reminder: a + in the rollout title bar means it's unopened and you'll need to click it to have it "roll out.")

4. Enter **4** inches for the Radius and **12** inches for the Height. Click the Create button. The cylinder object is created with its origin placed at the origin of the Home Grid.

5. Click the Zoom Extents All button at the lower right corner of the interface to get in close. Right-click the new cylinder object and select Properties from the pop-up menu. Select the See-Through option so you can see the gumball spheres you'll create.

6. Back in the Create panel, click the Sphere button and then, in the Keyboard Entry rollout, enter **0.5** inches in the Radius field. Click the Create button to create a sphere.

7. Now you have a crude approximation of the jar and the gumball. Clone the gumball and start filling the jar. When you're done, count all the gumballs. (It won't be easy , but this is what it takes if you want to win.)

Note   There is actually an easier way to do this. Using the Dynamics features of MAX, you can turn on border detection so the balls don't overlap and enable a Gravity Space Warp, so they settle realistically under the effects of gravity. Dynamics will be covered in Chapter 34,"Creating a Dynamic Simulation."

Figure 10-1 shows the filled jar.

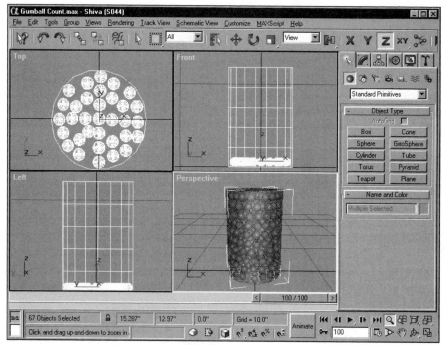

Figure 10-1: Recreating an approximation of a jar filled with gumballs using the Keyboard Entry rollout

Primitive Object Types

MAX includes many standard primitives and even more nonstandard primitives. These can all be created from the Create panel. There are two subcategories for creating primitives: Standard Primitives and Extended Primitives.

Standard Primitives

The Standard Primitives comprise many of the most basic and most used objects, including boxes, spheres, and cylinders.

Box

The Box primitive can be used to create regular cubes and boxes of any width, length, and height. Holding down the Ctrl key while dragging the box base creates a perfect square for the base. To create a cube, select the Cube option in the Creation Method rollout. This only requires a single click and drag to complete the cube.

The Length, Width, and Height Segment values indicate how many polygons make up each dimension. The default is only one segment.

Sphere

Spheres are seen everywhere from sports objects to planets in space. Spheres are also among the easiest primitives to create. After selecting the Sphere button, simply click and drag in a viewport. The Creation Method rollout offers two methods for creating spheres. The Edge method creates a sphere by dragging the diameter of the sphere, and the Center method defines the radius from the center outward.

In the Parameters rollout, the Segments value specifies the number of polygons that make up the sphere. The default of 32 produces a smooth sphere, and a value of 4 actually produces a diamond-shaped object. The Smooth option lets you make the sphere smooth or faceted. Faceted spheres are useful for identifying faces for modifications. Figure 10-2 shows three spheres. The one on the left has 32 Segments and the Smooth option turned on. The middle one also has 32 Segments, but with the Smooth option turned off. The one on the right has only 16 Segments with the Smooth option off.

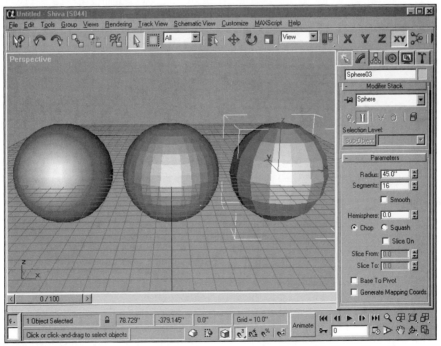

Figure 10-2: Sphere primitives of various Segment values with Smooth option on and off

The Parameters rollout also lets you create hemispheres. The hemisphere shape is set by the Hemisphere value, which can range from 0.0 to 1.0 with 0 being a full sphere and 1 being nothing at all. (A value of 0.5 would be a perfect hemisphere.) With the Hemisphere value specified, you now have two options with which to deal with the unused polygons that make up the originating sphere: the Chop option, which removes the unused polygons, and the Squash option, which retains the polygons but "squashes" them to fit in the hemisphere shape.

Figure 10-3 shows several hemispheres. They range from 0.25 to 0.5 in the middle and 0.75 at the right end. The top row uses the Chop option and the bottom row is set to Squash. Notice how many extra polygons are included in the bottom row.

Figure 10-3: Creating hemispheres with the Chop and Squash options

The Slice option enables you to dissect the sphere into slices (like segmenting an orange). The Slice From and Slice To fields accept values ranging from 0 to 360 degrees. Figure 10-4 shows three spheres that have been sliced. The left one is sliced from 0 degrees to 230 degrees, the second is sliced from 60 to 160, and the third is from 120 to –230. Finally, the Base to Pivot option determines whether the position of the pivot point will be at the bottom of the sphere or at the center.

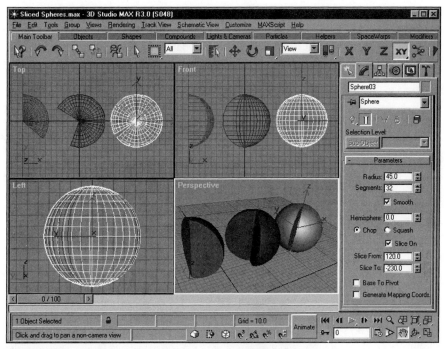

Figure 10-4: Using the Slice option to create sphere slices

New Feature The Slice feature is new to Release 3. You can slice many primitives including a sphere, cylinder, torus, cone, and tube.

Cylinder

A cylinder can be used in many places, for example, as a pillar in front of a home or as a car driveshaft. To create one, first specify a base circle and then a height. Like the sphere object, the cylinder also has two Creation Methods: The Edge method defines the diameter of the base circle, and the Center method specifies the Radius from the center out.

The default number of sides is 18, which produces a smooth cylinder. Height and Cap Segments values define the number of polygons that make up the cylinder sides and caps. The Smooth and Slice options work the same as they do with a sphere.

Tip If you don't plan on modifying the ends of the cylinder, make the Cap Segments equal to 1 to keep the model complexity down.

Torus

A *Torus* (also referred to as a "doughnut") is a ring with a circular cross section. To create a Torus, you need to specify two radii. The first is the value from the center of the Torus to the center of the ring and the second is the radius of the circular cross section. You can also use the Edge or Center Creation Methods to define these radii.

The default settings create a Torus with 24 segments and 12 sides. The Rotation and Twist options cause the sides to twist a specified value as the ring is circumnavigated. Figure 10-5 shows three Toruses with a Smooth setting of None. The one on the left has no Rotation or Twist value, the Middle one has a Rotation value of 120, and the one on the right has a Twist value of 360. The higher the number of segments, the rounder the Torus looks when viewed from above. The default of 24 is sufficient to create a smooth Torus. The number of sides defines the circular smoothness of the cross section.

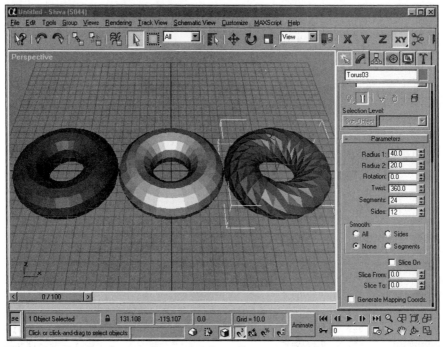

Figure 10-5: Using the Rotation and Twist options on a Torus

The Parameters rollout includes settings for four different Smooth options. Figure 10-6 shows each of these. The All option, shown in the upper left, smoothes all edges, and the None option, shown in the lower left, displays all polygons as faceted. The Sides option, shown in the upper right, smoothes edges between sides, resulting in a Torus with banded sides. The Segment option, shown in the lower right, smoothes between segment edges, resulting in separate smooth sections around the Torus.

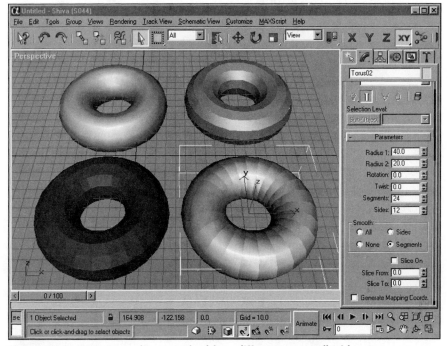

Figure 10-6: A Torus can be smoothed four different ways: All, Sides, None, or Segments.

The Slice options work with a Torus the same way as they do with the sphere and cylinder objects.

Teapot

Okay, let's all sing together, "I'm a little teapot, short and stout . . ." The teapot is another object that, like the sphere, is easy to create. Within the Parameters rollout, you can specify the number of Segments, whether the surface is smooth or faceted, and which parts to display, including Body, Handle, Spout, and Lid. Figure 10-7 shows the teapot in all its glory.

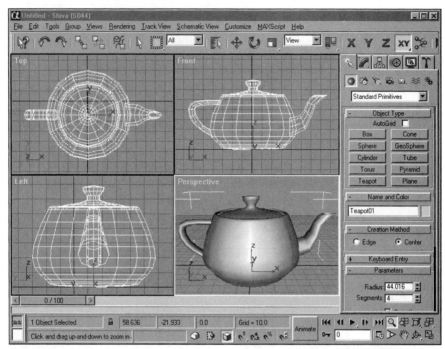

Figure 10-7: The ubiquitous teapot is very useful for a developer who is testing algorithms.

Note   You may recognize most of these primitives as standard shapes, with the exception of the teapot. The teapot has a special place in Computer Graphics. In early Computer Graphics development labs, the teapot was chosen as the test model for many early algorithms. It is still included as a valuable benchmark for Computer Graphics programmers.

Cone

The Cone object, whether used to create ice cream cones or megaphones, is exactly like the cylinder object except that the second cap can have a radius different from that of the first. Clicking and dragging to specify the base circle, dragging to specify the cone's height, and then dragging again for the second cap creates a Cone.

In addition to the two cap radii and the Height, parameter options include the number of Height and Cap Segments, the number of Sides, and the Smooth and Slice options.

GeoSphere

The GeoSphere object is a sphere that is more efficient than the normal sphere. One reason for this is that a GeoSphere uses triangle faces instead of square faces.

The two Creation Methods for a GeoSphere are Diameter and Center. These act the same as the previously discussed Edge and Center Creation Methods.

In the Parameters rollout are several Geodesic Base Type options, including Tetra, Octa, and Icosa. The Tetra type is based on a four-sided tetrahedron, the Octa type is based on an eight-sided Octahedron, and the Icosa type is based on the 20-sided Icosahedron. Setting the Segment value to 1 produces each of these Hedron shapes. Each type aligns the triangle faces differently.

GeoSpheres also have the Smooth, Hemisphere, and Base to Pivot options. Selecting the Hemisphere option changes the GeoSphere into a hemisphere, but there are no additional options like Chop and Squash. GeoSpheres also cannot be sliced.

Tutorial: Comparing spheres and geospheres

To prove that GeoSpheres are more efficient than Sphere objects, follow these steps:

1. Create a normal Sphere and sets its Segment value to **4**.

2. Next to the sphere object, create one of each of the GeoSphere types, also with Segment values of **4**.

Figure 10-8 shows these spheres as a comparison. The normal sphere, shown at the upper left, looks like a diamond, but the GeoSpheres still resemble spheres. Notice how the Icosa type GeoSphere, shown in the lower right, produces the smoothest sphere.

Tube

The Tube primitive is useful for any time you need a pipe object. It can also be used to create ring-shaped objects that have rectangular cross-sections. Creating Tube objects is very similar to the Cylinder and Cone objects. Tube parameters include two radii for the inner and outer tube wall. Tubes also have the Smooth and Slice options.

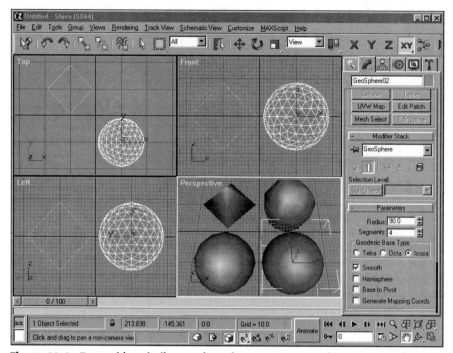

Figure 10-8: Even with a similar number of segments, GeoSpheres are much more spherical.

Pyramid

Pyramid primitives are constructed with a rectangular base and triangles at each edge that rise to meet at the top, just like they made in Egypt. Two different Creation Methods are used to create the base rectangle. The Base/Apex method creates the base by dragging corner to corner, and the Center method drags from the base center to a corner.

The Width and Depth parameters define the base dimensions, and the Height value determines how tall the pyramid is. You can also specify the number of segments for each dimension.

Plane

The Plane object enables you to model the Great Plains. The Plane primitive creates a simple plane that looks like a rectangle, but it includes Multiplier parameters that let you specify the size of the plane at render time. This makes it convenient to work in a viewport without having to worry about its actual dimensions.

The Plane primitive includes two Creation Methods: Rectangle and Square. The Square method creates a perfect square in the viewport when dragged. You can also define the Length and Width Segments, but the real benefits of the Plane object are derived from the use of the Render Multipliers.

The Scale Multiplier value determines how many times larger the plane should be at render time. Both Length and Width are multiplied by equal values. The Density Multiplier specifies the number of segments to produce at render time.

New Feature

The Plane object is new to Release 3 and is very useful for creating infinite ground planes.

Extended Primitives

The Extended Primitives are accessed by selecting Extended Primitives in the subcategory drop-down list in the Create panel. These primitives aren't as generic as the Standard Primitives, but are equally useful.

Hedra

Hedras, or *Polyhedra*, form the basis for a class of geometry defined by fundamental mathematical principles. Johannes Kepler used these polyhedra as the basis for his famous "Harmony of the Spheres" theory. The Hedra primitives available in MAX are Tetrahedron, Cube/Octahedron, Dodecahedron/Icosohedron, and two Star types called Star1 and Star2. From these basic Polyhedra, many different variations can be created.

The Family section options determine the shape of the Hedra. Each member of a Hedra pair is mathematically related to the other member. The Family Parameters include the P and Q values. These values change the Hedra between the two shapes that make up the pair. For example, if the family option is set to Cube/Octa, then a P value of 1 will display an Octagon, and a Q value of 1 will display a Cube. When both P and Q values are set to 0, the shape will become an intermediate shape somewhere between a Cube and an Octagon. Because both values are interrelated, only one shape of the pair can have a value at 1 at the same time. Both P and Q cannot be set to 1 at the same time.

Note

The Tetra, Star 1, and Star 2 options include two different kinds of shapes as a pair.

Figure 10-9 shows each of the basic Hedra Families in columns from left to right: Tetra, Cube/Octa, Dodec/Icos, Star1, and Star2. The top row has a P value of 1 and a Q value of 0, the middle row has both P and Q set to 0, and the bottom row sets P to 0 and Q to 1. Notice how the middle row shapes are a combination of the top and bottom rows.

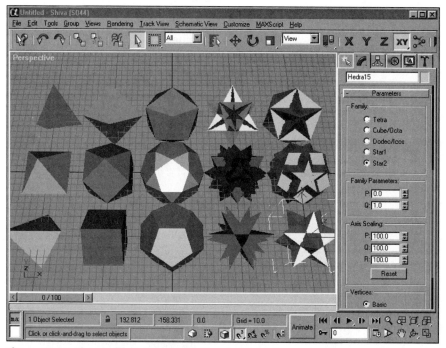

Figure 10-9: The Hedra Families with the standard shapes in the top and bottom rows and the intermediate shapes in the middle row

The relationship between P and Q can be described in this manner: When the P value is set to 1 and the Q value is set to 0, one shape of the pair is displayed. As the P value decreases, each vertex will become a separate face. The edges of these new faces will increase as the value is decreased down to 0. The same holds true for the Q value.

Tip   Altering the P and Q parameters can create many unique shapes. For each Hedra, try the following combinations: P-0, Q=0; P=1, Q=0; P=0, Q=1; P=0.5, Q=0.5; P=0.5, Q=0; P=0, Q=0.5. These represent the main intermediate objects.

As the geometry of the objects changes, the Hedra can have as many as three different types of polygons comprising the faces. Each type of face can be scaled, creating sharp points extending from each face. If only one unique polygon is used for the faces, then only one Axis Scaling parameter will be active. The Reset button simply returns the Axis Scaling value back to its default at 100. For example, using the R Axis Scaling value, pyramid shapes can be extended from a cube Hedra.

Figure 10-10 shows some results of using the Axis Scaling options. One of each family type has been created and displayed in the top row for reference. The bottom row has had the Q axis scaled to a value of 170. This causes one type of polygon face to be extended, thereby producing a new shape.

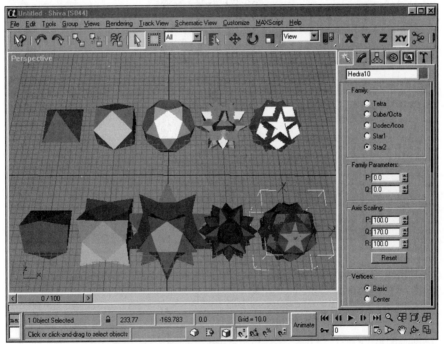

Figure 10-10: Hedras with extended faces, compliments of the Axis Scaling option

The Vertices parameter options add additional vertices and edges to the center of each extended polygon. There are three options: Basic is the default and doesn't add any new information to the Hedra, Center adds vertices to the center of each extended polygon, and Center and Sides add both center vertices and connecting edges for each face that is extended using the Axis Scaling options.

Way at the bottom of the Parameters rollout is the Radius value.

ChamferBox

A *chamfered* object is an object whose edges have been smoothed out, so a ChamferBox primitive is a box with beveled edges. The parameter that determines the amount of roundness applied to an edge is *Fillet*. In many ways this object is just a simple extension of the Box primitive.

The only additions in the Parameters rollout are two fields for controlling the Fillet dimension and the Fillet Segments. Figure 10-11 shows a normal box next to a ChamferBox. The ChamferBox has a Fillet value of 10 and the Smooth option is turned off.

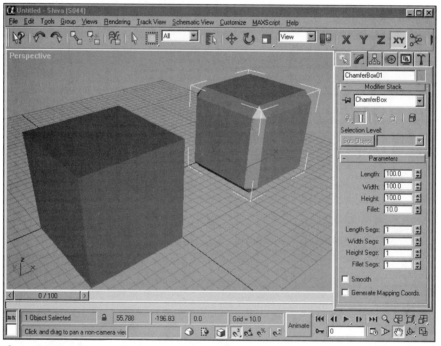

Figure 10-11: A Normal Box verses a ChamferBox. The only difference is the Fillet.

Oil Tank

Oil Tank seems like a strange name for a primitive. This object is essentially the Cylinder primitive with domed caps like you'd see on a diesel truck transporting oil. The Parameters rollout includes an additional option for specifying the Cap Height. The Height value can be set to indicate the entire height of the object with the Overall option, or the height to the edge of the domes using the Centers option. The only other new option is Blend, which smoothes the edges between the cylinder and the caps.

Figure 10-12 displays all the cylindrical primitive types. The top row includes the Standard Primitives: Cylinder, Cone, and Tube. The second row includes the Extended Primitives: Oil Tank, Spindle, ChamferCyl, and Capsule. These last three will be covered shortly.

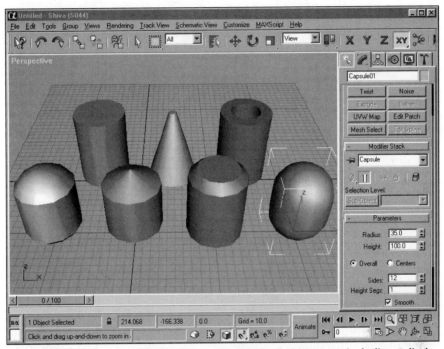

Figure 10-12: There are many different cylindrical primitive types including Cylinder, Cone, Tube, Oil Tank, Spindle, ChamferCyl, and Capsule.

Spindle

The Spindle primitive is the same as the Oil Tank primitive, except that the domed caps are replaced with conical caps. All other options in the Parameters rollout are identical to the Oil Tank primitive.

Gengon

The Gengon primitive creates and extrudes regular polygons such as triangles, squares, and pentagons. There is even an option to Fillet (or smooth) the edges. To specify which polygon to use, enter a value in the No of Sides field.

Figure 10-13 shows eight simple Gengons with different number of edges.

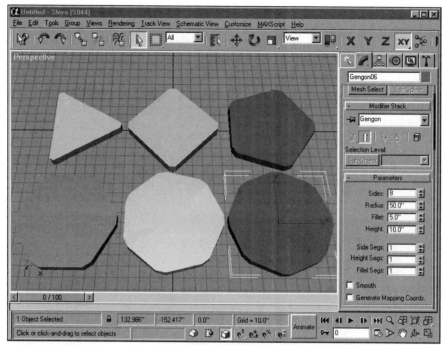

Figure 10-13: Gengon primitives are actually just extruded regular polygons.

RingWave

The RingWave primitive is a specialized primitive that can be used to create a simple gear or a sparkling sun. . It consists of two circles that make up a ring. The circle edges can be set to be wavy and even fluctuate over time. RingWaves can also be used to simulate rapidly expanding gases that would result from a planetary explosion. If you're considering a Shockwave effect, then you should look into using a RingWave primitive.

New Feature The RingWave primitive is new with Release 3.

The Radius setting and the inner edge define the outer edge by the Ring Width. This ring can also have a Height. The Radial and Height Segments and the number of Sides determine the complexity of the object.

The RingWave Timing controls set the expansion values. The Start Time is the frame where the ring begins at zero, the Grow Time is the number of frames required to reach its full size, and the End Time is the frame where the RingWave object stops expanding. The No Growth option prevents the object from expanding, and it remains the same size from the Start frame to the End frame. The Grow and Stay option causes the RingWave to expand from the Start Time until the Grow Time frame is reached, and then remain full-grown until the End Time. The Cyclic Growth begins expanding the objects until the Grow Time is reached. It then starts again from zero and expands repeatedly until the End Time is reached.

Cross-Reference

An example of the RingWave primitive is included in Chapter 19, "Working with Materials and Maps."

The last two sections of the Parameter rollout define how the inner and outer edges look and are animated. If the Edge Breakup option is On, then the rest of the settings are enabled. These additional settings control the number of Major and Minor Cycles, the Width Flux for these cycles, and the Crawl Time which is the number of frames to animate.

Figure 10-14 shows four animated frames of a RingWave object with both Inner and Outer Edge Breakup settings. Notice how the edges change over the different frames.

Figure 10-14: Four frames of a rapidly expanding and turbulent RingWave object

Torus Knot

A Torus Knot is similar to the Torus covered earlier, except that the circular cross-section follows a 3D curve instead of a simple circle. The method for creating the Torus Knot primitive is the same as that for creating the Torus. The Parameters rollout even lets you specify the base curve to be a circle instead of a knot. A knot is a standard, mathematically defined 3D curve.

Below the Radius and Segment parameters are the P and Q values. These values are where Torus Knots get really wild. The P value is a mathematical factor for computing how the knot winds about its vertical axis. The maximum value is 25, which makes it resemble a tightly wound spool. The Q value causes the knot to wind horizontally. It also has a maximum value of 25. Setting both values the same results in a simple circular ring.

Figure 10-15 shows some of the beautiful shapes that are possible by altering the P and Q values of a Torus Knot. The first Torus Knot in the upper left is the default with P=2 and Q=3; the second has P=2, Q=3; the third has P=1, Q=3; the fourth has P=10, Q=15; the fifth has P=15, Q=20; and the sixth has P=25, Q=25.

Figure 10-15: Various Torus Knots display the beauty of mathematics.

When the Base Curve is set to Circle, the P and Q values become disabled and the Warp Count and Warp Height fields become active. These fields control the number of ripples in the ring and their height. Figure 10-16 shows several possibilities. From top left to bottom right the settings are Warp Count=5, Warp Height=0.5; Warp Count=10, Warp Height=0.5; Warp Count=20, Warp Height=0.5; Warp Count=50, Warp Height=0.5; Warp Count=80, Warp Height=1.0; and Warp Count=100, Warp Height=-0.5.

ChamferCyl

The ChamferCyl primitive is very similar to the ChamferBox primitive, only applied to a cylinder instead of a box. The Parameters rollout includes some additional fields for handling the Fillet values. A ChamferCyl object was previously displayed in Figure 10-12.

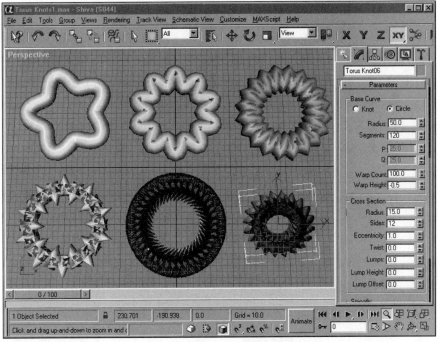

Figure 10-16: Torus Knots with a Circle Base Curve are useful for creating impressive rings.

Capsule

The Capsule primitive is a yet another primitive based on the cylinder, only this time with hemispherical caps. This object resembles the Oil Tank primitive very closely. The only real noticeable difference is in the border between the cylinder and caps. This object was previously displayed in Figure 10-12.

L-Ext

The L-Ext primitive stands for L-Extension. You can think of it as two rectangular boxes that are connected at right angles to each other. To create an L-Ext object, you need to first drag to create a rectangle that defines the overall area of the object. Next you drag to define the Height of the object, and, finally, you drag to define the width of each leg.

The Parameters rollout includes dimensions for Side and Front Lengths, Side and Front Widths, and the Height. You can also define the number of Segments for each dimension. Figure 10-17 shows both the L-Ext and C-Ext primitives.

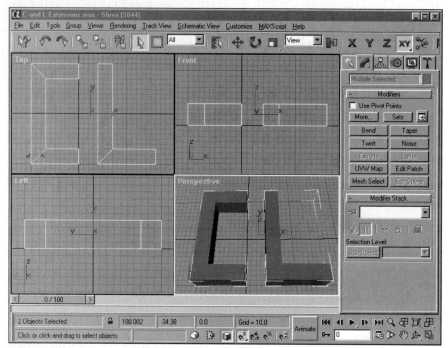

Figure 10-17: These primitives are great if your name is Clive Logan or Carrie Lincoln.

C-Ext

The C-Ext primitive is the same as the L-Ext primitive with an extra rectangular box. The C shape connects three rectangular boxes at right angles to each other.

The Parameters rollout includes dimensions for Side, Front and Back Lengths, Side, Front and Back Widths, and the Height. You can also define the number of Segments for each dimension.

Prism

The Prism primitive is essentially an extruded triangle. Each of the sides of the base triangle can have a different length.

Summary

Primitives are the most basic shapes and often provide a starting point for more ambitious modeling projects. The two classes of primitives — Standard and Extended — provide a host of possible objects. In this chapter, you

✦ Learned about the basics of creating primitives by dragging and entering keyboard values

✦ Explored all the various primitives in both the Standard and Extended subcategories

In the next chapter, you'll learn all about splines and shape objects.

✦   ✦   ✦

Working with Spline Shapes

Having covered creating primitive objects, let's move on to another simple object type—spline shapes. A *spline* is a special type of line that curves according to mathematical principles. In MAX, splines are used to create all sorts of shapes.

Spline shapes can be found on the Create panel under the Shapes category, and, just as with the Geometry category, there are several spline shape primitives. Spline shapes can be rendered, but they are normally used to create more advanced 3D geometric objects through the application of a Modifier-like Extrude of Lathe. Splines can be used to create animation paths as well as Loft and NURBS objects.

This chapter covers spline shapes and how to edit them to create additional objects.

Drawing in 2D

Shapes in MAX are unique from other objects because they are drawn in 2D, which confines them to a single plane. That plane is defined by the viewport used to create the shape. For example, drawing a shape in the Top view will constrain the shape to the XY plane, while drawing the shape in the Front view will constrain it to the ZX plane. Even shapes drawn in the Perspective view will be constrained to a plane.

2D shapes are usually produced in a drawing package like Adobe Illustrator or CorelDraw. MAX supports importing line drawings using the AI format.

While newly created or imported shapes are 2D and are confined to a single plane, splines can exist in 3D space. The Helix shape for example exists in 3D, having height as well as width values. Animation paths in particular need to move into 3D space. Later in the chapter, we'll explain how to edit these splines to make them 3D.

Understanding Spline Primitives

The spline primitives that are displayed in the Object Type rollout include many basic shapes like a rectangle, circle, and star. Once a shape is created, several new rollouts appear, including the Parameters rollout, enabling you to further adjust the shapes.

Above the Shape buttons are two checkboxes: AutoGrid and Start New Shape. AutoGrid creates a temporary Grid, which is centered on the surface of the nearest object under the mouse at the time of creation. This is helpful for starting a new spline on the surface of an object. AutoGrid is discussed in more detail in Chapter 8, "Transforming Objects."

The Start New Shape option will create a new object with every new shape drawn in a viewport. Leaving this option unchecked lets you create compound shapes which consist of several shapes used to create one object. Because compound shapes consist of several shapes, they cannot be edited using the Parameters rollout. For example, if you want to write out your name using splines, keep the Start New Shape option unselected to make all the letters part of the same object.

Just as with the Geometric primitives, every shape that is created is given a Name and a Color. You can change either of these in the Name and Color rollout.

Almost every primitive shape has a General rollout (Section is the exception). In the General rollout, you can define the number of Interpolation Steps or segments that make up the shape. Larger step values result in smoother curves. The default option is Adaptive, which automatically sets the number of steps to use. The Optimize option attempts to reduce the number of steps to produce a simpler spline.

The General rollout also contains an option for making a spline Renderable by giving it a thickness value. The spline thickness will not be displayed in the viewport, but only at render time. Renderable splines can include material maps. The Generate Mapping Coordinates automatically creates mapping coordinates if enabled. Later in the chapter, there is an example of Renderable Splines.

Note   By default, a renderable spline has a 12-sided circle as its cross-section.

Most spline primitives also include Creation Method and Keyboard Entry rollouts (Text and Star are the exceptions). The Creation Method rollout offers options for specifying different ways to create the spline by dragging, such as from edge to edge or from the center out. The Keyboard Entry rollout offers a way to enter exact position and dimension values. After the values are entered, the Create button is used to create the spline in the active viewport.

The Parameters rollout includes such basic settings for the primitive as Radius, Length, and Width. These settings can be altered immediately after an object is created. However, once an object has been be deselected, the Parameters rollout moves to the Modify panel, and any alterations to the shape must be done there.

Line

The Line primitive includes several Creation Method settings, enabling you to create hard, sharp corners or smooth corners. The Initial Type option can be set to either Corner or Smooth and will create a sharp or smooth corner for the first point created.

After clicking where the initial point is located, you can add additional points by clicking in the viewport. Dragging while creating a new point can make a point either a Corner, Smooth, or Bézier based on the Drag Type option selected. The curvature created by the Smooth corners option is determined by the distance between adjacent vertices, while the curvature created by the Bézier curves option can be controlled by dragging with the mouse a desired distance after the point is created. Bézier corners have control handles associated with them, enabling you to change their curvature. This feature will be covered later in the chapter.

Tip   Holding down the Shift key while clicking creates points that are vertically or horizontally in line with the previous point. Holding the Ctrl key down snaps new points at an angle from the last segment, as determined by the Angle Snap setting.

After creating all the points, you exit line mode by clicking the right mouse button — this creates an open spline. To create a closed spline, place your last point on top of the first point — this causes an alert box to appear, asking if you want to close the spline. Click Yes to create a closed spline, or No to continue adding points. Even after creating a closed spline, you can add additional points to the current selection to create a compound shape if the Start New Shape option isn't selected.

Figure 11-1 shows the creation of several splines using the various Creation Method settings. The spline in the upper left was created with all the options set to Corner, and the spline in the upper right was created with all the options set to Smooth. The lower left spline uses the Corner Initial Type and shows where dragging has smoothed many of the points. The lower left spline was created using the Bézier option.

In the Keyboard Entry rollout, points can be added by entering their X, Y, and Z dimensions and clicking the Add Point button. The spline can be closed at any time by clicking the Close button or kept open by clicking the Finish button.

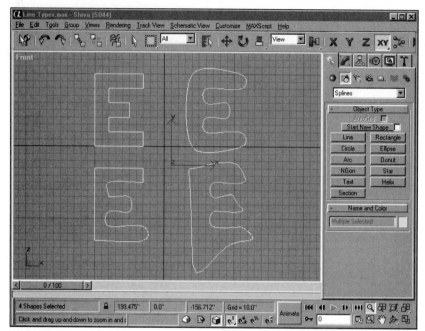

Figure 11-1: The Line shape can create various combinations of shapes with smooth and sharp corners.

Circle

The Circle button creates — you guessed it — circles. It includes Creation Method settings for Edge and Center and the only adjustable parameter in the Parameters rollout is the Radius. All other rollouts are the same as explained earlier in the chapter.

Arc

The Arc primitive has two Creation Methods. Use the End-End-Middle method to create an arc shape by clicking and dragging to specify the two end points and then dragging to complete the shape. Use the Center-End-End method to create an arc shape by clicking and dragging from the center to one of the end points and then dragging the arc length to the second end point.

Other parameters include the Radius and the From and To settings where you can enter the value in degrees for the start and end of the arc. The Pie Slice option connects the end points of the arc to its center to create a pie-sliced shape. The Reverse option lets you reverse the arc's direction.

Figure 11-2 shows a sampling of some of the arcs that can be created. The top arcs were created with the Center-End-End Creation Method, the lower arcs were created with the End-End-Middle Creation Method, and the four pie-shaped arcs used the Pie Slice option.

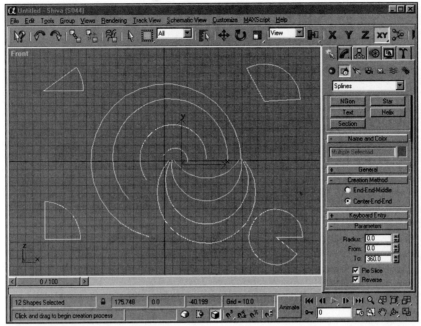

Figure 11-2: Arcs can be created in two different ways, and they can be turned into pie slices.

NGon

The *NGon* shape is very similar to the circle shape except that you can specify the Number of Sides and the Corner Radius. You can also specify whether the NGon is Inscribed or Circumscribed. Inscribed polygons are positioned within a circle that touches all the polygon's vertices. Circumscribed polygons are positioned outside of a circle that touches the mid-point of each polygon edge. The Circular option displays the inscribed or circumscribed circle.

Text

The Text shape can be used to add text outlines by typing. In the Parameters rollout you can specify Font, Justification, Style, Size, Kerning, and Leading values. There is also a text area where you can type the text to be created. The Text shape automatically updates when changed. To turn off automatic updating, select the Manual Update toggle.

> **Note**
>
> The list of available fonts will include only the Windows TrueType fonts and Type 1 Postscript fonts specified by the font path listed in the Configure Paths dialog box.

After setting the parameters and typing the text, the text will appear as soon as you click in one of the viewports. Figure 11-3 shows an example of some text.

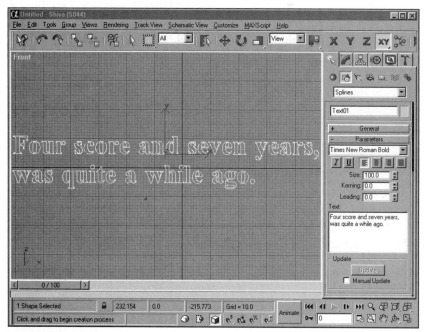

Figure 11-3: The Text shape can create text with several settings such as font, justification, and style.

Section

Section stands for cross-section. The Section shape is a cross-section of the edges of any 3D object that the Section's cutting-plane passes through. The process consists of dragging in the viewport to create a cross-sectioning plane. The cross-sectioning plane can then be moved, rotated, or scaled to obtain the desired crosssection. In the Parameters rollout is a Create Shape button. Clicking this button opens a dialog box where you can name the new shape. Additionally, one Section object can be used to create multiple shapes.

Note

Sections can only be made from intersecting a 3D object. If the cross-sectioning plane doesn't intersect the 3D object, then it won't create a shape. You cannot use the Section shape on shapes.

The Parameters rollout includes settings for updating the Section shape. You can update it when the Section Moves, when the Section is Selected, or Manually. You can also set the Section Extents to Infinite, Section Boundary, or None. The Infinite setting creates the cross-section spline as if the cross-sectioning plane were of infinite size, while the Section Boundary limits the plane's extents to the boundaries of the visible plane.

To give you an idea of what the Section shape can produce, Figure 11-4 shows the shapes resulting from sectioning a Cone object including a circle, an ellipse, a parabola, and a hyperbole.

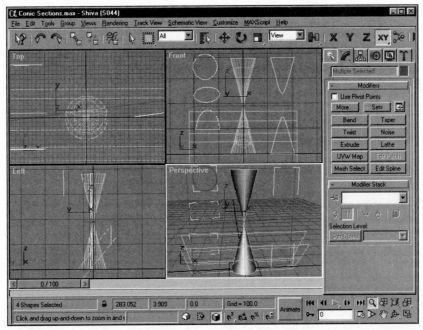

Figure 11-4: The Section object can be used to create the conic sections from a 3D cone.

Rectangle

The Rectangle shape produces simple rectangles. In the Parameters rollout, you can specify the Length and Width and also a Corner Radius.

Ellipse

Ellipses are simple variations of the Circle shape. They are defined by Length and Width values and can be created using the Edge or Center Creation Method.

Donut

As another variation of the Circle shape, the Donut shape consists of two concentric circles and can be created using the Edge or Center Creation Method. The parameters for this object are simply two radii.

Star

The Star shape also includes two radii values — the larger Radius value identifies the outer points of the Star shape, and the other Radius value specifies the inner points. There is also a Point setting to indicate the number of points. This value can range from 3 to 100. The Distortion value causes the inner points to rotate relative to the outer points and can be used to create some interesting new star types. The Fillet Radius 1 and Fillet Radius 2 values adjust the Fillet for the inner and outer points.

Figure 11-5 shows a sampling of what is possible with the Star shapes.

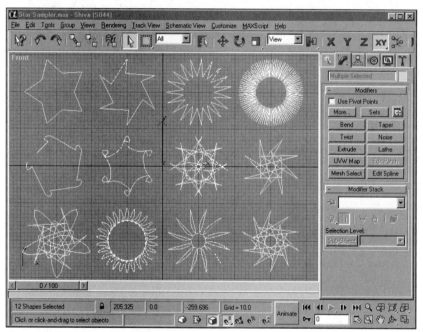

Figure 11-5: Using the Star shape is a lot like playing with a Spirograph.

Helix

A *Helix* is like a spring coil shape, and it is the one shape of all the Shape primitives that exists in 3D. Helix parameters include two radii for specifying the inner and outer radius. These two values can be equal to create a coil or unequal to create a spiral. There are also parameters for the Height and number of Turns. The Bias parameter causes the Helix turns to be gathered all together at the top or bottom of the shape. The CW and CCW options let you specify whether the Helix turns clockwise or counterclockwise.

Figure 11-6 shows a sampling of Helix shapes.

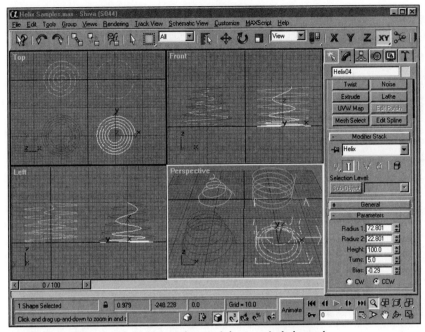

Figure 11-6: The Helix shape can be straight or spiral shaped.

Tutorial: Viewing the interior of a heart

As an example of the Section shape, let's explore a section of a Heart model. The model was created by Viewpoint Datalabs and is very realistic — so realistic in fact, it could be used to teach medical students the inner workings of the heart.

To create a spline from the crosssection of the heart, follow these steps:

1. Import the heart model by selecting File ➪ Import.

2. Open the Create panel, select the Shapes category, and click the Section button. Drag a plane in the Top viewport that is large enough to cover the heart. This will be your cross-sectioning plane.

3. Reorient the cross-sectioning plane to cross the heart at the desired angle. Use the transformation buttons as needed.

4. Open the Modify panel to view the Section object parameters. Click the Create Shape button and give the new shape the name **Heart Section**.

5. From the Select by Name dialog box, select the section by name, separate it from the model, and reposition it to be visible.

Figure 11-7 shows the resulting model and section.

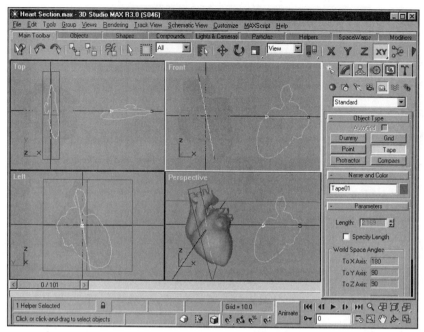

Figure 11-7: The Section shape can be used to view the interior area of the heart.

Tutorial: Drawing a company logo

One of the early uses for 3D graphics was to animate corporate logos, and MAX can still do this without any problems. The Shape tools can even be used to help design the logo. In this example, we'll design and create a simple logo using the Shape tools for the fictitious company named "Expeditions South."

To use the Shape tools to design and create a company logo, follow these steps:

1. Start by creating a four-pointed star. Click the Star button and drag in the Top view to create a shape. Change the parameters for this star as follows: Radius1 = **60**, Radius2 = **20**, and Points = **4**.

2. Select and move the star shape to the left side of the viewport.

3. Now, click the Text button. Change the font to Impact and the Size to **50**. In the Text area, type **Expeditions South** and include a line return and several spaces between the two words. Click in the Top Viewport.

4. Use the Select and Move button to reposition the text next to the Star shape.

5. Click the Line button and create several short highlighting lines around the bottom point of the star.

The finished logo is now ready to extrude and animate. Figure 11-8 shows the results.

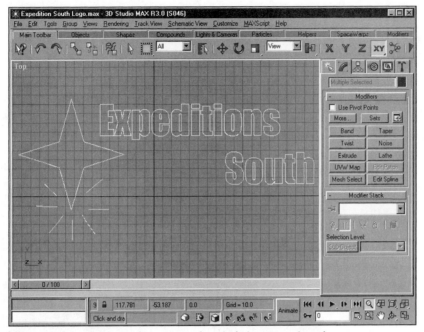

Figure 11-8: A Company logo created entirely in MAX using Shapes

Importing and Exporting Splines

In the previous example, we used MAX to design and create a logo. However, in most companies a professional creative team using advanced tools such as Illustrator will design the logo. Learning how to import files created externally will give you a jump-start on your project.

There will also be times, such as with the heart cross section, when you'll want to export splines from MAX to other drawing packages.

When importing vector-based files into MAX, only the lines are imported. MAX cannot import fills, blends, or other specialized vector effects. All imported lines are automatically converted to Bézier splines in MAX.

Tutorial: Importing vector drawings from Illustrator

Although MAX can draw splines, it takes a back seat to the vector functions available in Adobe Illustrator. If you have an Illustrator file, you can save it as an AI file and import it into MAX.

To import Adobe Illustrator files into 3D Studio MAX, follow these steps:

1. Within Illustrator, save your file as an AI file by selecting File ➪ Save As. Figure 11-9 shows a logo created using Illustrator.

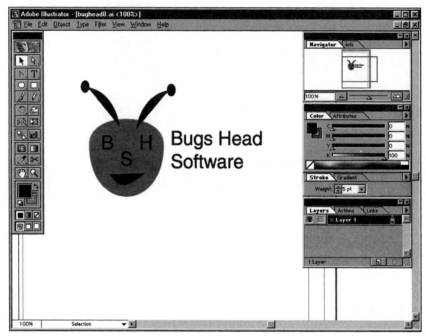

Figure 11-9: A Company logo created in Illustrator and ready to save and import into MAX

2. Open MAX and select File ➪ Import. This opens a file dialog box.

3. Select Abode Illustrator (AI) as the File Type. Locate the file to import and click OK.

4. The AI Import dialog box asks if you want to merge the objects with the current scene or replace the current scene. For our purposes, replace the current scene.

5. The Shape Import dialog box asks if you want to import the shapes as single or multiple objects. You will generally want to import the objects as a single object, but if you plan on assigning different materials to the various parts, then use the Multiple Objects option.

Figure 11-10 shows the logo after it has been imported into MAX. Notice that all the fills are missing.

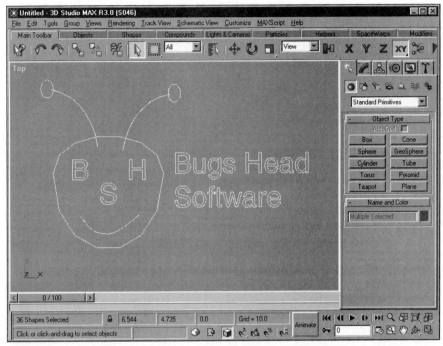

Figure 11-10: A company logo created in Illustrator and imported into MAX

Tutorial: Exporting a MAX-generated logo

When exporting MAX splines, you can choose to use either the File ➪ Export command or the File ➪ Export Selected command to limit the lines being exported.

Caution Be sure to not include any shapes that have been extruded, converted to Meshes, or altered from their original spline object type, or you will receive an error.

In this tutorial, we will export the Expeditions South logo that was created in MAX.

To export MAX splines to Adobe Illustrator, follow these steps:

1. Within MAX, open the logo file and select Edit ➪ Select All.

2. In order to maintain the spacing between different shape objects, you'll need to Attach all the splines into one object. To do this, open the Modify panel and click the Edit Spline button. This will make all the selected splines editable.

3. Deselect all the shapes and then reselect just one spline shape. In the Geometry rollout, click the Attach button and then click the remaining objects. This will attach all the shapes into one object ready to export.

4. Select File ➪ Export Selected, select Adobe Illustrator (AI) as the Save as Type, and save the file.

5. Open Illustrator and load the AI file by selecting File ➪ Open.

6. The scale will likely be off, so select View ➪ Fit to Window to see the imported splines.

Figure 11-11 shows the logo in Illustrator.

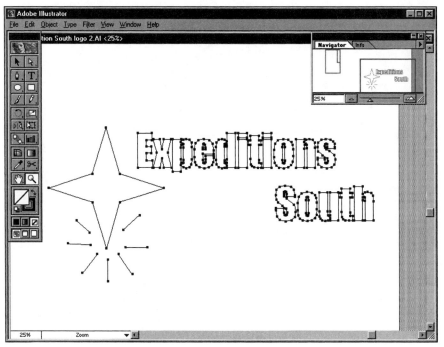

Figure 11-11: A company logo created in MAX and exported to Illustrator

Editing Splines

Before a spline can be edited, it must be converted to an Editable Spline. This can be done with the Edit Spline Modifier found in the Modify panel, or by right-clicking the spline shape and selecting Convert to Editable Spline from the pop-up menu.

Once the spline is converted to an Editable Spline, you can edit individual subobjects within the spline, such as Segments and Vertices. The drawback to using this Modifier is that you will no longer be able to change the parameters associated with the spline shape.

Note   When an object is created that contains two or more splines (such as creating splines with the Start New Shape option disabled), all the splines in the object are automatically converted into Editable Splines.

The General rollout in the Modify panel is the same for newly created shapes and ones being modified. The Interpolation Steps determine how many segments to include between vertexes. For shapes composed of straight lines (like the Rectangle and simple NGons), this isn't an issue, but for a shape with many sides (like a Circle, Ellipse, or Helix), the Steps value can have a big effect. The Optimize button eliminates all the extra vertices and segments associated with the shape. The Adaptive option automatically sets the number of steps to produce a smooth curve and will set the number of steps for straight segments to 0.

Making splines renderable

Splines normally will not show up in a rendered image, but using the Renderable option and assigning a thickness to a spline will make it appear in the rendered image. Figure 11-12 shows a rendered image of the Expeditions South logo after all shapes have been made Renderable and assigned a Thickness of 1.0. Because no materials have been used, the colors of the logo are the randomly assigned object colors.

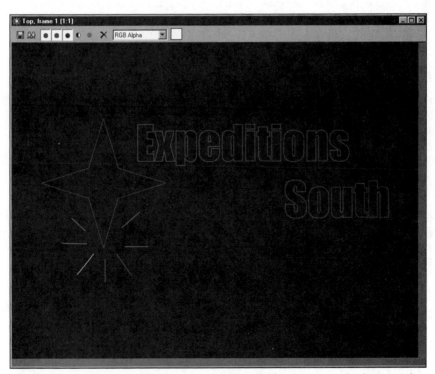

Figure 11-12: Using Renderable splines with a Thickness of 1.0, the logo can be rendered.

Selecting spline subobjects

When editing splines, you must choose the subobject level to work on. For example, when editing splines, you can work with Vertex, Segment, or Spline subobjects. Before you can edit spline subobjects, you must select them. To select the subobject type, click the Sub-Object button in the Modify panel and select a subobject type from the drop-down list. Alternatively, you can click the red-colored icons under the Selection rollout.

New Feature The subobject type icons under the Selection rollout are new to Release 3.

Clicking the Sub-Object button again exits subobject edit mode. Remember, you must exit this mode before you can select another object.

Tip The Sub-Object button turns yellow when selected to remind you that you are in subobject edit mode.

Many subobjects can be selected at once by dragging an outline over them. You can also select and deselect vertices by holding down the Ctrl key while clicking them. Holding down the Alt key will remove any selected vertices from the selection set.

Editing vertices

To edit a vertex, click the Edit Spline button in the Modify panel and, from the Sub-Object drop-down list, select Vertex, or click the Vertex button under the Selection rollout.

Once the Vertex subobject type is selected, you can use the Select and Move button in the main toolbar to move vertices. Moving a vertex around will cause the associated spline segments to follow.

With a vertex selected, you can change its type from Corner, Smooth, or Bézier by right-clicking, and select the type from the pop-up menu. Clicking the Bézier-type vertex will reveal two green-colored handles on either side of the vertex. Dragging these handles away from the vertex will alter the curvature of the segment.

Tip Holding down the Shift key while clicking and dragging on a handle will cause it to move independently of the other handle. This can be used to create sharp corner points.

After selecting several vertices, you can create a Named Selection Set by typing a name in the Name Selection Sets drop-down list in the main toolbar. These Selection Sets can then be Copied and Pasted onto other shapes. The Lock Handles option causes all selected Bézier handles to move together when one handle is moved. The Area Selection option selects all the vertices within a defined radius.

The Selection rollout also has the Show Vertex Numbers option to display all the vertex numbers of a spline or to show the numbers of only the selected vertices. This can be convenient for understanding how a spline is put together and to help you find noncritical vertices. Below these controls are the Selection Information, which displays the number of selected items and whether a spline is closed or not. Figure 11-13 shows several spline shapes and their vertex numbers.

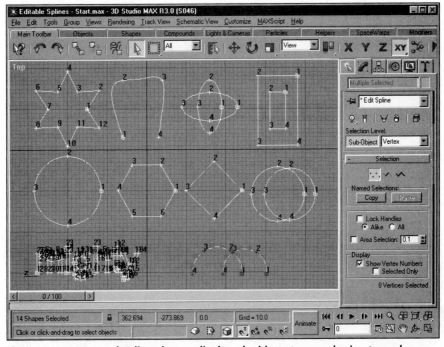

Figure 11-13: Several spline shapes displayed with vertex numbering turned on

New Feature Area Selection and Show Vertex Numbers are both new features in Release 3.

Much of the power of editing splines is contained within the Geometry rollout, including the ability to add new splines, attach objects to the spline, weld vertices, use Boolean operations, Trim and Extend, and many more. Some Geometry buttons may be disabled, depending on the subobject type that you've selected. For instance, the buttons described in the following sections apply only to the Vertex subobject.

New Feature Several buttons have been added to MAX in Release 3 to assist you in editing vertices, including Fuse, Cycle, CrossInsert, Fillet, Chamfer, Hide/Unhide, and Bind/Unbind.

Weld

When two vertices are selected and are within the specified Weld Threshold, they can be welded into one vertex using the Weld button. Several vertices can be welded simultaneously. Another way to weld vertices is to move one vertex on top of another. If they are within the threshold distance, a dialog box asks if you want them to be welded. Click the Yes button to weld them.

In Figure 11-14, the star shape (top row, far left) has had all its lower vertices first fused and then welded together. The Fuse button is similar to the Weld command, except it doesn't delete any vertices.

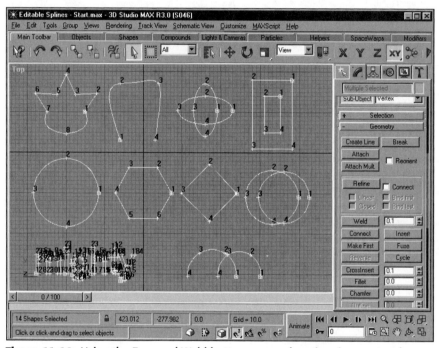

Figure 11-14: Using the Fuse and Weld buttons, several vertices in our star shape have been combined.

Connect

The Connect button lets you connect end vertices to each other to create a new line. This will only work on end vertices and not on connected points within a spline. To connect the ends, click the Connect button and drag the cursor from one endpoint to another (the cursor will change to a plus sign when it is over a valid endpoint) and release. To exit Connect mode, click the Connect button again or right-click anywhere in the viewport.

Figure 11-15 shows the results of the Connect button on our second shape (top row, second from left). A new line has connected the bottom two vertices.

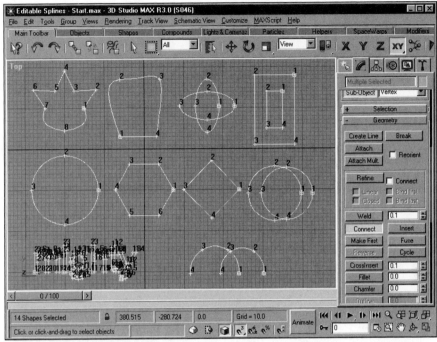

Figure 11-15: The Connect button can be used to connect end points of shapes.

Make First

The Show Vertex Numbers option displays the number of each vertex. The first vertex is identified with a square around it. The Make First button lets you change which vertex you want to be the first vertex in the spline. To do this, select a single vertex and click the Make First button. If more than one vertex is selected, MAX will ignore the command. If the selected spline is an open spline, an endpoint must be selected.

Note   The vertex number is important because it determines the first key for path animations and where Loft objects start.

Fuse

The Fuse button can be used to move the selected vertices to a single location. This is accomplished by selecting all the vertices to relocate and clicking the Fuse button. The average point between all the selected vertices becomes the new location. You can combine these vertices into one after they've been fused by using the Weld button.

Cycle

If a single vertex is selected, the Cycle button will cause the next vertex in the Vertex Number order to be selected. The Cycle button can be used on open and closed splines and can be repeated around the spline. The exact vertex number is shown in the Information displayed in the Selection rollout. This is very useful to locate individual vertices in groups that are close together, such as groups that have been fused.

Cross Insert

If two splines that are part of the same object overlap, the CrossInsert button can be used to create a vertex on each spline at the location where they intersect. The distance between the two splines must be closer than the Threshold value for this to work. Note that this button does not join the two splines; it only creates a vertex on each spline. Use the Weld button to join the splines. To exit this mode, right-click in the viewport or click the CrossInsert button again.

Figure 11-16 shows how the CrossInsert button can be used to add vertices at the intersection points of two elliptical splines (top row, third from the left). Notice how each ellipse now has eight vertices.

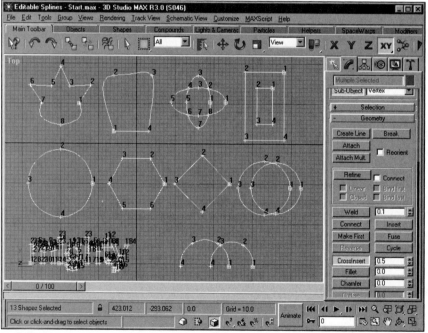

Figure 11-16: The CrossInsert button can add vertices to any overlapping splines of the same object.

Fillet

The Fillet button is used to round the corners of a spline where two edges meet. To use the Fillet command, click the Fillet button and then drag on a corner vertex in the viewport. The more you drag, the larger the Fillet. You can also enter a Fillet value in the Fillet spinner for the vertices that are selected. The Fillet has a maximum value based on the geometry of the spline. To exit Fillet mode, right-click in the viewport or click the Fillet button again.

> **Tip** Several vertices can be filleted at once by selecting them and then clicking the Fillet button and dragging the Fillet distance.

Chamfer

The Chamfer button works much like the Fillet button, except the corners are replaced with straight-line segments instead of smooth curves. To use the Chamfer command, click the Chamfer button and drag on a vertex to create the Chamfer. You can also enter a Chamfer value in the rollout. To exit Chamfer mode, right-click in the viewport or click the Chamfer button again.

Figure 11-17 shows both Fillets and Chamfers applied to the two rectangular shapes (top row, right side). Fillet has been applied to the larger rectangle shape and Chamfer to the smaller.

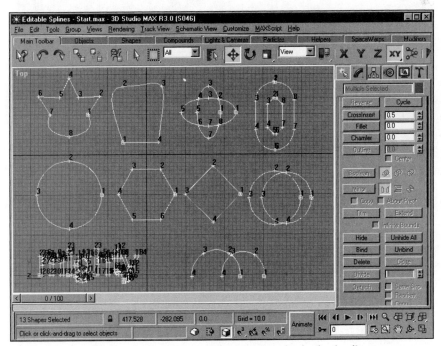

Figure 11-17: Fillets and Chamfers are used to alter the look of spline corners.

Hide/Unhide All

The Hide and Unhide All buttons are used to Hide spline subobjects. They can be used in any subobject mode. To hide a subobject, select the subobject and click the Hide button. To Unhide the hidden subobjects, click the Unhide All button.

Bind/Unbind

The Bind button is used to attach an end vertex to a segment. The bound vertex then cannot be moved independently, but only as part of the bound segment. The Unbind button removes the binding on the vertex and lets it move independently once again. To bind a vertex, click the Bind button and then drag from the vertex to the segment to bind to. To exit Bind mode, right-click in the viewport or click the Bind button again.

For Figure 11-18, I used the Break button to break the circle shape (second row, far left) at its right-most vertex. Then I used the Bind button to bind the number 1 vertex to the far segment. Any movement of the spline keeps this vertex bound to the segment.

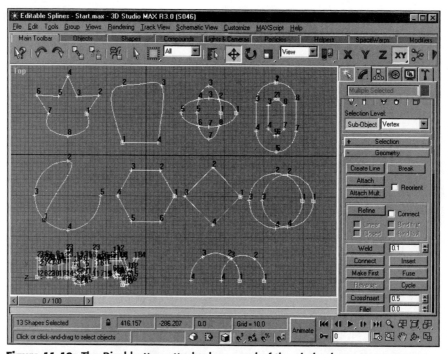

Figure 11-18: The Bind button attached one end of the circle shape to a segment.

Editing segments

To edit a segment, click the Edit Spline button in the Modify panel and, from the Sub-Object drop-down list, select Segment. Alternatively, you can click the Segment button under the Selection rollout.

Segments are the lines or edges that run between two vertices, and many of the editing options work in the same way as when editing Vertex subobjects. You can select multiple segments by holding down the Ctrl key while clicking the segments, or you can hold down the Alt key to remove selected segments from the selection set. Segments can also be copied when being transformed by holding down the Shift key. The cloned segments break away from the original spline while still remaining attached to it.

Segments can be changed from Lines to Curves by right-clicking the segment and selecting Line or Curve from the pop-up menu. Line segments created with the Corner type vertex option cannot be changed to Curves, but lines created with Smooth and Bézier type vertex options can be switched back and forth.

Several Geometry rollout buttons work exclusively on Segment subobjects such as the ones described in the following sections.

Break

Clicking the Break button and then clicking a vertex breaks the segment at that location by creating two separate endpoints. The Break button in the Geometry rollout can be used to add another vertex along a segment, thereby breaking the segment into two. You can exit Break mode by right-clicking in the viewport or by clicking the Break button again.

Figure 11-19 shows the hexagon shape (second row, second from left) separated into two shapes using the Break button.

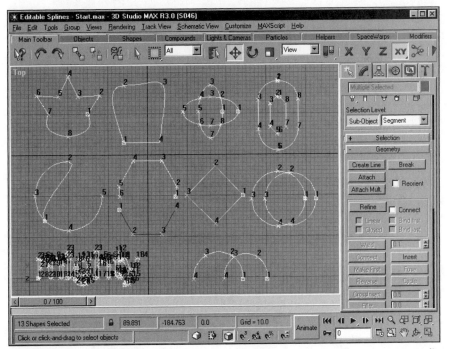

Figure 11-19: The Break button was used twice to break the hexagon into two splines.

Divide

When a segment is selected, the Divide button becomes active. This button adds the number of vertices specified to the selected segment or segments. Figure 11-20 shows the diamond shape (second row, second from right) after all four segments were selected, a value of 1 was entered into the spinner, and the Divide button was clicked.

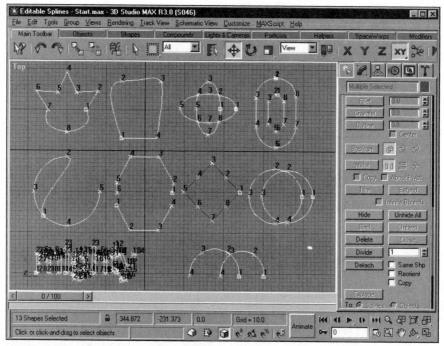

Figure 11-20: The Divide button adds segments to the spline.

Editing Spline subobjects

To edit a spline, click the Edit Spline button in the Modify panel and from the Sub-Object drop-down list, select Spline, or click the Spline button under the Selection rollout.

Transforming a spline object containing only one spline works the same way in subobject mode as it does in a normal transformation. Working in Spline subobject mode on a spline object containing several splines lets you transform individual splines. Right-clicking a spline in subobject mode opens a pop-up menu that lets you convert it between Curve and Line types. The Curve type option changes all vertices to Bézier type and the Line type option makes all vertices Corner type. Spline subobject mode includes many of the buttons previously discussed as well as some new ones in the Geometry rollout.

Reverse

The Reverse button is only available for Spline subobjects. It reverses the order of the vertex numbers. For example, a circle that is numbered clockwise from 1 to 4 would be numbered counterclockwise after using the Reverse button.

Outline

The Outline button creates a spline identical to the one selected, and that is offset based upon an amount specified by dragging or specified in the Offset value. The Center option creates an outline on either side of the selected spline, centered on the original spline. When the Center option is not selected, then an outline is created by offsetting a duplicate of the spline on only one side of the original spline. To exit Outline mode, click the Outline button again or right-click in the viewport.

Figure 11-21 shows the text for the word "mighty" after the Outline button was applied (bottom row, left side). I've turned off the vertex numbering to make this easier to see.

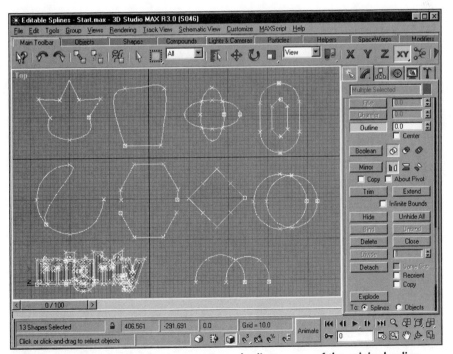

Figure 11-21: The Outline button creates a duplicate copy of the original spline and offsets it.

Boolean

A *Boolean* is a value that has only two states: on or off. With splines, Boolean operations can be used to combine or subtract overlapping areas. Booleans can also be used to combine or subtract 3D volumes (the concept is covered in Chapter 15, "Building Compound Objects").

The Boolean button works on overlapping closed splines and has three different options: Union, Subtraction, and Intersection. The splines must all be part of the same object. The Union option combines the areas of both splines, the Subtraction option removes the second spline's area from the first, and the Intersection option only keeps the areas that overlap.

To use the Boolean feature, select one of the splines and select one of the Boolean operation options. Then click the Boolean button and select the second spline. Depending on which Boolean operation you chose, the overlapping area will be deleted, the second spline will act to cut away the overlapping area on the first, or only the overlapping area will remain. To exit Boolean mode, right-click in the viewport.

Note   Boolean operations can only be performed on closed splines that are contained within the same object.

Figure 11-22 shows the results of the Subtraction operation on two overlapping circles.

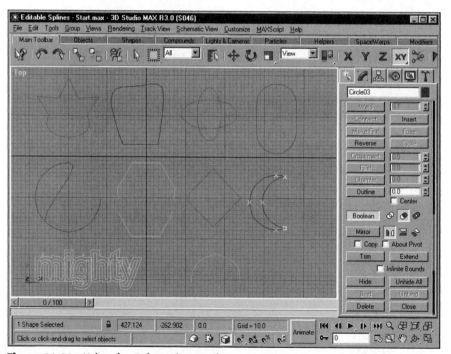

Figure 11-22: Using the Subtraction Boolean operation to create a crescent shape from two circles.

Mirror

The Mirror button can be used to mirror a spline object horizontally, vertically, or along both axes. To use this feature, select a spline object to mirror, then locate the Mirror button. To the right of the Mirror button are three smaller buttons, each of which indicates a direction: Mirror Horizontally, Mirror Vertically, and Mirror Both. Select a direction and then click the Mirror button. If the Copy option is selected, a new spline is created and mirrored. The About Pivot option causes the mirroring to be completed about the Pivot Point axes.

With the crescent shape from our Boolean operation still selected, clicking the Mirror button produces the results in Figure 11-23.

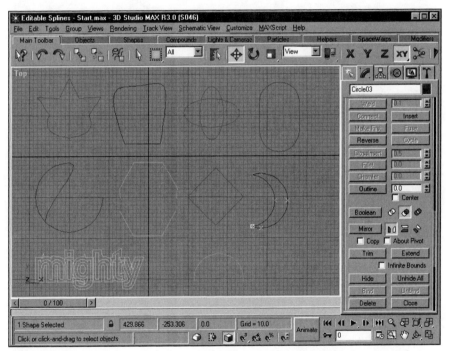

Figure 11-23: Mirroring a shape is as simple as clicking the Mirror button and selecting an axis.

Trim

The Trim button works on open splines contained within the same object. It cuts off any extending portion between two overlapping splines. The splines must be part of the same object. To use the Trim feature, select two overlapping splines and click the Trim button, then click the segment to trim. The spline you click will be trimmed back to the nearest intersecting point. To exit Trim mode, right-click in the viewport or click the Trim button again. This button only works in Spline subobject mode.

The Infinite Bounds option works for both the Trim and Extend buttons. When enabled, it treats all open splines as if they were infinite for the purpose of locating an intersecting point. Figure 11-24 displays the results of the Trim button on the two arcs (bottom row, right side).

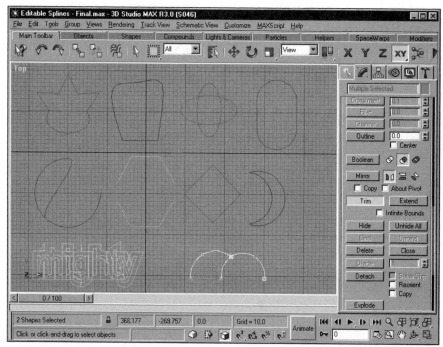

Figure 11-24: The Trim button can be used to cut away the excess of a spline.

Extend

The Extend button works in the reverse manner compared to the Trim button. The Extend button lengthens the end of a spline until it encounters an intersection. (There must be a spline segment to intersect.) To use the Extend command, click the Extend button, then click the segment to extend. The spline you click will be extended. To exit Extend mode, right-click in the viewport or click the Extend button again.

Close

The Close button completes an open spline and creates a closed spline by attaching a segment between the first and last vertices.

Explode

The Explode button performs the Detach command on all subobject splines at once. It separates each segment into a separate spline.

Controlling spline geometry

In addition to the subobject-specific buttons, there are several remaining buttons that work on several different types of subobjects.

Tip   The Create Line, Attach, and Attach Mult. buttons do not require that you be in subobject mode.

Create line

While editing splines, you can add new lines to a spline by clicking the Create Line button and then clicking between two vertices. The cursor will change when over a vertex. Several lines can be added at the same time. Right-click in the viewport to exit this mode.

Attach

The Attach button lets you attach any existing splines to the currently selected spline. The cursor changes when this mode is active. Clicking an unselected object will make it part of the current object. The Reorient option aligns the coordinate system of the spline being attached with the selected spline's coordinate system.

For example, using the Boolean button requires that objects be part of the same object. The Attach button can be used to attach several splines into the same object.

The Attach button can also be used in all three subobject modes.

Attach Mult.

The Attach Mult. button enables several splines to be attached at once. When the Attach Mult. button is clicked, the Attach Multiple dialog box (which looks a lot like the Select by Name dialog box) opens. Use this dialog box to select the objects you want to attach to the current selection. Click the Attach button when you're finished. A right-click in the viewport or another click of the Attach Mult. button exits Attach mode. This button can be used in all three subobject modes.

Insert

Insert adds vertices to a selected spline. Click the Insert button, then click the spline to place the new vertex. At this point you can reposition the new vertex and its attached segments — click again to set it in place. A single click will add a Corner type vertex, and a click and drag will add a Bézier type vertex.

After positioning the new vertex, you can add another vertex next to the first vertex by dragging the mouse and clicking. To add vertices to a different segment, right-click to release the currently selected segment but stay in Insert mode. To exit Insert mode, right-click in the viewport or click the Insert button to deselect it.

Refine

The Refine button adds vertices to a spline without changing the curvature, giving you more control over the details of the spline. The Connect option makes a new spline out of the added vertices. When the Connect option is enabled, then the Linear, Closed, Bind First, and Bind Last options become enabled. The Linear option creates Corner type vertices resulting in linear segments. The Closed option closes the spline by connecting the first and last vertices. The Bind First and Bind Last options bind the first and last vertices to the center of the selected segment. Refine is only available for Vertex and Segment subobject modes.

 New Feature

All the Refine options, including Connect, Linear, Closed, Bind First, and Bind Last, are new to Release 3.

Delete

The Delete button deletes the selected subobject. It can be used to delete vertices, segments, or splines. This button is available in all subobject modes.

Detach

The Detach button separates the selected subobjects from the rest of the object. When you click this button, the Detach dialog box opens, enabling you to name the new detached subobject. When segments are detached, you can select the Same Shape option to keep them part of the original object. The Reorient option realigns the new detached subobject to match the position and orientation of the current active grid. The Copy option creates a new copy of the detached subobject.

Detach can be used on either selected Spline or Segment subobjects.

Show Selected Segs

The Show Selected Segs option causes any selected segments to continue to be highlighted in Vertex subobject mode as well as Segment subobject mode. This helps you keep track of the segments that you are working on when moving vertices.

Tutorial: Spinning a spider's web

Now that you're familiar with the many aspects of editing splines, let's try to mimic one of the best spline producers in the world—the spider. The spider is an expert at connecting lines together to create an intricate pattern. (Luckily, we won't go hungry if this example fails.)

To create a spider web from splines, follow these steps:

1. First we need the edges to attach our web to. Pretend that the web is being built inside a tire swing. For our purposes, we'll skip building a tire model and focus on the inner, empty part of the tire. Create a circle shape in the Front view for the outer perimeter of this empty space.

2. Click the Min/Max Toggle to expand the Front view. In the Create panel, click the Line button. Make sure that the Creation Method types are both set to Corner. This will ensure that we get only straight lines.

3. Start by creating a series of lines that roughly intersect in the center of the circle and don't worry about overlapping the circle.

4. Then, starting at the center, use the Line shape to create a line that spirals outward, crossing the intersecting lines. Continue the spiral until you reach the outer edge of the circle.

5. Open the Modify panel and click the Edit Spline button. This will convert the spline into Editable Spline.

6. Click the Attach Mult. button in the Geometry rollout. Then select all the remaining lines and click Attach to make them into one object. The splines will be converted into Editable Splines as they are added to the spline object.

7. With the spline object selected, click the Sub-Object button and select Vertex. Then, open the Selection rollout and click the Show Vertex Numbers option.

8. While in Vertex subobject mode, click the CrossInsert button and follow the spiral spline around, clicking every intersection. You'll need to increase the CrossInsert threshold to around 1.0. The vertex numbers will change as you do this.

9. Next you'll want to weld together all the vertices close to one another. This can be done in one move by selecting all the vertices, setting the threshold to around 5.0, and clicking the Weld button. If the web is severely distorted, then undo the last command, lower the threshold, and try it again. If this fails to unite all the vertices, select the vertices at an intersection by dragging over them and clicking the Fuse button. Then click the Weld button.

10. The next task is to cut off the overlapping sections that run beyond the circle boundary. Select Spline in the Sub-Object drop-down list. Click the Trim button and then click the end of each spline that protrudes beyond the circle.

Figure 11-25 shows the finished spider web. (I have a new respect for spiders.)

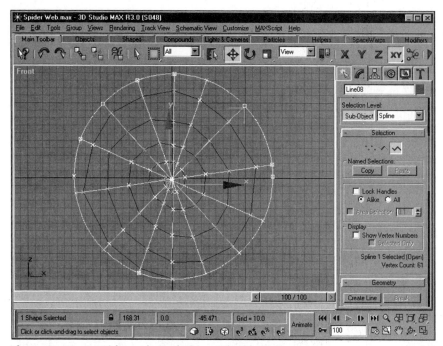

Figure 11-25: A spider web made from Editable Splines

Using the Shape Check Utility

The Shape Check utility is helpful in verifying that a shape doesn't intersect itself. Shapes that have this problem cannot be extruded, lofted, or lathed without problems. To use this utility, open the Utilities panel and click the More button. Select Shape Check from the Utilities dialog box list and click OK.

The Shape Check rollout includes only two buttons: Pick Object and Close. Click the Pick Object button and click the shape you want to check. Any intersection points will be displayed as red squares, and the response field will display "Shape Self-Intersects." If the shape doesn't have any intersections, then the response field reports, "Shape OK."

Note   The Shape Check utility can be used on normal splines and on NURBS splines.

Moving Splines to 3D

Although splines can be rendered, the real benefit of splines in MAX is to use them to create 3D object. There are many places where splines are used, and these will be discussed individually in the chapters to come, but I'll cover a few common methods here.

Cross-Reference There are many additional Modifiers that work with spline shapes. To learn about more of these, check out Chapter 9, "Modifying Objects."

Extruding splines

Because splines are drawn in a 2D plane, they already include two of the three dimensions. By adding a Height value to the spline, we can create a simple 3D object. The process of adding Height to a spline is called *extruding*.

The Extrude Modifier is located on the Modify panel. To use it, select a spline object and click the Extrude button. In the Parameters rollout, you can specify an Amount, which is the height value of the extrusion; the number of Segments; and the Capping options (*caps* fill in the surface at each end of the Extruded shape). You can also specify the final Output to be a Patch, Mesh, or NURBS object.

Figure 11-26 shows our capital *E*s that modeled the various vertex types extruded to a depth of 10.0.

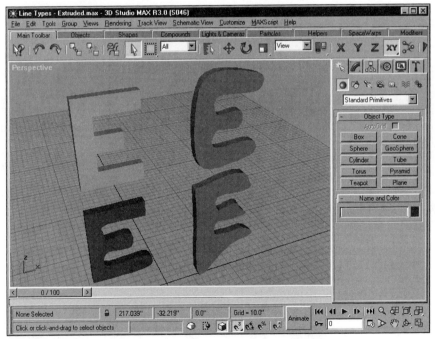

Figure 11-26: Extruding simple shapes adds depth to the spline.

Lathing splines

To the right of the Extrude button is the Lathe button. This button rotates the spline about an axis to create an object with a circular cross-section (such as a baseball bat). In the Parameters rollout you can specify the Degrees to rotate (a value of 360 will make a full rotation) and Cappings (which are unnecessary with a full 360-degree rotation). Additional options include Weld Core, which causes all vertices at the center of the lathe to be welded together, and Flip Normals, which realigns all the normals.

The Direction option determines the axis about which the rotation takes place. The rotation will take place about the object's Pivot Point. You can move the Pivot Point to affect the center of the rotation.

Caution   If your shape is created in the Top view, then lathing about the screen Z-axis will produce a thin disc without any depth.

Tutorial: Lathing a crucible

As an example of the Lathe Modifier, we'll create a crucible, although we could produce any object that has a circular cross section.

To create a crucible using the Lathe Modifier, follow these steps:

1. In the Create panel, click the Shape category button, and then click the Line button. Set the Creation Method types to Corner and Bézier.

2. In the Front viewport, create a rough profile of the crucible.

3. Open the Modify panel and click the Edit Spline button.

4. Click the Sub-Object button and select Vertex from the drop-down list.

5. Select any vertex that you wish to correct and adjust its position. Use the Bézier handles to modify the curvature.

6. Once you are comfortable with the profile, click the Sub-Object button again to exit subobject mode.

7. The next step is to locate the Pivot Point that we will lathe the line about. Open the Hierarchy panel and click the Pivot button at the top of the panel. The Pivot Point will be displayed.

8. To move the Pivot Point, click the Affect Pivot Only button, and then use the transform buttons to relocate the point to the edge of the spline. Click the Affect Pivot Only button again to exit this mode.

9. Return to the Modify panel and click the Lathe button. Set the Degrees value to **360**. Because you'll lathe a full revolution, you don't need to check the Cap options. In the Direction section, select the Y button (the Y-axis), and you're done.

Figure 11-27 shows the finished product. (This can easily be made into a coffee mug by adding a handle.)

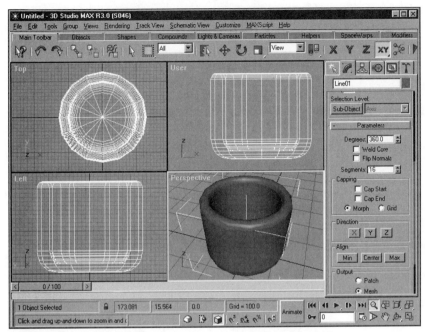

Figure 11-27: Lathing a simple profile can create a circular object.

Tutorial: Using the ShapeMerge compound object

Modifiers aren't the only commands that deal with shapes. The ShapeMerge object function (located in the Create panel under the Compound Objects subcategory) uses shapes to indent shapes in the surface of an object or cookie cutter completely through any object.

As an example of the ShapeMerge object function, let's work with the Bugs Head Software logo that we imported into MAX in an earlier example.

To use the ShapeMerge object to remove the center area from an extrusion, follow these steps:

1. Import the Bugs Head Software Logo file and select the logo to be imported as Multiple objects.

2. The first order of business is to close the spline that makes up the bug's mouth. To do this, select the mouth spline, then in the Modify panel, click the Edit Spline button. Click the Sub-Object button and select Spline, then click the Close button in the Geometry rollout. Exit subobject mode by clicking the Sub-Object button again.

3. Select the bug's head, the logo name, and all parts of the two antennae. (Be sure not to select the facial features or the interior shapes of the letters.) Open the Modify panel and click the Extrude button. Enter an Amount value of **0.3**.

4. Deselect all the objects and select the interior splines of the letter *B* that make up the bug's left eye. Open the Display Floater by selecting Tools ➪ Display Floater and click the Selected button under the Hide column to hide the interior portions of this letter.

5. Select the bug's head again. Then open the Create panel, select the Compound Objects subcategory, and click the ShapeMerge button.

6. Set the Operation to Cookie Cutter and click the Pick Shape button. Select the mouth and the letters used for the eyes and nose. Click the Pick Shape button again to exit pick mode. Deselect the bug's head.

7. Now, select each letter in the logo name that has an interior spline (such as the *B*) and click the ShapeMerge button again. Use the Pick Shape button and the Cookie Cutter operation to remove the centers of these letters. Click the Pick Shape button or select one of the other Select buttons to exit ShapeMerge mode.

8. Open the Display panel again and, in the Hide rollout, click Unhide All to redisplay the interior splines of the letter *B* that make up the bug's left eye. Select the two splines and in the Modify panel, click Extrude.

Figure 11-28 shows the finished logo. Notice that the letters have the interior sections removed.

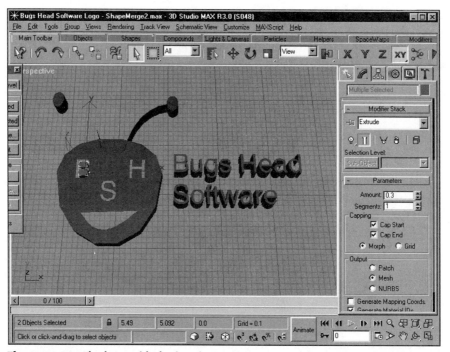

Figure 11-28: The logo with the interior centers removed from extruded letters using the ShapeMerge object

Creating Spline Paths

Another way to use splines is to create animation paths. Generally, these paths are not likely to be confined to a single plane. As an example we'll use a type of spline called a *Helix* to create an animation path in the next tutorial. The Helix doesn't stay within the 2D world, as the tutorial will show.

There are basically two ways to use splines for animation paths. One way would be to create a spline and have an object follow it using either the Path Controller or the Path Follow Space Warp function. The other way would be to animate an object and then edit the Trajectory path. A *Trajectory* is the spline path that an object follows when it is animated. To edit a Trajectory path, go to the Motion panel and click the Trajectories button. The Trajectories rollout includes buttons to convert splines to trajectories and to convert trajectories to splines. In either case, the spline editing features discussed in this chapter will be helpful.

The Path Controller will be covered in more detail in Chapter 32, "Animating with Controllers." For more details on using Trajectories, see Chapter 30, "Animation Basics."

Tutorial: Creating a bumblebee flight path

Now that your appetite's whetted for some animation, here's a simple animation done using a spline path and the Path Controller. In this tutorial, we'll use a simple Helix path and attach it to a Dragonfly model—the result will be a dizzy insect. The Dragonfly model was taken from the Sampler CD-ROM provided by Zygote Media.

The Dragonfly model, along with many other Zygote models, is included on the CD-ROM provided with this book.

To attach an object to a spline path, follow these steps:

1. Open the Create panel and click the Shapes category button.

2. Click the Helix button and drag the path in the Top viewport. In the Parameters rollout, set the Radius 1 value to **130**, Radius 2 to **0**, Height to **200**, and the number of Turns to **5**. This will create a path with a nice spiral shape.

3. Import the dragonfly model (dragfly.3DS) from the CD-ROM by selecting File ➪ Import. The 3DS Import dialog box opens. Select the option to merge with the current scene and click OK. At this point, a 3DS File Import warning window will appear asking if you want to set the current animation length to match the value stored in the imported 3DS animation file. Click No.

4. Group the dragonfly parts together and name the group **Dragonfly**.

5. In the Motion panel, open the Assign Controller rollout and select the Position: Bézier Position controller. Click the Assign Controller button directly under the Assign Position rollout title bar. This opens the Assign Position Controller dialog box.

6. In the dialog box list, select Path and click OK.

7. In the Path Parameters rollout, click the Pick Path button and then click the Helix path. The dragonfly will attach itself to the start of the Helix spline. In the Path Options section, select the Follow option.

8. In the Top view, rotate the dragonfly group so that the head is facing the path.

9. Click the Play Animation button in the Time Controls to see the dragonfly follow the path.

Figure 11-29 shows the dragonfly in its path up the spiral.

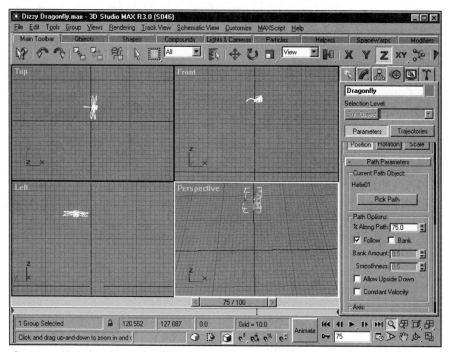

Figure 11-29: The dragonfly object has been attached to a spline path that it follows.

Using Spline Boolean Operations

Boolean operations were lightly touched upon earlier in the chapter, but they deserve more coverage as well as an example.

Caution   Spline Boolean operations can only be done to splines that are part of the same object and only between closed splines.

Spline Boolean operators

There are three spline Boolean operators: Union, Subtraction, and Intersection.

The Union operator combines the outlines of the two splines and includes all the overlapping areas.

The Subtraction operator does the opposite of the Union operator. It removes all the area of the second spline from the first. The outline is altered to follow the displaced area.

The Intersection operator discards all spline areas except where the two splines overlap.

See Chapter 15, "Building Compound Objects," for more information on Boolean modeling.

Tutorial: Routing a custom shelf

In Woodshop 101, you use a router to add a designer edge to doorframes, window frames, and shelving of all sorts. In Woodshop 3D, the Boolean tools will work nicely as we customize a bookshelf.

To create a custom bookshelf using spline Boolean operations, follow these steps:

1. In the Create panel, select the Shapes category and, in the Front view, create a simple triangle shape.

2. Click the Circle button and draw three circles like the ones shown in Figure 11-30.

3. Select one of the splines, and in the Modify panel, and click the Edit Spline button.

4. Select the triangle shape and click the Attach button. Then select the other three circles and attach them to the triangle to form a single object. (Boolean operations can only be performed on splines in the same object.) Click the Attach button again to exit Attach mode.

5. Click the Sub-Object button and select Spline from the drop-down list.

6. Click the Subtraction button next to the Boolean button (it's the middle one). Then select the triangle shape and click the Boolean button.

7. Click all three circles in turn to subtract their areas from the triangle. Right-click in the viewport to exit Boolean mode and remember to exit subobject mode also.

8. Back at the top of the Modify panel, select the Extrude Modifier and enter an Amount of **1000**. Select Zoom Extents All to resize your viewports and view your bookshelf.

Figure 11-31 shows the finished bookshelf ready to hang on the wall.

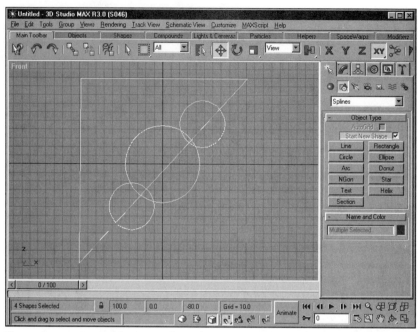

Figure 11-30: Preparing to use the Subtraction Boolean operator to create a fancy bookshelf

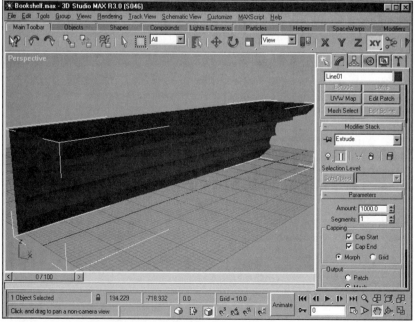

Figure 11-31: The finished bookshelf created with spline Boolean operations

Summary

As this chapter has shown, there is much more to splines than just points, lines, and control handles. Splines in MAX are one of the fundamental building blocks and the pathway to advanced modeling skills using NURBS.

This chapter covered the following spline topics:

✦ Understanding the various spline primitives

✦ Importing and exporting splines

✦ Editing splines

✦ Using the Shape Check Utility

✦ Moving splines to 3D using the Extrude, Lathe, and ShapeMerge functions.

✦ Creating spline paths for animation

✦ Using spline Boolean operations

As we leave splines behind, don't forget them because they will be important when we discuss more advanced objects such as meshes, which are covered in the next chapter.

✦   ✦   ✦

Working with Meshes

✦ ✦ ✦ ✦

In This Chapter

Parametric versus.
nonparametric
objects

Creating an Editable
Mesh object by
converting from other
object types

Using the Editable
Mesh features to
edit meshes

Modifying mesh
objects with
Modifiers

✦ ✦ ✦ ✦

M *eshes* are the default model type that most 3D-file types use. In this chapter, you'll learn about how to create and edit mesh objects, and you'll also get experience using some Modifiers that work with mesh objects.

Parametric versus Non-Parametric

All geometric primitives in MAX are Parametric. *Parametric* means that the geometry of the object is controlled by variables called *parameters*. Modifying these parameters modifies the geometry of the object. This is a powerful concept that gives parametric objects unlimited flexibility.

Non-parametric objects do not have this flexibility. Once a nonparametric object has been created, you cannot modify it by changing parameters. All mesh objects in MAX are nonparametric. Because meshes don't have parameters, they rely on Modifiers to change their geometry.

When a primitive object is converted to an Editable Mesh, it loses its parametric nature and can no longer be changed by altering its parameters. Editable Meshes do have their advantages though. You can edit subobjects such as vertices, edges, and faces of meshes, things that you cannot edit for a parametric object. Editable Meshes also have a host of functions that are specific to meshes. This will be covered in the coming sections.

Note   There are several Modifiers that maintain the parametric nature of an object and enable you to access the object's parameters. These include Edit Mesh, Mesh Select, Delete Mesh, Tessellate, Face Extrude, and Affect Region.

Primitive objects can be converted into Editable Mesh objects. This will change the object type at the bottom of the Modifier Stack to Editable Mesh. Figure 12-1 shows the Modifier Stack for two spheres. The sphere in the Stack on the left was converted to an Editable Mesh and then the Bend Modifier was applied. The sphere in the Stack on the right was not converted, but had the Bend Modifier applied. The right sphere is still parametric.

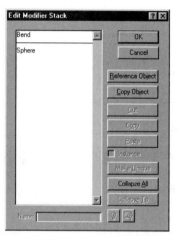

Figure 12-1: The Modifier Stacks for an Editable Mesh versus a normal primitive

Creating an Editable Mesh Object

There is no method in the Create panel for making mesh objects — mesh objects need to be converted from another object type or produced as the result of a Modifier. Object types that can be converted include shapes, primitives, Booleans, patches, and NURBS. Many models that are imported will appear as mesh objects. Most 3D formats, including 3DS and DXF, import as mesh objects.

Note   Even spline shapes can be converted to Editable Meshes, whether they are open or closed. Closed splines are filled with a polygon, while open splines are only a single edge and can be hard to see.

Before you can use many of the mesh editing functions discussed in this chapter, you'll need to convert the object to an Editable Mesh object. There are several ways to create an Editable Mesh.

Converting to an Editable Mesh

Perhaps the quickest and easiest way to create an Editable Mesh is to right-click an object and select Convert to Editable Mesh from the pop-up menu. Another way to convert an object is to click the Edit Stack button (in the Modify panel under the Modifier Stack rollout) provided no Modifiers have been applied. This will open a pop-up menu with the option to Convert to Editable Mesh.

Still another way to create an Editable Mesh is to Collapse the Modifier Stack. To do this, open the Edit Modifier Stack dialog box by clicking the Edit Stack button and then click the Collapse All button. A warning dialog box appears, notifying you that this action will delete all the creation parameters. Click Yes to continue with the collapse.

Tip
In addition to the Yes and No buttons, the warning dialog box includes a Hold/Yes button. This button will save the current state of the object to the Hold buffer and then apply the Collapse All function. If you have any problems, you can retrieve the object's previous state before the collapse was applied by selecting Edit ➪ Fetch.

Using the Collapse utility

There is also a Collapse utility found on the Utility panel. This utility will let you collapse an object or several objects to a Modifier Stack Result or to a Mesh object. Collapsing to a Modifier Stack Result doesn't necessarily produce a mesh but collapses the object to its base object state, which is displayed at the bottom of the Stack. Depending on the Stack, this could result in a Patch, Spline, or other object. You can also collapse to a Single Object or to Multiple Objects. The Boolean operations are available if you are collapsing several overlapping objects into one. Figure 12-2 shows the rollout for the Collapse utility.

Figure 12-2: The Collapse utility can collapse several objects at once.

Caution   Collapsing the Modifier Stack is not an action that you can undo. Before proceeding with the collapse, use the Edit ⇨ Hold command to provide a way to recover
before the collapse.

Editing a Mesh Object

Once an object has been converted to an Editable Mesh, you can alter its shape by
applying Modifiers, or you can work with the mesh subobjects. In the Modify panel
are many tools for controlling meshes and working with their individual subobjects,
which include Vertex, Edge, Face, Polygon, and Element.

Note   Open spline objects that have been converted to an Editable Mesh have only the
Vertex subobject mode available because they don't have any edges or faces.

Selecting Mesh Sub-Objects

Before you can edit mesh Sub-Objects, you must select them. To select a Sub-Object
type, click the Sub-Object button in the Modify panel and select a Sub-Object type
from the drop-down list. Alternatively, you can click one of the Sub-Object buttons
(the red-colored icons) in the Selection rollout.

New
Feature   The Sub-Object type icons in the Selection rollout are new to Release 3.

A third way to enter subobject edit mode is to right-click the Editable Mesh object.
This opens the pop-up menu where you select Sub-Object and, from the nested pop-
up menu, select the subobject type to edit.

Each of the mesh subobject modes has an associated keyboard shortcut (available
only when the Plug-In Keyboard Shortcut Toggle at the bottom of the screen is
selected). These shortcuts are listed in Table 12-1.

Table 12-1 Editable Mesh Sub-Object Keyboard Shortcuts	
Press This Key	*To Access This Mode*
1	Vertex subobject
2	Edge subobject
3	Face subobject
4	Polygon subobject
5	Element subobject
6	Object mode
+	Move up one mode
−	Move down one mode

To exit subobject edit mode, click the Sub-Object button again. Remember, you must exit this mode before you can select another object. The Sub-Object button turns yellow when selected to remind you that you are in Sub-Object edit mode.

Multiple subobjects can be selected at the same time by dragging an outline over them. You can also select multiple subobjects by holding down the Ctrl key while clicking them. The Ctrl key can also deselect selected subobjects while maintaining the rest of the selection. Holding down the Alt key will remove any selected vertices from the current selection set.

Holding down the Shift key while clicking and dragging on a subobject will clone it. During cloning, a dialog box appears that enables you to clone the subobject to the current element or as a separate object. You can also give the new object a name.

Selection Options

The By Vertex option selects all edges and faces that are connected to a vertex when the vertex is selected. Ignore Backfacing selects only those subobjects with normals pointing towards the current viewport. For example, if you are trying to select some faces on a sphere, only the faces on the side closest to you will be selected. If this option is off, then faces on both sides of the sphere are selected.

The Ignore Visible Edges option is only active in Polygon subobject mode. This button enables you to select all the polygons within a plane, as determined by the Planar Threshold value. If the Ignore Visible Edges option is not selected, the selection is limited to the edges of the polygon that is clicked on.

The Hide button hides the selected subobjects. Hidden object can be made visible again with the Unhide All button.

After selecting several subobjects, you can create a Named Selection Set by typing a name in the Name Selection Sets drop-down list in the main toolbar. These Selection Sets can then be copied and pasted onto other shapes.

At the bottom of the Selection rollout is the Selection Information, which is a text line that automatically displays the number and type of selected items.

Soft Selection

In subobject mode the Soft Selection rollout becomes available. Soft Selection selects all the subobjects surrounding the current selection and applies transformations to them to a lesser extent. For example, if a face is selected and moved a distance of 2, then with linear Soft Selection, the neighboring faces that aren't selected will move a distance of 1. The overall effect is a smoother transition.

The Use Soft Selection parameter enables or disables the Soft Selection feature. The Edge Distance option sets the range (the number of edges from the current selection) that Soft Selection will affect. The Affect Backfacing option applies the Soft Selection to selected subobjects on the backside of an object.

The Soft Selection Curve shows a graphical representation of how the Soft Selection is applied. The Falloff value defines the spherical region where the Soft Selection has an effect. The Pinch button sharpens the point at the top of the curve. The Bubble button has an opposite effect and widens the curve.

Figure 12-3 shows the Soft Selection rollout.

Figure 12-3: The Soft Selection rollout includes a curve that shows how the selection will be applied.

Editing Vertices

When working with an Editable Mesh object, once a Vertex Sub-Object type is selected and vertices are selected, you can transform them using the transform buttons in the main toolbar. When you move the vertices around, the mesh edges will follow.

Much of the power of editing meshes is contained within the Edit Geometry rollout. Features contained here include, among many others, the ability to create new vertices, attach objects to the mesh, weld vertices, Chamfer vertices. Some Geometry buttons will be disabled, depending on the Sub-Object that you've selected. For instance, the buttons described in the following sections apply only to the Vertex subobject.

Create

The Create button lets you add new vertices to a mesh object. To create a new vertex, click the Create button to enter Create mode. You can then click where you want the new vertex to be located. Click the Create button again or right-click in the viewport to exit Create mode.

Tip   With the Plug-in Keyboard Shortcut Toggle enabled at the bottom of the MAX window, you can press the C key to enter and exit Create mode.

Create mode works for all subobject types except edges.

Delete

The Delete button deletes the selected vertices. This button works for all the subobject types.

Caution   Deleting a vertex also deletes all faces and their edges connected to that vertex. This can cause holes in the geometry.

Attach

The Attach button is available with all subobject modes and even when you are not in subobject mode. When no subobject mode is selected, the Detach button (to the right) changes to an Attach List button. Clicking the Attach List button opens the Attach List dialog box where you can select from a list all the objects to attach. The list contains only objects that can be attached.

The Attach button is used to add objects to the current Editable Mesh object. This can be used to add Primitives, splines, patch objects, and other mesh objects. An object that is attached to a mesh object is automatically converted into an Editable Mesh.

To use this feature, select the main object and click the Attach button. Move the mouse over the object to be attached — the cursor will change over acceptable objects. Click the object to select it. Click the Attach button again or right-click in the viewport to exit Attach mode.

Detach

The Detach button separates the selected subobjects from the rest of the object. To use this button, select the subobject and click the Detach button. The Detach dialog box opens, enabling you to name the new detached subobject. You also have the options to Detach to Element or to Detach as Clone. All subobject modes except Edge have a Detach option.

Tip   If you enable the Plug-in Keyboard Shortcut Toggle (at the bottom of the MAX window), you can press the T key to enter and exit Detach mode.

Break

The Break button creates a separate vertex for adjoining faces that are connected by a single vertex.

New Feature This feature is new with Release 3.

In a normal mesh, faces are all connected by vertices — moving one vertex will change the position of all adjoining faces. The Break button enables you to move the vertex associated with each face independent of the others. The button is only available in Vertex subobject mode.

Tip If you enable the Plug-in Keyboard Shortcut Toggle (at the bottom of the MAX window), you can press the B key to break vertices away.

Figure 12-4 shows a hexagon shape with polygon faces that were joined at the center. The Break button was used to separate the center vertex into separate vertices for each face. The faces can be manipulated independently, as the figure shows.

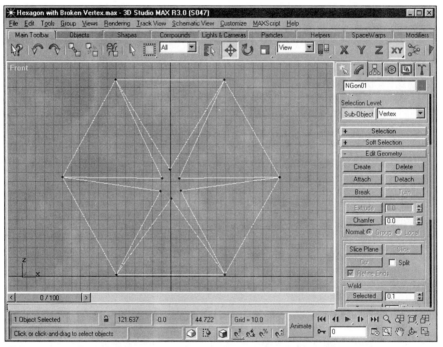

Figure 12-4: The Break button can be used to give each face its own vertex.

Chamfer

The Chamfer button, which is enabled in Vertex and Edge subobject modes, lets you cut the edge off a corner and replace it with a face. This existing corner vertex is deleted and automatically replaced with a face as well as vertices for each edge that was connected to the original corner vertex. The Chamfer amount is the distance the new face vertices move along the edge away from the original vertex position.

New Feature   The Chamfer button is new in Release 3.

To use this feature, select the Chamfer button, then click and drag the vertex to be chamfered or select a vertex and enter a value in the Chamfer spinner. If multiple vertices are selected, they all are chamfered equal amounts. If you click and drag on an unselected vertex, then the current selection is dropped and the new selection is chamfered.

Figure 12-5 shows the results of chamfering all the vertices of a cube at the same time.

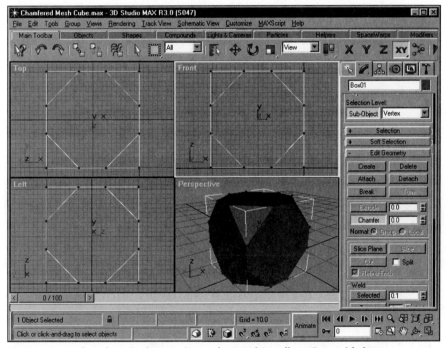

Figure 12-5: The Chamfer button is used to replace all vertices with faces.

Slice

The Slice Plane button lets you split the mesh object along a plane. When you click the Slice Plane button, a yellow slice plane gizmo will appear on the selected object. This gizmo can be moved, rotated, and scaled using the transform buttons. Once the plane is properly positioned and all options are set, click the Slice button to finish slicing the mesh. All intersected faces are split in two and new vertices and edges are added to the mesh where the Slice Plane intersects the original mesh.

The Slice Plane mode stays active until the Slice Plane button is deselected or until you right-click in the viewport; this feature enables you to make several slices in one session. The Slice Plane button is enabled for all subobject modes.

Tip   If you enable the Plug-in Keyboard Shortcut Toggle (at the bottom of the MAX window), you can press the C key to enable Slice mode. The Shift+C shortcut does the same thing as clicking the Sub-Object button.

The Split option doubles the number of vertices along the Slice Plane. Figure 12-6 shows a Slice Plane added to the chamfered cube from the previous figure.

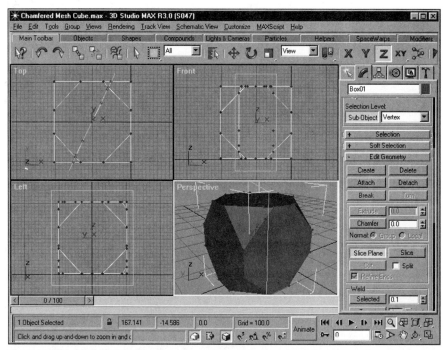

Figure 12-6: The Slice button creates new vertices and edges where the gizmo intersects with the mesh.

Weld Selected and Weld Target

The Weld Selected button works like the Weld function for splines. To use this feature, select two or more vertices and click the Weld button. If the vertices are within the threshold value specified by the spinner to the right of the button, they are welded into one vertex. If no vertices are within the threshold, an alert box opens and notifies you of this.

Tip   If you enable the Plug-in Keyboard Shortcut Toggle (at the bottom of the MAX window), you can press the W key to use the Weld Selected feature.

The Weld Target button lets you select a vertex and drag and drop it on top of another vertex. If the target vertex is within the number of pixels specified by the Target value, the vertices are welded into one vertex. To exit Weld Target mode, click the Target button again or right-click in the viewport.

Both of these buttons are available only in Vertex subobject mode.

Remove Isolated Vertices

The Remove Isolated Vertices button automatically deletes all isolated vertices associated with a mesh object, selected or not. Isolated vertices can result from deleting a face, or they could be inserted with the Create button and never connected. This is a helpful feature to clean up a mesh before applying any Modifiers.

 Tip

If you enable the Plug-in Keyboard Shortcut Toggle (at the bottom of the MAX window), you can press the R key to Remove Isolated Vertices.

View and Grid Align

The View and Grid Align buttons move and orient all selected vertices to the current active viewport or to the current construction grid.

Make Planar

A single vertex or two vertices don't define a plane, but three or more vertices do. If three or more vertices are selected, you can use the Make Planar button to make these vertices coplanar. Doing so will position the selected vertices so they lie in the same plane.

 New
Feature

The Make Planar button is new in Release 3.

Collapse

The Collapse button reduces several selected vertices into one. The position of the new vertex is the averaged position of the selected ones. This is similar to the Weld button, except that the selected vertices don't need to be within a Threshold value to be combined.

 Tip

If you enable the Plug-in Keyboard Shortcut Toggle (at the bottom of the MAX window), you can press the L key to Collapse selected vertices.

Surface Properties Rollout

The Surface Properties rollout lets you give selected vertices a Weight. Vertices with higher weight have a greater pull, like the gravity of a larger planet. Several Modifiers (such as MeshSmooth) use this weight.

Also within this rollout is the Edit Color color swatch, which enables you to assign a color to the selected vertices. You can then recall vertices with the same color by selecting the color in the Existing Color swatch and clicking the Select button. The RGB values match all colors within the Range defined by these values. For example, if the RGB Range values are all set to 255, then every vertex will be selected. The Edit Color swatch is available in all subobject modes except Edge.

Editing Edges

Edges are the lines that run between two vertices. Edges can be *closed*, which means that each side of the edge is connected to a face; or *open*, which means that only one face connects to the edge. Mesh edges, such as in the interior of a shape that has been converted to a mesh, can also be *invisible*.

You can select multiple edges by holding down the Ctrl key while clicking the edges or the Alt key to remove selected edges from the selection set. Edges can also be copied using the Shift key while transforming the edge. The cloned edge maintains connections to its vertices by creating new edges.

Many of the Edge subobject options work in the same way as the Vertex subobject options. The following Geometry rollout buttons work exclusively on Edge subobjects.

Divide

The Divide button adds a new vertex at the middle of the edge and splits the edge into two equal sections. When an edge is selected, the Divide button replaces the Break button used in Vertex subobject mode. To exit Divide mode, click the Divide button again or right-click in the viewport.

This button works in all subobject modes except Vertex.

Tip   If you enable the Plug-in Keyboard Shortcut Toggle (at the bottom of the MAX window), you can press the D key to enter Divide mode.

Turn

The Turn button rotates the hidden edges that break the polygon up into triangles (all polygonal faces include these hidden edges). For example, if a quadrilateral face has a hidden edge, which runs between vertices 1 and 3, then the Turn button would change this hidden edge to run between 2 and 4. This will affect how the surface is smoothed when the polygon is not coplanar. To exit Turn mode, click the Turn button again or right-click in the viewport.

This button is available only in Edge subobject mode.

Extrude

The Extrude button adds depth to an edge by extending it and creating a new face behind the extruded edge. For example, a square extruded from a patch grid would form a box with no lid. To use this feature, select an edge or edges and click the Extrude button; then drag in a viewport. The edges will interactively show the extrude depth. Release the button when you've reached the desired distance.

Alternatively, you can set an extrude depth in the Extrusion spinner. The Normal Group option extrudes all selected edges along the normal for the group (the normal runs perpendicular to the face) and the Normal Local option moves each individual edge along its local normal. To exit Extrude mode, click the Extrude button again or right-click in the viewport.

The Extrude button is enabled for all subobject modes except Vertex.

Tip If you enable the Plug-in Keyboard Shortcut Toggle (at the bottom of the MAX window), you can press Shift+E to enter Extrude mode.

Figure 12-7 shows a sphere that has been converted to an Editable Patch and had all its edges extruded.

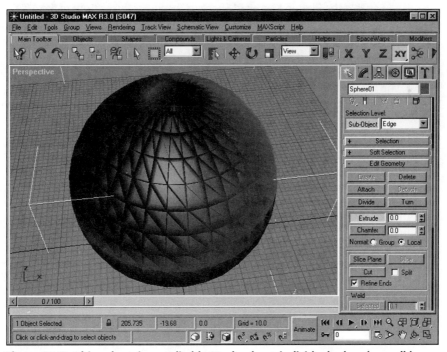

Figure 12-7: This sphere is an Editable Mesh whose individual edges have all been extruded.

Cut

The Cut button enables you to split an edge into two by cutting an existing edge. To use this feature, click the Cut button and then click and drag across the edges you wish to cut. If you drag across several faces, a new vertex and edge will be created at each intersection. You can also create a single vertex at any point along an edge by double- clicking. To exit this mode, right-click. Then right-click again to disable the Cut button.

The Split option creates two vertices at every junction, enabling these faces to be easily separated. The Refine Edges option maintains the continuous surface of the mesh by adding additional vertices to all adjacent faces to the cut. The Cut button is available in all subobject modes except Vertex.

Tip   If you enable the Plug-in Keyboard Shortcut Toggle (at the bottom of the MAX window), you can press the Shift+C key to enter Cut mode.

Select Open Edges

The Select Open Edges button locates and selects all open edges. This is a good way to find any holes in the geometry. This is another feature to help eliminate potential problems with a mesh object.

Tip   If you enable the Plug-in Keyboard Shortcut Toggle (at the bottom of the MAX window), you can press the O key to select any open edges.

Create Shape from Edges

The Create Shape from Edges button creates a new spline shape from selected edges. The Create Shape dialog box appears, enabling you to give the new shape a name. You can also select options for Smooth or Linear shape types and to Ignore Hidden Edges.

Surface Properties Rollout

The Surface Properties rollout includes Visible and Invisible buttons that can be used to make invisible edges between polygons visible. The Auto Edge button automatically makes all selected edges less than the Threshold value invisible if the Set and Clear Edge Vis option is selected. The Set option only makes invisible edges visible, and the Clear option only makes visible edges invisible.

Tip   If you enable the Plug-in Keyboard Shortcut Toggle (at the bottom of the MAX window), you can press the V key to make any selected edges visible and the I key to make any selected edges invisible. Pressing Shift+V is the same as pressing the Auto Edge button.

Editing Face, Polygon, and Element Sub-Objects

Meshes include two different types of faces: Face subobjects and Polygon subobjects. *Face subobjects* have only three edges. This is the simplest possible polygon, and all other polygons can be broken down into this type of face. *Polygon subobjects* are any faces with more than three vertices. A Polygon subobject includes two or more faces. A dashed line contained within the polygon designates these faces.

Tip   By using the Invisible button in Edge subobject mode, you can increase the size of a polygon subobject.

A mesh object can also contain several elements. The Element subobject mode includes all the same commands as the Face and Polygon subobject modes.

Transforming a face or polygon object works the same way in subobject mode as in normal transformations. The Geometry rollout includes many of the same buttons previously covered in the Vertex and Edge sections, but includes some additional features that only apply to Face and Polygon subobjects. These features are covered in the following sections.

Create

The Create button can be used to create new faces and/or polygons based on new or existing vertices. To create a new face, click the Create button — all vertices in the selected mesh will be highlighted. Next, click a vertex to start the face — after clicking two more vertices, a new face is created. You can also create a new vertex not based on any existing vertices by holding down the Shift key while clicking.

Polygons aren't limited to only three vertices. You can click as many times as you want to add additional vertices to the polygon. Click the first vertex, or double-click to complete the polygon.

Caution   The order in which the face vertices are selected is important in determining the direction of the face normal. If vertices are selected in a clockwise order, then the face normal will point inward. Counterclockwise vertex selection results in an outward pointing normal. If your newly created faces don't display in a view that is smooth shaded, then you probably have a normal pointing the wrong way. You can use the Normal Flip button in the Surface Properties rollout to correct this problem or create the face again, selecting the vertices in the opposite order.

Figure 12-8 shows a simple hexagon to which I've added several triangles using the Create button.

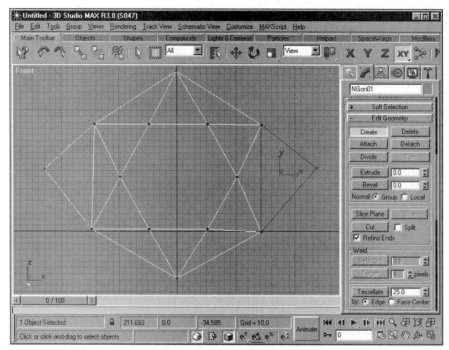

Figure 12-8: All the triangles exterior to the center hexagon were added using the Create button.

Bevel

The Bevel button extrudes the Face or Polygon subobject selection and then lets you bevel the edges. To use this feature, select a face or polygon and click the Bevel button; then drag up or down in a viewport to the Extrusion depth and release the button. Drag again to specify the Bevel amount. The Bevel amount determines the relative size of the extruded face.

The Normal Group option extrudes all selected faces or polygons along the normal for the group, and the Normal Local option moves each individual face or polygon along its local normal. To exit Bevel mode, click the Bevel button again or right-click in the viewport. The Bevel button is enabled for all subobject modes except Vertex and Edge.

Figure 12-9 displays a mesh pyramid that has been extruded with a value of 20 and beveled to a value of –20.

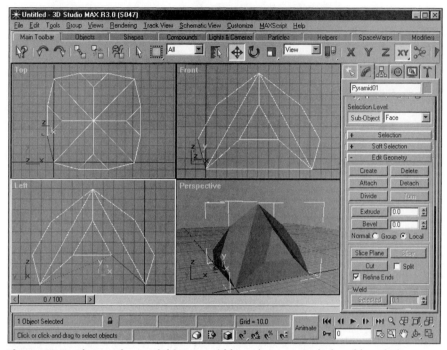

Figure 12-9: The top faces of this pyramid have been extruded and beveled.

Tessellate

The Tessellate button can be used to increase the resolution of a mesh by splitting a face or polygon into several faces or polygons. There are two options to do this: Edge and Face-Center.

The Edge method splits each edge at its midpoint. For example, a triangular face would be split into three smaller triangles. The Tension spinner to the right of the Tessellate button specifies a value that is used to make the tessellated face concave or convex.

The Face-Center option creates a vertex in the center of the face and also creates three new edges, which extend from the center vertex to each original vertex. For a square polygon, this option would create six new triangular faces. (Remember, a square polygon is actually composed of two triangular faces.)

In Figure 12-10, I tessellated the faces of a cube once using the Edge option and then again using the Face-Center option.

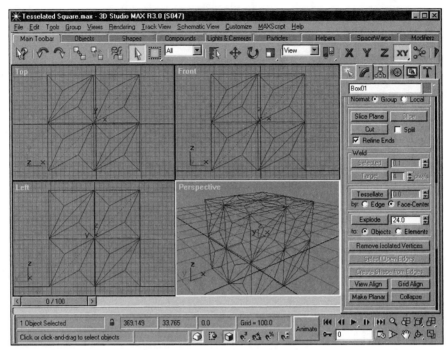

Figure 12-10: A cube tessellated twice using each option

Explode

The Explode button separates all selected faces or polygons into individual objects or elements. The spinner to the right sets the angle value of the faces to include in this operation. If the Objects option is selected, the Explode to Objects dialog box appears, enabling you to name the object.

Tip   If you enable the Plug-in Keyboard Shortcut Toggle (at the bottom of the MAX window), you can press the X key to explode the selected faces.

Surface Properties Rollout

The Surface Properties rollout includes the Show option to display the face normals. The normals appear as blue arrows extending perpendicularly from the center of each selected face. To the right is the Scale spinner, which enables you to adjust the length of the blue lines. The Flip and Unify buttons are used to control the direction of these normals. Flip reverses the direction of the normals of each selected face; Unify makes all normals face in the same direction based on the majority. The Flip Normal Mode button activates a mode where you can click individual faces and flip their normals. This mode stays active until you click the Normal Mode button again or right-click in the viewport.

The Surface Properties rollout also includes Material IDs and Smoothing Groups options.

The Material IDs option settings are used by the Multi/Sub-Object material type to apply different materials to faces or polygons within an object. By selecting a polygon subobject, you can use this option to apply a unique material to the selected polygon.

Cross-Reference   More information on the Multi/Sub-Object material can be found in Chapter 17, "Exploring the Material Editor."

The Smoothing Group option is used to assign a polygon to a unique Smoothing Group. To do this, select a patch and click a Smoothing Group number.

Tutorial: Modeling a clown head

Now that all the Editable Mesh features have been covered, lets use them to actually get some work done. In this example, you'll quickly deform a mesh sphere to create a clown face. This is done by selecting, moving, and working with some vertices.

To create a clown head by moving vertices, follow these steps:

1. In the Create panel, click the Geometry category and click the Sphere button. Then drag in the Top viewport to create a sphere.

2. Right-click the sphere and select Convert to Editable Mesh from the pop-up menu. This will automatically open the Modify panel.

3. Now, make a long, pointy nose by pulling a vertex outward from the sphere object. Click the Sub-Object button and select Vertex from the drop-down list. Then select the single vertex at the top of the sphere. Make sure the Select and Move button is selected, and in the Top viewport, drag the vertex along the Y-axis until it projects from the sphere.

4. Next, create the mouth by selecting and indenting a row of vertices. For this selection, open the Soft Selection rollout and click the Use Soft Selection option. Underneath the nose, select several vertices in a circular arc that make a smile and press the Spacebar to lock the selection. Then move the selected vertices along the negative Y-axis.

5. Unlock the mouth selection. For the eyes, select two sets of three vertices above the nose and lock the selection once again. With the Soft Selection still enabled, move the eye vertices in the Y-axis, but not as far as the nose.

6. Unlock the eyes selection. Select each eye set of vertices independently and click the Weld Selected button. (If the vertices aren't within the threshold, increase the threshold and try again.)

7. Select both sets of eye vertices and click the Chamfer button. Then drag in the viewport an intermediate distance back to the surface of the sphere.

There is more that we can do the clown face, but this gives you an idea. Figure 12-11 shows the clown head in a shaded view.

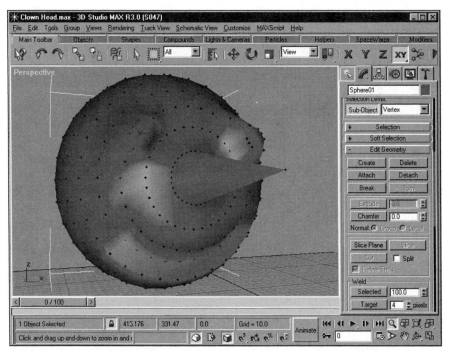

Figure 12-11: A clown head created from an Editable Mesh by selecting and moving vertices

Tutorial: Beveling a geometric hedra

The Hedra object that is found under the Extended Primitives subcategory can create some wonderful derivations, including a variety of stars and shapes. If these Hedra are converted into Editable Meshes, then even more shapes can be easily created. One such feature for Editable Meshes is the Bevel command.

To bevel a geometric Hedra, follow these steps:

1. Open the Create panel, click the Geometry category, select the Extended Primitives subcategory, and click the Hedra button. In the Parameters rollout, select the Dodec/Icos option and make the Q value **1.0**. Then drag in the viewport to create a dodecahedron shape.

2. Right-click the Hedra and select Convert to Editable Mesh from the pop-up menu. This will automatically open the Modify panel.

3. Click the Sub-Object button and select Polygon from the drop-down list. Then select one of the Hedra faces. In the Geometry rollout, click the Bevel button and enter **20** as the Extrusion amount and **–10** as the Bevel amount. Repeat this procedure for each face.

Figure 12-12 shows the dodecahedron after beveling each of its faces.

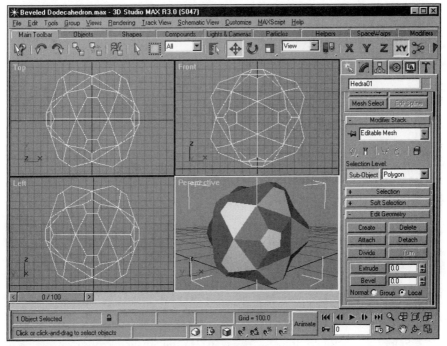

Figure 12-12: A dodecahedron with beveled faces

Tutorial: Cleaning up imported meshes

Almost all 3D formats are mesh formats, and importing mesh objects can sometimes create problems. By collapsing an imported model to an Editable Mesh, you can take advantage of several of the Editable Mesh features to clean up these problems.

Figure 12-13 shows a model that was exported from MetaCreation's Poser 3 using the 3DS format. Notice that the model's waist is black. It only appears this way because I've turned the Backface Cull option off in the Viewport Configuration dialog box. If it were turned on, his waist would be invisible. The problem here is that the normals for this object are pointing the wrong direction. This is a common problem for imported meshes, and we'll fix it in this tutorial.

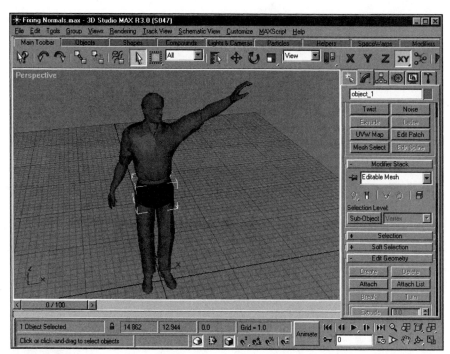

Figure 12-13: This mesh suffers from objects with flipped normals, which makes them invisible.

To fix the normals on an imported mesh model, follow these steps:

1. Import the human figure using the File ⇨ Import command.

2. Select the problem object — the waist. In the Surface Properties dialog box, select the Show Normals option and set the Scale value to a small number like **0.1**. Click the Sub-Object button and select Element from the drop-down list. Drag over the element to select it. Figure 12-14 shows all the normals for this element from the Top view. Notice all the normals that are pointing to the interior of the element.

3. With the elements still selected, click the Unify button in the Surface Properties dialog box and then click the Flip button until all normals are pointing outward. This fixes the problem, and the waist object is now a visible part of the mesh. The fixed mesh will look just like the original mesh without the ugly black pelvis.

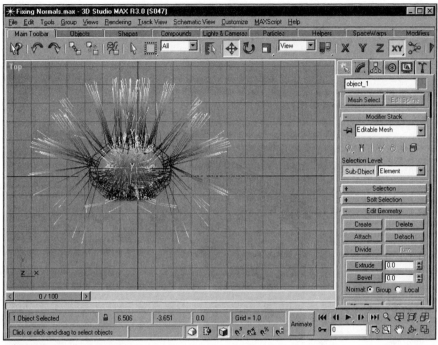

Figure 12-14: The Show Normals option of the Surface Properties rollout displays all the normals for an object.

Modifying Meshes

Most of the Modifiers available with MAX can be applied to mesh objects. The following sections will give you a sampling of how some of these Modifiers work.

Cross-Reference For more information on Modifiers, see Chapter 9, "Modifying Objects."

Using the Edit Mesh Modifier

When an object is converted to an Editable Mesh, its parametric nature is eliminated. However, if you use the Edit Mesh Modifier, you can still retain the same object type and its parametric nature while having access to all the Editable Mesh features. The Edit Mesh Modifier is one of the default Modifiers and can be found as a button at the top of the Modify panel.

For example, if you create a sphere and apply the Edit Mesh Modifier and then extrude several faces, you can still change the radius of the sphere by selecting the Sphere object in the Modifier Stack and changing the Radius value in the Parameters rollout.

Caution   When you switch the Stack back to the Sphere entry, a Warning dialog box appears, stating that a Modifier exists that depends on the topology of the object and that undesirable effects may follow. Depending on the type of features you've used, you may have problems with the geometry if you alter its parameters.

Using the Mesh Select Modifier

The Mesh Select Modifier includes a subset of the Editable Mesh features, including the Selection and Soft Selection rollouts. These rollouts enable you to pick a subobject selection that can be passed up the Stack to another Modifier. The Mesh Select Modifier is also one of the default Modifiers in the Modify panel.

For example, you can use the Mesh Select Modifier to select several vertices on an object. Then, if you select the Bend Modifier, the effect bends only the selected vertices. Any Modifiers that have been applied to subobject selections have an asterisk in front of the Modifier name listed in the Stack.

Using the Delete Mesh Modifier

The Delete Mesh Modifier deletes the current selection as defined by the Mesh Select Modifier. It can be used to delete a selection of vertices, edges, faces, polygons, or even the entire mesh if there is no subobject selection. The Delete Mesh Modifier has no parameters. It can be found in the Modifier dialog box by clicking the More button at the top of the Modify panel.

Note   Even if the entire mesh is deleted using the Delete Mesh Modifier, the object still remains. To completely delete an object use the Delete key.

Using the Cap Holes Modifier

The Cap Holes Modifier can instantly detect and fill holes that are sometimes found in the geometry of imported objects. A hole is caused by an edge that is only connected to a single face. This Modifier works best on holes that are planar, and attempts to correct nonplanar holes. This Modifier can be accessed from the Modifier dialog box.

For example, if you create an Extruded object without any caps, the Cap Holes Modifier can be used to create caps for that object.

Using the MeshSmooth Modifier

The MeshSmooth Modifier, located in the Modifier dialog box, smoothes the entire surface of an object by applying a chamfer function to both vertices and edges at the same time. This Modifier has the greatest effect on sharp corners and edges. It also includes options to control the Smoothing Strength, the Subdivision amount, and the Weighting of control vertices. You can also produce a NURMS object that is similar to NURBS in that it uses weighted control points to affect the surface.

Tutorial: Creating a heart-shaped NURMS

Here's an example just in time for Valentine's Day. Create a spline heart, extrude it, and then convert it to a NURMS object using the MeshSmooth Modifier.

To create a heart-shaped NURMS object, follow these steps:

1. Open the Create panel, click the Shapes category, and then click the Lines button. Set the Creation Method types to Bézier and draw a heart-shaped spline. Convert the spline to an Editable Spline by right-clicking the spline and selecting Convert to Editable Spline from the pop-up menu. Then edit the vertices until the curves look smooth using the Vertex subobject mode.

 Tip
An easier method is to draw only half the heart and then to mirror it using the Tools ⇨ Mirror command.

2. With the spline shape complete and selected, click the Extrude button in the Modify panel and enter an Amount value of **100**.

3. Click the More button at the top of the Modify panel to open the list of additional modifiers, select the MeshSmooth Modifier, and click OK. In the Parameters rollout, select the NURMS option (if it isn't already selected).

4. If you click the Sub-Object button and select Vertex, you'll notice that the transform buttons are all disabled. Changing the weight of its vertices alters a NURMS object. In the Parameters rollout, select the Display Control Mesh option, select the two vertices at the heart's top (the bottom of the crease), and increase the Weight value to **100**. This will cause the faces to gravitate toward the selected vertices.

Figure 12-15 shows the NURMS heart.

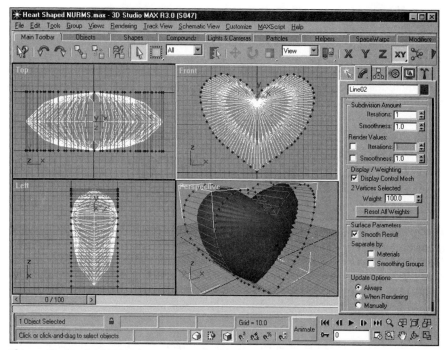

Figure 12-15: A NURMS heart created with the MeshSmooth Modifier

Summary

Meshes are probably the most common 3D modeling types. They can be created by converting objects to Editable Meshes or by collapsing the Stack. Editable Meshes in MAX have a host of features for editing meshes, as you learned in this chapter. You also found out that there are several Modifiers that work with meshes.

More specifically, in this chapter you've

   ✦ Learned the difference between parametric and nonparametric objects

   ✦ Created Editable Mesh objects by converting other objects or collapsing the Stack

   ✦ Discovered the features of the Editable Mesh object

   ✦ Modified mesh objects with Modifiers

In the next chapter, you'll learn about patch objects.

✦   ✦   ✦

Creating Patches

Patches are a modeling type that exists somewhere between polygon meshes and NURBS. They are essentially polygon surfaces stretched along a closed spline. Modifying the spline alters the surface of the patch.

This chapter describes how to create and use patches.

Introducing Patch Grids

Because patches have splines along their edges, a patch can be deformed in ways that a normal polygon cannot. For example, a polygon always needs to be co-planar, meaning that if you look at it on edge it appears as a line. A patch doesn't have this requirement and can actually bend, which permits greater control over the surface.

Creating a Patch Grid

Patches are usually named according to the number of vertices at their edges; for example, a Tri Patch has three vertices, a Quad Patch has four vertices, and so on. A Quad Patch is made up of 36 visible rectangular faces and a Tri Patch has 72 triangular faces, as shown in Figure 13-1.

To create patches, open the Create panel and select the Geometry category. In the Object-Type drop-down list, select Patch Grids. Under the Object Type rollout, two buttons will appear: Quad Patch and Tri Patch. To create a patch grid, select a button, click in a viewport, and drag to specify the dimensions of the grid.

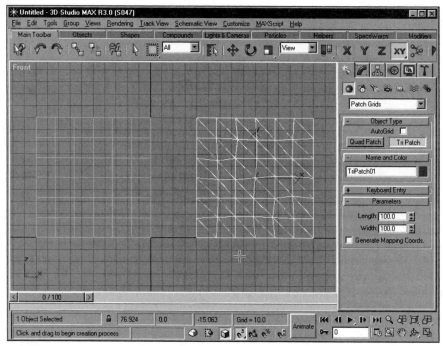

Figure 13-1: A Quad Patch and a Tri Patch

There is also a Keyboard Entry rollout that you can use to create patch grids with precise dimensions. To use this rollout, enter the grid's position coordinates and its dimensions and click the Create button. The X, Y, and Z coordinates define the location of the center of the grid.

Patch grid Parameters include Length and Width values as well as the number of Segments for each dimension. A Segment value of 1 will create 6 rows or columns of segments, so the total number of polygons for a Quad Patch will never drop below 36. Tri Patches do not have a Segments parameter. You can also select to automatically Generate Mapping Coordinates.

Newly created patches will always be flat.

Tutorial: Creating a checkerboard

In this tutorial, we'll create a simple checkerboard. To keep the white squares separate from the black squares, we'll use Quad and Tri Patches.

To create a checkerboard from patch surfaces, follow these steps:

1. Open the Create panel and click the Geometry category. Select Patch Grids from the drop-down list.

2. Right-click the 3D Snap Toggle at the bottom of the window to open the Grid and Snaps Settings dialog box. Click the Clear All button and select Grid Points. Close the dialog box and select the 2D Snap Toggle flyout (hold down the 3D Snap Toggle button until the flyout appears).

3. Click the Quad Patch button and, in the Top View, drag a perfect square over one construction-grid square (the grid square should have ten subdivisions).

4. Click the Tri Patch button and create another square next to the Quad Patch.

5. Select the Quad Patch, click its color swatch, and change its object color to black. Then select the Tri Patch and make its color white.

Caution

With the Tri Patch's object color set to white, it can be difficult to tell when it is selected.

6. Select both patches and clone them by selecting Edit ➪ Clone. Select the Copy option.

7. Activate the Select and Rotate button, then right-click it to access the Rotate Transform Type-In. Enter **180** in the Z-axis Offset field and press the Enter key. Close the Rotate Transform Type-In.

8. With the cloned grids still selected, click the Select and Move button and right-click it to open the Move Transform Type-In again. This time enter **100** in the Y-axis offset field and press Enter. Close the Move Transform Type-In.

9. You should now have a two-by-two grid of alternating black and white squares. Select all four squares and open the Array dialog box by selecting Tools ➪ Array.

10. In the Array dialog box, enter a value of **200** in the Incremental X-axis Move field, a value of **4** in both the 1D and 2D fields, and a value of **200** in the Y-axis Incremental Row Offset field. Then click OK.

Figure 13-2 shows the completed checkerboard. The next section covers how to edit individual patches.

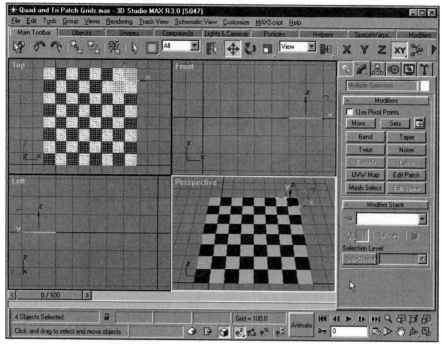

Figure 13-2: A checkerboard created using patch grids

Editing Patches

Once a patch grid has been created, you can alter its shape by applying Modifiers to it or you can work with the Patch's subobjects. The Modify panel has many tools for controlling patches and working with their individual subobjects. But, before you can access any of these tools, you'll need to convert the patch grid to an Editable Patch object or apply the Edit Patch Modifier.

Editable Patches versus the Edit Patch Modifier

The differences between Editable Patches and objects with the Edit Patch Modifier applied are subtle. The main difference between these two appears in the Modifier Stack. Editable Patch objects have the type Editable Patch displayed at the bottom of the Stack. This eliminates the parametric nature of the patch grid and creates a new object type.

Patch grids with the Edit Patch Modifier applied maintain their creation parameters and the Edit Patch Modifier is displayed in the Stack above the object type where it can be moved or removed at any time.

The other big difference is that the transformation of an Editable Patch subobject can be animated, while patch grids with the Edit Patch Modifier cannot.

Editable Patches and patch grids with the Edit Patch Modifier applied both access subobjects and their parameters in the same way. These will be covered in the next section.

Note The Editable Patch object actually requires less memory than using the Edit Patch Modifier and is the recommended method.

Converting to an Editable Patch

Editable Patches are composed of a surface applied over a frame of edges and vertices. These edges and vertices make up control points, and transforming these control points alters the patch surface.

To convert a patch grid into an Editable Patch, click the Edit Stack button before any Modifiers have been applied. This opens a small pop-up menu from which you can select Convert To Editable Patch. You can also right-click an object and select Convert to Editable Patch from the pop-up menu.

Primitive and mesh objects can also be converted to Editable Patches by right-clicking the object and selecting Convert to Editable Patch. Spline shapes can be converted to Editable Patch as well, but in a more roundabout way. First, convert the spline to a mesh object. If the spline is a closed spline, then a face will be created. Using the right-click menu again, convert the mesh object to an Editable Patch.

Another way to create an Editable Patch is to collapse the Stack of a patch grid. Click the Edit Stack button, and, from the small pop-up menu, select Edit Stack to open the Edit Modifier Stack dialog box. Select the Collapse All button and click OK.

Selecting Patch Sub-Objects

Editable Patches and the Edit Patch Modifier make patch subobjects accessible. The subobjects for patches include Vertex, Edge, and Patch.

Before you can edit patch subobjects, you must select them. To select a subobject type, click the Sub-Object button in the Modify panel and select a Sub-Object type from the drop-down list. Alternatively, you can click the red-colored icons under the Selection rollout.

New Feature   The Sub-Object type icons under the Selection rollout are new to Release 3.

A third way to enter subobject edit mode is to right-click the Editable Patch and select Sub-Object and the subobject type to edit from the pop-up menu.

Clicking the Sub-Object button again exits subobject edit mode. Remember, you must exit this mode before you can select another object.

Tip   The Sub-Object button turns yellow when selected to remind you that you are in subobject edit mode.

Many subobjects can be selected at once by dragging an outline over them. You can also select and deselect many subobjects by holding down the Ctrl key while clicking them. Holding down the Alt key will remove any selected vertices from the current selection set.

After selecting several vertices, you can create a Named Selection Set by typing a name in the Name Selection Sets drop-down list in the main toolbar. These Selection Sets can then be Copied and Pasted onto other patch objects. The Selection rollout also lets you filter which objects are displayed when selected — Vertices or Vectors. The Lock Handles option causes all selected Bézier handles to move together when one handle is moved.

Editing Vertices

Once Vertex subobject mode is selected, you can transform selected vertices using the transform buttons in the main toolbar, or you can move or rotate the selected vertices by transforming the handles, shown as small green squares. Dragging these handles will change the surface of the patch.

Patch vertices can be either of two types: Coplanar or Corner. Coplanar vertices maintain a smooth transition from vertex to vertex because their handles are locked. This causes the handles to always move so as to prevent any surface discontinuities. The handles of corner vertices can be dragged to create gaps and seams in the surface.

You can switch between these different vertex types by right-clicking a vertex while in vertex subobject mode and selecting the desired type from the pop-up menu.

Tip Holding down the Shift key while clicking and dragging on a handle will unlock the handles and automatically change the vertex type to Corner.

Much of the power of editing patches is contained within the Geometry rollout. You can use this rollout to attach new patches, weld and delete vertices, and bind and hide vertices. Some Geometry buttons may be disabled in Vertex subobject mode but are enabled in one of the other subobject editing modes.

Bind and Unbind

The Bind button can connect edge vertices of one patch to an edge of another patch, which is useful for connecting edges with a different number of vertices. Be aware that the two patches must be part of the same object. To use the Bind feature, click the Bind button, then drag a line from a vertex to the edge where it should join.

Caution If you're combining edges, weld the corner vertices together first. If you try to Bind a vertex before welding the corner vertices, then the Bind action won't work.

The Bind button attaches vertices to edges; to attach vertices to vertices, use the Weld button. The point of contact between the two patches will be seamless and the vertex will become part of the interior. The Bind button attaches vertices to edges. If you want to attach vertices to vertices, use the Weld button instead, as discussed in the next subsection.

To exit Bind mode, click the Bind button again or right-click in a viewport.

The Unbind button is used to detach vertices that have been connected using the Bind button.

New Feature The Bind and Unbind buttons are new to Release 3.

Weld

The Weld button enables you to take two or more vertices and weld them into one vertex. To use this feature, move the vertices close to one another, drag an outline over them to select them all, and then click the Weld button. You can tell if the weld has been successful by looking at the number of vertices selected at the bottom of the Selection rollout. If the Weld was unsuccessful, increase the Weld Threshold specified by the spinner and try again.

Figure 13-3 shows two inverted sloping patches that have been combined. The resolution of the patch on the right is twice that of the patch on the left. The Bind button was used to attach the center vertex to the edge of the other patch. Notice how the seam between the two patches is smooth.

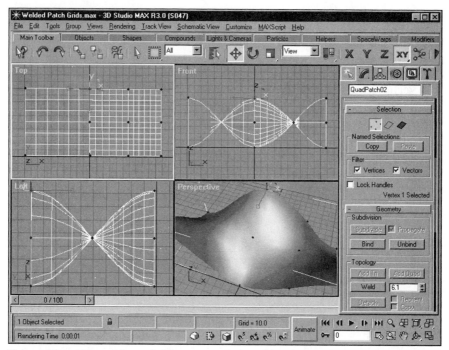

Figure 13-3: Two patches of different resolutions have been combined using the Weld and Bind buttons.

Attach

The Attach button is available with all subobject modes and even when you're not in subobject mode. It is used to add objects to the current Editable Patch object, such as primitives, mesh objects, and other patch objects. However, be aware that you cannot attach a spline.

To use this feature, select an object, click the Attach button, and move the mouse over the object to attach. The cursor will change over acceptable objects. Click the object to be attached. Click the Attach button again or right-click in the viewport to exit Attach mode. The Reorient option aligns the attached object's local coordinate system with the local coordinate system of the patch that it is being attached to.

Caution

Converting mesh objects to patch objects results in objects with many vertices.

Delete

The Delete button deletes the selected vertices and their control points. This button works for all the subobject types.

Caution

Deleting a vertex also deletes all faces and edges connected to that vertex. For example, deleting a single (top) vertex from a sphere that has been converted to an Editable Patch object leaves only a hemisphere.

Hide and Unhide All

The Hide and Unhide All buttons are used to hide and unhide vertices. They can be used in any subobject mode. To hide a subobject, select the subobject and click the Hide button. To Unhide the hidden subobjects, click the Unhide All button.

New
Feature

The Hide and Unhide All buttons are new to Release 3.

Surface Settings

The View Steps value determines the resolution of the patch grid that is displayed in the viewport. This resolution can be changed for rendering using the Render Steps value. The Interior Edges can be turned off altogether using the Show Interior Edges option.

A Quad patch with a View Steps value of 0 is a simple square. Figure 13-4 shows four spheres that have all been cloned from one, converted to Editable Patches, and set with different View Steps. From left to right, the View Steps values are 1, 2, 3, and 4.

Editing Edges

Edges are the lines that run between two vertices. You can select multiple edges by holding down the Ctrl key while clicking the edges or the Alt key to remove selected edges from the current selection set.

Many of the features in the Geometry rollout work in the same way as the Vertex subobjects, but the Geometry rollout also includes some features that are only enabled in Edge subobject mode, like the ones in the following sections.

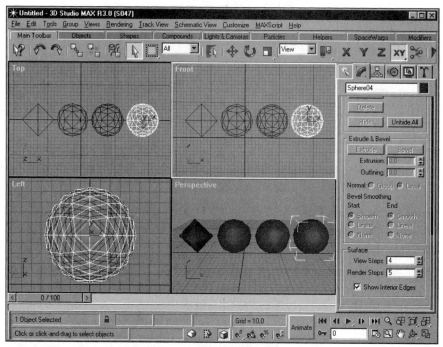

Figure 13-4: The only differences in these patch spheres are the View Steps values.

Subdivide

The Subdivide button is used to increase the resolution of a patch. This is done by splitting an edge into two separate edges divided at the original edge's center. To use this feature, select an edge or edges and click the Subdivide button. The Propagate option causes the edges or neighboring patches to be subdivided also. Using Subdivide without the Propagate option enabled can cause cracks to appear in the patch. The Subdivide button also works on patch subobjects.

In Figure 13-5, I've subdivided a Quad Patch edge five times both horizontally and vertically.

Add Tri and Add Quad

Quad and Tri Patches can be added to any open edge of a patch. To do this, select the open edge or edges and click the Add Tri or Add Quad button. The new patch extends along the current curvature of the patch. To add a patch to a closed surface, like a box, you'll first need to detach one of the patches to create an open edge. This feature provides a way to extend the current patch.

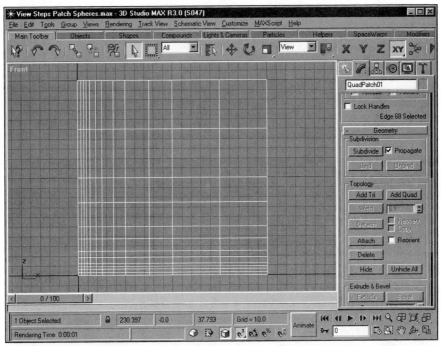

Figure 13-5: By subdividing edge subobjects, you can control where the greatest resolution is located.

Editing Patch Sub-Objects

Transforming a patch object containing only one patch works the same way for subobject mode as it works for normal transformations. Working with the Patch subobject on an object that contains several patches lets you transform individual patches. A key advantage of working with the Patch subobjects is controlling their Geometry using the buttons in the Geometry rollout. The following sections discuss the additional features available in Patch subobject mode.

Detach

The Detach button separates the selected subobjects from the rest of the object. Using this button opens the Detach dialog box, which enables you to name the detached subobject. The Reorient option realigns the detached subobject patch to match the position and orientation of the current active patch. The Copy option creates a new copy of the detached subobject.

Extrude

The Extrude button adds depth to a patch by replicating a patch surface and creating sides to connect the new patch surface to the original. For example, a square patch grid that is extruded forms a cube. To use this feature, select a patch, click the Extrude button, and then drag in a viewport — the patch will interactively show the extrude depth. Release the button when you've reached the desired distance.

Alternatively, you can specify an extrude depth in the Extrusion spinner. The Outlining value lets you resize the extruded patch. Positive outlining values cause the extrusion to get larger, while negative values reduce its size. The Normal Group option extrudes all selected patches along the normal for the group and the Normal Local option moves each individual patch along its local normal. To exit extrude mode, click the Extrude button again or right-click in the viewport.

Figure 13-6 shows a sphere that has been converted to an Editable Patch. Each of its eight patches have then been selected and extruded using a value of 50 with Smooth settings.

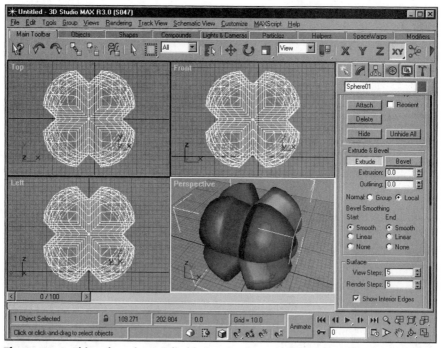

Figure 13-6: This sphere is an Editable Patch whose individual patches have been extruded.

Bevel

The Bevel button extrudes a patch and then lets you bevel the edges. To use this feature, select a patch, click the Bevel button, and then drag in a viewport to the Extrusion depth and release the button. Then drag again to specify the Outlining amount.

You can use the same options for the Bevel button as for the Extrude button described previously. In addition, the Bevel button includes Smoothing Options for the bevel. The Start and End Smoothing options can be set to Smooth, Linear, or None.

Figure 13-7 displays another version of the patch sphere. This one was extruded with the Bevel button and then an Outline value of −20 was entered.

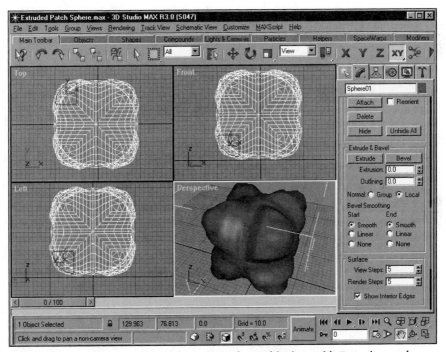

Figure 13-7: Another version of the same sphere, this time with Extrusion and Outlining values applied

Surface Properties Rollout

If patch subobject mode is selected, an additional rollout for assigning Material IDs and Smoothing Groups appears. Material IDs are used by the Multi/Sub-Object material type to apply different materials to different patches within an object. By selecting a patch subobject, you can use this control to apply a unique material to each patch.

You can also assign a patch to a unique Smoothing Group. To do this, select a patch and click a Smoothing Group number.

Tutorial: Modeling a shell

A patch object can be used to create a common beach shell, as we'll do in this tutorial.

To model a shell using a patch, follow these steps:

1. Start with a simple circle. In the Create panel, click the Shapes category button and then click the Circle button. Drag in the viewport to create a circle.

2. Open the Modify panel and click the Extrude button. In the Parameters section, enter a value of **5.0** in the Amount field and make sure both the Cap Start and Cap End options are enabled. You could select the Output to be Patch option, but for the purposes of this tutorial, select Mesh instead.

3. Right-click the object and select Convert to Editable Patch from the pop-up menu. This will create lines from a single vertex on one edge of the circle to all other vertices around its perimeter.

4. Click the Vertex icon to enter Vertex subobject mode. Then, select and move several neighboring vertices on each side of the main vertex to form a fan-shaped patch.

5. Once the neighboring vertices have been positioned, select them all and click the Weld button. If the vertices fail to be welded, increase the Weld Threshold and try again.

6. Click the Edge subobject icon in the Modify panel and select every other interior set of edges. Make sure that you select both the front and back edges. The Info line at the bottom of the Selection rollout will tell you what is selected. When you've got all the edges selected, press the Spacebar to lock the selection.

7. Click the Select and Move button and move the edges up in the Top view. This will create a zigzag pattern on the surface of the patch.

Figure 13-8 shows the competed shell.

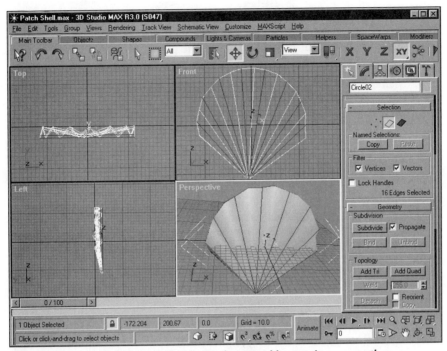

Figure 13-8: This shell is an Editable Patch created by moving every other interior edge.

Tutorial: Creating a patchwork quilt

When I think of patches, I think of a 3D MAX object type, but for many people, "patches" would instead bring to mind small scraps of cloth used to make a quilt. Because they share the same name, maybe we can use MAX patches to create a quilt.

To create a quilt using patches, follow these steps:

1. In the Create panel, click the Geometry category button and then in the subcategory drop-down list, select the Patch Grids subcategory.

2. Turn the 2D Snap Toggle on (found at the bottom of the window) and create a number of consecutive Tri Patch grids out in the Top view. (I made 54 patches to create a 6 × 9 patch grid, as you can see in the final quilt shown in Figure 13-9.)

Note

You could also use the Array tool to accomplish this.

3. Select the patch grid in the upper left corner, and from the right-click pop-up menu select Convert to Editable Patch. This will open the Modify panel.

4. Click the Attach button and attach all the patch grids by clicking each one individually. Click the Attach button again to exit Attach mode.

5. Open the Material Editor by selecting Tools ➪ Material Editor and click the first sample slot. Then click the Type button. This will open the Material/Map Browser. In the list of materials, locate and double-click the Multi/Sub-Object material. This will load it into the selected sample slot and display the Multi/Sub-Object Basic Parameters rollout in the Material Editor.

6. In the Multi/Sub-Object Basic Parameters rollout, click the color swatches to the right of the Material button to open the Color Selector. Select different colors for each of the first ten material ID slots.

7. Drag the Multi/Sub-Object material from its sample slot in the Material Editor and onto the patch object. Close the Material/Map Browser and the Material Editor.

8. In the Modify panel, select the Patch subobject and scroll to the bottom of the Modify panel to the Surface Properties rollout.

9. Assign each patch a separate Material ID by clicking a patch and changing the ID number in the rollout field.

10. Select all the patches by dragging an outline around them and click the Extrude button. Enter a value of **10** in the Amount field.

Figure 13-9 shows the finished quilt. Because it's a patch, you'll be able to drape it over objects easily.

Modifying Patches

When working with either a simple patch grid or an Editable Patch, you can still apply almost all available Modifiers. There are several Modifiers that are unique to patch objects, one of which is the Edit Patch Modifier. This section covers a few new Modifiers as applied to patch objects.

Tutorial: Creating a terrain

As a simple example of applying a Modifier to a patch grid, we'll create a terrain. Using a patch grid and the Noise Modifier, we can quickly create a hilly or jagged terrain.

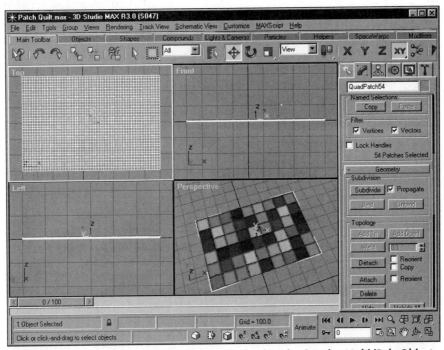

Figure 13-9: A quilt composed of patches and colored using the Multi/Sub-Object material

To create a terrain, follow these steps:

1. In the Create panel, click the Geometry category button and select the Patch Grids subcategory from the subcategory drop-down list.

2. Click the Quad Patch button and create a patch in the Top view. In the Parameters rollout, change the Length and Width Segments to **20** each. This will supply ample resolution for the terrain.

3. Open the Modify panel and click the Noise button. In the Parameters rollout, enter a Z Strength value of **200** for smooth, rolling hills or click the Fractal option for more rough and jagged peaks.

Figure 13-10 shows a sample terrain with gently rolling hills.

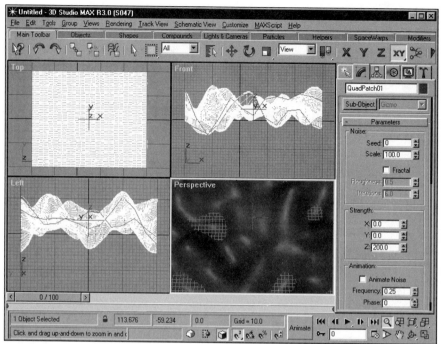

Figure 13-10: A terrain created from a patch grid and the Noise Modifier

Note   As an alternative way to create terrains, check out the new Terrain compound object covered in Chapter 15, "Building Compound Objects."

Edit Patch Modifier

The Edit Patch Modifier is represented differently in the Stack, but all the features of this Modifier are the same as those of the Editable Patch covered previously. If you want to animate the features of an Editable Patch, use the Edit Patch Modifier. The Edit Patch Modifier can even be applied to an Editable Patch.

Using the PatchDeform Modifier

The PatchDeform Modifier deforms an object to match the contours of a patch object. To use it, apply the Modifier to the object you want to deform, click the Pick Patch button in the parameters rollout, and then select a patch object.

Note This Modifier works the same way as the PathDeform and SurfDeform Modifiers, but deforms using a patch instead of a spline or NURBS object.

Tutorial: Deforming a car going over a hill

Have you seen those commercials that use rubber cars to follow the curvature of the road as they drive? In this tutorial, we'll use the PatchDeform Modifier to bend a car over a hill made from a patch.

To deform a car according to a patch surface, follow these steps:

1. First create a patch hill. In the Create panel, click the Geometry category button and select the Patch Grids subcategory. Click the Quad Patch button and drag in the viewport.

2. In the Modify panel click the Edit Stack button and select Convert to Editable Patch from the pop-up menu. Select the Vertex subobject mode and drag an outline over the two top vertices in the Top view. Click the Select and Move button and drag the vertices up along the Z-axis to form a hill. Click the Sub-Object button again to exit vertex subobject mode.

3. With the patch selected, select the Tools ⇨ Mirror command and mirror a Copy about the X-axis. Then drag the new patch in the Left view until the top edges match up.

4. Back in the Modify panel, click the Attach button and select both patches to combine them into one object (make sure the Reorient option isn't selected). Click the Attach button to deselect it, select the Vertex subobject mode again, drag an outline over the two overlapping vertices that lie along the center edges, and click the Weld button. Repeat this for the other two vertices on the opposite side.

5. Import a car model using the File ⇨ Import command. Viewpoint Datalabs created the model in this example. Position the car and scale it to roughly match the size of the patch. In the Modify panel, click the More button to open the Modifiers list. Select the PatchDeform Modifier and click OK.

6. In the Parameters rollout, click the Pick Patch button and select the patch object. An orange gizmo will appear under the car and the car will be bent around it. Set the U and V Percent values to 50 and the U and V Stretch values to 1.0. I've set the Deform Plane to the XY plane.

Figure 13-11 shows the results of this tutorial.

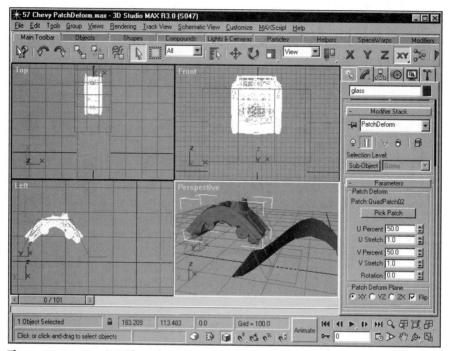

Figure 13-11: Our '57 Chevy hugs the road thanks to the PatchDeform Modifier

Using the Surface Tools Modifiers

The CrossSection and Surface Modifiers are Surface Tools, useful for creating organic, smooth surfaces. First, the CrossSection Modifier is used to combine several splines into a single spline object, and then the Surface Modifier is used to create a surface over a network of connected splines. The resulting surface is a patch object. Once the surface is created, you can apply the Edit Patch Modifier to further edit and refine the patch surface.

 New Feature   The Surface Tools are new to Release 3.

Tutorial: Modeling the Mercury space capsule

One of the early space capsules used in the space race was the Mercury space capsule. Although a lot of advanced technology was contained within the capsule, the exterior shape was relatively simple. Primitive shapes could be used to create the capsule, but in this tutorial, we'll create it using the Surface Tools.

To create a space capsule, follow these steps:

1. In the Create panel, click the Shapes category button and then click the Circle shape. Select the 2D Snap Toggle to snap the center of the circles to the same point. Drag in the Front viewport to create eight circles of the following sizes: one with a radius of **150, 145,** and **140**; two with radius values of **45**: two more at **25**; and one at **15.**

2. Click the Select and Move button and position the circles in the Top view from largest to smallest.

3. Select a circle on one end, right-click it, and select Convert to Editable Spline from the pop-up menu. Open the Modify panel, click the Attach button, and then click each individual circle in order (the order is important for the CrossSection Modifier). This will attach all the circles together into one Editable Spline object. Click the Attach button again to exit Attach model.

Tip   You can check the spline order by entering Spline subobject mode and selecting each spline. The spline number will be displayed at the bottom of the Selection rollout.

4. In the Modify panel, click the More button to open the additional Modifiers dialog box list and select the CrossSection Modifier. This will automatically connect all the splines in order by connecting their vertices. Select the Linear option in the Parameters rollout.

5. Click the More button and select the Surface Modifier from the additional Modifiers dialog box. This will create a surface that covers the spline framework. The surface that is created is a patch object. If the module looks inverted, select the Flip Normals option.

Figure 13-12 shows the completed Mercury space capsule. Using the Surface Tools to create patch objects results in objects that are easy to modify. You can change any patch subobjects by applying the Edit Patch Modifier and using the rollouts in the Modify panel.

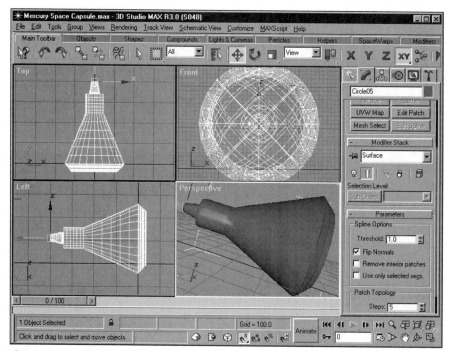

Figure 13-12: The Mercury space capsule, created using the CrossSection and Surface Modifiers

Summary

Patches don't have the overhead of NURBS objects and are better optimized than mesh objects. In this chapter, you learned how to create and edit patches and viewed a few Modifiers that work with patches.

More specifically, in this chapter, you've

✦ Learned to create Quad and Tri Patch grids

✦ Discovered the features of an Editable Patch object

✦ Modified patches with Modifiers such as the PatchDeform and Surface Tools Modifiers

Now that splines, meshes, and patches have been covered, we focus next on working with Loft objects. Loft objects are actually part of the Compound Objects subcategory, but they are important enough to get their own chapter. They will also be a good precursor to NURBS.

✦   ✦   ✦

Creating Loft Objects

Lofting is a term that comes from the shipbuilding industry. It describes a method for building ships, which creates and positions the cross-sections and then attaches a surface or skin along the length of the cross-sections. As you will discover in this chapter, you can create loft objects in MAX in much the same way.

Creating a Loft Object

To create a Loft object, you need to have at least two spline shapes: one shape that defines the path of the Loft and a second shape that defines its cross-section. Once the shapes are created, open the Create panel, click the Geometry category button and, from the subcategory drop-down, select Compound Objects. A Loft button will be enabled if two or more splines are present in the viewport.

Note There are many different Compound Objects. The others are discussed in Chapter 15, "Building Compound Objects."

Using the Get Shape and Get Path buttons

After you click the Loft button, the Creation Method rollout will display the Get Path and Get Shape buttons, which are used to specify which spline will be the path and which spline will be the cross-section. Select a spline and then click either the Get Path button or the Get Shape button. If you click the Get Shape button, the selected spline will be the path and the next spline shape you select will be the cross-section. If you click the Get Path button, the selected spline will be the shape and the next spline shape you select will be the path.

Note   After you click the Get Path or Get Spline button, though the cursor changes when you're over a valid spline, not all spline shapes can be used to create Loft objects. For example, you cannot use a spline created with the Donut button as a path.

When creating a Loft object with the Get Shape and Get Path buttons, you can specify either to Move the spline shape, or to create a Copy or an Instance of it. The Move option replaces both splines with a Loft object. The Copy option leaves both splines in the viewport and creates a new Loft object. The Instance maintains a link between the spline and the Loft object. This link enables you to modify the original spline. The Loft object will be updated automatically.

The vertex order of the path spline is important. The Loft object will be created starting at the vertex numbered 1.

Note   You can tell which vertex is the first by enabling Vertex Numbering in the Selection rollout of an Editable Spline.

Tutorial: Creating a simple loft

To understand the difference between making a shape a cross-section and making it a path, you can try this quick tutorial.

To create a simple loft, follow these steps:

1. In the Create panel, click the Shapes category button. Then select the Ellipse button and drag two simple ellipses in the Front view. Then click the Star button and create two stars in the Front view.

2. With the Create panel still open, click the Geometry category button and, from the subcategory drop-down, select Compound Objects. Select one of the ellipses and click the Loft button. In the Creation Method rollout, click the Get Path button and then click one of the stars. A new loft object will appear, one that uses the ellipse as the cross-section and the star as the path.

3. Select the other ellipse and click the Loft button again. This time, click the Get Shape button and select the second star shape. This will also create a Loft object, this time with a star cross-section and an elliptical path.

Notice in Figure 14-1, how different these two Loft objects are. The first followed the star spline with an oval cross-section and the second followed the oval spline with a star cross-section.

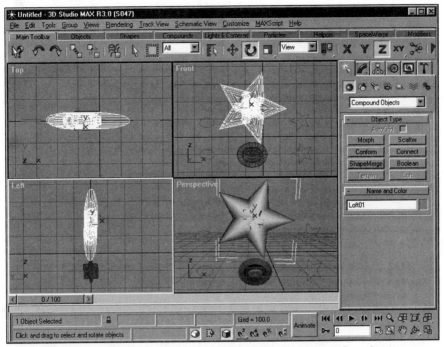

Figure 14-1: Two different Loft objects created from the same spline shapes

Controlling Loft Parameters

When a Loft object is created, several rollouts appear. These include the Surface Parameters, Path Parameters, and Skin Parameter rollouts.

Controlling Surface Parameters

All Loft objects include the Surface Parameters rollout. Using this rollout you can set the smoothing of the Loft object with two different options: Smooth Length and Smooth Width. You can use the Mapping options to control the mapping of textures by setting values for the number of times the map repeats over the Length or Width of the Loft. The Normalize option applies the map to the surface evenly or proportionately according to the shape's vertex spacing. You can set the Loft object to automatically generate Material and Shape Ids, and you can specify the output of the Loft to be either a Patch or Mesh.

Changing Path Parameters

The Path Parameters rollout will let you position several different cross-sectional shapes at different positions along the Loft path. The Path value indicates either the Distance or Percentage along the path where this new shape should be located. The Snap option, if turned on, enables you to snap to consistent distances along the path. The Path Steps option enables you to place new shapes at steps along the path where the vertices are located. Each path will have a different number of steps depending on its complexity.

The viewport displays a small yellow X at the location where the new cross-sectional shape will be inserted. At the bottom of the rollout are three buttons, which are illustrated and described in Table 14-1.

Table 14-1
Path Rollout Buttons

Toolbar Button	Name	Description
	Pick Shape	Selects a new cross-section spline to be inserted at the specified location
	Previous Shape	Moves to the previous cross-section shape along the Loft path
	Next Shape	Moves to the next cross-section shape along the Loft path

Setting Skin Parameters

The Skin Parameters rollout includes many options for determining the complexity of the Loft skin. You can specify whether to cap either end of the Loft using the Cap Start and/or Cap End options. The caps can be either Morph or Grid type.

This rollout also includes many options for controlling the look of the skin. These include the following:

✦ **Shape and Path Steps**—Set the number of segments that appear in each vertex's cross-sectional shape and between each division along the path. The straight segments are ignored if the Optimize Path option is selected.

✦ **Optimize Shapes and Paths**—Reduce the Loft's complexity by deleting any unneeded edges or vertices.

✦ **Adaptive Path Steps**—Automatically determine the number of steps to use for the path.

✦ **Contour** — Determines how the cross-sectional shapes line up with the path. If this option is enabled, the cross-section is aligned to be perpendicular to the path at all times. If disabled, this option will cause the cross-sectional shapes to maintain their orientation as the path is traversed.

✦ **Banking** — Causes the cross-section shape to rotate as the path bends.

✦ **Constant Cross-Section** — Scales the cross-sectional shapes in order to maintain a uniform width along the path. Turning this option off will cause the cross-sections to pinch at any sharp angles along the path.

✦ **Linear Interpolation** — Causes straight linear edges to appear between different cross-sectional shapes. Turning this option off will cause smooth curves to connect various shapes.

✦ **Flip Normals** — Used to correct difficulties that would appear with the normals. Many times the normals will be flipped accidentally when the Loft is created.

✦ **Quad Sides** — Creates four-sided polygons to connect to adjacent cross-section shapes with the same number of sides.

✦ **Transform Degrade** — Makes the loft skin disappear when subobjects are transformed. This will help you better visualize the cross-sectional area while it is being moved.

The Display options at the bottom of the Skin Parameters rollout give you the choice of displaying the skin in all viewports or displaying the Loft skin only in the viewports with shading turned on.

Tutorial: Designing a slip-proof hanger

As an example of creating a Loft object with different cross-sectional shapes, we'll design a new hanger that includes some rough edges along its bottom section to keep slacks from sliding off.

To design a hanger Loft object with different cross-sections, follow these steps:

1. In the Create panel, click the Shapes category button and then click the Line button. In the Front view, drag a rough outline of the hanger, starting at the hook at the top and continuing until it ends at the neck.

2. Open the Modify panel, click the Edit Spline button, and, from the Sub-Object drop-down, select Vertex mode. To open the pop-up menu right-click the first vertex and select Bézier. Then select each remaining vertex and edit it by dragging its green Bézier control handles until the hanger looks right.

3. Return to the Create panel, click the Shapes category button again, and use the Circle and Star buttons to create a small circle and a small six-sided star.

4. Click the Geometry category button again and select the Compound Objects subcategory from the drop-down list. Then select the hanger spline and click the Loft button. In the Creation Method rollout, click the Get Shape button and then click the small circle shape (make sure the Copy option is selected). This will loft the entire hanger with a circular cross section.

5. In the Path Parameters rollout, select the Path Steps option and increment the Path value until the yellow X marker in the viewport is positioned at the beginning of the hanger's bottom bar (at Step 53 for this tutorial). At this point, with the Get Shape button still active, click the small circular shape again. This will extend the circular cross section from the start at Step 0 to Step 53.

6. Increment the Path value by 1 to Step 54 and select the star shape. This will make the remainder of the hanger use a star-shaped cross section. Increment the Path value again to the end of the hanger's bottom bar (at Step 60) and select the star shape again to end the cross section.

Note   If you forget to start and end a section with the same cross section, the loft will blend between the two different cross sections.

7. Increment the Path value a final time to Step 61 and click the circular shape. Click the Get Shape button at the bottom of the Path Parameters dialog box to change the cross section of the hanger to the end of the path. Right-click in the viewport to exit Get Shape mode.

Figure 14-2 shows the finished designer hanger.

Using Deformations

When a Loft object is selected and the Modify panel is opened, the Deformation rollout appears. This rollout includes five buttons that let you Scale, Twist, Teeter, Bevel, and Fit the cross-section shapes along the path. All five buttons open similar graph windows that include control points and a line that represents the amount of the effect to apply. Next to each button is a toggle button with a light switch on it. This button enables or disables the respective effect.

The Deformation Window interface

All five deformation options use the same basic window and controls. The lines within the window represent the length of the path. As an example of the deformation window interface, Figure 14-3 shows the Scale Deformation window.

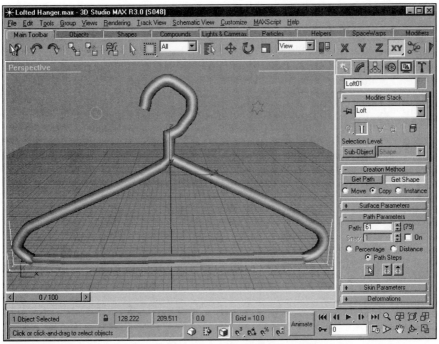

Figure 14-2: A lofted hanger created with two different cross-sectional shapes.

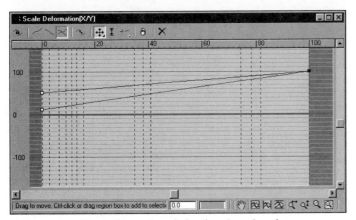

Figure 14-3: The Deformation dialog box interface lets you control the cross section over the length of the path.

Dragging the curve directly can modify the deformation curve. You can also insert control points at any location along the curve. These control points can be of one of three different types: Corner, Bézier Corner, or Bézier Smooth. Bézier type points have handles for controlling the curvature at the point. To change the point type, select the point and right-click. Then make your selection from the pop-up menu. The end points must always be either Corner or Bézier Corner type.

To move a control point, select and drag it or enter a horizontal and/or vertical value in the fields at the bottom of the window.

The buttons at the top of the Deformation window are described in Table 14-2.

Table 14-2 Deformation Dialog Box Buttons		
Toolbar Button	**Name**	**Description**
	Make Symmetrical	Links the two curves so that changes made to one curve are also made to the other
	Display X-Axis	Makes the line controlling the X-axis visible
	Display Y-Axis	Makes the line controlling the Y-axis visible
	Display XY axes	Makes both lines visible
	Swap Deform Curves	Switches the lines
	Move Control Point	Enables you to move control points and includes flyouts for horizontal and vertical movements
	Scale Control Point	Scales the selected control point
	Insert Corner Point Insert Bézier Point	Used to insert new points on a deformation curve
	Delete Control Point	Deletes the current control point

Toolbar Button	Name	Description
✕	Reset Curve	Returns the original curve
✋	Pan	Pans the curve as the mouse is dragged
⊠	Zoom Extents	Zooms to display the entire curve
⊠	Zoom Extents Horizontal	Zooms to display the entire horizontal curve range
⊠	Zoom Extents Vertical	Zooms to display the entire vertical curve range
◁▷	Zoom Horizontal	Zooms on the horizontal curve range
◻↕	Zoom Vertical	Zooms on the vertical curve range
🔍	Zoom	Zooms in and out as the mouse is dragged
🔍	Zoom Region	Zooms to the region specified by the mouse

Note   Several buttons are disabled on the Twist and Bevel Deformation windows because these dialog boxes have only one deformation curve.

At the bottom of the Deformation dialog boxes are two value fields. The value fields display the X and Y coordinate values for the currently selected point. The navigation buttons enable you to pan and zoom within the dialog box.

Scale Deformation

The Scale Deformation window can alter the relative scale of the Loft object at any point along its path. This window includes two lines — one red and one green. The red line displays the X-axis scale and the green line displays the Y-axis scale. By default, both lines are positioned equally at the 100 percent value. Specifying a value that is greater than 100 percent increases the scale and specifying a value that is less than 100 percent has the opposite effect.

Figure 14-4 shows a Scale Deformation applied to a lofted pillar.

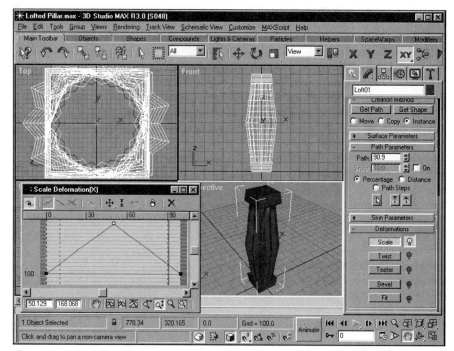

Figure 14-4: A Loft object with Scale Deformation applied along its length

Twist Deformation

The Twist Deformation rotates one cross section relative to the others and can be used to create an object that spirals along its path. This is similar to the Banking option, which can also produce rotations about the path.

The Twist Deformation window includes only one red line representing the rotation value. By default, this line is set to a 0-degree rotation value. Positive values result in counter-clockwise rotations, and negative values have the opposite effect.

Figure 14-5 shows a Twist Deformation applied to a lofted pillar.

Teeter Deformation

The Teeter Deformation rotates a cross section so that its outer edges move closer to the path. This is done by rotating the cross section about its local X- or Y-axis. The result is similar to that produced by the Contour option.

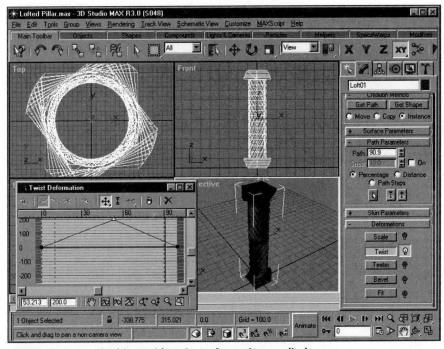

Figure 14-5: A Loft object with Twist Deformation applied

The Teeter Deformation window includes two lines — one red and one green. The red line displays the X-axis rotation, and the green line displays the Y-axis rotation. By default, both lines are positioned equally at the 0 degree value. Positive values result in counter-clockwise rotations, and negative values have the opposite effect.

Figure 14-6 shows a Teeter Deformation applied to a lofted pillar.

Bevel Deformation

The Bevel Deformation bevels the cross-section shapes. The Bevel Deformation window includes only one red line representing the amount of bevel that is applied. By default, this line is set to a 0 value. Positive values increase the bevel amount, which equals a reduction in the shape area, and negative values have the opposite effect.

The Bevel Deformation window can also be used to select three different types of beveling: Normal, Adaptive Linear, and Adaptive Cubic. The buttons for these three beveling types are illustrated and described in Table 14-3 and can be selected from a flyout at the right end of the window.

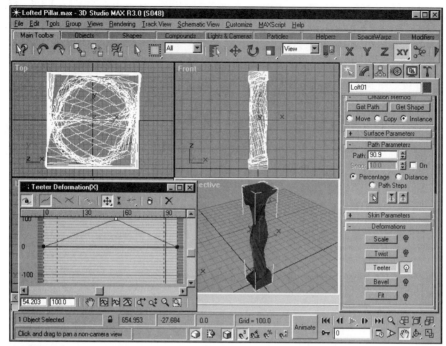

Figure 14-6: A Loft object with Teeter Deformation applied

Table 14-3
Bevel Deformation Buttons

Toolbar Button	Name	Description
	Normal Bevel	Produces a normal bevel with parallel edges, regardless of the path angle
	Adaptive (Linear)	Alters the bevel linearly, based on the path angle
	Adaptive (Cubic)	Alters the bevel using a cubic spline based on the path angle

Figure 14-7 shows a Bevel Deformation applied to a lofted pillar.

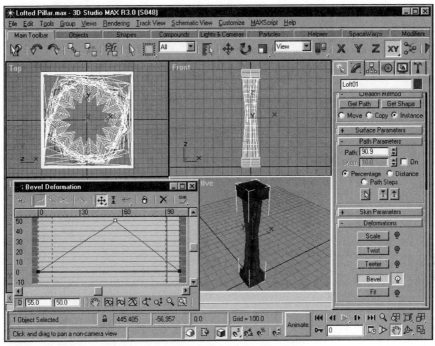

Figure 14-7: A Loft object with Bevel Deformation applied

Fit Deformation

The Fit Deformation window lets you specify a profile for the outer edges of the cross-section shapes to follow. This window includes two lines — one red and one green. The red line displays the X-axis scale, and the green line displays the Y-axis scale. By default, both lines are positioned equally at the 100 percent value. Specifying a value that is greater than 100 percent increases the scale, and specifying a value that is less than 100 percent has the opposite effect.

The Fit Deformation window includes eight buttons unique to it that are used to control the profile curves. These buttons are illustrated and described in Table 14-4.

Table 14-4
Fit Deformation Dialog Box Buttons

Toolbar Button	Name	Description
⟷	Mirror Horizontally	Mirrors the selection horizontally
↕	Mirror Vertically	Mirrors the selection vertically
↰	Rotate 90 degrees CCW	Rotates the selection 90 degrees counterclockwise
↵	Rotate 90 degrees CW	Rotates the selection 90 degrees clockwise
🖰	Delete Control Point	Deletes the selected control point
✕	Reset Curve	Returns the curve to its original form
🖰	Delete Curve	Deletes the selected curve
🖉	Get Shape	Selects a separate spline to use as a profile
✎	Generate Path	Replaces the current path with a straight line
⁺🖰	Lock Aspect	Maintains the relationship between height and width

Figure 14-8 shows a Fit Deformation applied to a lofted pillar. The Fit shape used is positioned to the right of the pillar in the Perspective view. It was loaded using the Get Shape button.

Modifying Loft Subobjects

When a Loft object is selected, you can work with its subobjects in the Modify panel. The subobjects for a Loft include Path and Shape. The Path subobject opens the Path Commands rollout. This rollout has only a single button — Put — for creating a copy of the Loft path. If this button is clicked, the Put To Scene dialog box appears enabling you to give the path a name and select to create it as a Copy or an Instance.

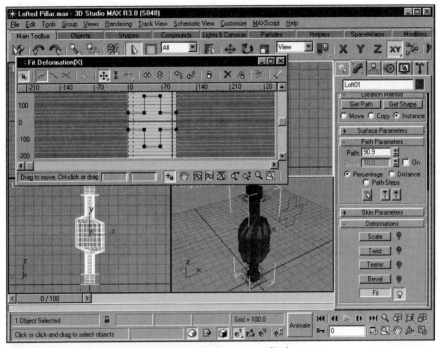

Figure 14-8: A Loft object with Fit Deformation applied

If your path is created as an Instance, you can edit the instance to control the Loft path.

The Shape subobject opens the Shape Commands rollout. This rollout also includes a Put button along with some additional controls. The Path Level value adjusts the shape's position on the path. The Compare button opens the Compare dialog box, which is discussed in the following section. The Reset button returns the shape to its former state before any rotation or scaling had taken place, and the Delete button deletes the shape entirely.

> **Note** You cannot delete a shape if it is the only shape in the Loft object.

The Shape Commands rollout also includes six Align buttons for aligning the shape to the Center, Default, Left, Right, Top, and Bottom. For the Loft object local coordinates, Left and Right move the shape along the X-axis, and Top and Bottom move it along the Y-axis.

Comparing shapes

The Compare dialog box superimposes selected cross-sectional shapes included in a Loft object on top of one another to check their center alignment. The button in the upper left corner is the Pick Shape button. This button lets you select which shapes to display in the dialog box. The button to its right is the Delete Shape button for removing a shape from the dialog box.

Figure 14-9 shows the Compare dialog box with the two shapes from the pillar example selected. Notice how the first vertices on these two shapes are in different locations. This causes the strange twisting at both the top and bottom of the pillar.

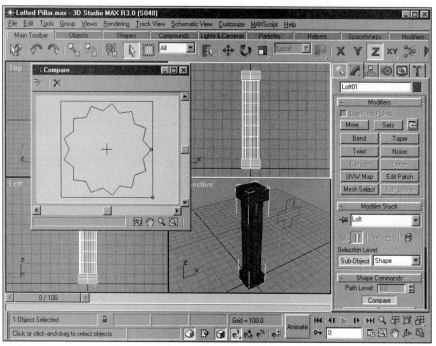

Figure 14-9: The Compare dialog box can be used to align shapes included in a Loft.

Tip

You can align these two vertices by subdividing the square shape in Edit Spline mode and selecting a new first vertex with the Make First button.

While the Compare dialog box is open, the Align buttons in the Shape Commands rollout are still active and can be used to move and position the shapes. The first vertex on each shape is shown as a small square. If these vertices aren't correctly aligned on top of one another, then the resulting Loft object will have skewed edges.

The lower right corner of the dialog box includes buttons to View Extents, Pan, Zoom, and Zoom Region.

Editing Loft paths

The original shapes that were used to create the Loft object can be edited at any time. These updates will also modify the Loft object. The shapes, if not visible, can be selected using the Select by Name button. The shapes maintain their base parameters or they can be converted to an Editable Spline.

Figure 14-10 shows our pillar Loft after its star shape has been modified. For this figure, the Fillet Radius 2 value has been set to 20.

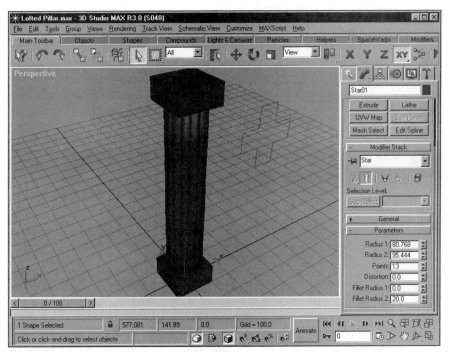

Figure 14-10: A modified pillar accomplished by changing the base parameters of the star cross-section shape

Tutorial: Creating drapes

Modeling home interiors is a task commonly performed by professional architects and interior designers, but creating the drapes can be tricky. In this tutorial, we'll create some simple drapes using a Loft Object.

To create drapes using a Loft object, follow these steps:

1. In the Create panel, click the Shapes category button and then click the Line button. In the Creation Method rollout, set the Initial Type to Corner and the Drag Type to Bézier. In the Top view, click and drag from the left to the right, creating a random spline that resembles the cross section of a drape. Be sure to drag after each click to make the vertices flow into one another.

2. Open the Modify panel and click the Spline subobject icon. Then in the Geometry rollout, click the Outline button and enter a value of **2**. This will duplicate the spline and offset it by 2. The Outline button will also connect the ends to produce a closed spline. Use a larger value for thicker drapes.

3. Return to the Create panel and click the Line button again. Then create a vertical line in the Left view for the height of the drape.

4. Click the Geometry category button and select the Compound Objects subcategory from the drop-down. The straight line should still be selected, so click the Loft button, click the Get Shape button, and then click the cross-section shape.

5. Open the Modify panel and, under the Skin Parameters rollout, turn off the Contour and Banking options.

6. Use the Deformation functions to add more control to the drapes, such as tying them together as shown in Figure 14-11.

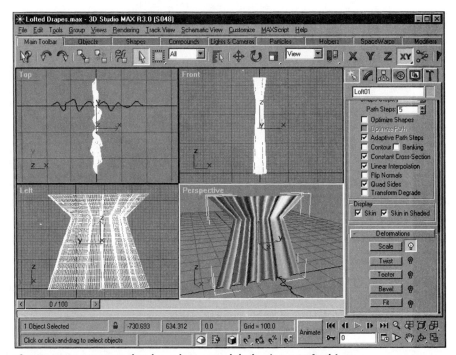

Figure 14-11: Drapes that have been modeled using a Loft object

Loft Objects versus Surface Tools

Loft objects can be created completely from 2D shape splines — one open spline is typically used as the Loft path and other, closed splines are used as the cross sections. You can have several different cross sections, and these can change as you travel the path. Loft cross sections aren't required to have the same number of vertices, and you can modify the scale and rotation of the cross sections with the Deformation options.

The Surface Tools, which include the CrossSection and Surface Modifiers, provide a new way to model that is similar to lofting. The CrossSection Modifier takes several cross- section shapes and connects their vertices with additional splines to create a spline framework. The Surface Modifier can then be used to cover this framework with a skin.

Understanding the differences

Although similar in nature, Loft objects and the Surface Tools have different subtleties and strengths.

One difference is that the CrossSection Modifier connects spline cross-sections according to their order. This can cause strange results if the order is incorrect. A Loft always follows a path, so the cross section order isn't a problem.

Another difference is that Surface Tools give you more control over the surface of a created object. Because the underlying structure is a series of splines, new branches and objects can be added without much difficulty. This can be hard to do with Loft objects.

As a general guideline, Loft objects are better suited to modeling rigid objects with relatively uniform cross sections, while the Surface Tools are better for modeling more organic model types.

Tutorial: Modeling a vacuum hose

To get a better understanding of the differences between Loft objects and Surface Tools, let's model the end of a vacuum hose using these two methods. Both will use the same cross-section shapes, but the results will be a little different.

To model a vacuum hose using a Loft object and Surface Tools, follow these steps:

1. In the Create panel, select the Shapes category button, click the Circle button, and then create two circles in the Top view. Next, click the Rectangle button and create two rectangles in the Top view. Make the first rectangle larger than both of the circles and make the second one much larger still. In the Parameters rollout, use the Corner Radius spinner to round the corners on both rectangles.

2. In the Top view, use the Select and Move button to position the shapes on top of one another. Now, select the smaller rectangle and in the Left or Front View, move it to a position a short distance above the larger rectangle. Then select a circle and move it to a position a short distance above the rectangles. Follow this by moving the remaining circle to a position a good distance above the other objects. Rotate the circle so that it forms a 45-degree angle with the construction grid. Once the shapes are correctly positioned, select them all and copy them using Tools ➪ Mirror and move the new set to the side.

3. First, let's create the Loft version. To create a path, click the Line button in the Create panel and click at roughly the center of each shape in the Left or Front view. Right-click when finished to end the line.

4. With the path selected, click the Geometry category button and select Compound Objects from the subcategory drop-down. Click the Loft button and in the Creation Method rollout, click the Get Shape button and then click the top circle.

5. In the Path Parameters rollout, select the Path Steps option and increment the Path value until the yellow X has traveled down the path to the center of the second circle. Then click the second circle. Increment the Path value to move the yellow X down to the center of the smaller rectangle and then select it. Increment the Path value a final time to move the yellow X to the center of the large rectangle and select it to complete the Loft object.

6. For the Surface Tools version, we'll work on the mirrored shapes. Select the top circle and right-click it to open a pop-up menu. Choose Convert to Editable Spline. Open the Modify panel and, in the Geometry rollout, click the Attach button. Then select the shapes in order from top to bottom.

7. Click the More button at the top of the Modify panel to open the additional Modifiers list dialog box and select the CrossSection Modifier. Splines will be drawn to connect all the shapes. Click the More button again and select the Surface Modifier to complete the model.

Figure 14-12 shows the resulting models with the Loft object on the right and the Surface Tools model on the left. Notice how the Loft object is twisted. This is because the Loft object automatically aligned the vertices of the different shapes. This can be fixed using the Loft Deformation options.

The Surface Tools model has a small bump at the neck of the extension. This is caused by the mesh being rotated to line up the vertices between the circle and the rectangles. From this example, you can see that each method has its advantages and disadvantages.

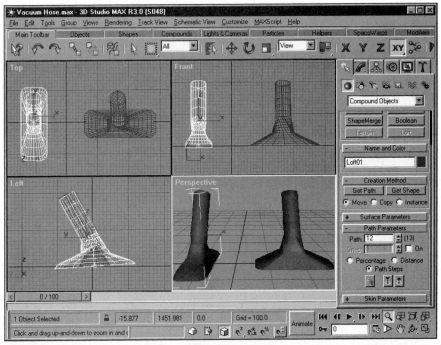

Figure 14-12: Two vacuum hose models created using a Loft object and Surface Tools

Summary

Loft objects are unique objects created from spline shapes that are used as the loft path and the cross section. Loft objects can be used to create some interesting objects.

In this chapter, you've

✦ Created a Loft object

✦ Discovered how to control Loft parameters

✦ Learned to use Loft deformations

✦ Modified Loft subobjects

✦ Learned the difference between Loft Objects and Surface Tools

In the next chapter, you'll learn about modeling with *compound objects*.

✦   ✦   ✦

Building Compound Objects

C H A P T E R

15

So far in Part III, we have covered a variety of different modeling types. The Compound Objects category includes several additional modeling types that don't seem to fit anywhere else. As you will see in this chapter, these modeling types provide several new and unique ways to model objects.

Understanding Compound Object Types

The Compound Objects subcategory includes several unique object types. You can access these object types by clicking the Geometry category button in the Create panel and by selecting Compound Objects in the subcategory drop-down list. All of the object types included in the Compound Object subcategory are displayed as buttons at the top of the Create panel. They include the following:

✦ **Morph** — Consists of two or more objects with the same number of vertices. These vertices are interpolated from one object to the other over several frames.

✦ **Scatter** — Randomly scatters a source object about the scene. You can also select a Distribution object that defines the volume or surface where the objects scatter.

✦ **Conform** — Wraps the vertices of one object onto another. This can be used to simulate a morph between objects with different numbers of vertices.

✦ **Connect**—Connects two objects with open faces by joining the holes with additional faces.

✦ **ShapeMerge**—Lets you embed a spline into a mesh object or subtract the area of a spline from a mesh object.

✦ **Boolean**—Created by performing Boolean operations on two or more overlapping objects. The operations include Union, Subtraction, Intersection, and Cut.

✦ **Terrain**—Creates terrains from the elevation contour lines like those found on topographical maps.

✦ **Loft**—Sweeps a cross-section shape along a spline path.

Cross-Reference Loft objects were the topic of Chapter 14, "Creating Lofted Objects," so they will not be covered in this chapter.

Modeling with Boolean Objects

When two objects overlap, you can perform different Boolean operations on them to create a unique object. The Boolean operations include Union, Subtraction, Intersection, and Cut. The Union operation combines two objects into one. The Subtraction operation subtracts the overlapping portions of one object from another. The Intersection operation retains only the overlapping sections of two objects, and the Cut operation can cut an object like the Subtraction operator, while letting the cut piece remain.

Note Unlike many CAD packages that deal with solid objects, MAX's Booleans are applied to surfaces, so if the surfaces of the two objects don't overlap, the Boolean operation has no effect.

All Boolean operations are layered in the Stack. You can revisit an operation at any time and make changes to it.

Tip It is a good idea to collapse the Stack after all operations have been performed.

Union

The Union operation combines two objects into one. To Union two objects, select an object and click the Boolean button. Under the Parameters rollout, the selected object will be referred to as Operand A. Now, in the Pick Operand rollout, click the Pick Operand B button and select a second object in the viewport. (Operand B can be a Copy, Instance, a Reference, or a Move object.) To apply the Boolean operation, click the Union option.

Figure 15-1 shows a sphere and a cube that have been joined using the Union operator.

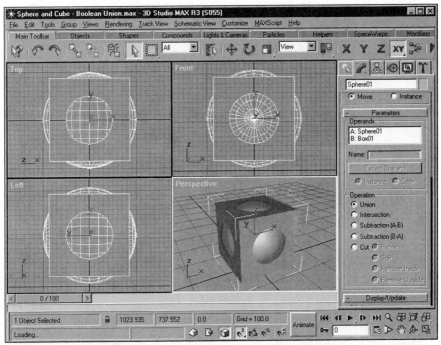

Figure 15-1: A Boolean object resulting from the Union of a cube with a sphere

Subtraction

The Subtraction operation subtracts the overlapping portions of one object from the other. For this operation, the order in which the objects are selected is important. Subtracting object A from object B gives you a different object from what you get when you subtract object B from object A.

Figure 15-2 shows the sphere and the cube that have been subtracted using the Subtraction A–B operator and Figure 15-3 shows the Subtraction B–A operator.

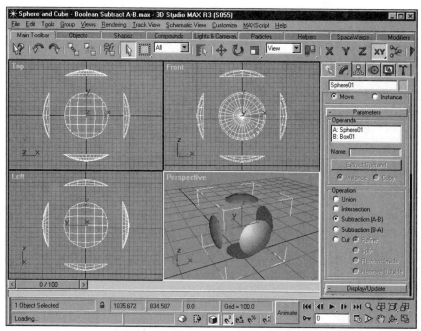

Figure 15-2: A Boolean object resulting from the A–B Subtraction of cube and sphere

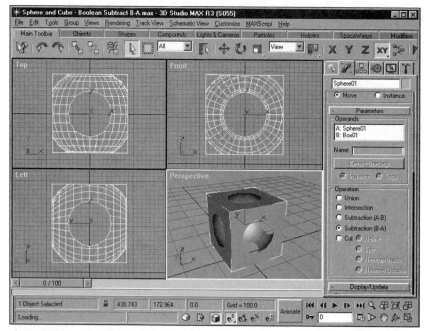

Figure 15-3: A Boolean object resulting from the B–A Subtraction of the cube and a sphere

Intersection

The Intersection operation creates an object from the overlapping sections of two objects. For this operation it isn't important which object is A and which is B.

Figure 15-4 shows the intersection of a sphere and a cube object using the Intersection operator.

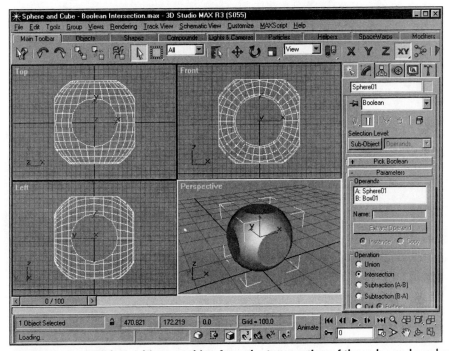

Figure 15-4: A Boolean object resulting from the Intersection of the cube and a sphere

Cut

The Cut operation is similar to the Slice Modifier except it uses another object instead of a slice plane gizmo, and only Operand A is modified in the process. The Cut operation has several options including Refine, Split, Remove Inside, and Remove Outside.

New Feature   The Cut Boolean operation is new in Release 3.

The Refine option marks the selected object with new edges where it intersects Operand B. The Split option actually divides the mesh object into separate elements. Figure 15-5 shows a sphere that was cut by a cube object. After the Boolean Cut operation, the object was converted to an Editable Mesh object and, using element subobject mode, various elements were selected and moved away from the rest of the sphere. The Backface Cull option was also disabled in the Object Properties dialog box so you could see the holes.

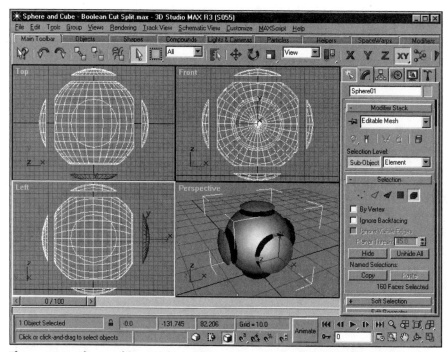

Figure 15-5: The resulting Boolean object when the Cut operation is used on two objects

The Remove Inside and Remove Outside options are variations of the Split option. They remove the inner or outer portion. These options work like the Subtraction and Intersection options, except the Cut operation leaves holes in the base geometry.

Tips for working with Booleans

Working with Boolean objects can be difficult. If you try to perform a Boolean operation on an ill-suited object, the results could end up being erratic. As you prepare objects for Boolean operations, keep the following points in mind:

✦ Avoid meshes with long, skinny polygon faces. All faces should have roughly equal lengths and widths. The ratio of edge length to width should be less than 4 to 1.

✦ Avoid curved lines where possible. Curved lines have the potential of folding back on themselves, which will cause problems. If you need to use a curve, try not to intersect it with another curve; keep the curvature to a minimum.

✦ Unlink any objects not involved in the Boolean operation. Linked objects, even if they don't intersect, can cause problems.

✦ If you're having difficulty getting a Boolean operation to work, try applying the XForm Modifier (found in the additional Modifiers list) to combine all the transformations into one. Then collapse the Stack and convert the objects to Editable Mesh objects. This will remove any Modifier dependencies.

✦ Make sure that your objects are complete closed surfaces with no holes, overlapping faces, or unwelded vertices. You can check these criteria by applying the STL-Check Modifier or by looking at all sides of the objects in a viewport with Smooth Shading enabled.

✦ Make sure that all surface normals are consistent — inconsistent normals will cause unexpected results. You can use the Normal Modifier to unify and flip all normals on an object. The Show Normals option in the viewport can also help.

Tutorial: Creating a Lincoln Log set

In the household where I grew up, we had sets of Legos and of a lesser-known construction set known as Lincoln Logs that let you to create buildings using notched logs that fit together. Using a Subtraction operation, you can create your own virtual set of Lincoln Logs.

To use Boolean objects to create a log cabin, follow these steps:

1. In the Create panel, click the Cylinder button, and then drag in the Left viewport to create a cylinder. In the Parameters rollout, set a Radius value of **10** and a Height of **200**.

2. Click the Box button and in the Top view, create a box with a Length of **30**, Width of **20**, and a Height of **20**.

3. Clone the Box object three times and position two of the objects at each end of the log at a distance of **10** from the end, top, and bottom.

4. Select the Cylinder object, and then select the Compound Objects subcategory from the drop-down list and click the Boolean button. In the Operation section, select the Subtraction (A–B) option. Then in the Pick Boolean rollout, click the Pick Operand B button and select one of the Box objects.

5. Repeat the Subtraction operation on the other three boxes by clicking the Select button and performing Step 4 again. When finished, you should have a cylinder with four notches.

Note If you simply click the Pick Operand B button again, the first notch will be replaced by the second operation.

6. Clone the single log by selecting Edit ⇨ Clone and then selecting the Copy option. Move the cloned log along the negative Y-axis a distance of 160. The easiest way to do this is to select the Select and Move button and right-click it to open the Move Transform Type-In dialog box. In the Absolute World field, enter **−160** as the Y-axis value. This will position two logs next to one another to form the bottom layer of the house.

7. Select both logs and open the Array dialog box by selecting the Tools ⇨ Array command. In the Incremental Move row, enter **10** for the Z-axis. In the Incremental Rotate row, enter **90** for the Z-axis. In the Array Dimensions section, enter a Count value of **16**. Click the OK button. This will stack several layers of logs.

8. Select one log and use the right-click pop-up menu to convert that log to an Editable Mesh. Open the Modify panel and click the Attach button, and then select every log to combine them all into a single object. Click the Attach button again to exit attach mode when you're done.

9. In the Create panel, click the Geometry category button, select the Box button, and create a Box object with the following dimensions: Length of **40**, Width of **40**, and Height of **80**. Then position the Box where the front door should be.

10. Return to the Compound Objects subcategory, select the logs, and click the Boolean button. Then click the Pick Operand B button again and select the Box. The rollout will remember and retain the last options selected including the Subtract (A–B) operation.

11. To add a roof, select the Extended Primitives subcategory and click the Prism button. Drag in the Left view to create a prism object that covers the logs.

Figure 15-6 shows our Boolean log cabin — ready for the virtual pioneers.

Morphing Objects

Morph Objects are used to create a Morph animation by interpolating the vertices in one object to the vertex positions of a second object. The original object is called the *Base object* and the second object is called the *Target object*. The Base and Target objects must be either mesh or patch objects, and they must have the same number of vertices. One Base object can be morphed into several targets.

Tip To ensure that the Base and Target objects have the same number of vertices, create a copy of one object and modify it to be a target. Be sure to avoid the Modifiers such as Tessellate and Optimize that will change the number of vertices.

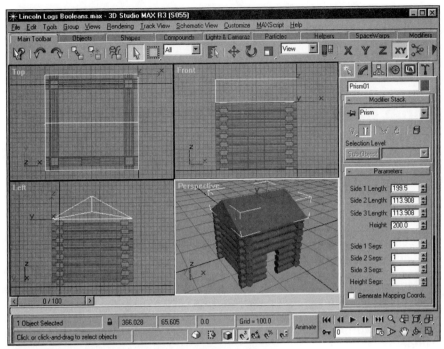

Figure 15-6: A log cabin built using Boolean objects

To morph a Base object into a Target, select the Base object and open the Create panel. Select the Compound Objects subcategory and click the Morph button. Then click the Pick Target button and select a Target object in the viewport. Pick Target options include Copy, Instance, Reference, and Move. (The Move option deletes the original object that is selected.) The Target object will be displayed under the Current Targets rollout in the Morph Targets list.

Each Morph object can have several Target objects. The Pick Target button can be used to select several targets, and the order in which these targets appear in the list is the order in which they are morphed. To delete a Target object, select it from the list and click the Delete Morph Target button. Beneath the list is a Name field where you can change the name of the selected Target object.

Creating Morph keys

With a Target object selected in the Morph Targets list, you can drag the Time Slider to a frame and set a Morph key by clicking the Create Morph Key button found at the bottom of the panel. This sets the number of frames used to interpolate among the different morph states. Morph keys can be set with or without the Animate button enabled.

Tip   If the Morph object changes dramatically, set the Morph Keys to include enough frames to interpolate smoothly.

If a frame other than 0 is selected when a Target object is picked, a Morph Key is automatically created.

Morph Objects versus the Morph Modifier

MAX includes two different ways to morph an object. You can create a Morph object or apply the Morph Modifier to an existing object. The Morph object is different from the Morph Modifier, but the results are the same; however, there are some subtle differences between these two.

A Morph object can include multiple Morph targets, but it can only be created once. Each target can have several Morph Keys, which makes it easy to control. For example, you could set an object to morph to a different shape and return to its original form with only two Morph Keys.

The Morph Modifier, on the other hand, can be applied multiple times and works well with other Modifiers, but the control for each Modifier is buried in the Stack. The Parameter options available for the Morph Modifier are much more extensive than for the Morph object, and they include channels and support for the Morph material.

For the best of both worlds, apply the Morph Modifier to a Morph object.

Tutorial: Morphing a sword into a plowshare

The Bible speaks of a time of peace when swords will be beaten into plowshares. In this tutorial, we'll try to hasten this peaceful time, by doing just that—virtually of course.

To morph a sword into a plowshare, follow these steps:

1. Import the sword model, which was created by Zygote Media. Name the model **sword**.

Note   You can find this model and all other models used in the tutorials on the book's CD-ROM.

2. Clone the sword model twice using the Edit ➪ Clone command. The clones will be positioned directly on top of the original sword. Name the first clone **puddle** and the second one **plowshare**.

3. Select the puddle object, open the Modify panel, and click the More button. Select the Melt Modifier and set the Melt Amount to **750** and the Solidity to **Jelly**.

4. Select the plowshare object, and then click the Sub-Object button and select Vertex from the subobject list. Then drag an outline over the vertices along the top of the blade. Click the Select and Move button and move these vertices to form a plowshare model.

Caution Be careful not to delete or weld any vertices, or the morph object can't be created.

5. Select the original sword object, open the Create panel, select the Compound Objects subcategory, and click the Morph button. Drag the Time Slider to frame 50. In the Pick Targets rollout, click the Pick Target button and select the puddle object. Next, drag the Time Slider to frame 100 and select the plowshare object.

The sword object will now morph into a puddle and then into a modified plowshare object. For Figure 15-7, I cloned the original and final objects and placed them on either side of the morphing object.

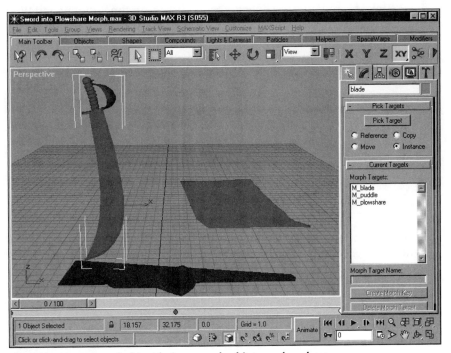

Figure 15-7: A sword object being morphed into a plowshare

On the CD-ROM You can see the final animation of this morph on the CD-ROM.

Creating Conform Objects

Conform objects mold one object over the surface of another. The object that is modified is called the *Wrapper object*. The other object is known as the *Wrap-To object*. These objects need to be either mesh objects or objects that can be converted to mesh objects.

Note   Another way to mold one object over the surface of another is with the Conform Space Warp. This Space Warp is covered in Chapter 25, "Deforming Objects with Space Warps."

To create a Conform object, select an object to be the Wrapper object, open the Create panel, and select the Compound Objects subcategory. Then click the Conform button. To select the Wrap-To object, click the Pick Wrap-To Object button in the Parameters rollout and choose one of the options below the button (Reference, Move, Copy, or Instance).

In the Parameters rollout, the Objects section lists both the Wrapper and Wrap-To objects. There are also Name fields for changing the names of both objects.

The Wrapper Parameters section includes two adjustable values: Default Projection Distance, which is the distance that the Wrapper moves if it doesn't intersect with the Wrap-To object, and Standoff Distance, which is the distance between the Wrapper and the Wrap-To object. There is also the Use Selected Vertices option, which causes only the selected vertices passed up the Stack to be moved.

Tip   In the Update section, you can enable the Hide Wrap-To Object option. This is the key to morphing between objects with different numbers of vertices.

Setting a Vertex Projection Direction

The Parameters rollout also includes controls for specifying the Vertex Projection Direction settings. You can select to project the vertices based on the current active viewport with the Use Active Viewport option. If the view changes, the Recalculate Projection button can be used to compute the new projection direction. Figure 15-8 shows a Conform object created using an Active Viewport projection. The Perspective view has been rotated since the projection was set.

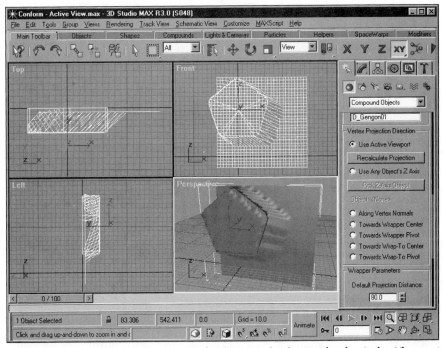

Figure 15-8: A Conform object created using a projection set by the Active Viewport

You can also use the local Z-axis of any object in the scene as the projection direction. The Pick Z-Axis Object button lets you select the object to use. Once you have selected it, rotating this object can alter the projection direction. The name of the object is displayed below the Pick Z-Axis Object button.

Other projection options include Along Vertex Normals, Towards Wrapper Center, Towards Wrapper Pivot, Towards Wrap-To Center, and Towards Wrap-To Pivot. The Along Vertex Normals option sets the projection direction opposite the Wrapper's normals. The other options set the direction toward the center or pivot of the Wrapper or Wrap-To objects. Figure 15-9 shows the projection resulting from the Along Vertex Normals option.

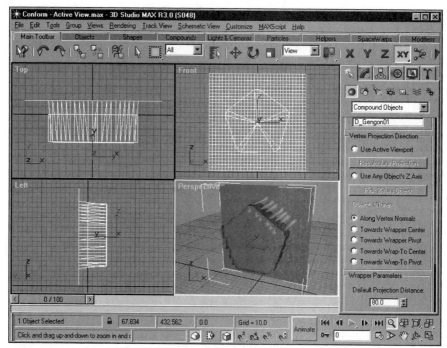

Figure 15-9: A Conform object created using a projection set by the Along Vertex Normals

Tutorial: Building a masquerade mask

When it's time for the ball and you need a masquerade mask, the Conform object works very well.

To create a facial mask using the Conform object, follow these steps:

1. Import the general model, which was created by Viewpoint Datalabs, and delete all parts of the model except for the face.

2. Open the Create panel and select the Patch Grids subcategory. Click the Quad Patch button and then drag a grid in the Front view that completely covers the general's face. In the Parameters rollout, increase the resolution of the grid by entering a value of **12** in both the Length and Width Segment fields.

3. With the grid selected, move it in the Top view until it is positioned in front of the face. The grid will be the Wrapper object and the face will be the Wrap-To object.

4. With the face object selected, select the Compound Objects subcategory in the Create panel and click the Conform button. Under the Parameters rollout, go to the Vertex Projection Direction section and select the Along Vertex Normals option. Then click the Pick Wrap-To Object button, select the Move option beneath it, and finally, select the face model.

The patch grid object molds over the top of the face as shown in Figure 15-10.

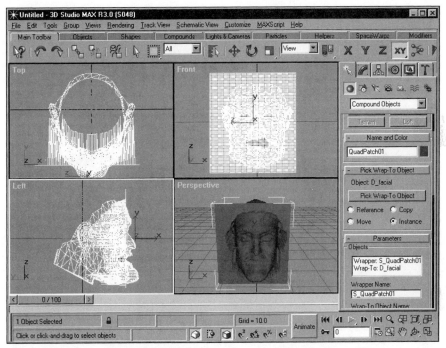

Figure 15-10: A patch grid being conformed to the front of a face object

Creating Connect Objects

A Connect object is useful for building a connecting bridge between two separate objects. Each object must have an open face or hole that specifies where the two objects are to be connected.

To use this object, delete a face on two Editable Mesh objects and then position the holes across from each other. Select one of the objects. In the Create panel, select Compound Objects subcategory from the drop-down list. Click the Connect button, and then click the Pick Operand button and select the second object. The Connect object will build the additional faces required to connect the two holes.

If multiple holes exist between the objects, the Connect object will attempt to patch them all. You can also use the button several times to connect a single object to multiple objects.

 Caution   The Connect object doesn't work well with NURBS objects.

Figure 15-11 shows a normal Connect object without any smoothing options.

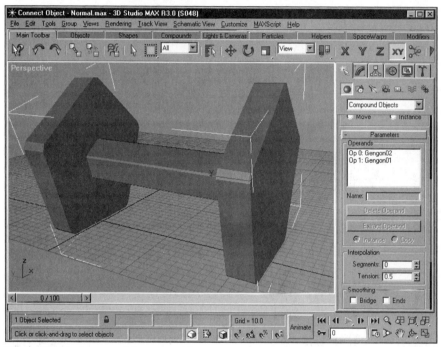

Figure 15-11: A normal Connect object

The Parameters rollout includes a list of all the Operands or objects involved in the connection. You can delete any of these with the Delete Operand button. The Extract Operand button lets you separate the Operand object from the Connect object.

In the Interpolation section, the Segments value is the number of segments used to create the bridge section, and the Tension value is the amount of curvature to use in an attempt to smooth the connected bridge.

The Bridge Smoothing option smoothes the faces of the bridge, and the Ends option smoothes where the bridge and the original objects are connected. Figure 15-12 shows the same object that was shown in the previous figure, this time with the Bridge Smoothing option enabled.

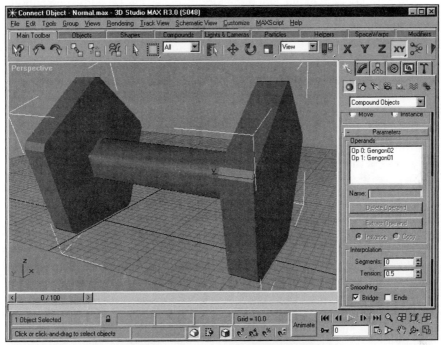

Figure 15-12: A Connect object with Bridge Smoothing applied

Tutorial: Creating a barbell

The Connect object is best used between two symmetrical copies of an object that need to be attached, as with a table or bridge. For this tutorial, we'll use the Connect object to create the center rod of a barbell.

To connect two weights to form a barbell, follow these steps:

1. Open the Create panel, select the Standard Primitives subcategory, and click the Cylinder button. Drag a cylinder in the Left view to a Radius of **100** and a Height of **100**. Create a second cylinder with a Radius of **15** and a Height of **−10** that shares the same center.

2. In the Create panel, select the Compound Objects subcategory. Select the larger cylinder object and click the Boolean button. Select the Cut and Refine options, click the Pick Operand B button, and then select the smaller cylinder. This will add a circular face to the center of the larger cylinder.

3. Right-click the cylinder and select the Convert to Editable Mesh command from the pop-up menu. Open the Modify panel, click the Polygon subobject icon and in the Perspective view, and select the interior circular face (you may need to rotate the view). Click the Delete button or press the Delete key on the keyboard. An alert box will ask if you want to Delete Isolated Vertices. Click the Yes button.

4. Select the Cylinder object and select the Tools ⇨ Mirror command. In the Mirror: World Coordinates dialog box, select the X Mirror axis, enter an Offset of **200**, and choose Copy as the Clone Selection. Click the OK button.

5. Back in the Create panel, select one of the Cylinder objects, click the Connect button, click the Pick Operand button, and select the other object. The open faces of the two objects will be connected.

Figure 15-13 shows the resulting barbell.

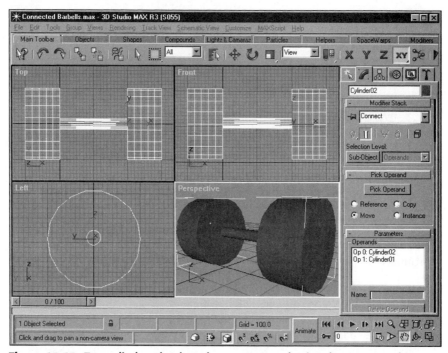

Figure 15-13: Two cylinders that have been connected using the Connect object

Tutorial: Creating simple straight hair

Many human models need hair because, let's face it, not everyone is bald. There are some amazing plug-ins available for creating hair, but the Connect object can be used to create straight spiked hair, which will work in some cases.

To create some simple straight hair using the Connect object, follow these steps:

1. Open the Create panel, click the GeoSphere button, and create a GeoSphere in one of the viewports. With the GeoSphere still active, set the Segments to **10** in the Parameters rollout to create some small regular faces.

2. Click the Pyramid button and create a small pyramid above the GeoSphere object.

3. Select and convert both objects to Editable Mesh objects, using the right-click pop-up menu. Deselect the pyramid and select the GeoSphere.

4. Open the Modify panel, select the Polygon subobject mode, and, in the Top view, select 50 or so random faces on the top half of the GeoSphere. (Use the Ctrl key to add to the selection.) Click the Delete button or press the Delete key on the keyboard to remove these faces. Click the Sub-Object button to exit subobject mode, deselect the GeoSphere, and select the pyramid. Select the Polygon subobject mode again, and remove a single face on the pyramid object. Click the Sub-Object button again to exit subobject mode.

5. Holding down the Shift key, select and move the pyramid object to clone about 50 new pyramids around the top half of the GeoSphere. Select one of the pyramids and click the Select List button. From the Select by Object dialog box, select all the listed pyramid objects and click OK.

6. Select the GeoSphere and open the Create panel. Select the Compound Objects subcategory and click the Connect button. Click the Pick Operand button and randomly select the pyramids. This will create random objects between each open face pair.

Figure 15-14 shows the resulting straight spiky hair.

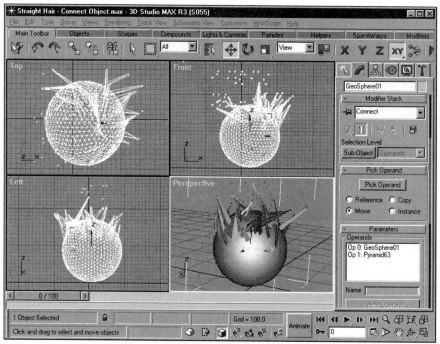

Figure 15-14: A Connect object can be used to create straight hair segments.

Creating a Scatter Object

A Scatter object spreads multiple copies of the object about the scene or within a defined area. The object that is scattered is called the *Source object* and the area where the scatter objects can be placed is defined by a *Distribution object*.

Note   Particle Systems, discussed in Chapter 24, "Creating and Controlling Particle Systems," can also create many duplicate objects, but you have more control over the placement of objects with a Scatter object.

To create a Scatter object, open the Create panel, select the Compound Objects subcategory, and click the Scatter button. The selected object becomes the Source object. A rollout is then opened where you can select the Distribution object or use defined transforms.

Under the Scatter Objects rollout, the Objects section lists the Source and Distribution objects. There are also Name fields for changing the names of either object. The Extract Operand button is only available in the Modify panel—it lets you select an operand from the list and make a copy or instance of it.

Working with Source objects

The Source object is the object that is to be duplicated. Figure 15-15 shows a Pyramid primitive scattered over a spherical Distribution object with 100 duplicates. The Perpendicular and Distribute Using Even options are set.

Figure 15-15: A Scatter object made of a sharp Pyramid spread over an area defined by a sphere

In the Scatter Objects rollout are several parameters for controlling the Source Object. In the Source Object Parameters rollout, the Duplicates value specifies how many objects to scatter. You can also specify a Base Scale and the Vertex Chaos values. The Base Scale is the value that the object is scaled to before being scattered. All new objects are scaled equally to this value. The Vertex Chaos button randomly distributes the object vertices.

The Animation Offset defines the number of frames between a new duplicate and the previous one.

Note   If you look closely at a Scatter object, you'll notice that both the Source and Distribution objects will have the same object color. To color them differently use the Multi/Sub-Object Material.

Working with Distribution objects

To select a Distribution object, click the Pick Distribution Object button and select an object in the viewport (make sure the Use Distribution Object option is selected in the Scatter Objects rollout). The Distribution object can be specified as a Copy, an Instance, a Reference, or a Move.

Under the Distribution Object Parameters rollout are several options for controlling the Distribution object. The Perpendicular option causes the Source objects to be aligned perpendicular to the Distribution object. If the perpendicular option is disabled, the orientation will remain the same as that of the default Source object. Figure 15-16 shows the same Scatter object as in the previous figure, with the Perpendicular option disabled.

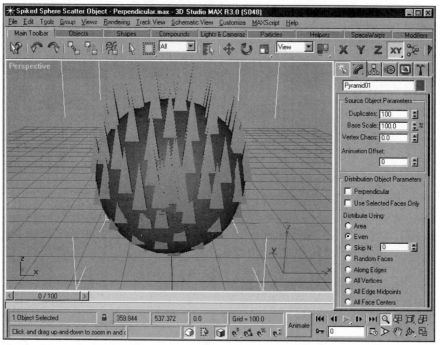

Figure 15-16: A Scatter object with the Perpendicular option disabled

The Use Selected Faces Only option enables you to select the faces over which the duplicates are positioned. The Selected Faces are those passed up the Stack by the Mesh Select Modifier.

Other Distribution Object Parameter options include Area, Even, Skip N, Random Faces, Along Edges, All Vertices, All Edge Midpoints, All Face Centers, and Volume. The Area option evenly distributes the objects over the surface area, and the Even option places duplicates over every other face. The Skip N option lets you specify how many faces to skip before placing an object. The Random Faces and Along Edges options randomly distribute the duplicates around the Distribution object. The All Vertices, All Edge Midpoints, and All Face Centers options ignore the Duplicates value (that specifies the number of duplicates) and place a duplicate at every vertex, edge midpoint, and face.

Figure 15-17 shows the Scatter object with the All Vertices option set.

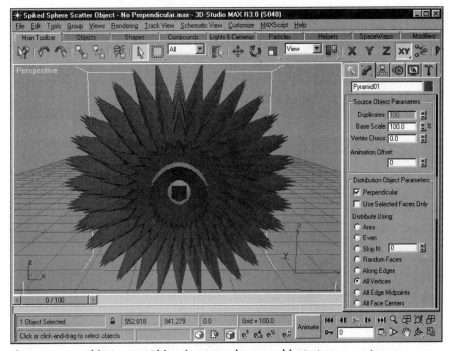

Figure 15-17: This Scatter Object is set to place an object at every vertex.

All of the options described thus far place the duplicates on the surface of the object, but the Volume option scatters the duplicates inside the Distribution object's volume.

Setting Transforms

The Transforms rollout is used to specify the individual transformation limits of the duplicate objects. For example, if the Z-axis value is set to 90, then each new duplicate will be randomly rotated about its local Z-axis at a distance somewhere between -90 and 90.

These transformations can be used with a Distribution object or by themselves if the Use Transforms Only option is selected under the Scatter Objects rollout. The

Use Maximum Range option causes all three axes to adopt the same value. The Lock Aspect Ratio option maintains the relative dimensions of the Source object to ensure uniform scaling.

Speeding updates with a Proxy

Working with a large number of duplicates can slow the viewport updates down to a crawl. To speed up these updates, select the Proxy option in the Display rollout. This will replace each duplicate with a wedge-shaped object.

Another way to speed the viewport updates is to use the Display spinner. Using this spinner you can select a percentage of the total number of duplicates to display in the viewport. The rendered image will still use the actual number specified.

The Hide Distribution Object option lets you make the Distribution object visible or invisible. The Seed value is used to determine the randomness of the objects.

Loading and siaving Presets

With all the various parameters, the Load/Save Presets rollout enables you to Save, Load, or Delete various Presets. Saved Presets can be used with another Source object.

Tutorial: Filling a box with spiders

When I was a kid, my brothers and I always had a terrarium full of snakes, lizards, or spiders. Mom was okay with this as long as we remembered the one key rule — keep the lid on. Well, kids will be kids and at times we forgot. Then it was spiders everywhere (and you thought this effect was only good for horror flicks).

To scatter spiders across the surface of a box, follow these steps:

1. Import the spider model, which was created by Zygote Media. To work with the spider model, combine all its parts into a single mesh. The easiest way to do this is to select a single part, right-click, and convert it to an Editable Mesh from the pop-up menu. Then, in the Modify panel, click the Attach button and attach each part.

Note   If you're attaching objects with materials, an alert box will give you some options for dealing with these materials.

2. In the Create panel, click the Geometry category button, select Standard Primitives subcategory from the drop-down list, and click the Box button. In the Keyboard Entry rollout, enter the values of **50** for the Length, **100** for the Width, and **50** for the Height, and then click the Create button. This results in a solid box.

3. Click the Select and Scale button and hold down the Shift key while dragging to create a slightly smaller box. This will create a copy of the first box. Position the smaller box so that it fits inside the larger one and extends slightly above it in the Front view.

4. Select the larger box and in the Create panel, select the Compound Objects subcategory from the drop-down list and click the Boolean button. Under the Parameters rollout, select the Subtraction A–B option and then click the Pick Operand B button. Now click the smaller box to create a terrarium.

5. Select the spider object and click the Scatter button. At the top of the rollouts, click the Pick Distribution Object button and click the box object. In the Source Object Parameters, enter **20** in the Duplicates field. Make sure that the Perpendicular and Area options are selected and that the Hide Distribution Object is not selected. This will cause the spiders to be spread across the surface of the box.

Figure 15-18 shows the spiders creeping about. Notice how the box and spiders are all part of the same object and have the same object color.

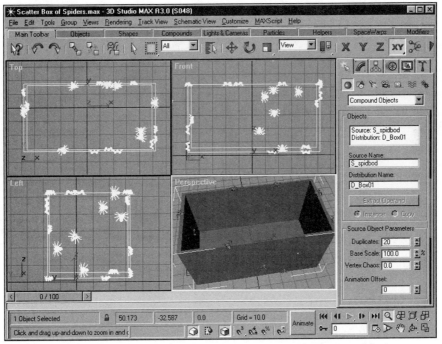

Figure 15-18: Spiders spread over the box surface using the Scatter object

Tutorial: Jungle vine

Using the Vertex Chaos value, you can simulate the effect of jungle vines growing thick upon the surface of an object.

To cover an object with jungle vines, follow these steps:

1. Open the Create panel and click the Cylinder button. Drag in the Top view to create a cylinder. Set the Radius to **30** and the Height to **250**. Also in the Top view, create a sphere with a Radius of **5** and set its object color to dark green.

2. With the sphere object selected, select the Compound Objects subcategory and click the Scatter button. Then click the Pick Distribution Object button and select the cylinder.

3. In the Scatter Objects rollout, set the number of Duplicates to **500** and the Vertex Chaos value to **5** (lower the number of Duplicates if necessary).

Figure 15-19 shows the resulting overgrowth.

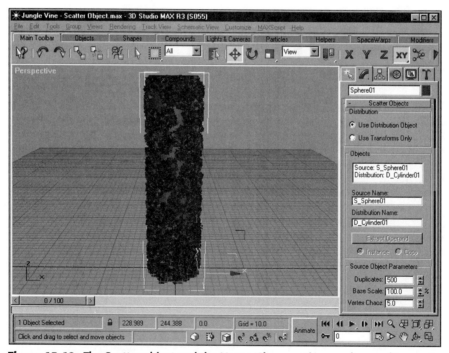

Figure 15-19: The Scatter object and the Vertex Chaos option can be used to create the look of jungle vines growing on a pillar.

Creating a ShapeMerge Object

The ShapeMerge object enables you to use a spline shape as a cookie cutter to extract a portion of a mesh object. This button is only enabled if a mesh object and a spline exist in the scene. To use this object, select a mesh object and click the Pick Shape button, and then select a spline shape.

The spline shape is always projected toward its negative Z-axis. By rotating and positioning the spline before selecting it, you can apply it to different sides of an object. Multiple shapes can be applied to the same mesh object.

The Parameters rollout displays each mesh and shape object in a list. You can also rename either object using the Name field. The Extract Operand button lets you separate either object as an Instance or a Copy.

Cookie Cutter and Merge options

The Operations group includes options for cutting the mesh, including Cookie Cutter and Merge. The Cookie Cutter option cuts the shape out of the mesh surface, and the Merge option combines the spline with the mesh. You can also Invert the operation to remove the inside or outside of the selected area.

Like the Boolean Subtraction operations, the Cookie Cutter option can remove sections of the mesh, but it uses the area defined by a spline instead of a volume defined by a mesh object. The Merge option is useful for marking an area for selection, as we did in the barbell tutorial earlier in the chapter. We could have specified the inner connection faces using a ShapeMerge object with the Merge option.

Figure 15-20 shows a ShapeMerge object with the Merge option selected, and Figure 15-21 shows the same object with the Cookie Cutter option selected.

Tip The Merge option can be used to create a precise face object that can be used with the Connect object.

The Output Sub-Mesh Selection option lets you pass the selection up the Stack for additional Modifiers. Options include None, Face, Edge, and Vertex.

Cross-Reference Chapter 11, "Working with Spline Shapes," includes an example where the ShapeMerge object is used to remove the interior section of several extruded letters.

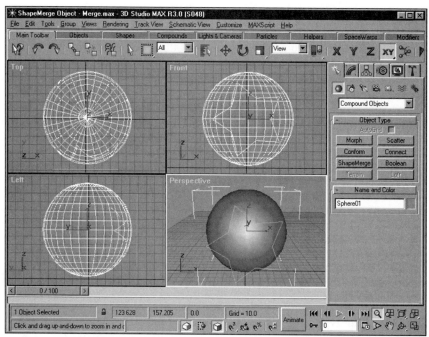

Figure 15-20: A ShapeMerge object using the Merge option

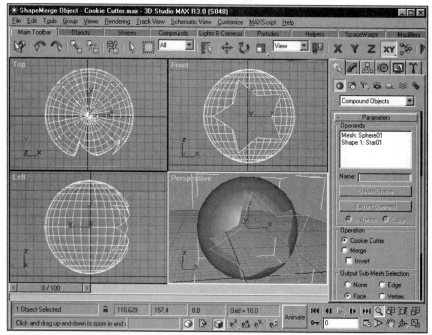

Figure 15-21: A ShapeMerge object using the Cookie Cutter option

Tutorial: Creating a letter cube

Using the ShapeMerge object you can create a Letter Cube object with letters cut out of each side.

To create a Letter Cube, follow these steps:

1. In the Create panel under the Extended Primitives subcategory, select the Chamfer Box button. Drag in the viewport to create a box, and in the Parameters rollout, enter a value of **50** for the Length, Width, and Height, and a value of **5** for Fillet.

2. Select the Shapes category and click the Text button. Then, in the Front view, create letters to be placed on each side. Make sure to create each letter as a separate object by deselecting it before creating the next one. (For this example, I used the Impact font and created the letters A, B, C, D, E, and F.)

3. Use the transform buttons to position the letters. Place a letter in front of each side so that its negative Z-axis points at each face.

4. With all the letters in place, select the cube and open the Create panel. Select the Compound Objects subcategory, click the ShapeMerge button, and click the Pick Shape button. Then select each letter shape — the letters will each be added to the list of operands. In the Operation section, select the Cookie Cutter option, and the ShapeMerge object will be completed.

Tip   To see the backsides of the faces, right-click the object, select Properties from the pop-up menu, and disable the Backface Cull option.

Figure 15-22 shows the completed Letter Cube. Figure 15-23 shows the same cube with the Invert option selected.

Creating a Terrain Object

The Terrain object is a great new object that enables you to create terrains from splines representing elevation contours. These contour splines can be created in MAX or imported using a format like AutoCAD's DWG. If the splines are created in MAX, make sure that they are attached to each other as one object, in the order in which they will eventually be attached. The splines all need to be closed splines.

New Feature   The Terrain object is new in Release 3.

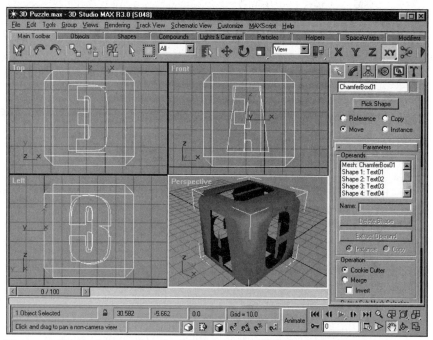

Figure 15-22: A Letter Cube created with the ShapeMerge feature

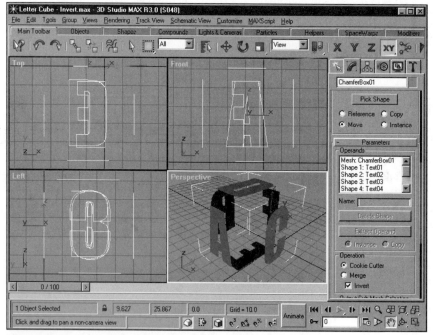

Figure 15-23: The Letter Cube with the Invert option applied

To create a Terrain, create splines at varying elevations, select all the splines, and click the Terrain button. The Pick Operand button can be used to select additional splines to add to the Terrain object. All splines in the object become Operands and are displayed in the Operands list.

The Form group includes three options that determine how the terrain is formed: Graded Surface, Graded Solid, and Layered Solid. The Graded Surface option displays a surface grid over the contour splines, the Graded Solid adds a bottom to the object, and the Layered Solid displays each contour as a flat, terraced area.

The Display group includes options to display the Terrain mesh, the Contour lines, or Both. You can also specify how you want to update the terrain.

The Simplification rollout lets you alter the resolution of the terrain by selecting how many vertical and horizontal vertices to use. Options include using all vertices, half of the vertices, or a quarter of the vertices.

Coloring Elevations

The Color by Elevation rollout displays as reference the Maximum and Minimum Elevations. In between these is a Reference Elevation value, which is the location where the landmass meets the water. Entering a Reference Elevation and clicking the Create Defaults button automatically creates several separate color zones. New zones can be added, modified, or deleted using the Add, Modify, or Delete Zone button.

Each color zone can be accessed from a list. To change a zone's color, select it and click the color swatch. Colors can be set to Blend to the Color Above or to be Solid to Top of Zone.

Tutorial: Creating an island terrain

In this tutorial, we'll create a simple island. The Color by Elevation rollout makes it easy to distinguish the water from the land.

To create an island using the Terrain object, follow these steps:

1. In the Create panel, click the Shapes category button and then click the Ellipse button. Drag in the Top view to create several ellipses of various sizes.

2. In the Left view, select and move the ellipses so that the largest one is on the bottom and the smallest one is on top. Create two small hills by including two ellipses at the same level.

3. Return to the Create panel, click the Geometry category button, and then select the Compound Objects subcategory. Select all the ellipses and click the Terrain button. Joining all the ellipses will form the island.

4. In the Color by Elevation rollout, select a Reference Elevation of 5, just above the Minimum Elevation value, and click the Create Defaults button. In the Color Zone section, set all Zones to Blend to the Color Above except for the Zone with the lightest blue.

Figure 15-24 shows the final terrain. As an alternative, you could create a small tree and use the Scatter object tool to populate the terrain with trees.

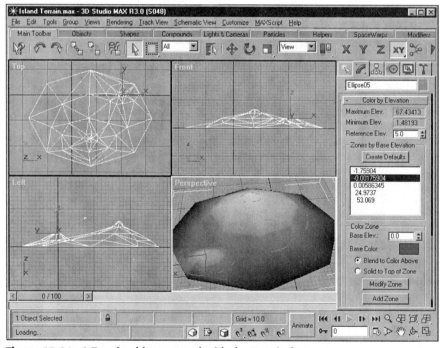

Figure 15-24: A Terrain object created with the Terrain feature

Tutorial: Covering the island with trees

In this final tutorial, we'll add trees to our island using the Scatter object, which will give us a chance to combine two Compound Object types.

To add trees to the island with the Scatter object, follow these steps:

1. With the island terrain from the last tutorial available, open the Create panel and create a simple cone object. At the base of this object, create a cylinder to serve as the tree's stump.

2. Select the cone object and convert it to an Editable Mesh using the right-click pop-up menu. Then click the Attach button and select the cylinder — this will make the tree objects one connect mesh.

3. With the tree object selected, select the Compound Object's subcategory and click the Scatter button. Click the Pick Distribution Object button and select the island terrain. Set the number of Duplicates to **100** and disable the Perpendicular option — this will cause all the trees to stand upright. Select the Random Faces option — this will make the trees denser around the hills where there are more faces.

Figure 15-25 shows the island with the trees.

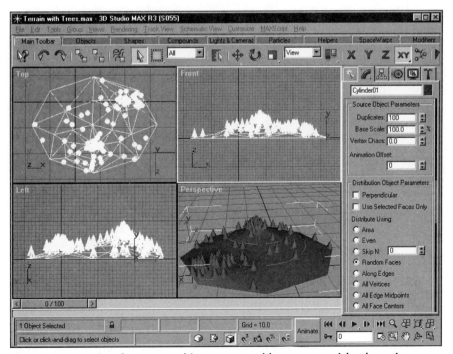

Figure 15-25: Using the Scatter object we can add trees to our island terrain.

Summary

Compound objects provide several additional modeling types to our bulging modeling toolkit. These special-purpose types can be used to model many different objects. In this chapter, you

✦ Learned about the various compound object types

✦ Modeled with Boolean objects

✦ Morphed objects with the same number of vertices

✦ Created a Conform object with differing number of vertices

✦ Created a Connect object to join two objects

✦ Created a Scatter object

✦ Used splines and mesh objects to create a ShapeMerge object

✦ Created a Terrain object using splines

The next chapter introduces modeling with NURBS.

✦   ✦   ✦

Working with NURBS

◆ ◆ ◆ ◆

In This Chapter

Understanding
NURBS curves
and surfaces

Converting primitives
to NURBS surfaces

Creating point and
CV curves and
surfaces

Using the NURBS
Creation Toolbox

Working with NURBS

◆ ◆ ◆ ◆

NURBS is an acronym for Non-Uniform Rational B-Splines.
They are the ideal modeling tool for creating organic
characters because they are easy to work with, they give you
good interactive control, they blend together seamlessly, and
the surfaces remain smooth even when distorted. NURBS are
superior to polygonal modeling methods for building
streamlined mechanical models or models with smooth
flowing contours.

In this chapter we explore different methods of NURBS model
construction and then look at some advanced NURBS tutorials.

Understanding NURBS Curves and Surfaces

There are two kinds of NURBS curves: CV curves and point
curves. CV (control vertex) curves are the most commonly
used NURBS curves. *CV curves* have a *CV control lattice* with
points that let you control the shape of an individual curve or
the entire surface.

The *point curve* is similar to a CV curve except that the NURBS
curve passes through the control vertices. Point curves give
you more intuitive control over the shape of a curve or
surface, but they are not as stable as CV curves, and point
surfaces do not have as many modification options.

Figure 16-1 shows a NURBS point curve on the left and a
NURBS CV curve on the right.

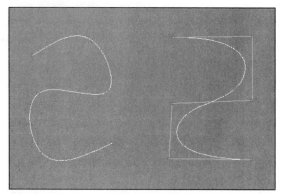

Figure 16-1: NURBS curves come in two different types: CV and point curves.

NURBS CV surfaces and point surfaces can be created from the respective NURBS curves using the Surface Creation tools. These tools are discussed in detail later in the chapter. *CV surfaces* can be modified by moving the control vertices that surround the surface or by adjusting the weight of the individual CVs. *Point surfaces* have no lattice and are shaped directly by moving the points on the surface.

Tip   When building a model such as a human head, it is often easier to use point surfaces because you can adjust the surface interactively, and you avoid the confusion of having a complex control vertex lattice floating on top of your model, obscuring the area you are working on.

NURBS surfaces can also be created by converting MAX's standard primitives to NURBS surfaces, or by creating flat NURBS planes commonly called *NURBS patches*.

Creating NURBS

NURBS models can be created by converting standard primitive objects to NURBS, by creating NURBS surface rectangles (NURBS patches), or by drawing NURBS curves and covering them with a skin to generate surfaces. These various methods are discussed in the following sections.

Converting objects to NURBS

To convert a standard primitive object to a NURBS object, select the primitive object, open the Modify panel, and then click the Edit Stack button in the Modifier Stack rollout. This opens a pop-up menu where you can select the Convert To

NURBS option. Another option for converting primitives is to right-click the primitive object and select the Convert To NURBS option from the pop-up menu.

The primitive, when converted to a NURBS surface object, has a lattice of control vertices attached for manipulating its surface. Figure 16-2 shows two spheres. The one on the left is a normal primitive sphere, and the one on the right has been converted to a NURBS surface.

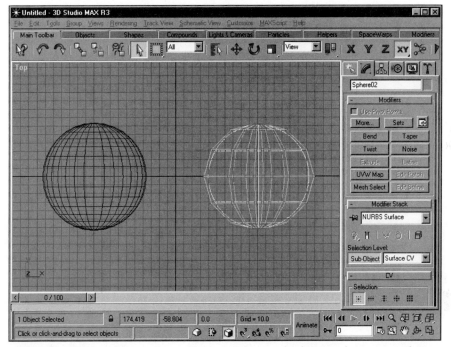

Figure 16-2: Standard primitives, like the sphere on the left, can be converted to NURBS surfaces.

Caution   Be aware that extended primitive objects and modified standard primitive objects cannot be converted to NURBS.

Another method to convert a standard primitive to a NURBS object is to attach it to a NURBS object. To do this, select the NURBS object, open the Modify panel, and under the General rollout click the Attach button and select the polygon object to attach. Any object that is attached to a NURBS object is automatically converted to a NURBS object.

Some Modifiers, such as the Lathe Modifier, give you the option of creating a patch, mesh, or NURBS as the output type. However, once a lathed object has been output as a polygonal mesh or a patch object, it can no longer be converted to a NURBS object.

Splines can also be converted to NURBS curves, but not all types of splines will convert to one-piece NURBS curves. For example, a line created using the Corner Initial Type and Drag Type options will convert to a series of separate NURBS curves. If you want the spline to convert to a single curve, you must set the Drag Type option to Smooth or Bézier. Of the many types of splines available in the Shapes category, only the Helix cannot be converted to a NURBS curve. The Rectangle, N-Gon, and Text shapes yield segmented NURBS curves, and closed shapes such as the Circle, Star, Ellipse, and Donut yield one-piece NURBS curves when converted.

Note If you plan to use multiple-piece curve shapes as cross sections in a 1- or 2-rail sweep (discussed later in the chapter) or as NURBS Extrusion curves, it is important to consider whether a curve is closed or not. To function properly, multiple-piece curve shapes need to be welded into a single NURBS curve after conversion.

Creating a rectangular NURBS surface

Flat rectangular point and CV surfaces can be made by opening the Create panel, clicking the Geometry category button, and selecting NURBS Surfaces from the subcategory drop-down menu. Then, to create the surface, you simply click and drag to make a rectangular shape in any viewport; when you release the mouse button, the surface is built. These rectangles, also referred to as NURBS patches, are easy to form into shapes by moving, scaling, and rotating the CVs. A large model can be built by assembling a group of these NURBS patches and attaching them with various NURBS surface tools.

Creating NURBS curves

To create a NURBS curve, open the Create panel, click the Shapes category button, and from the subcategory drop-down list select NURBS Curves. Click either Point Curve or CV Curve, and then click and drag in the viewport to set the first point and begin drawing the curve. After each click, drag the mouse to a new location and click again to continue extending the curve, and then right-click to end the curve. Notice that NURBS curves are automatically smoothed, but, unlike splines, they do not have Bézier control handles to adjust their shape. You can adjust the shape of a NURBS curve by moving the control vertices or by adjusting the weights (strengths of attraction) of individual CVs.

Figure 16-3 shows the Create CV Curve rollout, which becomes available when the CV Curve option is chosen. Using this rollout, you can set the Interpolation Steps value. The Optimize and Adaptive options automatically reduce the number of points required for the curve. You can also use this rollout to make the curve renderable. Renderable curves require a Thickness value. The Generate Mapping Coords. (Coordinates) option automatically generates mapping coordinates as the curve is created. The Automatic Reparamerization options include None, Chord Length, and Uniform. The Chord Length and Uniform options use different algorithms to determine the spacing of the CVs.

Figure 16-3: The Create CV Curve rollout is used to set some preliminary curve parameters.

The Create Point Curve rollout has the same parameters as the Create CV Curve rollout, except that there are no Reparamerization options.

Forming surfaces from NURBS curves

NURBS surfaces can be created from NURBS curves using the various buttons found in the Create Surfaces rollout in the Modify panel. These buttons are covered in the section that follows.

When a surface is created from two or more NURBS curves using the buttons in the Create Surfaces rollout, the surface is displayed in the form of U and V isoparms. *Isoparms* are lines that span the distance from one curve to the next and establish the NURBS surface. Isoparms are displayed in the viewport as green lines when a NURBS surface is selected.

Editing NURBS

Editing and modeling NURBS curves and surfaces into desired shapes can be done using the rollouts in the Modify panel, using the tools in the NURBS Creation Toolbox, or by working with the NURBS subobjects.

NURBS rollouts

When a NURBS curve is selected, several rollouts are available. The first of these is the General rollout, shown in Figure 16-4. This rollout includes buttons to attach and import NURBS. There are also the buttons Attach Multiple and Import Multiple, which let you select from a dialog box several objects to attach or import. When attaching NURBS, you have the option of reorienting the attached object.

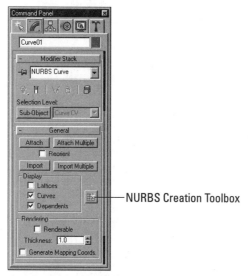

—NURBS Creation Toolbox

Figure 16-4: The General rollout for curves enables you to set the display options.

The General rollout also includes a Display section where you can select which elements get displayed. For curves, the options include Lattices, Curves, and Dependents. For surfaces, the options include Surfaces, Surface Trims, and Transform Degrade, and you can also choose the surface display to be a Tessellated Mesh or a Shaded Lattice. Next to the Display section is the NURBS Creation Toolbox button. This button opens a floating window of buttons that make it easy to work with NURBS. The NURBS Creation Toolbox buttons are covered in the next section.

When you're working with NURBS curves, the General rollout has options for making NURBS curves renderable with a given thickness and automatically generating mapping coordinates.

For NURBS surfaces, the Display Line Parameters rollout, shown along with the General rollout for NURBS surfaces in Figure 16-5, lets you specify the number of U and V isoparms to use to display the NURBS surface. These isoparms are the lines that make the NURBS object visible in the viewport.

Figure 16-5: The General and Display Line Parameters rollouts for NURBS surfaces

When you're working with NURBS surfaces, the Surface Approximation and Curve Approximation rollouts, shown in Figure 16-6, let you control the surface details for both the viewport and the renderer. For Base Surface, Surface Edge, and Displaced Surface, you can set Tessellation Method. There are three Tessellation Presets: Low, Medium, and High. These presets set the parameters for the various tessellation methods, with Low representing the values that produce the lowest-quality surface. You can also select which tessellation method to use — Regular, Parametric, Spatial, Curvature, or Spatial and Curvature. Each of these methods uses a different algorithm to compute the surface.

The Merge value determines the space between surfaces that should be combined to eliminate gaps when the surface is rendered. In most cases, the default value is acceptable for eliminating surface gaps. The Advanced Parameters button opens an additional dialog box of parameters that are used by the Spatial, Curvature, and Spatial and Curvature tessellation methods. The Clear Surface Level button eliminates all Surface Approximation settings.

Figure 16-6: The Surface Approximation and Curve Approximation rollouts let you choose the tessellation method and interpolation steps.

The Curve Approximation rollout lets you select the number of interpolation steps to use. You can also select the Optimize or Adaptive option. These options define the number of segments that are used to represent the curve.

The final three rollouts for NURBS objects are Create Points, Create Curves, and Create Surfaces. The buttons included in these rollouts work in the same fashion as the icon buttons found in the NURBS Creation Toolbox, which is covered next.

The NURBS Creation Toolbox

Clicking the NURBS Creation Toolbox button in the General rollout opens the toolbox shown in Figure 16-7. Clicking the button a second time closes the toolbox. This toolbox is divided into three sections: Points, Curves, and Surfaces.

Tip You can also open the NURBS Creation Toolbox by using the Ctrl+T keyboard shortcut.

Each of these sections includes buttons that create dependent subobjects. Dependent subobjects are objects that depend on other points, curves, or surfaces. When the parent object is changed, the dependent subobjects are changed also.

Figure 16-7: The NURBS Creation Toolbox lets you work with NURBS points, curves, and surfaces.

The Points section includes buttons for creating dependent NURBS points. These point types and their respective buttons are described in Table 16-1.

Table 16-1
Points NURBS Creation Toolbox Buttons

Toolbar Button	Name	Description
	Create Point	Creates a free independent point
	Create Offset Point	Creates a point that is offset from another point
	Create Curve Point	Creates a point that is on a curve
	Create Curve-Curve Point	Creates a point that intersects two curves
	Create Surf Point	Creates a point that is on a surface
	Create Surface Curve Point	Creates a point that intersects a curve and a surface

Creating freestanding or dependent NURBS points gives you another way to build curves. When one of these buttons is selected, the cursor changes when it is positioned over a place where the point can be created. For example, clicking the Create Surf Point button causes the cursor in the viewport to change when it is over a NURBS surface.

The Curves section includes many more buttons than the Points section. These buttons can be used to create dependent NURBS curves. Table 16-2 describes each of these buttons.

Table 16-2
Curves NURBS Creation Toolbox Buttons

Toolbar Button	Name	Description
	Create CV Curve	Creates a CV curve
	Create Point Curve	Creates a point curve
	Create Fit Curve	Creates a point curve that fits the selected points
	Create Transform Curve	Creates a copy of a curve that is transformed
	Create Offset Curve	Creates a copy of the original curve that is larger or smaller and moved to one side according to the distance setting
	Create Blend Curve	Blends or smoothly connects the ends of two NURBS curves
	Create Mirror Curve	Creates a mirrored copy of the original curve in the selected axis at a user-set distance
	Create Chamfer Curve	Creates a bevel where two curves meet
	Create Fillet Curve	Creates a radius line to make a smooth transition between two curves that cross each other
	Create Surface-Surface Intersection Curve	Creates a curve along the edge created when two NURBS surfaces intersect each other
	Create U Iso Curve	Creates a dependent curve from the U isoparm that make up the NURBS surface
	Create V Iso Curve	Creates a dependent curve from the V isoparm that make up the NURBS surface
	Create Normal Projected Curve	Projects a curve on a NURBS surface by projecting along a surface normal
	Create Vector Projected Curve	Projects a curve on a NURBS surface by projecting along a vector
	Create CV Curve on Surface	Enables the user to create a CV curve directly on a NURBS surface

Toolbar Button	Name	Description
	Create Point Curve on Surface	Enables the user to create a point curve directly on a NURBS surface
	Create Surface Offset Curve	Creates a curve that is offset from a surface curve
	Create Surface Edge Curve	Creates a curve that lies on the surface edge

Dependent curve subobjects can be created from points, curves, or surfaces. The cursor indicates when these can be created. Some dependent curves require two objects. For example, the Create Blend Curve button can attach two curves together. Selecting the first and then selecting the second does this. Each curve is highlighted blue as it is selected. The curves must be part of the same object.

The Surfaces section includes buttons for creating dependent NURBS surfaces. Table 16-3 describes each of these buttons.

Table 16-3
Surfaces NURBS Creation Toolbox Buttons

Toolbar Button	Name	Description
	Create CV Surface	Creates a CV surface
	Create Point Surface	Creates a point surface
	Create Transform Surface	Creates a copy of a surface that is transformed
	Create Blend Surface	Connects one surface to another with a smooth surface between them
	Create Offset Surface	Creates a copy of the original curve that is moved to one side according to the distance setting
	Create Mirror Surface	Creates a mirrored copy of the original surface in the selected axis at a user-set distance
	Create Extrude Surface	Creates a NURBS surface at right angles to the construction plane

Continued

	Table 16-3 *(continued)*	
Toolbar Button	**Name**	**Description**
	Create Lathed Surface	Creates a NURBS surface by rotating a curve about an axis
	Create Ruled Surface	Creates a straight surface that joins the edges of two separate surfaces; one edge can be curved and the other straight
	Create Capped Surface	Creates a surface that closes the edges of a closed surface
	Create U Loft Surface	Creates a surface by linking multiple closed curved contours along the U axis
	Create UV Loft Surface	Creates a surface by linking multiple closed curved contours along the U and V axes
	Create 1-Rail Sweep	Creates a surface using an edge defined by one curve with a cross section defined by another
	Create 2-Rail Sweep	Creates a surface using an edge defined by two curves with a cross section defined by another
	Create a Multisided Blend Surface	Creates a surface by blending several curves and surfaces
	Create a Multicurved Trimmed Surface	Creates a surface that is trimmed by several curves that form a loop
	Create Fillet Surface	Creates a surface with rounded corners where the surfaces meet

The buttons included in the NURBS Creation Toolbox give you a wide variety of possible NURBS objects to work with. Many of these NURBS objects are used in the tutorials later in this chapter.

Using NURBS subobject editing tools

MAX provides you with many tools that can be used to edit the various NURBS points, curves, and surfaces. To access these tools, select a NURBS object, open the Modify panel, click the Sub-Object button, and from the drop-down list select the subobject that you want to work with. The rollouts present the available editing tools. For example, if you select CV Surface from the subobject drop-down list, you can then adjust the position of the control vertices (or points on a point surface),

using MAX's standard transform buttons to change the shape of any
NURBS surface.

The rollouts change depending on the type of NURBS object and subobject selected.
The tools in these rollouts let you select and name specific areas, as well as hide,
delete, break, and detach NURBS elements, and even work with a Soft Selection.

Many details of these various subobject tools are demonstrated in the tutorials
that follow.

Working with NURBS

You'll learn many of the details of working with NURBS as you dive in and start
building NURBS objects. This section includes several tutorials that can help as you
try to grasp the power and flexibility of modeling with NURBS.

**On the
CD-ROM**

An additional advanced NURBS tutorial for creating a head model can be found on
the CD-ROM, along with the examples used in the tutorials in this chapter.

Lofting a NURBS surface

U Loft is one of the most versatile NURBS surface tools — it can be used to create
simple or very complex surfaces. In the following tutorial, we create a spoon by
U Lofting a NURBS surface over a series of point curve cross sections.

Tutorial: Creating a NURBS spoon

Lofting a skin over a series of cross-section curves can create NURBS surfaces. In
this tutorial, we create the point curves necessary for modeling a NURBS spoon.
Then we use the U Loft tool to skin the surface and create the finished spoon.

To create a NURBS spoon using the U Loft feature, follow these steps:

1. Load the spoon.jpg cross-section template image from the CD-ROM as a
   background image into both the Front and the Top viewports.

2. In the Create panel, click the Shapes category button, select NURBS Curves
   from the subcategory drop-down list, and then click the Point Curve button.

3. Maximize the Front viewport, and then locate the cross-section curve with
   points marked *A* through *L* that represents the shape of the large bell-shaped
   portion of the spoon. Click the point nearest the letter *A*, and then drag the
   cursor to the point marked *B* and click again to start the point curve.

4. Continue clicking in a clockwise direction until you get to the point marked *L*,
   and then click the *A* point again. The CV Curve dialog box will open, asking if
   you want to close the curve — click Yes to finish the curve.

5. Repeat the process to create all curves.

Tip   Another method for creating the curves is to create one of the smaller spoon handle cross-section curves, and then clone it and scale it to create the other cross-section curves.

6. Now maximize the Top viewport. Press the *H* hot key to open the Select Object by Name dialog box, and select the cross sections one at a time and move them into position to match the side and top views of the spoon. Each of the cross sections will look like a single white line when selected. They are numbered 1 through 10 on the template.

7. When the cross sections are correctly positioned, as shown in Figure 16-8, select one of the curves and open the Modify panel. In the General rollout, click the Attach Multiple button to open the Attach Multiple dialog box, click the All button to select all the curves, and then click the Attach button to attach all the curves to the first curve you selected.

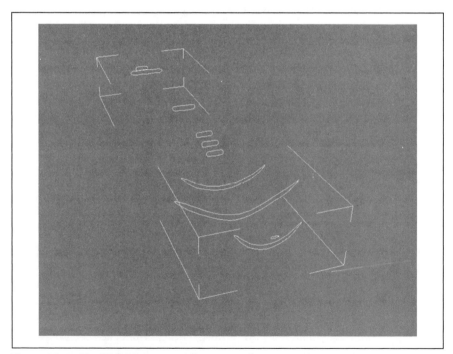

Figure 16-8: The NURBS cross-section curves for a spoon

8. You are now ready to U Loft the spoon's surface. Select any of the NURBS curves, and then in the Modify panel under the General rollout, click the NURBS Creation Toolbox icon (the small green icon to the right of the Display section) to open the NURBS toolbox window. From the window, in the

Surfaces section, select the Create U Loft Surface icon. The cursor will change to a pointer accompanied by the U Loft Surface icon. (Notice that when you place the cursor over a cross section, it changes to a cross and the curve turns blue.)

Note   You can also create this surface using the U Loft button found in the Create Surfaces rollout.

9. Click the smallest cross section at the tip of the spoon marked with the number *1*, and then drag to the curve marked *2*, and click again. The first section of the U Lofted NURBS surface is then generated as indicated by the green isoparm lines displayed in the viewport.

10. Continue clicking each curve in sequential order until you have lofted the entire spoon. After you've clicked the final section, right-click to exit this mode.

11. To view the U Loft, right-click the viewport name and select Smooth and Highlights. If the spoon remains transparent, go to the Modify panel, and at the bottom of the U Loft Surface rollout select the Flip Normals option to see the NURBS surface.

12. Now cap the ends by returning to the NURBS toolbox window, selecting the Create Cap Surface tool, and clicking each small end curve.

Figure 16-9 shows the completed NURBS spoon.

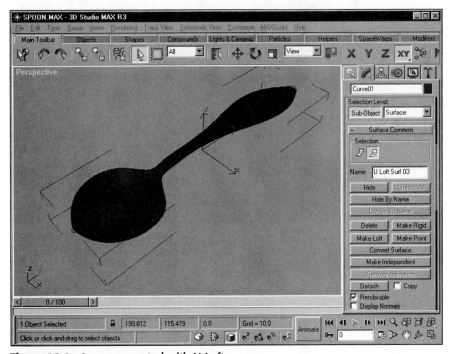

Figure 16-9: A spoon created with U Loft

UV Loft surface

A UV Loft surface can have more complex contours than a U Loft surface. As an example, Figure 16-10 shows a chair seat that has been UV Lofted using three curves in the U direction and five curves in the V direction, thus enabling the surface to be contoured to fit a human being without the user having to go back later and modify it by moving control vertices. The long center and right-side contour U curves were cloned from the original left-side curve, and then moving CVs modified the center curve. The short cross-section V curves were cloned from the original curve at the top of the seat back, modified into shape by moving CVs, and moved into position so that the ends and centers touched the U contour curves. The curves were then attached and the surface was UV Lofted.

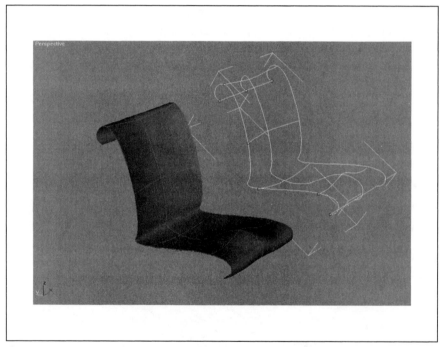

Figure 16-10: A UV Loft surface lofted from two sets of curves

This is a very useful technique for building mechanical shapes, automobiles, and spaceships and for modeling product designs.

Lathing a NURBS surface

Lathing a NURBS curve works the same way as lathing a spline using the NURBS Modifier. You simply need to select a curve, click the Lathe button in the Create Surface rollout, and then click the curve. You can change the Degrees value and the axis of rotation in the Lathe Surface rollout that appears under the Create Surfaces rollout in the Modify panel.

Tutorial: Lathing a NURBS CV curve to create a vase

In this tutorial we create a NURBS CV curve profile shape. This curve is then used with the Lathe Modifier to create a vase.

To create a NURBS CV curve, follow these steps:

1. To draw the first NURBS curve, we use a template image as a pattern for the shape of the vase. To load the template image, select Views ➪ Viewport Background to open the Viewport Background dialog box. Click the Files button to open the Select Background Image dialog box, and then locate the vase.jpg image file in the Front view, select it, and click Open to return to the Viewport Background dialog box.

2. In the Viewport drop-down list at the bottom of the Viewport Background dialog box, select Front. Then select both the Match Bitmap option and the Lock Zoom/Pan option. Click OK to exit the Viewport Background dialog box. The vase template drawing that is displayed on your screen is shown in Figure 16-11.

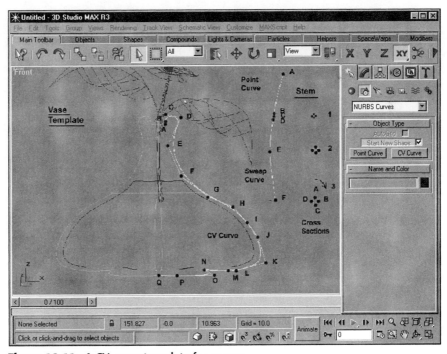

Figure 16-11: A CV curve template for a vase

3. Maximize the Front viewport. To begin drawing the CV curve, open the Create panel, click the Shapes category button, and then from the subcategory drop-down list select NURBS Curves.

4. Under the Object Type rollout, select CV Curve.

5. The background image shows a point marked *A*. Click this point to start the CV curve, and release the mouse button. Then drag the cursor to point *B* and click the mouse button again to place the second CV curve point.

6. Continue clicking all the points in order. After clicking the last point (*P*), right-click to end NURBS curve creation. You should now have a CV curve that matches the background template curve.

7. With the CV curve still selected, open the Modify panel and click the Lathe button in the Create Surfaces rollout. The Lathe Surface rollout will appear at the bottom of the Modify panel; enter a value of **360** in the Degrees field and click the Y-axis button. Then click the CV curve to complete the lathe. Click the Lathe button again to exit lathe mode.

Figure 16-12 shows the completed vase produced using the Lathe tool.

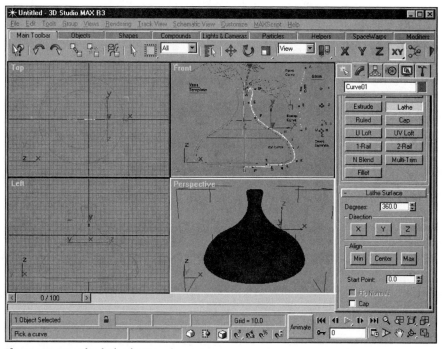

Figure 16-12: The lathed CV surface vase

Creating a 1- and 2-rail sweep surface

The 1-rail sweep surface tool lets you create a NURBS surface by using one NURBS curve to act as a side rail, and one or more profile shape curves to sweep along the rail to generate the surface. A 2-rail sweep surface is similar, except that it uses two NURBS curves as side rails.

Tutorial: Creating a flower stem

Now that we have carefully constructed a flower vase, we need to create some flowers to place in the vase. We start with the flower stem.

To create a NURBS Point surface using a 1-rail sweep, follow these steps:

1. Load the vase.jpg template image from the previous tutorial into the Front viewport background if it is not already loaded.

2. Locate the vertical curved line that is labeled "Stem" in the template image. This is the template for the 1-rail sweep curve that you make into a flower stem.

3. To begin drawing the Point curve, click the Shapes category button in the Create panel, and then in the subcategory drop-down menu select NURBS Curves.

4. Under the Object Type rollout, click the Point button. Then in the Front viewport, click the point on the stem template marked *A* to start the point curve. Drag the cursor to point *B* and click the mouse to place the second point. Continue clicking all the points in order. After clicking the last point (*F*), right-click to end the NURBS curve creation. You should now have a point curve that matches the stem template curve.

5. Next to the stem are three circles with points marked *A* through *D*. Click those points in order for each circle, but instead of right-clicking to end the curve, click the *A* point again. The CV Curve dialog box opens, asking if you want to close the curve—select Yes.

6. To create a NURBS surface, first reposition the three circular stem cross sections so that they are at a right angle to the long stem curve. They must all be oriented in the same direction and should touch the rail on one edge. (The stem will not skin correctly if the shape is too far away from the rail.)

7. Now, select the long stem curve. Open the Modify panel (if it isn't open already) and click the Attach Multiple button to open the Attach Multiple dialog box. Select the three circular stem cross-section curves and then click the Attach button.

8. Open the Create Surfaces rollout and click the 1-Rail (Sweep) button.

9. In the prompt line MAX will ask you to "Pick a curve for the Rail" — click the long stem curve. Then the prompt line will ask you to "Pick a curve for cross-section 1" — click the bottom cross section and then repeat (following the prompt line) for the middle and top cross sections. Right-click to end the creation of the 1-rail sweep.

The NURBS skin is generated on the stem as shown in Figure 16-13.

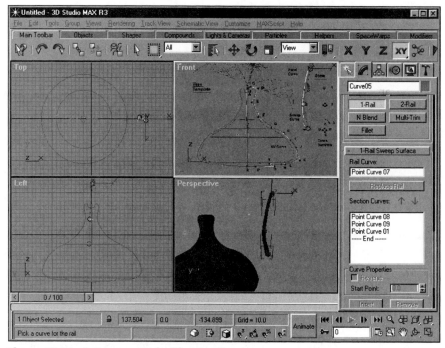

Figure 16-13: A stem created with a 1-rail sweep

Sculpting a rectangular NURBS surface

NURBS patches are a quick way to create a surface that can be sculpted using the subobject elements, such as a control lattice. For each subobject type, there are many different tools that can be used to form the patch.

Tutorial: Creating a NURBS leaf

In this tutorial we create a NURBS CV surface plane that is sculpted into a leaf for the NURBS flower. To do this, we work in the Surface CV subobject level and use the Select and Move transform tool to move CVs and sculpt the NURBS rectangle into a leaf shape.

To create a rectangular NURBS CV surface, follow these steps:

1. In the Create panel, click the Geometry category button and select NURBS Surfaces from the subcategory drop-down list. Click the CV Surf button and in the Create Parameters rollout, increase the Length CVs to 6 and Width CVs to **6**; then click the Generate Mapping Coords. check box.

2. In the Top viewport, click and drag to create the NURBS surface. In the Create Parameters rollout, set both the Length and Width to **180**. Still in the Top viewport, rotate the NURBS surface 45 degrees using the Select and Rotate tool so that it looks like a diamond shape.

3. Select the NURBS surface. In the Modify panel, click the Sub-Object button to enable the default Surface CV subobject mode.

4. The CV lattice is displayed in the Top viewport. Select the Non-Uniform Scale tool, constrain it to the X-axis, and then drag-select the middle horizontal row of CVs. Scale them down (narrower) to 85%.

5. Select the middle three horizontal rows of CVs (including the one just scaled) and scale them down to 90%. Then select the middle five horizontal rows and scale them down to 90%. This gently rounds the outside contours of the NURBS surface.

6. In the Front viewport you should see the edge of the NURBS surface. Maximize the viewport, and then select the Rotate tool, constrain it to the Z-axis, and select the right half of the CVs but do not select the CVs at the very center. Rotate the CVs upward 60 degrees.

7. Repeat the select-and-rotate process with the CV on the left half of the center, but do not alter the CVs at the very center. The leaf should now be U-shaped.

8. Click the Move tool, constrain it to the Y-axis, and then select the center row of CVs and move them downward –40 units to make a deep V shape.

Figure 16-14 shows the NURBS leaf with the control lattice visible.

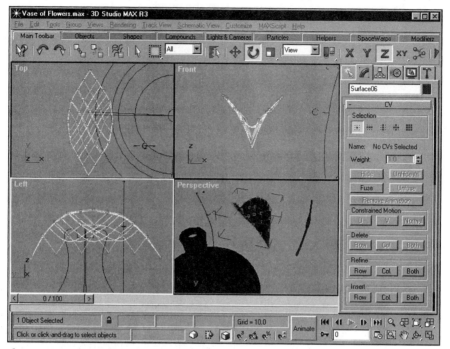

Figure 16-14: Translating CVs to sculpt a NURBS leaf

Tutorial: Sculpting a flower petal

Continuing to build our flower, we now sculpt a second rectangular NURBS surface into the shape of a flower petal. In this case the center CVs of the surface are raised to create a soft rounded shape. We then sculpt one end of the NURBS rectangle into a blossom petal shape, and then scale and clone it to create three more petals.

To sculpt the flower petal shape, follow these steps:

1. In the Create panel, click the Geometry category button and select NURBS Surfaces from the subcategory drop-down. Click the CV Surf button, and in the Keyboard Entry rollout, create a NURBS rectangular surface 80 units long and 80 units wide, with 6 Length CVs and 6 Width CVs.

2. Select the Rotate tool, and in the Top view rotate the surface 45 degrees. In the Modify panel, click the Sub-Object button to enable the Surface CV mode.

3. Select the Non-Uniform Scale tool, constrain to the X-axis, and then select the center horizontal row of CVs and scale it down (narrower) to 86%. This rounds the outside corners of the petal.

4. Drag-select the six CVs that make up the upper tip of the petal. Non-uniform-scale the triangle of CVs in the Y-axis down to 35% to blunt the point at the top of the petal.

5. Click and drag a selection box around all the CVs in the center of the petal (don't select any CVs on the edges). You can use the Ctrl key to add CVs to the selection and the Alt key to remove CVs from the selection. In the Front viewport, select the Move tool and move the CVs upward 6 units in the Y-axis to round the top of the petal.

6. In the Top viewport select the lower half of the center vertical row of CVs, press the Lock Selection icon (or press the spacebar), and then in the Front viewport use the Move tool to move the CVs 7 units downward in the Y-axis. This makes a groove halfway down the center of the petal. Unlock the selection set.

7. To clone the petal, turn off subobject mode, and then activate the Top viewport. Select World from the Reference Coordinate System drop-down. Click the Mirror icon to open the Mirror: Screen Coordinates dialog box, and then clone the petal by selecting the Y-axis and Copy options. Move the new petal downward in the Y-axis so that the points of the petals touch.

8. Now clone the petals again, but smaller. Select the Uniform Scale button, select both petals in the Top viewport, and then press the Shift key and scale the petals down to 40% to create smaller cloned versions of the petals. Lock the selection set, click Rotate, and then rotate the small petals 90 degrees to finish the blossom.

Figure 16-15 shows the completed flower.

To finish the flower and vase model, you need to merge all the parts of the flower vase project into one scene. Clone and position the leaves next to the stem. Position the stem in the throat of the vase at a slight angle. Position the leaves midway up the stem, and then place the flower at the top of the stem, at right angles to the leaves. Finally, texture-map all objects, applying a glass material to the vase, dark green to the leaves and stem, and a pink and white radial gradient to each petal of the blossom. Put a reflection map on the table, and create a second lathed object inside the vase to simulate colored water. The final rendering of the finished flower is shown in Figure 16-16.

Chapter 17, "Exploring the Material Editor," explains how to add materials to the final model.

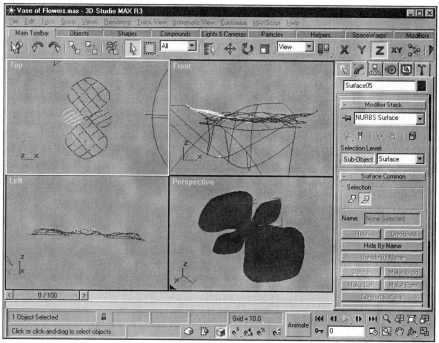

Figure 16-15: Flower petals that were sculpted using NURBS

Figure 16-16: A vase and flower built completely from NURBS

Summary

NURBS are an ideal method for modeling if you require free-flowing models. In this chapter you've:

✦ Discovered how to convert primitives to NURBS objects

✦ Created CV and point curves

✦ Created NURBS surfaces from curves

✦ Learned to edit NURBS curves and surfaces

✦ Lofted surfaces from point and CV curves

✦ Used NURBS subobject tools

This concludes the modeling part of the book. The next part covers materials and maps, beginning with a chapter on the Material Editor.

✦   ✦   ✦

Materials and Maps

Exploring the Material Editor

Materials are used to dress, color, and paint objects. Just as materials in real life can be described as scaly, soft, smooth, opaque, or blue, materials applied to 3D objects can mimic properties such as color, texture, transparency, shininess, and so on.

In this chapter, you'll learn the basics of working with materials and all the features of the Material Editor for creating and applying these materials to objects.

Understanding Material Properties

Up until now, the only material property that has been applied to an object has been the default object color, randomly assigned by MAX. The Material Editor can add a whole new level of realism using materials that simulate many different types of physical properties such as the ones discussed in the following sections.

Note   Many of these material properties aren't visible until the scene is actually rendered.

Colors

Color is probably the simplest material property and the easiest to identify. However, unlike the object color defined in the Create and Modify panels, there isn't a single color swatch that controls an object's color.

Consider a basket of shiny red apples. When you shine a bright blue spotlight on them, all the apples turn purple. So, even if the apples are assigned a red material, the final color in the image might be very different.

Within the Material Editor are several different color swatches that control different aspects of the object's color. The following list describes the types of color swatches that are available.

✦ **Ambient** — Defines an overall background lighting that affects all objects in the scene, including the color of the object when it is in the shadows. This color can often be locked to the Diffuse color so that they are changed together.

✦ **Diffuse** — The surface color of the object surface in normal, full light. The normal color of an object is typically defined by its Diffuse color.

✦ **Specular** — The color of the highlights where the light is focused on the surface of a shiny material.

✦ **Self-Illumination** — The color that the object glows from within. This color takes over any shadows on the object.

✦ **Filter** — The transmitted color caused by light shining through a transparent object.

✦ **Reflect** — The color that is reflected by a Raytrace material to other objects in the scene.

✦ **Luminosity** — Causes an object to glow with the defined color. It is similar to Self-Illumination color, but can be independent of the Diffuse color.

✦ **Transparency** — The color that is applied to materials behind a transparent Raytrace material. It is similar to Filter color but is available only for Raytrace materials.

✦ **Extra Lighting** — Applied to Raytrace materials to increase the effect of Ambient light on a particular material. This can be used to simulate radiosity.

✦ **Translucency** — The color of an object that scatters light. It is available for Raytrace materials.

✦ **Fluorescence** — Makes materials glow like fluorescent colors under a black light. It is available for Raytrace materials.

If you ask someone the color of an object, he or she would respond by identifying the Diffuse color, but all these properties play an important part in bringing a sense of realism to the material. Try applying very different, bright materials to each of these color swatches and notice the results. The object will look unique, but not very realistic.

Tip

For realistic materials, your choice of colors depends on the scene lights. Indoor lights have a result different from an outdoor light like the sun. You can simulate objects in direct sunlight by giving their Specular color a yellow tint and their Ambient color a complementary, dark, almost black or purple color. For indoor objects, make the Specular color bright white and use an Ambient color that is the same as the Diffuse color, only much darker.

Opacity and transparency

Opaque objects are objects that you cannot see through, such as rocks and trees. *Transparent objects*, on the other hand, are objects that you can see through, like glass and clear plastic. MAX's materials include several controls for adjusting these properties, including Opacity and several Transparency controls.

Opacity is the amount that an object refuses to allow light to pass through it. It is the opposite of transparency and is typically measured as a percentage. An object with 0 percent opacity is completely transparent, and an object with an opacity of 100 percent doesn't let any light through.

Transparency is the amount of light that is allowed to pass through an object. Because this is the opposite of opacity, transparency can be defined by the opacity value. There are several options for controlling the transparency including Falloff, Amount, and Type. These controls will be discussed later.

Reflection and refraction

A *reflection* is what you see when you look in the mirror. Shiny objects will reflect their surroundings. By defining a material's reflection values, you can control how much it reflects its surroundings. A mirror, for example, will reflect everything, but a rock won't reflect at all.

Refraction is the bending of light as it moves through a transparent material. The amount of refraction a material produces is expressed as a value on the Index of Refraction.

The *Index of Refraction* is the amount that light bends as it goes through a transparent object. For example, thick glasses will bend light farther than thin ones and will therefore have a higher Index of Refraction value. The default Index of Refraction value is 1.0. Water has a value of 1.3, glass a value of around 1.5, and solid crystal a value of around 2.0.

Shininess and specular highlights

Shiny objects such as polished metal or clean windows will include highlights where the lights reflect off their surface. These highlights are called *specular highlights* and are determined by the Specular settings. These settings include Specular Level, Glossiness, and Soften values.

The *Specular Level* is a setting for the intensity of the highlight. The *Glossiness* determines the size of the highlight — higher values result in a smaller highlight. The *Soften* value thins the highlight by lowering its intensity and increasing its size.

A rough material has the opposite properties of a shiny material and almost no highlights. The *Roughness* property sets how quickly the Diffuse color blends with the Ambient color. Cloth and fabric materials will have a high Roughness value, and plastic and metal Roughness values will be small.

Other properties

There are several miscellaneous properties that MAX uses to help define Standard materials, including Diffuse Level and Metalness.

The *Diffuse Level* property controls the brightness of the Diffuse color. Decreasing this value darkens the material without affecting the specular highlights.

The *Metalness* property controls the metallic look of the material.

Raytrace properties

Several of the properties discussed thus far are only available for Raytrace materials. There are also several properties that are unique to Raytrace materials, including Translucency and Fluorescence.

Translucency is similar to transparency in that it lets light pass through an object, but it also scatters the light so that other objects cannot be seen through the translucent object; an example of such a translucent object would be frosted glass.

Raytrace materials can also simulate *Fluorescence*, which is the ability to reflect light in fluorescent colors under a black light.

Working with the Material Editor

The *Material Editor* is the interface where materials are defined, created, and applied. You can access the Material Editor by selecting Tools ➪ Material Editor, clicking the Material Editor button on the main toolbar, or by using the **M** keyboard shortcut.

Using the Material Editor controls

At the top of the default Material Editor window are six sample slots that display a preview of available materials. Surrounding these slots are button icons for controlling the appearance of these sample slots and interacting with materials. Figure 17-1 shows the Material Editor.

The button icons to the right and below the sample slots control how the materials appear in the editor. These buttons are defined in Table 17-1.

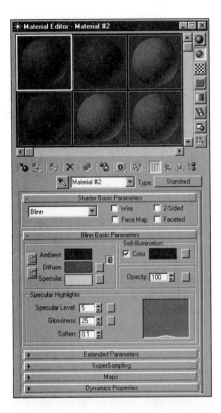

Figure 17-1: The Material Editor window is used to store and work with materials.

Table 17-1
Material Editor Buttons

Toolbar Button	Name	Description
	Sample Type	Controls the type of object displayed in the sample slot. The default object is a sphere. Other options available as flyouts include a Cylinder and a Cube. You can also select a custom object to use as the preview object.
	Backlight	Turns backlighting in the sample slots on or off.
	Background	Displays a checkered background image behind the material. This helps when displaying a transparent material.

(Continued)

	Table 17-1 *(continued)*	
Toolbar Button	*Name*	*Description*
	Sample UV Tiling	Sets UV tiling for the map in the sample slot. The default is 1x1. Additional options available as flyouts are 2x2, 3x3, and 4x4. This setting only affects maps.
	Video Color Check	Checks the current material for colors that are unsupported by the NTSC and PAL formats.
	Make Preview, Play Preview, Save Preview	Used to generate, view, and save material preview renderings. These animated material previews enable you to see the effect of an animated material before rendering.
	Options	Opens the Material Editor Options dialog box. This dialog box includes settings for enabling material animation, loading a custom background, defining the light intensity and color of sample slots, and selecting the number of sample slots.
	Select by Material	Selects all objects using the current material. This button opens the Select Objects dialog box with those objects selected.
	Get Material	Opens the Material/Map Browser for selecting materials.
	Put Material in Scene	Updates the materials in the scene after materials have been edited.
	Assign Material to Selection	Paints the selected object with the selected material.
	Reset Map/ Mtl to Default Settings	Removes any modified properties and resets the material properties to their defaults.
	Make Material Copy	Creates a copy of the current material in the active sample slot.
	Put to Library	Opens a simple dialog box that lets you rename the material and saves it into the current open library.
	Material Effects Channel	Sets a unique channel ID for applying post-processing effects. This button includes channels 1–15 as flyouts. A material with channel 0 means no effect will be applied.
	Show Map in Viewport	Displays 2D material maps on objects in the viewports.

Toolbar Button	Name	Description
	Show End Result	Displays the material in the sample slot with all levels applied. If this button is disabled, you will see only the level that is currently selected.
	Go to Parent	Moves you up one level for the current material. This applies only to Compound Objects with several levels.
	Go Forward to Sibling	Selects the next maps or material at the same level.
	Material/Map Navigator	Opens the Material/Map Navigator dialog box. This dialog box displays a tree of all the levels for the current material.
	Pick Material From Object	Enables you to select a material from an object in the scene and load the material into the current sample slot.
Map #2 ▼	Material drop-down list	Lists the elements in the current material. You can change the material or map name by typing a new name in this field.
Bitmap	Type button	Displays the current material or map type that is being used. Clicking this button opens the Material/Map Browser where you can select a new material or map type.

Below the material name and type button is where the rollouts for the current material are opened. These rollouts will change depending on the material type and will be discussed along with the various material types.

Using the sample slots

The Material Editor includes twenty-four sample slots that display materials and map previews. Each of these sample slots contains one material or map. The materials are rendered using the Scanline renderer, but a different rendering engine can be specified in the Options dialog box. Only one sample slot can be active at a time—the active slot is outlined with a white border. Click one of the material slots to select it.

Note   Sample slots cannot be empty—they always contain a material of some kind.

Sample slots are temporary placeholders for materials and maps. An actual scene can have hundreds of materials. By loading a material into a sample slot, you can change its parameters, apply it to other materials, or save it to a library for use in other scenes.

Twenty-four slots are available, but the default layout displays only six. You can access the other eighteen slots using the scroll bars. You can also change the number of displayed slots. To change the number of slots, right-click any of the materials and select 2x3, 3x5, or 4x6 from the pop-up menu. These options are also available in the Options dialog box. Figure 17-2 shows the Material Editor with twenty-four sample slots displayed.

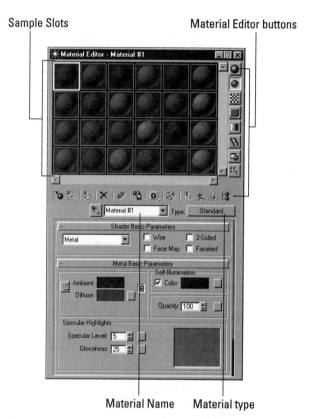

Sample Slots   Material Editor buttons

Material Name   Material type

Figure 17-2: You can set the number of sample slots in the Material Editor to display 6, 15, or 24 slots.

Tip   The 24 default sample slots that are available when the Material Editor is opened are loaded from the medit.mat file in the \matlibs subdirectory. To load your own materials, save them into this file.

Using the right-click pop-up menu

When you right-click the active sample slot, a pop-up menu appears. From this menu you can select several commands. The Drag/Copy command is a toggle setting. When enabled, it leaves a copy of the material when it's dragged to another slot. The Drag/Rotate command lets you rotate the material object in the sample slot when you drag with the mouse. Dragging on the object rotates it about its X- and Y-axes, and dragging from the corner of the sample slot rotates it about its Z-axis. Holding down the Shift key constrains the rotation about a single axis. The Reset Rotation command resets the material object to its original orientation.

The Render Map command opens the Render Map dialog box, shown in Figure 17-3. This dialog box renders the current map as a bitmap or an animation file and enables you to save the file. From this dialog box you can select the Range of frames to include and the Dimensions of the rendered file.

Figure 17-3: The Render Map dialog box lets you render and save a map applied to a material.

Note   Render maps can be saved as AVI, BMP, Kodak Cineon, EPS, FLC, JPEG, PNG, MOV, SGI, RLA, RPF, TGA, and TIF files.

The Options command opens the Material Editor Options dialog box discussed in the next section.

The Magnify command opens the material in a magnified window. You can also open this window by double-clicking the sample slot. The window can be resized to view the material at any size, and it can be set to automatically update when changes are made. If the Auto option is disabled, you can update the material by clicking the Update button. Figure 17-4 shows the magnified window.

The 2x3, 3x5, and 4x6 Sample Windows commands set the number of sample slots that are displayed.

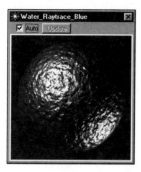

Figure 17-4: Materials can be opened in a magnified window by double-clicking them.

Using different sample objects

The Sample Type displayed in the sample slots can be changed among sphere, cube, and cylinder using the Sample Type button at the top right of the Material Editor window.

The Options button opens the Material Editor Options dialog box where you can designate a custom sample object. This dialog box is discussed in more detail in the "Setting Material Editor Options" section later in this chapter. The sample object must be contained in a .max file. To create a sample object, create and save a MAX scene with a single object that fits inside a 100-unit cube.

The scene can also include custom lights and cameras. The object must have Mapping Coordinates enabled. These can be enabled by selecting the Generate Mapping Coordinates option for objects like primitives or by applying the UVW Map Modifier. Once the object is loaded using the Options dialog box, you'll need to select the object from the Object Type flyout.

Figure 17-5 shows the Material Editor with several custom samples loaded.

Dragging materials

You can drag and drop materials in MAX, such as between the various sample slots. The materials in a sample slot can be also be dragged and dropped onto object within the viewport. Dropping a material onto an object automatically assigns the material to that object.

You can also drag materials from the sample slots back and forth among the Material/Map Browser, the Asset Manager Utility, and any rollouts where maps can be specified, such as the Environment Map button, the Projector Light button, and the Displace Modifier Map button.

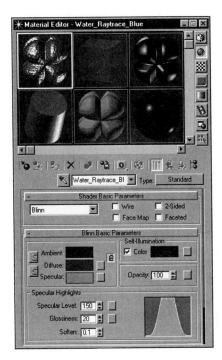

Figure 17-5: You can load a custom sample object to be displayed in the sample slots.

Renaming materials

Every material has a name that appears underneath the sample slots. You can rename a material by typing a new name in the material name box. This name will appear in the Material/Map Navigator dialog box and in the Track View. With Release 3, MAX no longer restricts material names to 16 characters. When a material is saved to a Library, a dialog box opens that enables you to rename the material.

Caution

If you drag a material from one sample slot to another, a copy is made with the same name as the original. If one of these materials is changed and then applied to the scene, a warning dialog box will appear stating that a material with the same name already exists in the scene. It also gives you the option of replacing or renaming the material.

Applying standard materials

When a material is selected, it can be applied to the selected object with the Assign Material to Selection button. Alternatively, you could drag a material from its sample slot and drop it on an object.

Note   When a material is assigned to an object in the scene the material becomes "Hot." A *Hot material* is automatically updated in the scene when the material parameters change. Hot materials have white corner brackets displayed around their sample slots.

New materials are loaded into the sample slots by clicking the Get Material button—this opens the Material/Map Browser. Click the Mtl Editor radio button to see a list of standard materials. Materials are indicated with a blue sphere icon, and material maps have a green parallelogram next to them. To select a new material, double-click it. The new material will be loaded into the selected sample slot.

Tip   Another easy way to apply a material is to simply drag it from one of the Material Slots onto an object in a viewport. This automatically applies the material to the object.

Setting Material Editor options

As mentioned earlier in this chapter, you can open the Material Editor Options dialog box by clicking the Options button to the right of the sample slots. You can also open this dialog box by right-clicking a sample slot and selecting Options from the pop-up menu. Figure 17-6 shows this dialog box.

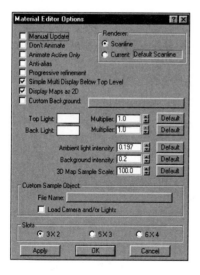

Figure 17-6: The Material Editor Options dialog box offers many options for controlling the Material Editor window.

The Material Editor Options dialog box includes options that control how the materials are displayed in the sample slots. These options are as follows:

✦ **Manual Update** — Doesn't update any changes in the sample slot until the slot is clicked on.

✦ **Don't Animate** — Causes materials not to animate when an animation is played or the Time Slider is dragged. It does, however, update these materials to the current frame.

✦ **Animate Active Only** — Animates only the active sample slot if it contains an animated material. This option is only available when the Don't Animate option is selected.

✦ **Anti-alias** — Enables anti-aliasing for all sample slots.

✦ **Progressive refinement** — Causes materials to be rendered progressively. This causes the material to appear quickly as blocky sections and then slowly in more detail. This gives you a rough idea of how the material looks before the rendering is finished.

✦ **Simple Multi Display Below Top Level** — Displays several different areas for only the top level when a Multi/Sub-Object material is applied.

✦ **Display Maps as 2D** — Displays stand-alone maps in 2D and not on the sample object. This is helpful to know when you're looking at a map versus a material.

✦ **Custom Background** — Enables you to use a custom background behind the sample slots. The background can be loaded using the button to the right of the option. Once changed, the new background is used in all sessions.

Also, within the Material Editor Options dialog box, you can select the renderer you want to use to render the materials in the sample slots. The Scanline option is the default option. The Current option lets you select to use the renderer that is specified in the Preferences dialog box. The Scanline renderer is always an option, regardless of the current renderer.

This dialog box also offers options to adjust the color and intensity of the Top and Back lights used to render the materials in the sample slots. The Ambient Light Intensity value controls the brightness of the Ambient light in the sample slots. The Background Intensity value sets the brightness of the background — a value of 0 produces a black background and 1 produces a white background. The 3D Map Sample Scale option scales the sample objects for all slots.

The Custom Sample Object button is for loading a Custom Sample Object (as discussed in the earlier sections) as well as options for specifying the number of sample slots. Any of these settings can be reset to their original values by clicking the Default button.

Using the Material/Map Browser

Whenever you change material types, choose a new map, or click the Get Material button the Material/Map Browser is opened. This is a separate dialog box, shown in Figure 17-7, where all the material and map types are stored. This dialog box also lets you access and manage material libraries.

Figure 17-7: The Material/Map Browser lets you select new material and map types.

The Material/Map Browser includes several browse options including Material Library, Material Editor, Active Slot, Selected, Scene, and New. The New option is the default. You can also limit it to show only materials, only maps, or both, and you can restrict the browser to show only a specific type of map.

The buttons above the material list enable you to display the materials and maps in different ways. For example, Figure 17-8 shows the View Small Icons option.

View list and icons   View small icons

View list   View large icons

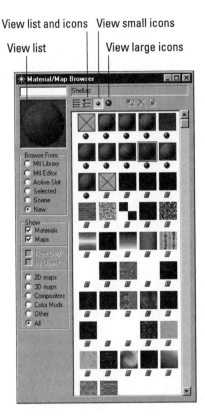

Figure 17-8: The Material/Map Browser includes several display modes, such as View Small Icons.

Working with additional material libraries

When a MAX scene is created and new materials are applied, the materials are saved along with the MAX file. To be able to share materials between scenes, you can save them into an additional library.

Libraries of preset materials can be created, loaded, and saved. Once a library is created, you can add materials to and delete materials from it.

On the CD-ROM

A sample material library is included on the CD-ROM, along with the models used in this chapter's tutorials.

To load a library, click the Get Material button in the Material Editor to open the Material/Map Browser, shown in Figure 17-9. In the Browse From section, select the Mtl Library option and click the Open button. You can also merge an external library with the current one. The Save and Save As buttons let you save new library sets.

Delete from library

Update scene materials from library   Clear material library

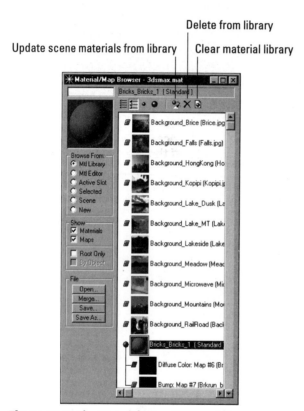

Figure 17-9: The Material/Map Browser lets you work with saved material libraries.

Material libraries are saved as MAT files. These files include all the parameter settings for the materials and can be viewed as text files with the File Insert ➪ View File command. You can look for additional material libraries on the supplementary CD-ROMs that ship with MAX.

Figure CI-1: Suburbs 2000 by Dawid Michalczyk

Figure CI-2: "Memories of Alexander Green" by Victoria Brace

Figure CI-3: "Chateau Brumal" by Molly Barr

Figure CI-4: "Phint (A gift to my Wife, Angela)" by Joe Poppa

Figure CI-5: "Schumettering über Rose (Butterfly above Rose)" by Takara Ookami

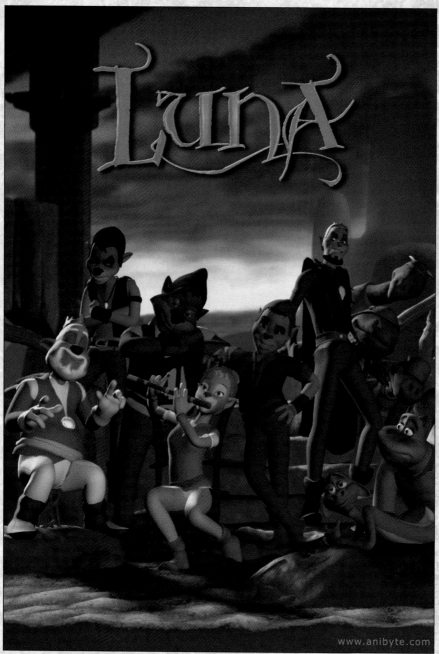

www.anibyte.com

Figure CI-6: "Luna" by Victor Garrido

Figure CI-7: "Forest Girl" by Virgins Lands, Germany

Figure CI-8: "Energy Rifle" by Arild Wiro

Figure CI-9: "School of Fish II" by Ian Dale

Figure CI-10: "Woman World" by Szymon Masiak

Figure CI-11: "Lost World" by Paul Rance

Figure CI-12: "The Number Forest" by Van Spragins, Christopher Sherrill, Cythina Levine, Steven Marshall, Arnaldo Laboy, and Joey Elardy for Zenimation

Figure CI-13: "The Traveler" by Tim Wallace

Figure CI-14: "Telescope" by Gary Butcher

Figure CI-15: "Einstein's Legacy" by Michael Lawso

Figure CI-16: "Soccer Ball" by Thomas Suurland

Above the material list, three additional buttons become enabled when a material library is opened. These buttons let you update the scene, delete the selected material from the library, and clear the entire library.

Tutorial: Coloring Easter eggs

Everyone loves Spring with its bright colors and newness of life. One of the highlights of the season is the tradition of coloring Easter eggs. In this tutorial, we'll use virtual eggs, — no messy dyes and no "egg salad" sandwiches for the next two weeks.

To create our virtual Easter eggs and apply different colors to them, follow these steps:

1. First we'll create the egg. Open the Create panel and click the Sphere button. Drag in the Top view to create a sphere object. Then click and hold the mouse down on the Select and Uniform Scale button in the main toolbar and select the Select and Non-Uniform Scale flyout. Then click the sphere in the Left view and drag upward to elongate the sphere object along the Z-axis.

2. Open the Modify panel and click the Taper button. Then enter **-0.35** in the Amount field and press Enter on the keyboard to apply this value. This will taper the sphere to create a real looking egg.

3. Open the Array dialog box by selecting Tools ⇨ Array. Enter a value slightly greater than the sphere Radius value in the Incremental X-axis Move field. Then enter the same value in the Incremental Row Offset field after entering a 1D Count of **6** and a 2D Count of **2**. Click OK. This will create a dozen eggs in two rows of six. All the eggs will have the same object color at this point.

4. Open the Material Editor by selecting Tools ⇨ Material Editor (or you can press the M key).

5. Increase the number of sample slots by right-clicking the active material and selecting 5 X 3 Sample Windows from the pop-up menu.

6. Select the first sample slot and click the Diffuse color swatch in the rollout below it. From the Color Selector that appears, drag the cursor around the color palette until you find the color you want, then click Close.

7. In any viewport, select an egg and then click the Assign Material to Selection button in the Material Editor.

8. Repeat Steps 6 and 7 for all the eggs.

Figure 17-10 shows the assortment of eggs we just created.

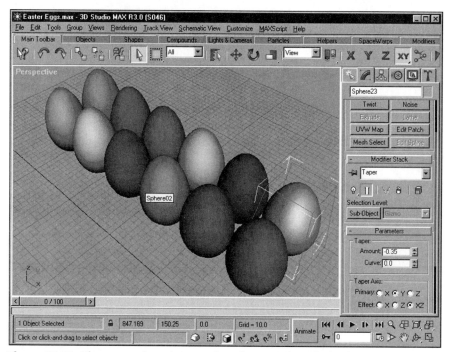

Figure 17-10: These eggs have been assigned materials with different Diffuse colors.

Using Standard Materials

Standard materials are the default MAX R3 material type. They provide a single, uniform color determined by the Ambient, Diffuse, Specular, and Filter color swatches. Standard materials can use any of several different Shaders. *Shaders* are algorithms used to compute how the material should look, given its parameters.

Standard materials also have parameters for controlling highlights, transparency, and self-illumination. These materials include the following rollouts: Shader Basic Parameters, Basic Parameters (based on the Shader type), Extended Parameters, SuperSampling, Maps, and Dynamic Properties. By modifying these parameters you can create really unique materials. With all the various rollouts, even a Standard material has an infinite number of possibilities.

Using shading types

MAX R3 includes several different Shader types. These Shaders are all available in a drop-down list in the Shader Basic Parameters rollout. Each Shader type will display different options in its respective Basic Parameters rollout, as previously shown in Figure 17-1.

Shaders and the Shader rollout are new in Release 3.

The Shader Basic Parameters rollout also includes several options for shading the material, including Wire, 2-Sided, Face Map, and Faceted. Wire mode causes the model to appear as a wireframe model. 2-Sided makes the material appear on both sides of the face and should be used in conjunction with the Wire option. The Face Map mode applies maps to each single face on the object. Faceted ignores the smoothing between faces.

Each of the various Shaders will be covered in the following sections.

Blinn

This is the standard default Shader. It renders simple circular highlights and smoothes adjacent faces.

The Blinn Shader includes color swatches for setting Ambient, Diffuse, Specular, and Self-Illumination colors. To change the color, click the color swatch and select a new color in the Color Selector dialog box.

 You can drag colors among the various color swatches. When you do, a Copy or Swap Colors dialog box will enable you to copy or swap the colors.

The Lock buttons to the left of the color swatches can be used to lock the colors together so that a change to one automatically changes the other. Ambient can be locked to Diffuse, and Diffuse can be locked to Specular.

The small square buttons to the right of the Ambient, Diffuse, Specular, Self-Illumination, Opacity, Specular Level, and Glossiness controls are shortcut buttons for adding a map in place for the respective parameter. Clicking these buttons opens the Material/Map Browser where you can select the map type.

When a map is loaded and active, it will appear in the Maps rollout and an uppercase letter M will appear on this button. When a map is loaded but inactive, a lowercase m appears. Once a map is applied, these buttons will open to make the map the active level and display its parameters in the rollouts. Figure 17-11 shows these map buttons.

 More about maps and the various map types will be covered in Chapter 18, "Using Material Maps."

Self-Illumination can use a color if the Color option is enabled. If this option is disabled, a spinner appears that enables you to adjust the amount of default color used for illumination. Materials with a Self-Illumination value of 100 or a bright color like white will lose all shadows and highlights and appear to glow from within. To remove the effect of Self-Illumination, set the spinner to 0 or the color to black.

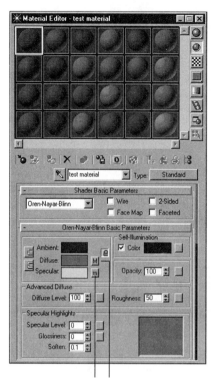

Figure 17-11: Maps can be specified by clicking the square buttons to the right of the color swatches and values.

Inactive map   Active map

The Opacity spinner sets the level of transparency of an object. A value of 100 makes a material completely opaque, while a value of 0 makes the material completely transparent. Use the Background button to view the effects of the Opacity setting.

Specular Highlights are the bright points on the surface where the light is reflected at a maximum value. The Specular Level value determines how bright the highlight is. Its values can range from 0, where there is no highlight, to 100, where the highlight is at a maximum. The graph to the right of the values displays the intensity per distance for a cross section of the highlight. The Specular Level defines the height of the curve or the value at the center of the highlight where it is the brightest. This value can be overloaded to accept numbers greater than 100. Overloaded values create a larger, wider highlight.

The Glossiness value determines the size of the highlight. A value of 100 produces a pinpoint highlight, and a value of 0 increases the highlight to the edges of the graph. The Soften value doesn't affect the graph, but it spreads the highlight across the area defined by the Glossiness value. It can range between 0 (wider) to 1 (thinner).

Figure 17-12 shows a material with a Blinn Shader applied.

Figure 17-12: A material with a Blinn Shader applied. Notice the circular highlights.

Phong

The Phong Shader creates smooth surfaces like Blinn without the quality highlights, but it renders more quickly than the Blinn Shader does. The parameters for the Phong Shader are identical to those for the Blinn Shader. The differences between Blinn and Phong are very subtle, but Blinn can produce highlights for lights at low angles to the surface, and its highlights are generally softer.

Anisotropic

The Anisotropic Shader is characterized by noncircular highlights. An Anisotropic value is the difference between the two axes that make up the highlight. A value of 0 is circular, but higher values increase the difference between the axes and the highlights are more elliptical.

New Feature

The Anisotropic shading type is new to Release 3.

Most of the parameters for this Shader are the same as those for the Blinn Shader, but several parameters of the Anisotropic type are unique. The Diffuse Level value determines how bright the Diffuse color appears. This is similar to Self-Illumination, but it doesn't affect the specular highlights or the shadows. Values can range from 0 to 400.

Compared with the Blinn Shader, the highlight graph, shown in Figure 17-13, looks very different. That is because it is displaying two highlight components that intersect at the middle. The Specular Level value still controls the height of the curve and the Glossiness still controls the width, but the Anisotropy value changes the width of one axis relative to the other creating elliptical highlights. The Orientation value rotates the highlight.

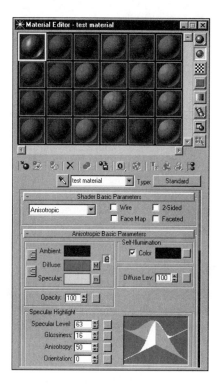

Figure 17-13: The Specular highlight graph for an Anisotropic Shader includes two bell-shaped curves that intersect.

Figure 17-14 shows a material with the Anisotropic Shader applied. This material has an Anisotropic value of 75.

Figure 17-14: A material with the Anisotropic Shader applied. The highlights are now elliptical.

Multi-Layer

The Multi-Layer Shader includes two Anisotropic highlights. Each of these highlights can have a different color. All parameters for this Shader are the same as the Anisotropic Shader described previously, except that there are two Specular Layers.

New Feature The Multi-Layer shading type is new to Release 3.

One additional parameter — Roughness — is included with the Multi-Layer Shader. This parameter defines how well the Diffuse color blends into the Ambient color. When Roughness is set to a value of 0, an object appears the same as with the Blinn Shader, but with higher values, up to 100, the material grows darker.

Figure 17-15 shows a material with a Multi-Layer Shader applied.

Figure 17-15: A material with a Multi-Layer Shader applied. There are now two crossing highlights.

Oren-Nayar-Blinn

The Oren-Nayar-Blinn Shader is useful for creating materials for matte surfaces such as cloth and fabric. The parameters are identical to the Blinn Shader with the addition of the Diffuse Level and Roughness values. The rollout for this shader was shown previously in Figure 17-11.

Metal

The Metal Shader simulates the luster of metallic surfaces. The Highlight curve has a shape that is different from that of the other Shaders. It is rounder at the top and doesn't include a Soften value. You also cannot specify a Specular color. All other parameters are similar to those of the Blinn Shader.

Figure 17-16 shows a material with a Metal Shader applied.

Figure 17-16: A material with a Metal Shader applied. The Metal Shader generates its own highlights.

Strauss

The Strauss Shader provides another alternative for creating metal materials. There are only four parameters for this Shader: Color, Glossiness, Metalness, and Opacity. The Glossiness controls the entire highlight shape. The Metalness value makes the material appear more metal-like by affecting the primary and secondary highlights. Both of these values can range between 0 and 100.

New Feature

The Strauss shading type is new to Release 3.

Extended Parameters

The Extended Parameters rollout, shown in Figure 17-17, includes Advanced Transparency, Reflection Dimming, and Wire controls. It is the same for all Shaders.

The Advanced Transparency controls can set the Falloff to be In, Out, or with a specified Amount. The In option increases the transparency as you get further inside the object, and the Out option does the opposite. The Amount value sets the transparency for the inner or outer edge.

Figure 17-18 shows two materials that use the Transparency Falloff options. The material on the left uses the In option and the one on the right uses the Out option. Both are set at Amount values of 100.

There are three transparency types: Filter, Subtractive, and Additive. The Filter type multiples the Filter color with any color surface that appears behind the transparent object. With this option, you can select a Filter color to use. The Subtractive and Additive types subtract from or add to the color behind the transparent object. Figure 17-19 shows, from left to right, the Filter, Subtractive, and Additive transparency types.

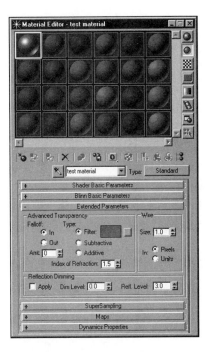

Figure 17-17: The Extended Parameters rollout includes Advanced Transparency, Reflection Dimming, and Wire settings.

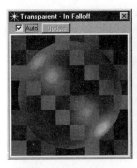
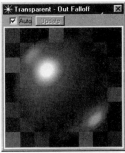

Figure 17-18: Materials with the In and Out Falloff options applied.

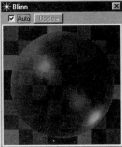

Figure 17-19: The three different transparency types are Filter, Subtractive, and Additive.

The Index of Refraction is a measure of the amount of distortion caused by light passing through a transparent object. Different physical materials have different Index of Refraction values. The amount of distortion also depends on the thickness of the transparent object. The Index of Refraction for water is 1.33 and for glass 1.5. The default of 1.0 has no effect.

The Wire section lets you specify a wire Size or thickness. This is used if the Wire mode is enabled in the Shaders rollout. The size can be measured in either Pixels or Units. Figure 17-20 shows three spheres with different Wire values.

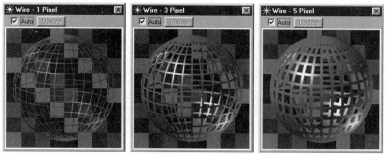

Figure 17-20: Three spheres with Wire values of 1, 3, and 5.

Reflection Dimming controls how intense a reflection is. It can be enabled using the Apply option. The Dim Level setting controls the intensity of the reflection within a shadow, and the Refl Level sets the intensity for all reflections not in the shadow.

SuperSampling

Pixels are small square dots that collectively make up the entire screen. At the edges of objects where the material color changes from the object to the background, these square pixels can cause jagged edges to appear. These edges are called *artifacts* and can ruin an image. *Anti-aliasing* is the process through which these artifacts are removed by softening the transition between colors.

SuperSampling is an additional Anti-aliasing pass that can improve image quality. There are several SuperSampling methods to choose from.

New Feature   The SuperSampling rollout is new in Release 3.

SuperSampling is only calculated if the Anti-Aliasing option in the Render Scene dialog box is enabled. The Raytrace material has its own SuperSampling pass and doesn't need SuperSampling enabled.

Caution Using SuperSampling can greatly increase the time it takes to render an image.

In a SuperSampling pass, the colors at different points around the center of a pixel are sampled. These samples are then used to compute the final color of each pixel. The four available SuperSampling methods are

✦ **Adaptive Halton** — Takes semirandom samples along both the pixel's X-axis and Y-axis. It can take from 4 to 40 samples.

✦ **Adaptive Uniform** — Takes samples at regular intervals around the pixel's center. It takes from 4 to 26 samples.

✦ **Hammersley** — Takes samples at regular intervals along the X-axis, but takes random samples along the Y-axis. It takes from 4 to 40 samples.

✦ **MAX 2.5 Star** — Takes four samples along each axis.

The first three methods enable you to select a Quality setting. This setting specifies the number of samples to be taken. The more samples taken, the higher the resolution, but the longer it takes to render. The two Adaptive methods (Adaptive Halton and Adaptive Uniform) offer an Adaptive option with a Threshold spinner. This takes more samples if the change in color is within the Threshold value. The SuperSample Texture option includes maps in the SuperSampling process along with materials.

Maps

A *map* is a bitmap image that is pasted on an image. The Maps rollout, shown in Figure 17-21, includes a list of the maps that you can apply to an object. Using this rollout you can enable or disable maps, specify the intensity of the map in the Amount field, and load maps. Clicking the Map buttons opens the Material/Map Browser.

Cross-Reference Maps will be covered in more detail in Chapter 18, "Using Material Maps."

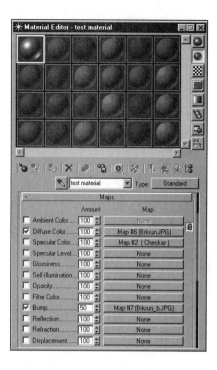

Figure 17-21: The Maps rollout lets you select, enable and control the map Amount.

Dynamic Properties

The properties in the Dynamic Properties rollout are used along with the Dynamics utility in simulations. These properties define how the object is animated during collisions. If these properties are not specified for an object, then the default material settings, which are similar to steel, are used.

The Dynamic Properties rollout includes only the following three values:

✦ **Bounce Coefficient**—Determines how high an object will bounce after a collision. The default of 1.0 is equal to a normal elastic collision. A ball with a value greater than 1, for example, will continue to bounce higher with each impact.

✦ **Static Friction**—Determines how difficult it is to start an object moving when pushed across a surface. Objects with high Static Friction values will require a lot of force to move.

✦ **Sliding Friction**—Determines how difficult it is to keep an object in motion across a surface. Ice, for example, would have a low Sliding Friction value, because once it starts moving, it will continue easily.

For more information on dynamic simulations, check out Chapter 34, "Creating a Dynamic Simulation."

Tutorial: Coloring a dolphin

As a quick example of applying materials, we'll take a dolphin model created by Zygote Media and position it over a watery plane. We'll then apply custom materials to both objects.

To add materials to a dolphin, follow these steps:

1. Import the dolphin model using the File ⇨ Import command. Then open the Create panel and click the Plane button. Drag in the Top view to create a Plane object. Set the Scale Multiplier value of the Plane to **100**. Then position the dolphin above the plane.

2. Open the Material Editor by selecting Tools ⇨ Material Editor, or by pressing the M key.

3. In the Material Editor, select the first sample slot, and in the Name field (to the right of the Pick Material from Object button) rename the material **Dolphin Skin**. Click the Diffuse color swatch and select a light gray color. Then click the Specular color swatch and select a light yellow color. Click the Close button to exit the Color Selector. In the Specular Highlights section, increase the Specular Level to **45**.

4. Drag the "Dolphin Skin" material from the first sample slot to the second sample slot and name it **Ocean Surface**. Click the Diffuse color swatch and select a light blue color. Set the Specular Level and Opacity values to **80**. In the Maps rollout, click the None button to the right of the Bump selection. This will open the Material/Map Browser. Then double-click the Noise selection.

5. Drag the "Ocean Surface" material onto the plane object in the Top viewport. Then drag the "Dolphin Skin" material onto the dolphin model.

This model also includes separate objects for the eyes, mouth, and tongue. These objects could have different materials applied to them, but they are so small in this image that we won't worry about them.

6. Select the Rendering ⇨ Environment command and then click the Background Color swatch and change it to a light sky blue.

Figure 17-22 shows the resulting image.

Figure 17-22: A dolphin over the water with applied materials

Using Raytrace Materials

Raytracing is a rendering method that calculates image colors by following imaginary light rays as they move through a scene. These rays can travel through transparent objects and reflect realistically off shiny materials. The results are stunning realistic images, but the drawback is the amount of time it takes to render using Raytrace materials. Scenes with lots of lights and reflecting materials will take even longer.

Raytrace materials also support special effects such as fog, color density, translucency, and fluorescence. They include the following rollouts, shown in Figure 17-23 (some of which are similar to the Standard materials): Raytrace Basic Parameters, Extended Parameters, Raytracer Controls, Maps, and Dynamic Properties.

Note   Raytracing can take a long time to complete. As an alternative, a Reflect/Refract map can be used to simulate raytracing.

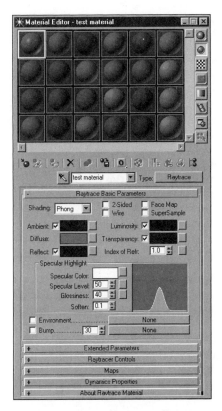

Figure 17-23: The Raytrace material includes several material properties that are unique to this material type.

Raytrace Basic Parameters

The Raytrace material doesn't have a Shader rollout. Instead, shading is determined by a drop-down list at the top of the Basic Parameters rollout. The options include Phong, Blinn, Metal, and Constant. The first three are similar to the Shaders with the same names for Standard materials and the last is like Phong shading with Faceted enabled. The Shading options are the same as those for Standard materials except Faceted is replaced by SuperSample, which completes an additional anti-aliasing pass.

The colors for a Raytrace material are different from their Standard material counterparts — only the Diffuse color is similar. All the other color swatches can be switched between a color swatch and a value by enabling the checkbox to the left of the label. The spinners can range between 0 and 100, which equate to black or white.

The Ambient color is different from that for the Standard material although it is named the same. For Raytrace materials, the Ambient value is the amount of ambient light that is absorbed. A setting of white is like locking a Standard material's Diffuse and Ambient colors together.

The Reflect color is the color that is added to reflections. For example, if the background color is set to yellow and the Reflect color is red, then the reflections for this object will be tinted orange. This is different from the Specular highlight color, which is set in the Specular Highlight group.

The Luminosity color makes an object glow with this color, similar to the Self-Illumination color for the Standard material. In fact, when the Luminosity setting is disabled, the text label changes to Self-Illumination.

The Transparency color sets the color that filters light passing through the transparent material. When the color swatch is white, the material is transparent, and when it is black, the material is opaque.

At the bottom of the Raytrace Basic Parameters rollout are two map options for Environment and Bump maps. These maps, which are also included in the Maps rollout, are here for convenience. The Environment map for Raytrace materials overrides the global Environment Map set in the Environment dialog box. The Environment map will only be visible if the Reflect color is enabled or its value is not 0. Figure 17-24 shows a sphere with an Environment Map of a mountain meadow applied. The image is taken from Corel's Photo CD library.

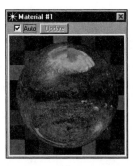

Figure 17-24: A sphere with an Environment Map reflected off a Raytrace material

Cross-Reference For more information on Environment, Bump, and other maps, see Chapter 18, "Using Material Maps."

Extended Parameters

The Extended Parameters rollout, shown in Figure 17-25, holds the settings for all the special material effects that are possible with the Raytrace material. Only the Wire settings are the same as for the Standard material.

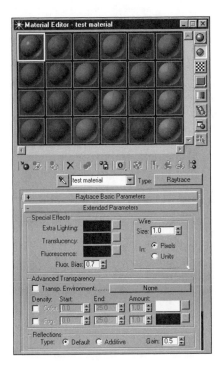

Figure 17-25: The Extended Parameters rollout includes a Special Effects section.

The Extra Lighting color swatch increases the effect of Ambient light. It can increase the ambient light for a single object or subobject area and can be used to simulate radiosity. *Radiosity* is a rendering method that creates realistic lighting by calculating how light reflects off objects.

Translucency lets light penetrate an object, but the objects on the other side are unclear, or semitransparent. This effect can be used to create frosted glass. Figure 17-26 shows a Translucent material with Transparency set at 50.

Figure 17-26: A Translucent sphere

Fluorescence makes materials glow like fluorescent colors under a black light. The Fluorescence Bias field, which can range between 0 and 1, controls this effect.

The Advanced Transparency group includes a shortcut for the Transparent Environment map. This map is refracted through a transparent object and is only visible if the Environment map is enabled. Figure 17-27 shows the results of applying a Transparency Environment map.

Figure 17-27: A sphere with a Transparency Environment map

Raytrace materials that are transparent can also have Color and Fog Density settings. Color Density can be used to create tinted glass — the amount of color depends on how thick the object is and the Amount setting. The Start value is where the color starts and the End value is the distance at which the color reaches a maximum.

Fog Density works the same way as Color Density and is based on object thickness. This effect can be used to create smoky glass.

The Reflections section offers a Default Reflection Type and an Additive Reflection Type. The Default type layers the reflection on top of the current Diffuse color, and the Additive type adds the reflection to the Diffuse color. The Gain value controls the brightness of the reflection and can range between 0 and 1.

Raytracer Controls

Raytracing can take a long time, but the Raytracer Control rollout, shown in Figure 17-28, lets you control several Raytracer options that can speed up the process. You can use this rollout to turn Raytrace Reflections or Refractions on or off. The Falloff values determine the distance at which the reflections or refractions fade to black. The Bump Map Effect increases or decreases the effect of bump maps on the reflections or refractions.

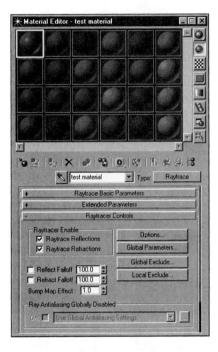

Figure 17-28: The Raytracer Controls rollout lets you set the raytracing options.

The Options button opens the Raytracer Options dialog box, shown in Figure 17-29. This dialog box includes Global and Local options. Global settings apply to all Raytrace materials, and Local applies only to the current selection. The options are Enable Raytracing, Anti-aliasing, Self Reflect/Refract, Atmosphere, Reflect/Refract Material ID, Objects Inside Raytraced Objects, Atmosphere Inside Raytraced Objects, and Color Density/Fog.

The Global Parameters button under the Options button in the Raytracer Controls rollout opens the Global Raytracer Settings dialog box. This dialog box, shown in Figure 17-30 controls the actual Raytracing engine, which affects all Raytrace materials. The Maximum Depth setting tells the Raytracer how long to follow each ray, or you can set a Cutoff Threshold. (Lower numbers speed up render times.) You can also specify a color or background to use for rays that reach the Max Depth, which is useful for identifying lost rays.

Figure 17-29: The Raytracer Options dialog box lets you enable and disable many raytracing effects.

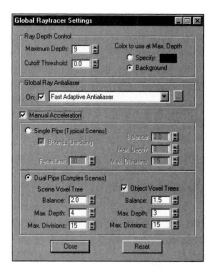

Figure 17-30: The Global Raytracer Settings dialog box offers settings that can greatly speed up render times.

The Global Ray Antialiaser group includes a drop-down list with two options: Fast Adaptive Anti-aliaser and Multi-resolution Adaptive Anti-aliaser. Each selection has a dialog box that can be opened with settings for Blur and Defocus. If SuperSampling is used in the same material, this option isn't needed, and vice versa. These options can also be selected for individual materials from within the Raytrace Controls rollout.

The Global Raytracer Settings dialog box also includes two Manual Acceleration options: Single Pipe and Dual Pipe. These options enable you to set how the Raytracer divides and processes different portions of the scene. The Single Pipe option is used for typical scenes, while the Dual Pipe option is used for more complex scenes.

One of the easiest ways to increase the speed of the Raytracer is to reduce the number of objects that it has to deal with. The Global Exclude and Local Exclude buttons open the Exclude/Include dialog box. From within this dialog box you can select objects to be excluded from the Raytracer. Global affects all Raytrace materials in a scene and Local only affects the current material.

The Exclude/Include dialog box includes two panes. The pane on the left lists all the objects within the scene and the one on the right lists the objects to Include or Exclude, depending on which option is selected. Figure 17-31 shows this dialog box with half the scene object excluded from the Raytracer.

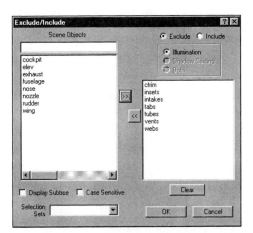

Figure 17-31: The Exclude/Include dialog box lets you select objects to be removed from the Raytracer.

Note   The same Exclude/Include dialog box is used to exclude objects from the effects of lights.

Additional rollouts

Raytrace materials include three additional rollouts: Maps, Dynamic Properties, and About Raytrace Material. The Maps rollout works the same for Raytrace materials as it does with Standard materials, but the Raytrace material includes several different maps (covered in Chapter 18, "Working with Material Maps"). The Dynamic Properties rollout for Raytrace materials is identical to the Dynamic Properties rollout for Standard materials. The About Raytrace Material rollout lists the creators and release versions of this material.

Tutorial: Coming up roses

Raytrace examples often include glasses or vases because shiny, highly reflective glass surfaces show off the effects of Raytracing best. Zygote Media has an object that is perfect for this task—a vase of roses. (Zygote also created the table used in this tutorial.)

To apply Raytrace materials to a vase of roses, follow these steps:

1. Import the roses model along with a table model and position the roses on the table.

2. Open the Create panel and click the Plane button. Drag in the Top and Front views to create two plane objects, set their Scale Multiplier values to **50**, and position them under and behind the table to form the floor and wall.

3. Open the Material Editor, select the first sample slot, and name the material **Raytrace Glass**. Click the Type button and double-click the Raytrace material type in the Material/Map Browser. Deselect the Transparency option and set its value to **100**. Set the Index of Refraction to **1.5** and raise the Specular Level to **100**. Select the vase object and click the Assign Material to Selection button.

4. Select the second sample slot and name it **Leaves**. In the Shader Basic Parameters rollout, select the Oren-Nayar-Blinn Shader from the drop-down list. Then click the Diffuse color swatch and select a dark green color. Set the Diffuse Level, Opacity, and Roughness to **100** and the Specular Level to **10**. Then select the stems and leaves and apply this material.

5. Select the third sample slot, click the Pick Material from Object tool to the left of the Name field, and then click the roses. This will load the material already applied to the roses into the sample slot. Disable the Faceted option and reapply the material using the Assign Material to Selection button.

6. Select the fourth sample slot and click the square button to the right of the Diffuse color swatch to open the Material/Map Browser. Double-click the Wood map to apply this map instead of the Diffuse color and to display the map parameter rollouts. Set the Y-axis Tiling value to **20** in the Coordinates rollout. Then click the Go to Parent button and, in the Blinn Basic Parameters rollout, increase the Specular Level to **75**. Name the material **Tabletop** and drag the material to the tabletop.

7. In a graphics program like Adobe Photoshop, create and save a 200 × 200 image with some repeating colored vertical stripes that can be used as wallpaper. Select the fifth sample slot and click the map button to the right of the Diffuse color. In the Material/Map Browser, double-click the Bitmap selection. This will load a File dialog box where you can locate the wallpaper image. In the Coordinates rollout, set the U coordinate Tiling value to **100** and drag the material to the wall plane object.

Figure 17-32 shows the rendered image.

Figure 17-32: A rendered image with Raytrace materials applied to the vase and table

Using Matte/Shadow Materials

Matte/Shadow materials can be applied to objects to make portions of the model invisible. This lets any objects behind the object or in the background show through. Objects with Matte/Shadow materials applied can also cast and receive shadows. The effect of these materials is only visible when the object is rendered.

Matte/Shadow Basic Parameters

You can apply a Matte/Shadow material by clicking the Type button and selecting the Matte/Shadow from the Material/Map Browser. Matte/Shadow materials only include a single rollout: the Matte/Shadow Basic Parameters, shown in Figure 17-33.

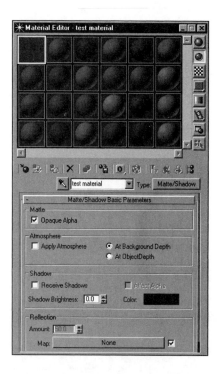

Figure 17-33: The Matte/Shadow Basic Parameters rollout includes controls for Atmospheres, Shadows, and Reflections.

The Opaque Alpha option causes the matte material to appear in an alpha channel. This essentially is a switch for turning Matte objects on and off.

Atmosphere effects like fog and volume light can be applied to Matte materials. The At Background Depth option applies the fog to the background image. The At Object Depth option applies the fog as if the object were rendered.

The Receive Shadows section enables shadows to be cast on a Matte object. You can also specify the Shadow Brightness and color. Increasing Shadow Brightness values makes the shadow more transparent. The Affect Alpha option makes the shadows part of the alpha channel.

Matte objects can also have Reflections. The Amount spinner controls how much reflection is used, and the Map button opens the Material/Map Browser.

Tutorial: Ballooning in New York

Touring New York City can be exhilarating and exasperating at the same time, but the real way to tour New York City is by balloon (or by virtual balloon). This way, you won't have to worry about the crowds or bustle, but it might be a little difficult to take the subway. In this tutorial, we'll visit the Statue of Liberty in a balloon and use a Shadow/Matte material to fly the balloon behind the statue.

To use a Matte/Shadow material to hide geometry, follow these steps:

1. First create a balloon. This is done easily using the Line tool and the Lathe Modifier. Use the Line button to draw the outline of a balloon and another outline of its basket. Then use the Lathe Modifier about the Y-axis to create the balloon and the basket objects. Add some additional cylinders as ropes to connect the balloon to the basket.

2. In an image-editing program like Adobe Photoshop, create and save an image with four horizontally striped colors to apply as a map to the balloon.

3. Back in MAX, open the Material Editor by pressing the M keyboard shortcut. Select the first sample slot and name the material **Balloon Fabric**. Then click the map button to the right of the Diffuse color swatch. In the Material/Map Browser, double-click the Bitmap selection. This will load a file dialog box. Locate the image you created in the image-editing program and click the Open button. After loading the bitmap, enter **75** as the W Angle in the Coordinates rollout to apply the map at an angle. Drag the sample slot to the balloon to apply the map. Use the Show Map in Viewport button to see the applied results.

4. Next comes the background image. This tutorial uses a Statue of Liberty image taken from the Corel World Landmarks Photo CD. Select the Rendering ⇨ Environment command and click the Environment Map button to open the Material/Map Browser. Double-click Bitmap to open a file dialog box. Locate the image in the file dialog box and click OK.

5. To see the same Statue of Liberty image as the viewport background, select Views ⇨ Viewport Background to open the Viewport Background dialog box. Select the Use Environment Background and Display Background options.

6. The next step is to create a mask for the Statue of Liberty. To do this, load the Statue of Liberty image in a drawing program like Adobe Illustrator and use the Auto-Trace tool to convert the outline of the statue to splines. Save the traced image as an AI file called **Statue of Liberty Mask**.

7. Back in MAX, import the AI file using the File ⇨ Import command. You will need to scale and rotate the outline to match the background image in the viewport. Use the Tools ⇨ Align to View command to orient the outline at the same angle at the Perspective view.

Caution

If you use the Viewport Navigation buttons, such as Zoom Extents, the mask will no longer be correctly aligned. If this happens accidentally, use the Views ⇨ Undo command.

8. Open the Modify panel and click the Edit Spline button. This will convert the imported splines to Editable Splines. In the Selection rollout, click the Sub-Object button and select Segment from the drop-down list. Then select and delete all the segments that don't make up the statue, such as the background lines. Then, select Spline Sub-Object mode and click the Close button to close the spline. With the spline closed, exit subobject mode by clicking the Sub-Object button again, and then click the Extrude button. Enter an Amount of **5**. If any holes exist in the statue, use the Cap Holes Modifier to close them up.

9. With the mask object in place, open the Material Editor and select the first sample slot. Name the slot **Statute of Liberty Matte** and click the Type button. Select the Matte/Shadow material by double-clicking it. Then apply it to the mask object.

10. Position the balloon in the viewport so it covers the Statue of Liberty in the Perspective view. Make sure that the balloon is behind the mask object.

Figure 17-34 shows the resulting image.

Figure 17-34: A rendered balloon object behind an object with a Matte/Shadow material applied.

Using Compound Materials

Compound materials combine several different materials into one. You select a compound object type by clicking the Type button in the Material Editor and then selecting the material type from the Material/Map Browser.

Whenever Compound materials are selected, the Replace Material dialog box appears, asking if you want to discard the old material or make the old material a submaterial. This enables you to change a normal material into a Compound material while retaining the current material.

Cross-Reference More examples of Composite material types can be found in Chapter 19, "Creating Custom Materials."

Navigating materials

Composite materials will usually include several different levels. For example, a Top/Bottom material includes two materials for both the top and bottom. Each of these submaterials could then include another Top/Bottom material and so on. The Material/Map Navigator dialog box (accessed by clicking the Material/Map Navigator button) displays the material as a hierarchical list. This list lets you easily choose the level you wish to work with. Figure 17-35 shows the Material/Map Navigator dialog box.

Figure 17-35: The Material/Map Navigator shows all the levels of a complex material.

Blend

The Blend material blends two separate materials on a surface. The Blend Basic Parameters rollout, shown in Figure 17-36, includes buttons for loading the two submaterials. The checkboxes to the right of these buttons enable or disable each submaterial. The Interactive option enables you to select one of the submaterials to be viewed in the viewports.

The Mask button lets you load a map to specify how the submaterials are mixed. White areas on the map are well blended and black areas don't blend at all. As an alternative to a mask, the Mix Amount determines how much of each submaterial to display. A value of 0 displays only Material 1 and a value of 100 displays only Material 2.

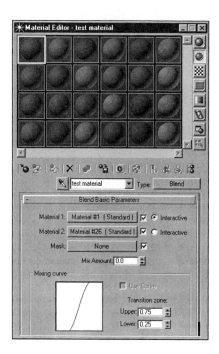

Figure 17-36: The Blend material can include a mask to define the areas that are blended.

The Mixing Curve defines the transition between edges of the two materials. The Upper and Lower spinners are used to control the curve.

Composite

The Composite material mixes up to 10 different materials by adding, subtracting, or mixing the opacity. The Composite Basic Parameters rollout, shown in Figure 17-37, includes buttons for the Base Material and 10 additional materials that can be composited on top of the base material. The materials are applied from top to bottom.

New Feature   The Composite material type is new to Release 3.

Each material can be enabled or disabled using the checkbox to the left. The buttons labeled with an A, S, and M are used to specify the opacity type: Additive, Subtractive, or Mix. The Additive option brightens the material by adding the background colors to the current material. The Subtractive option has the opposite effect and subtracts the background colors from the current material. The Mix option blends the materials based on their Amount values.

To the right of the A, S, and M buttons is the Mix amount. This value can range from 0 to 200. At 0, none of the materials below it will be visible. At 100, full compositing occurs. Values greater than 100 cause transparent regions to become more opaque.

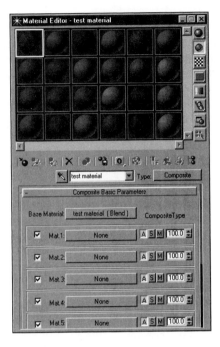

Figure 17-37: Composite materials are applied from top to bottom with the last layer being placed on top of the rest.

Double Sided

The Double Sided material specifies different materials for the front and back of object faces. There is also an option to make the material translucent.

The Double Sided Basic Parameters rollout includes two buttons for both the Facing and Back materials. The Translucency value sets how much of one material shows through the other.

Figure 17-38 shows a sample slot with this material applied.

Figure 17-38: A rendered sphere with a Double Sided material applied. Notice how the back wires are a different color from the front wires.

Top/Bottom

The Top/Bottom material assigns different materials to the top and bottom of an object. The Top and Bottom areas are determined by the direction that the face normals point. These normals can be according to the World or Local coordinate system. You can also Blend the two materials.

The Top/Bottom Basic Parameters rollout includes two buttons for loading the Top and Bottom materials. The Swap button can be used to switch the two materials. Using World Coordinates enables you to rotate the object without changing the material positions. Local Coordinates tie the material to the object.

The Blend value can range from 0 to 100, with 0 being a hard edge and 100 being a smooth transition. The Position value sets the location where the two materials meet. A value of 0 represents the bottom of the object and displays only the top material. A value of 100 represents the top of the object, and only the Bottom material is displayed.

Figure 17-39 shows a magnified sample slot with the Top/Bottom material applied.

 **Figure 17-39:** A sphere with different materials applied to the top and the bottom

Shellac

The Shellac material is added on top of the Base material. The Shellac Basic Parameters rollout includes only two buttons for each material along with a Color Blend value. There is no upper limit for the Blend value.

 New Feature   The Shellac material type is new to Release 3.

Multi/Sub-Object

The Multi/Sub-Object material can be used to assign several different materials to a single object via the material IDs. The Mesh Select Modifier can be used to select each subobject area to receive the different materials.

At the top of the Multi/Sub-Object Basic Parameters rollout, shown in Figure 17-40, there is a Set Number button that lets you select the number of subobject materials to include. This number is displayed in a text field to the right of the button. Each submaterial is displayed as a separate area on the sample object in the sample slots.

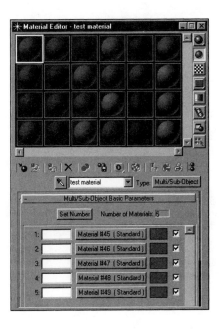

Figure 17-40: The Multi/Sub-Object material defines materials according to material IDs.

Each submaterial includes an index number listed to the left, a Name field where you can type the name of the submaterial, a button for selecting the material, a color swatch for creating solid color materials, and a checkbox for enabling or disabling the submaterial.

Once a Multi/Sub-Object material is applied to an object, use the Mesh Select Modifier to make a subobject selection. In the Material rollout for this subobject selection, choose a Material ID to associate with a submaterial ID.

Figure 17-41 shows the sample slot with a Multi/Sub-Object material applied.

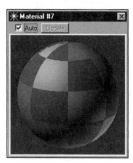

Figure 17-41: The rendered sample slot shows the Multi/Sub-Object material with six different colors.

Chapter 13, "Using Patches," includes a tutorial where the Multi/Sub-Object material is applied to a quilt.

Morpher

The Morpher material type works with the Morpher Modifier to change materials as an object morphs. This material can only be used on an object that has the Morpher Modifier in its Stack. The Morpher Modifier includes a button called Assign New Material for loading the Material Editor with the Morpher Material type.

The Morpher material type is new to Release 3.

The Choose Morph Object button in the Parameters rollout, shown in Figure 17-42, opens a dialog box that is used to bind the Morpher Material to an object with the Morpher Modifier applied. The Refresh button updates all the channels. The Base Material is the material used before any channel effects are used.

The Morpher material includes 100 channels that correlate to the channels included in the Morpher Modifier. Each channel can be turned on and off. The Mixing Calculation option determines how often the blending is calculated. The Constantly setting can slow the system down.

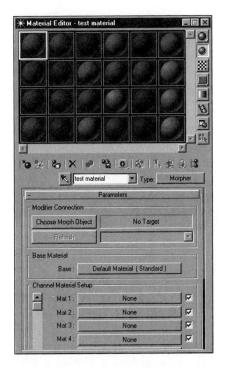

Figure 17-42: The Morpher material lets you define materials for each Morph channel.

Tutorial: Surfing the waves

As an example of a Compound material, we'll apply the Top/Bottom material to a surfboard. Viewpoint Datalabs created the Surfboard model used in this tutorial.

To apply a Top/Bottom Compound material to a surfboard, follow these steps:

1. Import the surfboard model and position it in the scene. Create a plane object, scale it to 500, and apply the "Ocean Surface" material from the earlier tutorial to it.

2. In the Material Editor, select the second sample slot and click the Type button. From the Material/Map Browser, select the Browse From New option and double-click the Top/Bottom material.

3. When the Replace Material dialog box appears, select the Discard Old Material option. Type the name **Surfboard** for the new material. Then click the Top Material button, name the material **Surfboard Top**, and change the Diffuse color to White. In the material drop-down list, select Surfboard and then click the Bottom Material button. Give this material the name **Surfboard Bottom** and change the Diffuse color to Black.

4. Click the Material/Map Navigator button to view the hierarchy of the material. Then drag this material to the surfboard object.

Figure 17-43 shows the resulting image.

Figure 17-43: A rendered image of a surfboard with the Top/Bottom Compound material applied

Summary

Materials can add a lot to the realism of your models. Learning to use the Material Editor enables you to create a variety of unique materials, as you saw in this chapter. This chapter also presented the various material types, including Standard, Raytrace, Matte/Shadow, and Compound materials. In this chapter, you've

✦ Learned about various material properties

✦ Worked with the Material Editor buttons and sample slots

✦ Used the Material/Map Browser

✦ Discovered the basics of using Standard materials

✦ Learned about Raytrace, Matte/Shadow, and Compound materials

The next chapter delves into the topic of Material Maps.

✦   ✦   ✦

Using Material Maps

In This Chapter

Understanding
mapping coordinates
and tiling

Exploring all the map
types, including 2D
maps, 3D maps,
compositors, color
modifiers, and others

Mapping using the
Maps rollout

Another way to enhance an object with materials is to use a map—but not a roadmap; these maps are closer to bitmaps, with patterns that can be applied to the surface of an object. Some maps wrap an image onto objects, but others, such as displacement and bump maps, modify the surface based on the map's intensity.

Maps were used in several of the examples in the previous chapter, but they weren't discussed in any detail. This chapter will present the details of using maps.

Understanding Maps

To understand a material map, think of this example. Cut the label off a soup can, scan it into the computer, and save the image as a bitmap. You could then create a cylinder with roughly the same dimensions as the can, load the scanned label image as a material map, and apply it to the cylinder object to simulate the original soup can.

There are different types of maps. Some maps wrap images about objects, while others define areas to be modified by comparing the intensity of the pixels in the map. An example of this is a *bump map*. A standard bump map would be a grayscale image—when mapped onto an object, lighter color sections would be raised to a maximum of pure white and darker sections would be indented to a minimum of black. This enables you to easily create surface textures, such as an orange rind, without having to model them.

Still other uses for maps include background images called *environment maps* and *projection maps* that are used with lights.

For information on Environment Maps, see Chapter 35, "Working with Backgrounds, Environments, and Atmospheric Effects." Projection maps are covered in Chapter 21, "Lighting Special Effects."

Maps that are used to create materials are all applied using the Material Editor. The Material/Map Browser lists all the available maps in several different categories. These maps have many common features and will be covered in the following sections.

Setting mapping coordinates

Every map that is applied needs to have mapping coordinates that define how the map lines up with the object and affects the look of the object. For example, with the soup can label, you'll probably want to align the top edge of the label with the top edge of the can, but you could position the top edge at the middle of the can.

All map coordinates are based on a UVW coordinate system that equates to the familiar XYZ coordinate system, except that it is named uniquely so as not to be confused with transformation coordinates. These coordinates are required for every object that a map is applied to. In most cases, you can generate these coordinates automatically when you create an object by selecting the Generate Mapping Coordinates option in the object's parameter rollout.

Editable Meshes don't have any default mapping coordinates, but you can generate mapping coordinates using the UVW Map Modifier. This Modifier is discussed in Chapter 19, "Creating Custom Materials."

When an object that uses maps is rendered, MAX will look for the map in the same place it was loaded from in the Material Editor. If it cannot be found, the Missing Map Files dialog box (shown in Figure 18-1) appears. The dialog box includes Continue, Cancel, and Browse buttons. The Browse button will let you locate the missing image.

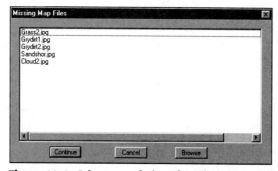

Figure 18-1: Prior to rendering, the Missing Map Files dialog box displays all objects that don't have mapping coordinates.

Tiling a map

Maps can also be tiled across the surface of an object. Tiling positions several single image maps next to one another. You will often want to use tiled images that are seamless, or that repeat from edge to edge.

Figure 18-2 shows an image tile that is seamless. The horizontal and vertical seams line up. Below the tile, three more tiles have been positioned next to each another. This tile was created using Fractal Design Painter 3D.

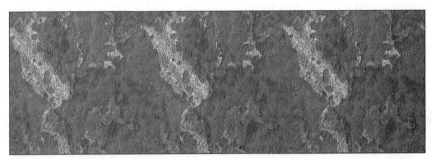

Figure 18-2: Seamless image tiles are a useful way to cover an entire surface with a small map.

Material Map Types

Maps are typically used along with materials. Most material maps can be opened from the Material/Map Browser. Figure 18-3 shows this Browser filtered to display the available maps.

There are several different types of maps. In the Material/Map Browser you can use the options in the Show group to filter the types of maps to be displayed. Options include 2D Maps, 3D Maps, Compositors, Color Mods, Other, and All. These map divisions can only be selected if the New option is selected in the Browse From section.

Note
This chapter describes all the default map types in MAX R3, but it doesn't include any tutorials. You'll get a chance to use these maps in several of the tutorials in other chapters in this book; Chapter 19, "Working with Materials and Maps," includes many mapping examples.

Figure 18-3: The Material/Map Browser can list all the maps available for assigning to materials.

Common parameters

There are several rollouts that many maps have in common. These include Coordinates, Noise, Time, and Output. In addition to these rollouts, each individual map type has its own parameters rollout.

The Coordinates rollout

Whenever a map is included as part of a material, the Coordinates rollout, shown in Figure 18-4, appears. This rollout controls how the map lines up with the object. Common settings include Offset, Tiling, and Angle rotation values for each dimension, though there are variances. For example, 2D Maps have only the U and V values, while 3D maps have U, V, and W dimensions.

The Map Channel spinner lets you specify map channels, which you can use to apply several maps to a single object. The Blur and Blur Offset values affect the bluriness of the image. The Blur value blurs the image based on its distance from the view, while the Blur Offset value blurs the image regardless of its distance.

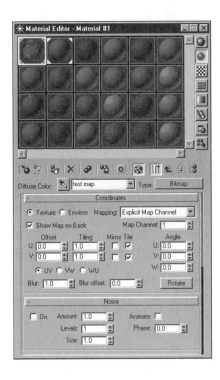

Figure 18-4: The Coordinates rollout lets you offset and tile a map.

The Noise rollout

The Noise rollout, previously shown in Figure 18-4, adds *noise* to the map. The Amount value is the strength of the noise function that is applied with a value range from 0 for no noise through 100 for maximum noise. This noise function can be disabled at any time, using the On option.

The Levels value defines the number of times the noise function is applied. The Size value determines the extent of the noise function based on the geometry. You can also Animate the noise. The Phase value controls how quickly the noise changes over time.

The Time rollout

Maps, such as Bitmaps, that can load animations also include a Time rollout for controlling animation files. In this rollout, you can choose a Start Frame and the Playback Rate. The default Playback Rate is 1.0—higher values run the animation faster, and lower values run it slower. You can also set the animation to Loop, Ping-Pong, or Hold the last frame.

The Output rollout

The Output rollout includes settings for controlling the final look of the map. The Invert option creates a negative version of the image. The Clamp option prevents any colors from exceeding a value of 1.0 and prevents maps from becoming self-illuminating if the brightness is increased.

The Alpha From RGB Intensity option generates an alpha channel based on the Intensity of the map. Black areas will become transparent and white areas opaque.

The Output Amount value controls how much of the map should be mixed when it is part of a composite material. The RGB Offset value can be used to increase or decrease the map's tonal values. The RGB Level value can increase or decrease the saturation level of the map. The Bump Amount value is only used if the map is being used as a bump map — it determines the height of the bumps.

The Enable Color Map option enables the Color Map graph at the bottom of the Output rollout. This graph displays the tonal range of the map. Adjusting this graph affects the highlights, midtones, and shadows of the map. Figure 18-5 shows a Color Map graph.

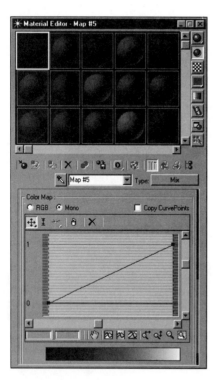

Figure 18-5: The Color Map graph enables you to adjust the highlights, midtones, and shadows of a map.

The left end of the graph equates to the shadows, and the right end is for the highlights. The RGB and Mono options let you display the graphs as independent red, green, and blue graphs or as a single combined graph. The Copy CurvePoints option will copy any existing points from Mono mode over to RGB mode and vice versa. The buttons across the top of the graph are used to manage the graph points.

2D maps

A two-dimensional map can be wrapped onto the surface of an object or used as an environment map for a scene's background image. 2D maps only appear on the surface because they have no depth. The Bitmap map is perhaps the most common 2D map. It enables you to load any image, which can be wrapped around an object's surface in a number of different ways.

In the Coordinates rollout for 2D Maps, you can specify whether the map will be a texture map or an environment map. The Texture option applies the map to the surface of an object as a texture. The Mapping types for Texture include Explicit Map Channel, Vertex Color Channel, Planar from Object XYZ, and Planar from World XYZ. The Environ option creates an Environment Map, and its Mapping types include Spherical Environment, Cylindrical Environment, Shrink-Wrap Environment, and Screen.

The Show Map on Back option causes planar maps to project through the object and be rendered on the object's back.

The U and V coordinates define the X and Y positions for the map. For each coordinate, you can specify an Offset value, which is the distance from the origin. The Tiling value is the number of times to repeat the image and is only used if the Tile option is selected. The Mirror option inverts the map. The UV, VW, and WU options apply the map onto different planes.

You can also rotate the map about each of the U, V, and W axes. Enter the angle to rotate and then click the Rotate button.

Adobe Photoshop plug-in

This map type lets you use Photoshop plug-ins to apply to an image. The Browse button lets you specify the path where MAX should look for plug-ins. The current Category and Filters will be displayed in drop-down lists. Many plug-ins use the Foreground and Background colors and the Alpha Plane in their processing. These can be input in the Adobe Photoshop Plug-In Parameters rollout, shown in Figure 18-6.

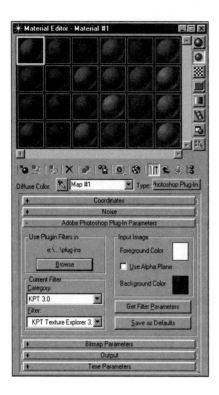

Figure 18-6: The Adobe Photoshop Plug-In Parameters rollout lets you use installed Photoshop plug-ins to create textures.

The Get Filter Parameters button opens the plug-in interface where you can set the various parameters for the plug-in. You can save these settings with the Save as Defaults button.

The Adobe Photoshop Plug-In map also includes a Bitmap Parameters rollout with the same settings as the Bitmap map.

Cross-Reference

Adobe Photoshop and Premiere plug-ins can also be applied during post production in the Video Post dialog box. More information on both of these plug-ins can be found in Chapter 39, "Using the Video Post Interface."

Adobe Premiere video filters

The Adobe Premiere Video Filter Parameters map rollout includes a Filter Path button to set the Path where MAX should look for any filters installed on your system. The available filters are displayed in a list. Several filters can be applied to the Filter Input map simultaneously. The parameters for the filters can be set using the Setup at Start button.

Bitmap

The Bitmap type opens the Select Bitmap Image File dialog box where you can locate an image file. Various image and animation formats are supported; these include AVI, BMP, CIN, GIF, IFL, IPP, FLC, JPEG, MOV, PNG, PSD, RGB, RLA, TGA, TIF, and YUV.

If you need to change the bitmap file, click the Bitmap button at the top of the Bitmap Parameters rollout and select the new file. The Reload button can update the bitmap if you've made changes to bitmap image by an external program.

The Bitmap Parameters rollout includes three different Filtering options: Pyramidal, Summed Area, and None. These methods perform a pixel averaging operation to anti-alias the image. The Summed Area option requires more memory but produces better results.

You can also specify the output for a mono channel or for an RGB channel. For maps that only use the monochrome information in the image (such as an opacity map), the Mono Channel as RGB Intensity or Alpha option can be used. For maps that use color information (for example, a diffuse map), the RGB Channel can be RGB (full color) or Alpha as Gray.

The Cropping/Placement controls enable you to crop or place the image. *Cropping* is the process of cutting out a portion of the image, and *Placing* is resizing the image while maintaining the entire image. The View Image button opens the image in a Cropping/Placement dialog box, shown in Figure 18-7. The rectangle is available within the image when Crop mode is selected. The handles of this rectangle can be moved to specify the crop region.

Tip When the Crop option is selected, a UV button is displayed in the upper right of the Cropping/Placement dialog box. Clicking this button changes the U and V values to X and Y pixels.

You can also adjust the U and V parameters, which define the upper left corner of the cropping rectangle, and the W and H parameters, which define the crop or placement width and height. The Jitter Placement option works with the Place option to randomly place and size the image.

Note The U and V values are a percentage of the total image. For example, a U value of 0.25 will position the image's left edge at a location that is 25 percent of the distance of the total width from the left edge of the original image.

If the bitmap has an alpha channel, you can specify whether it is to be used with the Image Alpha option, or you can define the alpha values as RGB Intensity or as None. You can also select to use Premultiplied Alphas. *Premultiplied Alphas* are alpha channels that have already been multiplied by each separate RGB channel. By premultiplying, you won't need to multiply the channels when compositing the image.

Figure 18-7: Viewing an image in the Cropping/Placement dialog box enables you to set the crop marks.

Bricks

The Bricks map creates brick patterns. The Standard Controls rollout contains a Preset Type drop-down list with a list of preset brick patterns. These patterns are popular brick patterns including Common Flemish, English, Stack, Fine Stack, Running, Fine Running, and Half Running. There is also a Custom option that lets you define your own brick pattern.

In the Advanced Controls rollout under both the Bricks and Mortar Setup sections, you can use a custom Texture map and color. You can specify the Horizontal and Vertical Count of the Bricks and the Mortar's Horizontal and Vertical Gaps as well as Color and Fade Variance values for both. The Mortar's Horizontal and Vertical Gaps can be locked to always be equal. For Mortar, you can also define the Percentage of Holes. Holes are where bricks have been left out. There is also a Rough value for controlling the roughness of the mortar.

The Random Seed value controls the randomness of the patterns, and the Swap Texture Entries exchange the brick texture with the mortar texture.

In the Stacking Layout section, the Line Shift and the Random Shift values are used to move each row of bricks a defined or random distance.

The Row and Column Editing section offers options that let you change the number of bricks Per Row or Column and the Change in each row or column.

Figure 18-8 shows three different Brick map styles.

Figure 18-8: From the Standard Controls rollout, you can select from several preset Brick styles, including Running Bond, English Bond, and Fine Running Bond.

Checker

The Checker map creates a checkerboard image with two colors. The Checker Parameters rollout includes two color swatches for changing the checker colors. You can also load maps in place of each color. The Swap button switches the position of the two colors and the Soften value blurs the edges between the two colors.

Figure 18-9 shows three Checker maps with Tiling values of 2 for the U and V directions and Soften values of 0, 0.2, and 0.5

 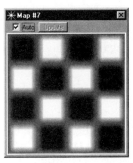 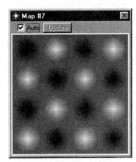

Figure 18-9: The Checker map can be softened as these three maps are with Soften values of 0, 0.2, and 0.5.

Gradient

The Gradient map creates a gradient image using three colors. The Gradient Parameters rollout includes a color swatch and map button for each color. The center color can be positioned at any location between the two ends using the Color 2 Position value spinner. The value can range from 0 through 1. The rollout lets you choose between Linear and Radial gradient types.

The Noise Amount adds noise to the gradient if its value is nonzero. The Size value scales the noise effect, and the Phase controls how quickly the noise changes over time. There are three types of noise that you can select: Regular, Fractal, and Turbulence. The Levels value determines how many times the noise function is applied. The High and Low Threshold and Smooth values set the limits of the noise function to eliminate discontinuities.

Figure 18-10 shows linear and radial Gradient maps.

Figure 18-10: A Gradient map can be linear or radial.

Gradient Ramp

This is an advanced version of the Gradient map that can use many different colors. The Gradient Ramp Parameters rollout includes a color bar with several flags along its bottom edge. You can add flags by simply clicking along the bottom edge. Flags can also be dragged or deleted.

 New Feature   The Gradient Ramp map is new in Release 3.

To define the color for each flag, right-click the flag and then select Edit Properties from the pop-up menu. This will open the Flag Properties dialog box, shown in Figure 18-11, where you can select a color to use.

Figure 18-11: The Flag Properties dialog box enables you to specify a color and its position to use in the Gradient Ramp.

The Gradient Type drop-down in the Gradient Ramp Parameters rollout offers various Gradient Types, including 4 Corner, Box, Diagonal, Lighting, Linear, Mapped, Normal, Pong, Radial, Spiral, Sweep, and Tartan. You can also select from several different Interpolation Types including Custom, Ease In, Ease In Out, Ease Out, Linear, and Solid.

The Noise controls work just like the Gradient Map parameters.

Figure 18-12 shows several of the gradient types available for the Gradient Ramp map.

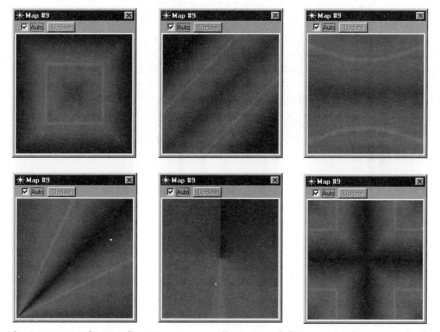

Figure 18-12: The Gradient Ramp map offers several different gradient types including (from top left to bottom right) Box, Diagonal, Normal, Pong, Spiral, and Tartan.

Paint

This map works with Discreet Logic's paint* plug-in package that enables users to paint directly on object.

Note   To use this map type, you must have the paint* plug-in made by Discreet Logic installed. If the plug-in isn't installed, the text, "Error: Paint Engine DLL Not Found" is displayed at the top of the Paint Parameters rollout.

The Project button lets you load a file to paint on. These files are limited to the types that paint* supports, such as their standard IPP files. The Edit button loads the paint* interface.

In the Live Edit section, the Unwrap Selected button places marking on the bitmap image to show where the mapping coordinates are located. The UV button lets you change from among UV, VW, and UW coordinate systems. The Track Time button lets you change the current frame, which enables you to paint materials that change over time. The Paint button changes the viewport cursor to enable you to interactively paint in the viewport.

The Paint map also includes a Time rollout, similar to the Bitmap map, for filtering and controlling animation frames.

Swirl

The Swirl map creates a swirled image of two colors — Base and Swirl. The Swirl Parameters rollout includes two color swatches and map buttons to specify these colors. The Swap button switches the two colors. Other options include Color Contrast, which controls the contrast between the two colors; Swirl Intensity, which defines the strength of the swirl color; and Swirl Amount, which is how much of the Swirl color gets mixed into the Base color.

Note   All maps that use two colors include a Swap button for switching between the colors.

The Twist value sets the number of swirls. Negative values cause the swirl to change direction. The Constant Detail value determines how much detail is included in the swirl.

With the Swirl Location X and Y values you can move the center of the swirl. As the center is moved far from the materials center, the swirl rings become tighter. The Lock button causes both values to change equally. If the lock is disabled, then the values can be changed independently.

The Random Seed sets the randomness of the swirl effect.

Figure 18-13 shows the Swirl map with three different Twist values. From left to right, the Swirl values are 1, 5, and 10.

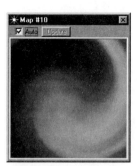 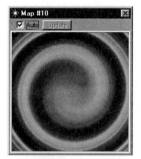 

Figure 18-13: The Swirl map combines two colors in a swirling pattern.

3D maps

3D Maps are procedurally created, which means that these maps are more than just a grouping of pixels; they are actually created using a mathematical algorithm. This algorithm defines the map in three-dimensions, so that if a portion of the object were to be cut away, the map would line up along each edge.

The Coordinates rollout for 3D maps is similar to the Coordinates rollout for 2D maps with a few exceptions; differences include Coordinate Source options of Object XYZ, World XYZ, Explicit Map Channel, and Vertex Color Channel. There are also Offset, Tiling, and Angle values for the X, Y, and Z axes as well as Blur and Blur offset options.

Cellular

The Cellular 3D map creates patterns of small objects referred to as cells. In the Cell Color section of the Cellular Parameters rollout, you can specify the color for the individual cells or apply a map. Setting the Variation value can vary the cell color.

In the Division Colors section, two color swatches are used to define the colors that appear in between the cells. This space will be a gradient between the two colors.

In the Cell Characteristics section, you can control the shape of the cells by selecting Circular or Chips, a Size, and how the cells are Spread. The Bump Smoothing value smoothes the jaggedness of the cells. The Fractal option causes the cells to be generated using a fractal algorithm. The Iterations value determines the number of times that the algorithm is applied. The Adaptive option determines automatically the number of iterations to complete. The Roughness setting determines how rough the surfaces of the cells are.

The Size value affects the overall scale of the map, while the Threshold values specify the specific size of the individual cells. Settings include Low, Mid, and High.

Figure 18-14 shows two Cellular maps: one with Circular cells (on the left) and the other with Chips cells (on the right).

Figure 18-14: The Cellular map creates small, regular-shaped cells.

Dent

The Dent 3D map works as a bump map to create indentations across the surface of an object. In the Dent Parameters rollout, the Size value sets the overall size of the dents. The Strength value determines how deep the dents are, and the Iterations sets how many times the algorithm is to be computed. You can also specify the colors for the dent map. The default colors are black and white. Black defines the areas that are indented.

Figure 18-15 shows two spheres with the Dent map applied as bump mapping. The sphere on the left has a Size value of 100, and the one on the right has a Size value of 500.

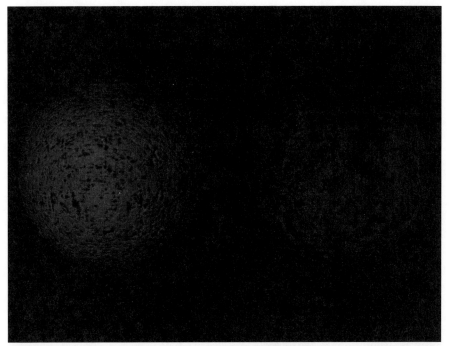

Figure 18-15: The Dent map causes dents in the object when applied as bump mapping.

Falloff

The Falloff 3D map creates a grayscale image based on the direction of the surface normals. Areas with normals that are parallel to the view are black, and areas whose normals are perpendicular to the view are white. This map is usually applied as an opacity map, giving you greater control over the opacity of the object.

The Falloff Parameters rollout includes two color swatches, a Strength value of each, and an optional map. There are also drop-down lists for setting the Falloff Type and the Falloff Direction. Falloff Types include Perpendicular/Parallel, Towards/Away, Fresnel, Shadow/Light, and Distance Blend. The Falloff Direction options include Viewing Direction (Camera Z-axis); Camera X-Axis; Camera Y Axis; Object; Local X, Y, and Z Axis; and World X, Y, and Z Axis.

In the Mode Specific Parameters section, there are several parameters that are based on the Falloff Type and Direction. If Object is selected as the Falloff Direction, then a button that lets you select the object becomes active. The Fresnel Falloff Type is based on the Index of Refraction and provides an option to override the material's Index of Refraction value. The Distance Blend Falloff Type offers values for Near and Far distances.

The Falloff map also includes a Mix Curve graph and rollout that give you precise control over the falloff gradient. The graph controls are the same as those for the Color Map graph, which was previously shown in Figure 18-5, and that was discussed in the "The Output Rollout" section earlier in the chapter.

Figure 18-16 shows two spheres with the Falloff map applied as opacity mapping. The sphere on the left uses the Perpendicular/Parallel Falloff Type with a Falloff Direction based on the Viewing Direction. The sphere on the right uses the Fresnel Falloff Type with a Local Y-Axis Falloff Direction. The Mix Curve has also been adjusted to provide some banding.

Figure 18-16: The Falloff map, when applied as opacity mapping, results in transparent areas based on the object normals.

Marble

The Marble 3D map creates a marbled material with random colored veins. The Marble Parameters rollout includes two color swatches: Color #1 is the vein color and Color #2 is the base color. You also have the option of loading maps for each color. The Swap button switches the two colors. The Size value determines how far each vein is from each other, and the Vein Width defines the vein thickness.

Figure 18-17 shows two spheres with the Marble map applied. The sphere on the left has a Vein Width value of 0.1, and the one on the right has a Vein Width of 0.025.

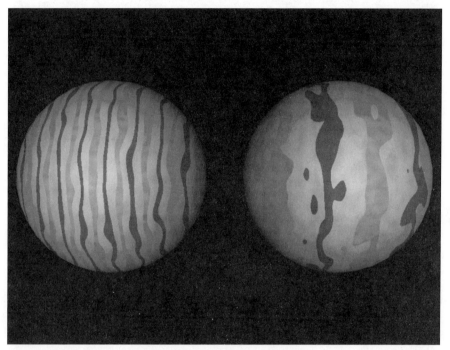

Figure 18-17: The Marble map creates a marbled surface.

Noise

The Noise 3D map randomly alters the surface of an object using two colors. The Noise Parameters rollout offers three different Noise types: Regular, Fractal, and Turbulence. Each type uses a different algorithm for computing noise. The two color swatches let you alter the colors used to represent the noise. You also have the option of loading maps for each color. The Swap button switches the two colors, and the Size value scales the noise effect. To prevent discontinuities, the High and Low Noise Threshold can be used to set noise limits.

Figure 18-18 shows two spheres with the Noise map applied. The sphere on the left uses the Fractal noise type and the one on the right uses the Turbulence noise type.

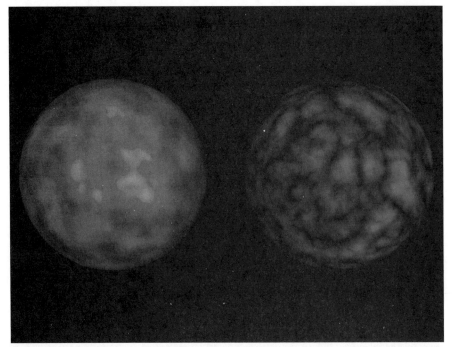

Figure 18-18: The Noise map produces a random noise pattern on the surface of the object.

Particle Age

The Particle Age map is used with particle systems to change the color of particles over their lifetime. The Particle Age Parameters rollout includes three different color swatches and age values.

Cross-Reference   The Particle Age map is covered in more detail in Chapter 24, "Creating and Controlling Particle Systems."

Particle MBlur

The Particle MBlur map is also used with particle systems. This map is used to blur particles as they increase in velocity. The Particle Motion Blur Parameters rollout includes two colors — the first color is the one used for the slower portions of the particle, and the second color is used for the fast portions. When you apply this map as an opacity map, the particles are blurred. There is also a Sharpness value to determine the amount of blur.

The Particle MBlur map is covered in more detail in Chapter 24, "Creating and Controlling Particle Systems."

Perlin Marble

This map creates marble textures using a different algorithm. Perlin Marble is more chaotic and random than the Marble map. The Perlin Marble Parameters rollout includes a Size parameter, which adjusts the size of the marble pattern, and a Levels parameter, which determines how many times the algorithm is applied. The two color swatches determine the base and vein colors, or you can assign a map. There are also values for the Saturation of the colors, and the Swap button switches the colors.

Figure 18-19 shows two spheres with the Perlin Marble map applied. The sphere on the left has a Size value of 50, and the one on the right has a Size value of 200.

Figure 18-19: The Perlin Marble map creates a marble pattern with random veins.

Planet

The Planet map is especially designed to create random areas of land and water. The Planet Parameters rollout includes three color swatches for the water areas and five color swatches for the land areas. These colors are displayed successively to simulate the elevation of the map. Other options include the Continent Size, the Island Factor (which determines the number of islands), an Ocean percentage, and a Random Seed. There is also an option to Blend Water and Land.

Figure 18-20 shows two spheres with the Planet map applied. The sphere on the left has a Continent Size value of 20, and the one on the right has a Continent Size value of 60.

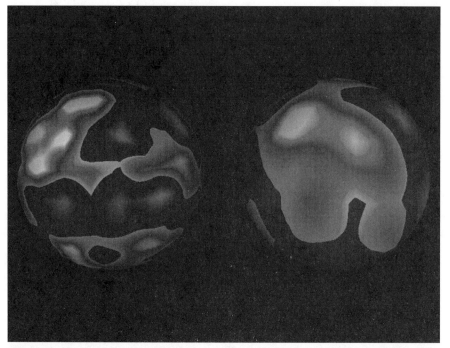

Figure 18-20: The Planet map can be used to create planets with landmasses and oceans.

Smoke

The Smoke map can create random fractal-based patterns such as those you'd see in smoke. In the Smoke Parameters rollout, you can set the Size of the smoke areas and the number of Iterations (how many times the fractal algorithm is computed).

The Phase value shifts the smoke about, and the Exponent value produces thinner, wispy lines of smoke. The rollout also includes two colors for the smoke particles and the area in between the smoke particles, or you could load maps instead.

Figure 18-21 shows two spheres with the Smoke map applied as diffuse and opacity mapping. The sphere on the left has a Size value of 20 and the one on the right has a Size value of 40.

Figure 18-21: The Smoke map simulates the look of smoke when applied as opacity mapping.

Speckle

The Speckle map produces small randomly positioned specks. The Speckle Parameters rollout lets you control the Size and color of the specks. Two color swatches are for the base and speck colors.

Figure 18-22 shows two spheres with the Speckle map applied. The sphere on the left has a Size value of 60, and the one on the right has a Size value of 120.

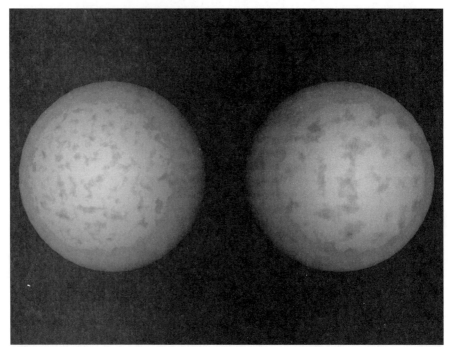

Figure 18-22: The Speckle map paints small random specks on the surface of an object.

Splat

The Splat map can create the look of covering an object with splattered paint. In the Splat Parameters rollout, you can set the Size of the splattered areas and the number of Iterations, which is how many times the fractal algorithm is computed. The Threshold value determines how much of each color to mix. The rollout also includes two colors for the splattered sections, or you could load maps instead.

Figure 18-23 shows two spheres with the Splat map applied. The sphere on the left has a Size value of 20 and the one on the right has a Size value of 60.

Stucco

The Stucco map generates random patches of gradients that create the look of a stucco surface if applied as a bump map. In the Stucco Parameters rollout, the Size value determines the size of these areas. The Thickness value determines how blurry the patches are, which changes the sharpness of the bumps for a bump map. The Threshold value determines how much of each color to mix. The rollout also includes two colors for the patchy sections, or you could load maps instead.

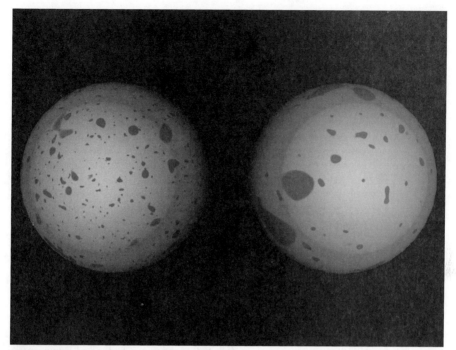

Figure 18-23: The Splat map splatters paint randomly across the surface of an object.

Figure 18-24 shows two spheres with the Stucco map applied as bump mapping. The sphere on the left has a Size value of 10, and the one on the right has a Size value of 20.

Water

This map creates wavy, watery looking maps and can be used as both a diffuse and a bump map to create a water surface. There are several values for setting the wave characteristics in the Water Parameters rollout, including the number of Wave Sets, the Wave Radius, the minimum and maximum Wave Length, the Amplitude, and the Phase. There is also an option to Distribute the waves as 2D or 3D, and there is a Random Seed value.

Figure 18-25 shows two spheres with the Water map applied as diffuse and bump mapping. The sphere on the left uses the 3D Distribution option, and the one on the right uses the 2D Distribution option.

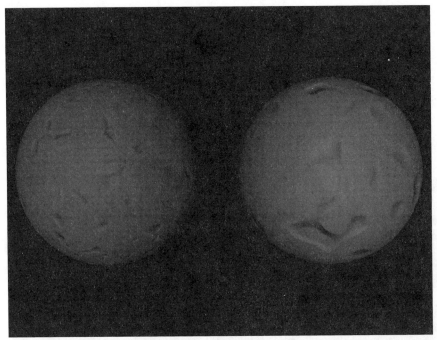

Figure 18-24: The Stucco map creates soft indentations when applied as bump mapping.

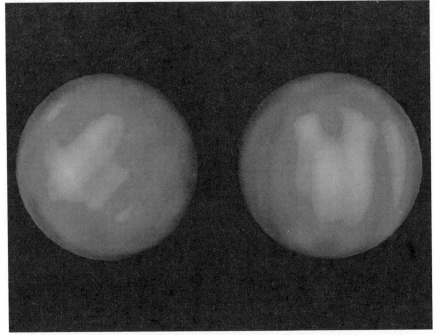

Figure 18-25: The Water map can be used to create watery surfaces.

Wood

The Wood map produces a two-color wood grain. The Wood Parameters rollout options include Grain Thickness, Radial, and Axial Noise. You can select the two colors to use for the wood grain.

Figure 18-26 shows two spheres with the Wood map applied. The sphere on the left has a Grain Thickness of 7 and the one on the right has a Grain Thickness of 20.

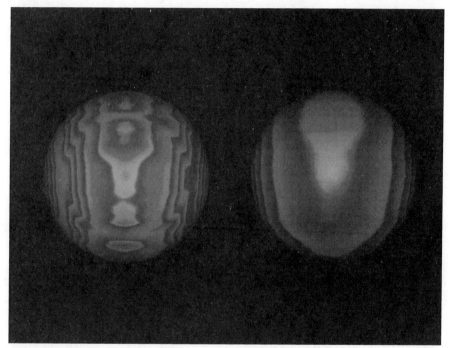

Figure 18-26: The Wood map creates a map with a wood grain.

Compositors

Compositor maps are made from combining several maps into one. Compositor map types include Composite, Mask, Mix, and RGB Multiply.

Composite

Composite maps combine a specified number of maps into a single map using the alpha channel. The Composite Parameters rollout enables you to specify the number of maps and has buttons for loading each.

The sphere on the left in Figure 18-27 uses a Composite map with a Brick and Gradient map. The alpha channel of the gradient fades the brick's texture from top to bottom.

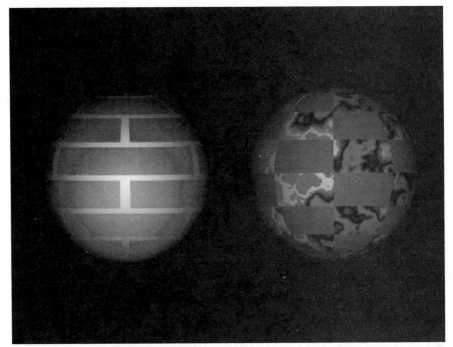

Figure 18-27: The Composite and Mask maps can use multiple maps.

Mask

In the Mask Parameters rollout, you can select one map to use as a Mask and another one to display through the holes in the mask simply called Map. There is also an option to Invert the Mask.

The sphere on the right in Figure 18-27 uses a Mask map. The Map is set to Perlin Marble, and the Mask is set to Checker with Tiling values of 4.

Mix

The Mix map can be used to combine two maps or colors. It is similar to the Composite map, except that it uses a Mix Amount value to combine the two colors or maps instead of using the alpha channel. In the Mix Parameters rollout, the Mix Amount value of 0 includes only Color #1, and a value of 100 includes only Color #2. You can also use a Mixing Curve to define how the colors are mixed. The curve shape is controlled by altering its Upper and Lower values.

Figure 18-28 shows two spheres with the Mix map applied. The sphere on the left combines the Cellular and Marble maps and the one on the right combines Wood and Splat.

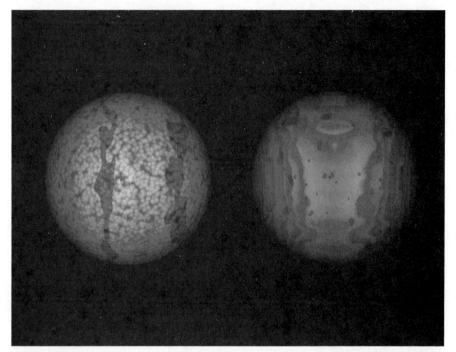

Figure 18-28: The Mix map lets you combine two maps and define the Mix Amount.

RGB Multiply

The RGB Multiply map multiplies the RGB values for two separate maps and combines them to create a single map. Did you notice in the previous figure how the Mix map fades both maps? The RGB Multiply map keeps the saturation of the individual maps by using each map's alpha channel to combine the maps.

The RGB Multiply Parameters rollout includes an option to use the Alpha from either Map #1 or Map #2 or to Multiply the Alphas.

Figure 18-29 shows two spheres with the RGB Multiply map applied. These spheres use the same submaps as in the previous figure, only this time their alpha channels are multiplied.

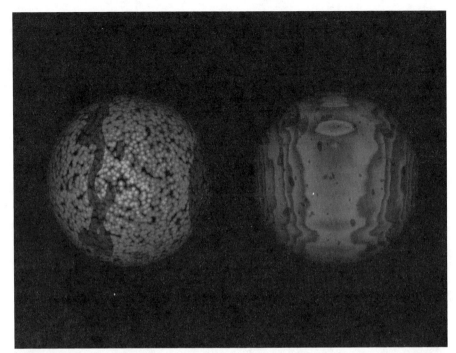

Figure 18-29: The RGB Multiply map combines maps at full saturation using alpha channels.

Color modifiers

This group of maps can be used to change the color of different materials. Code Modifier map types include Output, RGB Tint, and Vertex Color.

Output

The Output map provides a way to add the functions of the Output rollout to maps that don't include an output rollout. These features are the same as those discussed in the "The Output Rollout" section already discussed.

RGB Tint

The RGB Tint map includes color swatches for the red, green, and blue channel values. Adjusting these colors alters the amount of tint in the map. For example, setting the red color swatch in the RGB Tint Parameters rollout to white and the green and blue color swatches to black would create a map with a heavy red tint. You can also load maps in place of the colors.

Vertex Color

The Vertex Color map makes the vertex colors assigned to an Editable Mesh visible when the object is rendered. For more information on assigning vertex colors to an Editable Mesh, see Chapter 12, "Working with Meshes."

Caution   This map doesn't work on vertex colors assigned using the Vertex Colors utility.

Reflection and refraction

These maps are actually grouped into a category called *Other*, but they all deal with reflection and refraction effects. Maps in this category include Flat Mirror, Raytrace, Reflect/Refract, and Thin Wall Refraction.

Flat Mirror

The Flat Mirror map reflects the surroundings using a coplanar group of faces. In the Flat Mirror Parameters rollout, you can select a Blur amount to apply. You can specify whether to Render the First Frame Only or Every Nth Frame. There is also an option to Use the Environment Map or to apply to Faces with a given ID.

Note   Flat Mirror maps are applied to selected coplanar faces only.

The Distortion options include None, Use Bump Map, and Use Built-In Noise. If the Bump Map option is selected, you can define a Distortion Amount. If the Noise option is selected, you can choose Regular, Fractal, or Turbulence noise types with Phase, Size, and Levels values.

Figure 18-30 shows a model being reflected off a simple patch object with a Flat Mirror map applied to it.

Figure 18-30: A Flat Mirror map causes the object to reflect its surroundings.

Raytrace

The Raytrace map is an alternative to the Raytrace material discussed in the previous chapter and, as a map, can be used in places where the Raytrace material cannot. The Raytrace map includes several different rollouts. In the Raytracer Parameters rollout, shown in Figure 18-31, the Trace Mode determines how the rays are cast through the scene. Options include Auto Detect, Reflection, and Refraction. You can also use the Environment Settings or specify a color or map to use for the Background.

When you click the Options button in the Raytracer Parameters rollout, the Raytracer Options dialog box is displayed, as shown in Figure 18-32. This dialog box lets you enable or disable many Raytracer Options at the Local and Global level.

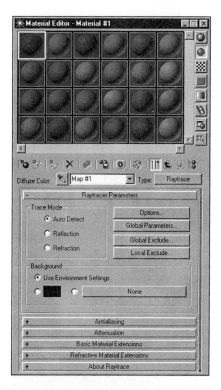

Figure 18-31: The Raytracer Parameters rollout includes buttons for controlling the Raytracer.

Figure 18-32: The Raytracer Options dialog box lets you specify which features to enable.

The Global Parameters button on the Raytracer Parameters rollout opens the Global Raytracer Settings dialog box, shown in Figure 18-33, where you can select Ray Depth Control settings including the Maximum Depth and the Cutoff Threshold. You can also select either the Multiresolution Adaptive Anti-aliaser or the Fast Adaptive Anti-aliaser as the Global Ray Anti-aliaser, or you can load a third-party anti-aliaser. By default the Acceleration settings are automatic, but you can select to use Manual Acceleration, which includes options for Single or Dual Pipe processing.

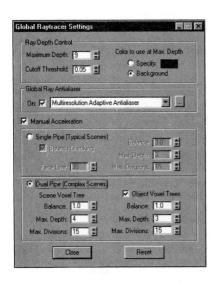

Figure 18-33: The Global Raytracer Settings dialog box lets you specify the settings for the raytracing engine.

The Global Exclude and Local Exclude buttons on the Raytracer Parameters rollout open the Exclude/Include dialog box where you can select which items to include or exclude in the raytracing calculations.

Back in the Material Editor, the Anti-aliasing rollout includes controls for overriding the Global Anti-aliasing Settings. You can also copy the Global settings to Local and vice versa. There are also controls for making the attenuation adaptive and controls for setting Blur features.

The Attenuation rollout lets you select from one of several Falloff Types. The options include Linear, Inverse Square, Exponential, and Custom Falloff. You can also set values for the Start and End distances. The Custom Falloff type lets you set a graph by adjusting Near, Far, and two Control values.

The Basic Material Extensions rollout lets you set the Reflectivity/Opacity Map and its strength. You can also set a Basic Tinting color or map. The Refractive Material Extensions rollout includes setting for specifying the Color Density (Filter color) and Fog.

Figure 18-34 shows a place setting created by Zygote Media that includes a wineglass with a Raytrace map applied.

Figure 18-34: The Raytrace map can be used to raytrace only select objects.

Reflect/Refract

Reflect/Refract maps are yet another way to create reflections and refractions on objects. These maps work by producing a rendering from each axis of the object, like one for each face of a cube. These rendered images, called *cubic maps*, are then projected onto the object.

These rendered images can be created automatically or loaded from prerendered images using the Reflect/Refract Parameters rollout. Using automatic cubic maps is easier, but they take considerably more time. If the Automatic option is selected, you can select to render the First Frame Only or Every Nth Frame. If the From File option is selected, then you are offered six buttons that can load cubic maps for each of the different directions.

The Reflect/Refract Parameters rollout can also specify the Blur settings and the Atmospheric Ranges.

Figure 18-35 shows a model of a '57 Chevy created by Viewpoint Datalabs, with a Reflect/Refract map applied to its bumper.

Figure 18-35: The Reflect/Refract map is applied to the chrome bumper of a '57 Chevy.

Thin Wall Refraction

The Thin Wall Refraction map simulates the refraction caused by a piece of glass, such as a magnifying glass. The same result is possible with the Reflect/Refract map, but the Thin Wall Refraction map achieves this result in a fraction of the time.

The Thin Wall Refraction Parameters rollout includes options for setting the Blur, the frames to render, and Refraction values. The Thickness Offset determines the amount of offset and can range from 0 through 10. The Bump Map Effect value changes the refraction based on the presence of a bump map.

The Maps Rollout

Now that you've seen all the different types of maps that are available, we'll revisit the Material Editor and Maps rollouts introduced in the previous chapter and cover them in more detail.

The Maps rollout is where maps are applied to the various materials. To use a map, click the Map button—this opens the Material/Map Browser where you can select the map to use. The Amount spinner sets the intensity of the map, and there is an option to enable or disable the map. For example, a white material with a red Diffuse map set at 50 percent Intensity will result in a pink material.

The available maps in the Maps rollout depend on the type of material and the Shader that you are using. Raytrace materials have many more available maps than the Standard material. Some of the common mapping types found in the Maps rollout will be discussed in this section.

 New Feature   The Diffuse Level, Roughness, Anisotropy, Orientation, and Metalness mapping options are new to Release 3.

Ambient mapping

Ambient mapping replaces the ambient color component of the base material. This can be used to make an object's shadow appear as a map. Diffuse mapping (discussed next) also affects the Ambient color. A lock button in the Maps rollout enables you to lock these two mappings together.

Diffuse mapping

Diffuse mapping replaces the diffuse color component of the base material. This is the main color used for the object. When you select a map such as Wood, the object appears to be created out of wood. As mentioned previously, diffuse mapping can also affect the Ambient color if the lock button is selected.

Diffuse Level mapping

Diffuse Level mapping changes the diffuse color level from 0, where the map is black, to a maximum, where the map is white. This mapping is only available with the Anisotropic, Oren-Nayar-Blinn, and Multi-Level Shaders.

Roughness mapping

Roughness mapping sets the roughness value of the material from 0, where the map is black, to a maximum, where the map is white. This mapping is only available with the Oren-Nayar-Blinn and Multi-Level Shaders.

Specular mapping

Specular mapping replaces the specular color component of the base material. This enables you to include a different color or image in place of the specular color. This is different from the Specular Level and Glossiness mappings, which also affect the specular highlights.

Specular Level mapping

Specular Level mapping controls the intensity of the specular highlights from 0, where the map is black, to 1, where the map is white. For the best effect, apply this mapping along with the Glossiness mapping.

Glossiness mapping

Glossiness mapping defines where the specular highlights will appear. This can be used to make an object appear older by diminishing certain areas. Black areas on the map show the nonglossy areas, and white areas are where the glossiness is at a maximum.

Self-Illumination mapping

Self-Illumination mapping makes certain areas of an object glow and, because they glow, they won't receive any lighting effects, such as highlights or shadows. Black areas represent areas that have no self-illumination, and white areas receive full self-illumination.

Opacity mapping

Opacity mapping determines which areas are visible and which are transparent. Black areas for this map will be transparent, and white areas will be opaque. This mapping works in conjunction with the Opacity value in the Basic Parameters rollout. Transparent areas, even if perfectly transparent, still receive specular highlights.

Filter color mapping

Filter color mapping is used to color transparent areas for creating materials such as colored glass. White light that is cast through an object using filter color mapping will be colored with the filter color.

Anisotropy mapping

Anisotropy mapping can control the shape of an anisotropy highlight. This mapping is only available with the Anisotropic and Multi-Level Shaders.

Orientation mapping

Orientation mapping is used to control an anisotropic highlight's position. Anisotropic highlights are elliptical, and this mapping can position them at a different angle. Orientation mapping is only available with the Anisotropic and Multi-Level Shaders.

Metalness mapping

Metalness mapping controls how metallic an area looks. It specifies metalness values from 0, where the map is black, to a maximum, where the map is white. This mapping is only available with the Strauss Shader.

Bump mapping

Bump mapping uses the intensity of the bitmap to raise or indent the surface of an object. The white areas of the map are raised, and darker areas are lowered. Although bump mapping appears to alter the geometry, it actually doesn't affect the surface geometry.

Reflection mapping

Reflection mapping reflects images off the surface as a mirror does. There are three different types of Reflection mapping: Basic, Automatic, and Flat Mirror. Basic reflection mapping simulates the reflection of an object's surroundings. Automatic reflection mapping projects the map outward from the center of the object. Flat-Mirror reflection mapping reflects a mirror image off a series of coplanar faces.

Reflection mapping doesn't need mapping coordinates because they are based on world coordinates and not on object coordinates. Therefore, the map will appear different if the object is moved — which is how reflections work in the real world.

Refraction mapping

Refraction mapping bends light and displays images through a transparent object, in the same way as the view of a room through a glass of water. The amount of this effect is controlled by a value called the Index of Refraction. This value is set in the parent material's Extended Parameters rollout.

Displacement mapping

Displacement mapping, unlike bump mapping, can be used to actually change the geometry of an object. The white areas of the map are pushed outward, and the dark areas are pushed in. The amount of the surface that is displaced is based on a percentage of the diagonal that makes up the bounding box of the object. Displacement mapping can only be applied to patches, Editable Meshes, and NURBS objects. For other object types, you can use displacement mapping only after the Disp Approx Modifier has been applied.

Displacement mapping isn't visible in the viewports unless the Displace NURBS (for NURBS objects) or the Displace Mesh (for Editable Meshes) Modifiers have been applied.

Summary

We've covered a lot of ground in this chapter because there are a lot of different maps. Learning to use these maps will make a big difference in the realism of your materials.

In this chapter you've learned about

- ✦ The basics of mapping coordinates and tiling
- ✦ All the different map types in several different categories, including 2D, 3D, Compositors, Color Mods, and Reflection/Refraction
- ✦ The various mapping possibilities provided in the Maps rollout

In the next chapter, you'll gain some experience using the various materials and maps.

✦   ✦   ✦

Working with Materials and Maps

At this point, you should have no difficulty relating to the familiar adage about teaching a man to fish versus giving him a fish, because you've now learned the basics of materials and maps. With a basic understanding of these fundamental building blocks, you can create an unlimited number of materials.

This chapter covers several aspects of material creation that haven't been covered yet and includes several examples of working with custom materials.

Creating New Materials

Any time you adjust a material or a map parameter, a new material is created, and the material's sample slot is updated. Although newly created materials are saved along with the scene file, you can make them available for reuse by including them in a library.

Building a new material library

Materials can be saved to a new library or to the default library. To add a material to the current library, select the material's sample slot and click the Put in Library button. This will open a simple dialog box in which you can name the material and add the selected material to the current library.

To see which library is current, open the Material/Map Browser by clicking the Get Material button. Select the

Mtl Library option in the Browse From section—the library name will be shown in the Title Bar. The File section includes four buttons for opening, merging, and saving material libraries. Figure 19-1 shows a library of materials used in this book. This material library is called "3dsmax r3 Bible."

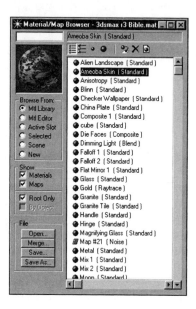

Figure 19-1: The Material/Map Browser can open additional material libraries.

The 3dsmax r3 Bible material library can be found on the book's CD-ROM.

Tutorial: Creating space textures

"Space . . . the final frontier." Space is a great place to start creating and using new materials. With objects floating in space, you don't need to worry about lining things up, and it is easy to model planets because they are made from simple spheres—the materials are what make it look good. So, as an example of creating new materials, let's create several new "space" materials.

In this tutorial, you'll learn how to make textures for the sun, a moon, and several different planets.

To create several planetary textures, follow these steps:

> **1.** Start by creating five spheres.

2. Open the Material Editor, select the first sample slot, and name the material **Sun**. Click the map button to the right of the Diffuse color swatch to open the Material/Map Browser, and double-click the Noise map. In the Noise Parameters rollout, select the Fractal option and set the Size to **20** and the Levels to **10**. Choose an orange color for Color #1 and black for Color #2. Next, open the Maps rollout and drag the Noise map from the Diffuse mapping to the Self Illumination mapping. A small dialog box will open, enabling you to Copy the map as an Instance or a Copy or Swap the maps. Select the Copy option and click OK.

Tip   Double-click the sample slot to open a magnified view of the material. This will let you see the details up close.

3. Select the second sample slot and name it **Planet 1**. Then click the map button to the right of the Diffuse color swatch to open the Material/Map Browser again and double-click Planet. In the Planet Parameters rollout, select three shades of blue for the Water Colors and five shades of green for the Land Colors. Set the Continent Size to **20** and enable the Blend Water/Land option.

4. Select the third sample slot and name it **Planet 2**. Then click the map button to the right of the Diffuse color swatch to open the Material/Map Browser and double-click Planet. In the Planet Parameters rollout, select shades of orange and brown for both the water and landmass of this planet. Set the Continent Size to **40** and enable the Blend Water/Land option.

5. Select the forth sample slot and name it **Planet 3**. Then click the map button to the right of the Diffuse color swatch and select the Planet map. For this planet, select different shades of red. Set the Continent Size to **80**, the Island Factor to **40**, and the Ocean Percent to **20,** and disable the Blend Water/Land option.

6. Select the fifth sample slot and name it **Planet 4**. Then click the Diffuse color map button and select Swirl from the Material/Map Browser. Select two colors for the Swirl and set the Swirl Intensity to **5.0**. For the Swirl color, click the map button and select the Noise map. For the Noise map, set the Size value to **30** and select the Turbulence option.

7. Select the sixth sample slot and name it **Moon**. Then click the Diffuse color map button and select Smoke from the Material/Map Browser. Set the Size value to **20** and click the map button for Color #1. Select the Noise map. Set the Size value to **25** and select the Turbulence option.

8. Select the sixth sample slot and name it **Star Background**. Then click the Diffuse color map button and select Noise. Set the Size value to **2.0**, the High value to **0.5**, and the Levels to **2.0**. Click the Swap button until Color #2 is black. In the Output rollout, set the Output Amount to **2.0**.

9. Apply these materials to the various spheres and assign the Star Background as an Environment Map using the Rendering Í Environment dialog box.

Figure 19-2 shows the resulting solar system.

Figure 19-2: Using a variety of techniques, you can create an assortment of different space textures.

Tutorial: Aging objects for realism

I don't know if your toolbox is well-worn like mine — it must be the hostile environment that it is always in (or all the things I keep dropping in and on it). To render a toolbox with nice specular highlights just doesn't feel right. This tutorial shows a few ways to age an object so that it looks older.

To add maps to make an object look old, follow these steps:

1. Create a toolbox model using extruded splines.

2. Open the Material Editor and select the first sample slot. Select the Metal Shader. For the Diffuse color, select a nice shiny red and increase the Specular Level and Glossiness. Name the material **Toolbox**.

3. In the Maps rollout, click the button for the Glossiness mapping and select the Splat map from the Material/Map Browser. Set the Size value to **100** and change Color #1 to a rust color and Color #2 to white.

4. With the Maps rollout still open, click the Bump mapping button and select the Dent map from the Material/Map Browser. Set the Size value to **200** and Color #1 to black and Color #2 to white.

5. At the top of the Material Editor, select the second sample slot and name it **Hinge**. Select the Metal Shader for this material also and increase the Specular Level slightly. Also change the Diffuse color to a light gray. Click the map button next to the Glossiness value and choose the Noise map. Set the Noise map to Fractal with a Size on **10**.

6. Drag the "Toolbox" material to the toolbox object and the "Hinge" material to the hinge and the handle.

Note Bump and glossiness mappings will not be visible until the scene is rendered. To see the material's results, select Rendering ➪ Render and click the Render button.

Figure 19-3 shows the well-used toolbox.

Figure 19-3: This toolbox shows its age with Glossiness and Bump mappings.

Animating Materials

Materials can be animated if their properties are altered while the Animate button is active. MAX will interpolate between the values as the animation progresses. The material must be consistent for the entire animation — you cannot change materials at different keys, you can only alter the existing materials parameters.

If you want to change materials as the animation progresses, you can use one of the materials that combines multiple materials, such as the Blend material. This material includes a Mix Amount value that can change at different keyframes. The next tutorial shows how to use the Blend material in this manner.

Several maps include a Phase value, including all maps that have a Noise rollout. This value provides the means to animate the map. For example, using a Noise map and changing the Phase value over many keys will animate the noise effect.

Tutorial: Dimming lights

Occasionally you'll want to change materials in a scene to gradually alter it in some way, such as dimming a light. This can be easily accomplished with the Blend material.

To create a light that dims with time, follow these steps:

1. Create a bulb object and select it.

2. Open the Material Editor and select the first sample slot. Then click the Type button and select the Blend material from the Material/Map Browser. Give the material the name **Dimming Light**.

When using composite materials, a dialog box will appear asking if you want to discard the old material or keep it as a submaterial. If you choose to keep it, the current material in the sample slot will become one of the maps for the composite material.

3. Click the Material 1 button and give the material the name **Light On**. Set the Diffuse color to yellow and the Self Illumination to yellow. Then click the Go Forward to Sibling button.

Composite materials such as Blend include several submaterials. When one of these submaterials is selected, you can move quickly to the other submaterials by clicking the Go Forward to Sibling button. To access the root material, click the Go to Parent button.

4. Name the second material **Light Off** and select a gray Diffuse color. Then click the Go to Parent button to return to the Blend material.

5. With the Time Slider at frame 0, click the Animate button. Then drag the Time Slider to frame 100 and change the Mix Amount to **100**. Click the Animate button again to deactivate it. This will cause the material to change gradually from the "Light On" material to the "Light Off" material. By dragging the Time Slider, you'll be able to see the material in the sample slot change.

Note   Another way to view the dimming material is to click the Make Preview button. This will open the Create Material Preview dialog box, shown in Figure 19-4. Select the Active Time Segment option and click OK. The material will render every frame and automatically open and play the material preview.

Figure 19-4: The Create Material Preview dialog box can render the entire range of frames or a select number of frames.

6. Click the Assign Material to Selection button to assign the material to the bulb object.

Figure 19-5 shows a simple lamp object with a dimming sphere in its center.

Using IFL files

Anyplace where you can load a bitmap map, you can also load an animation file such as an AVI or a FLC file. Another way to create animated material is with IFL files.

Note   If you're using an animated file as a material, you can produce a material preview by clicking the Make Preview button to open the Create Material Preview dialog box. The preview can then be played or saved using the flyout buttons under the Make Preview button.

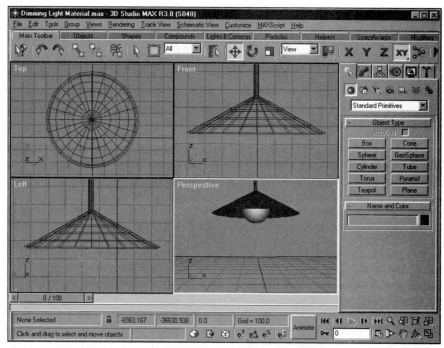

Figure 19-5: This lamp object will dim as the animation proceeds.

IFL files are text files that list which images should appear and for which frames. They are saved with the .IFL extension and can be loaded using the Bitmap map. To create an IFL file, open a text editor and type the name of the image followed by the number of frames that it should appear for. Be sure to include a space between the name and the number of frames. The images will be displayed in the order they are listed and repeated until all frames have been displayed. Once applied, the IFL file will be visible in the sample slot if you drag the Time Slider, or you could create a material preview.

Tip

You can also use the * and ? wildcard characters within an IFL file. For example, **flyby*** will include any image file that begins with "flyby," and **flyby?** will include any image file that begins with "flyby" and has one additional character.

Generating IFL files with the IFL manager utility

If you don't want to create text files by yourself, you can use the IFL Manager Utility to generate IFL files for you. To use this utility, open the Utilities panel and click the More button. Then select the IFL Manager utility and click OK.

In the IFL Manager rollout, the Select button opens a File dialog box where you can select a sequential list of images to include in an IFL file. Once a list of images is selected, you can specify the Start and End images. You can cause the images to be displayed in reverse by placing a greater number in the Start field than is in the End field. The Every Nth field can specify to use every Nth image. The Multiplier field is used to specify how many frames each image should appear.

The Create button opens a File dialog box where you can save the IFL file. The Edit button opens an IFL text file in the system's default text editor for editing.

Tutorial: What's on TV?

Animated files such as AVI and FLC can be opened and mapped to an object to animate the texture, but you can also use IFL files.

To create an IFL file that will be mapped on the front of a television model, follow these steps:

1. Open a graphics editor such as Adobe Photoshop and create an image of some television static to use in the IFL file. We will also use several images rendered from the "Quick-Start" tutorials you performed at the beginning of this book.

2. Open a text editor and type the following:

```
; these frames will be positioned on a television screen.
static.tif 20
Fighter Jet Fly-By -frame74.tif 2
Fighter Jet Fly-By -frame75.tif 2
Fighter Jet Fly-By -frame76.tif 2
Fighter Jet Fly-By -frame77.tif 2
Fighter Jet Fly-By -frame78.tif 2
Fighter Jet Fly-By -frame79.tif 2
Fighter Jet Fly-By -frame80.tif 2
Fighter Jet Fly-By -frame81.tif 2
Fighter Jet Fly-By -frame82.tif 2
Fighter Jet Fly-By -frame83.tif 2
static.tif 60
```

Note The first line of text is referred to as a *comment line*. You enter comments into the IFL file by starting the line with a semicolon (;) character.

3. Save the file as **tv.ifl**. Make sure that your text editor doesn't add the extension ".TXT" on the end of the file.

Caution The IFL file as described above will look for the image files in the same directory as the IFL file. Make sure that the images are included in this directory.

4. Import the television model (created by Zygote Media) and select the front screen object.

5. Open the Material Editor and select the first sample slot. Name the material **Television Screen.** Click the map button to the right of the Diffuse color swatch. Double-click the Bitmap map. In the File dialog box, locate the "tv.ifl" file and click OK. Then click the Assign Material to Selection button to apply the material to the screen.

Tip   To see the map in the viewport, click the Show Map in Viewport button. This button makes the frames of the IFL file visible in the viewport.

6. Because the screen object is a mesh object, you'll need to use the UVW Map Modifier to create some mapping coordinates for the map. Open the Modify panel and click the UVW Map button. Set the mapping option to Planar. Then click the Sub-Object button and transform the planar gizmo until it covers the screen.

Figure 19-6 shows one frame of the television with the IFL file applied.

Figure 19-6: IFL files can be used to animate materials via a list of images.

Applying Multiple Materials

Most complex models are broken down into multiple parts, each distinguished by the material type that is applied to it. For example, a car model would be separated into windows, tires, and the body, so that each part could have a unique material applied to it.

Using Material IDs

There may be times when you'll want to apply multiple materials to a single part. Selecting subobject areas and using Material IDs can do this.

Many of the standard primitives have Material IDs automatically assigned — spheres get a single material ID, while boxes get six (one for each side) and cylinders get three (one for the cylinder and one for each end cap). In addition to the standard primitives, Editable Mesh objects can be assigned Material IDs. These Material IDs can also be assigned to any object or subobject using the Material Modifier. These Material IDs correspond to the various materials specified in the Multi/Sub-Object material.

Note   These Material IDs shouldn't be confused with the Material Effect IDs, which are selected using the Material Effect flyout buttons under the sample slots. Material IDs are used only with the Multi/Sub-Object material type, whereas the Effect IDs are used with the Render Effects and Video Post dialog boxes for adding effects such as glows to a material.

Tutorial: Mapping die faces

As an example of mapping multiple materials to a single object, consider a die. It wouldn't make sense to split the cube object that makes up the die up into several different parts, so we'll use the Multi/Sub-Object material instead.

To create a die model, follow these steps:

1. Open Adobe Photoshop and create six images with the dots of a die on them. These images should be the same size.

2. Open the Create panel, click the Box button, and select the Cube options in the Creation Method rollout. Then drag in the Top view to create a cube object.

3. Open the Material Editor and select the first sample slot. Name the material **Die Faces** and click the Type button. Select the Multi/Sub-Object material from the Material/Map Browser. Select to discard the current map and click OK.

4. In the Multi/Sub-Object Basic Parameters rollout, click the Set Number button and enter a value of **6**.

5. Name the first material **face 1** and click the material button to open the parameter rollouts for the first material. Then click the map button to the right of the Diffuse color swatch to open the Material/Map Browser and double-click the Bitmap map. In the Select Bitmap Image File dialog box, choose the image with one spot and click Open.

6. Back in the Material Editor, click the Go to Parent button twice to return to the Multi Sub-Object Basic Parameters rollout and repeat Step 5 for each of the die faces.

7. When the Multi/Sub-Object material is defined, select the cube object and click the Assign Material to Selection button. Then click the Show Map in Viewport button to see the material applied to the cube.

Note   Because the cube object used in this example is a box primitive, we didn't need to assign the Material IDs to different subobject selections. The box primitive automatically assigned a different Material ID to each face of the cube. When Material IDs do need to be assigned, they can be specified in the Surface Properties rollout for Editable Meshes.

8. To smooth the edges of the die, open the Modify panel, click the More button, and select the MeshSmooth Modifier. In the Parameters rollout, select the Classic Type and set the Strength value to **0.1**.

Figure 19-7 shows two dice being rolled.

Material Modifiers

In Chapter 9, "Modifying Objects," the basic Modifiers were presented. In this section, you'll get a chance to use several material-specific Modifiers in a variety of tutorials.

Tutorial: Using the UVW Map Modifier to apply decals

The UVW Map Modifier was already used in the television example earlier in this chapter, but it's worth exploring further. Once mapping coordinates have been applied either automatically or with the UVW Map Modifier, the UVW XForm Modifier can be used to move, rotate, and scale the mapping coordinates.

Most objects can automatically generate mapping coordinates — with the exception of meshes. For meshes, you need to use the UVW Map Modifier. The UVW Map Modifier includes seven different mapping options. Each mapping option wraps the map in a different way. The options include Planar, Cylindrical, Spherical, Shrink Wrap, Box, Face, and XYZ to UVW.

Figure 19-7: These dice have different bitmaps applied to each face.

In this tutorial, we'll use the UVW Map Modifier to apply a decal to a rocket model. Zygote Media created the rocket model.

To use the UVW Map Modifier, follow these steps:

1. In an image-editing program such as Adobe Photoshop, create a 300 × 600 image with a white background and type the word **NASA** in black capital letters. Set the background color to be transparent, and save the image as a .GIF file.

Note

The GIF file format can make areas of the image transparent. These transparent areas become the alpha channel when loaded into MAX.

2. Open the Material Editor and select the first sample slot. Name the material **NASA Logo**. Click the Diffuse color swatch and select a white color. Then click the map button to the right of the Diffuse color swatch, and from the Material/Map Browser, double-click the Bitmap map. Locate the NASA image created in Step 1 and click Open. This will load the bitmap image and display the Bitmap parameters in the rollouts. In the Coordinates rollout, deselect the Show Map on Back option and enter a value of **–90** in the W Angle field. This will rotate the letters vertically. Then, in the Bitmap Parameters rollout, select the Image Alpha option.

3. Import the rocket model and select the white section. Open the Modify panel and click the Element subobject button at the top of the Selection rollout. Then select the bottom white section and click the Detach button. This will open a simple Detach dialog box where you can name the detached part. Name it **Stage 2**, make sure that the Detach To Element and Detach as Clone options are not selected, and click OK. Then click the Sub-Object button to exit subobject mode.

4. At the top of the Modify panel, click the UVW Map button. Select the Cylindrical Mapping option, but don't select the Cap option.

5. With the cylinder section selected, open the Material Editor again, select the first sample slot, and click the Assign Material to Selection button.

6. In order to see the rocket clearly against its background, open the Environment dialog box with the Rendering ⇨ Environment command and select a light blue color for the background color.

Figure 19-8 shows the resulting image.

Figure 19-8: The UVW Map Modifier can be used to apply decals to objects.

Tutorial: Random marquee lights

The MaterialByElement Modifier enables you to change material IDs randomly. In this tutorial, we'll reproduce the effect of lights randomly turning on and off on a marquee by using the Multi/Sub-Object material together with the MaterialByElement Modifier.

To create a randomly lighted marquee, follow these steps:

1. Create spheres arranged in a rectangle.

2. Right-click one of the spheres and convert it to an Editable Mesh object. Then open the Modify panel and click the Attach button. Select each additional sphere to make all the spheres part of the same object. Click the Attach button again to disable it when you're through.

3. Open the Material Editor and select the first sample slot. Then click the Type button and select the Multi/Sub-Object material from the Material/Map Browser. Select to discard the current material and click OK. Give the material the name **Random Lights**.

4. In the Multi/Sub-Object Basic Parameters rollout, click the Set Number button and change its value to **2**. Then click the Material 1 button, and, in the Material roll-down, give the material the name **Light On**. Set the Diffuse color to yellow and the Self Illumination to yellow. Then click the Go Forward to Sibling button to access the second material.

5. Name the second material **Light Off** and select a gray Diffuse color. Then click the Go to Parent button to return to the Multi/Sub-Object material.

6. Click the Assign Material to Selection button to assign the material to the spheres.

7. With the spheres selected, click the More button at the top of the Modify panel to open the list of additional Modifiers. Select the MaterialByElement Modifier and click OK. In the Parameters rollout, select the Random Distribution option and set the ID Count to **2**.

Figure 19-9 shows the marquee with its random lights. (I've always wanted to see my name in lights!)

Using the Unwrap UVW Modifier

The Unwrap UVW Modifier lets you control how a map is applied to an object. This is accomplished by creating planar maps for various sides of an object and then editing the mapping coordinates in the Edit UVWs dialog box, shown in Figure 19-10.

Figure 19-9: This marquee is randomly lighted thanks to the MaterialByElement Modifier.

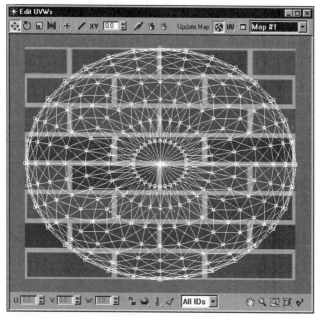

Figure 19-10: The Edit UVWs dialog box lets you control how different planar maps line up with the model.

The edited mapping coordinates can be saved and loaded. Saved mapping coordinate files have the .UVW extension. The buttons in the Edit UVWs dialog box are shown and described in Table 19-1.

Table 19-1
Edit UVW Dialog Box Buttons

Buttons	Name	Description
	Move, Move Horizontal, Move Vertical	Moves the selected vertices when dragged.
	Rotate	Rotates the selected vertices when dragged.
	Scale, Scale Horizontal, Scale Vertical	Scales the selected vertices when dragged.
	Mirror Horizontal, Mirror Vertical	Mirrors the selected vertices about the center of the selection.
	Expand Selection, Contract Selection	Adds or subtracts all adjacent vertices to the current selection.
	Falloff Type	Enables you to select a falloff type including Linear, Sinusoidal, Slow Out, and Fast Out.
	World Falloff Space, Texture Falloff Space	Sets the falloff coordinate system.
0.0	Falloff Distance	Determines the distance before the color changes.
	Break Selected Vertices	Splits the selected vertices into two.
	Target Weld	Enables you to drag selected vertices to a single vertex for welding.
	Weld Selected	Welds all the selected vertices together.

Continued

Table 19-1 *(continued)*		

Buttons	Name	Description
Update Map	Update Map	Updates the map in the viewport.
[icon]	Show Map	Toggles the display of the map in the dialog box.
UV	Coordinates	Displays the vertices for the UV, UW, and WU axes.
[icon]	Unwrap Options	Opens the Unwrap Options dialog box for setting preferences.
Map #4 ▼	Pick Texture	Displays a drop-down list of all the maps applied to this object. New maps can be displayed using the Pick Texture option.
U: 0.49 V: W:	U, V, W values	Displays the coordinates of the selected vertex. These values can be used to move a vertex.
[icon]	Lock Selected Vertices	Locks the selected vertices and prevents additional vertices from being selected.
[icons]	Hide, Unhide	Hides or unhides the selected vertices.
[icons]	Freeze, Unfreeze	Freezes or unfreezes the selected vertices.
[icon]	Filter Selected Faces	Displays vertices for only the selected faces.
[icon]	All IDs	Filters selected Material IDs.

The buttons in the lower right corner of the Edit UVWs dialog box work just like the Viewport Navigation buttons described in earlier chapters.

The Unwrap Options dialog box, shown in Figure 19-11, lets you set the Line and Selection Colors as well as the preferences for the Edit UVWs dialog box. You can set the map resolution or use the Use Bitmap Resolution option. There is also a setting for the Weld Threshold and options to constantly update, show selected vertices in viewport, and snap to the middle pixel.

Figure 19-11: The Unwrap Options dialog box sets the preferences for the Edit UVWs dialog box.

Tutorial: Controlling the mapping of teddy bear's head

The teddy bear model created by Viewpoint Datalabs is fairly simplistic, but you can add details to it using planar maps. In this tutorial, we'll add and edit the mapping coordinates for the teddy bear's eyes using the Unwrap UVW Modifier.

To control how planar maps are applied to the head of a teddy bear, follow these steps.

1. Open Adobe Photoshop and create a new 300 × 300 file with a light brown background. Use the Ellipse tool to draw two eyes and save the file as **Teddy Bear Eyes.tif**.

2. Import the Viewpoint Datalabs teddy bear model. Select and zoom in to the head of the model.

3. Open the Modify panel and click the UVW Map button. This will apply a planar map to the teddy bear's head. Click the Sub-Object button and rotate the gizmo until it is parallel with the Front view. Then click the Sub-Object button again to deselect it.

4. Open the Material Editor and select the first sample slot. Name the material **Teddy Bear Head**. Then click the Diffuse color map button and double-click the Bitmap map. In the Select Bitmap Image File dialog box, locate the "Teddy Bear Eyes.tif" file and click OK. Then apply this material to the teddy bear's head object.

5. Click the More button at the top of the Modify panel to open the additional Modifiers list, select the Unwrap UVW, and click OK. In the Parameters rollout, click the Edit button. This will open the Edit UVWs dialog box, shown in Figure 19-12.

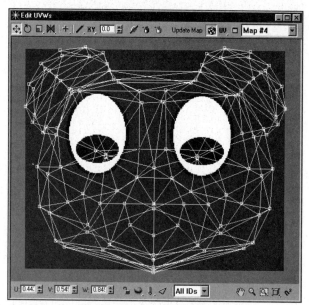

Figure 19-12: The Edit UVWs dialog box lets you transform the mapping coordinates by moving the vertices.

6. In the Edit UVWs dialog box, drag the mouse over all the vertices that immediately surround the white section of the eyes to select them (or you could hold down the Ctrl key and click them individually). These vertices will turn red when selected. Then click the Move button and move all these vertices to the center of the eyes. Try to move all the vertices so that they maintain symmetry. To check the results of the edits, close the Edit UVWs dialog box and enable Smooth Shading in the Front viewport by right-clicking the Front viewport title and selecting Smooth + Highlights. Figure 19-13 shows the results of the new mapping coordinates.

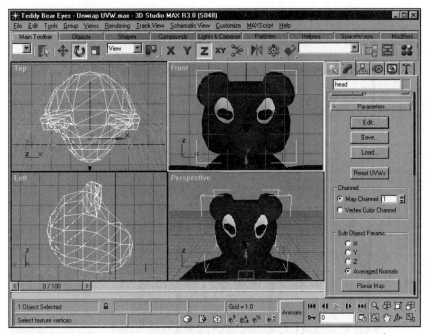

Figure 19-13: The position of this teddy bear's eyes has been set using the Unwrap UVW Modifier.

Painting vertices

A unique way to color objects is with the Vertex Paint Modifier. This Modifier lets you paint on an object by specifying a color for each vertex. If adjacent vertices have different colors assigned, then a gradient is created across the face. The benefit of this coloring option is that it is very efficient and requires almost no memory.

Note   The Assign Vertex Color utility works a little differently. It converts any existing material colors to vertex colors. To use this utility, select an object, choose a Light Model (Scene Lights or Diffuse lighting), and click the Assign to Selected button.

Tutorial: Marking heart tension

As an example of using the Vertex Paint Modifier, imagine a doctor who has a 3D model of the human heart. While discussing the results of the latest test with a patient, the doctor can color parts of the heart model to illustrate the various points.

To color on a human heart using the Vertex Paint Modifier, follow these steps:

1. Import the Viewpoint Datalabs heart model.

2. Select a portion of the heart model and open the Modify panel. Click the More button and select the Vertex Paint Modifier.

3. In the Parameters rollout, select the red color, select both the VertCol and Shaded button, and click the Paint button. Then drag the mouse over the surface of the Perspective view.

Figure 19-14 shows the resulting color.

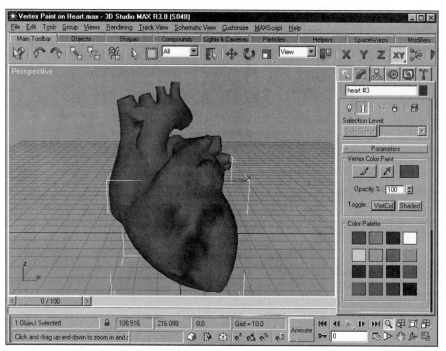

Figure 19-14: The Vertex Paint Modifier can apply color to an object by assigning a color to its vertices.

Using Maps to Change Geometry

Materials that use a bump mapping can make the surface of an object appear to change, but the actual geometric surface doesn't change. There are some maps, however, that actually can change the geometry of an object. The Displacement map is an example of this kind of map.

Modeling with displacement maps

The Displacement map can actually change a geometry's surface via a grayscale map. In the follow tutorials, we'll create landscapes using a grayscale image.

Tutorial: Creating an alien landscape

A Displacement map determines surface height based on the gradient value, making black pixels low and white pixels high. To illustrate this, we'll use a Displacement map to create an alien landscape.

To create a landscape using a Displacement map, follow these steps:

1. Open Adobe Photoshop and create a grayscale bitmap that will represent the landscape. The peaks should be white and the valleys should be black (this is best accomplished with a feathered brush). Apply the Blur filter and save the bitmap.

2. Open MAX and create a Quad Patch grid in the Top view with 20 by 20 segments.

3. Open the Material Editor and select the first sample slot. Name the material **Alien Landscape**.

4. In the Maps rollout, click the Displacement map button to open the Material/Map Browser and double-click the Bitmap map. In the Select Bitmap Image File dialog box, locate the prepared gradient file and click OK.

5. Drag the material onto the Patch grid object to apply it.

6. Select the Patch grid object and open the Modify panel. Click the More button to open the additional Modifiers list, select the Disp Approx. Modifier, and click OK. The displacement will be visible when the scene is rendered.

7. To view the displacement in the viewport you'll need to apply the Displace Modifier. In the Parameters rollout, click the Map button to open the Material/Map Browser. In the Browse From section, select the Selected option and double-click the Displacement Map. Next set the Strength value to **10**. The displacement will be visible in the viewports.

Summary

This chapter concludes the Materials and Maps part of the book. In the previous two chapters we skimmed quickly over several features and examples that we were able to explore more fully in this chapter. Along the way, I hope you've learned some tricks that will help you unravel the complexities of working with materials and maps.

In this chapter you:

- ✦ Learned how to create new materials and build a material library
- ✦ Animated materials using IFL files
- ✦ Applied multiple materials to an object with Material IDs
- ✦ Explored several material Modifiers, including the MaterialByElement, UVW Map, Unwrap UVW, and Vertex Paint Modifiers
- ✦ Modeled objects with Displacement maps

In the next part we'll move on to using lights and cameras, beginning with a close look at how to control lights in Chapter 20.

✦   ✦   ✦

Lights
and Cameras

◆ ◆ ◆ ◆

In This Part

◆ ◆ ◆ ◆

Controlling Lights

Lights play an important part in the visual process. Have you ever looked at a blank page and been told it was a picture of a polar bear in a snow blizzard or looked at a completely black image and been told it was a rendering of a black spider crawling down a chimney covered in soot? The point of these two examples is that with too much or not enough light, you can't really see anything.

Light in the 3D world figures into every rendering calculation, and 3D artists often struggle with the same problem of too much or not enough light. This chapter covers creating and controlling lights in your scene.

The Basics of Lighting

Lighting plays a critical part of any MAX scene. Understanding the basics of lighting can make a big difference. Most all MAX scenes typically use one of two types of lighting: natural light or artificial light. *Natural light* is used for outside scenes and uses the sun and moon for its light source. *Artificial light* is usually reserved for indoor scenes where light bulbs provide the light.

Natural and artificial light

Natural light is best created using lights that have parallel light rays coming from a single direction—this type of light can be created using a Direct Light. The intensity of natural light is also dependent on the time, date, and location of the sun—this can be controlled precisely using MAX's Sunlight System feature.

The weather can also make a difference in the light color. In clear weather, the color of sunlight is pale yellow; in clouds sunlight has a blue tint; and in dark, stormy weather, sunlight is dark gray. The colors of light at sunrise and sunset are more orange and red. Moonlight is typically white.

Artificial light is typically produced with multiple lights of lower intensity. The Omni light is usually a good choice for indoor lighting because it casts light rays in all directions from a single source. Standard white fluorescent lights usually have a light green or light blue tint.

A standard lighting method

When lighting a scene, it is best not to rely on a single light. A good lighting method includes one key light and several secondary lights.

A spotlight is good to use for the main key light. It should be positioned in front of and slightly above the subject, and it should usually be set to cast shadows, because it will be the main shadow-casting light in the scene.

The secondary lights are used to fill in the lighting gaps and holes. You can position these at floor level on either side of the subject, with the intensity set at considerably less than the key light, and set to cast no shadows.

One additional light can be placed behind the scene to backlight the subjects. This light should be very dim and also cast no shadows.

From the user's perspective, all the objects in the scene will be illuminated, but the casual user will identify only the main spotlight as the light source, because it casts shadows.

Figure 20-1 shows a standard lighting model using a key light, two secondary lights, and a backlit light. This model will work for most standard scenes, but if you wish to highlight a specific object, additional lights will be needed.

Backlit light   Backlit light

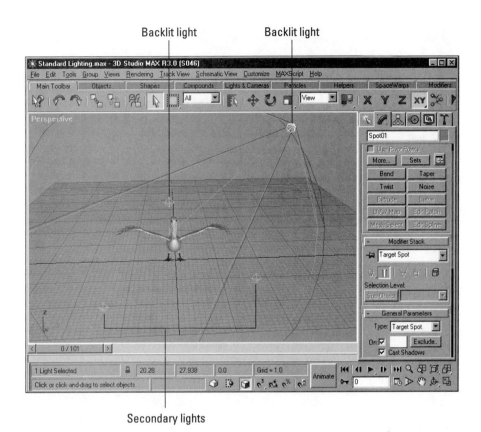

Secondary lights

Figure 20-1: A standard lighting model includes a key light, two secondary lights, and a backlit light.

Figure 20-2 shows a rendered image in the upper left that uses the standard lighting model from the previous figure. The upper right image uses only a single key light. The lower left image shows the standard lighting model with the key light turned off, and the lower right image uses MAX's default lighting.

The final type of light to keep in mind is ambient light. *Ambient light* is not from a direct source but is created by light that is deflected off walls and objects. It provides overall lighting to the entire scene and keeps shadows from becoming completely black.

Figure 20-2: An image rendered using the standard lighting model (upper left), a single key light (upper right), no key light (lower left), and default lighting (lower right).

Shadows

Shadows are the area behind an object where the light is obscured. MAX supports two types of shadows: Shadow Maps and Ray Traced Shadows. *Shadow Maps* are actual bitmaps that the renderer produces and combines with the finished scene to produce an image. These maps can have different resolutions, but higher resolutions require more memory. Shadow Maps typically create more realistic, softer shadows.

Ray Traced Shadows are calculated by following the path of every light ray striking a scene. This process takes a significant amount of processing cycles, but can produce very accurate, hard-edged shadows. Ray Tracing enables you to create shadows for objects that Shadow Maps can't, such as transparent glass.

Figure 20-3 shows several images rendered with the different shadow types. The image in the upper left includes no shadows. The upper right image uses a Shadow Map set to a Size of 512. The lower left image uses a Shadow Map set to a Size of 4096, and the lower right image uses Ray Traced Shadows. The last two images took considerably longer to create. Viewpoint Datalabs created the pelican model shown in this figure.

Figure 20-3: Images rendered with different shadow types, including no shadow (upper left), a 512 Shadow Map (upper right), a 4096 Shadow Map (lower left), and Ray Traced Shadows (lower right).

Understanding Light Types

MAX includes several different types of lights. The main difference in these types is how the light rays are cast.

Default lighting

So, you get MAX installed, and you eagerly start the application, throw some objects in a scene, and render it . . . and you'll be disappointed in the output, because you forgot to put lights in the scene. Right? Wrong! MAX is smart enough to place default lighting in the scene that does not have any light.

The default lighting disappears as soon as a light is created in a scene (even if the light is turned off). When all the lights in a scene are deleted, default lighting magically reappears. So you can always be sure that your objects will be rendered using some sort of lighting. Default lighting actually consists of two lights — the first light is positioned above and to the left, and the bottom light is positioned below and to the right.

The Viewport Configuration dialog box, shown in Figure 20-4, has an option to enable default lighting for any viewport or set the default lighting to use only one light. This dialog box can be opened by selecting Customize ⇨ Viewport Configuration or by right-clicking the viewport title and selecting Configuration from the pop-up menu.

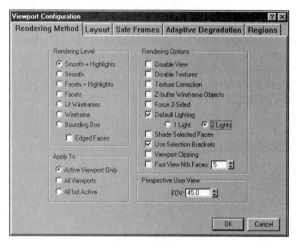

Figure 20-4: The Viewport Configuration dialog box includes an option to use Default Lighting with one or two lights.

If you wish to access the default lights in your scene, you can use the Views ⇨ Add Default Lights to Scene command. This will convert the default lights into actual light objects that you can control and reposition.

Ambient light

Ambient light is a general lighting that uniformly illuminates the entire scene. It is caused by light that bounces off other objects. Using the Environment dialog box, you can set the ambient light color. You can also set the Default ambient light color in the Rendering panel of the Preference Settings dialog box. This color is the darkest color that can appear in the scene, generally in the shadows.

In addition to these global ambient settings, each material can have an ambient color selected in the Material Editor.

Omni light

The Omni light is like a light bulb—it casts light rays in all directions. The two default lights are omni lights.

Spot light

Spotlights are directional—they can be pointed and sized. There are two different types of spotlights available in MAX: a Target Spot and a Free Spot. A Target Spot light consists of a light object and a target marker at which the spotlight points. A Free Spot light has no target, which enables it to be rotated in any direction using the Select and Rotate transform button. Spotlights always are displayed in the viewport as a cone with the light positioned at the cone apex.

Note Both Target Spot and Target Direct lights are very similar in functionality to the Target Camera object. The Target Camera object is discussed in Chapter 22, "Controlling Cameras."

Direct light

Direct lights cast parallel light rays in a single direction, like the sun. Just like spotlights, direct lights come in two types: a Target Direct light and a Free Direct light. The position of the Target Direct light always points toward the target, which can be moved within the scene using the Select and Move button. A Free Direct light can be rotated to determine where it points. Direct lights are always displayed in the viewport as cylinders.

Creating and Positioning Light Objects

MAX R3, in its default setup, can create five different types of light. Each of them has different properties and features. To create a light, just open the Create panel and click the Lights category button. Then click the button for the type of light you wish to create and drag in a viewport to create it. The five light types are Target Spot, Target Direct, Omni, Free Spot, and Free Direct. Figure 20-5 shows each of the light types.

Omni and Free lights are created with a single click, but Target lights are created by clicking at the light's position and dragging to the position of the target.

Target Spot light   Target Direct light

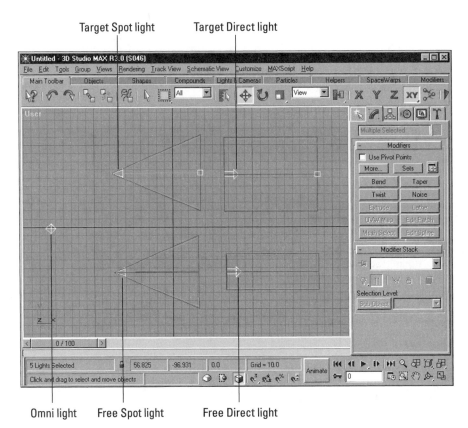

Omni light   Free Spot light   Free Direct light

Figure 20-5: A complete set of lights, including Omni, Target Spot, Free Spot, Target Direct, and Free Direct.

Transforming lights

Lights can be transformed just like other geometric objects; however, not all transformations are available for all the light types. An Omni light, for example, cannot be scaled. To transform a light, click one of the transformation buttons and select and drag the light.

Target lights can have the light and the target transformed independently, or you can select both the light and target by clicking the line that connects them. Target lights can be rotated and scaled only if the light and target are selected together. Scaling a Target light will increase its cone or cylinder. Scaling a Target Direct light with only the light selected increases the diameter of the light's beam, but if the light and target are selected, then the diameter and distance are scaled.

An easy way to select or deselect the target is to right-click the light and select Select Target from the pop-up menu.

All transformations work on free lights.

Setting highlights

Another way to aim a camera is with the Tools ⇨ Place Highlight command. To use this command, select a light to move and select the command, or click the Place Highlight button, which is a flyout of the Align button. Then, in a viewport, drag an object, and a blue arrow will display the face normal. When you've located the point where you want the highlight to be positioned, release the mouse. The selected light will be repositioned to place the highlight at the selected location.

Viewing a Scene from a Light

Viewports can be configured to display the view from any light, with the exception of an Omni light. To do this, right-click the viewport title and select Views and the light name at the top of the pop-up menu.

Tip The keyboard shortcut for making the active viewport a Light view is the $ key. If more than one light exists, then the Select Light dialog box appears and lets you select which light to use.

Light viewport controls

When a viewport is changed to show a light view, the Viewport Navigation buttons in the lower right corner of the screen change into Light Navigation Controls. These controls are described in Table 20-1.

Note Many of these controls are identical for viewports displaying lights or cameras.

If you hold down the Ctrl key while using the Light Hotspot or Falloff buttons, the distance between the hotspot and falloff cones is maintained. The Hotspot cone cannot grow any larger than the Falloff cone.

You can constrain any light movements to a single axis by holding down the Shift key. The Ctrl key causes the movements to increase rapidly.

For Free Lights, an invisible target is determined by the distance computed from the other light properties. The Shift key can be used to constrain rotations to be vertical or horizontal, and the Ctrl key speeds the rotation speed.

Note Changes in the normal viewports can be undone using the Views ⇨ Undo command, but light viewport changes are undone with the regular Edit ⇨ Undo command.

Table 20-1		
Light Navigation Control Buttons		

Toolbar Button	Name	Description
	Dolly, Target, Both	Moves the light, its target, or both the light and its target closer to or further away from the scene in the direction it is pointing.
	Light Hotspot	Adjusts the angle of the light's hotspot, which is displayed as a blue cone.
	Roll Light	Spins the light about its local Z-axis.
	Zoom Extents All, Zoom Extents All Selected	Zooms in on all objects or the selected objects until they fill the viewport.
	Light Falloff	Changes the angle of the light's Falloff cone.
	Truck Light	Moves the light perpendicular to the line of sight.
	Orbit, Pan Light	The Orbit button rotates the light around the target, whereas the Pan Light button rotates the target around the light.
	Full Screen Toggle	Makes the current viewport fill the screen. Clicking this button a second time returns the display to several viewports.

Tutorial: Lighting a lamp

To practice using lights, let's try to get a lamp model to work as it should.

To add a light to a lamp model, follow these steps:

1. Import the lamp model created by Zygote Media. It looks like a standard living room lamp that you could buy in any department store.

2. Create an Omni light by opening the Create panel and clicking the Lights category. Click the Omni button and click again in any viewport.

3. Use the Select and Move transform button to position the light object inside the lamp's light bulb.

4. Create a ground plane by clicking the Plane button in the Geometry category of the Create panel and increase the Scale Multiplier value to **25**. The size of the Plane object doesn't matter, because it will be scaled automatically when rendered.

5. Create two additional Plane objects and position them at right angles to each other for the walls. Set the Scale Multiplier to **25** for each of these Planes. Figure 20-6 shows the model all ready to render with the Omni light object selected.

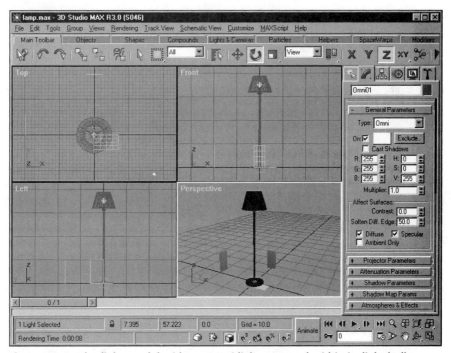

Figure 20-6: The light model with an Omni light centered within its light bulb

The resulting image is shown in Figure 20-7. Notice how the light intensity is greater at places closer to the light.

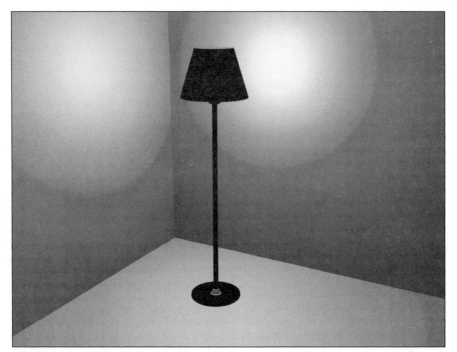

Figure 20-7: The rendered lighted-lamp image

Altering Light Parameters

Lights affect every object in a scene and can really make or break a rendered image, so it shouldn't be surprising that each light comes with many controls and parameters.

General parameters

If you're looking for a light switch to turn lights on and off, look no farther than the Modify panel. When a light is selected, the General Parameters rollout appears, shown in Figure 20-8. The options contained in this rollout enable you to turn the lights on and off, select a light color and intensity, and determine how a light affects object surfaces.

The Type drop-down list lets you change the type of light instantly, so that you can switch from Omni light to Spot light without a lot of work. This provides an easy way to look at the results of using a different type of light. If you change the type of light, you'll lose the settings for the previous light.

Figure 20-8: The General Parameters rollout includes the light's on/off switch among other commands.

 New Feature The ability to change light types quickly is new in Release 3.

To the right of the on/off switch is a color swatch. Clicking this switch opens a Color Selector where you can choose a new light color. The RGB and HSV values provide an alternative method for selecting a light color.

The Exclude button opens the Exclude/Include dialog box, where you can select objects to be included or excluded from illumination and/or shadows. The pane on the left includes a list of all the current objects in the scene. To exclude objects from being lit, select the Exclude option; then select the objects to be excluded from the pane on the left, and click the double arrow icon pointing to the right to move the objects to the pane on the right.

Figure 20-9 shows the Exclude/Include dialog box. This dialog box also recognizes any Selection Sets you've previously defined. They can be selected from the Selection Sets drop-down list.

Back in the light's General Parameters rollout, the Multiplier value is the light intensity. A light with a Multiplier set to 2 will be twice as bright as a light with its Multiplier set to 1.

 Caution Higher Multiplier values will make a light appear white regardless of the light color.

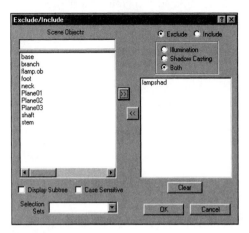

Figure 20-9: The Exclude/Include dialog box lets you set which objects are excluded or included from being illuminated.

Options in the Affect Surface section control how light interacts with an object's surface. The Contrast value alters the contrast between the diffuse and the ambient surface areas. The Soften Diffuse Edge value blurs the edges between the diffuse and ambient areas of a surface. The Diffuse and Specular options let you disable these properties of an object's surface. When the Ambient Only option is turned on, the light affects only the ambient properties of the surface. (The Diffuse, Specular, and Ambient properties are discussed in detail in Chapter 17, "Exploring the Material Editor.")

New Feature

The Affect Surface section is new in Release 3.

Attenuation parameters

Attenuation is a property that determines how light fades over distance. An example of this is a candle set in a room. The further you get from the candle, the less the light shines.

There are three basic parameters used to simulate realistic attenuation. These parameters are displayed in the Attenuation Parameters rollout, shown in Figure 20-10. Near Attenuation sets the distance at which the light begins to fade, and Far Attenuation sets the distance at which the light falls to 0. Both these properties are ranges that include Start and End values. The third parameter sets the Decay value — a method that simulates attenuation using a mathematical formula to compute the drop in light intensity over time.

Figure 20-10: The Attenuation Parameters rollout lets you set Near and Far Attenuation values and settings for Decay.

Selecting the Use option enables the Near and Far Attenuation values — each has a Start and End value that sets the range for this attenuation type. The Show option makes the attenuation distances and decay values visible in the viewports. There are three types of decay from which you can choose: None, Inverse, and Inverse Square. The Inverse type decays linearly with the distance away from the light. The Inverse Square type decays exponentially with distance.

Tip

The Inverse Square type approximates real lights the best, but it is often too dim for computer graphic images. You can compensate for this by increasing the Multiplier value.

Spot and directional light parameters

The Spotlight Parameters rollout, shown in Figure 20-11, includes values to set the angular distance of both the Hot Spot and Falloff cones. You can also set the light shape to be circular or rectangular. For a rectangular-shaped spotlight, you can control the aspect ratio. You can use the Bitmap Fit button to make the aspect ratio match a particular bitmap.

The Directional Light Parameters rollout, which appears for Direct light types, is identical to the Spotlight Parameters rollout and also includes settings for the Hot Spot and Falloff values.

Figure 20-11: The Spotlight Parameters rollout includes settings for the Hot Spot and Falloff cones.

Projection maps

Any light can be used as a projector — the location of this option depends on the type of light. For Spot and Direct lights, this option can be found in their respective rollouts, as shown previously in Figure 20-11. For Omni lights, a Projector Parameters rollout can be used. In any of these rollouts, selecting the Map option enables you to use the light as a projector. You can select a map to project by clicking the button to the right of the map option. You can drag a material map directly from the Material/Map Browser onto the projector map button.

Projection maps will be covered in more detail in Chapter 21, "Lighting Special Effects."

Shadow parameters

All light types have a Shadow Parameters rollout, shown in Figure 20-12. This rollout, just like the General Parameters rollout, has an On/Off switch. This switch lets you specify whether a light casts shadows or not.

You can also select from a drop-down list whether the shadows are created using a Shadow Map or Ray Traced Shadows. If the Shadow Map option is selected in the Shadow Parameters rollout, the Shadow Map Params (Parameters) rollout appears below it (as shown in the previous figure). This rollout includes controls for the Bias, Size, and Sample Range of the map.

Figure 20-12: The Shadow Parameters rollout controls shadow settings, including turning them on and off.

If the Ray Traced Shadows option is selected in the Shadow Parameters rollout, the Ray Traced Shadows Parameters rollout appears below it. This simple rollout includes only two values: Bias and Max Quadtree Depth. The Bias settings cause the shadow to move toward or away from the object that casts the shadow. The Max Quadtree Depth determines the accuracy of the shadows by controlling how long the ray paths are followed.

Note   Depending on the number of objects in your scene, shadows can take a long time to render. Enabling Ray Traced Shadows for a complex scene can greatly increase the render time.

Back in the main Shadow Parameters rollout, you can defer to the global settings by selecting the Use Global Settings option. This option helps to maintain consistent settings across several lights. It applies the same settings to all lights, so that changing the value for one light changes that same value for all lights that have this option selected.

You can also select a shadow color by clicking the color swatch. The default color is black.

New Feature   Being able to specify shadow colors is new in Release 3.

The Dens setting stands for "Density" and controls how dark the shadow appears. Lower values produce light shadows, and higher values produce dark shadows. This can also be a negative value.

The Map option, like the Projection Map, can be used to project a map along with the shadow color. The Light Affects Shadow Color option alters the Shadow Color by blending it with the light color if selected.

In the Atmosphere Shadows section, the On button lets you determine whether atmospheric effects, such as fog, can cast shadows. You can also control the Opacity and the degree to which atmospheric colors blend with the Shadow Color.

New Feature   Atmosphere Shadows is new to Release 3.

When a light is selected and the Modify panel is opened, one additional rollout is available—the Atmospheres and Effects rollout. This rollout is a shortcut to the Environment dialog box, where you can specify atmospheric effects such as fog and volume lights.

Cross-Reference   Atmospheric effects will be presented in Chapter 35, "Working with Backgrounds, Environments, and Atmospheric Effects."

Tutorial: Creating twinkling stars

Surely there is some poetry somewhere that speaks of dotting the sky with stars. In this tutorial, I'll be showing you how to do just that using a view full of Omni lights positioned close to a Plane object.

Cross-Reference   Starfields can also be created using the Video Post dialog box, as shown in Chapter 39, "Using the Video Post Interface."

To create a background of controllable stars, follow these steps:

1. Open the Create panel and select the Lights category. Then click the Omni button and click in the Top viewport to create about 30 to 50 lights. Each light will be a separate star.

2. Next, click the Geometry category and click the Plane button. Then drag in the Top view to create a simple plane object. The size of the plane doesn't matter, but the Scale Multiplier should be set to **50**. Change the Object Color swatch for the plane object to dark blue.

3. With the Select and Move button, select the Plane object and right-click the Select and Move button to access the Move Transform Type-In dialog box. In this dialog box, enter **–1.0** in the Z-axis field. This will move the Plane object barely underneath all the Omni lights.

4. Click the Select by Name button in the main toolbar, and in the Select Objects dialog box, select all the Omni lights. Then open the Modify panel and click the Noise button. This will apply the Noise Modifier to all the lights. In the Strength field for the Z-axis, enter **5** and select the Animate Noise option with a Frequency of 1.0.

5. When you render the animation, set the render viewport to the Top view.

Although a black and white figure doesn't really do the rendered image justice, Figure 20-13 shows the scene set-up in MAX.

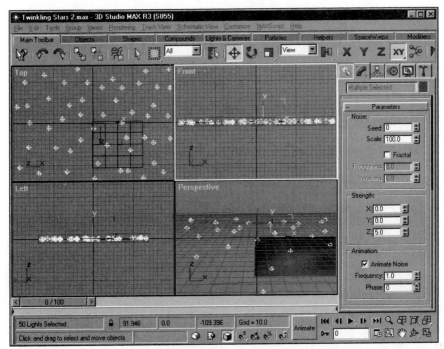

Figure 20-13: Countless Omni lights positioned close to a Plane object can create a realistic starfield with animated twinkling stars.

Using the Sunlight System

The Sunlight system, accessed through the Systems category of the Create panel, creates a light that simulates the sun for a specific geographic location, date, time, and compass direction.

To create a Sunlight System, open the Create panel and click the Systems category button. Then click the Sunlight button and drag the mouse in a viewport. A Compass helper object will appear. Click again and a Direct light representing the sun is created. Figure 20-14 shows the Compass helper created as part of the Sunlight System.

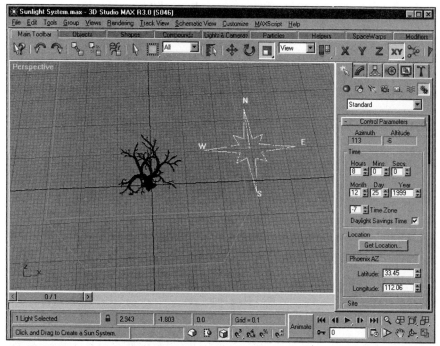

Figure 20-14: The Compass helper provides an orientation for positioning the sun in a Sunlight System.

Using the Compass helper

The Compass helper is useful when working with a Sunlight System. It can be used to define the map directions of North, East, South, and West. The Sunlight System uses these directions to orient the system light. This helper is not renderable and is created automatically when a sunlight object is defined.

Once a Sunlight System is created, you can alter the sun's position by transforming the Compass helper. This will cause the direct light object to move appropriately. You cannot transform the Direct light by itself.

Tip

You can change the settings for the light that is the sun by selecting the light from the Select by Name dialog box and opening the Modify panel. The sun light object uses Ray Traced Shadows by default.

Understanding Azimuth and Altitude

Azimuth and Altitude are two values that help define the location of the sun in the sky. Both are measured in degrees. *Azimuth* refers to the compass direction and can range from 0 to 360, with 0 degrees being North, 90 degrees being East, 180 degrees being South, and 270 degrees being West. *Altitude* is the angle in degrees between the sun and the horizon. This value ranges typically between 0 and 90, with 0 degrees being either sunrise or sunset and 90 when the sun is directly overhead.

Specifying date and time

The Time section of the Control Parameters rollout lets you define a time and date. The Time Zone value is the number of offset hours for your current time zone. You can also set the time to be converted for Daylight Savings Time.

Specifying location

Clicking the Get Location button in the Control Parameters rollout opens the Geographic Location dialog box, shown in Figure 20-15, which displays a map or a list of cities. Selecting a location using this dialog box automatically updates the Latitude and Longitude values. In addition to the Get Location button, you can enter Latitude and Longitude values directly in the Control Parameters rollout.

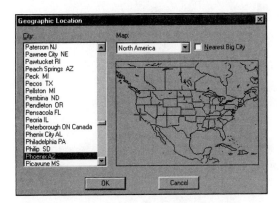

Figure 20-15: The Geographic Location dialog box lets you specify where you want to use the Sunlight System. There are many different cities to choose from.

Tutorial: Animating a day in 20 seconds

The Sunlight System can be animated to show an entire day from sunrise to sundown in a short number of frames. In this tutorial, we'll focus on an old tree positioned somewhere in Phoenix, Arizona, on Christmas. The tree certainly won't move, but watch its shadows.

To use the Sunlight System to animate shadows, follow these steps.

1. Import a tree model, created by Zygote Media, using the File ⇨ Import command.

2. Add a Sunlight System by selecting the Systems category in the Create panel and clicking the Sunlight button. Then drag in the Top view to create the compass helper. In the Control Parameters, enter **12/25/2000** for the Date and an early morning hour for the Time.

3. Click the Get Location button, locate Phoenix in the Cities list, and click OK. Rotate the compass helper in the Top view so that north is pointing toward the top of the viewport.

4. Click the Animate button and move the Time Slider to frame 100.

5. In the Control Parameters rollout, change the Time value to an evening hour. Then click the Animate button again to disable animation mode.

Tip   You can tell when the sun comes up and goes down by looking at the Altitude value for each hour. A negative Altitude value indicates that the sun is below the horizon.

Figure 20-16 shows a snapshot of this quick day. The upper left image shows the animation at frame 20, the upper right image shows it at frame 40, the lower left image shows it at frame 60, and the final image shows it at frame 80.

Figure 20-16: Several frames of an animation that shows a tree scene from sunrise to sunset

Summary

I hope you have found this chapter enlightening. (Sorry about the bad pun, but I need to work them in where I can.) There are many different lights in MAX, each with plenty of controls. Learning to master these controls can take you a long way toward increasing the realism of the scene. In this chapter, you've

- ✦ Learned the basics of lighting
- ✦ Discovered MAX's light types
- ✦ Created and positioned light objects
- ✦ Learned to change the viewport view to a light
- ✦ Used the Sunlight System

This chapter was just enough to get us started on the topic of lights. The next chapter will present several examples of the types of special effects that can be created using lights.

✦   ✦   ✦

Lighting Special Effects

The basics of lights were introduced in the previous chapter, but there is so much more you can do with lights. In this chapter, we'll explore the use of lights at a deeper level and look at some interesting examples of special effects that are possible with lights.

Using Volume Lights

When light shines through fog, smoke, or dust, the beam of the light becomes visible. The effect is known as a *Volume Light*. To add a Volume Light to a scene, select the Rendering ⇨ Environment command to open the Environment dialog box. Then click the Add button in the Atmosphere rollout to open the Add Atmospheric Effect dialog box and select Volume Light. The parameters for the volume light will be presented in the Volume Light Parameters rollout.

You can also access the Volume Light effect from the Atmospheres and Effects rollout in the Modify panel when a light is selected.

 Cross-Reference Other atmospheric effects are covered in Chapter 35, "Working with Backgrounds, Environments, and Atmospheric Effects."

Volume light parameters

At the top of the Volume Light Parameters rollout, shown in Figure 21-1, is a Pick Light button, which enables you to select a light to apply the effect to. Several lights can be selected, and they will be shown in a drop-down list. Lights can be removed from this list with the Remove Light button.

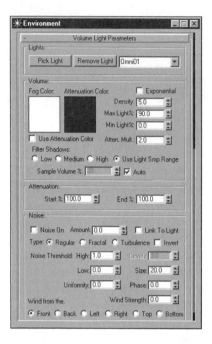

Figure 21-1: The Volume Light Parameters rollout in the Environment dialog box lets you choose which lights to include in the effect.

In the Volume section, the Fog Color swatch lets you select a color for the fog that is seen within the light. This color is combined with the color of the light. The Attenuation Color is the color the fog appears to have at a distance far from the light source. This color also combines with the Fog Color and is best set to a dark color.

The Density value determines the thickness of the fog. The Exponential option causes the density to increase exponentially with the distance. The Max and Min Light Percentage values determine the amount of glow that the volume light causes, and the Attenuation Multiplier controls the strength of the attenuation color.

You have four options for filtering shadows: Low, Medium, High, and Use Light Smp Range. The Low option renders shadows quickly but isn't very accurate. The High option takes a while but produces the best quality. The Use Light Smp Range option bases the filtering on the Sample Volume value and can be set to Auto. The Sample Volume can range from 1 to 10,000. The Low option has a Sample Volume value of 8; Medium, 25; and High, 50.

The Start and End Attenuation values are percentages of the Start and End range values for the light's attenuation. These values have an impact only if attenuation is turned on for the light.

The Noise settings help determine the randomness of Volume Light. Noise effects can be turned on and given an Amount. You can also Link the noise to the light instead of using world coordinates. Noise types include Regular, Fractal, Turbulence, and Invert. The Noise Threshold limits the effect of noise. Wind settings affect how the light moves as determined by the wind's direction, Wind Strength, and Phase.

Figure 21-2 shows several volume light possibilities. The upper left image shows a lamp with a volume light effect applied to a simple spotlight, and the upper right image shows the light with shadows activated. The lower left image shows the volume light with the Density value doubled, and the lower right image includes some Turbulent Noise.

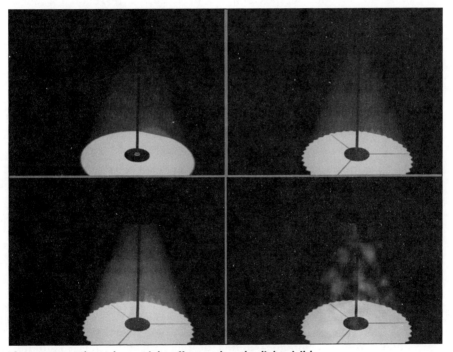

Figure 21-2: The Volume Light effect makes the light visible.

Tutorial: Showing car headlights

One popular way to use volume lights is to display the headlights of cars. For this tutorial, we're going to once again use the '57 Chevy model created by Viewpoint Datalabs.

To display the headlights of a car, follow these steps:

1. Import the '57 Chevy model and position it in the scene.

2. Open the Material Editor, select the first sample slot, and name the material **Headlights**. Then click the Pick Material from Object eyedropper button and click the left headlight. This will load the currently assigned material into the first sample slot. Create a bright yellow Self-Illumination color and reassign the material.

3. In the Create panel, click the Lights category, and then click the Target Spot button and drag in the Left viewport to create a spotlight object. Select and move the spotlight and the target to be positioned to look as if a light is shining out from the left headlight. Open the Modify panel and, in the Spotlight Parameters rollout, set the Hotspot value to **20** and the Falloff to **25**. In the Atmospheres and Effects rollout, click the Add button, select Volume Light from the Add Atmosphere or Effect dialog box that appears, and click OK.

Note When a light is added to the scene, the default lights are automatically turned off. To provide any additional lighting, add some Omni lights above the car.

4. Select the Volume Light effect in the list within the Atmospheres and Effects rollout and click the Setup button. This will open the Environment dialog box, where you can edit the Volume Light parameters for the newly created light. Set the Density value to 100.

5. Now, create the second headlight. To do this, select both the first spotlight object and its target, and create a cloned copy by holding down the Shift key while moving it toward the right headlight. Position the second spotlight so that it shines outward from the right headlight.

Figure 21-3 shows the resulting car with its two headlights illuminated.

Tutorial: Creating laser beams

Laser beams are extremely useful lights. From your CD-ROM drive to your laser printer, lasers are found throughout a modern-day office. They are also great to use in fantasy and science fiction images. Laser beams can be created easily using direct lights and the Volume Light effect. In this tutorial, we'll add some lasers to the laser truck model created by Viewpoint Datalabs.

To add some laser beams to a scene, follow these steps:

1. Import the laser truck model and add a ground floor, using the Plane object with a Scale Multiplier set to **100**.

2. Open the Create panel, select the Lights category, and add a Free Direct light to the end of one of the laser guns. Scale the light down until the cylinder is the size of the desired laser beam.

Figure 21-3: The car now has headlights, thanks to spotlights and the Volume Light effect.

3. With the light selected, open the Modify panel and, in the Atmospheres and Effects rollout, click the Add button and double-click the Volume Light selection. Then select the Volume Light option in the list, and click the Setup button to open the Environment dialog box. Change the Fog Color to red, and make sure the Use Attenuation Color is disabled.

4. In the Top view, clone the direct light three times and move the cloned lights in front of the other guns.

5. With the direct lights added to the scene, the default lights will be deactivated, so you'll need to add some Omni lights above the truck model to illuminate it. To do this, open the Create panel, select the Lights category, and click the Omni button. Then click above the car in the Front view three times to create three lights. Set the Multiplier on the first light to **1.0**, and position it directly above the model. Set the other two lights to **0.5**, and position them on either side of the truck and lower than the first light.

Figure 21-4 shows the resulting laser beams shooting forth from the laser truck.

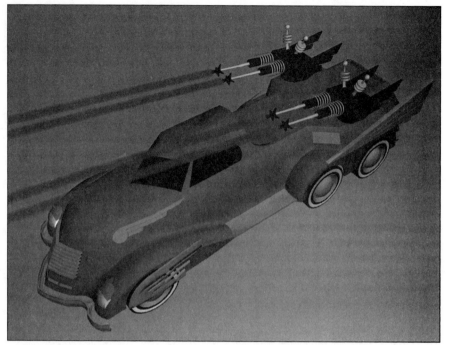

Figure 21-4: Laser beams can be created using direct lights and the Volume Light effect.

Using Projector Maps and Raytraced Shadows

If a map is added to a light in the Parameters rollout, the light becomes a projector. Projector maps can be simple images, animated images, or black and white masks to cast shadows. To load a projector map, select a light, open the Modify panel, and under the Spotlight Parameters rollout, click the Projector Map button and select the map to use from the Material/Map Browser.

Raytraced shadows take longer to render than the Shadow Maps option, but the shadows will always have a hard edge and be an accurate representation of the object.

Tip Shadows for wire-frame objects can be created only by using raytraced shadows.

In the Shadow Parameters rollout, you can select whether shadows are computed using Shadow Maps or Ray Traced Shadows. Using the latter selection lets you project a transparent object's color onto the shadow.

Tutorial: Projecting a trumpet image on a scene

As an example of a projector light, we'll create a musical scene with several musical notes and project the image of a trumpet on them.

To project an image onto a rendered scene, follow these steps:

1. First we'll create the mask to project. Import the trumpet model created by Viewpoint Datalabs and position it so its complete side can be seen in the Left viewport. Using the Material Editor, change the Diffuse color swatch to white and apply the material to the trumpet. Select Rendering ➪ Render, set the resolution to 640 × 480, and select the Left viewport. Then click the Render button. This will render the side view of the trumpet in the Virtual Frame Buffer. Click the Save File button in the Virtual Frame Buffer, and save the file as **trumpet.tif**.

2. Open the trumpet image in Adobe Photoshop and select all black areas. Then invert the selection and color the selection white. Save this file as **Trumpet Mask.tif**.

3. Back in MAX, reset the scene with the File ➪ Reset command. Create several musical notes and position them around the scene. Create a Plane object in the Top viewport and set its Scale Multiplier value to **100**.

4. Open the Create panel and select the Lights category. Click the Target Spot button and drag to create two lights in the Top viewport. Position the first spotlight to be perpendicular to the scene and to shine down on it from above. Open the Modify panel and, in the Spotlight Parameters rollout, click the Projector Map button and double-click Bitmap from the Material/Map Browser. Locate and select the "Trumpet Mask.tif" file and click Open. This will project a silhouette of a trumpet onto the scene. Use the second spotlight to light the music notes.

Figure 21-5 shows the musical notes with the trumpet projection map.

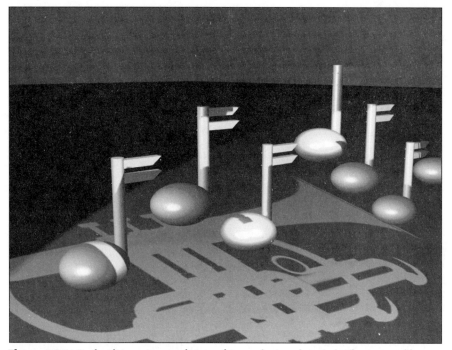

Figure 21-5: Projection maps can be used to project an image in the scene, like this trumpet.

Tutorial: Creating a stained-glass window

When a light that uses raytraced shadows shines through an object with transparent materials, the Filter color of the material is projected onto objects behind. In this tutorial, we will create a stained-glass window and shine a light through it using raytraced shadows.

To create a stained-glass window, follow these steps:

1. First we'll need to create the stained-glass window. Open the Create panel and select the Shapes category. Click the Line button and draw the outline of the window and the silhouette of a fish. Then click the Text button and enter the word **FISH** with the Arial font, size 50. Click the Front view to place the text within the window outline. Then use the Select and Move button to position the shapes.

2. Next, we'll need to combine all these shapes into one object. We'll do this using the ShapeMerge compound object. With the window outline selected, open the Create panel, select the Geometry category, choose the Compound Object subcategory, and click the ShapeMerge button. In the Pick Operand rollout, click the Pick Shape button and select the Move option. Then in the Parameters rollout, select the Merge option and click the fish and text shapes in the Front viewport. This will combine all the objects into one.

3. Open the Material Editor and select the first sample slot. Name the material **fish stained glass**. Then click the Type button and double-click the Multi/Sub-Object material. In the Multi/Sub-Object Basic Parameters rollout, click the Set Number button and enter a value of **3**. Type the name **window** for the first material, **fish** for the second material, and **text** for the third material. Click the first material button and select a blue color for the Diffuse color swatch, set the Opacity value to **50**, and drag the blue color from the Diffuse color swatch to the Filter color swatch in the Extended Parameters rollout. Click the Go Forward to Sibling button to access the second material, and change its Diffuse and Filter colors to red and its Opacity to **50**. Click the Go Forward to Sibling button again, and change the third material's Diffuse and Filter colors to black and its Opacity to **50**.

4. Right-click the window in the Front view, and select the Convert to Editable Mesh option from the pop-up menu. Then open the Modify panel and click the Polygon Sub-Object button in the Selection rollout. Select the fish shape and, in the Surface Properties rollout, change the Material ID to **2**. Then select each of the text letters and change their Material IDs to **3**. Click the Polygon Sub-Object button again to exit subobject mode. Then apply the Multi/Sub-Object material to the window.

5. Open the Create panel, select the Geometry category and the Standard Primitives subcategory, and click the Plane button. Create a floor for the scene by dragging a small plane object in the Top view and setting its Scale Multiplier to **100**.

6. In the Create panel, select the Lights category and click the Target Spot button. Then drag in the Left view from a position to the right and above the window to the window — this will create a target spotlight that shines through the stained-glass window onto the floor behind it. In the General Parameters rollout, make sure the Cast Shadows option is selected. In the Shadow Parameters rollout, enable the On option, and select Ray Traced Shadows from the drop-down list.

Figure 21-6 shows the stained-glass window with the colored shadow cast on the scene floor.

Figure 21-6: A stained-glass window effect created with raytraced shadows

Creating Electricity and Neon

In addition to the light types, lighting in a scene can be provided by self-illuminating an object and using a glow effect. Self-illuminating an object is accomplished by applying a material with a Self-Illumination value greater than 0 or a color other than black. Glows can be created using the Render Effects dialog box or the Video Post dialog box.

Cross-Reference

For more information on applying glows, see Chapter 37, "Using Render Effects," and Chapter 39, "Using the Video Post Interface."

Tutorial: Creating shocking electricity from a plug outlet

Working with a faulty electrical outlet can be a shocking experience. In this tutorial, we'll create an electric arc that runs from an outlet to a plug. To create the effect of electricity, you can use a renderable spline with several vertices and apply the

Noise Modifier to make it dance around. The light can be set using a self-illuminating material and a Glow render effect.

To create an electric arc that runs between an outlet and a plug, follow these steps:

1. Create models of an electrical plug and an outlet, and position them within the scene.

2. Open the Create panel, click the Shapes category button, and then click the Line button. In the Top view, click the initial vertex at the plug and then in a crooked path click to create several other vertices leading to the outlet. Right-click to end the line.

3. With the line selected, open the Modify panel and in the General rollout, select the Renderable option and set the Thickness to **3 pixels**. Click the Sub-Object button, select Vertex, and select all the middle vertices. Then select the Noise button at the top of the panel. In the Parameters rollout, enable the Fractal option, set the Strength values to **50** for all axes, enable the Animate Noise button, and set the Frequency to **20**. Then click the Animate button, drag the Time Slider to frame 100, and enter a value of **720** in the Phase field. Click the Animate button again to deactivate it. Click the Play Animation button to see the electric arc dance.

4. Open the Material Editor and select the first sample slot. Select a yellow Diffuse color and an equally bright yellow for the Self-Illumination color. Set the Material Effects Channel to **1** by clicking the Material Effects ID button and holding it down until a pop-up array of numbers appears, and then drag to the number 1 and release the mouse. Drag this new material to the electric arc.

5. Open the Render Effects dialog box by selecting Rendering ⇨ Effects. Click the Add button, select the Lens Effects option, and click OK. Then select Lens Effects from the list and double-click Glow in the Lens Effects Parameters rollout. Select Glow from the list and, in the Glow Element rollout, set the Size to **1** and the Intensity value to **50**. Then open the Options panel, set the Effects ID to **1**, and enable it.

Figure 21-7 shows the resulting electric arc.

Tutorial: Creating neon

The Glow render effect can also be used to create neon signs. The letters for these signs can be simple renderable splines, as this tutorial will show.

Figure 21-7: Electricity can be created using a simple spline, the Noise Modifier, and the Glow render effect.

To create a neon sign, follow these steps:

1. Open the Create panel, select the Shapes category, and click the Lines button. Then click the Front view and create the word **Blues** in a cursive style. Then click the Rectangle button and surround the letters with a rectangle shape with a Corner Radius value of **20**. Select the letters, open the Modify panel, click the Attach button, and select the rectangle shape.

2. In the Modify panel under the General rollout, select the Renderable option, and set the Thickness value to **5**.

3. Open the Material Editor, select the first sample slot, and name it **Blue Neon**. Set its Diffuse color to blue and its Self-Illumination color to dark blue. Set the Material Effects Channel to **1**, and apply the material to the sign.

4. In the Create panel, select the Geometry category and click the Plane button. Drag in the Front view to create a plane object and set the Scale Multiplier to **5**. Position the plane object to the left of the sign object in the Left view.

5. Open the Material Editor, select the second sample slot, and name the material **brick wall**. Click the map button to the right of the Diffuse color swatch and double-click the Bricks selection from the Material/Map Browser. Apply this material to the plane object.

6. In the Create panel, click the Box button and drag in the Front view to create a box that surrounds the blue splines (which will be the backing for the sign). With the Select and Move button, drag the box object so that it is positioned between the plane object and the splines. Set the box's object color to black.

7. Open the Rendering Effects panel and click the Add button. Double-click the Lens Effects option to add it to the Effects list. In the Lens Effects rollout, double-click the Glow option and select it in the list to enable its rollouts. In the Lens Effects Globals rollout, set the Size and Intensity values to 1. In the Glow Element rollout, set the Size to **10** and the Intensity to **100**, and make sure the Glow Behind option is selected. For the neon color, set the Use Source Color to **100**. Finally, open the Options panel and set the Effects ID to **1** and enable it.

Note   As an alternative to using the source color, you could set the Use Source Color value to 0 and set the Radial Color swatch to blue. This gives you more control over the glow color.

Figure 21-8 shows the rendered neon effect.

Figure 21-8: The glow of neon lights, easily created with Render Effects

Summary

This chapter covered a miscellaneous collection of lighting effects. In it, you learned to do the following:

✦ Use the Volume Light atmospheric effect

✦ Add projection maps to lights

✦ Use raytraced shadows to create a stained-glass window

✦ Create electricity and neon effects

In the next chapter, we'll cover the basics of controlling cameras.

✦   ✦   ✦

Controlling Cameras

The benefit of cameras is that they can be positioned anywhere within a scene to offer a custom view. Camera views can be opened in a viewport and can also be used to render images or animated sequences. This chapter covers many aspects of working with cameras in MAX.

Understanding Cameras

If you're a photography hobbyist or like to take your video camera out and shoot your own footage, then many of the terms in this section will be familiar to you. The cameras used in MAX to get custom views of a scene behave in many respects identically to real-world cameras.

MAX and real-world cameras both work with different lens settings, which are measured and defined in millimeters. You can select from a variety of preset Stock Lenses, including 35mm, 80mm, and even 200mm. MAX cameras also offer complete control over the camera's focal length, Field of View, and perspective for wide-angle or telephoto shots. The big difference is that you never have to worry about focusing a lens, setting flashes, or loading film.

Light coming into a camera is bent through the camera lens and focused on the film, where the image is captured. The distance between the film and the lens is known as the *focal length*. This distance is measured in millimeters and can be changed by switching to a different lens. On a camera that shoots 35mm film, a lens with a focal length of 50mm produces a view similar to what your eyes would see. A lens with a focal length less than 50mm is known as a wide-angle lens because it displays a wider view of the scene. A lens longer than 50mm is called a telephoto lens because it has the ability to give a closer view of objects for more detail, as a telescope does.

Field of View is directly related to focal length and is a measurement of how much of the scene is visible. It is measured in degrees. The shorter the focal length, the wider the field of view.

When we look at a scene, objects appear larger if they are up close than they would lying at a farther distance. This effect is referred to as *perspective* and helps us to interpret distances. As mentioned, a 50mm lens gives a perspective similar to what our eyes give. Images taken with a wide Field of View look distorted because the effect of perspective is increased.

Creating a Camera Object

To create a camera object you'll need to open the familiar Create panel and click the Cameras category button. There are two different types of cameras that you can create: a Free camera and a Target camera.

Camera objects are visible as icons in the viewports, but they aren't rendered. The camera icon looks like a box with a smaller box on front of it, which represents the lens or front end of the camera. Both the Free and Target camera types can include a cone that shows where the camera is pointing. The Top view in Figure 22-1 shows the two cameras — the camera on the left is a Free Camera and the one on the right is a Target Camera. The bottom two views are the views from these cameras.

Free Camera

The Free Camera object offers a view of the area that is directly in front of the camera and is the better choice if the camera will be animated. When a Free Camera is initially created, it points at the negative Z-axis of the active viewport. The single parameter for Free Cameras defines a Target Distance — the distance to an invisible target about which the camera can orbit.

Target Camera

A Target Camera always points at a controllable target point some distance in front of the camera. Target Cameras are easy to aim and are useful for situations where the camera won't move. To create this type of camera, click a viewport to position the camera and drag to the location of its target. The target can be named along with the camera. When created, MAX will automatically name the target by attaching ".target" on the end of the camera name. You can change this default name by typing a different name in the Name field.

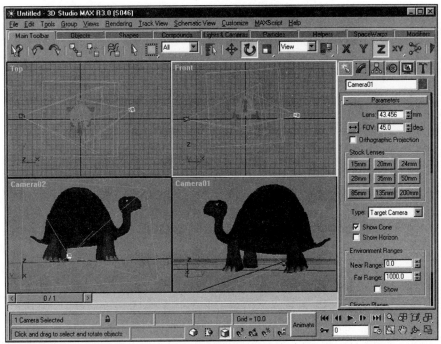

Figure 22-1: A turtle as seen by two different cameras, one on either side

Creating a Camera View

Any viewport can be changed to show a camera's viewpoint. To do this, right-click the viewport's title, and select View and the camera's name from the pop-up menu. Any movements done to the camera are reflected immediately in the viewport.

Another way to select a camera for a viewport is to press the C key. This keyboard shortcut will make the active viewport into a camera view. If several cameras exist in a scene, then the Select Camera dialog box appears, from which you can select a camera to use.

The camera object icons can be turned off using the Display panel. In the Display panel, under the Hide by Category rollout, select the Cameras option. When selected, the camera icons will not be visible in the viewports.

Tip   Cameras are usually positioned at some distance away from the rest of the scene. Their distant position can make scene objects appear very small when the Zoom Extents button is used. If the visibility of the camera icons is turned off, the Zoom Extents will not include them in the zoom. You could also enable the Ignore Extents option in the Object Properties dialog box.

Controlling a Camera

I was once on a ride at Disneyland when a person behind me decided to blatantly disregard the signs not to take photographs. As he leaned over to snap another picture, I heard a fumbling noise, a faint, "Oh no," and then the distinct sound of his camera falling into the depths of the ride. (That was actually more enjoyable than the ride. It served him right.) As this example shows, controlling a camera can be difficult. This chapter will offer many tips and tricks for dealing with the cameras in MAX, and you won't have to worry about dropping them.

Camera Viewport Controls

The camera view in a viewport is controlled by means of the Camera Navigation controls located in the lower right corner of the screen. These controls replace the viewport controls when a camera viewport is selected and are different from the normal viewport controls. The Camera Navigation controls are identified and defined in Table 22-1.

Note   Many of these controls are identical to the controls for lights.

Note   You can constrain the movements to a single axis by holding down the Shift key. The Ctrl key causes the movements to increase rapidly. For example, holding down the Ctrl key while dragging the Perspective tool magnifies the amount of perspective applied to the viewport.

Changes in the normal viewports can be undone using the Views ➪ Undo command, but camera viewport changes are undone with the regular Edit ➪ Undo command.

Table 22-1
Camera Navigation Control Buttons

Control Button	Name	Description
	Dolly, Target, Dolly Camera + Target	Moves the camera, its target, or both the camera and its target closer to or farther away from the scene in the direction it is pointing.
	Perspective	Increases or decreases the viewport's perspective by dollying the camera and altering its Field of View.
	Roll Camera	Spins the camera about its local Z-axis.
	Zoom Extents All, Zoom Extents All Selected	Zooms in on all objects or the selected objects by reducing the Field of View until they fill the viewport.
	Field of View	Changes the width of the view, similar to changing the camera lens or zooming without moving the camera.
	Truck Camera	Moves the camera perpendicular to the line of sight.
	Orbit, Pan Camera	The Orbit button rotates the camera around the target, and the Pan button rotates the target around the camera.
	Full Screen Toggle	Makes the current viewport fill the screen. Clicking this button a second time returns the display to several viewports.

Setting Camera Parameters

When a camera is first created, you can modify the camera parameters directly in the Create panel as long as the new camera is selected. Once the camera object has been deselected, modifications can be made in the Modify panel's Parameters rollout for the camera, shown in Figure 22-2.

Figure 22-2: The Parameters rollout lets you specify Lens values or choose from a selection of Stock Lenses.

Lens settings and Field of View

The first parameter in the Parameters rollout sets the Lens value or more simply, the camera's focal length in millimeters.

The second parameter, FOV (which stands for Field of View), sets the width of the area that the camera displays. The value is specified in degrees and can be set to represent a Horizontal, Vertical, or Diagonal distance using the flyout button to its left.

New Feature

The FOV direction flyouts are new to Release 3.

The Orthographic Projection option displays the camera view in a manner similar to any of the orthographic viewports such as Top, Left, or Front. This eliminates any perspective distortion of objects farther back in the scene and displays true dimensions for all edges in the scene.

Professional photographers and film crews use standard Stock Lenses in the course of their work. These lenses can be simulated in MAX by clicking one of the Stock Lens buttons. Preset Stock Lenses include 15, 20, 24, 28, 35, 50, 85, 135, and 200mm lengths. The Lens and FOV fields will be automatically updated on Stock Lens selection.

Camera type and display options

The Type option enables you to change a Free Camera to a Target Camera and back at any time.

New Feature
The Type option is new in Release 3.

The Show Cone option enables you to display the camera's cone, showing the boundaries of the camera view. The Show Horizon option sets a horizon line, which is a dark gray line where the horizon is located.

Environment ranges and clipping planes

The Near and Far Range values are used to specify the volume within which atmospheric effects like fog and volume lights are to be contained. The Show option causes these limits to be displayed as yellow rectangles within the camera's cone.

Clipping planes are used to designate the closest and farthest object that the camera can see. In MAX they are displayed as red rectangles in the camera cone. The Clip Manually option lets you specify the Near Clip Plane to be something less than 3 units. Figure 22-3 shows a camera with both Environment Ranges and Clipping Planes specified. Notice how the Far Clipping Plane intersects the turtle vertically and displays only the sections closest to the camera.

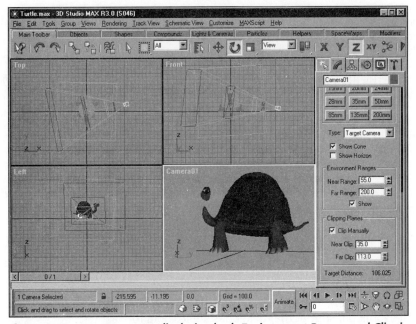

Figure 22-3: A camera cone displaying both Environment Ranges and Clipping Planes. Clipping Planes are the rectangles with diagonals.

Aiming a Camera

In addition to the Camera Navigation buttons, you can use the Transformation buttons on the main toolbar to reposition a camera. To move a camera, select the camera object and click the Select and Move button. Then drag in the viewports to move the camera.

Using the Select and Rotate transformation changes the direction that a camera points, but only Free Cameras will rotate in all directions. When applied to a Target Camera, the rotate transformation only spins the camera about the axis pointing to the target. Target Cameras are aimed by moving their targets.

Caution   Don't try to rotate a Target Camera so that it is pointing directly up or down, or the camera will flip.

The target for a Target Camera can be selected by selecting its camera object, right-clicking to open the pop-up menu, and selecting Select Target.

Another way to aim a camera is with the Tools ➪ Align Camera command. Then in a viewport, click an object face and hold the mouse button down, and the normal to the object face that is currently under the cursor icon will be displayed as a blue arrow. When you've located the point at which you want the camera to point, release the mouse button. The camera will be repositioned to point directly at the selected point on the selected face along the normal.

Cameras can be automatically positioned to match any view that a viewport can display, including lights and the Perspective view. To do this, select a camera, then activate the viewport with the view that you want to match, and select View ➪ Match Camera to View. The camera will be moved to display this view.

Note   If you use the Match Camera to View command while a camera view is the active viewport, the two cameras will be positioned on top of each other.

Tutorial: Watching a rocket

Because cameras can be transformed like any other geometry, they can also be set to watch the movements of any other geometry. In this tutorial, we'll aim a camera at a distant rocket and watch it as it flies past us and on into the sky. Zygote Media created the rocket model used in this tutorial.

To aim a camera at a rocket as it hurtles into the sky, follow these steps:

1. Load a rocket model using the File ➪ Import command. Once imported, group the entire rocket using the Group ➪ Group command. Give it the name, **rocket**.

2. In the Left view, position the rocket so that it is at the bottom of the viewport, and zoom out so that the rocket has some room to blast off.

3. Create a Target Camera in the Left view and position it about two thirds of the way up along the rocket's path and to the right a distance. (Don't worry about targeting it right now.) Set the Field of View value to **2.0** degrees. The corresponding Lens value is around 1031mm.

4. Click the Animate button, move the Time Slider to 100, and translate the rocket up to the top of the Left viewport. If you click the Play Animation button, the rocket should move vertically for 100 frames.

5. With the Animate button still enabled, drag the Time Slider back to 0 and position the camera's target on the rocket at its starting location. Then drag the Time Slider to frame 100 and position the camera's target once again on top of the rocket at the top of the screen. Then, turn the Animate button off.

6. To view the scene from the camera's viewpoint, right-click the Perspective viewport title and select Views ⇨ Camera01. Then click the Play Animation button to see how well the camera follows the target. If you need to, position the target on the rocket halfway through its motion at frame 50.

7. To add a simple environment to the scene, open the Environment dialog box by selecting Rendering ⇨ Environment, and select a light blue background color. Then open the Create panel, select the Geometry category and click he Plane button. In the Top view, create a plane object and set the Scale Multiplier to **500**. Set the object color for this plane object to brown. This will make an effective ground plane.

Figure 22-4 shows some frames from this animation.

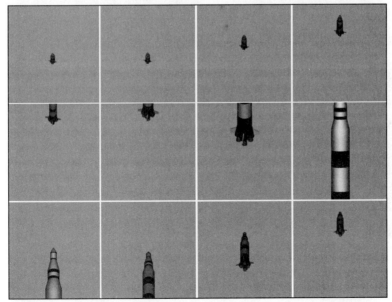

Figure 22-4: Positioning the camera's target on the rocket enables the camera to follow the rocket's ascent.

Tutorial: Setting up an opponent's view

There is no limit to the number of cameras that you can place in a scene. In Chapter 8, "Transforming Objects," there was an example of re-creating a chess game, in which we had one camera that showed the board from the White player's perspective. The Align Camera command will enable us to create a similar view from the Black player's perspective.

To create a new aligned view from the Black player's perspective, follow these steps:

1. Open the "Chess Game.max" file from within the directory containing the examples for Chapter 8.

2. Open the Create panel, select the Cameras category, and click the Target Camera button. Then give the new camera the name **Black Camera**.

3. Position the new target camera behind the Black player's pieces roughly symmetrical to the other camera.

4. With the new camera selected, drag the target point and position it on top of the other camera's target point somewhere below the center of the board.

To see the new camera view, right-click the Perspective viewport title and select View ⇨ Black Camera. Figure 22-5 shows the view from this camera.

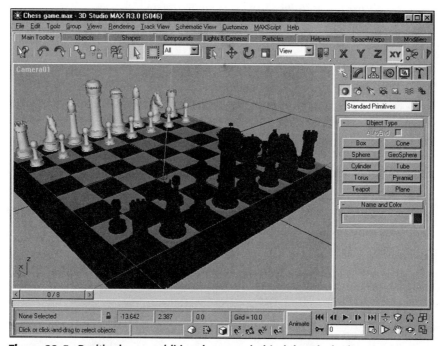

Figure 22-5: Positioning an additional camera behind the Black player's pieces offers the opponent's view.

Using the Look At Controller

The Look At Controller can be used to let cameras follow objects as they move around a scene. In fact, it is the default transform controller for Target Camera objects.

Look At Controller parameters

When the Look At Controller is assigned, you can create and delete transformation keys using the Look At Parameters rollout, shown in Figure 22-6. You can also set the camera to look at any of the axes in the scene, but perhaps the most useful button is the Pick Target button. This button enables you to select a specific object in the scene that the camera will continue to follow. This object can be a Dummy object.

Figure 22-6: The Look At Parameters rollout lets you pick a target object to follow.

When the Look At Controller is assigned, the Create Key button for rotation changes to Roll. This is because the camera is locked to point at the assigned object and cannot rotate, but only roll about the axis.

Tutorial: Watching a dragonfly fly

Back in Chapter 11, "Working with Spline Shapes," there was an example of a dragonfly that was attached to a spiral path. To follow the dragonfly around his path, we could clone the original path and offset it so that it is slightly behind the dragonfly and then use a Path Controller to attach a camera to this cloned path. This would create a camera that would follow the dragonfly on its spiral path, but this wouldn't be much different from the example in Chapter 11. Instead, in this tutorial we'll use the Look At Controller to watch the dragonfly as it circles about the spiral.

To have a camera watch the motions of an object with the Look At Controller, follow these steps:

1. Open the Dizzy Dragonfly.max file from the CD-ROM. This file can be found along with the examples for Chapter 11, "Working with Spline Shapes."

2. In the Create panel, click the Cameras category button and create a Free Camera in any viewport.

3. With the camera selected, open the Motion panel and under the Assign Controller rollout, select the Transform Controller track in the Controller list. Click the Assign Controller button (directly beneath the Assign Controller bar).

4. From the Assign Transform Controller dialog box list, select Look At and click OK.

5. In the Look At Parameters rollout, click the Pick Target button and select the dragonfly object in the scene.

6. Move the camera up to the peak of the spiral and prepare to get really dizzy.

7. To see the movements of the dragonfly as it flies around, add a plane object with a Scale Multiplier of **10** in the Top view. Then use the Material Editor to apply a checkered map to the plane object and use the Environment dialog box to change the background color to light green.

Figure 22-7 shows one frame of the dragonfly spinning along its path.

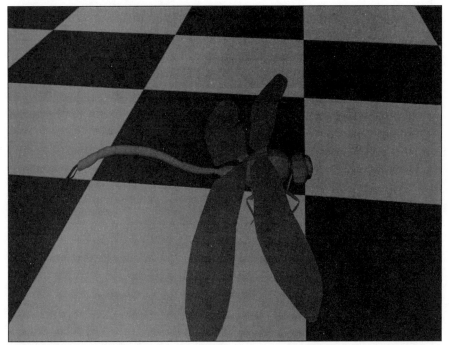

Figure 22-7: The camera in this scene follows the dragonfly on its path using the Look At Controller.

Summary

Cameras can offer a unique look at your scene. They can be positioned and moved anywhere. This chapter discussed how cameras work and how to control and aim them at objects. In this chapter, you've

- ✦ Learned the basics of cameras
- ✦ Created a camera object and view
- ✦ Discovered how to control a camera
- ✦ Changed camera parameters
- ✦ Aimed a camera at objects
- ✦ Used the Look At Controller

The next chapter covers the Camera Match and Camera Tracker utilities.

✦   ✦   ✦

Camera Matching and Tracking

At times you'll want to integrate your rendered images with existing background images and animations. To do this, MAX includes two unique features: the Camera Match and the Camera Tracker utilities.

The Camera Match utility can fit rendered scenes into an existing background image by matching the camera's position to the perspective of the image.

Just as the Camera Match utility can match rendered images to a background object, the Camera Tracker utility can be used to match scene objects to an animated background.

This chapter describes both of these powerful utilities and gives you some practice using them.

Using the Camera Match Utility

The Camera Match tool is used to align a camera's position to the background image. You can find this tool under the Utilities panel. Before you can use this tool, you need to load a bitmap image as a background. This can be done using the Environment dialog box that can be opened using the Rendering ⇨ Environment command.

Chapter 35, "Working with Backgrounds, Environments, and Atmospheric Effects," provides more details on loading and working with background images.

Once a bitmap image is loaded as an environment map, make the background visible in the viewport by selecting Views ➪ Viewport Background to open the Viewport Background dialog box. Here, you can specify a background source image or use the environment map you just loaded.

Setting Camera Match points

Once a background image is loaded and visible in the viewport, you need to create CamPoints in the scene. These CamPoints identify specific locations within the bitmap and help match them to scene dimensions. To create the CamPoints, open the Create panel, click the Helpers category button, and select the Camera Match subcategory.

The Camera Match utility needs to have at least five CamPoints defined before it can create a camera. These CamPoints should be positioned in the scene at precise coordinates that match the background image. For example, if the distance between two points is four feet, then create the CamPoints such that their distance is four units from each other. In the Keyboard Entry rollout, you can create new CamPoints by entering exact XYZ values.

To help keep the CamPoints straight, you can name each CamPoint by typing a name in the Name field. This helps when you try to identify each point in the Camera Match utility.

After positioning the CamPoints, open the Utility panel and click the Camera Match button. The CamPoint Info rollout includes a list of CamPoints. Each CamPoint needs to be assigned an XY position that matches its 3D location to a 2D position on the background bitmap. To assign these positions, click the Assign Position button, select a CamPoint from the list, and click the location in the viewport where this point should be positioned. You can also enter the X and Y coordinate values for the selected position in the X and Y fields in the CamPoint Info rollout.

As you line up the CamPoint positions, the bottom of the Camera Match rollout shows the current camera error. If the error value is greater than 5, the camera can't be created. The Use This Point option can disable a CamPoint without deleting it, which can help you pinpoint the CamPoint that is misaligned.

The Create Camera button creates a camera after all the CamPoints have been correctly positioned. The Modify Camera lets you realign CamPoints and change the current camera position. The Iterations value determines the number of calculations required to position the camera; if your error values are too high, try reducing this number and creating the camera again. The Freeze FOV option prevents the FOV from changing as a camera is created.

Tutorial: Driving in Rome

The streets of Rome are narrow and intricate — maybe because they need to wind around all the ancient structures. In this tutorial, they provide a perfect opportunity to practice using the Camera Match utility.

To match a camera view to a background image, follow these steps:

1. Start by loading a background image for the scene. Select Rendering ⇨ Environment to open the Environment dialog box, click the Environment Map button to open the Material/Map Browser, and double-click the Bitmap selection. This opens the Select Bitmap Image File dialog box, enabling you to select the background image. Locate the Temple of Saturn Rome image, and click Open. Back in the Environment dialog box, click the Use Map option, and close the dialog box.

2. To view the background image in a viewport, select the Views ⇨ Viewport Background command to open the Viewport Background dialog box. Select the User Environment Background and the Display Background options for the Perspective viewport, and click OK.

3. The next step is to assign CamPoints throughout the scene using the CamPoint helper objects. Open the Create panel, click the Helper category button, and then select the Camera Match subcategory. Click the CamPoint button, and click in the Perspective view six times to create six CamPoints. Then select the first CamPoint, and click the Select and Move button. Then open the Move Transform Type-In by selecting the Tools ⇨ Transform Type-In command. Give the CamPoints the names and dimensions in the following list. Enter the dimensions in the Absolute column.

   - Left base of pillar: X = 0, Y = 0, Z = 0
   - Right base of pillar: X = 10, Y = 0, Z = 0
   - Left edge of wall: X = –10, Y = 0, Z = 0
   - Right edge of wall: X = 20, Y = 0, Z = 0
   - Right end of structure: X = 0, Y = 20, Z = 0
   - Top of pillar: X = 0, Y = 0, Z = 30

Note

Although accurate measurements are better, these dimensions are relative approximations (because I didn't have time to fly to Rome with a tape measure).

4. Once the six CamPoints have been positioned, click the Camera Match utility in the Utilities panel. In the CamPoint rollout is a list of the CamPoints that you've created. For each CamPoint in the list, click the Assign Point button, select the point, and click the background image where it is located. The following list has the exact dimensions that you can use to check your placement. When you're finished, click the Assign Position button again to exit position selection mode.

- Left base of pillar: X = 279, Y = 324
- Right base of pillar: X = 322, Y = 346
- Left edge of wall: X = 236, Y = 306
- Right edge of wall: X = 372, Y = 370
- Right end of structure: X = 358, Y = 305
- Top of pillar: X = 278, Y = 144

5. Once all CamPoints have been positioned, click the Create Camera button. If the current camera error value is less than 5, a camera appears in the scene. You can update the CamPoint positions by clicking the Assign Position button, selecting a CamPoint from the list, and clicking the new location, or by changing the X and Y values. Click the Modify Camera button after moving the CamPoint's position to realign the camera. Figure 23-1 shows the camera in the Perspective view after it has been matched.

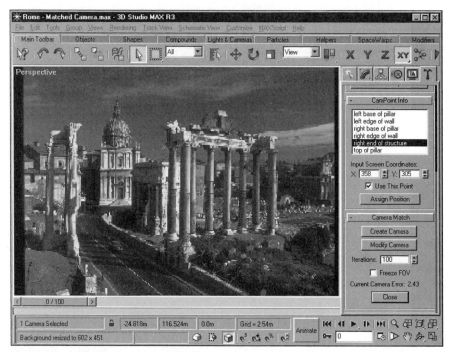

Figure 23-1: The Perspective view after our camera has been matched to the background bitmap

6. Change the Perspective viewport to display the matched camera by pressing the C key on the keyboard.

7. Import the Porsche model created by Viewpoint Datalabs. After grouping the model and scaling it down, position it in the Camera viewport on the road. Turn off the construction grid by pressing the G key on the keyboard. Figure 23-2 shows our current scene from the matched camera perspective.

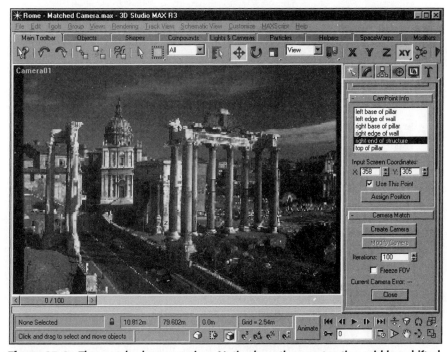

Figure 23-2: The matched camera view. Notice how the construction grid has shifted.

Figure 23-3 shows a sample test rendering of the scene, which can be used to check placement. The final scene will need the lights and materials changed, but the placement looks good.

Using the Camera Tracker Utility

The Camera Tracker utility matches scene objects to an animated background. As with the Camera Match utility, the Camera Tracker utility is accessed from the Utilities panel. Click the More button to open the Utilities dialog box and select it from the list of additional utilities.

Figure 23-3: A test rendering of the car model positioned in a scene and viewed from a matched camera

Loading a movie file

One of the first tasks is to load a movie file to track. This can be done using the Movie File button (initially labeled "none") found in the Movie rollout, shown in Figure 23-4. This button opens the Browse Image for Input dialog box, where you can select a movie file to load. Usable formats include AVI, MOV, FLC, and IFL. Once a movie file is selected, the button's label changes to the name of the movie file. The Movie rollout also includes a Display Movie button to view a single frame of the movie. The Show Frame value lets you display a specific frame of the movie.

The Deinterlace option can be set to off, odd, or even and, if enabled, deinterlaces a video file using odd or even lines. This enables you to view interlaced video segments whose individual frames include only odd or even lines. The Fade Display option fades the movie by 50 percent so the tracker gizmos can be clearly seen. (Tracker gizmos are explained in the next section.)

Figure 23-4: The Movie rollout lets you load and view a movie file.

The Movie rollout also includes buttons to Save, Save As, and Load camera tracker setting files, which are saved with the .MOT extension. The Auto Load/Save Setting option automatically saves these files in the same directory as the movie file; they are automatically updated anytime any of the settings change.

Working with trackers

The Camera Tracker utility uses CamPoints, just as the Camera Match utility does. CamPoints can be set up in the same manner discussed in the previous section. The Camera Tracker utility requires a minimum of six CamPoints and at least two that are in separate planes.

These CamPoints become the motion trackers for the utility. Motion trackers are points that are followed throughout the animation. These points are used to compute the camera's path. These trackers are displayed and controlled using the Motion Trackers rollout, shown in Figure 23-5. To add a tracker to the list, click the New Tracker button. This places the tracker gizmo in the list. The parameters for the gizmo can be changed and the gizmo can be moved as needed.

The Scene Object button lets you select a CamPoint or some other object as the object to track. You can also specify values for Match Weights and Max Move per Frame. The higher the Match Weights value, the more consistent the track points will be in the scene.

The Set Start and Set Stop buttons let you set the frames at which the tracking starts and stops. If a tracking object moves out of the scene, click the Set Stop button at the frame where it disappears.

Figure 23-5: The Motion Tracker rollout lets you add trackers to the scene.

Using the tracker gizmo

The tracker gizmo looks like two boxes within each other. The crosshairs mark the center of the tracking object, the inner box (called the Feature Selection box) marks the edges of the tracking object, and the outer box (called the Motion Search box) determines the search area in which the tracker gizmo looks for the object in each frame.

Figure 23-6 shows the tracker gizmo.

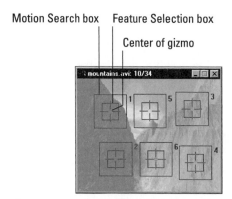

Figure 23-6: The tracker gizmo is used to track objects through several frames.

Stepping through frames

The Movie Stepper rollout, shown in Figure 23-7, is used to step through the animation frames. This is useful to ensure that the tracking objects are visible throughout the entire animation. You can also use this rollout to manually set the tracking.

Figure 23-7: The Movie Stepper rollout lets you step through the movie frames.

The Movie Frame spinner displays the current frame. The buttons under the frame number let you move forward or backward through the frames. These buttons can move to the beginning frame, back ten frames, back one frame, forward one frame, forward ten frames, or to the last frame.

The Feature tracking button, when enabled, computes the tracking locations; the tracker gizmos move to their tracked positions if the positions have already been tracked. The Step Keyframes option lets you move between keyframes instead of frames using the stepping buttons. The Show Track option displays the path traveled by each tracker as a line.

Note
Red track lines indicate that the tracker has been tracked. White track lines are trackers that haven't been tracked.

The Live Camera Match option moves the camera as you reposition the tracker gizmos. The Sync Animation option causes the time slider and the viewports to update along with the Movie Stepper buttons.

Caution
Be aware that updating the viewports with the Sync Animation option can slow down the system substantially.

The Error Threshold rollout, also shown in Figure 23-7, lets you set the maximum allowable error values for Match Error, Variance Delta, and Jump Delta. If the tracking exceeds these values, an error appears in the Tracking Error Review list in the Batch Track rollout.

Automating the tracking process

Once the parameters have been set up, the Complete Tracking button in the Batch Track rollout, shown in Figure 23-8, can be used to start the tracking process. As tracking proceeds, any errors are captured and displayed in the Tracking Error Review list. After reviewing the errors, go to the Movie Stepper rollout to correct them, and run the tracking process again. This iterative process produces the best results.

Figure 23-8: The Batch Track rollout lets you initiate the tracking process.

The Complete Tracking button initiates the tracking process. This process tracks only those frames that haven't been tracked yet. The Check Status button checks for errors and for any frames that haven't been tracked. Any errors are displayed in the Tracking Error Review list, and the tracks that haven't been completed are displayed next to the Incomplete label.

Note   Each error listed displays the tracker number, the frame number, an error code, and the threshold value. Possible error codes include "me" for match error; "vd" for color variance error, and "jd" for jump error.

The Next button moves to the next error in the list, and the Clear button removes an error from the list.

The Position Data rollout, also shown in Figure 23-8, lets you clear, show, or export the tracking data for the selected tracker, the enabled trackers, or all trackers. The Show Data button opens the data in a text window, shown in Figure 23-9. Exported data can be saved as an Excel spreadsheet in the .CSV format or as text with the .DAT extension.

```
: Untitled - MAXScript                                          _ □ ✕
File  Edit  Search  Help
  10, 147.0, 142.0, 132.0, 127.0, 162.0, 157.0, 117.0, 112.0, 177.0, 17:
  11, 147.0, 146.0
  12, 159.0, 139.0
  13, 162.0, 142.0
  14, 166.0, 150.0
  15, 173.0, 160.0, 158.0, 145.0, 188.0, 175.0, 143.0, 130.0, 203.0, 19
  16, 186.0, 173.0
  17, 196.0, 161.0, 181.0, 146.0, 211.0, 176.0, 166.0, 131.0, 226.0, 19.
  18, 183.0, 146.0
  19, 168.0, 159.0
  20, 182.0, 173.0, 167.0, 158.0, 197.0, 188.0, 152.0, 143.0, 212.0, 20
  21, 189.0, 172.0
  22, 203.0, 157.0

 |
```

Figure 23-9: The Show Data button in the Position Data rollout displays the tracking data in a text window.

Matching the camera

Once all the tracking positions have been established, you need to select a camera to match the tracking data. In the Match Move rollout, shown in Figure 23-10, is a Camera button (initially labeled "none"). Click this button to select the camera to use.

Note   The camera specified in the Match Move rollout must be a free camera.

While matching the camera, you can specify which camera parameters to include in the process. Options include FOV, Pan, Tilt, Roll, Dolly, Truck H (horizontal), and Truck V (vertical). You can also specify the Movie Start and Animation Start frames, as well as the Frame Count. The Reset Ranges button resets the Movie Start, Animation Start, and Frame Count values to their defaults.

Figure 23-10: The Match Move rollout lets you select a camera to match to the racking data.

The Animate Displays option updates the viewport frame by frame with the camera match. The Generate Keyframes option creates keys for each frame of the match. When you're all ready, the Match Move button starts the Match Move process. The Maximum Pixel Error displays the tracking error for each frame. To view all the error values in a text window, click the Show Errors button.

Smoothing the camera motion

Once the camera is matched to the tracking data, its motion might be a little erratic and bumpy. You can smooth its motion using the Move Smoothing rollout, shown in Figure 23-11. This rollout lets you select which options to include in the smoothing calculations: Rotation, Position, Roll, Pan, Tilt, FOV, Dolly, Truck Horizontal, or Truck Vertical.

There are two smooth types that you can choose from: Straight Line Average and Low Pass Filter with a Smooth Amount. You can also smooth just the Match Move Range or All Frames. With the options set, click the Smooth button to initiate the smoothing calculations.

Tutorial: Tracking a flyby camera's motion

As an example of the Camera Tracker utility, I've located a scenic flyby animation that was created using VistaPro. This animation flies over a terrain landscape. The Camera Tracker utility can be used to duplicate the camera motion for this animation sequence.

Figure 23-11: The Move Smoothing rollout lets you smooth the camera motion.

To track a camera's motion through a landscape animation, follow these steps:

1. First you need to create a free camera. Open the Create panel, select the Cameras category, and click the Free button. Then click in the Top view to create a camera.

2. Next, access the Camera Tracker utility by opening the Utilities panel, clicking the More button, and double-clicking the Camera Tracker selection. In the Movie rollout, click the Movie button and load the mountains.avi file. Click the Display Movie button to open the movie file in a separate window; this window will show the camera trackers once they've been added to the scene.

3. To position the CamPoints, it is helpful to view the animation in the view-port background. To load the animation as the scene background, select the Rendering ➪ Environment command to open the Environment dialog box. Click the Environment Map button, and double-click the Bitmap selection in the Material/Map Browser. Locate and open the mountains.avi file, and close the Environment dialog box. Then select the Front view, and select the Views ➪ Viewport Background command. In the Viewport Background dialog box, select the Use Environment Background and Display Background options, and click OK. Click the Max/Min Toggle to maximize the Perspective view.

Tip Press the G key to hide the home grid.

4. The loaded animation includes 19 frames. You can set this range by clicking the Time Configuration button and entering a value of **19** for the length.

5. The next step is to position at least six CamPoints in the scene. Open the Create panel, click the Helpers category button, select the Camera Match subcategory, and click the CamPoint button. Because this is a rendered scene, you need to approximate the CamPoint positions, but it is best if you can use accurate measurements. Create six CamPoints in the Front view, and name these CamPoints as in the following list. Then, using the Move Transform Type-In dialog box, position the CamPoints using the listed dimensions.

- Left dome: X = 0, Y = 0, Z = 0
- Center dome: X = 20, Y = 0, Z = 0
- Right dome: X = 40, Y = 0, Z = 0
- Left peak: X = 50, Y = 65, Z = 70
- Right valley: X = 70, Y = 65, Z = 50
- Right peak: X = 80, Y = 65, Z = 75

Figure 23-12 shows the six CamPoints for the first frame.

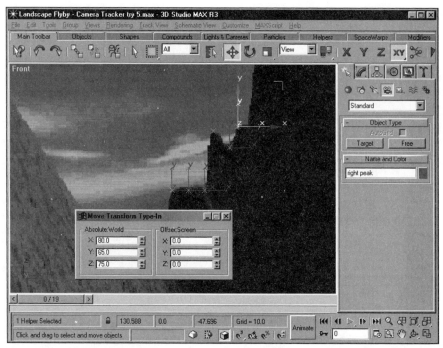

Figure 23-12: The CamPoints identify locations to be tracked.

6. Back in the Utilities panel, open the Motion Trackers rollout, and click the New Tracker button. A new tracker is added to the list. Next, click the Scene Object button, and select the right peak CamPoint. The CamPoint name is added to the motion tracker list. Repeat these steps until all CamPoints have been added to the list. Once all the trackers have been added to the Motion Trackers rollout, click the Save As button in the Movie rollout, and name the file **mountain.mot**.

7. Gizmos for all six motion trackers are positioned on top of each other in the movie window. To reposition them, select a tracker in the list, and move it to its correct location in the movie window by dragging the small green dot. Resize the inner Feature Selection box to just surround the feature. Repeat this for all six trackers. Figure 23-13 shows the movie window with all motion trackers in position.

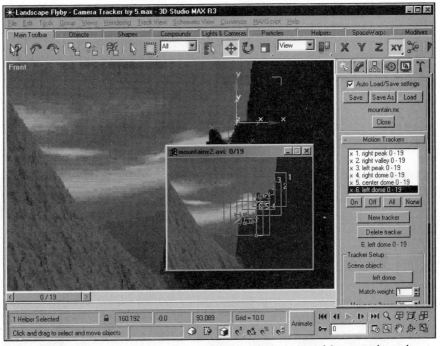

Figure 23-13: These motion trackers will follow their assigned features throughout the animation.

8. In the Batch Track rollout, click the Complete Tracking button. This computes the tracking position for each frame. When the tracking is finished, click the Check Status button to see a list of errors. Errors can be eliminated in several ways. You might need to increase the error thresholds, or you can manually set the tracking position by enabling the Feature Tracking option in the Movie Stepper rollout and repositioning the tracker for the frame in error. After making corrections, click the Check Status button again to update the error list.

9. When all the errors are eliminated, open the Match Move rollout, click the Camera button, and select the camera that you created at the start of this tutorial. Then click the Match Move button.

Note

Because you approximated the positions of the CamPoints, your Match Move computations most likely have some errors. When an error occurs, a dialog box appears stating the error and asking whether you wish to continue. If the animation motion is roughly in a straight line, as it is in this example, you can get by with a few errors.

10. Change the Perspective view to the Camera view by right-clicking the viewport title and selecting Views ➪ Camera01 from the pop-up menu. Then generate a preview animation using the Rendering ➪ Make Preview command. Check the motion of the camera. You can synchronize the viewport with the movie window by selecting the Sync Animation option in the Movie Stepper rollout.

11. If the camera motion needs to be smoothed, open the Move Smoothing rollout, and click the Smooth button.

Figure 23-14 shows the movie window with its trackers. Notice how the Camera01 viewport is synchronized with the movie window.

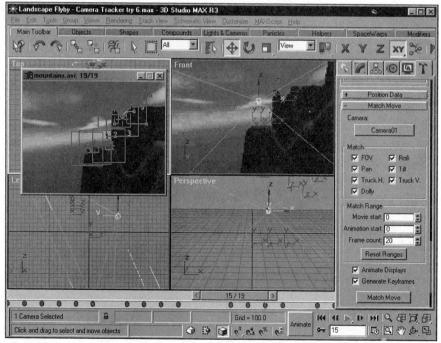

Figure 23-14: Once tracked, the camera follows the animation's path.

Pinning objects

Once the tracked data is captured, you can select an object to follow the path that is positioned in front of the camera. This technique is called *pinning*. In the Object Pinning rollout, shown in Figure 23-15, select a tracker from the drop-down list and click the Object to Pin button. Then select the object to pin in the viewport. You can also set a Pin Range, the Pin Space (Screen or Grid), and Pin Mode (Absolute or Relative). To complete the pinning, click the Pin button.

Figure 23-15: The Object Pinning rollout can position an object in front of the camera path.

Tutorial: Pinning a jet in front of the camera

In this tutorial, we use the object-pinning function to add a jet to the flyby scene.

To pin a jet model in front of the tracked camera, follow these steps:

1. Import the jet model, and position it in front of the camera. Group the model with the Group ➪ Group command. Name the group **jet.**

2. In the Utilities panel, open the Object Pinning rollout, click the Object to Pin button, and select the Relative Pin Mode option. Then select the jet model.

Figure 23-16 shows the scene with a jet model positioned in front of the camera. The jet model will follow the same relative path as the camera.

Figure 23-16: This jet model was pinned in front of the camera using the same camera track.

Summary

The Camera Match and Camera Tracker utilities enable you to match your scene's position and motion to a background image or animation. This can be very helpful in creating realistic images and animations.

In this chapter, you've

✦ Learned to use the Camera Match utility to match a camera to a background image

✦ Controlled a camera's position using the Camera Tracker utility

✦ Pinned an object in front of the camera path

This is the last chapter on lights and cameras. In the next part of the book we investigate particle systems and Space Warps, beginning with a chapter that covers creating and controlling particle systems.

✦   ✦   ✦

Particle Systems and Space Warps

◆ ◆ ◆ ◆

In This Part

◆ ◆ ◆ ◆

Creating and Controlling Particle Systems

Every object that is added to the scene will slow down MAX to a small degree, because MAX needs to keep track of every object. If thousands of objects are added to a scene, not only will MAX slow down noticeably, but the objects will become difficult to identify. For example, if you had to create thousands of simple snowflakes for a snowstorm scene, the system would become unwieldy, and the number wouldn't get very high before you ran out of memory.

Particle systems are objects that combine large numbers of objects into a single system that is easy to manage and control. This chapter discusses using these special systems and how to control them.

Understanding the Various Particle Systems

A *particle* is a small, simple object that is duplicated en masse, like snow, rain, or dust. Just as in real life, MAX includes many different types of particles that can vary in size, shape, texture, color, and motion. These different particle types are included in various *particle systems*. MAX includes the following particle systems:

> ✦ **Spray**—Simulates drops of water. These drops can be Drops, Dots, or Ticks. The particles travel in a straight line from the emitter's surface after they are created.

✦ **Snow** — Similar to the Spray system, with the addition of some fields to make the particles Tumble as they fall. You can also render the particles as a Six Pointed shape that looks like a snowflake.

✦ **Super Spray** — An advanced version of the Spray system that can use different mesh objects, closely packed particles called MetaParticles, or an instanced object as its particles. Super Spray is useful for rain and fountains. Binding it to the Path Follow Space Warp can create waterfalls.

✦ **Blizzard** — An advanced version of the Snow system that can use the same mesh object types as the Super Spray system. Binding the system to the Wind Space Warp can create storms.

✦ **PArray** — Can use a separate Distribution Object as the source for the particles. For this system, you can set the particle type to Fragment and bind it to the PBomb Space Warp to create explosions.

✦ **PCloud** — Confines all generated particles to a certain volume. A good use of this is to reproduce bubbles in a glass or cars on the road.

Creating a Particle System

All of the various particle systems can be located under the Create panel. To access these systems, click the Geometry category and select the Particle Systems subcategory from the drop-down list. All the particle systems will then appear as buttons.

With the Particle Systems subcategory selected, click the button for the type of particle system you want to use, and then click in a viewport to create the particle system emitter icon. The *emitter* is an icon that looks like a plane or a sphere and defines the location in the system where the particles all originate. Attached to the icon is a single line that indicates the direction in which the particles move when generated. This points toward the construction grid's negative Z-axis when first created.

Figure 24-1 shows the emitter icons for each particle system type. Along the top from left to right are Spray, Snow, and Super Spray, and on the bottom from left to right are Blizzard, PArray, and PCloud.

These icons can be transformed using the standard transform buttons and can be moved, rotated, and scaled. Rotating an emitter changes the direction in which the particles initially move.

Once an icon is created, you can set the number, shape, and size of the particles and define their motion in the Parameter rollouts. To apply a material to the particles, simply apply the material to the system's icon.

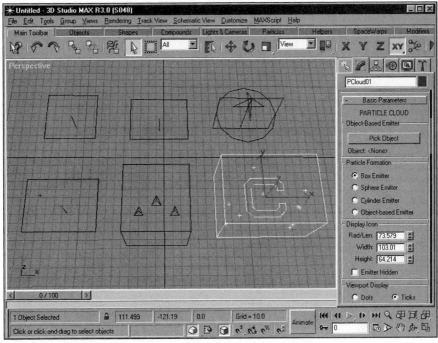

Figure 24-1: The emitter icons for each particle system type

Setting Particle Parameters

You can set the parameters for the MAX particle systems in the Create panel when they are first created or in the Modify panel at any time. Each of the simpler systems, Spray and Snow, has a single Parameters rollout, whereas the advanced versions of these systems, Super Spray and Blizzard, include multiple Parameters rollouts. The PArray and PCloud systems have similar multiple rollouts, with a few subtle differences. The following sections describe how to use these rollouts to set the parameters for each of the six particle systems.

Spray parameters

The Spray Parameters rollout, shown in Figure 24-2, includes values for the number of particles to be included in the system. These values can be different for the viewport and renderer. You can also specify the drop size, initial speed, and variation. The variation values can alter the initial speed and direction.

Figure 24-2: The Spray Parameters rollout holds the parameters for the Spray particle system.

Spray particles can be Drops, Dots, or Ticks, which affect how the particles look only in the viewport. Drops appear as streaks, Dots are simple points, and Ticks are small plus signs. You can also set how the particles are rendered — as Tetrahedron objects or as Facing objects (square faces that always face the viewer).

Note   The Facing option is visible only in the Perspective view.

The Timing values determine when the particles appear and how long the particles stay around. The Start Frame is the first frame where particles begin to appear, and the Life value determines the number of frames in which the particles are visible. Once a particle's lifetime is up, it disappears. The Birth Rate value lets you set how many new particles appear in each frame — you can use this setting or select the Constant option. The Constant option determines the Birth Rate value by dividing the total number of particles by the number of frames.

The emitter dimensions specify the width and height of the emitter. You can also hide the emitter with the Hide option.

Note   The Hide option hides the emitter only in the viewports. Emitters are never rendered.

Snow parameters

The parameters for the Snow particle system are similar to the Spray particle system, except for a few unique settings. Snow can be set with a Tumble and Tumble Rate. The Tumble value can range from 0 to 1, with 1 causing a maximum amount of rotation. The Tumble Rate determines the speed of the rotation.

The Render options are also different for the Snow particle system. There are three options: Six Point, Triangle, and Facing. The Six Point option renders the particle as a six-pointed star. Triangles and Facing objects are single faces.

Super Spray parameters

The Super Spray particle system includes several rollouts, which are covered in the following sections.

Super Spray basic parameters

The Super Spray particle system emitter is a simple icon with a cylinder and an arrow that points in the direction in which the particles will travel. Using the Basic Parameters rollout, shown in Figure 24-3, you can control their axis and plane angles and how far from the direction axis the particles are allowed to appear. The Spread values set the distance from this center axis that particles can be created. If these values are left at 0, then the particle system emits a single, straight stream of particles.

Figure 24-3: The Basic Parameters rollout lets you specify how the particles appear in the viewports.

The icon size can be set or the icon can be hidden in the viewport. You can also set the particles to be displayed in the viewport as Dots, Ticks, Meshes, or Bounding Boxes. The Percentage value is the number of the total particles that are visible in the viewport and should be kept low to ensure rapid viewport updates.

Particle Generation rollout

The Particle Generation rollout, shown in Figure 24-4, is where you set the number of particles to include in a system as either a Rate or Total value. The Rate value is the number of particles per frame that are generated. The Total value is the number of particles generated over the total number of frames.

Figure 24-4: The Particle Generation rollout specifies the number of particles to include in a system.

In the Particle Motion group, the Speed value determines the initial speed and direction of particles. The Variation value alters this initial speed as a percentage of the Speed value. The Divergence value is the angular amount by which the initial direction can be altered.

In the Particle Timing group, you can set when the emitting process starts and stops. Using the Display Until value, you can also cause the particles to continue displaying after the emitting has stopped. The Life value is how long particles stay around, which can vary based on another variation setting.

When an emitter is animated (such as moving back and forth), the particles can clump together where the system changes direction. This clumping effect is called *puffing.* The Subframe Sampling options help reduce this effect. There are three options: Creation Time, Emitter Translation, and Emitter Rotation. Each of these helps prevent puffing for different types of motion.

Caution The Subframe Sampling options increase the rendering time and should be used only if necessary.

The particle size can be specified along with a variation value. You can also cause the particles to grow and fade for a certain number of frames.

The Seed value helps determine the randomness of the particles. Clicking the New button automatically generates a new Seed value.

Particle Type rollout

The Particle Type rollout, shown in Figure 24-5, lets you define the look of the particles. At the top of the rollout are three Particle Type options: Standard Particles, MetaParticles, and Instanced Geometry.

Figure 24-5: The Particle Type rollout lets you define how the particles look.

Standard particles

If you select Standard Particles as the particle type, you can select which geometric shape you want to use from the Standard Particles section. The options are Triangle, Special, Constant, Six Point, Cube, Facing, Tetra, and Sphere.

The Special type consists of three intersecting planes, which are useful if you apply maps to them. The Facing type is also useful with maps; it creates a simple, square face that always faces the view. The Constant type maintains the same pixel size regardless of the distance from the camera or view. Six Point renders each particle as a 2D six-pointed star. All other types are common geometric objects.

MetaParticles

The MetaParticles option makes the particles Metaballs. *Metaballs* are viscous spheres that, like mercury, flow into each other when close. These particles take a little longer to render but are effective for simulating water and liquids.

Selecting the MetaParticles option in the Particle Types section enables the MetaParticle Parameters group. In this group are options for controlling how the MetaParticles behave. The Tension value determines how easily objects blend together. MetaParticles with a high tension resist merging with other particles. This value can be varied with the Variation value.

Because MetaParticles can take a long time to render, the Evaluation Coarseness settings enable you to set how computationally intensive the rendering process is. This can be set differently for the viewport and the renderer. The higher the value, the quicker the results. You can also set this to Automatic Coarseness. The One Connected Blob option speeds the rendering process by ignoring all particles that aren't connected.

Instanced Geometry

If the Instanced Geometry option is selected as the particle type, you can select an object to use as the particle. Figure 24-6 shows the section in the Particle Type rollout that appears when this option is selected. To choose an object to use as a particle, click the Pick Object button, and then select an object from the viewport. If the Use Subtree Also option is selected, then all child objects are also included.

Figure 24-6: The Particle Type rollout includes settings for selecting a separate object to use as a particle.

The Animation Offset Keying determines how an animated object that is selected as the particle is animated. The None option animates all objects the same, regardless of when they are born. The Birth option starts the animation for each object when it is created, and the Random option offsets the timing randomly based on the Frame Offset value. For example, if you have selected an animated bee that flaps its wings as the particle and you select None as the Animation Offset Keying option, all the bees flap their wings in concert. Selecting the Birth option instead starts them flapping their wings once they are born, and selecting Random offsets each instance differently.

For materials, the Time and Distance values determine the number of frames or the distance traveled before a particle is completely mapped. Materials can be applied to the icon that appears when the particle system is created. The Get Material From button lets you select the object from which to get the material. The options include the icon and the Instanced Geometry.

Rotation and Collision rollout

The Rotation and Collision rollout, shown in Figure 24-7, contains several controls to alter the rotation of individual particles. The Spin Time is the number of frames required to rotate a full revolution. The Phase value is the initial rotation of the particle. Both of these values can be varied.

Figure 24-7: The Rotation and Collision rollout can control how objects collide with one another.

You can also set the axis about which the particles rotate. Options include Random, Direction of Travel/MBlur, and User Defined. The Stretch value under the Direction of Travel option causes the object to elongate in the direction of travel. The User Defined option lets you specify the degrees of rotation about each axis.

Interparticle collisions are computationally intensive and can easily be enabled or disabled with the Enable option. You can also set how often the collisions are calculated. The Bounce value determines the speed of particles after collisions as a percentage of their collision speed. The Bounce value can be varied with the Variation value.

New Feature   Interparticle collisions are a new feature in Release 3.

Object Motion Inheritance rollout

The settings on the Object Motion Inheritance rollout, shown in Figure 24-8, determine how the particles move when the emitter is moving. The Influence value defines how closely the particles follow the emitter's motion; a value of 100 has particles follow exactly, and a value of 0 means they don't follow at all.

Figure 24-8: The Object Motion Inheritance rollout sets how the particles inherit the motion of their emitter.

The Multiplier value can exaggerate or diminish the effect of the emitter's motion. Particles with a high multiplier can actually precede the emitter.

Bubble Motion rollout

The Bubble Motion rollout, also shown in Figure 24-8, simulates the wobbling motion of bubbles as they rise in a liquid. There are three values to define this motion, each with variation values. Amplitude is the distance that the particle moves from side to side. Period is the time that it takes to complete one side-to-side motion cycle. The Phase value defines where the particle starts along the amplitude curve.

Particle Spawn rollout

The Particle Spawn rollout, shown in Figure 24-9, sets options for spawning new particles when a particle dies or collides with another particle. If the setting is None, colliding particles bounce off one another, and dying particles simply disappear. The Die After Collision option causes a particle to disappear after it collides. The Persist value sets how long the particle stays around before disappearing. The Variation value causes the Persist value to vary by a defined percentage.

Figure 24-9: The Particle Spawn rollout can cause particles to spawn new particles.

The Spawn on Collision, Spawn on Death, and Spawn Trails options all enable the Spawn controls and define when particles spawn new particles. The Spawns value is the number of times a particle can spawn other particles. The Affects value is the percentage of particles that can spawn new particles; lowering this value creates some duds that do not spawn. The Multiplier determines the number of new particles created.

Caution

The Spawn Trails option causes every particle to spawn a new particle at every frame. This can very quickly create an enormous number of particles and should be used with caution.

The chaos settings define the direction and speed of the spawned particles. A Direction Chaos value of 100 gives the spawned particles the freedom to travel in any direction, whereas a setting of 0 moves it in the same direction as its originator.

The Chaos Speed Factor is the difference in speed between the spawned particle and its originator. This factor can be faster or slower than the original. Selecting the Both option speeds up some particles and slows others randomly. You can also choose to have spawned particles use their parent's velocity or use the factor value as a fixed value.

The Scale Chaos Factor works similarly to the Chaos Speed Factor, except that it scales particles to be larger or smaller than their originator.

The Lifespan Value Queue, shown in Figure 24-10, lets you define different lifespan levels. Original particles have a lifespan equal to the first entry in the queue. The particles that are spawned from those spawned particles last as long as the second value, and so on. To add a value to the list, enter the value in the Lifespan spinner, and click the Add button. The Delete button removes values from the list, and the Replace button switches value positions.

Figure 24-10: The Lifespan Value Queue changes the spawning particle over time.

If Instanced Geometry is the selected particle type, you can fill the Object Mutation Queue with additional objects to use at each spawn level. These are objects that appear once a particle is spawned. To pick a new object to add to the queue, use the Pick button. You can select several objects, and they are used in the order in which they are listed.

Load/Save Presets rollout

Each particle configuration can be saved and loaded using the Load/Save Presets rollout, shown in Figure 24-11. To save a configuration, type a name in the Preset Name field, and click the Save button. All saved presets are displayed in the list. To use one of these preset configurations, select it, and click the Load button.

Figure 24-11: The Load/Save Presets rollout enables you to save different parameter settings.

Note   A saved preset is valid only for the type of particle system used to save it. For example, you cannot save a Super Spray preset and load it for a Blizzard system.

Blizzard parameters

The Blizzard particle system uses the same rollouts as the Super Spray system with some different options. For example, the Basic Parameters rollout includes dimensions for the Blizzard icon and an option to hide the emitter. You can also select to view the particles in the viewport as Dots, Ticks, Meshes, or Bounding Boxes. The Percentage of Particles value is the number of the total particles to display in the viewport.

In the Particle Generation rollout, you'll find values for Tumble and Tumble Rate. These options enable you to tumble snowflakes realistically.

Another difference is the Emitter Fit Planar option under the Material Mapping group of the Particle Type rollout. This option sets particles to be mapped at birth, depending on where they appear on the emitter.

The other big difference is that the Blizzard particle system has no Bubble Motion rollout, because snowflakes don't make very good bubbles.

PCloud parameters

The PCloud particle system includes the same rollouts as the Super Spray system with some subtle differences.

The options on Basic Parameters rollout, shown in Figure 24-12, are unique to this system. This system can use a separate mesh object as an emitter. To select this emitter object, click the Pick Object button, and select the object to use. This button is active only if the Object-based Emitter option is selected. If it is selected, the button icon displays the word "Fill" until an object is selected using the Pick Object button. Other options include Box, Sphere, and Cylinder Emitter. For these emitters, the Rad/Len, Width, and Height values are active for defining its dimensions.

Figure 24-12: The Basic Parameters rollout for the PCloud particle system lets you choose the shape of the emitter.

Particles can appear in the viewport as Dots, Ticks, Meshes, or Bounding Boxes; the Percentage value determines how many of the total particles to display.

In addition to these differences in the Basic Parameters rollout, several Particle Motion options in the Particle Generation rollout are different for the PCloud system as well. Particle Motion can be set to either a random direction, a specified vector, or in the direction of a reference object's Z-axis.

PArray parameters

The final particle system is the PArray system. Many of the rollouts for this system are the same as the ones previously discussed. There are some interesting differences, starting with the Basic Parameters rollout, shown in Figure 24-13.

Figure 24-13: The Basic Parameters rollout for the PArray particle system lets you select the location where the particles form.

Like the PCloud system, the PArray system can also select separate objects as emitters. This is done with the Pick Object button. You can also select the location on the object where the particles are formed. Options include Over Entire Surface, Along Visible Edges, At All Vertices, At Distinct Points, and At Face Centers. For the At Distinct Points option, you can select the number of points to use.

The Use Selected Sub-Object option forms particles in the locations selected with the Pick Object button, but only within the subobject selection passed up the stack.

This is useful if you want to emit particles only from a certain selection of a mesh, such as a dragon's mouth or the end of a fire hose.

The other options in the PArray system's Basic Parameters rollout are the same as in the other systems.

The Particle Generation rollout includes a Divergence value. This value is the angular variation of the velocity of each particle from the emitter's normal.

The Particle Type rollout for the PArray system contains a new particle type: Object Fragments. This type breaks the selected object into several fragments. Object Fragment settings include a Thickness value. This value gives each fragment a depth. If the value is set to 0, the fragments are all single-sided polygons.

Also in the Particle Type rollout, the All Faces option separates each individual triangular face into a separate fragment. An alternative to this is to use the Number of Chunks option, which enables you to divide the object into chunks and define how many chunks to use. A third option splits an object up based on the smoothing angle, which can be specified.

In the Material section of the Particle Type rollout, you can select material IDs to use for the fragment's inside, outside, and backside.

Working with Particle Systems

Particle systems are usually used to create special effects, and with the vast number of parameters that can be set, the possibilities are limitless. This section presents several particle system examples.

Chapter 26, "Particle System Special Effects," includes several additional particle system examples.

Tutorial: Creating rain and snow

One of the simplest uses for particle systems is to simulate rain or snow. In this tutorial, you'll use the Spray system to create rain and then learn how to use the Snow system to create snow.

To create a scene with rain using the Spray particle system, follow these steps:

1. Load the umbrella model created by Zygote Media.

2. Open the Create panel, click the Geometry category button, and then select the Particle Systems subcategory. Click the Spray button, and drag the icon in the Top viewport to cover the entire scene. Position the icon above the objects, and make sure the vector is pointing down toward the scene objects.

3. Open the Modify panel, and in the Parameters rollout, set the Render Count to **1000** and the Drop Size to **2**. Keep the default speed of 10, and select the Drops option; this makes the particles appear as streaks. Select the Tetrahedron Render method, and set the Start and Life values to **0** and **100**, respectively.

Tip

To cover the entire scene with an average downpour, set the number of particles to 1000 for a 100-frame animation.

4. Open the Material Editor and drag a light-blue-colored material to the particle system icon.

Figure 24-14 shows the results.

Figure 24-14: Rain created with the Spray particle system

Creating a snowstorm is very similar. To create a snowstorm, use the Snow particle system with the same number of particles. Use a white material with some self-illumination added. In the Parameters rollout, set the Flake Size to **6**, and use the Six Point Render option. Figure 24-15 shows a scene with these settings.

Figure 24-15: A simple snowstorm created with the Snow particle system

Using MetaParticles

One of the particle types in the Particle Type rollout is MetaParticles. These particles are like blobs of liquid that flow together. The MetaParticles type is available for the Super Spray, Blizzard, PArray, and PCloud particle systems.

Tutorial: Spilling soda from a can

MetaParticles are a good option to use to create drops of liquid, like those from a soda can.

To create liquid flowing from a can, follow these steps:

1. Import the soda can model created by Zygote Media. Position the can so that it is angled on its side.

2. Open the Create panel, click the Geometry category button, and select the Particle Systems subcategory from the drop-down list. Then click the Super Spray button, and drag the icon in the Front viewport. Position the icon so its

origin is at the opening of the can and the directional vector is pointing outward.

3. Open the Modify panel, and in the Basic Parameters rollout, set the Off Axis and Off Plane Spread values to **40**. In the Particle Generation rollout, keep the default Rate and Speed values, but set the Speed Variation to **50** to alter the speed of the various particles. Set the Particle Size to **20**. In the Particle Type rollout, select the MetaParticles option, set the Tension value to **1**, and make sure the Automatic Coarseness option is selected.

4. Open the Material Editor, and drag a purple-colored material with sharp highlights to the particle system icon.

Figure 24-16 shows MetaParticles spilling from a soda can at frame 25. The particles for this figure were created using the Super Spray system with a particle size of 20 and Automatic Coarseness enabled.

Figure 24-16: MetaParticles emitting from the opening of a soda can

Using a geometry object as a particle

Using the Particle Type rollout, you can select an object to use as the particle. To do this, simply select the Instanced Geometry option, click the Pick Object button, and select the object to use in the viewport.

Caution Using complicated objects as particles can slow down a system and increase the rendering time.

Enabling particle collisions

In the Rotation and Collisions rollout is an option to enable interparticle collisions. This option causes objects to bounce away from one another when their object boundaries overlap.

Caution This is another option that can increase the rendering time of a scene.

Tutorial: Basketball shooting practice

When an entire team is warming up before a basketball game, the space around the basketball hoop is quite chaotic — with basketballs flying in all directions. In this tutorial, we use a basketball object as a particle and spread it around a hoop. (Watch out for flying basketballs!)

To use a basketball object as a particle, follow these steps:

1. Import the basketball and basketball hoop models created by Zygote Media. Position the hoop so that it is facing the Perspective view. Select the basketball object and group it with the Group ⇨ Group command. Give it the name **Basketball**.

2. Open the Create panel, and select the Particle Systems subcategory. Then click the Super Spray button, and drag the icon in the viewport. Position the icon in the Front view so that its origin is above and slightly in front of the hoop and the directional vector is pointing down.

3. Open the Modify panel, and in the Basic Parameters rollout, set the Off Axis Spread value to **90** and the Off Plane Spread value to **40**; this randomly spreads the basketballs around the hoop. In the Viewport Display group of the Basic Parameters rollout, select the BBox option. Set the Percentage of Particles to **100** percent to see the position of each basketball object in the viewport.

Note Because the basketball is a fairly complex model, using the Mesh option severely slows down the viewport update.

4. In the Particle Generation rollout, select the Use Total option, and enter **30** for the value. (This is a reasonable number and not uncommon during warm-ups.) Set the Life value to **100** because we don't want basketballs to disappear.

5. In the Particle Type rollout, select the Instanced Geometry option, and click the Pick Object button. Make sure the Use Subtree Also option is selected to get the entire group, and then select the basketball group in the viewport. At the bottom of this rollout, select the Instanced Geometry option, and click the Get Material From button to give all the particles the same material as the original object.

6. In the Rotation and Collisions rollout, set the Spin Time to **100** to make the basketballs spin as they move about the scene. Set the Spin Axis Control to Random. Also enable the Collisions option, and set the Calculation Interval to **1** and the Bounce value to **100**; this prevents the basketballs from overlapping one another.

Figure 24-17 shows a rendered image of the scene at frame 30 with several basketballs bouncing chaotically around a hoop.

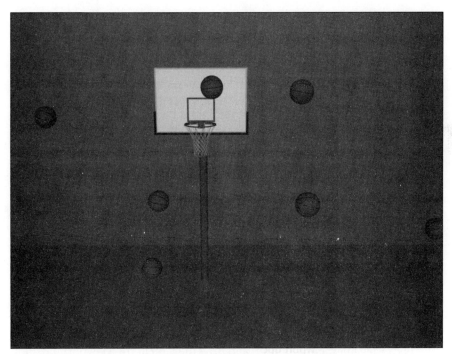

Figure 24-17: Multiple basketball particles flying around a hoop

Using mapped materials

Using material maps on particles is another way to add detail to a particle system without increasing its geometric complexity. All materials and maps available in the Material Editor can be applied to particle systems. To apply them, select the particle system icon, and click the Assign Material to Selection button in the Material Editor.

Cross-Reference For more details on using maps, see Chapter 18, "Using Material Maps."

There are two map types that are specifically designed to work with particle systems: Particle Age and Particle MBlur. These maps can be found in the Material/Map Browser.

Using the Particle Age map

The Particle Age map parameters include three different colors that can be applied at different times, depending on the Life value of the particles. Each color includes a color swatch, a map button, an Enable checkbox, and an Age value for when this color should appear.

This map typically is applied as a Diffuse map because it affects the color.

Using the Particle MBlur map

The Particle MBlur map changes the opacity of the front and back of a particle, depending on the color values and sharpness specified in its parameters rollout. This results in an effect of blurred motion if applied as an Opacity map.

Caution MBlur does not work with the Constant, Facing, MetaParticles, or PArray object fragments.

Tutorial: Creating a fire-breathing dragon

The Particle Age and MBlur maps work well for adding opacity and colors that change over time, such as hot jets of flames, to a particle system. A good example of this is the breath from a fire-breathing dragon. In this tutorial, we use a dragon model created by Viewpoint Datalabs.

To create a fire-breathing dragon, follow these steps:

1. Import the dragon model using the File ➪ Import command.

2. Open the Create panel, and select the Particle Systems subcategory. Then click the Super Spray button, and drag the icon in the viewport. Position the icon so that its origin is right in the dragon's mouth and the directional vector is pointing outward and down.

3. Open the Modify panel, and in the Basic Parameters rollout, set the Off Axis Spread value to **20** and the Off Plane Spread value to **90**; this focuses the flames shooting from the dragon's mouth. In the Particle Generation rollout, use the default values, except for the Particle Size, which you should set to **50**. In the Particle Type rollout, select the Standard Particles option and select the Sphere type.

4. Open the Material Editor, and select the first sample slot. Name this material **Dragon's Breath**, and click the map button to the right of the Diffuse color. From the Material/Map Browser that opens, select the Particle Age map. In the Particle Age Parameters rollout, select red, orange, and yellow colors for the ages 0, 50, and 100.

5. Select the Dragon's Breath material from the drop-down list, and click the map button to the right of the Opacity setting. Select the Particle MBlur map. In the Particle MBlur Parameters rollout, make Color #1 white and Color #2 black with a Sharpness value of **2.0**. Then drag this material onto the particle system icon.

Figure 24-18 shows the dragon at frame 30 with its fiery breath.

Figure 24-18: A fire-breathing dragon created using the Particle Age and MBlur maps

Using an object as an emitter

In the PArray system, you can select a geometry object to be used as an emitter. You can specify the precise location where the particles are emitted, including the entire surface, only along edges, at all vertices, at distinct points, or from the face centers. You can also select to use a subobject that is passed up the stack.

To select the object to use as an emitter, click the Pick Object button in the Basic Parameters rollout, and select an object in the scene.

Tutorial: Magic butterfly wings

In this tutorial, we create the effect of sparkling magic dust floating from butterfly wings using the PArray particle system with the butterfly wings as emitters.

To emit particles from butterfly wings, follow these steps:

1. Import the butterfly model created by Zygote Media using the File ⇨ Import command.

2. Open the Create panel, and select the Particle Systems subcategory. Click the PArray button, and drag in the Top view to create the system.

3. In the Basic Parameters rollout, click the Pick Object button, and select the butterfly wings. In the Particle Generation rollout, set the Emit Stop value to **100**. In the Particle Type rollout, select the Standard Particles and the Sphere options.

4. Open the Material Editor, select the first sample slot, and name the material **Magic Dust**. Click the Diffuse color swatch, and select a light-blue color. Then drag the blue color from the Diffuse color swatch to the Self-Illumination color swatch. Set the Material Effects Channel to **1**. Drag the material to the PArray icon.

5. In the Create panel, select the Standard Primitives subcategory, and click the Plane button. Then drag in the Front view to create a background plane. Set the Scale Multiplier to **50** and the object color to dark green.

6. Open the Rendering Effects dialog box with the Rendering ⇨ Effects command, and click the Add button. Double-click the Lens Effects option to select it. In the Lens Effects Parameters rollout, double-click the Star option in the left pane. In the Star Element rollout, set the Size to **2**, the Width to **0**, and the Intensity to **100**. Then open the Options panel, select the Image Centers option, and enable the Effects ID option with a setting of **1**.

Figure 24-19 shows the butterfly at frame 30 with sparkling magic particles being emitted from its wings.

Figure 24-19: The wings of this magic butterfly are the emitters for the particle system.

Summary

This chapter presented particle systems and showed how you can use them. The chapter also took a close look at each system, including Spray, Snow, Super Spray, Blizzard, PArray, and PCloud. In this chapter, you

- ✦ Learned about the various systems and their parameters
- ✦ Created a particle system for producing rain and snow
- ✦ Created a particle system using MetaParticles
- ✦ Specified an object to use as a particle and an object to use as an emitter
- ✦ Used the Particle Age and Particle MBlur maps on particles

In the next chapter, you'll learn how to add unseen forces to the scene using Space Warps.

✦   ✦   ✦

Using Space Warps

Space Warps are a way to add forces to a scene that can act on an object. Space Warps are not renderable and must be bound to an object to have an effect. A single Space Warp can be bound to several objects.

This chapter discusses the various Space Warp types and how to use them.

Creating and Binding Space Warps

Space Warps sound like a special effect from a science fiction movie, but actually they are nonrenderable objects that let you affect another object in many unique ways to create special effects.

You can think of Space Warps as the unseen forces that control the movement of objects in the scene. Space Warp types include Gravity, Wind, and Wave. Several Space Warps, such as Push and Motor, deal with dynamic simulations and can define forces in real-world units. Some Space Warps can deform an object's surface, others provide the same functionality as some modifiers, and some work only with particle systems.

In many ways, Space Warps are similar to modifiers, but modifiers typically apply to individual objects, whereas Space Warps can be applied to many objects at the same time and are applied to world space coordinates. This ability to work with multiple objects makes Space Warps the preferred way to alter particle systems.

Creating a Space Warp

Space Warps are found in the Create panel under the Space Warps category. From the subcategory drop-down list, you can select from five different subcategories. Each subcategory has buttons to enable several different Space Warp options. To create a Space Warp, click a button, and then click and drag in a viewport.

When a Space Warp is created, an icon is placed in the scene. This icon can be transformed as other objects can, by using the standard transformation buttons. The size and position of the Space Warp icon often affects its results. Once a Space Warp is created, it affects only the objects to which it is bound.

Binding a Space Warp to an object

A Space Warp's influence is felt only by its bound objects; several objects can be bound to a single Space Warp, and a single object can be bound to many different Space Warps. The Bind to Space Warp button is found on the main toolbar next to the Unlink button. After clicking the Bind to Space Warp button, drag from the Space Warp to the object to which you wish to link it.

All Space Warp bindings appear in the modifier stack at the topmost level. You can use the Edit Modifier Stack dialog box to copy and paste Space Warps between objects.

Some Space Warps can be bound only to certain types of objects. The Supports Objects of Type rollout lists the supported objects.

Space Warp Types

Just as there are many different types of forces in nature, there are many different Space Warp types. These appear in several different subcategories based on their function.

There are a couple of rollout features that appear for all Space Warps, including an Icon Size value. This value sets the size of the icons used to represent the Space Warp.

The sections that follow explain all the various Space Warp types and their parameters.

Geometric/Deformable

Geometric/Deformable Space Warps are used to deform the geometry of an object. Space Warps in this subcategory include FFD (Box), FFD (Cyl), Wave, Ripple, Displace, Conform, and Bomb. Figure 25-1 shows the Space Warp icons that are included in the Geometric/Deformable subcategory. These Space Warps are covered in the following sections.

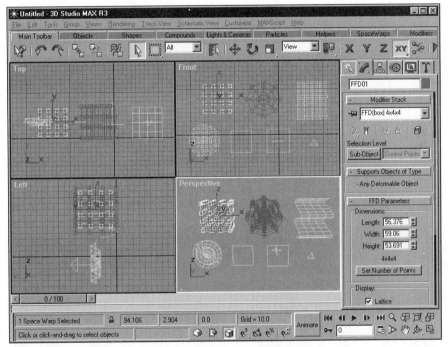

Figure 25-1: The Geometric/Deformable Space Warps

FFD (Box)

The FFD (Box) Space Warp shows up as a lattice of control points in the shape of a box; you can move these control points to deform an object. The bound object deforms to fit within the modified lattice.

The dimensions for the FFD lattice, including Length, Width, and Height, can be set in the FFD Parameters rollout. The Set Number of Points button enables you to specify the number of points to be included in the FFD lattice.

You can also select to display the lattice or the source volume, or both. If the Lattice option is disabled, only the control points are visible. The Source Volume option shows the original lattice before any vertices were moved.

There are two deform options: Only In Volume and All Vertices. The Only In Volume option limits the vertices that can be moved to the interior vertices only. If the All Vertices option is selected, the Falloff value determines the point at which vertices are no longer affected by the FFD. Falloff values can range between 0 and 1. The Tension and Continuity values control how tight the lines of the lattice are when moved.

The three buttons at the bottom of the FFD Parameters rollout help in the selection of control points. If the All X button is selected, when a single control point is selected, all the adjacent control points along the X-axis are also selected. This makes it easier to select an entire line of control points. The All Y and All Z buttons work in a similar manner in the other dimensions.

Figure 25-2 shows a stepladder model created by Zygote Media being deformed with an FFD (Box) Space Warp. To move the control points, select the Space Warp object, open the Modify panel, and click the Sub-Objects button. This enables the single subobject selection Control Points, which let you alter the control points individually.

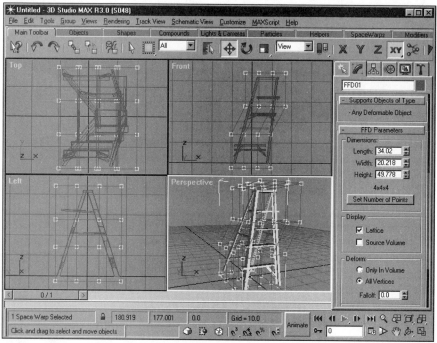

Figure 25-2: A stepladder being deformed with the FFD (Box) Space Warp

Tip   If the All Vertices option is selected, the Space Warp icon can be positioned anywhere within the scene.

FFD (Cyl)

The FFD (Cyl) Space Warp works just like the FFD (Box) Space Warp, except that it is in the shape of a cylinder and its dimension parameters include only Radius and Height.

Figure 25-3 shows the FFD (Cyl) Space Warp at work. Once the Space Warp is modified, you can move it around to alter different sections of the geometry. In this figure, the Space Warp is positioned at the right edge of the ladder, so the right edge is deformed. Moving the Space Warp to the left edge would deform the left edge.

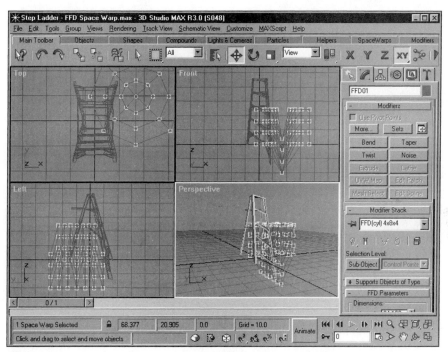

Figure 25-3: The FFD (Cyl) Space Warp deforms the geometry that it touches.

Wave

The Wave Space Warp creates linear waves in the objects to which it is bound. This effect is the same as that created by the Wave modifier. Parameters in the rollout help define the shape of the wave. Amplitude 1 is the wave's height along the X-axis, and Amplitude 2 is the wave's height along its Y-axis. The Wave Length value defines how long each wave is. The Phase value determines how the wave starts at its origin. The Decay value sets how quickly the wave dies out. A value of 0 maintains the same amplitude for the entire wave.

The Sides and Segments values determine the number of segments for the X- and Y-axes. The Division value changes the icon's size without altering the wave effect.

Figure 25-4 shows a Wave Space Warp applied to a simple Box primitive. Notice that the Space Warp icon is smaller than the box, yet it affects the entire object.

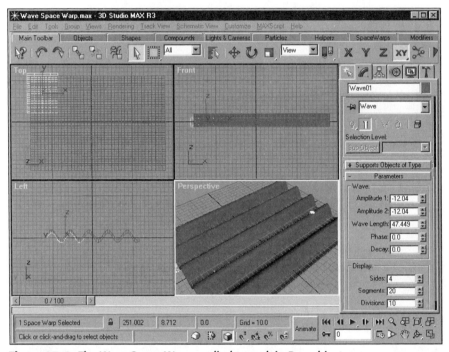

Figure 25-4: The Wave Space Warp applied to a plain Box object

 Caution   Be sure to include enough segments in the bound object, or the effect won't be visible.

Ripple

The Ripple Space Warp also produces waves, but these waves are radial and form concentric circles. The parameters for this Space Warp are the same as those for the Wave Space Warp.

Figure 25-5 uses the Ripple Space Warp to deform a simple box. The position of the Space Warp icon determines the center point for the rippling waves.

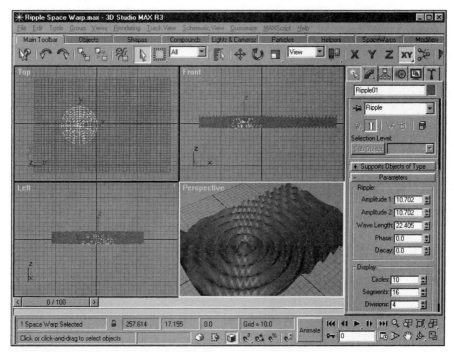

Figure 25-5: The Ripple Space Warp generates concentric circular waves.

Displace

The Displace Space Warp is like a force field: it pushes objects and is useful when applied to a particle system. The strength of the displacement can be defined with Strength and Decay values or with a grayscale bitmap.

The Strength value is the distance that the geometry is displaced and can be positive or negative. The Decay value causes the displacement to decrease as the distance increases. The Luminance Center is the grayscale point where no displacement occurs; any color darker than this center value is moved away and any brighter areas move closer.

The Bitmap and Map buttons let you load images to use as a displacement map; the amount of displacement corresponds with the brightness of the image. There is also a Blur setting for blurring the image. These maps can be applied with different mapping options, including Planar, Cylindrical, Spherical, and Shrink Wrap. You can also adjust the Length, Width, and Height dimensions and the U, V, and W Tile values.

Note The Displace Space Warp is similar in function to the Displace modifier. The Displace modifier is discussed in Chapter 9, "Modifying Objects."

Figure 25-6 shows two Displace Space Warps with opposite Strength values.

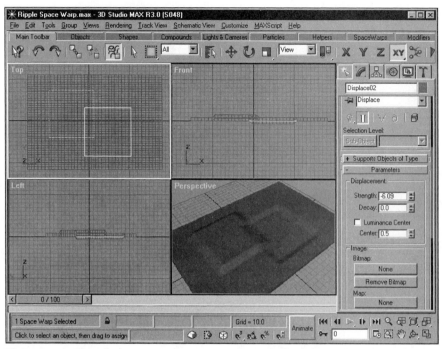

Figure 25-6: The Displace Space Warp can raise or indent the surface of an object.

Conform

The Conform Space Warp pushes all object vertices until they hit another target object called the Wrap To Object, or until they've moved a preset amount. The Conform Parameters rollout includes a Pick Object button that lets you pick the Wrap To Object. The object vertices move no further than this Wrap To Object.

You can also specify a Default Projection Distance and a Standoff Distance. The Default Projection Distance is the maximum distance that the vertices move if they don't intersect with the Wrap To Object. The Standoff Distance is the separation amount maintained between the Wrap To Object and the moved vertices. There is also an option to Use Selected Vertices that moves only a subobject selection.

Note The Conform Space Warp is similar in function to the Conform compound object that is covered in Chapter 15, "Building Compound Objects."

Figure 25-7 shows a simple box being deformed with the Conform Space Warp. A sphere has been selected as the Wrap To Object.

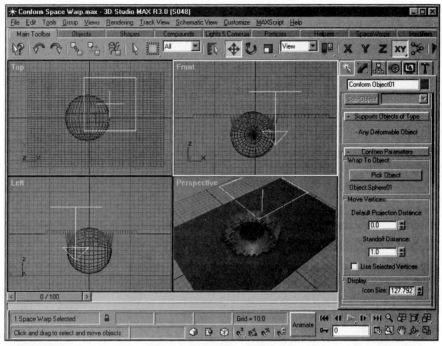

Figure 25-7: The Conform Space Warp wraps the surface of one object around another object.

Bomb

The Bomb Space Warp causes an object to explode from its individual faces. The Strength value is the power of the bomb and determines how far objects travel when exploded. The Spin value is the rate at which the individual pieces rotate. The Falloff value defines the boundaries of faces affected by the bomb. Object faces beyond this distance remain unaffected. The Falloff On option must be selected for the Falloff value to work.

The Min and Max Fragment Size values set the minimum and maximum number of faces caused by the explosion.

The Gravity value determines the strength of gravity and can be positive or negative. Gravity always points toward the world's Z-axis. The Chaos value can range between 0 and 10 to add variety to the explosion. The Detonation value is the number of the frame where the explosion should take place, and the Seed value alters the randomness of the event.

Figure 25-8 shows frame 20 of an explosion produced by the Bomb Space Warp.

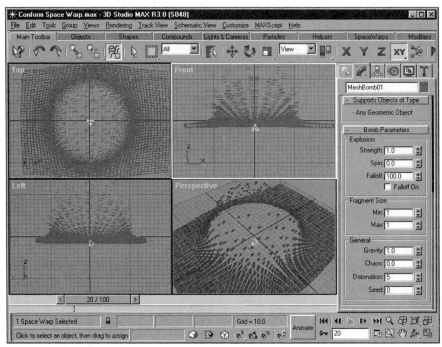

Figure 25-8: The Bomb Space Warp causes an object to explode.

Note   The Bomb Space Warp is seen over time. At frame 0, the object shows no effect.

Particles and Dynamics

The Particles and Dynamics subcategory of Space Warps is designed to be used with particle systems and dynamic simulations. Space Warps in this subcategory include Gravity, PBomb, Wind, Push, and Motor. Figure 25-9 shows the Space Warp icons in the Particles and Dynamics subcategory. These Space Warps are covered in the following sections.

Gravity

The Gravity Space Warp adds the effect of gravity to a scene. This causes objects to accelerate in the direction specified by the Gravity Space Warp. The Parameters rollout includes Strength and Decay values. There are also options to make the gravity planar or spherical. The Range Indicators can be turned on to display a plane or sphere where the gravity is half its maximum value.

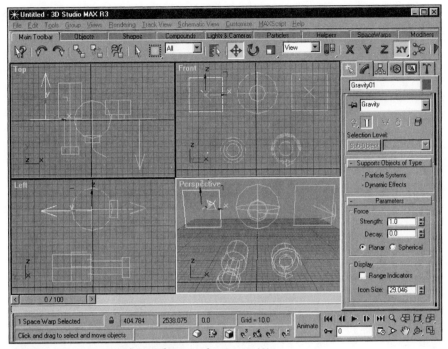

Figure 25-9: The Particles and Dynamics Space Warps

PBomb

The PBomb (particle bomb) Space Warp is similar to the Bomb Space Warp, except that it is designed specifically for the PArray particle system. To blow up an object with the PBomb Space Warp, create an object, make it a PArray emitter, and then bind the PBomb Space Warp to the PArray.

Cross-Reference

More information on the PArray particle system can be found in Chapter 24, "Creating and Controlling Particle Systems."

Basic parameters for this Space Warp include three different blast symmetry types: Spherical, Cylindrical, and Planar. You can also set the Chaos value as a percentage.

In the Explosion Parameters section, the Start Time is the frame where the explosion takes place, and the Duration defines how long the explosion forces are applied. The Strength value is the power of the explosion.

A Range value can be set to determine the extent of the explosion. It is measured from the center of the Space Warp icon. If the Unlimited Range option is selected, the Range value is disabled. The Linear and Exponential options change how the explosion forces die out. The Range Indicator option displays the effective blast range of the PBomb.

Figure 25-10 shows a box selected as an emitter for a PArray. The PBomb is bound to the PArray and not to the box object. The Speed value for the PArray has been set to 0, and the Particle Type is set to Fragments. Notice how the PBomb's icon determines the center of the blast.

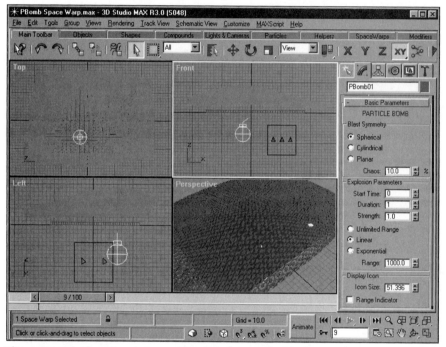

Figure 25-10: The PBomb Space Warp can be used with the PArray particle system to create explosions.

Wind

The Wind Space Warp, like the Gravity Space Warp, causes objects to accelerate. The Wind Space Warp includes additional parameters for adding Turbulence to the effect.

The Parameters rollout includes the same options as the Gravity Space Warp, with the addition of Turbulence, Frequency, and Scale values. The Turbulence value randomly moves the objects in different directions, and the Frequency value controls how often these random turbulent changes occur. Larger Scale values cause turbulence to affect larger areas, but smaller values are more wild and chaotic.

Figure 25-11 shows the Wind Space Warp pushing the particles being emitted from a Super Spray particle system.

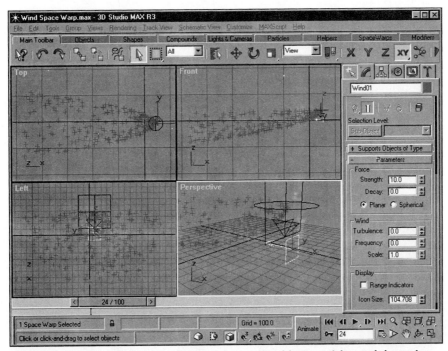

Figure 25-11: The Wind Space Warp can be used to blow particles and dynamic objects.

Push

The Push Space Warp accelerates objects in the direction of the Space Warp's icon from the large cylinder to the small cylinder. Using the Parameters rollout, you can specify the force Strength in units of newtons or pounds.

The On and Off Time sets the frames where the force is applied and disabled, respectively.

The Feedback On option causes the force to change as the object's speed changes. When this option is off, the force stays constant. You can also set a Target Speed, which is the speed at which the force begins to change if the Feedback option is enabled. The Reversible option causes the force to change directions if the Target Speed is reached, and the Gain value is how quickly the force adjusts.

The push force can also be adjusted with Periodic Variations, which cause the push force to increase and then decrease in a regular pattern. You can define two different sets of Periodic Variation parameters: Period 1, Amplitude 1, Phase 1; and Period 2, Amplitude 2, Phase 2.

For particle systems, you can enable and set a Range value. The Push Space Warp doesn't affect particles outside this distance.

Figure 25-12 shows the Push Space Warp pushing the particles being emitted from the Super Spray particle system. Notice that the Feedback On and Periodic Variation options are both enabled.

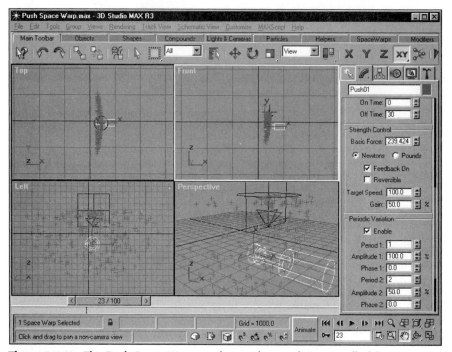

Figure 25-12: The Push Space Warp can be used to apply a controlled force to particles and dynamic objects.

Motor

The Motor Space Warp applies a rotational torque to objects. This force accelerates objects radially instead of linearly. Many parameters for this Space Warp are similar to those for the Push Space Warp. The Strength value is a measurement of torque in newton-meters, foot-pounds, or inch-pounds.

You can also enable Feedback and define Target Revolution units in revolutions per hour (RPH), revolutions per minute (RPM), or revolutions per second (RPS).

Figure 25-13 shows the Motor Space Warp twisting the particles being emitted from the Super Spray particle system in the direction of the icon's arrow.

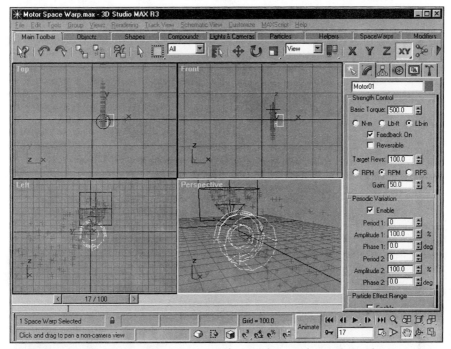

Figure 25-13: The Motor Space Warp can be used to apply a twisting force to particles and dynamic objects.

Modifier-Based

Modifier-Based Space Warps produce the same effects as the standard modifiers, but because they are Space Warps, they can be applied to many objects simultaneously. Space Warps in this subcategory include Bend, Twist, Taper, Skew, Noise, and Stretch. All Modifier-Based Space Warp icons are simple box shapes. The parameters for all Modifier-Based Space Warps are identical to the modifiers of the same name.

Cross-Reference For details on modifiers and their parameters, see Chapter 9, "Modifying Objects."

These Space Warps include a Gizmo Parameters rollout with values for the Length, Width, and Height of the gizmo. You can also specify the deformation decay. The Decay value causes the Space Warp's effect to diminish with distance from the bound object.

The Modifier-Based Space Warp's gizmo can be repositioned as a separate object, but the normal modifiers require that you select the gizmo subobject in order to reposition it. Unlike modifiers, Space Warps don't have any subobjects.

Figure 25-14 shows the icons for the Modifier-Based Space Warps. Notice how they all use the same box-shaped icon.

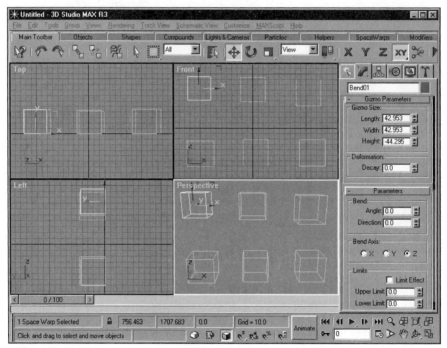

Figure 25-14: The Modifier-Based Space Warps

Bend

The Bend Space Warp brings two ends of an object closer together by bending the object. Figure 25-15 shows the Bend Space Warp being applied to a flat box object with an Angle of 35.

Twist

The Twist Space Warp rotates both ends of an object in opposite directions. Figure 25-16 shows the Twist Space Warp being applied to a flat box object with an Angle of 10. Notice that the Space Warp doesn't need to encompass the box.

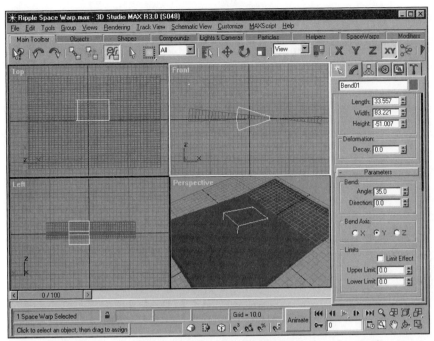

Figure 25-15: The Bend Space Warp can bend an object around any axis.

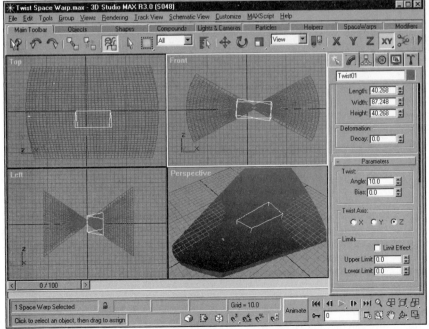

Figure 25-16: The Twist Space Warp twists an object around any axis.

Taper

The Taper Space Warp scales one end of an object. Figure 25-17 shows the Taper Space Warp being applied to a flat box object with an Amount of 0.4 about the X-axis.

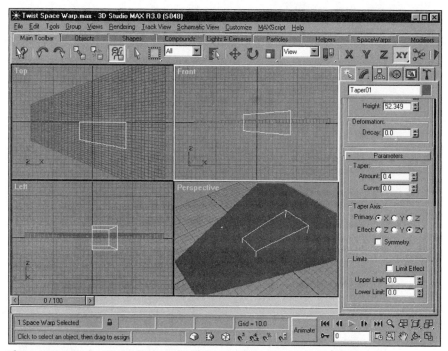

Figure 25-17: The Taper Space Warp tapers one end of an object.

Skew

The Skew Space Warp moves one end of an object while keeping the other end stationary. Figure 25-18 shows the Skew Space Warp being applied to a flat box object with an Amount of 40.

Noise

The Noise Space Warp randomly perturbs the location of individual vertices along an axis or axes. Figure 25-19 shows the Noise Space Warp being applied to a flat box object with Strength of 200 along the Z-axis. The Fractal option is also enabled with an Iterations value of 6.

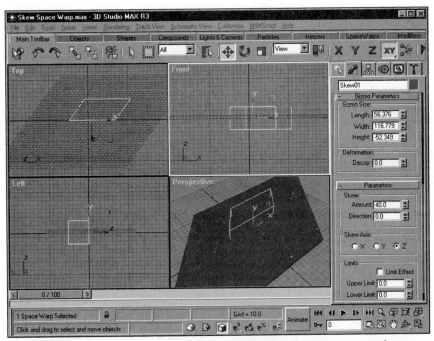

Figure 25-18: The Skew Space Warp skews an object by moving one end.

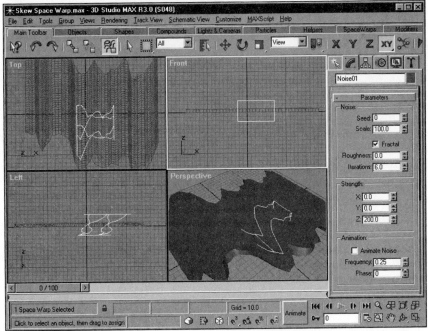

Figure 25-19: The Noise Space Warp randomly positions each vertex of an object.

Stretch

The Stretch Space Warp elongates the object along one axis while simultaneously reducing it along the other axes. Figure 25-20 shows the Stretch Space Warp being applied to a flat box object with a Stretch value of 0.2 along the X-axis.

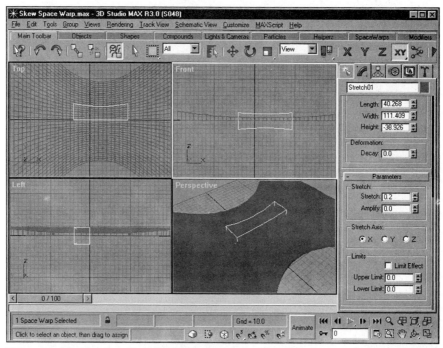

Figure 25-20: The Stretch Space Warp stretches an object along an axis.

Particles Only

The Particles Only group of Space Warps applies only to particle systems. Space Warps in this subcategory include POmniFlect, SOmniFlect, UOmniFlect, Deflector, SDeflector, UDeflector, and Path Follow. Figure 25-21 shows the Space Warp icons that are included in the Particles Only subcategory. These Space Warps are covered in the following sections.

 New Feature The POmniFlect, SOmniFlect, and UOmniFlect Space Warps are new to Release 3.

POmniFlect

The POmniFlect Space Warp is a planar deflector that defines how particles reflect and bounce off other objects. Its Parameters rollout includes a Timing section with Time On and Time Off values and a Reflection section.

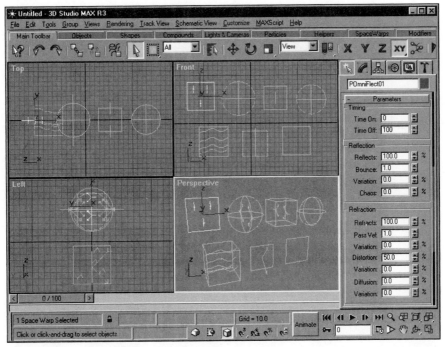

Figure 25-21: The Particles Only Space Warps

In addition to reflection, particles bound to this Space Warp can be refracted through an object. The values entered in the Refraction section of the Parameters rollout change the velocity and direction of a particle. The Refracts value is the percentage of particles that are refracted. The Pass Vel (velocity) is the amount that the particle speed changes when entering the object; a value of 100 maintains the same speed. The Distortion value affects the angle of refraction; a value of 0 maintains the same angle, and a value of 100 causes the particle to move along the surface of the struck object. The Diffusion value spreads the particles throughout the struck object. Each of these values can be varied using its respective Variation value.

Note If the Refracts value is set to 100 percent, no particles are available to be refracted.

You can also specify the Inherit Velocity value. In the Spawn Effects Only section, the Spawns and Pass Velocity values control how many particle spawns are available and their velocity upon entering the struck object.

Figure 25-22 shows a POmniFlect Space Warp bound to a Super Spray particle system. The Reflect percentage for the Space Warp is set to 50, and the remaining particles are refracted through the Space Warp's plane.

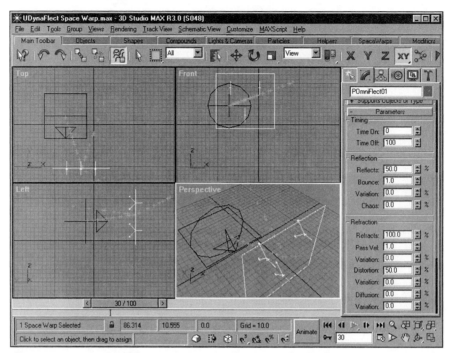

Figure 25-22: A POmniFlect Space Warp reflecting and refracting particles emitted from the Super Spray particle system

SOmniFlect

The SOmniFlect Space Warp is just like the POmniFlect Space Warp, except it is spherical in shape. Figure 25-23 shows an SOmniFlect Space Warp bound to a Super Spray particle system. The Reflect percentage for the Space Warp is set to 50, and the remaining particles are refracted. Notice how the particles are also reflecting off the opposite side of the sphere.

UOmniFlect

The UOmniFlect Space Warp is another deflector, but this one can assume the shape of another object. The Parameters rollout includes a Pick Object button that is used to select an object to use as a deflector.

In the Common section, you can also set a Friction value and an Inherit Velocity value, which causes objects to be reflected at odd angles and velocities.

Figure 25-24 shows a UOmniFlect Space Warp bound to a Super Spray particle system with a tube object selected as the deflector. The Reflect percentage for the Space Warp is set to 50, and the remaining particles are refracted through the Space Warp's plane.

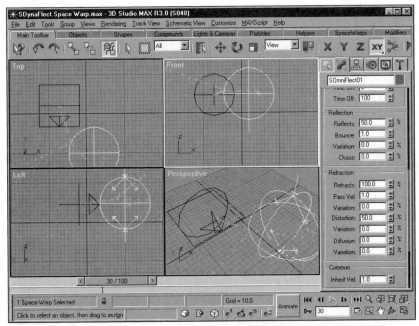

Figure 25-23: An SOmniFlect Space Warp reflecting and refracting particles emitted from the Super Spray particle system

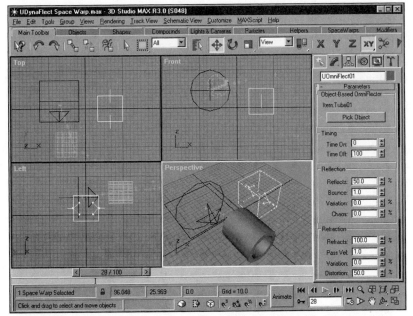

Figure 25-24: A UOmniFlect Space Warp reflecting and refracting particles emitted from the Super Spray particle system through a tube object

Deflector

The Deflector Space Warp is a simplified version of the POmniFlect Space Warp. Its parameters include Bounce, Width, and Length.

SDeflector

The SDeflector Space Warp is a simplified version of the SOmniFlect Space Warp. It includes values for Bounce, Variation, Chaos, and Inherit Velocity.

UDeflector

The UDeflector Space Warp is a simplified version of the UOmniFlect Space Warp. It has a Pick Object button for selecting the object to act as the deflector and all the same parameters as the SDeflector Space Warp, with the addition of a Friction value.

Path Follow

The Path Follow Space Warp causes particles to follow a path defined by a spline. The Basic Parameters rollout for this Space Warp includes a Pick Shape Object button for selecting the spline path to use. You can also specify a Range value or the Unlimited Range option. The Range distance is measured from the path to the particle.

In the Motion Timing section, the Start Frame value is the frame where the particles start following the path, the Travel Time is the number of frames required to travel the entire path, and the Last Frame is where the particles no longer follow the path. There is also a Variation value to add variety.

The Basic Parameters rollout also includes a Particle Motion section with two options for controlling how the particles proceed down the path: Along Offset Splines and Along Parallel Splines. The first causes the particles to move along splines that are offset from the original and the second moves all particles from their initial location along parallel path splines. The Constant Speed option makes all particles move at the same speed.

Also in the Particle Motion section is the Stream Taper value. This value is the amount by which the particles move away from the path over time. Options include Converge, Diverge, or Both. Converging streams move all particles closer to the path, and diverging streams do the opposite. The Stream Swirl value is the number of spiral turns that the particles take along the path. This swirling motion can be Clockwise, Counterclockwise, or Bi-directional. The Seed value determines the randomness of the stream settings.

Figure 25-25 shows a Path Follow Space Warp bound to a Super Spray particle system. A Helix shape has been selected as the path.

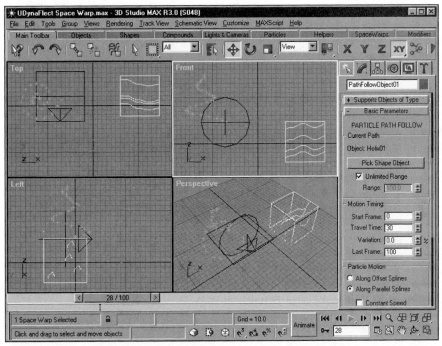

Figure 25-25: A Path Follow Space Warp bound to an emitter from the Super Spray particle system and following a Helix path

Dynamics Interface

Dynamics Interface Space Warps can be used with dynamic systems and particle systems. Space Warps in this subcategory include PDynaFlect, SDynaFlect, and UDynaFlect. Figure 25-26 shows the Space Warp icons that are included in the Dynamics Interface subcategory. These Space Warps are covered in the following sections.

New Feature The PDynaFlect, SDynaFlect, and UDynaFlect Space Warps are new to Release 3.

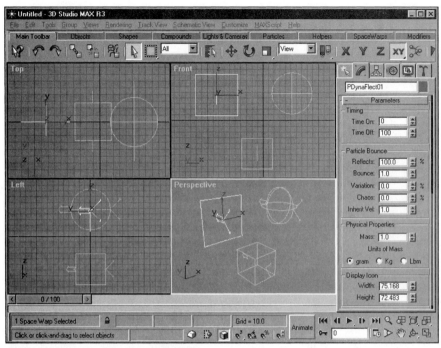

Figure 25-26: The Dynamics Interface Space Warps

PDynaFlect

The PDynaFlect Space Warp enables particles to affect other objects in a scene. It is planar in shape.

In the Particle Bounce section of the PDynaFlect Parameters rollout, the Reflects, Bounce, Variation, and Chaos values control how particles reflect off a surface. The Reflects value determines the percentage of particles that are reflected. The Bounce value is a multiplier that defines a change in the particle's velocity after the impact: values greater than 1 cause the particle to move faster after the impact. The Variation value causes each particle to bounce with a different value, and the Chaos value changes the randomness of the angle at which the particles leave the object. The Inherit Velocity value determines how much of the particle's velocity is inherited by the object being struck. This causes the struck object to move when the particles hit it.

In the Physical Properties section, you can specify the mass of the bound particle in units of grams, kilograms (Kg), or pounds-mass (Lbm).

Figure 25-27 shows a Super Spray particle system emitting a straight line of particles at a PDynaFlect Space Warp. The PDynaFlect Space Warp is set to reflect 100 percent of the particles.

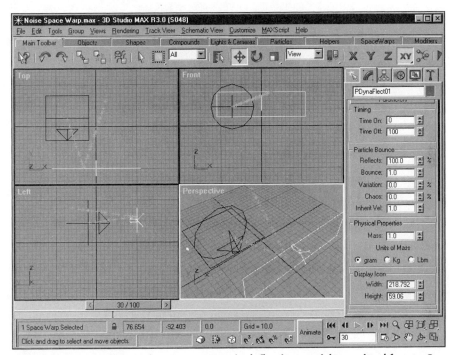

Figure 25-27: The PDynaFlect Space Warp is deflecting particles emitted from a Super Spray particle system.

SDynaFlect

The SDynaFlect Space Warp is similar to the PDynaFlect Space Warp, except its shape is spherical. Figure 25-28 shows a Super Spray particle system emitting a straight line of particles at an SDynaFlect Space Warp.

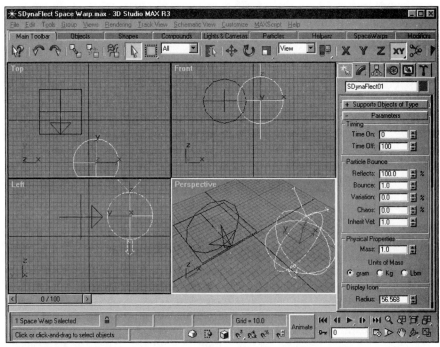

Figure 25-28: An SDynaFlect Space Warp deflecting particles emitted from a Super Spray particle system

UDynaFlect

The shape of this deflector Space Warp can be any other object. Its Parameter rollout includes a Pick Object button used to select the object to use as a deflector. You can also set a Friction value, which causes objects to be reflected at odd angles and velocities.

Figure 25-29 shows a Super Spray particle system emitting a string of particles at a tube object. The tube was selected to be a deflector for the UDynaFlect Space Warp using the Pick Object button.

Working with Space Warps

To conclude this chapter, let's look at some examples that use Space Warps. With all these Space Warps and their various parameters, the possibilities are endless. These examples are only a small representation of what is possible.

Cross-Reference

More examples of Space Warps combined with particle systems are presented in the next chapter, "Particle System Special Effects."

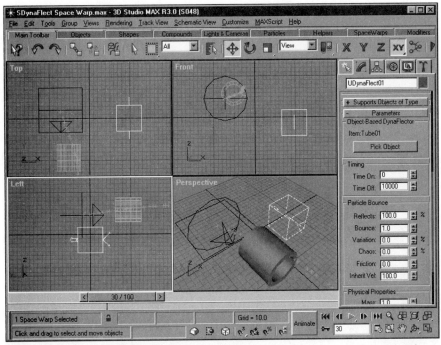

Figure 25-29: A UDynaFlect Space Warp using a tube object as a deflector for the particles emitted from a Super Spray particle system

Tutorial: Creating pond ripples

For this tutorial, we'll position a patch object so it aligns with a background image and apply the Ripple Space Warp to it.

To add ripples to a pond, follow these steps:

1. Open the Create panel, click the Geometry category button, and then select the Patch Grids subcategory. Click the Quad Patch button, and drag in the Top view to create a patch. In the Parameters rollout, set the Length and Width values to **500** and the Segment values to **20**.

2. In the Create panel, select the Space Warps category button, and then click the Ripple button. Drag in the Top view to create a Space Warp object. In the Parameters rollout, set the Amplitudes to **2**, the Wave Length to **30**, and the Decay to **0.2**. Then click the Bind to Space Warp button, and drag from the Space Warp to the patch object.

3. Select Rendering ➪ Environment to open the Environment dialog box. Click the Environment Map button to open the Material/Map Browser, and double-click the Bitmap option. In the Select Bitmap Image File dialog box that opens, locate the bridge background image. This image is from the Corel Photo CD collection.

4. To see the background image in the viewport, select the Perspective view, and then select the Views ➪ Viewport Background command. In the Viewport Background dialog box, select the Use Environment Map and the Display Background options, and click OK.

5. Position the Perspective view so that only the top half of the bridge is visible at the water line.

Figure 25-30 shows the resulting image.

Figure 25-30: A ripple in a pond produced using the Ripple Space Warp

Tutorial: Shattering glass

When glass shatters, it is very chaotic, sending pieces in every direction. For this tutorial, we'll shatter a glass mirror on a wall. The wall will keep the pieces from flying off, and most pieces will fall straight to the floor.

To shatter glass, follow these steps:

1. First create a wall and floor. Open the Create panel, select the Geometry category button, click the Plane button, and then create two plane objects in the Top and Front view to be the wall and floor. In the Modify panel, give each plane object a Scale Multiplier value of **100**.

2. Next, create a mirror using patch objects for single-faced pieces that are similar to an actual mirror. In the Create panel, select the Patch Grids subcategory button, and click the Tri Patch button. Then drag a rectangular patch in the Front view. Create a clone of the patch to act as the mirror's backfacing, and then create a third patch that is slightly larger than the first to act as the mirror's frame. Position the last two patches behind the first.

3. In the Create panel, select the Particle Systems subcategory, and click the PArray button. Then drag in the Front viewport to create the PArray icon. In the Basic Parameters rollout, click the Pick Object button and select the first patch object. In the Viewport Display section, select the Mesh option. In the Particle Generation rollout, set the Speed and Divergence to **0**. Also set the Emit Start to **30** and the Life value to **100**, so it matches the last frame. In the Particle Type rollout, select the Object Fragments option, and set the Thickness to **1.0**. Then in the Object Fragment Controls section, select the Number of Chunks option with a Minimum value of **30**. In the Rotation and Collision rollout, set the Spin Time to **100** and the Variation to **50**. These settings cause the patch to emit 30 object fragments with a slow, gradual rotation.

4. Select the Space Warps category button, and choose the Particles and Dynamics subcategory from the drop-down list. Click the PBomb button, and create a PBomb Space Warp in the Top view, then center it above the Mirror patch. In the Modify panel, set the Blast Symmetry option to Spherical with a Chaos value of **50** percent. Set the Start Time to **30** with a Strength value of **0.2**. Then click the Bind to Space Warp button, and drag from the PBomb Space Warp to the PArray icon.

5. In the Create panel, click the Gravity button, and create a Gravity Space Warp in the Front view. Position the Gravity Space Warp so that the icon arrow is pointing down. In the Modify panel, set the Strength value to **0.1**. Then bind this Space Warp to the PArray icon.

6. In the Create panel, select the Dynamics Interface subcategory from the drop-down list, and click the PDynaFlect button. Drag this Space Warp in the Top view, and make it wide enough to be completely under the mirror object. Rotate the PDynaFlect Space Warp so that a single large arrow is pointing up at the mirror. Position it so that it lies in the same plane as the plane object that makes up the floor. In the Modify panel, set the Reflects value to **100** percent and the Bounce value to **0**. Bind this Space Warp to the PArray as well; this keeps the pieces from falling through the floor.

7. Use the Sphere button to create a simple sphere, and position it in front of the mirror. Click the Animate button, and move the Time Slider to frame 30. Move the sphere until it contacts the mirror. Then drag the Time Slider to 100, and

move the sphere away from the mirror. Click the Animate button again to disable it.

8. With the sphere selected, move the Time Slider to frame 30, right-click the small oval key in the Track Bar (the Track Bar is directly under the Time Slider), and select the Sphere01 Position option. Click the In and Out buttons, and select the second option (Ease In and Ease Out) for both; this causes the sphere to bounce off the mirror.

Figure 25-31 shows the mirror immediately after being struck by a ball.

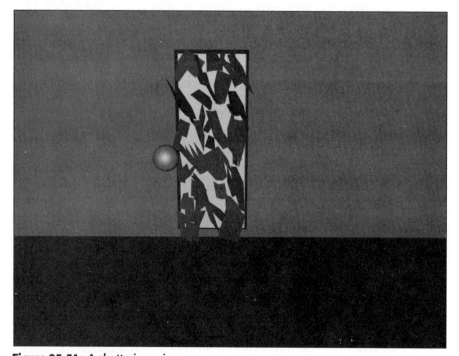

Figure 25-31: A shattering mirror

Summary

Space Warps are useful for adding forces and effects to objects in the scene. In this chapter you

✦ Learned how to create Space Warps

✦ Discovered how to bind Space Warps to objects

✦ Explored in depth all the various Space Warps in several categories

✦ Experimented with some Space Warps to create pond ripples and shatter glass

In the next chapter, we'll combine Space Warps with particle systems to create some additional special effects.

✦   ✦   ✦

Particle System Special Effects

✦ ✦ ✦ ✦

In This Chapter

Exploding a planet

Blowing away a
dandelion puff

Playing with
fireworks

Spraying particles

✦ ✦ ✦ ✦

Some of the most amazing special effects are made possible by combining particle systems with Space Warps. In the last two chapters we've seen isolated examples of each, and this chapter will give you a chance to combine these two to create some interesting effects.

Tutorial: Exploding a Planet

Combining a PBomb with a PArray and a Ringwave object for a shockwave can create an attention-getting explosion.

To explode a planet, follow these steps:

1. Starting in the Create panel, create a GeoSphere and clone it. In the Modify panel, set the Segments value for the cloned Geosphere to **20**.

2. Returning to the Create panel, select the Extended Primitives from the subcategory drop-down list, and click the Ringwave button. Drag in the Front view to create a Ringwave object. Under Parameters, set the Radius to **45** and the Ring Width to **20**. Enable the Grow and Stay option and set the Start Time to **25**, the Grow Time to **10**, and the End Time to **100**. Enable both the Inner and Outer Edge Breakup options. Position the RingWave object so its center coincides with the Geospheres.

3. Select Particle Systems from the subcategory drop-down list and click the PArray button. Create a PArray object in the Front viewport. Then, click the Pick Object button and select the first Geosphere. In the Viewport Display section, select the Mesh particles option. In the Particle Generation rollout, set the Speed to **10** and the Variation

to **100**. Then, set the Emit Start to **30** and the Display Until and Life values to **100**. In the Particle Type rollout, select Object Fragments and set the Thickness to **100** and the number of Chunks to **20**. In the Material Mapping and Source section, select the Picked Emitter option and then set values of **1**, **2**, and **3** for the Outside ID, the Edge ID, and the Backside ID. In the Rotation and Collision rollout, set the Spin Time to **50** with a Variation of **100**.

4. Drag again in the Front viewport to create a second PArray. Under the Basic Parameters rollout, click the Pick Object button and select the second Geosphere. In the Particle Generation rollout, set the Speed to **10** and the Variation to **100**. Then, set the Emit Start value to **25** and the Life value to **30**. In the Particle Type rollout, select Object Fragments, set the Thickness to **1**, and select the All Faces option. In the Material Mapping and Source section, select the Icon option. In the Rotation and Collision rollout, set the Spin Time to **20**. This PArray will be used to create the initial dust cloud.

5. Select the Space Warps category button and choose Particles and Dynamics from the subcategory drop-down. Click the PBomb button and create two PBomb objects, then click the Bind to Space Warp button in the main toolbar and drag from the first PBomb to the first PArray and from the second PBomb to the second PArray. Open the Modify panel and select each PBomb in turn, setting the Start Time for the first PBomb to **30** and the second to **25**. Position both PBomb icons so they are within the Geospheres.

Tip   Make the two PBomb icons different sizes so they are easier to select.

6. Open the Material Editor and select the first sample slot. Name this material **Starfield Background**. Click the Type button, select the New option in the Browse From section, and double-click the Noise selection. In the Noise Parameters rollout, select the Fractal option with a High Noise Threshold value of **0.3**, a Levels value of **2**, and a Size value of **0.1**. In the Output rollout, set the Output Amount to **3**. Then, open the Environment dialog box by selecting Rendering ➪ Environment and drag the starfield map to the Environment map button.

7. Select the second sample slot and name it **Dust**. Click the map button next to the Diffuse color swatch to open the Material/Map Browser and select a Noise map. In the Noise Parameters rollout, set the Size value to **25**. Then click the Go to Parent button to return to the Material Editor. Click the map button next to the Opacity value to open the Material/Map Browser and select the Mask map. In the Mask Parameters rollout, click the Map button and select another Noise map. Then click the Go to Parent button to return to the Mask Parameters rollout and click the Mask button. In the Material/Map Browser, select the Gradient option. In the Coordinates rollout, set the Blur value to **5** and, in the Gradient Parameters rollout, enable the Radial option as the Gradient Type. Set the Noise Amount to **0.5** and the Size value to **20**. Then apply this material to the second PArray.

8. Select the third sample slot and name it **Planet Fragments**. Click the Type button to open the Material/Map Browser and select the Multi/Sub-Object material. Click the Set Number button and select a value of **3**. Click the first map button and then click the Map button to the right of the Diffuse color swatch. In the Material/Map Browser, double-click the Planet selection, and then click the Go to Parent button twice to return to the root material. For the second material button, drag a tan-colored material from the sample slots to the second map button, and for the third material, drag a gray-colored material to the third map button. Then apply this material to the first GeoSphere.

9. Select the fourth sample slot and name it **Shockwave**. Set the Opacity to **75**. Click the map button next to the Diffuse color swatch to open the Material/Map Browser and select a Gradient Ramp map. Right-click each of the gradient flags in turn, selecting Edit Properties from the pop-up menu and adjusting the flag colors to create a gradient that goes from white to orange to red to blue. Select a Gradient Type of Radial with Linear Interpolation. Select the Turbulence option for Noise and apply this material to the Ringwave object. Use the Select by Name button to select the RingWave object.

Figure 26-1 shows the resulting planet as the explosion first starts.

Figure 26-1: Exploding a planet with a PBomb and a Ringwave

Tutorial: Blowing a Dandelion Puff

Space Warps can be used with other types of objects besides particle systems. The Scatter Object, for example, can quickly create many unique objects that can be controlled by a Space Warp. In this tutorial, we'll create a simple, crude dandelion puff that can blow away in the wind.

To create and blow away a dandelion puff, follow these steps:

1. Open the Create panel and click the GeoSphere button. Drag in the Front view to create a GeoSphere object. (We'll use a GeoSphere because its faces are regularly spaced as opposed to a normal sphere, which has more faces at the poles and fewer at the equator.) Clone the GeoSphere using the Edit ⇨ Clone command.

2. Click the Box button and drag in the Front view to create a box. In the Parameters rollout, set the Length, Width, and Height values to **100**, **5**, and **5**. Create another box in the Top view with the dimensions of **50**, **5**, and **5**, and position it so the box ends touch. Then clone the second box twice and rotate and position the clones in the Top view so that they are at 120 degrees from each other. Right-click the main box and select Convert to Editable Mesh from the pop-up menu. Open the Modify panel and click the Attach button. Then select the three additional boxes to make one complete mesh object.

3. Open the Create panel. Select the Compound Objects selection from the drop-down list, and click the Scatter button. Click the Pick Distribution Object button and select the GeoSphere to join the puff object with the GeoSphere. In the Scatter Objects rollout, select the Perpendicular and All Face Centers options. In the Transforms rollout, enter an X-axis Rotation value of **180** and a Z-axis Local Translation value of **–50** to position the puff so it protrudes outward from the GeoSphere.

4. In the Create panel, click the Space Warps category and click the Bomb button. Click in the Front view and position the Bomb icon to the left and slightly below the dandelion object. In the Bomb Parameters rollout, set the Strength to **10**, the Spin to **100**, and the Min and Max Fragment Size value to **24**. This is the total number of faces included in the dandelion object.

Figure 26-2 shows one frame of the dandelion puff being blown away.

Tutorial: Creating a Fireworks Fountain

Fireworks are essentially just lots of particles with a short life span and a high amount of self-illumination. (Tell yourself that next time you watch a fireworks display.)

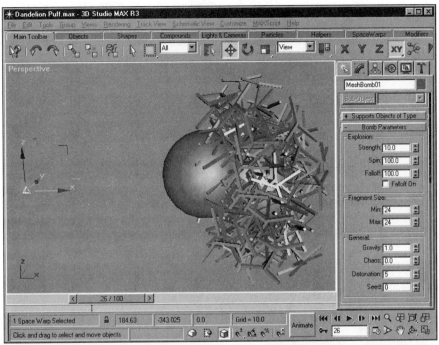

Figure 26-2: Space Warps can be used on Scatter objects as well as particle systems.

To create a fireworks fountain using a particle system, follow these steps:

1. Create a cylinder object to be the base of the fireworks fountain.

2. Select the Particle Systems subcategory and click the Super Spray button. Drag in the Top view and position the system at the top of the cylinder with the direction arrow pointing toward the sky.

3. Open the Modify panel and set the Off Axis Spread to **45** and the Off Plane Spread to **90**. In the Particle Generation rollout, set the number of Particles to **2000** with a Speed of **20** and a Variation of **100**. Set the Emit Start to **0** and the Emit Stop to **100**: set the Display Until to **100** and the Life to **25** with a Variation of **20**. The Size of the particles should be **5**.

4. Return to the Create panel, select the Space Warps category button, and select Particles and Dynamics from the subcategory drop-down. Click the Gravity button and drag in the Top view. Then position a Gravity Space Warp above the cylinder with the direction arrow pointing downward. Open the Modify panel and set the Gravity Strength to **0.5**.

5. Open the Material Editor and select the first sample slot. Name the material **Spark** and set the Diffuse and Self-Illumination colors to bright yellow. Click and hold the Material Effects Channel button and select the 1 button. Apply the "Spark" material to the Super Spray particle system.

6. Open the Rendering Effects dialog box by selecting Rendering ➪ Effects. Click the Add button, select the Lens Effects option, and click OK. Then select Lens Effects from the list and double-click the Glow in the Lens Effects Parameters rollout. Select Glow from the list and, in the Glow Element rollout, set the Size to **0.3** and the Intensity value to **110**. Then (still in the Glow Element rollout) open the Options panel, set the Effects ID to **1**, and enable it.

7. Select the Super Spray icon and right-click it to open the pop-up menu, then select the Properties menu option. In the Object Properties dialog box, select the Object Motion Blur option.

Figure 26-3 shows sparks emitting from the fireworks fountain.

Figure 26-3: The Glow Render Effect can be used to create firework sparks.

Tutorial: Adding Spray to a Spray Can

What good is a spray can without any spray? In this tutorial, we'll create a spray can model and then use the Super Spray particle system to create the spray coming from it. (This particle system could also be used to add a name to the spray can label.)

To create a stream of spray for a spray can, follow these steps:

1. Create a spray can model using a cylinder for the can base and the nozzle and a lathed spline for the top of the can.

2. Select the Particle Systems subcategory button and click the Super Spray button. Drag in the viewport to create the Super Spray icon and position it at the mouth of the nozzle. Set the Off Axis Spread to **20** and the Off Plane Spread to **90**. In the Particle Generation rollout, set the Emit Rate to **1000**, the Speed to **20**, and the Life to **30**. Set the Size of the particles to **5**.

3. Open the Material Editor and click the first sample slot. Name the material **Spray Mist**. Change the Diffuse color to white. Open the Maps rollout and change the Diffuse map amount to **50**. Then click the map button to the right of the color swatch to open the Material/Map Browser and select the Noise map. Click the Go to Parent button, and then click the Opacity map button to open the Material/Map Browser and select the Mask map. In the Mask Parameters rollout, click the Map button and from the Material/Map Browser, select another Noise map, and then click the Go to Parent button. Click the Mask button and, from the Material/Map Browser, select a Gradient map. Set the Gradient Type to Radial, the Amount to **0.5**, and the Size to **20**. Then apply this material to the Super Spray icon.

Figure 26-4 shows the fine spray from an aerosol can.

Figure 26-4: Using a mostly transparent material, you can create a fine mist spray.

Summary

This chapter didn't really present any new material, but expanded on the previous two chapters with some additional examples. Several of these examples used both Space Warps and particle systems. In this chapter you created the following effects:

✦ An exploding planet with PBomb and PArray

✦ A dandelion puff blowing in the wind

✦ A fireworks fountain

✦ A spray can with the Super Spray particle system

This concludes the Particle Systems and Space Warps part of the book. In the next part, we'll start looking at various model systems, beginning with a chapter on linking.

✦   ✦   ✦

Model Systems

Building Linked Hierarchies

A linked hierarchy attaches, or links, one object to another and makes it possible to transform the attached object by moving the one it is linked to. For example, the arm is a classic example of a linked hierarchy—when the shoulder rotates, so do the elbow, wrist, and fingers. Establishing linked hierarchies can make moving, positioning, and animating many objects easy.

Understanding Parent, Child, and Root Relationships

There are several terms used by MAX to describe the relationships between objects. A *parent object* is an object that controls any secondary, or child, objects linked to it. A *child object* is an object that is linked to and controlled by a parent. A parent object can have many children, but a child can have only one parent. Additionally, an object can be both a parent and a child at the same time.

A *hierarchy* is the complete set of related objects that includes these types of relationships. *Ancestors* are all the parents above a child object. *Descendants* are all the children below a parent object. The *root object* is the top parent object that has no parent and controls the entire hierarchy.

Each hierarchy can have several branches or subtrees. Any parent with two or more children represents the start of a new branch.

Note The default hierarchies established using the Link tool are referred to as *forward-kinematics systems,* in which control moves forward down the hierarchy from parent to child. In forward-kinematics systems, the child has no control over the parent. An *inverse kinematics system* (covered in Chapter 29, "Creating an Inverse Kinematics System") enables child objects to control their parents.

All objects in a scene, whether linked or not, belong to a hierarchy. Objects that aren't linked to any other objects are, by default, a child of the *world object,* which is an imaginary object that holds all objects.

Tip The world object can be viewed in the Track view and is labeled Objects. Individual objects are listed under the Objects track by their object name.

There are several ways to establish hierarchies using MAX. The simplest method is to use the Link and Unlink button found on the main toolbar. The Hierarchy panel in the Command panel provides access to valuable controls and information about established hierarchies. To create complex hierarchies, the bones system can help. Each of these various methods is covered in this chapter.

Building Links between Objects

The main toolbar includes two buttons to build a hierarchy: Link and Unlink. The order of selection defines which object becomes the parent and which becomes the child.

Linking objects

The Link command always links children to the parents. To remind you of this order, remember that a mother can have many children but a child can't have more than one mother.

To link objects, click the Link button in the main toolbar. This places you in Link mode, which continues until you turn it off by selecting another button, such as the Select button or one of the Transform buttons. When you're in Link mode, the Link button is highlighted light green.

With the Link button highlighted, click an object, which will be the child, and drag a line to the target parent object. The cursor arrow changes to the link icon when it is over a potential parent. When the mouse button is released, the parent object flashes once, and the link is established. If you drag the same child object to a different parent, the link to the previous parent is replaced by the link to the new parent.

Once linked, all transformations applied to the parent are applied equally to its children about the parent's pivot point. A *pivot point* is the center about which the object rotates.

Unlinking objects

The Unlink button is used to destroy links, but only to the parent. For example, if a selected object has both children and a parent, clicking the Unlink button destroys the link to the parent but not the links to its children.

To eliminate all links for an entire hierarchy, double-click an object and click the Unlink button. Double-clicking an object selects the object along with all its children.

Tutorial: Creating a solar system

Because the planets in the solar system all rotate about the sun, a solar system is a good model to show the benefits of linking. Once all planets are linked to the sun, the entire system can be repositioned simply by moving the sun.

To create a solar system of spheres that are linked together, follow these steps:

1. Open the Create panel, select the Geometry category button, and then click the Sphere button. Create ten spheres all in a line with the relative sizes of the sun and the planets.

2. Click the Link button in the main toolbar, and drag a line from each planet to the sun object.

3. Select the Select and Rotate button, and rotate the sun. At different places in the rotation, stop and select a planet and click the Unlink button.

4. Continue to rotate the sun object until all the planets have been unlinked at various locations around the sun.

5. Finish by selecting the Link button again, linking all the planets back to the sun, and rotating the sun again. Now all the planets lie at separate angles around the sun, but they all rotate together.

Figure 27-1 shows the planets as they orbit about the sun. The Link button made it possible to rotate all the planets simply by rotating their parent.

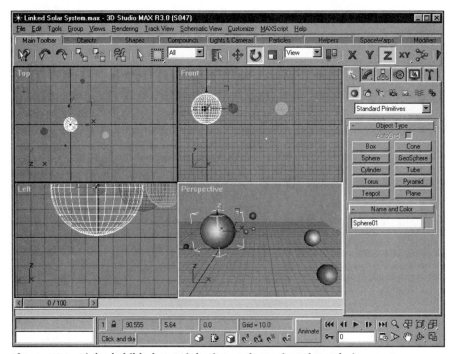

Figure 27-1: Linked child planets inherit transformations from their parent sun.

Displaying Links and Hierarchies

Once links have been established, there are several places to get information about the links in a scene. The Display panel holds a control for displaying links in the viewports.

The Select Objects dialog box, opened with the Select by Name button, displays all objects as a hierarchical list. The Schematic and Track views both display hierarchical lists as well.

Displaying links in the viewport

Links between objects can be seen in the viewports by selecting the Display Links option in the Link Display rollout of the Display panel, as shown in Figure 27-2.

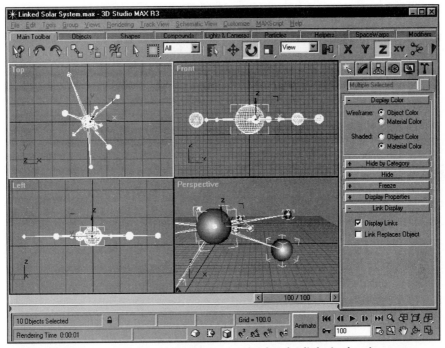

Figure 27-2: The Link Display rollout lets you display the links in the viewports.

The Display Links option shows links as lines that run between the pivot points of the objects with a diamond-shaped marker at the end of each line; these lines and markers are the same color as the object.

The Link Display rollout also offers the option to turn each individual link on or off. Another alternative is to select the Link Replaces Object option, which removes the objects and displays only the link structure. This removes the complexity of the objects from the viewports and lets you work with the links directly. Although this makes the objects disappear, you can still transform the objects using the link markers.

Figure 27-3 shows the solar system we created in the previous tutorial with the Display Links and Link Replaces Objects options turned on for all links.

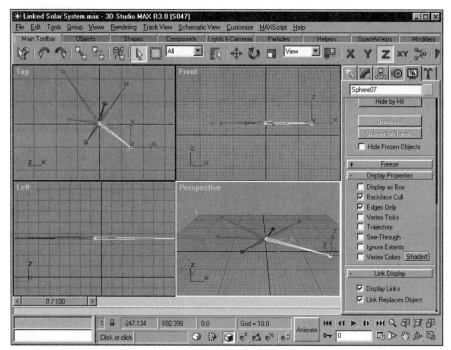

Figure 27-3: The solar system example with all links visible and objects turned off

Viewing hierarchies

The Select Objects dialog box and the Schematic and Track views can display the hierarchy of objects in a scene as an ordered list, with child objects indented under parent objects.

Clicking the Select by Name button in the main toolbar opens the Select Objects dialog box; click the Display Subtree option to see all the children under the selected object. Figure 27-4 shows the Select Objects dialog box with the Display Subtree option selected.

The Schematic view presents a graph in which objects are represented by rectangles with their hierarchical links drawn as lines running between them.

The Schematic view is covered in detail in Chapter 28, "Using Schematic View."

The Track view displays a lot of scene details in addition to the object hierarchy. In the Track view, the hierarchy can be expanded and contracted easily to focus on just the section you want to see or select.

For more information on using the Track view, see Chapter 31, "Working with Track View.

Figure 27-4: The Select Objects dialog box indents all child objects under their parent.

Working with Linked Objects

If your animation starts sending objects hurtling off into space, chances are that you've got a linked object that you didn't know about. Understanding object hierarchies and being able to transform those hierarchies are the keys to efficient animation sequences.

All transformations are done about an object's pivot point. These pivot points can be moved and reoriented as needed by clicking the Pivot button under the Hierarchy panel.

There are several additional settings for controlling links under the Hierarchy panel that are available by clicking the Link Info button. This button opens two rollouts, Locks and Inherit, which can be used to limit an object's transformations and specify the transformations it inherits. The following sections cover these techniques in detail.

Selecting hierarchies

A hierarchy needs to be selected before it can be transformed, and there are several ways to select a hierarchy. The easiest method is to simply double-click an object. Double-clicking the root object selects the entire hierarchy, and double-clicking an object within the hierarchy selects it and all of its children.

Another way to select hierarchies is by right-clicking an object and selecting the Select Children or Deselect Children command from the pop-up menu. This enables you to quickly select only parts of a hierarchy.

Once an object in a hierarchy is selected, pressing the Page Up and Page Down keyboard shortcuts selects its parent or child objects.

Using pivot points

An object's pivot point is the center about which the object is rotated and scaled and about which most modifiers are applied. Pivot points are created by default when an object is created and are usually created at the center of the object. A pivot point can be moved and oriented in any direction, but repositioning the pivot cannot be animated. Pivot points exist for all objects, whether they are part of a hierarchy or not.

Caution   Try to set your pivot points before animating any objects in your scene. If you relocate the pivot point after animation keys have been placed, all transformations are modified to use the new pivot point.

Positioning pivot points

To move and orient a pivot point, open the Hierarchy panel and click the Pivot button, shown in Figure 27-5. At the top of the Adjust Pivot rollout are three buttons; each button represents a different mode. The Affect Pivot Only mode causes any transformation to be applied to the pivot point only. The Affect Object Only mode causes the object to be transformed, but not the pivot point; the Affect Hierarchy Only mode allows an object's links to be moved.

Figure 27-5: The Pivot button under the Hierarchy panel includes controls for affecting the pivot point.

Note   Using the Scale transformation while one of these modes is selected alters the selected object but has no effect on the pivot point or the link.

Aligning pivot points

Below the mode buttons are three more buttons that are used to align the pivot points and that are active only when a mode is selected. These buttons include Center to Object/Pivot, Align to Object/Pivot, and Align to World. The first two buttons switch between Object and Pivot, depending on the mode that is selected.

The Center to Object/Pivot button moves the object or the pivot point so that their centers are aligned. The Align to Object/Pivot button rotates the object or pivot point until the object's local coordinate system and the pivot point are aligned. The Align to World button rotates either to the world coordinate system.

Under these three alignment buttons is another button labeled Reset Pivot, which is used to reset the pivot point to its original location.

Transforming linked objects

When an object is selected and transformed, any child objects are transformed along with it. All transformations are based on the Selection Center as designated on the main toolbar. However, a child object is transformed independently of its parent object.

As an object is moved or rotated, the distance between the object and its children stays constant. When that object is scaled, the distance between it and its children is also scaled.

To transform a parent object without transforming the children, open the Hierarchy panel, and click the Pivot button. In the Adjust Transform rollout (shown previously in Figure 27-5) is a button labeled Don't Affect Children, which enables you to transform a parent object without transforming the children.

The Adjust Transform rollout includes two other buttons — Reset: Transform and Reset: Scale. The Reset: Transform button realigns an object's local coordinate to match the world coordinate system. This realignment applies only to the selected object and not to its children.

The Reset: Scale button is used to reset the scale values for an object that has been scaled using nonuniform scaling. Nonuniform scaling can cause problems for child objects that inherit this type of scaling, and the Reset: Scale button can remedy this by resetting its values. When the scale is reset, there is no visible change to the object, but if you open the Scale Transform field while the scale is being reset, you see the absolute local values being set back to 100 each.

Tip   If you are using an object that has been nonuniformly scaled, it is best to use Reset: Scale before the item is linked.

Locking transformations

Once you have an object in the exact position you want, you can prevent any future transformations to it by using the Locks rollout. To open this rollout, click the Link Info button of the Hierarchy panel. The rollout, shown in Figure 27-6, includes nine checkboxes — one for each axis and transformation type. To lock a specific transformation along a certain axis, select the appropriate checkbox.

Figure 27-6: The Locks rollout can prevent an object from being transformed.

The Locks rollout displays unselected X, Y, and Z checkboxes for the Move, Rotate, and Scale transformations. By selecting the checkboxes, you limit the axes about which the object can be transformed. For example, if you check the X and Y boxes under the Move transformation, the object is able to move only in the Z direction of the local coordinate system.

Note   These locks work regardless of the Axis Constraint settings in the main toolbar.

Inheriting transformations

The Inherit rollout, like the Locks rollout, includes checkboxes for each axis and each transformation, except here all the transformations are selected by default. By deselecting a checkbox, you specify which transformations an object does not inherit from its parent.

For example, suppose a child object is created and linked to a parent and the X Move Inherit checkbox is deselected. As the parent is moved in the Y or Z directions, the child follows, but if the parent is moved in the X direction, the child does not follow. If a parent doesn't inherit a transformation, then its children don't either.

Using the Link Inheritance utility

The Link Inheritance utility works in the same way as the Inherit rollout of the Hierarchy panel, except that it can be applied to multiple objects at the same time. To use this utility, open the Utility panel, and click the More button. In the Utilities dialog box, select the Link Inheritance utility, and click OK. The rollout for this utility is identical to the Inherit rollout discussed in the previous section.

Linking to dummies

Dummy objects are useful as root objects for controlling the motion of hierarchies. By linking a hierarchy to a dummy object, you can control all the objects by moving the dummy.

To create a dummy object, open the Create panel and click the Helpers category button. Within the Object Type rollout is the Dummy button; click it, and then click in the viewport where you want the dummy object to be positioned. Dummy objects are not rendered.

Tutorial: Creating the two-cars-in-a-sphere stunt

Have you ever seen the circus act where two motorcycles race around the inside of a wire sphere without colliding? Well, we're going to do that stunt one better — we're going to do it with cars.

To perform this stunt, we'll create two dummy objects in the center of the sphere, link a car model to each, and rotate the dummy objects. The car we'll be using is the '57 Chevy model created by Viewpoint Datalabs (which we've used in previous chapters).

To link and transform objects using a dummy object, follow these steps:

1. Import the '57 Chevy model. Group the car with the Group ⇨ Group command and name it **57 Chevy**. Clone the car using the Edit ⇨ Clone command.

2. Create a large sphere in the center of the viewport. Scale and position the cars on opposite sides inside the sphere, with one car vertically positioned and the other horizontally positioned.

3. Select the sphere, open the Modifier panel, and click the More button to open the additional Modifiers list. Select the Lattice modifier. In the Parameters rollout, select the Apply to Entire Object option and the Both option to create struts and joints. Set the Strut Radius to **3.0** and the Joint Radius to **5.0**.

4. Open the Material Editor and select the first sample slot. Name the material **Transparent Sphere**. In the Extended Parameters rollout, select the Falloff In option and set the Amount value to **80**. Also select the Additive Type option, and drag the material to the sphere object.

5. Open the Create panel, select the Helpers category button, and click the Dummy button. Then create two dummy objects in the center of the sphere; make them different sizes so that they are easier to select.

Tip

To make the cars move consistently around the sphere, you need to align the center of the sphere with the centers of the two dummy objects. To do this, select the two dummy objects, and select the Tools ⇨ Align command. Then select the sphere object. This opens the Align Selection dialog box. Select the X, Y, and Z Position options and the Center options for both the Current and Target Objects, and then click OK.

6. Click the Link button in the main toolbar, and drag a line from one of the cars to one of the dummy objects.

Tip

Because both the cars and the dummy objects are inside the sphere, it can be difficult to create the link between them. To simplify this process, select and right-click the sphere object, select Properties from the pop-up menu, and select the Hide option in the Properties dialog box. This hides the sphere so that you can create the links between the cars and the dummy objects. Deselect the Hide option to make the sphere visible again.

7. Select one of the dummy objects and open the Hierarchy panel. Click the Link Info button to display the Locks rollout. For the first dummy object, lock the Rotate X- and Z-axes, and for the other dummy object, lock the Rotate X- and Y-axes.

8. Click the Animate button, and drag the Time Slider to frame 100. Rotate each dummy object several revolutions. Then deselect the Animate button and click the Play Animation button to see the results.

By linking the motions of the cars to dummy objects, you don't have to worry about moving the individual cars' pivot points, and, by locking their rotations, you can guarantee that they won't wander and crash into one another. Figure 27-7 shows a frame from the final animation.

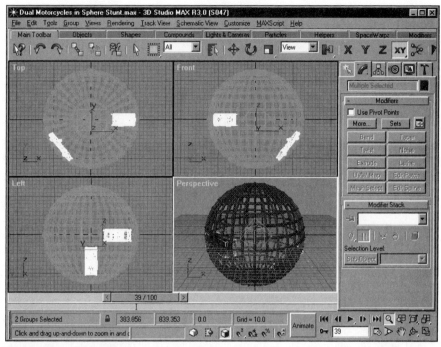

Figure 27-7: With links to dummy objects and transformation locks, these cars can complete the stunt safely.

Building a Bones System

In some instances, it is easier to establish a hierarchy of objects before linking objects together. By building the hierarchy first, you can be sure of the links between objects. One way to build this hierarchy is to use a *bones system*. A bones system consists of many bone objects that are linked together. These bone objects are not rendered and can be assigned the IK Controller for controlling their motion.

To create a bones system, open the Create panel, click the Systems category button, and then click the Bone button. Now click in a viewport to create a root bone, then click a short distance away to create another bone, and repeat this a few more times. Each subsequent click creates another bone linked to the previous one. When you're finished adding bones, right-click to exit bone-creation mode. In this manner, you've created a long chain of bone objects all linked together.

These bones are actually linked joints. Moving one bone pulls its neighbors in the chain along with it. Bones can also be rotated and scaled. Scaling a bones system affects the distance between the bones.

To branch the hierarchy of bones, simply click the link joint or line; this automatically selects and connects any additional bones to the previous bone. Click the Bone button again to create a new bone. Then continue to click to add new bones to the branch.

In the Bones Parameters rollout, shown in Figure 27-8, are three options for applying the IK Controller. You can automatically Assign to Children, Assign to Root, and Create End Effector. Select both the Assign to Children and the Assign to Root options to assign the IK Controller to all bones in the system. If the Assign to Children option is deselected, then the Assign to Root and Create End Effector options are disabled. An End Effector is an imaginary point that controls the placement of the last bone in the chain; it is added to the last bone in a link and is represented by a blue plus sign.

Figure 27-8: The Bones Parameters rollout lets you specify which bones get assigned the IK Controller.

More on the IK Controller is covered in Chapter 29, "Creating an Inverse Kinematics System."

Assigning bone colors

By default, all bone objects and their links appear as yellow objects in the viewports. This color can be changed for individual bones by clicking the color swatch next to the name of the bone.

You can also change the default color for all new bones by choosing Customize ⇨ Preferences Settings, then opening the Color panel, and selecting a new color.

Using an automatic bones system

You can create a hierarchy of bones based on an existing linked hierarchy structure. To create this automatic bones system, open the Create panel, select the Systems category button, and then click the Bone button. Click the Pick Root button in the Bones Parameters rollout (shown previously in Figure 27-8), and click the root object of the link to which you want to add bones.

The Auto Link option automatically links the objects in the original hierarchy to the new bone objects. The Copy Joint Parameters option copies the Rotational or Sliding IK joint parameters to the object. The Match Alignment option matches the bone object's coordinate system to the object's local coordinate system.

Tutorial: Adding bones to a linked teddy bear

Models such as vehicles and life forms have a natural link order and often come already linked. The automatic bones feature is very convenient for these types of models. In this tutorial, we'll import a teddy bear model created by Viewpoint Datalabs. The bear already has links established, and if we intend to animate this bear using the IK Controller, we need to apply some bones.

To apply bones to a linked model, follow these steps:

1. Import the model, and then click the Select by Name button in the main toolbar to open the Select Objects dialog box. To view the current hierarchy, select the Display Subtree option. A breakdown of the hierarchy is displayed in the list. Locate the root object for the model, which is the body object.

2. Open the Create panel, and click the Systems category button. Then click the Bone button; the Bones Parameters rollout appears.

3. Click the Pick Root button, and then click the root object in the viewport. Bones are created for all links.

Figure 27-9 shows the bear with the bone structure in place. Bones are created at the pivot point of each child object.

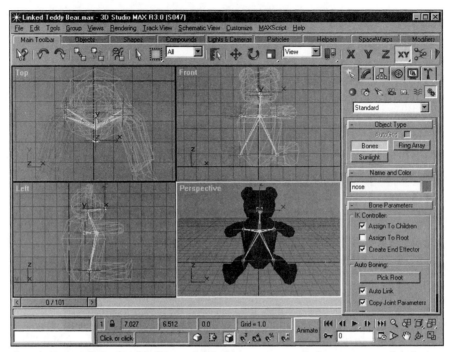

Figure 27-9: A linked teddy bear model after an automatic bones system has been applied

Animating Links

Links can be tricky to animate because linking cannot be animated. Child objects that are transformed move with their parent, but if the child object is unlinked, all animation caused as a result of the link goes away.

For example, if merry-go-round horses are linked to the center of the ride, they rotate consistently if the center parent object is rotated. If one of the horses is unlinked, however, it no longer moves with the rest of the horses and remains static for the entire animation.

Note   Once an animation sequence has been created, enabling the transformation locks in the Hierarchy panel has no effect on the current animation.

Although the process of linking and unlinking cannot be animated, the Link Controller provides a mechanism to switch links halfway through an animation. This enables you to stop the movement of an object even though its parent keeps moving.

Using the Link Controller

For an animated object to switch its link from one parent to another halfway through an animation, you need to use the Link Controller. To apply it, open the Motion panel, and select the Transform controller in the Assign Controller rollout. Next click the Assign Controller button (the small button above the Assign Controller rollout), select Link Control from the list, and click OK. This makes the Link Parameters rollout appear.

The Link Parameters rollout, shown in Figure 27-10, includes Add Link and Delete Link buttons, a list of linked objects, and the Start Time field. To switch the link of an object, enter for the Start Time the frame where you want the link to switch, or drag the Time Slider and click the Add Link button. Then select the new parent object.

Figure 27-10: The Link Parameters rollout lets you change parent objects at different times.

Note   If a link is created using the Link Controller, the object is not recognized as a child in any hierarchies

The Delete key becomes active when a link is selected in the list.

Tutorial: Skating a figure eight

Rotating about a static point is easy enough — just link the object to a dummy object and rotate the dummy object. The figure-eight motion is more complex but can be done with the Link Controller.

To move an object in a figure eight, follow these steps:

1. Import the figure skater model, and create two dummy objects using the Helpers category button in the Create panel.

2. Position the skater model above two equally spaced dummy objects in the Top view.

3. Click the Animate button, drag the Time Slider to frame 100, and rotate the first dummy object two full revolutions. An easy way to do this is to click the Select and Rotate button and right-click it again to open the Rotate Transform field. Enter **720** in the Offset: Screen Z-axis field.

4. Select the second dummy object, and rotate it two full revolutions in the opposite direction. Enter **–720** in the Z-axis field. Click the Animate button again to deactivate it.

5. Select the figure skater model, and open the Motion panel. Select the Transform controller and click the Assign Controller button. From the list, select Link Control, and click OK.

6. In the Link Parameters rollout, click the Add Link button. Click the first dummy object, and set the Start Time value to **0**. Then click the second dummy object, and set the Start Time to **25**. Finally, click the first dummy object again, and set the Start Time to **75**.

Note   Another way to accomplish this same motion is to create a spline of a figure eight and use the Path Controller. This method is described in more detail in Chapter 11, "Working with Spline Shapes.

Figure 27-11 shows the skater as she makes her path around the two dummy objects.

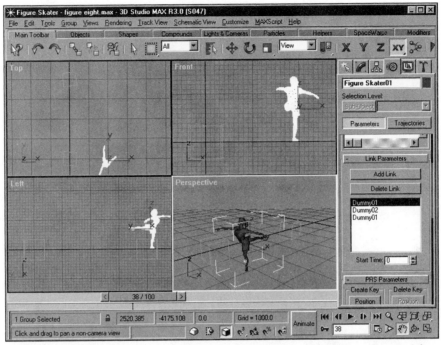

Figure 27-11: With the Link Controller, the figure skater can move in a figure eight by rotating about two different dummy objects.

Summary

Using links correctly can save you from having to duplicate and manually control the placement of many objects. In this chapter, you learned how to create linked structures and the basics of using them. More specifically, you

- ✦ Learned about parent, child, root relationships
- ✦ Built links between objects using the Link and Unlink buttons
- ✦ Viewed links in the viewport
- ✦ Discovered how to move Pivot Points
- ✦ Created a bones system
- ✦ Animated links using dummy objects
- ✦ Used the Link Controller to change parents

This knowledge is important as a preparation for working with inverse kinematics, which is covered later in this book. But first we'll take a look at a new, valuable tool introduced in Release 3 that enables you to view and organize your hierarchies: the Schematic view.

✦   ✦   ✦

Using Schematic View

S chematic view is a new tool in Release 3 that is designed to enable you to select, manage, and navigate among scene objects. It can also be used to rename objects, link objects, or even access an object's modifier stack.

Every object in the Schematic view is displayed as a rectangular box. These boxes, or nodes, are connected to show the relationships among them. They can be rearranged, and the customized views can be saved for later access.

New Feature The Schematic view and all its features are new to Release 3.

Using the Schematic View Window

The Schematic view window is accessed via the Schematic View menu command or by clicking its button in the main toolbar. When the window opens, it floats on top of the MAX interface and can be moved by dragging its title bar. The window is modeless and lets you access the viewports and buttons in the interface beneath it.

The Schematic View menu

The Schematic View menu options enable you to manage several different views. The Schematic View ⇨ New Schematic View command opens the Schematic view window to its default view, shown in Figure 28-1. Enter a name in the View Name Entry field at the top of the window to save the current view.

The Schematic View ⇨ Open Schematic View command opens the current Schematic view window. If several views exist, a dialog appears enabling you to select the view you want to open.

Tip The Schematic view window can be opened within a viewport window by right-clicking the viewport title and selecting Views ⇨ Schematic from the pop-up menu.

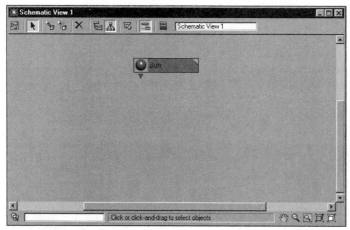

Figure 28-1: The default Schematic view window, showing the root object in the scene

The Schematic View ⇨ Delete Schematic View command opens a Schematic View dialog that displays all the saved views. Select the view you want to delete, and then click the Delete button.

The Schematic view interface

The Schematic view window has buttons across the top of the window. These buttons are shown in Table 28-1 and are described in the following sections.

Table 28-1
Schematic View Buttons

Toolbar Button	Name	Description
	Filters	Opens the Schematic View Settings dialog, where you can toggle which items are displayed or hidden.
	Select	Used to select object nodes.
	Link	Enables you to create links between objects in the Schematic view window. It is also used to copy modifiers and materials between objects.
	Unlink Selection	Destroys the link between the selected object and its parent.

Toolbar Button	Name	Description
✕	Delete Objects	Deletes the selected object in both the Schematic view and in the viewports.
🗂	Hierarchy Mode	Displays all child objects indented under their parents.
🔺	References Mode	Displays all object references and instances. This mode displays all materials and modifiers associated with the objects.
🗖	Synchronize Selection	Synchronizes the selected objects in the Schematic view window with the corresponding object viewports, and vice versa.
🗖	Auto-Arrange Graph Nodes	Automatically rearranges the object nodes into a sensible display to ensure that all objects are visible.
🗖	Toggle Visibility Downstream	Causes all child nodes of the current selection to be hidden. Clicking this button again displays all nodes.
Schematic View 1	View Name Entry Field	Enter a name into this field to name the current display. Named displays show up underneath the Schematic View menu.
🔍	Zoom Selected Viewport Object	Zooms in on the nodes that correspond to the selected viewport objects.
Sun	Search Name Entry Field	Locate an object node by typing its name.
✋	Pan	Move the node view by dragging in the window.
🔍	Zoom	Zoom by dragging the mouse in the window.
🔍	Region Zoom	Zoom to an area selected by dragging an outline.
🗖	Zoom Extents	Increases the window view until all nodes are visible.
🗖	Zoom Extents Selected	Increases the window view until all selected nodes are visible.

> **Tip**
> There are several keyboard shortcuts that work within the Schematic view window. Select Customize ➪ Preferences and click the Keyboard tab to see a list of the currently defined shortcuts. Select the Schematic View option, and the keyboard shortcuts are displayed.

Schematic View settings

The Filters button opens the Schematic View Settings dialog, shown in Figure 28-2, where you can set which items are displayed or hidden. Object categories that can be displayed or hidden include Base Objects, Modifiers, Materials, Maps, Assigned Controllers, and Bone Objects. You can also specify to show only the selected, visible, or animated objects.

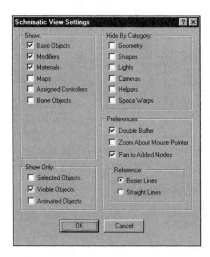

Figure 28-2: The Schematic View Settings dialog lets you display or hide various categories of objects.

The Schematic View Settings dialog also includes several preference settings. These preference settings include Double Buffer, which enables a double-buffer display and helps improve the viewport update performance. The Zoom About Mouse Pointer preference enables zooming by using the scroll wheel on your mouse or by pressing the middle mouse button while holding down the Ctrl key. The Pan to Added Nodes preference automatically resizes and moves the nodes to enable you to view any additional nodes that have been added.

The Reference options let you specify reference lines as Bézier or straight lines.

Selecting nodes

The Select button lets you select objects within the window and in the viewports by double-clicking the object node. Multiple objects can be selected by dragging an outline over them. Holding down the Ctrl key while clicking an object node selects or deselects it.

Different objects can be selected in the viewports and in the Schematic view at the same time. The node of an object selected in the Schematic view turns yellow, while the nodes of objects selected in the viewports are outlined in white. Nodes can be selected in the Schematic view but not selected in the viewports, and vice versa. The Synchronize Selection button synchronizes selections in the Schematic view and the viewports.

Working with Schematic View Nodes

Every object displayed in the scene (as determined by the Filter dialog) has a *node* — a simple rectangular box that represents the object. Each node contains an icon representing the type of object, the object name, and the object color or material, which is shown in the upper-right corner of the rectangular box.

Figure 28-3 shows two nodes close up. The arrow to the right of the Sphere node points to other objects that are instances of this object. If an arrow appears to the right of the node rectangle, then the object has a shared reference somewhere in the scene. Click the arrow to select and highlight all instances and references. These arrows can appear for any instances, including objects, materials, modifiers, and more.

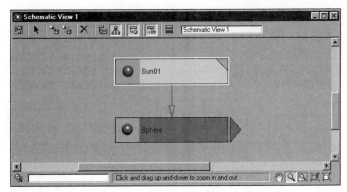

Figure 28-3: Schematic view nodes contain object information, including type, name, color, hierarchy, and references.

Hierarchical relationships are shown as red lines that connect the nodes. Figure 28-3 shows the Sphere object as a node that is part of the Sun01 hierarchy. Other hierarchical elements can include materials, modifiers, controllers, and more. Using the Toggle Visibility Downstream button, you can display or hide these subnodes. When all downstream nodes are hidden, a red arrow appears underneath the node. Clicking this red arrow displays the subnodes.

Rearranging nodes

Nodes can be moved and rearranged in any order. To move a node, simply click and drag it to a new location. When a node is dragged, all selected nodes move together, and any links follow the node movement. Figure 28-4 shows the solar system hierarchy after its nodes have been rearranged.

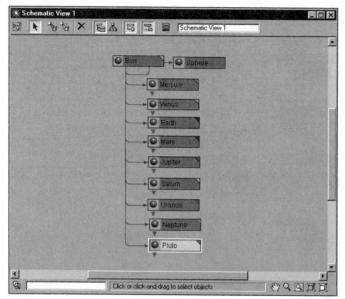

Figure 28-4: The planet nodes have been rearranged in their correct order.

Note Nodes for NURBS objects display the NURBS subobject as well as the actual object. Using Schematic view, you can select and rename these subobjects.

Node colors

Nodes have a color scheme to help identify them. Selected nodes are yellow. Material nodes are fuchsia, modifier nodes are green, geometry objects are light blue, camera nodes are dark green, controller nodes are salmon, Helper nodes are blue, light object nodes are dark yellow, and map nodes are pink.

The Preference Settings dialog can be used to change the node colors. You can access this dialog by selecting Customize ➪ Preferences. These colors are listed in the Other Views section and begin with SV in the drop-down list.

Renaming objects

In the Schematic view window, objects can be renamed quickly and conveniently. To rename an object, click a selected node and click again to highlight the text. When the text is highlighted, you can type the new name for the object.

Changing the object color

The upper-right corner of the node rectangle shows the object color or the material color if one has been assigned. Because the Schematic view window is modeless, you can click the color swatch in the Command Panel to change the object color or access the Material Editor to change the material color. Another method to change the object color is to right-click the node to open the pop-up menu, select Properties, and change the color in the Object Properties dialog.

Deleting nodes

To delete a node, select the node and click the Delete Objects button in the Schematic View toolbar or press the Delete key. If several nodes are selected, they are all deleted.

Creating a hierarchy

To create a hierarchy, use the Link button in the Schematic View toolbar. The Link button works the same way here as it does on the main toolbar—selecting the child node and dragging a line from the child node to its parent makes a link.

The Unlink button destroys the link between any object and its immediate parent. Remember that every child object can have only one parent.

Copying materials between objects

In the Schematic view, materials can only be copied between objects—you cannot apply new materials from the Material Editor to Schematic view nodes. To copy a material, select the material node for one object, click the Link button, and drag the material to the other object.

Materials and modifiers show up only if they are selected in the Schematic View Settings dialog. You can access this dialog by clicking the Filters button.

Figure 28-5 shows one material being copied to another.

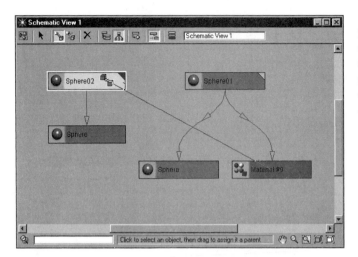

Figure 28-5: The Schematic view window enables you to copy materials from one object to another.

Copying and reordering modifiers

To view the modifiers that are associated with an object, click the arrow at the bottom of the node rectangle. A modifier can be copied to other objects by selecting it from the list, clicking the Link button, and then dragging the modifier to its destination and releasing the mouse. A dialog appears asking whether you want to Copy, Move, or Instance the modifier. Figure 28-6 shows this process.

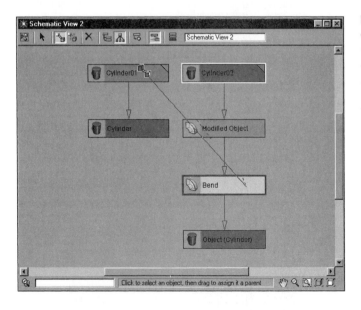

Figure 28-6: Copying a modifier from one object to another can be done in the Schematic view.

The same procedure can be used to reorder modifiers within an object stack. To do this, select the modifier to move, click Link, and drag the selected modifier to the modifier directly below which you want it to appear.

Tutorial: Building an inverted solar system

The solar system provides an orderly example of a linked hierarchy. In this tutorial, we'll turn the tables by reordering the planets using the Schematic view.

To create a hierarchy using the Schematic view, follow these steps:

1. In the Create panel, click the Sphere button and create 11 spheres in a viewport. You'll need a sphere for each of the nine planets, one for the sun, and one for the earth's moon.

2. Open the Schematic view by selecting Schematic View ➪ New Schematic View, and click the Hierarchy Mode button.

3. Rename each sphere by clicking its node and then clicking again to highlight the name. Give the spheres the following names: **Nus, Yrucrem, Sunev, Htrae, Noom, Sram, Retipuj, Nrutas, Sunaru, Enutpen, and Otulp** (which are simply the planet names spelled backwards).

4. Select the Nus node, and move it to the top of the window. Then select all the remaining nodes, click the Link button, and drag a link from the planets to the Nus node to attach them.

5. Select the Noom node, click the Link button, and drag this node to the Htrae node. Creating this new link automatically destroys the previous link. Figure 28-7 shows the final hierarchy.

6. If the nodes are all messed up, you can organize them by clicking the Auto-Arrange Graph Nodes button. You may need to click twice, once to deselect it and a second time to select it again. This causes all the nodes to be arranged neatly within the Schematic view window.

You can now edit the spheres in the viewports to correct the size and distance. Because this is an inverted solar system, remember to place Otulp closest to the Nus and Yrucrem the furthest from the Nus.

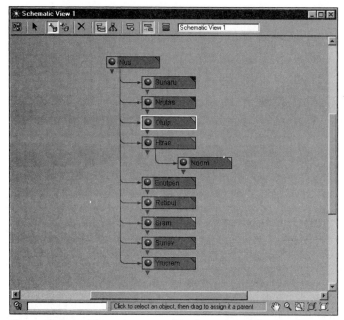

Figure 28-7: A hierarchy created in the Schematic view by linking nodes together

Summary

As objects are positioned in a scene and animated, it can sometimes be difficult to locate objects for modification. The Schematic view offers a unique way to look at all the objects that make up a scene and provides an easy way to select, organize, and understand all the parts that make up a scene.

In this chapter, you

✦ Learned about the Schematic view window interface

✦ Positioned the Schematic view nodes

✦ Renamed objects and changed an object's color

✦ Created a hierarchy

✦ Copied materials and modifiers between objects

Now that you've seen the basics of creating hierarchies and the Schematic view, the next chapter presents the concept and techniques of inverse kinematics.

✦   ✦   ✦

Creating an Inverse Kinematics System

N ow that you've learned about creating linked hierarchies, you're ready to learn about inverse kinematics systems.

Understanding Inverse Kinematics

Kinematics is a branch of mechanics that deals with the motions of a system of objects. In MAX, these systems are defined by links between objects. Once a system is built, the motions of that system can be solved using kinematics. These solutions can then be used to animate the system of objects.

Forward versus inverse kinematics

Forward kinematics causes objects at the bottom of a linked structure to move along with their parents. For example, consider the linked structure of an arm, where the upper arm is connected to a forearm, which is connected to a hand, and finally to some fingers. Using forward kinematics, the lower arm, hand, and fingers all move when the upper arm is moved.

Having the linked children move with their parent is what you'd expect and want, but say the actual object that you wanted to place is the hand. *Inverse kinematics* (IK) enables child objects to control their parent objects. So, using inverse kinematics, you can drag the hand to the exact position you want, and all other parts in the system will follow.

Inverse kinematics can be enabled or disabled using the Inverse Kinematics Toggle button in the main toolbar. When this button is disabled, forward kinematics is in effect; when the button is enabled, inverse kinematics is used.

Inverse kinematics methods

MAX includes three different ways to use inverse kinematics: Interactive IK, Applied IK, and the IK Controller.

Interactive IK

Interactive IK is the method that is used when the Inverse Kinematics Toggle on the main toolbar is enabled. This method lets you position an IK system at different frames, whereupon MAX will interpolate all the keyframes between the various keys. This method isn't as precise, but it uses a minimum number of keys.

Applied IK

Applied IK applies a solution over a range of frames, computing the keys for every frame. This is accomplished by linking the IK system to an object that it follows. This method is more precise than the interactive IK method.

IK Controller

The third way to animate with inverse kinematics is to assign an IK Controller to the system. Using an IK Controller gives the precision of the applied IK method with fewer keys. The IK Controller will be covered in detail later in this chapter.

Creating an Inverse Kinematics System

Before you can animate an inverse kinematics system, you'll need to build and link the system, define joints by positioning pivot points, and define any joint constraints you want.

Building and linking a system

The first step to creating an inverse kinematics system is to create and link several objects together. Links can be created using the Link button in the main toolbar.

With the linked system created, position the child object's pivot point at the center of the joint between it and its parent. For example, the joint between an upper and lower arm would be at the elbow, so this is where the pivot point for the lower arm should be located.

Creating linked systems and moving pivot points are covered in Chapter 27, "Building Linked Hierarchies."

Once the linked system is created and you've correctly positioned your pivot points, open the Hierarchy panel and click the IK button. This will open several rollouts that let you control the IK system, including the Object Parameters rollout shown in Figure 29-1.

Figure 29-1: The Object Parameters rollout lets you control the binding of an IK system.

Selecting a Terminator

Because child objects in an inverse kinematics system can cause their parents to move, moving a child could cause unwanted movements all the way up the system to the root object. For example, pulling on the little finger of a human model could actually move the head. To prevent this, you can select an object in the system to be a Terminator.

A *Terminator* is the last object in the IK system that is affected by the child's movement. Making the upper arm a Terminator would prevent the finger's movement from affecting any objects above the arm.

To set a Terminator, select an object and then enable the Terminator option in the Object Parameters rollout.

For Interactive IK mode, you can also enable the Auto Termination option included in the Auto Termination rollout, shown in Figure 29-2. The Number of Links Up value sets the Terminator a specified number of links above the current selection.

Figure 29-2: The Auto Termination and Sliding Joints rollouts help define the joint constraints.

Defining joint constraints

The next step is to define the joint constraints, which are specified in the Sliding Joints and Rotational Joints rollouts, shown in Figure 29-2. By default, each joint has six degrees of freedom, meaning that the two objects that make up the joint can each move or rotate along the X-, Y-, or Z-axes. Figure 29-2 shows the settings for only one sliding joint axis. The axis settings for all other sliding and rotational joints are identical. Defining joint constraints enables you to constrain these motions in order to prevent unnatural motions, such as an elbow bending backwards. To constrain an axis, select the object that includes the pivot point for the joint and, in the appropriate rollout, locate the section for the axis that you want to restrict and deselect the Active option. If an axis' Active option is deselected, the axis is constrained. You can also limit the motion of joints by selecting the Limited option.

When the Limited option is selected, the object can move only within the bounds set by the From and To values. The Ease option causes the motion of the object to slow as it approaches either limit. The Spring Back option lets you set a rest position for the object — the object will return to this position when pulled away. The Spring Tension sets the amount of force that the object uses to resist being moved from its rest position. The Damping value sets the friction in the joint, which is the value with which the object resists any motion.

Note   As you enter values in the From and To fields, the object will move to that value to show visually the location specified. You can also hold down the mouse on the From and To values to cause the object to move temporally to its limits. These settings are based on the current Reference Coordinate system.

Copying, pasting, and mirroring joints

Defining joint constraints can be work—work that you wouldn't want to have to duplicate if you didn't have to. The Copy and Paste buttons in the Object Parameters rollout enable you to copy Sliding Joints or Rotational Joints constraints from one IK joint to another.

To use these buttons, select an IK system and click the Copy button; then select each of the joints to be constrained in a similar manner, and click the Paste button. There is also an option to mirror the joints about an axis. This is useful for duplicating an IK system for opposite arms or legs of a human or animal model.

Binding objects

When using applied IK, you need to bind an object in the IK system to a follow object. The IK joint that is bound to the follow object will then follow the follow object around the scene. The bind controls are located in the Hierarchy panel under the Object Properties rollout. To bind an object to a follow object, click the Bind button in the Object Properties rollout and select the follow object.

In addition to binding to a follow object, IK joints can also be bound to the world for each axis by position and orientation. This causes the object to be locked in its current position so that it won't move or rotate along the axis that is selected. You can also assign a Weight value. When the IK computations determine that two objects need to move in opposite directions, the solution will favor the object with the largest Weight value.

The Unbind button eliminates the binding.

Understanding precedence

When MAX computes an IK solution, the order in which the joints are solved will determine the end result. The Precedence value (located in the Object Parameters rollout) lets you set the order in which joints are solved. To set the precedence for an object, select the object and enter a value in the Precedence value setting. MAX will compute the object with a higher precedence value first.

The default joint precedence for all objects is 0. This assumes that the objects furthest down the linkage will move the most. The Object Parameters rollout also includes two default precedence settings. The Child to Parent button sets the precedence value for the root object to 0 and increments the precedence of each level under the root by 10. The Parent to Child button sets the opposite precedence, with the root object having a value of 0 and the precedence value of each successive object decreasing by 10.

Tutorial: Building an extensible arm linkage

As an example of a kinematics system, we'll design a simple arm linkage composed of six struts. To the end of this linkage, we'll attach a rubber spider on a string. (This contraption will be perfect for surprising your coworkers in the office.)

To create an inverse kinematics system for an extensible arm, follow these steps:

1. First we'll want to build all the objects for the linkage. Each strut can be constructed from an extruded rectangle. Start with a Rectangle shape (Shapes category) in the Left view with a Length of **100** and a Width of **10**. Set the Rounded Corners value to **3**. Then open the Modify panel and click the Extrude button. Under the Parameters rollout, enter an Amount value of **5**.

2. The next step is to clone the single strut and position it above and overlapping one end of the first strut. To do this, clone the strut with the Edit ⇨ Clone command. Then select the Select and Move button, and right-click to open the Move Transform Type-In. Enter a Y Offset value of **90** and a Z Offset value of **5**. Then close the Type-In dialog box.

3. To duplicate the other struts, select both struts and then select Tools ⇨ Array to open the Array dialog box. In the Incremental section, enter a value of **180** in the Move row for the Y-axis and a Count value of **3** for the 1D dimension, and click OK. This will create all six struts.

4. Create a cylinder with a Radius of **0.2** and a Length of **100**, and then position one end at the end of the last strut. This cylinder will be the string that attaches the spider to the linkage. Then import the spider model and position it at the other end of the cylinder. Select all the spider parts and group them using the Group ⇨ Group command. Name the group **Spider**.

5. The next step is to position all the pivot points for the system. These pivot points will be positioned at the joint locations. To move the pivot points, open the Hierarchy panel and click the Pivot button. Then click the Affect Pivot Only button and move the pivot point for each strut from the center location to the end of the strut where it overlaps with the previous strut. Move the pivot point for the cylinder to the location where it touches the strut. (The spider pivot can stay in the center of the object.) Click the Affect Pivot Only button again to turn it off when you're finished.

6. Now we need to link the system. Select the Link button from the main toolbar and link the spider to the cylinder by selecting the spider and dragging from the spider to the cylinder. The spider then becomes the child to the cylinder. Next link the cylinder to the last strut and so on back to the first strut. To check the linking, open the Schematic View and click the Toggle Visibility Downstream icon to see all the nodes. It should look something like Figure 29-3.

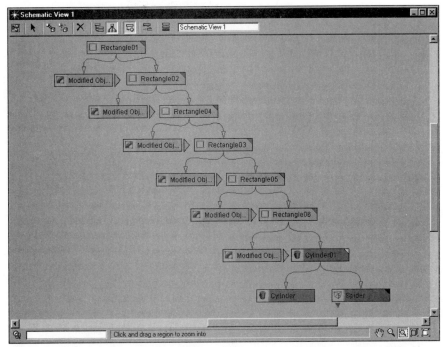

Figure 29-3: Schematic View provides a quick way to check your system links.

7. Next we need to define the joint constraints for the system. With the Hierarchy panel still open, click the IK button. In the Object Parameters rollout, select the first strut and enable the Terminator, Bind Position, and Bind Orientation options — this will prevent the first strut from moving anywhere. In the Sliding and Rotational Joint rollouts, deactivate all the axes except for the Rotational Z-axis. When this is done, the Active box for the Rotational Z-axis will be the only one selected. Then click the Copy buttons for both joint types in the Object Parameters rollout, select the other struts, and click both Paste buttons. This will copy the joint constraints from the first strut to the other strut objects. For the cylinder object, make all Rotational Joint axes active.

8. To test the system, click the Inverse Kinematics Toggle and select and move the spider. All the struts will rotate as the spider moves.

Figure 29-4 shows the struts bending to follow the spider as it is moved downward.

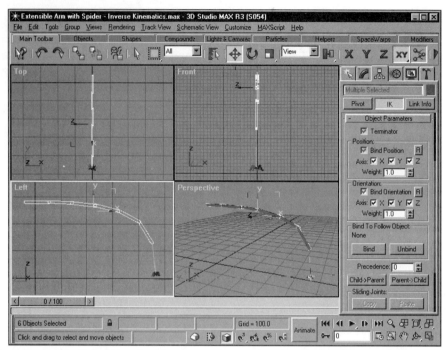

Figure 29-4: The objects in this scene are part of an inverse kinematics system.

Animating IK Systems

The animation process is different for the Interactive and Applied IK methods. Interactive IK interpolates positions between two different keys, whereas Applied IK computes positions for every key.

Animating using interactive IK

Once your IK system is established, animating using the Interactive IK method is simple. First you need to enable both the Inverse Kinematics Toggle button on the main toolbar and the Animate button. Then reposition the system in a different frame, and MAX will automatically interpolate between the two positions and create the animation keys.

Animating using applied IK

To animate using the Applied IK method, you need to bind one or more parts of the system to a follow object, which can be a dummy object or an object in the scene. This binding is done by clicking the Bind button in the Object Parameters rollout or the Hierarchy panel and selecting an object. Once the system has a follow object, select an object in the system. Open the Hierarchy panel and, in the Inverse Kinematics rollout, shown in Figure 29-5, click the Apply IK button. MAX will then compute the keys for every frame between the Start and End frames specified in the rollout. The Apply IK button will start the computation process that will set all the animation keys for the range of frames indicated.

Figure 29-5: The Inverse Kinematics rollout lets you set the Start and End frames for the IK solution.

The Apply Only to Keys option will force MAX to solve IK positions for only those frames that currently have keys. The Update Viewports option displays the solution positions in the viewport as the keys are computed. The Clear Keys option erases all existing keys prior to finding a solution.

Tutorial: Animating the arm linkage using interactive IK

Now that we have built the arm linkage, it would be a waste not to animate this system. In this tutorial, we'll animate the linkage using the interactive IK method.

To animate an IK system using the interactive IK method, follow these steps:

1. With the IK linkage set up, click the Inverse Kinematics Toggle button on the main toolbar and click the Animate button. Then drag the Time Slider to frame 100.

2. Select the spider object at the end of the linkage and move it to the left in the Left view using the Select and Move button. The rest of the linkage will follow.

3. Click the Play Animation button to see the linkage move between the two positions.

Figure 29-6 shows the spider at frame 100. As expected, the linkage followed the spider's move.

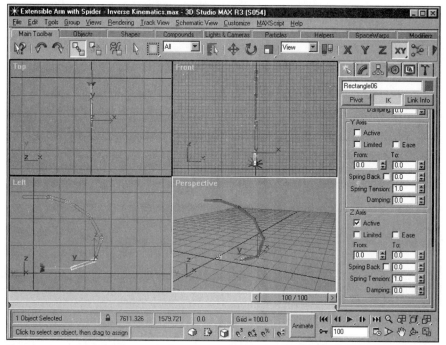

Figure 29-6: Setting keys with the Inverse Kinematics Toggle button enabled can interactively animate IK systems.

Tutorial: Animating a simple propeller system

Machines are good examples of a kinematics system, so in this tutorial, we'll create a simple gear-and-propeller system.

To create an inverse kinematics system with a propeller, follow these steps:

1. First we'll want to build all the objects for this system. To create the gear, open the Create panel, click the Geometry category button and select Extended Primitives from the subcategory drop-down list. Click the RingWave button and drag in the Front view to create the RingWave object. While it is still active, set the Radius to **50**, the Ring Width to **40**, and the Height to **10**. Under the RingWave Timing, select the No Growth option. Enable the Outer Edge Breakup with **12** Major Cycles and a Width Flux value of **15**, and then disable the Inner Edge Breakup. Name the gear **Gear1**.

2. Use cylinder and box primitives to build a handle and the shaft and disc. Position these in the center of the gear. Name the shaft object **Shaft**.

3. Use the Line button in the Shapes category to draw the outline of a propeller blade, and then extrude this shape using the Extrude button with an Amount of **4**. Then apply the Twist Modifier with an Angle of **60** about the Z-axis. Position the single propeller at the top of the disc on the end of the shaft. Next move the propeller's pivot point to the center of the disc by opening the Hierarchy panel, selecting Pivot, clicking the Affect Pivot Only button, and moving the pivot downward in the Top view to the center of the disc. Click the Affect Pivot Only button again to exit pivot mode. Open the Array dialog box by selecting Tools ➪ Array and enter **90** in the Rotate row. Enter a count of **4** in the 1D field and click OK.

4. To simplify the model, attach all the handle parts into a single mesh object. To do this, select and right-click one of the parts of the handle and select Convert to Editable Mesh from the pop-up menu. Then open the Modify panel, click the Attach button, and select the other parts of the handle. Click the Attach button again when you're finished. Repeat this step for the propeller and disc objects. Name the handle object **Handle** and the propeller object **Propeller**.

5. The model is now ready to be linked. Click the Link button in the main toolbar. Then drag from each child object to its parent. Connect the handle to the gear, the gear to the shaft, and the shaft to the propeller.

6. Next we need to position all the pivot points for each object. Open the Hierarchy panel and click the Pivot button. Because we will be dealing with rotational motions only, we need only make sure that the pivot for each part is positioned at the center of each part. If any pivots need to be moved, click the Affect Pivot Only button and move them using the Select and Move button. Be sure to disable the Affect Pivot Only button when you're done.

7. With the Hierarchy panel still open, click the IK button. We'll next constrain the motions of the parts by selecting the handle object. All Sliding Joints can be deactivated, and only the Z-axis Rotational Joint needs to be activated. To do this, make sure a check mark is next to the Active option. Once this is set for the handle object, click the Copy button for both joint types, select the gear object, and click Paste to copy these constraints. Then select the shaft object, click both Paste buttons again, and repeat this process for the propeller.

8. Next we need to create and bind a follow object. Open the Create panel, select the Helpers category button, and then click the Dummy button. Click and drag in the Front view to create the dummy object, and then center it behind the handle object. Click the Animate button, drag the Time Slider to frame 100, and rotate the dummy object about its Z-axis. Click the Animate button again to disable it. Open the Hierarchy panel, select the handle object, click the Bind button in the Object Properties rollout, and drag from the handle to the dummy object.

9. Finally, in the Inverse Kinematics rollout, select the Update Viewports and Clear Keys options and then click the Apply IK button. This will compute the positions and set keys for every frame.

Figure 29-7 shows the propeller system.

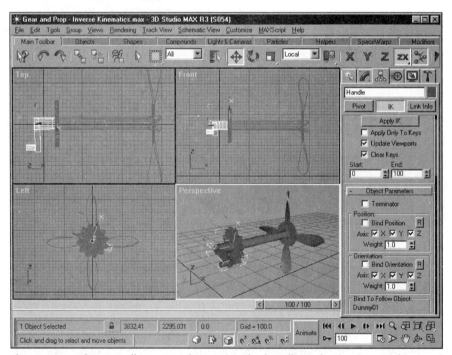

Figure 29-7: The propeller rotates by turning the handle and using inverse kinematics.

IK Preference Settings

The Preference Settings dialog box includes a panel for Inverse Kinematics, shown in Figure 29-8. Using this panel, you can set the Position and Rotation Thresholds for both applied and interactive IK methods. The Position and Rotation Threshold values determine how close the moving object must be to the defined position for the solution to be valid.

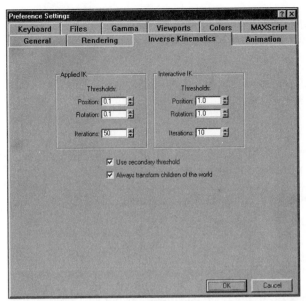

Figure 29-8: The Inverse Kinematics panel of the Preference Settings dialog box lets you set the global Threshold values.

Tip Because the Applied IK method is more accurate, you'll want to set its Threshold values lower than those of the Interactive IK method.

You can also set an Iterations limit for both methods. The Iterations value is the maximum number of times the calculations are performed. This limits the time that MAX spends looking for a valid solution. The Iterations settings control the speed and accuracy of each IK solution.

Caution If the Iterations value is reached without a valid solution, MAX will use the last calculated iteration.

The Use Secondary Threshold option provides a backup method to determine whether MAX should continue to look for a valid solution. This method should be used if you want MAX to bail out of a particularly difficult solution rather than to continue to try to find a solution.

The Always Transform Children of the World option enables you to move the root object when it is selected by itself but constrains its movement when any of its children are moved.

Using IK Controllers

The third IK method is to assign an IK Controller. The IK Controller works with the Bones system. When a Bone is created, it can be assigned a slave IK Controller. All slave IK Controllers are controlled by a master IK Controller.

Chapter 27, "Building Linked Hierarchies," explained how to build a Bones system.

When bones are created, you can specify that they get assigned the IK Controller by selecting the Assign to Children or Assign to Root option in the Bone Parameters rollout, shown in Figure 29-9. The Assign to Root option automatically assigns the IK Controller to all the root's children. If this is disabled, then the normal default Controller gets assigned. The Create End Effector option makes the last child in the chain an end effector. This end effector is the object that you move to control the IK chain. It is displayed as crossing blue axes. The end effector can also be selected in the IK Controller Parameters rollout.

Figure 29-9: The Bone Parameters rollout lets you automatically assign the IK Controller.

The IK Controller Parameters rollout, shown in Figure 29-10, can be accessed in the Motion panel if a bone is selected. Any parameter changes will affect all bones in the current structure. In the Threshold section, the Position and Rotation values set how close the end effector must be to its destination before the solution is complete. In the Solutions section, the Iterations value determines the maximum number of times the solution is attempted. These Threshold and Iteration values are the same as those in the Preference Settings dialog box, except they affect only the current linkage. The Start and End Time values set the frame range for the IK solution.

Figure 29-10: The IK Controller Parameters rollout sets the boundaries of the IK solution.

The Show Initial State option displays the initial state of the linkage and enables you to move it by dragging the end effector object. The Lock Initial State option prevents any linkage other than the end effector from moving.

The Update section enables you to set how the IK solution is updated with Precise, Fast, and Manual options. The Precise option solves for every frame, Fast solves for only the current frame, and Manual solves only when the Update button is clicked. The Display Joints options determine whether joints are Always displayed or only When Selected.

When you first create a Bones system, an end effector is set to the last joint automatically. In the End Effectors section, at the bottom of the IK Controller Parameters rollout, you can set any joint to be a Positional or Rotational end effector. To make a bone an end effector, select the bone and click the Create button. If the bone already is an end effector, then the Delete button is active. You can also link the bone to another parent object outside of the linkage with the Link button. The linked object will then inherit the transformations of this new parent.

The Delete button in the Joints section will delete a joint if clicked. If a bone is set to be an end effector, the Position or Rotation button will display the Key Info parameters for the selected bone.

Summary

Inverse kinematics provides a unique way to control and animate hierarchical structures by transforming the child node. In this chapter, you've

- ✦ Learned the basic concepts behind inverse kinematics
- ✦ Explored the difference between interactive and applied IK methods
- ✦ Created and animated an inverse kinematics system
- ✦ Used the IK settings in the Preferences Settings dialog box
- ✦ Learned how to use the IK Controller

This concludes the model systems part of the book. Later, you'll have a chance to put all these concepts to the test as you learn to create and control characters. But first, we'll start with animation basics in the next chapter.

✦   ✦   ✦

Animation

Animation Basics

✦   ✦   ✦   ✦

✦   ✦   ✦   ✦

In this chapter, we'll start discussing what is probably one of the main reasons that you decided to learn 3D Studio MAX in the first place — animation.

MAX includes many different tools to create animations. This chapter covers the easiest and most basic of these tools.

Using the Animate Button

It isn't just a coincidence that the largest button in the entire MAX interface is the Animate button found at the bottom of the window. This button enables you to create animation sequences easily by simply moving objects with the transform buttons or changing parameters in the Modify panel.

Note
The Track View can be used to tell you if a parameter can be animated or not. Every track that is displayed with a green triangle icon is animatable.

Only when the Animate button is active can animation sequences be created by moving objects. When active, the button is bright red, and the border around the active viewport also turns red to remind you that you are in animate mode.

Tip
You can set the Time Slider bar to be red as well by adding the following to the 3dsmax.ini file:

```
[RedSliderWhenAnimating]
Enabled=1
```

Working with Keys

With the Animate button enabled, every transformation or parameter change creates a key or marker that defines where and how an object should look at that specific frame. Complex animations can be generated with only a handful of keys. Figure 30-1 shows the Animate button, the Time Slider, the Track Bar, and Time Controls.

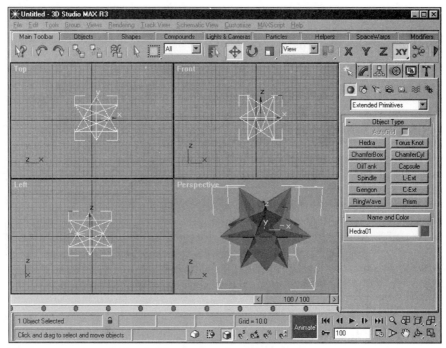

Figure 30-1: Controls for creating basic animations

When the first key is created, MAX automatically goes back and creates a key for frame 0 that holds the object's original position or parameter. By moving the Time Slider, you can set the frame at which to set a key. Upon setting the key, MAX will then interpolate all the positions and changes between the keys. As an example, let's say you have a sphere at the left edge of the viewport that you want to see move to the right. If the Animate button is enabled, the Time Slider is moved to frame 50, and the sphere at the left edge of the viewport is moved to the right edge of the viewport, and then two keys will be created. The first key, at frame 0, defines the sphere's position at the left edge of the viewport, and the second key, at frame 50, defines the sphere's position at the right edge of the viewport. As this animation is playing, the sphere will move across the screen in a straight line between the two positions.

Each frame can hold several different keys, but only one for each type of transform and each parameter. Considering the sphere in our example, at frame 50 this sphere could hold separate keys for position, rotation, and scaling as well as one key for each of the parameters associated with the sphere such as Radius or the Smooth option.

Another way to create keys is to right-click the Time Slider button. This opens the Create Key dialog box, shown in Figure 30-2, where you can set Position, Rotation, and Scale keys for the currently selected object.

Figure 30-2: The Create Key dialog boxes enable you to create a Position, Rotation, or Scale key quickly.

Next to the Animate button is a small key icon that enables and disables key mode. In key mode, the Previous and Next Frame buttons change to Previous and Next Key buttons, enabling you to move quickly between keys. In key mode, the arrows on either side of the Time Slider also move between keys.

Using the Track Bar

The MAX interface includes a simple way to work with keys using the new Track Bar, which is situated directly under the Time Slider. The Track Bar displays a marker for every key for the selected object. (For complete control over all the keys, you would use the Track View dialog box, which is covered in Chapter 31, "Working with Track View.")

 New Feature   The Track Bar is new to Release 3.

Using the Track Bar, you can move, copy, and delete keys. The Track Bar only shows key markers for the currently selected object or objects, with each marker displayed as a small oval-shaped dot. When the mouse is moved over the top of these markers, the cursor changes to a plus sign and you can select it by clicking — selected markers will turn white. To view all the keys associated with the marker, right-click the marker; a pop-up menu appears, displaying the list of keys. Figure 30-3 shows what this pop-up menu looks like.

 Note   In the pop-up menu, a check mark next to a key indicates that the key is shared with another instance.

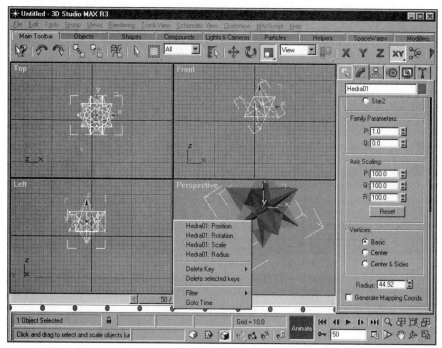

Figure 30-3: Right-clicking the markers on the Track Bar presents a list of keys.

The marker pop-up menu also offers options for deleting selected keys or filtering the keys. In addition, there is a Goto Time command, which automatically moves the Time Slider to the key's location when selected.

To move a key marker, simply select and drag it to its new location. Holding down the Ctrl key lets you select multiple key markers, and holding down the Shift key lets you clone the selected key markers. You can also select multiple key markers by clicking an area of the Track Bar that contains no keys and then dragging an outline over all the keys you wish to select.

To delete a key marker with all its keys, right-click to open the pop-up menu and use the Delete Key ➪ All command, or select the key marker and press the Delete key.

Viewing and Editing Key Values

At the top of the marker's right-click pop-up menu is a list of current keys for the selected object. When you select one of these keys, a key information dialog box opens. This dialog box displays different controls depending on the type of key that is selected. Figure 30-4 shows the dialog boxes for the Position, Rotation, Scale, and Radius keys.

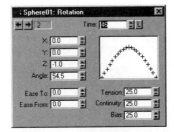

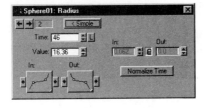

Figure 30-4: Key dialog boxes enable you to change the key parameters.

Note   Key-specific dialog boxes can also be accessed in the Motion panel for a selected object by clicking the Parameters button.

Within each of these key dialog boxes is a Time value that shows the current frame. Next to the Time value are two arrows that enable you to move easily to the other keys in the scene. The dialog box also includes several text fields, where you can change the key parameters.

Several of the key dialog boxes (such as those for the Position, Scale, and Radius keys in Figure 30-4) also include flyout buttons for selecting Key Tangents. Key Tangents determine how the animation moves into and out of the key. For example, if the In Key Tangent is set to Slow and the Out Key Tangent is set to Fast, the object will approach the key position in a slow manner but accelerate as it leaves the key position. The arrow buttons on either side of the Key Tangent buttons can copy the current Key Tangent selection to the previous or next key.

There are six different types of Tangents: Smooth, Linear, Step, Slow, Fast, and Custom. The default type is Smooth, which produces straight, smooth motion. The Linear type moves at a constant rate between keys. The Step type causes discontinuous motion between keys; it occurs only between matching In-Out pairs. Slow decelerates as you approach the key, whereas Fast accelerates. The Custom type lets you control the Tangent handles in function curves mode.

Controlling Time

The Time Slider provides an easy way to move through the frames of an animation. To do this, just drag the Time Slider in either direction. The Time Control buttons include controls for jumping to the Start or End of the animation, or to step forward or back by a single frame. You can also jump to an exact frame by entering the frame number in the frame number field.

The default scene starts with 100 frames, but this is seldom what you actually need. You can change the number of frames at any time by clicking the Time Configuration button, which is to the right of the frame number field. Clicking this button opens the Time Configuration dialog box, shown in Figure 30-5. You can also access this dialog box by right-clicking any of the Time Control buttons.

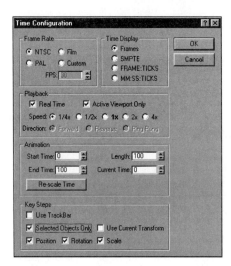

Figure 30-5: The Time Configuration dialog box lets you set the number of frames to include in a scene.

Within this dialog box, you can set the Start Time, End Time, Length, and Current Time values. These values are all interrelated, so setting the Length and the Start Time, for example, automatically changes the End Time. These values can be changed at any time without destroying any keys. For example, if you have an animation of 500 frames and you set the Start and End Time to 30 and 50, the Time Slider will control only those 21 frames. Keys before or after this time are still available and can be accessed by resetting the Start and End Time values to 0 and 500.

The Re-scale Time button fits all the keys into the active time segment by stretching or shrinking the number of frames between keys. You can use this to resize the animation to the number of frames defined by Start and End Time values.

The Key Steps group lets you set which key objects are navigated using key mode. If Use Track Bar is selected, key mode will only move through the keys on the Track Bar. If the Selected Objects Only option is selected, key mode will only jump to the keys for the currently selected object. You can also filter to move between Position, Rotation, and Scale keys. The Use Current Transform option will locate only those keys that are the same as the current selected transform button.

Setting frame rate

Frame rate provides the connection between the number of frames and time. It is measured in frames per second. There are four Frame Rate options available in the Time Configuration dialog box (previously shown in Figure 30-5): NTSC, Film, PAL, and Custom. The NTSC (National Television Standards Committee) standard for television frame rate (30 frames per second) is used throughout most of the world except Europe, which uses the PAL (Phase Alternative Line) standard, whose frame rate is 25 frames per second. The Film standard is 24 frames per second, and the Custom option lets you set your own rate.

Once a frame rate is selected, you can set the Time Display to Frames, SMPTE, Frame:Ticks, or MM:SS:Ticks (Minute and Seconds). *SMPTE* is a standard time measurement used in video and television. A *Tick* is $1/4800$th of a second.

Setting speed and direction

The Playback controls in the Time Configuration dialog box (previously shown in Figure 30-5) let you set the Speed at which the animation plays. Speed options include 1/4x, 1/2x, 1x, 2x, and 4x. You can also set the Direction of the animation to be Forward, Reverse, or Ping Pong. The Active Viewport Only option plays the animation only in the active viewport instead of in all viewports. The Real Time option causes the animation to drop frames in order to maintain the specified frame rate. The Direction options aren't available if the Real Time option is selected.

Using the Motion Command Panel

The Motion panel includes settings and controls for animating objects. At the top of the Motion panel are two buttons: Parameters and Trajectories.

Setting parameters

The Parameters button on the Motion panel lets you assign Controllers and create and delete keys. *Controllers* are like mini animation sequences that can be defined through the Parameters rollout, shown in Figure 30-6. These Controllers are assigned by selecting the position, rotation, or scaling track and clicking the Assign Controller button to open a list of applicable Controllers that you can select.

Figure 30-6: The Parameters section of the Motion panel lets you assign Controllers and create keys.

Cross-Reference

Controllers are discussed in detail in Chapter 32, "Animating with Controllers."

Below the Assign Controllers rollout is the PRS Parameters rollout, where you can create and delete Position, Rotation, and Scale keys. You can create keys whether or not the Animate button is enabled.

Below the PRS Parameters rollout are two Key Info rollouts: Basic and Advanced. Figure 30-7 shows these rollouts, which include the same key-specific information that can be accessed by right-clicking keys in the Track Bar.

Using trajectories

A *trajectory* is the actual path that the animation follows. When you click the Trajectories button in the Motion panel, the trajectory is shown as a spline with each key displayed as a node. The trajectory and its nodes can then be edited by clicking the Sub-Object button at the top of the Motion panel, shown in Figure 30-8. The only subobject available is Keys. With the subobject button enabled, you can use the transform buttons to move and reposition the trajectory nodes. You can also add and delete keys with the Add Key and Delete Key buttons.

Figure 30-7: The Key Info rollouts in the Motion panel include the parameters for the selected key.

Figure 30-8: The Trajectories rollout in the Motion panel enables you to see the animation path as a spline.

For more control over the trajectory path, you can convert the path to a normal editable spline with the Convert To button. You can also convert a spline into a trajectory with the Convert From button.

To use the Convert From button, select an object, click the Convert From button, and then click a spline path in the scene. This will create a new trajectory path for the selected object. The first key of this path will be the selected object's original position, and the second key will be located at the spline's first vertex position. Additional keys will be added as determined by the Samples value listed in the Sample Range group. All these new keys will be equally spaced between the Start and End times. The selected spline will be traversed from its initial vertex around the spline in order to the last vertex.

The Collapse button at the bottom of the Trajectories rollout will reduce all transform keys into a single editable path. For example, an object with several Controllers assigned can be collapsed, thereby reducing the complexity of all the keys.

Caution   If you collapse all keys, you will not be able to alter their parameters via the rollouts.

Animating Objects

Many different objects in MAX can be animated, including geometric objects, cameras, lights, and Space Warps. You can also animate parameters such as materials. In this section, we'll look at several different types of objects and parameters that can be animated.

Animating cameras

Cameras can be animated using the standard transform buttons previously described. When animating a camera that actually moves in the scene, it is best to use a Free Camera. A Target Camera can be pointed by moving its target, but you risk it being flipped over if the target is ever directly above the camera. If you want to use a Target Camera, attach both the camera and its target to a Dummy object using the Link button and move the Dummy object.

Two useful Controllers when animating cameras are the Path Controller and the Look At Controller. The Path Controller can make a camera follow a spline path. (You can see an example of this in Chapter 11, "Working with Spline Shapes.") The Look At Controller can direct the focus of a camera to follow an object as the camera or the object moves through the scene.

Animating lights

The process for animating lights includes many of the same techniques as that for animating cameras. For moving lights, use a Free Spot light or attach a Target Spot light to a Dummy object. The Look At and Path Controller can be used with lights also.

If you need to animate the sun at different times in the day, use the Sunlight System, which is discussed in Chapter 20, "Controlling Lights."

To flash lights on and off, enable and disable the On parameter at different frames and assign a Step Tangent. To dim lights, just alter the Multiplier value.

Animating materials

Changing an object's parameters at different frames with the Animate button enabled can be used to animate materials. Maps and their mapping coordinate systems can also be controlled in this manner.

You can also animate materials by applying an animated bitmap as a material. This can be done using an AVI, FLC, or IFL file. For more detail on these material types, see Chapter 17, "Exploring the Material Editor."

Tutorial: Following a dart

As a simple example of using the Animate button, we'll follow a dart on its path to a dartboard with a flying camera.

To animate a camera to follow a dart, follow these steps:

1. Import the dart and dartboard models created by Zygote Media. The dart should be positioned in the center of the dartboard.

2. From the Create panel, add two Plane objects with Scale Multiplier values set to **500** for the wall and the floor. Move the dartboard and dart about halfway up the wall.

3. Select the dart object, move the Time Slider to frame 100, open the Motion panel, click the Parameters button and, under the PRS rollout in the Create Key section, click the Position button. This will create the key for the dart's final destination.

4. Move the Time Slider back to frame 0, click the Animate button, and move the dart some distance away from the dartboard. Drag the Time Slider to see the dart move towards the dartboard.

5. Drag the Time Slider back to frame 100 and, with the Animate button still enabled, rotate the dart about its local Z-axis several times. This creates the keys to make the dart spin as it flies through the air. Click the Animate button to disable it.

6. With the dart still selected, click the Trajectories button in the Motion panel. Click the Sub-Object button, and then the Add Key button. Click the middle of the trajectory path in the Left view to create a new key. With the new key selected, click the Select and Move button, and drag the new key upward in the Left view to form an arc in the path.

7. Click the Animate button again, zoom in on the dart at frame 100, and rotate the dart object about its local Z-axis to be parallel with the path. Then do the same for the dart at frame 0. Disable the Animate button again.

8. Open the Create panel, click the Camera category button, and click the Free Camera button. Then click in the scene behind the dart at frame 0 to create the camera.

9. Select the dart again and back in the Motion panel, click the Trajectories button and then the Convert To button to create a duplicate of the path. Then select the new path by selecting it from the Select Objects dialog box and, in the Left view, move it to the right so that it is behind the dart. This will be the path we'll have the camera follow.

10. Select the camera object and click the Parameters button. Under the Assign Controller rollout, select the Transform track, and click the Assign Controller button to open the Assign Transform Controller dialog box. Select the Look At Controller and click OK. Then select the Position track, click the Assign Controller button and, from the Assign Position Controller dialog box, select the Path Controller and click OK. In the Look At Parameters rollout, click the Pick Target button and select the dart. In the Path Parameters rollout, click the Pick Path button, and select the new path spline that was moved behind the dart.

11. Right-click the Perspective view title and select Views ⇨ Camera01 to change this view to the camera's perspective. Drag the Time Slider to view the animation from the camera's view.

Tip   If you can't see the dart at frame 0, select the camera and open the Modify panel. In the Parameters rollout, enable the Clip Manually option and set the Near Clip value to 0.

Figure 30-9 shows the dart as it's flying toward the dartboard.

Figure 30-9: One frame of the dart animation

Summary

This chapter covered the basics of animating objects in MAX. More specifically, in this chapter you've learned how to

✦ Use the Animate button

✦ Work with keys and the Track Bar

✦ View and edit key values

✦ Control time

✦ View parameters and trajectories in the Motion panel

✦ Create a simple object animation

After this brief introduction to animation, you're ready to move on to the Track View, which offers the ability to control every aspect of an animation.

✦   ✦   ✦

Working with the Track View

The Track View is a display of all the details of the current scene, including all the parameters and keys. This view lets you manage and control all these parameters and keys without having to look in several different places.

The Track View also includes additional features that enable you to edit key ranges, add and synchronize sound to your scene, and control animation controllers using function curves.

The Track View Interface

The Track View window can be opened using the Track View ⇨ Open Track View command or by clicking the Open Track View button on the main toolbar. Once the Track View is opened, you can give it a unique name using the Name field at the right end of the Track View window toolbar. These named views are then listed in the Track View menu. Any Track Views that are named are saved along with the scene file.

The Track View dialog box can be viewed within any of the viewports by right-clicking the viewport title and selecting Views ⇨ Track ⇨ New or the name of an existing view from the pop-up menu.

Track View toolbar

No single dialog box in MAX uses more buttons than the Track View window, shown in Figure 31-1. This is because the Track View has numerous functions.

Tool bar   Track hierarchy

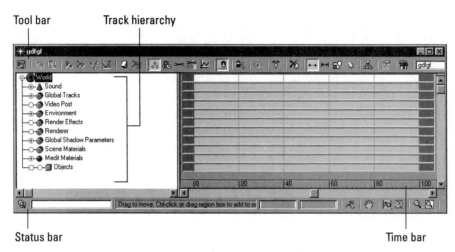

Status bar   Time bar

Figure 31-1: The Track View dialog box offers a complete hierarchical look at your scene.

The Track View toolbar contains two types of buttons: global and dynamic. The global buttons are described in Table 31-1. These buttons always stay the same. The dynamic buttons, on the other hand, change depending on the mode in which you are working; each of these buttons is discussed along with its corresponding mode in the "Track View Modes" section later in this chapter.

Table 31-1
Global Track View Toolbar Buttons

Toolbar Button	Name	Description
	Filters	Opens the Filter dialog box, where you can specify which tracks will appear.
	Copy Controller	Copies the selected track for pasting elsewhere.
	Paste Controller	Pastes the last copied track.
	Assign Controller	Enables you to assign a controller to the selected track.
	Delete Controller	Removes the current controller.

Toolbar Button	Name	Description
	Make Controller Unique	Changes an instanced track to one that is unique.
	Parameter Out-of-Range Types	Opens the Parameter Curve Out-of-Range Types dialog box, where you can make tracks loop and cycle.
	Add Note Track	Adds a note track to the current track for recording information.
	Delete Note Track	Deletes an associated note track.
	Edit Keys	Enables edit keys mode.
	Edit Time	Enables edit time mode.
	Edit Ranges	Enables edit ranges mode.
	Position Ranges	Enables position ranges mode.
	Function Curves	Enables function curves mode.
	Snap Frames	Causes moved tracks to snap to the nearest frame.
	Lock Selection	Prevents any changes to the current selection.
	Track View Utilities	Opens a dialog box of available Track View utilities.

Tracks

Below the toolbar is a hierarchical list of all the tracks. The track names are listed in the pane on the left, while the pane on the right displays the time range, keys, or function curves, depending on the mode. You can pan the left pane by clicking and dragging on a blank section of the pane: the cursor changes to a hand to indicate when you can pan the pane.

Below the right pane is the Time Ruler, which displays the current time as specified in the Time Configuration dialog box.

Tip   You can drag the Time Ruler vertically in the right pane.

Each track can include several subtracks. To display these subtracks, click the plus sign (+) to the left of the track name. To collapse a track, click the minus sign (–).

Note   You can also select, expand, and collapse tracks using the right-click pop-up menu.

The hierarchy includes many different types of tracks. An icon appearing to the left of a track's name identifies its type. Table 31-2 describes the various track types and the icons that identify them.

Table 31-2
Track Icons

Track Icons	Name	Description
●	World	The root of the scene. This holds all tracks.
▲	Sound	Enables you to add sound to the scene.
◉	Container	Can hold several different tracks.
●	Materials	Indicates materials.
▨	Maps	Indicates maps.
▣	Objects	Indicates objects that are visible in the viewports.
▷	Controllers	Indicate controllers.
◆	Modifiers	Indicates modifiers.
▷	Note Tracks	Marks note tracks.

By default, every scene includes the following tracks: World, Sound, Global Tracks, Video Post, Environment, Render Effects, Renderer, Global Shadow Parameters, Scene Materials, Medit Materials, and Objects.

The Shift, Ctrl, and Alt keys make it possible to select and deselect multiple tracks. To select a contiguous range of tracks, select a single track, then select another track while holding down the Shift key. This selects the two tracks and all tracks in between. Hold the Ctrl key down while selecting tracks to select multiple tracks that are not contiguous. The Alt key removes selected items from the selection set.

Status bar

At the bottom edge of the Track View window is the status bar, which includes several fields and buttons for displaying information and navigating the window, as shown in Figure 31-2. Starting from the left is the Zoom Selected Object button. Next is the Select by Name field, where a name can be typed to locate any tracks with that name. To the right of the Select by Name field is the Prompt Line, which displays instructions about what is expected next.

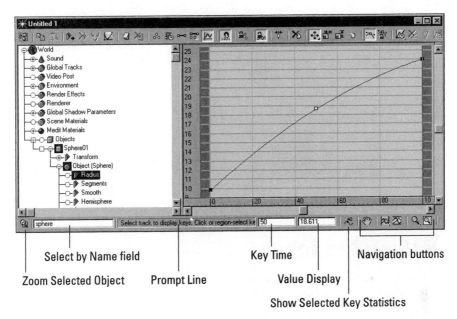

Figure 31-2: The Track View status bar includes buttons for navigating the window.

Note

> The Select by Name field can also use wildcard characters such as * (asterisk) and ? (question mark) to find several tracks.

The Key Time and Value Display fields display the current time and value. You can enter values in these fields to change the value for the current time. You can also enter an expression in these fields in which the variable *n* equals the key time or value. For example, to specify a key value that is 20 frames from the current frame, enter **$n + 20$** (where you supply the current value in place of *n*). You can also include any function valid for the Expression controller, such as sin( ) or log( ).

Cross-Reference

> The functions that are part of the Expression controller are presented in Chapter 33, "Using Expressions."

The status bar buttons are described in Table 31-3.

Table 31-3
Status Bar Buttons

Status Bar Button	Name	Description
	Zoom Selected Object	Places current selection at the top of the hierarchy.
	Show Selected Key Statistics	Displays the frame number and values next to each key.
	Pan	Pans the view.
	Zoom Horizontal Extents	Displays the entire horizontal track.
	Zoom Value Extents	Displays the entire vertical track.
	Zoom, Zoom Time, Zoom Values	Zooms in and out of the view.
	Zoom Region	Zooms within a region selected by dragging the mouse.

Track View Modes

The Track View includes five different modes that enable you to work with keys, time, ranges, position ranges, and function curves. The mode is set using the buttons on the Track View toolbar.

Edit keys mode

The edit keys mode is the default mode when the Track View is opened. It displays keys as small ovals and range bars for each track. Keys appear only within controller tracks.

This mode can be used to add, delete, move, align, slide, and scale the keys. You can also add and delete Visibility Tracks, which make an object visible or invisible, using edit keys mode. Figure 31-3 shows Track View in edit keys mode.

 Tip   The keyboard shortcut for this mode is the P key.

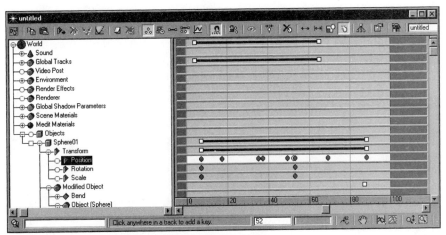

Figure 31-3: Edit keys mode lets you work with keys.

In edit keys mode, several new buttons appear in the Track View main toolbar. These buttons are described in Table 31-4.

Table 31-4 Edit Keys Mode Buttons		
Toolbar Button	**Name**	**Description**
	Add Visibility Track	Adds a track to an object for controlling its visibility.
	Align Keys	Moves all selected keys to the same location.
	Delete Keys	Deletes the selected keys.
	Move Keys	Enables you to move the selected keys.
	Slide Keys	Enables you to slide the selected keys.
	Scale Keys	Enables you to scale the selected keys.
	Add Keys	Enables you to add new keys to a track.
	Modify Subtree	Causes changes to a parent to affect its children.
	Properties	Displays a dialog box of properties associated with the track.

Edit time mode

Edit time mode lets you work with time sections. Keys and range bars are also displayed but cannot be edited. Edit time mode lets you copy and paste time ranges between several different tracks, regardless of type. Figure 31-4 shows Track View in edit time mode. The functions of this mode are discussed later in the chapter in the "Editing Time" section.

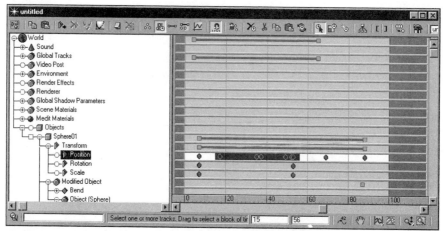

Figure 31-4: Edit time mode lets you work with blocks of time.

Tip   The keyboard shortcut for this mode is the F2 key.

In edit time mode, the buttons described in Table 31-5 become available.

Table 31-5
Edit Time Mode Buttons

Toolbar Button	Name	Description
	Delete Time	Deletes the selected block of time.
	Cut Time	Deletes the selected block of time and places it on the clipboard for pasting.
	Copy Time	Makes a copy of the selected block of time on the clipboard for pasting.
	Paste Time	Inserts the current clipboard time selection.
	Reverse Time	Reverses the order of the selected time block.

Toolbar Button	Name	Description
	Select Time	Enables you to select a block of time by clicking and dragging.
	Scale Time	Scales the current time block.
	Insert Time	Inserts an additional amount of time.
	Exclude Left End Point	Leaves the left end point out of the current time block.
	Exclude Right End Point	Leaves the right end point out of the current time block.
	Modify Subtree	Causes changes to a parent to affect its children.
	Reduce Keys	Optimizes the current time selection by eliminating unnecessary keys.

Edit ranges mode

In edit ranges mode, all tracks appear as range bars. This makes it easy to scale or slide the track, but you cannot edit the keys. Figure 31-5 shows Track View in edit ranges mode. There are no new buttons added to the toolbar in edit ranges mode, except the Modify Subtree button, which was explained earlier.

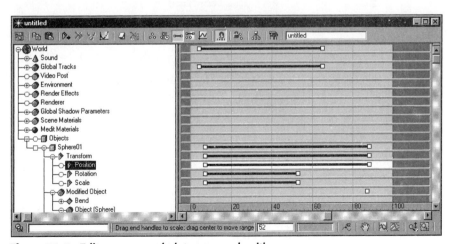

Figure 31-5: Edit ranges mode lets you work with ranges.

Tip   The keyboard shortcut for this mode is the F3 key.

Position ranges mode

This mode also shows all tracks as range bars. In this mode, a range bar can be moved and scaled independently of its keys, ignoring any keys that are out of range. The Recouple Ranges button is added to the toolbar in this mode and can be used to line the keys up with the range again. The left end of the range aligns with the first key and the right end aligns with the last key.

Tip   The keyboard shortcut for this mode is the F4 key.

Figure 31-6 shows the Track View in position ranges mode. All other buttons for this mode are global and are covered earlier in the chapter.

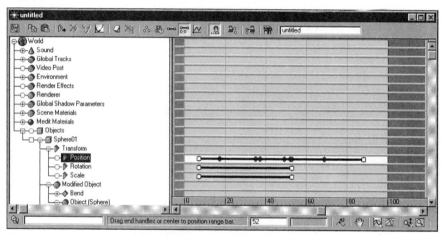

Figure 31-6: Position ranges mode lets you move the ranges without moving the keys.

Function curves mode

Function curves are graphs of a controller's value over time. In function curve mode you can alter the shape of these curves. Each key represents a vertex on the curve. You can edit and add new keys to each curve. If a key is added to a track without any controller, a new controller is automatically assigned to the track. Figure 31-7 shows Track View in function curves mode. The toolbar has been dragged to the left to show its far end.

Tip   The keyboard shortcut for this mode is the F5 key.

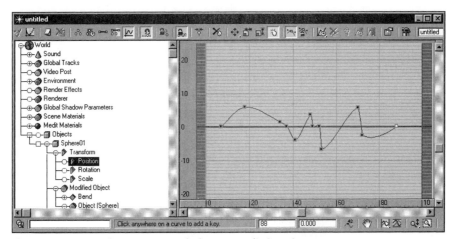

Figure 31-7: Function curves mode lets you edit function curves.

Function curves mode enables several new buttons, which are described in Table 31-6.

Table 31-6
Function Curves Mode Buttons

Toolbar Button	Name	Description
	Freeze Nonselected Curves	Prevents editing of unselected curves.
	Align Keys	Moves all selected keys to the same location.
	Delete Keys	Deletes the selected keys.
	Move Keys, Move Horizontal, Move Vertical	Moves the selected function curve point.
	Scale Keys	Scales the selected keys' positions horizontally.
	Scale Values	Scales the selected keys' values vertically.
	Add Keys	Enables you to add keys to the function curve.

Continued

Table 31-6 (continued)

Toolbar Button	Name	Description
	Show Tangents	Displays the Bézier curve handles.
	Lock Tangents	Prevent the curve handles from moving.
	Apply Ease Curve Apply Multiplier Curve	Applies an ease or multiplier curve.
	Delete Ease/Multiplier Curve	Removes the ease or multiplier curve.
	Enable Ease/Multiplier Curve Toggle	Turns the ease or multiplier curve on or off.
	Multiplier Out-of-Range Types	Opens a dialog box where you can select an out-of-range type.
	Properties	Displays a dialog box of properties associated with the track.

Working with Keys

Keys define the main animation points in an animation. MAX interpolates all the positions and values between the key points to generate the animation. Using the Track View and edit keys mode, you can edit these animation keys with precision. (The buttons that are used to edit keys were previously described in Table 31-4.)

Adding and deleting keys

With edit keys mode enabled and an animation track selected, you can add a key by clicking the Add Keys button and clicking the location where the new key should appear. Each new key is set with the interpolated value between the existing keys.

To delete keys, select the keys, and click the Delete Keys button or press the Delete key on the keyboard. By selecting the track name and pressing the Delete key, you can delete all keys in a track.

Moving, sliding, and scaling keys

The Move Keys button lets you select and move a key to a new location. You can clone keys by holding down the Shift key while moving a key.

The Slide Keys button lets you select a key and move all adjacent keys in unison to the left or right. If the selected key is moved to the right, all keys from that key to the end of the animation slide to the right. If the key is moved to the left, then all keys to the beginning of the animation slide to the left.

The Scale Keys button lets you move a group of keys closer together or farther apart. The scale center is the current frame. The Shift key can be used to clone keys while dragging.

Aligning keys

Selected keys can be moved to the current time using the Align Keys button. This feature works in both edit keys and function curves modes.

Editing keys

To edit the key parameters for any controller, you can click the Properties button; this opens the Key Info dialog box for most controllers. You can also get access to these dialog boxes by right-clicking a key and selecting Properties from the pop-up menu.

Using visibility tracks and the Level of Detail utility

When an object track is selected, you can add a visibility track using the Add Visibility Track button or the Object Properties dialog box. This track enables you to make the object visible or invisible. The selected track is automatically assigned the Bézier controller, but you can change it to an On/Off controller if you want that type of control. You can use function curves mode to edit the visibility track.

The visibility track can be used with the Level of Detail utility to present different resolutions of an object, depending on its distance from the camera. This is especially helpful for game environments where you need a quick-rendering scene.

Note   The Level of Detail feature is part of the VRML implementation, which is one standard that enables 3D graphics over the Web.

Tutorial: Using the Level of Detail utility

Why waste all the rendering power to animate a detailed object that will be only a few millimeters in size in the final image? The Level of Detail utility can display objects of different resolutions. This is a standard feature of game development and online rendered scenes.

For this tutorial, we use the high-resolution cow model created by Viewpoint Datalabs.

To use the Level of Detail utility, follow these steps:

1. Import the cow model and select the "hide" part. This is the part with the highest number of polygons. Name the object **high res hide**.

2. Create two clones of the hide using the Edit ⇨ Clone command, making sure that the clones are copies and not instances. (Using the Clone command instead of the Shift key maintains the position for all three cows.) Name the first clone **med res hide** and the second clone **lo res hide**.

3. Using the Select by Name dialog box, select the "med res hide" model. Open the Modify panel, click the More button to open the additional Modifiers list, and select the Optimize Modifier. Click OK. From the Parameters rollout, apply the Optimize Modifier. Set the Face Threshold to **10**, and press the Enter key to apply it to the model. Select the "lo res hide" model and repeat the process you used with the "med res hide" model, except apply the Optimize Modifier to it with a Face Threshold of **30**.

4. Select all three cow hides, and group them with the Group ⇨ Group command. Give the group the name **cow hide**.

5. Now open the Utilities panel, click the More button, and from the additional utilities list, double-click the Level of Detail utility.

6. Make sure the "cow hide" group is still selected. Then under the Level of Detail rollout, click the Create New Set button. The three hides now appear in the list field. The utility automatically sets some threshold values for each clone. The low-resolution hide appears if the hide is less than 31.5 percent of the Output Size, the medium-resolution hide appears if the hide is between 31.5 and 63.3 percent of the Output Size, and the high-resolution hide appears if the hide is larger than 63.3 percent. Entering new Min and Max Size values can change these threshold values.

Figure 31-8 shows the cow in the viewport and the Level of Detail utility in the Command Panel.

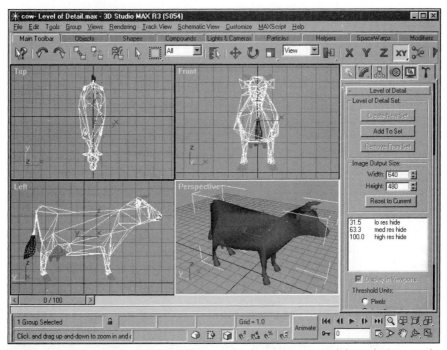

Figure 31-8: The Level of Detail utility can display different model resolutions as the model changes size.

Using the Randomize Keys utility

The Randomize Keys utility lets you generate random time or key positions with an offset value. To access this utility, open the Track View and click the Track View Utilities button (located on the Track View menu bar) to open the Track View Utilities dialog box. Select Randomize Keys from the list of utilities and click OK; this opens the Randomize Keys utility dialog box, shown in Figure 31-9.

Figure 31-9: The Randomize Keys utility can create random key positions and values.

In this dialog box, you can specify positive and negative shift values for both Time and Value. Click the Apply button to apply the randomization process.

Editing Time

In some cases, directly working with keys isn't what you want to do. For example, if you need to change the animation length from six seconds to five seconds, you'll want to work in Track View's edit time mode. To switch to this mode, click the Edit Time button in the Track View toolbar. (The buttons used in this mode are described in Table 31-5.)

Selecting time and the Select Keys by Time utility

Before you can scale, cut, copy, or paste time, you need to select a track and then select a time block. To select a section of time, click the Select Time button and drag the mouse over the time block.

The Select Keys by Time utility lets you select all the keys within a given time block by entering the frame or time values. To use this utility, click the Track View Utilities button to open the Track View Utilities dialog box, and select the Select Keys by Time utility from the list. Then in the Select Keys by Time dialog box, enter the Start and End values to complete the selection.

Deleting, cutting, copying, and pasting time

Once a block of time is selected, you can delete it by clicking the Delete Time button. Another way to delete a block of time is to use the Cut Time button, which removes the selected time block but places a copy of it on the clipboard for pasting. The Copy Time button also adds the time block to the clipboard for pasting, but it leaves the selected time in the track.

Once a time block has been copied to the clipboard, it can be pasted to a different location within the Track View. The track where it is pasted must be of the same type as the one from which it was copied.

All keys within the time block are also pasted, and you can select whether they are pasted relatively or absolutely. Absolute pasting adds keys with the exact values as the ones on the clipboard. Relative pasting adds the key value to the current initial value at the place where the key is pasted.

The Exclude Left End Point and Exclude Right End Point buttons can be enabled when pasting multiple sections next to each other. By excluding either end point, the time block loops seamlessly.

Reversing, inserting, and scaling time

The Reverse Time button flips the keys within the selected time block.

The Insert Time button lets you insert a section of time anywhere within the current track. To insert time, click and drag to specify the amount of time to insert; all keys beyond the current insertion point slide to accommodate the inserted time.

The Scale Time button scales the selected time block. This causes all keys to be pushed closer together or farther apart.

Reducing keys

The Reduce Keys button enables you to optimize the number of keys used in an animation. The applied IK method and the Dynamics utility calculate keys for every frame in the scene, which can increase your file size greatly. By optimizing with the Reduce Keys button, you can reduce the file size and complexity of your animations.

Chapter 34, "Creating a Dynamic Simulation," includes an example of reducing keys.

Clicking the Reduce Keys button opens the Reduce Keys dialog box, shown in Figure 31-10. The threshold value determines how close to the actual position the solution must be to eliminate the key.

Figure 31-10: The Reduce Keys dialog box lets you optimize the number of keys in an animation.

Setting Ranges

The position ranges mode enables you to move ranges without moving keys. For example, this mode lets you remove the first several frames of an animation without moving the keys.

Adjusting Function Curves

When an object is moving through the scene, it can sometimes be difficult to estimate the exact point where its position changes direction. Function curves provide this information by presenting a controller's value as a function of time. Each key is a vertex in the curve.

Function curves mode lets you edit and work with these curves for complete control over the animation parameters. (The buttons used with this mode are described in Table 31-6.)

Inserting new keys

Function curves with only two keys are always linear. You can add some curvature to the line with the addition of another point or key. To add another key, click the Add Keys button, and then click the curve where you want to place the key.

If the curve contains multiple curves, such as a curve for the RGB color values, then a point is added to each curve.

Moving keys

The Move Keys button enables you to move individual keys by dragging them. It also includes flyouts for constraining the key movement to a horizontal or vertical direction.

Scaling keys and values

The Scale Keys button moves the selected keys toward or away from the current time. This moves keys only horizontally.

The Scale Values button moves the selected keys toward or away from the zero value. This moves keys only vertically.

Working with tangents

Function curves for the Bézier controller have tangents associated with every key. To view and edit these tangents, click the Show Tangents button. These tangents are lines that extend from the key point with a handle on each end. By moving these handles, you can alter the curvature of the curve around the key.

The key dialog box, which can be opened by selecting a key and clicking the Properties button or by right-clicking the key, lets you specify two different types of tangent points: Continuous and Discontinuous. Continuous tangents are points with two handles that are on the same line. The curvature for continuous tangents is always smooth. Discontinuous tangents have any angle between the two handle lines. These tangents form a sharp point.

 Tip   Holding down the Shift key while dragging a handle lets you drag the handle independently of the other handle.

The Lock Tangents button lets you change the handles of several keys at the same time. If this button is disabled, adjusting a tangent handle affects only the key of that handle.

Applying ease and multiplier curves

Ease curves can be applied to smooth the timing of a function curve. Multiplier curves can be applied to alter the scaling of a function curve. Ease and multiplier curves can be used to automatically smooth or scale an animation's motion. Each of these buttons adds a new track and function curve to the selected controller track. Figure 31-11 shows the Track View after ease and multiplier curves have been applied.

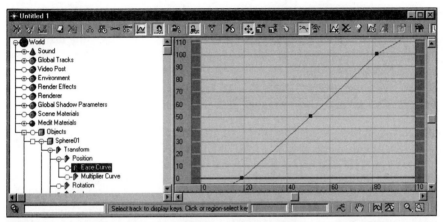

Figure 31-11: When ease and multiplier curves are added to a track, they become subtracks.

Note   Not all controllers can have an ease or multiplier curve applied.

These tracks and curves can be deleted using the Delete Ease/Multiplier Curve button. You can also enable or disable these curves with the Enable Ease/Multiplier Curve Toggle button.

Once an ease or multiplier curve has been applied, you can assign the type of curve to use with the Ease Curve Out-of-Range Types button. This button opens the Ease Curve Out-of- Range Types dialog box, shown in Figure 31-12. The dialog box includes seven different ease curves. By clicking the buttons below the types, you can specify an ease curve for the beginning and end of the curve. The seven ease types include Constant, Cycle, Loop, Ping Pong, Linear, Relative, and Identity. For an explanation of these types, see the section "Using Out-of-Range Types" later in this chapter.

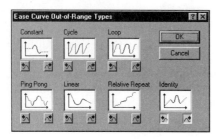

Figure 31-12: The Ease Curve Out-of-Range Types dialog box lets you select the type of ease curve to use.

Note

In the Ease Curve Out-of-Range Types dialog box, there is an option that isn't present in the Parameter Curve Out-of-Range Types dialog box. The Identity option begins or ends the curve with a linear slope that produces a gradual, constant rate increase.

Tutorial: Animating a hyper pogo stick

As an example of working with function curves, we'll create a pogo stick that hops progressively higher.

To animate a hyper pogo stick using function curves, follow these steps:

1. Start by creating a pogo stick model from several cylinders, boxes, and a rendered helix shape. Also create a ground plane using the plane primitive. Position the pogo stick so that it touches the ground plane.

2. Link all the parts to the center pole object using the Link button.

3. Open the Track View, and locate the pogo stick group's Position track (this track can be found under the Objects, Cylinder01, Transform tracks). Click the Assign Controller button to open the Assign Position Controller dialog box. Select the Bézier Position Controller, and click OK.

4. Click the Function Curves button to display the function curve for this track. Notice that there are three different curves: one red, one blue, and one green. These colors correspond to the default coordinate axes displayed in the lower-left corner of the viewport, so red is the X-axis, green is the Y-axis, and blue is the Z-axis.

5. Click the Add Keys button, and then click six different points along any one of the curves. Points are added on all three lines regardless of which line is clicked.

6. Next click the Move Keys button, and drag the second, fourth, and sixth points for the Z-axis (blue line) upward at increasing heights to create three peaks. Also, drag each point on the X-axis (red line) upward to form a straight line of increasing slope. These curves define the motions of the pogo stick, which will bounce up and down along the Z-axis and gradually move to the right along the X-axis. Figure 31-13 shows the function curves.

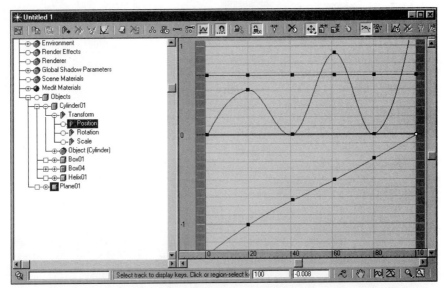

Figure 31-13: The function curves define the motions of the pogo stick object.

7. If you click the Play Animation button at this point, you won't see any motion. This is because the values are so small. Notice how the values in Figure 31-13 range between –1 and 1. This can be fixed by scaling the values. Click the Scale Values button, select all the nonzero points on the X- and Z-axis curves by holding down the Ctrl key and dragging the points upward. Use the Zoom Value Extents button to resize the window, and continue to drag until the first peak is around 200. Figure 31-14 shows the results after scaling the values.

Figure 31-15 shows the pogo stick as it bounces along its way.

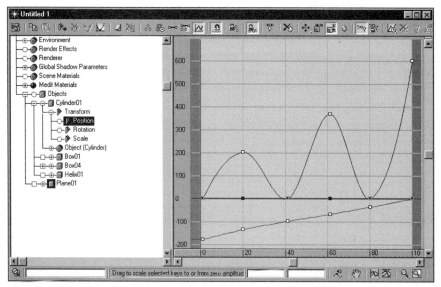

Figure 31-14: After you scale the values, the motions are visible in the viewports.

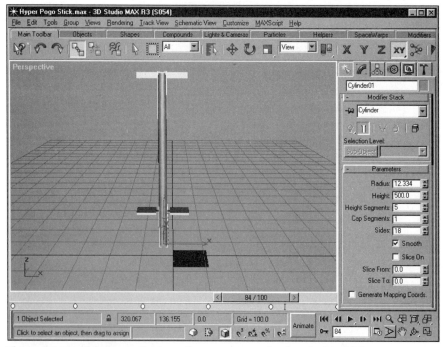

Figure 31-15: This pogo stick's motion was created using the Track View.

Filtering Tracks

With all the information included in the Track View, it can be difficult to find what you need. The Filters button on the left end of the Track View window toolbar can help. Clicking this button opens the Filters dialog box, shown in Figure 31-16.

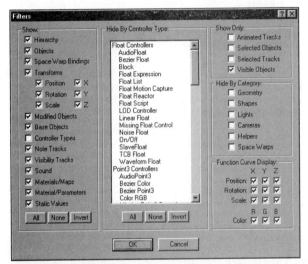

Figure 31-16: The Filters dialog box lets you focus on the specific tracks.

Tip   Right-clicking the Filters button reveals a quick list of filter items.

Using this dialog box, you can limit the number of tracks that are displayed in the Track View. The Hide by Controller Type lists all the available controllers. Any controller types selected from this list do not show up in the Track View. You can also elect to not display objects by selecting Hide Object by Category.

The Show Only group includes options for displaying only the Animated Tracks, Selected Objects, Selected Tracks, Visible Objects, or any combination of these. For example, if you wanted to see the animation track for a selected object, select the Animated Tracks option and click the OK button, then open the Filters dialog box again, select Selected Objects, and click OK.

You can also specify whether the function curve display includes the Position, Rotation, and Scale components for each axis or the RGB color components.

Working with Controllers

Controllers offer an alternative to manually positioning keys. Each controller can automatically control a key's position or a parameter's value. The Track View window toolbar includes three buttons for working with controllers. The Copy Controller and Paste Controller buttons let you move existing controllers between different tracks, and the Assign Controller button lets you add a new controller to a track.

 Cross-Reference Chapter 32, "Animating with Controllers," covers all the various controllers.

Although the buttons are labeled Copy Controller and Paste Controller, they can be used to copy different tracks. Tracks can only be copied and pasted if they are of the same type. You can copy only one track at a time, but that single controller can be pasted to multiple tracks. A pasted track can be a copy or an instance, and you have the option to replace all instances. For example, if you have several objects that move together, using the Replace All Instances option when modifying the track for one object modifies the tracks for all objects that share the same motion.

All instanced copies of a track change when any instance of that track is modified. To break the linking between instances, you can use the Make Controller Unique button.

Clicking the Assign Controller button opens the Assign Controller dialog box, where you can select the controller to apply. If the controller types are similar, the keys are maintained, but a completely different controller replaces any existing keys in the track.

Using Out-of-Range Types

Using the edit ranges mode, you can make the range of a selected track smaller than the range of the whole animation. These tracks then go out of range at some point during the animation. The Parameters Curve Out-of-Range Types button is used to tell the track how to handle its out-of-range time.

 Note You can also apply an out-of-range curve to a select range of frames using the Create Out-of-Range Keys utility. This utility is available via the Track View Utilities button.

The Parameters Curve Out-of-Range Types button opens the Param(eters) Curve Out-of-Range Types dialog box, shown in Figure 31-17.

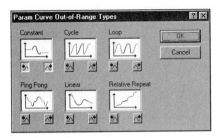

Figure 31-17: The Param Curve Out-of-Range Types dialog box lets you choose how to handle out-of-range values.

This dialog box includes six different options:

✦ **Constant**—Holds the value constant for all out-of-range frames

✦ **Cycle**—Repeats the track values as soon as the range ends

✦ **Loop**—Repeats the range values, like the Cycle option, except the beginning and end points are interpolated to provide a smooth transition

✦ **Ping Pong**—Repeats the range values in reverse order once the range end is reached

✦ **Linear**—Projects the range values in a linear manner when out of range

✦ **Relative Repeat**—Repeats the range values offset by the distance between the start and end values

Adding Note Tracks

Note tracks can be added to any track and can be used to attach information about the track. The Add Note Track button is used to add a note track, which is marked with a yellow triangle and cannot be animated.

After a note track has been added in the left pane, use the Add Keys button to position a note key in the track pane by clicking in the note track. This adds a small note icon. Right-clicking the note icon opens the Notes dialog box, where you can enter the notes, as shown in Figure 31-18. Each note track can include several note keys.

The Notes dialog box includes arrow controls that can be used to move between the various notes. The field to the right of the arrows displays the current note key number. The Time value displays the frame where a selected note is located, and the Lock Key option locks the note to the frame so it can't be moved or scaled.

The Delete Note Track button can be used to delete a selected note track.

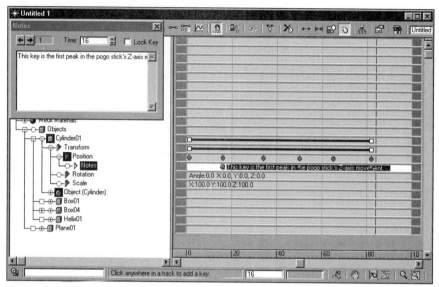

Figure 31-18: The Notes dialog box lets you enter notes and position them next to keys.

Synchronizing to a Sound Track

One of the default tracks for any scene is the sound track. Included in the Sound hierarchy is the metronome track. You can also set up a sound file using the Sound Options dialog box, shown in Figure 31-19. You can open this dialog box by right-clicking in the right pane of the sound track.

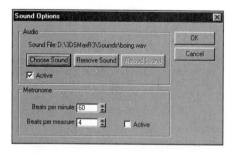

Figure 31-19: The Sound Options dialog box lets you select a sound to play during the animation.

Using the Sound Options dialog box

You can use the Audio section of the Sound Options dialog box to load a sound or remove an existing sound. The Active option causes the sound file to play when the animation is played. The Choose Sound button can load AVI, WAV, and FLC file types. The dialog box also includes buttons to Remove Sound and Reload Sound. The Active option enables the sound file.

You can also set up a regular metronome beat with two tones. For a metronome, you can specify the beats per minute and the beats per measure. The first option sets how often the beats occur, and the second option determines how often a different tone is played. This dialog box also contains an Active option for turning the metronome on and off.

Tutorial: Adding sound to an animation

As an example of adding sound to an animation, we revisit the hyper pogo stick and synchronize its animation to a sound clip.

To synchronize an animation to a sound clip, follow these steps:

1. In the Track View window, right-click in the right pane of the sound track to open the Sound Options dialog box. In the Sound Options dialog box, click the Choose Sound button. Then locate the boing.wav file, and click OK. Make sure the Active option is selected. The sound file appears as a waveform in the Track View, as shown in Figure 31-20.

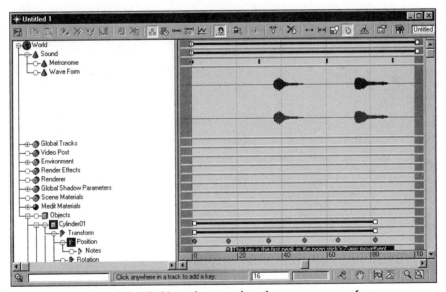

Figure 31-20: Sounds loaded into the sound track appear as waveforms.

Note

The Open Sound dialog box includes a play button that lets you play the sound before loading it.

2. Click the Edit Keys button, and move the keys to line up with the waveforms in the sound track.

3. Click the Play Animation button, and the sound file will play with the animation.

Summary

Using Track View, you have access to all the keys, parameters, and objects in a scene in one convenient location. In this chapter, you've

✦ Learned the Track View interface, including the toolbar, track panes, and status bar

✦ Learned about the different Track View modes for editing keys, time, ranges, and function curves

✦ Discovered how to work with keys, times, and ranges

✦ Controlled and adjusted function curves

✦ Selected specific tracks using the Filter dialog box

✦ Assigned controllers

✦ Explored the different out-of-range types

✦ Added Notes to a track

✦ Synchronized animation to a sound track

The next chapter explores the various controller types that are available in MAX.

✦   ✦   ✦

Animating with Controllers

In This Chapter

Understanding the various Controller types

Assigning Controllers using the Motion panel and the Track View

Setting default Controllers

Examining the various Controllers

Experimenting with Controllers

Controllers store and manage the key values for all animations in MAX. When an object is animated using the Animate button, a Controller is automatically assigned. The assigned Controller can be changed or altered using the Motion panel or the Track View. This chapter explains how to work with Controllers and examines all the various Controllers that are available.

Understanding Controller Types

Controllers are plug-ins that set the keys for animation sequences. Every object and parameter that is animated has a Controller assigned, and almost every Controller has parameters that can be altered to change its functionality. Some Controllers present these parameters as rollouts in the Motion panel, and others use a Properties dialog box.

In MAX, there are five basic Controller types and one specialized Controller type. The type depends on the type of values the Controller works with. The types include:

◆ **Float Controllers** — Used for all parameters with a single numeric value, such as Wind Strength and sphere Radius

◆ **Point3 Controllers** — Consist of color components for red, green, and blue, such as Diffuse and Background colors

◆ **Position Controllers** — Control the position coordinates for objects, consisting of X, Y, and Z values

◆ **Rotation Controllers** — Control the rotation values for objects along all three axes

◆ **Scale Controllers** — Control the scale values for objects as percentages for each axis

✦ **Transform Controllers**—A special Controller type that applies to all transforms (position, rotation, and scale) at the same time, such as the Look At, Link, and PRS Controllers

Assigning Controllers

For a Controller to be able to set keys, it must be assigned to a track. Controllers can be assigned automatically by creating or animating objects, using the Motion panel, or using the Track View. Each of these methods is explained in the following sections.

Automatically assigned Controllers

Many Controllers are automatically assigned when an object is created. For example, the IK Controller is automatically assigned when a Bones system is created. This Controller understands the Bones system and manages its movement.

Other automatically assigned Controllers are the Barycentric Morph, Master Point, and Slave Controllers. The Barycentric Morph Controller is automatically assigned when a morph compound object is created. The Master Point Controller is automatically assigned to any vertices or control points subobjects that are animated. The Slave Controller is assigned to any tracks that are included as part of a Block Controller. Each of these Controllers is discussed in detail later in the chapter.

Any parameter or object that is animated while the Animate button is active is also assigned a default Controller. These default Controllers and their parameters can be changed in the Animation panel of the Preference Settings dialog box, as explained later in this chapter.

Assigning Controllers in the Motion panel

The top of the Motion panel includes two buttons: Parameters and Trajectories. Clicking the Parameters button opens the Assign Controller rollout, which contains a list of the Controllers assigned to the currently selected object's Position, Rotation, and Scale transformation tracks.

 Cross-Reference   The Trajectories button is discussed in Chapter 30, "Animation Basics."

To change a transformation track's Controller, select the track and click the Assign Controller button positioned directly above the list. This opens an Assign Controller dialog box that is specific to the track you selected.

For example, Figure 32-1 shows the Assign Position Controller for a Position track. At the bottom of the dialog box, the default Controller type is listed. Select a new Controller from the list and click OK. This new Controller now is listed in the track, and the Controller's rollouts appear beneath the Assign Controller rollout.

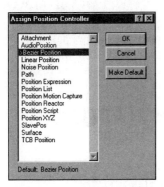

Figure 32-1: The Assign Controller dialog box lets you select a Controller to assign.

Assigning Controllers in Track View

The Track View can also be used to assign Controllers. To do this, locate and select the track to apply a Controller to, and click the Assign Controller button in the Track View toolbar. This opens an Assign Controller dialog box where you can select the Controller to use.

Cross-Reference

Chapter 31, "Working with the Track View," covers the details of the Track View.

You can also use the Track View toolbar to copy and paste Controllers between tracks, but you can paste Controllers only to similar types of tracks. When you paste Controllers, the Paste dialog box, shown in Figure 32-2, lets you choose to paste the Controller as a copy or as an instance. Changing an instanced Controller's parameters changes the parameters for all instances. The Paste dialog box also includes an option to replace all instances. This option replaces all instances of the Controller whether they are selected or not.

Figure 32-2: The Paste dialog box lets you paste a Controller as a copy or an instance.

Setting Default Controllers

When you assign Controllers using the Track View, the Assign Controller dialog box includes the option Make Default. With this option, the selected Controller becomes the default for the selected track.

You can also set the global default Controller for each type of track by selecting Customize ➪ Preferences, selecting the Animation panel, and then clicking the Set Defaults button. This opens the Set Controller Defaults dialog box, where you can set the default parameter settings, such as the In and Out curves for the Controller. To set the default Controller, select a Controller from the list and click the Set button; this opens a Controller-specific dialog box where you can adjust the Controller parameters. The Animation panel also includes a button to revert to the original settings.

 Note   Changing a default Controller will not change any currently assigned Controllers.

Examining the Various Controllers

Now that you've learned how to assign a Controller, let's take a look at the available Controllers. MAX includes a vast assortment of Controllers, and more Controllers can be added as plug-ins.

Earlier in the chapter, six specific Controller types were mentioned. These types define the type of data that the Controller works with. The following sections cover the various Controllers according to the types of tracks they work with.

 Note   Looking at the function curves for a Controller provides a good idea of how it can be controlled, so many of the figures that follow show the various function curves for the different Controllers.

General default Controllers

These Controller types include some of the common default Controllers and can typically be assigned to a wide variety of parameters and tracks.

Bézier Controller

The Bézier Controller is the default Controller for most parameters. It enables you to interpolate between values using an adjustable Bézier spline. By dragging its tangent vertex handles you can control the spline's curvature. Tangent handles produce a smooth transition when they lie on the same line, or you can create an angle between them for a sharp point.

Figure 32-3 shows the Bézier Controller assigned to a Position track. Notice that there are separate splines for each axis.

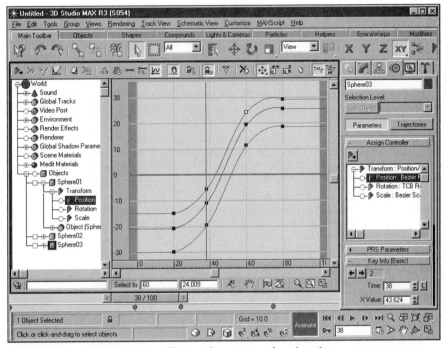

Figure 32-3: The Bézier Controller produces smooth animation curves.

The Bézier Controller parameters are displayed in the Motion panel under two rollouts: Key Info (Basic) and Key Info (Advanced).

At the top of the Key Info (Basic) rollout are two arrows and a field that shows the key number. The arrows let you move between the Previous and Next keys. Each vertex shown in the function curve represents a key. The Time field displays the frame number where the key is located. The Time Lock button next to the Time field can be set to prevent the key from being dragged in Track View. The value fields show the values for the selected track; the number of fields changes depending on the type of track that is selected.

At the bottom of the Key Info (Basic) rollout are two flyout buttons for specifying the In and Out curves for the key. The arrows to the sides of these buttons move between the various In/Out curve types. The curve types include Smooth, Linear, Step, Slow, Fast, Custom, and Tangent Copy.

Cross-Reference   These various In/Out curve types are described in Chapter 30, "Animation Basics."

The In and Out values in the Key Info (Advanced) rollout are enabled only when the Custom curve type is selected. These fields let you define the rate applied to each axis of the curve. The Lock button changes the two values by equal and opposite amounts. The Normalize Time button averages the positions of all keys. The Constant Velocity option interpolates the key between its neighboring keys to provide smoother motion.

TCB Controller

The TCB Controller produces curved animation paths similar to the Bézier Controller, except it uses the values for Tension, Continuity, and Bias to define their curvature.

The parameters for this Controller are displayed in a single Key Info rollout. Like the Bézier Controller rollouts, the TCB Controller rollout includes arrows and Key, Time, and Value fields. It also includes a graph of the TCB values; the red plus sign represents the current key's position while the rest of the graph shows the regular increments of time as black plus signs. Changing the Tension, Continuity, and Bias values in the fields below the graph changes its shape. Right-clicking the track and selecting Properties from the pop-up menu opens the TCB graph dialog box, shown in Figure 32-4.

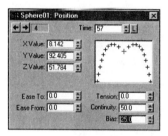

Figure 32-4: This dialog box shows and lets you control a curve defined by the Tension, Continuity, and Bias values.

The Tension value controls the amount of curvature: high Tension values produce a straight line leading into and away from the key, and low Tension values produce a round curve. The Continuity value controls how continuous, or smooth, the curve is around the key: the default value of 25 produces the smoothest curves, while high and low Continuity values produce sharp peaks from the top or bottom. The Bias value controls how the curve comes into and leaves the key point: high Bias values cause a bump to the right of the key, and low Bias values cause a bump to the left.

The Ease To and Ease From values control how quickly the key is approached or left.

Tip

Enabling the trajectory path by clicking the Trajectory button in the Motion panel lets you see the changes to the path as they are made in the Key Info rollout.

Figure 32-5 shows three TCB curves assigned to the Position track of an object.

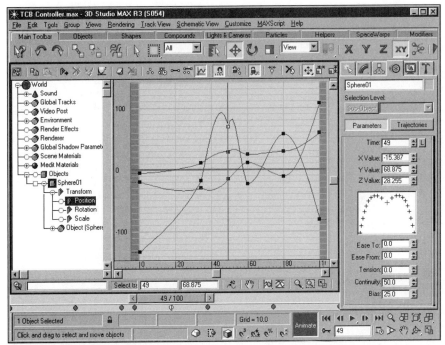

Figure 32-5: The TCB Controller offers a different way to work with curves.

Linear Controller

The Linear Controller interpolates between two values to create a straight line. The Linear Controller doesn't include any parameters and can be applied to time or values. Figure 32-6 shows the curves from the previous example after the Linear Controller is assigned—all curves have been replaced with straight lines.

Noise Controller

The Noise Controller applies random variations in a track's values. In the Noise Controller dialog box, shown in Figure 32-7, the Seed value determines the randomness of the noise, and the Frequency value determines how jagged the noise is. You can also set the Strength along each axis—the > (greater than) 0 option for each axis makes the noise values remain positive.

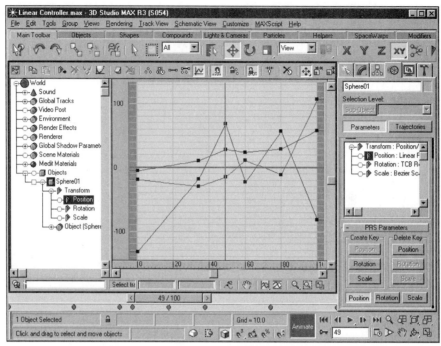

Figure 32-6: The Linear Controller uses straight lines.

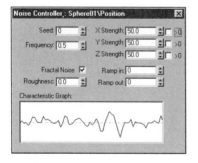

Figure 32-7: The Noise Controller lets you set the noise strength for each axis.

There is also an option to enable Fractal Noise with a Roughness setting. The Ramp in and Ramp out values determine the length of time before or until the noise can reach full value. The Characteristic Graph gives a visual look at the noise over the range.

Figure 32-8 shows the Noise Controller assigned to the Position track.

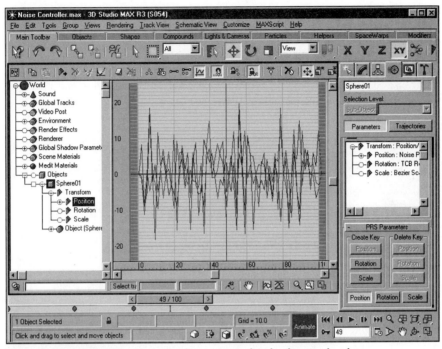

Figure 32-8: The Noise Controller lets you randomly alter track values.

Audio Controller

The Audio Controller can control an object's transform, color, or parameter value in response to the amplitude of a sound file. The Audio Controller dialog box, shown in Figure 32-9, includes Choose Sound and Remove Sound buttons for loading or removing sound files.

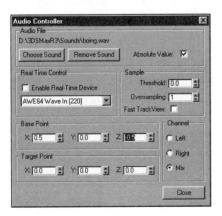

Figure 32-9: The Audio Controller dialog box lets you change values based on the amplitude of a sound file.

The Real Time Control drop-down list lets you specify a device to control the system. To control the sound input, you can specify a Sample Threshold and Oversampling rate. You can also set Base Point and Target Point values for each axis. The Channel options let you specify which channel to use: Left, Right, or Mix.

Figure 32-10 shows the Audio Controller assigned to the Position track. The boing.wav file is used to affect the position of the object.

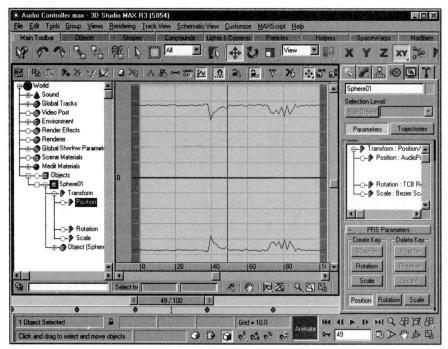

Figure 32-10: The Audio Controller changes the positional value based on the amplitude of the sound file.

Position Controllers

Position tracks can use a variety of Controllers from Bézier to Noise, but there are also several Controllers that can only be used with the Position track.

Position XYZ Controller

The Position XYZ Controller splits position transforms into three separate tracks, one for each axis. Each axis has a Bézier Controller applied to it, but each component track can be assigned a different Controller. The Position XYZ Parameters rollout lets you switch between the component axes.

Figure 32-11 shows the Position XYZ Controller assigned to a Position track with a Noise Controller assigned to each position component track. The X Position track has been given a strength of 10, the Y Position track has been given a strength of 30, and the Z Position track has been given a strength of 50.

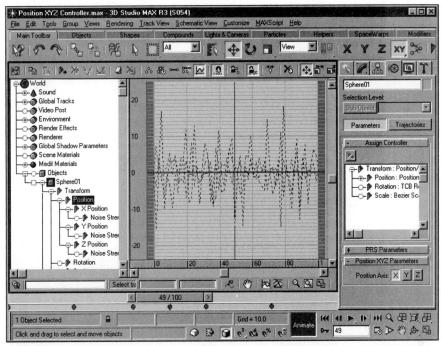

Figure 32-11: The Position XYZ Controller splits each position axis into different components.

Path Controller

The Path Controller lets you select a spline path for the object to follow. The object will be locked to the path and will follow it even if the spline is changed.

See Chapter 11, "Working with Spline Shapes," for an example of the Path Controller.

The Path Parameters rollout includes a Pick Path button for specifying the spline to use as the path. The Path Options include a % Along Path value for defining the object's position along the path. This value ranges from 0 at one end to 100 at the other end. The Follow option causes the object to be aligned with the path as it moves, and the Bank option causes the object to rotate to simulate a banking motion.

The Bank Amount value sets the depth of the bank, and the Smoothness value determines how smooth the bank is. The Allow Upside Down option lets the object spin completely about the axis, and the Constant Velocity option keeps the speed regular. At the bottom of the Path Parameters rollout, you can select the axis to use.

Figure 32-12 shows the Path Controller assigned to the Position track. Notice the Percent, Bank Amount, and Smoothness subtracks underneath the Position track in the hierarchy list.

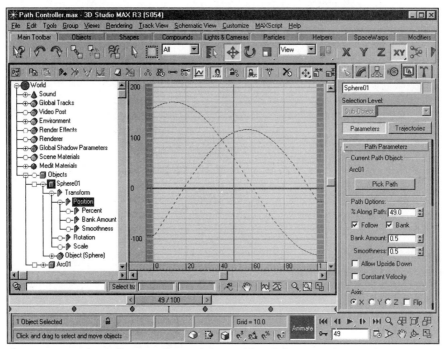

Figure 32-12: The Path Controller makes an object follow a path.

Surface Controller

The Surface Controller moves an object so it is on the surface of another object. This Controller can be used only on parametric objects such as primitives, patches, and NURBS objects.

In the Surface Controller Parameters rollout is a Pick Surface button that enables you to select the surface to attach to. You can also select specific U and V Position values. Alignment options include No Alignment, Align to U, Align to V, and a Flip toggle.

Figure 32-13 shows the Surface Controller assigned to the Position track of a second sphere added to the scene.

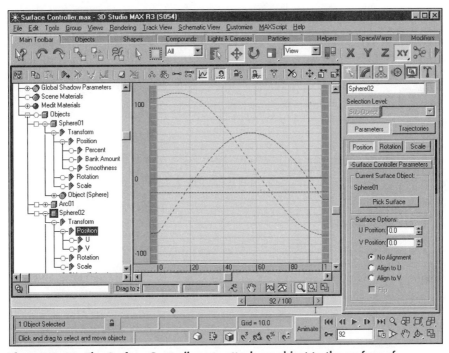

Figure 32-13: The Surface Controller can attach an object to the surface of another object.

Attachment Controller

The Attachment Controller determines an object's position by attaching it to the face of another object. This lets you attach an object to the surface of another object. At the top of the Attachment Parameters rollout is a Pick Object button for selecting the object to attach to. There is also an option to align the object to the surface. The Update section lets you manually or automatically update the attachment values.

The Key Info section displays the key number and lets you move between the various keys. The Time value is the current key value. In the Face field, you can specify the exact number of the face to attach to. To set this face, click the Set Position button and drag over the target object. The A and B values represent Barycentric coordinates for defining how the object lies on the face. You can change these coordinate values by entering values or by dragging the red crosshairs in the box underneath the A and B values.

The TCB section sets the Tension, Continuity, and Bias values for the Controller. You can also set the Ease To and Ease From values. Figure 32-14 shows a second sphere object that has been attached to the first. The first sphere is following a path.

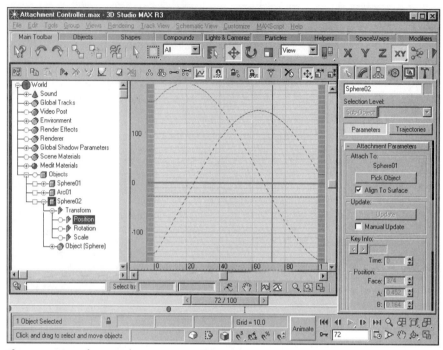

Figure 32-14: The Attachment Controller sticks one object to the surface of another.

Rotation Controllers

The Rotation tracks use a variety of Controllers, many of them common to the Position track. This section lists the Controllers that can be used only with the Rotation track.

Smooth Rotation Controller

The Smooth Rotation Controller automatically produces a smooth rotation. This Controller doesn't add any new keys but simply changes the timing of the existing keys to produce a smooth rotation. It does not have any parameters.

Euler XYZ Rotation Controller

The Euler XYZ Rotation Controller lets you control the rotation angle along the X, Y, and Z axes based on a single float value for each frame. Euler rotation is different from MAX's default rotation method (which is quaternion rotation and not as smooth). The main difference is that Euler rotation gives you access to the function curves. Using these curves you can smoothly define the rotation motion of the object.

Note Euler XYZ Rotation values are in radians instead of degrees. Radians are much smaller values than degrees. A full revolution is 360 degrees or 2 times Pi radians, so one degree equals about 0.0174 radians.

The Euler Parameters rollout lets you choose the Axis Order, which is the order in which the axes are calculated. You can also choose which axis to work with.

Figure 32-15 shows the X Rotation track for the Euler XYZ Controller.

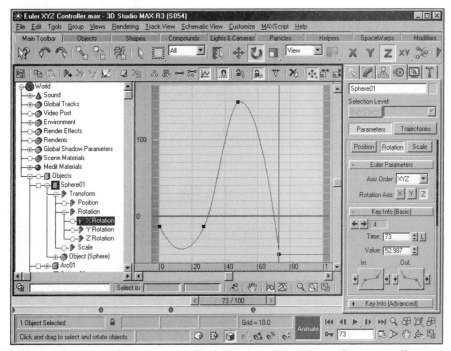

Figure 32-15: The Euler XYZ Controller lets you assign separate float Controllers to each axis.

Local Euler XYZ Rotation Controller

The Local Euler XYZ Rotation Controller works just like the Euler XYZ Rotation Controller, except the object is rotated relative to the local object's coordinates.

New Feature The Local Euler XYZ Rotation Controller is new to Release 3.

The Scale XYZ Controller

There is one Controller that can be used only in Scale tracks. The Scale XYZ Controller breaks scale transforms into three separate tracks, one for each axis. This enables you to precisely control the scaling of an object along separate axes. This is a better alternative to using Select and Non-Uniform Scale from the main toolbar because it is independent of the object geometry.

New Feature   The Scale XYZ Controller is new to Release 3.

The Scale XYZ Parameters rollout lets you select which axis to work with.

Figure 32-16 shows the X Scale track for the Euler XYZ Controller.

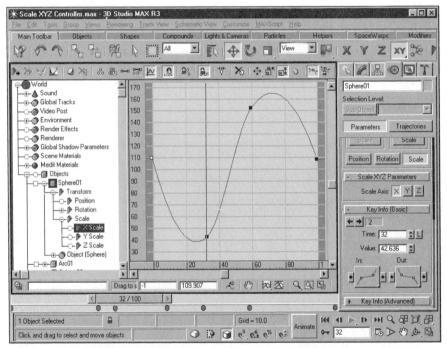

Figure 32-16: The Scale XYZ Controller lets you control the scale along each axis.

Transform Controllers

Transform Controllers work with the Position, Rotation, and Scale tracks all at the same time and are accessed by selecting the Transform track in the Motion panel and then clicking the Assign Controller button.

PRS Transform Controller

The PRS Transform Controller is the default Controller for all transforms. PRS stands for Position, Rotation, and Scale. This Controller includes a Bézier Controller for the Position and Scale tracks and a TCB Controller for the Rotation track.

The PRS Parameters rollout, shown in Figure 32-17, lets you create and delete keys for Position, Rotation, and Scale transforms. The Position, Rotation, and Scale buttons control the fields that appear in the Key Info rollouts positioned below the PRS Parameters rollout.

Figure 32-17: The PRS Parameters rollout is the default transform Controller.

Look At Controller

The Look At Controller is applied to all the transform tracks and looks at an object as it moves around the scene. This Controller affects the Position and Scale tracks, but the Rotation track is controlled by the Roll Angle value.

Cross-Reference

An example of the Look At Controller can be found in Chapter 22, "Controlling Cameras."

The Look At Parameters rollout includes Create Key buttons for Position, Roll, and Scale tracks. It also includes a Pick Target button that enables you to select an object to look at, as well as axis options. The Position, Rotation, and Scale buttons determine which fields appear in the Key Info rollouts below the Look At Parameters rollout.

Caution   The object using the Look At Controller flips when the target point is positioned directly above or below the object's pivot point.

Figure 32-18 shows the function curve for the Roll Angle track that replaces the Rotation track. The rotation of the object is controlled by the position of the Look At Target.

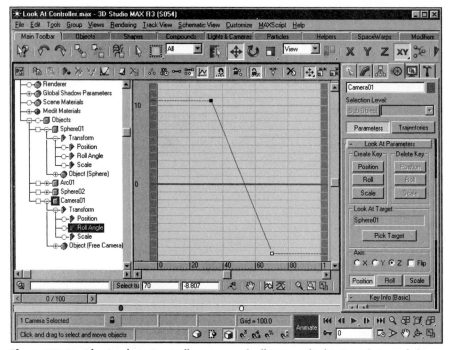

Figure 32-18: The Look At Controller automatically controls the Rotation track for you.

Link Controller

The Link Controller can transfer hierarchical links between objects. This Controller can cause a child's link to be switched during an animation.

Cross-Reference   An example of the Link Controller can be found in Chapter 27, "Building Linked Hierarchies."

All links are kept in a list in the Link Parameters rollout. You can add links to this list with the Add Link button or delete links with the Delete Link button. The Start Time field specifies when the selected object takes control of the link. The object listed in the list is the parent object, so the Start Time setting determines when each parent object takes control. This Controller also includes the PRS Parameters and Key Info rollouts.

Caution   Link Controllers cannot be used with IK systems.

Figure 32-19 shows the Link Controller in use. Sphere01 and Sphere03 move in opposite directions, and Sphere02 has the Link Controller assigned. Sphere02 changes its link from Sphere01 to Sphere03 at frame 50 as specified in the Link Parameters rollout.

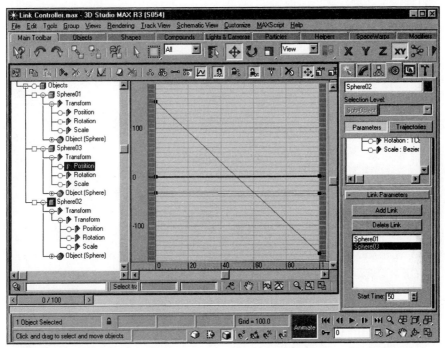

Figure 32-19: The Link Controller lets you change links between objects during an animation.

Float Controllers

Float Controllers work with parameters that use float numbers such as a sphere's Radius or plane object's Scale Multiplier value. Float values are numbers with a decimal value, such as 2.3 or 10.99. A Float Controller is assigned to any parameter that is animated. Once it is assigned, you can access the function curves and keys for this Controller in the Track View and also in the Track Bar.

On/Off Controller

The On/Off Controller works on tracks that hold a binary value, such as the Visibility track, and can be used to turn the track on and off or to enable and disable options. In the Track View, each On section is displayed in blue, with keys alternating between on and off. There are no parameters for this Controller.

Figure 32-20 shows a Visibility track that has been added to a sphere object. This track was added using the Add Visibility Track button in Edit Keys mode. Keys can be added with the Add Keys button. Each new key will toggle the track on and off.

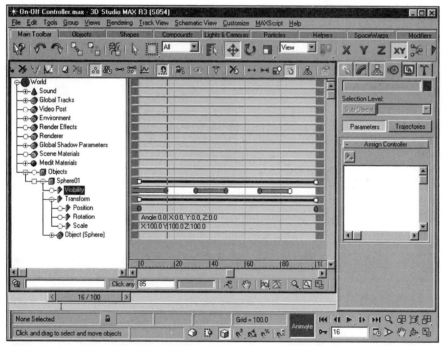

Figure 32-20: The On/Off Controller lets you make objects appear and disappear.

Waveform Controller

The Waveform Controller can produce regular periodic waveforms such as a sinusoidal wave. Several different waveform types can make up a complete waveform. The Waveform Controller dialog box, shown in Figure 32-21, includes a list of all the combined waveforms. To add a waveform to this list, click the Add button.

Once a waveform in the list is selected, you can give it a name and edit its shape using the buttons and values. Preset waveform shapes include Sine, Square, Triangle, Sawtooth, and Half Sine. You can also invert and flip these shapes.

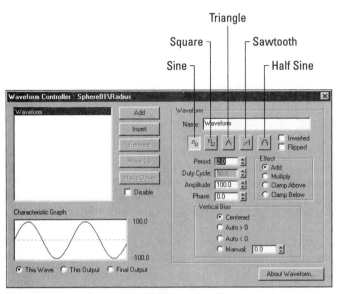

Figure 32-21: The Waveform Controller dialog box lets you produce sinusoidal motions.

The Period value defines the number of frames required to complete one full pattern. The Amplitude value sets the height of the wave, and the Phase value determines its location at the start of the cycle. The Duty Cycle value is used only for the square wave to define how long it stays enabled.

You can use the Vertical Bias options to set the values range for the waveform. Options include Centered, which sets the center of the waveform at 0; Auto > 0, which causes all values to be positive; Auto < 0, which causes all values to be negative; and Manual, which lets you set a value for the center of the waveform.

The Effect option determines how different waveforms in the list are combined. They can be added, multiplied, clamped above, or clamped below. The Add option simply adds the waveform values together, and the Multiply option multiplies the separate values. The Clamp Above or Clamp Below option forces the values of one curve to its maximum or minimum while not exceeding the values of the other curve. The Characteristic Graph shows the selected waveform, the output, or the final resulting curve.

Figure 32-22 shows the Characteristic Graph for each Effect option when a sine wave and a square wave are combined.

Figure 32-23 shows the Waveform Controller set to produce a sinusoidal curve assigned to the Radius track of a sphere object. This causes the size of the sphere to alternatively grow large and small.

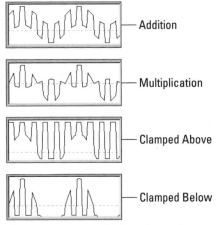

— Addition

— Multiplication

— Clamped Above

— Clamped Below

Figure 32-22: Combining sine and square waves with the Add, Multiply, Clamp Above, and Clamp Below Effect options

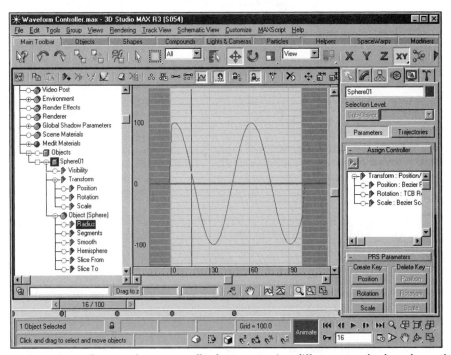

Figure 32-23: The Waveform Controller lets you assign different standard mathematical curves to track values.

The Color RGB Controller

The Color RGB Controller can be used to animate colors. Color values are different from regular float values in that they include three values that represent the amounts of red, green, and blue (referred to as *RGB values*) that are present in the color. This data value type is known as Point3.

The Color RGB Controller splits a track with color information into its component RGB tracks. You can use this Controller to apply a different Controller to each color component and also to animate any color swatch in MAX.

Figure 32-24 shows the function curves for the Color RGB Controller assigned to the Background Color track under the Environment track, including subtracks for Red, Green, and Blue. The figure shows the Noise Controller that is assigned to the Red track.

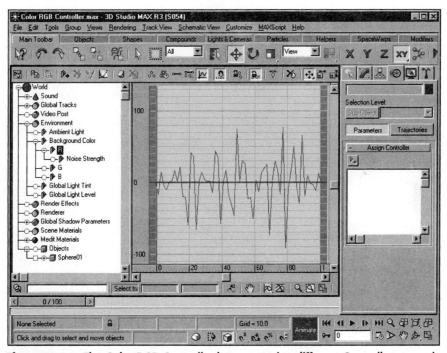

Figure 32-24: The Color RGB Controller lets you assign different Controllers to each color component.

Morph Controllers

There are two specialized Controllers for working with morph objects: Cubic Morph and Barycentric Morph.

Cubic Morph Controller

The Cubic Morph Controller can be assigned to a morph compound object. The track for this object can be found under the Objects track. A subtrack of the morph object is the Morph track, which holds the morph keys.

The Cubic Morph Controller uses Tension, Continuity, and Bias values to control how targets blend with one another. These TCB values can be accessed in the Key Info dialog box by right-clicking any morph key or by right-clicking the Morph track and selecting Properties from the pop-up menu.

Tip   You can also access the TCB values by right-clicking the keys in the Track Bar.

Figure 32-25 shows the Morph track with the Cubic Morph Controller applied. The Key Info dialog is also open and displayed.

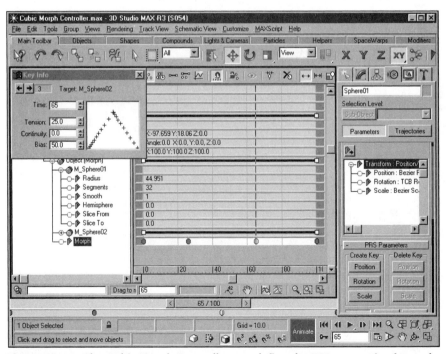

Figure 32-25: The Cubic Morph Controller can define the TCB properties for each morph key.

Barycentric Morph Controller

The Barycentric Morph Controller is automatically applied when a morph compound object is created. Keys are created for this Controller based on the morph targets set in the Modify panel under the Current Targets rollout for the morph compound object. These keys can be edited using the Barycentric Controller Key Info dialog box, shown in Figure 32-26, which can be opened by right-clicking a morph key in the Track View or in the Track Bar.

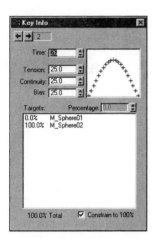

Figure 32-26: The Barycentric Morph Controller Key Info dialog box lets you set weights for different morph keys.

The main difference between the Cubic Morph Controller and the Barycentric Morph Controller is that the latter can have weights applied to the various morph keys.

The Barycentric Morph Controller Key Info dialog box includes a list of morph targets. If a target is selected, its Percentage value sets the influence of the target. The Time value is the frame where this key is located. The TCB values and displayed curve control the Tension, Continuity, and Bias parameters for this Controller. The Constrain to 100% option causes all weights to equal 100% — changing one value will change the other values proportionally if this option is selected.

Special-purpose Controllers

Other types of Controllers consist of miscellaneous collections that don't fit into the previous categories. Many of these Controllers combine several Controllers into one, such as the List and Block Controllers; others include separate interfaces, such as the Expression and Script Controllers, for defining the Controller's functions.

List Controller

The List Controller can be used to apply several Controllers at once. This enables you to produce smaller, subtler deviations, such as adding some noise to a normal Path Controller.

When the List Controller is applied, the default track appears as a subtrack along with another subtrack labeled Available. By selecting the Available subtrack and clicking the Assign Controller button, you can assign additional Controllers to the current track.

All subtrack Controllers are included in the List rollout of the Motion panel. You can also access this list by right-clicking the track and selecting Properties from the pop-up menu. The order of the list is important, as it defines which Controllers are computed first.

The Set Active button lets you specify which Controller can be interactively controlled in the viewport; the active Controller is marked with an arrow, which is displayed to the left of the name. You can also cut and paste Controllers from and to the list. Because you can use the same Controller type multiple times, you can distinguish each one by entering a name in the Name field.

Figure 32-27 shows the List Controller assigned to the Position track of a sphere. Listed are the default Controller (Bézier Position) and an Available track. The Noise Controller was added by selecting the Available track and clicking the Assign Controller button. Notice in the function curves how the noise is secondary to the Bézier motion.

Block Controller

The Block Controller combines several tracks into one block so they can be handled all together. This Controller is located in the Global Tracks track. If a track is added to a Block Controller, a Slave Controller is placed in the track's original location.

 New Feature   The Block Controller is new to Release 3.

To add a Block Controller, select the Available track under the Block Control track or the Global Tracks track, and click the Assign Controller button. From the Assign Constant Controller dialog box that opens, select Master Block (Master Block is the only selection) and click OK. Right-click the Master Block track to open the Master Block Parameters dialog box, shown in Figure 32-28.

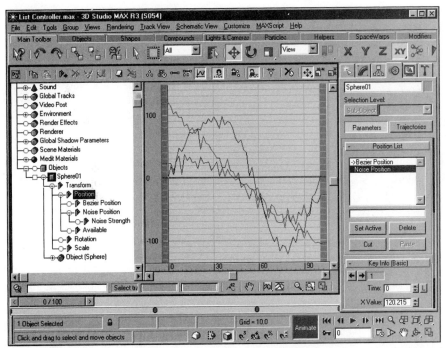

Figure 32-27: The List Controller lets you assign multiple Controllers to a single track.

Figure 32-28: The Master Block Parameters dialog box lists all the tracks applied to a Block Controller.

In the Master Block Parameters dialog box, you can add a track to the Block Controller with the Add button. All tracks added are displayed in the list on the left. You can give each track a name by using the Name field. You can also use the Add Selected button to add any selected tracks. The Replace button lets you select a new Controller to replace the currently selected track. The Load and Save buttons enable you to load or save blocks as separate files.

The Add button opens the Track View Pick dialog box, shown in Figure 32-29. This dialog box displays all valid tracks in a darker color to make them easier to see, while graying out invalid tracks.

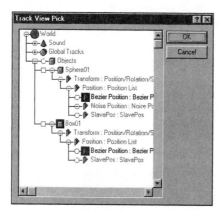

Figure 32-29: The Track View Pick dialog box lets you select the tracks you want to include in the Block Controller.

Select the tracks that you want to include and click the OK button. This opens the Block Parameters dialog box, shown in Figure 32-30, where you can name the block, specify Start and End frames, and choose a color. Click OK when you've finished with this dialog box.

Figure 32-30: The Block Parameters dialog box lets you name a block.

Back in the Master Block Parameters dialog box, clicking the Load button opens a file dialog box where you can load a saved block of animation parameters. After the parameters have been loaded, the Attach Controls dialog box opens, as shown in Figure 32-31. This dialog box includes two panes. The Incoming Controls pane on the left lists all motions in the saved block. By clicking the Add button, you can add tracks from the current scene to which you can copy the saved block motions.

Because the saved motions in the Incoming Controls pane match up with the Copy To entries in the right pane, the Add Null button adds a space in place of a specific track if you don't want a motion to be copied. The Match by Node button matches tracks by means of the Track View Pick dialog box.

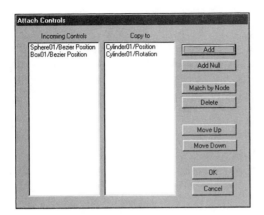

Figure 32-31: The Attach Controls dialog box lets you attach saved tracks to the Block Controller.

Figure 32-32 shows a Block Controller with several motions included. The MasterBlock track also includes a Blend subtrack for defining how the various tracks interact.

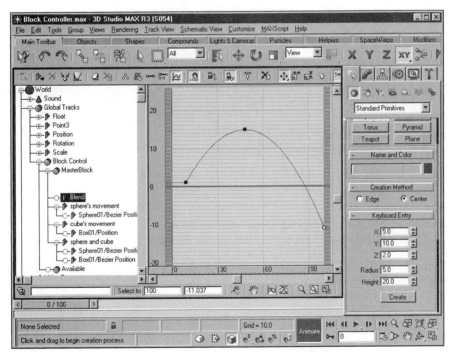

Figure 32-32: The Block Controller lets you combine several tracks into a single global track.

Expression Controller

The Expression Controller can define a mathematical expression that controls the track values. This expression can use the values of other tracks and basic mathematical functions such as sines and logarithms to control animation keys.

Cross-Reference The Expression Controller is covered in Chapter 33, "Using Expressions."

Script Controller

The Script Controller is similar to the Expression Controller, except that it can work with the MAXScript lines of code. Right-clicking a track with the Script Controller assigned and selecting Properties opens the Script Controller dialog box, shown in Figure 32-33.

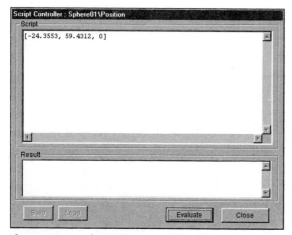

Figure 32-33: The Script Controller dialog box runs scripts to generate animation keys.

This dialog box includes a Script pane and a Result pane along with buttons to save and load scripts. Once a script is loaded, the Evaluate button executes the script.

Cross-Reference For more information on MAXScript, see Chapter 41, "Using MAXScript."

IK Controller

The IK Controller works on a Bones system for controlling the bone objects of an IK system. The IK Controller includes many different rollouts for defining joint constraints and other parameters.

The IK Controller is covered in Chapter 29, "Creating an Inverse Kinematics System."

Master Point Controller

The Master Point Controller controls the transforms of any point or vertex subobject selections. The Master Point Controller gets added as a track to an object whose subobjects are transformed. Subtracks under this track are listed for each subobject. The keys in the Master track are colored green.

The Master Point Controller is new to Release 3.

Right-clicking a green master key opens the Master Track Key Info dialog box, shown in Figure 32-34. This dialog box shows the key number with arrows for selecting the previous or next key, a Time field that displays the current frame number, and a list of all the vertices. Selecting a vertex from the list displays its parameters at the bottom of the dialog box.

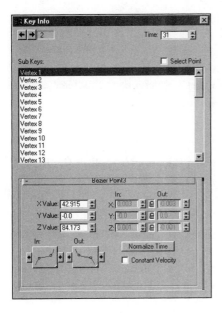

Figure 32-34: The Master Track Key Info dialog box lets you change the key values for each vertex.

Figure 32-35 shows the Master Point Controller that was automatically assigned when a selection of vertex subobjects was moved with the Animate button enabled. A separate track is created for each vertex.

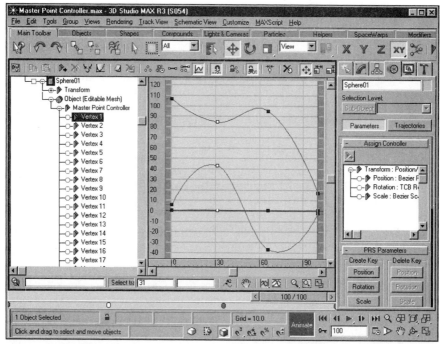

Figure 32-35: The Master Point Controller defines tracks for each subobject element that is animated.

Reactor Controller

The Reactor Controller changes its values as a reaction to another Controller. This is different from the Attachment Controller in that the motions don't need to be in the same direction. For example, you can have one object rise as another object moves to the side.

New Feature   The Reactor Controller is new to Release 3.

Once the Reactor Controller is assigned to a track, you can define the reactions using the Reaction Parameters dialog box, shown in Figure 32-36. To open this dialog box, select and right-click the track to which the Reactor Controller is assig-ned, and then select Properties from the pop-up menu.

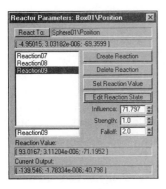

Figure 32-36: The Reactor Parameters dialog box lets you set the parameters of a reaction.

The React To button opens the Track View Pick dialog box. All reactions are kept in a list. To add a reaction to the list, click the Create Reaction button. The Delete Reaction button deletes the selected reaction from the list. The Set Reaction Value button lets you specify the value for the reaction. These values are displayed in the Reaction Value field. Each reaction can have an Influence, Strength, and Falloff value.

Figure 32-37 shows position function curves that result from the Reactor Controller.

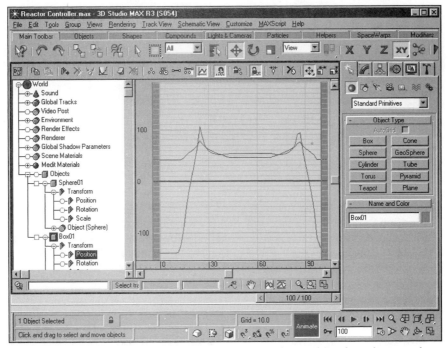

Figure 32-37: The Reactor Controller lets you control one object based on another.

Motion Capture Controller

The Motion Capture Controller enables you to control an object's transforms using an external device such as a mouse, keyboard, joystick, or MIDI device. This Controller works with the Motion Capture utility to capture motion data.

After the Motion Capture Controller is assigned to a track, right-clicking the track and selecting Properties from the pop-up menu opens the Motion Capture dialog box, shown in Figure 32-38. This dialog box lets you select the devices to use to control the motion of the track values. For example, in Figure 32-38 the X and Y positions of the sphere are controlled by the mouse, and the Z position is controlled by the A key.

Figure 32-38: The Motion Capture Controller lets you control track values using external devices.

The Motion Capture dialog box only defines which device controls which values. The actual capturing of data is accomplished using the Motion Capture utility. Selecting the Motion Capture utility in the Utilities panel displays the Motion Capture rollout, shown in Figure 32-39. This rollout includes buttons to start, stop, and test the data capturing process.

Before you can use the Start, Stop, and Test buttons, you need to select the tracks to capture from the Tracks list. The Record Range section lets you set the Preroll, In, and Out values, which are the frame numbers to include. You can also set the number of samples per frame. The Reduce Keys option, if enabled, removes any unnecessary keys.

Figure 32-39: The Motion Capture rollout includes controls for capturing motion data.

Controller Examples

Now that you've seen all the Controllers and learned about their various parameters, we examine a few Controllers in the following tutorials. Controller examples are included in other chapters of this book as well.

Tutorial: Rotating gears with the Reactor Controller

Many mechanical devices use gears, and animating these gears can be tricky because adjacent gears rotate in opposite directions. Animating by linking the gears together causes one gear to rotate around the other one. This motion can be done by animating the rotation of every gear individually, or you could use the Reactor Controller to make the gears work like they are supposed to — which is what we do in this tutorial.

To rotate gears using the Reactor Controller, follow these steps:

1. Create a gear object using the RingWave primitive by setting Radius to **50** and Ring Width to **40** with the No Growth option selected. Enable the Outer Edge Breakup option with **12** Major Cycles and a Flux Width of **15**. Clone the gear as a copy and position its clone so that the teeth intermesh.

2. Select the first gear, click the Animate button, and drag the Time Slider to frame 100. Then select the Select and Rotate button and right-click it to open the Rotate Transform Type-In. Enter a value of **180** in the Z-axis Offset.

3. Open the Track View and locate the Rotation track for the second gear. Select this track and click the Assign Controller button. Select the Rotation Reactor option and click OK.

4. Right-click the Rotation track and select Properties to open the Reactor Parameters dialog box. Drag the Time Slider back to frame 0. Click the React To button, select the Rotation track for the first gear, and click OK. This creates a reaction in the list.

5. Drag the Time Slider to frame 100 and click the Create Reaction button. This creates another reaction in the list. Click the Edit Reaction State button to enable it. Then select the second gear, select and right-click the Select and Rotate button, and enter **–180** in the Z-axis Offset.

Figure 32-40 shows the two gears and the Reactor Parameters dialog box. The second gear rotates in the opposite direction of the first gear.

Tutorial: Rolling a tire over a hill with the Surface Controller

Moving a vehicle across a landscape can be a difficult procedure if you need to place every rotation and position key, but with the Surface Controller it becomes easy. In this tutorial, we use the Surface Controller to roll a tire over a hill.

To roll a tire over a hill with the Surface Controller, follow these steps:

1. Open the Create panel and make a tire object in the Front view using a tube object. Then make the spokes from boxes and place them using the Array dialog box, and make a hub from a cylinder object. Make a hill by creating a patch grid, deforming it to form one-half of a hill, mirroring it, and then attaching the two pieces together. Position the tire at the base of the hill.

2. Create a dummy object from the Helpers category, and link the tire object to it as a child; this causes the tire to move along with the dummy object. Position the dummy object's pivot point at the bottom of the tire and at the base of the hill.

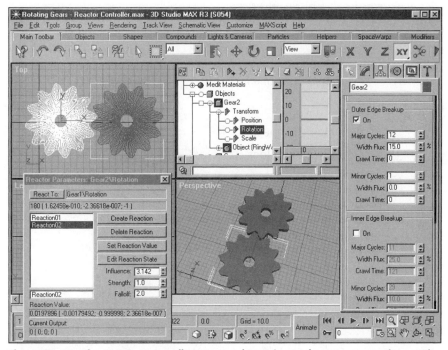

Figure 32-40: The Reactor Controller was used to animate these two opposite-rotating gears.

3. Select the dummy object, open the Motion panel, and select the Position track in the Assign Controller rollout. Click the Assign Controller button, select the Surface Controller, and click OK; this adds U and V Bézier Float Controllers as subtracks.

4. In the Surface Controller Parameters rollout, click the Pick Surface button and select the patch grid hill. Select the Align to V and Flip options to position the dummy and tire objects at the top of the hill. Set the V Position value to **50** to move the tire to the center of the hill.

5. Click the Animate button, drag the Time Slider to frame 100, and change the U Position to **100**. Click the Animate button again to deactivate it, and click the Play Animation button to see the tire move down the hill.

Figure 32-41 shows the tire as it moves down the hill. In the Top view you can see the function curves for this motion.

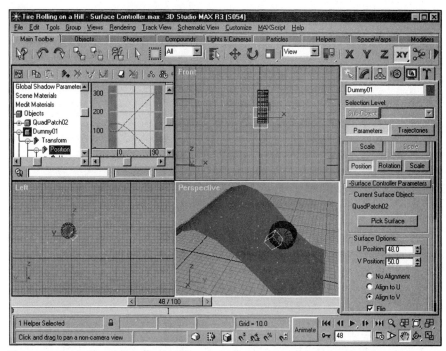

Figure 32-41: The Surface Controller can animate one object moving across the surface of another.

Tutorial: Drawing with a pencil using the Motion Capture Controller

Some motions, such as drawing with a pencil, are natural motions for our hands but become very difficult to animate using keyframes. In this tutorial, we use the Motion Capture Controller and utility to animate the natural motion of drawing with a pencil.

To animate a pencil drawing on paper, follow these steps:

1. Open the Create panel and make a simple pencil object from a cylinder and a cone primitive. Link the cone to the cylinder and create a box object to be the paper. Position the pencil above the paper.

2. Open the Motion panel and select the Position track. Then click the Assign Controller button and double-click the Position Motion Capture selection. Right-click the Position track and select Properties from the pop-up menu to open the Position Motion Capture dialog box. Click the X Position button and double-click the Mouse Input Device selection. Then click the Y Position button and double-click the Mouse Input Device selection again. In the Mouse Input Device rollout, select the Vertical option, and then close the dialog box.

3. Open the Utilities panel and click the Motion Capture button. In the Motion Capture rollout, select the Position track and get the mouse ready to move. Then click the Start button and move the mouse as if you were drawing. The Motion Capture utility will create a key for each frame.

4. Click the Play Animation button to see the results.

Figure 32-42 shows the scene after the Motion Capture has computed all the frames.

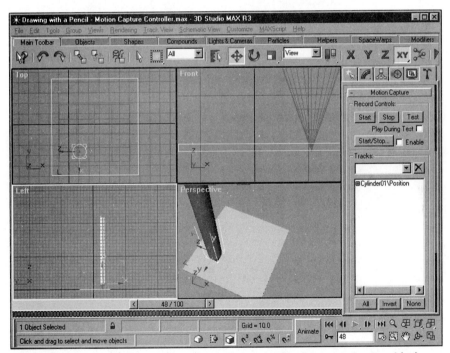

Figure 32-42: The Motion Capture Controller and utility let you animate with the mouse, keyboard, joystick, or a MIDI device.

Summary

If you're an animator, you should thank your lucky stars for Controllers. Controllers offer power flexibility for animating objects — and just think of all those keys that you don't have to set by hand.

In this chapter, you've:

✦ Learned about the various Controller types

✦ Discovered how to assign Controllers using the Motion panel and the Track View

✦ Set default Controllers in the Preference Settings dialog box

✦ Examined the various Controllers in several different categories

✦ Tried out a few examples of using Controllers

In the next chapter, we focus on one particularly useful Controller — the Expression Controller. This Controller enables you to animate objects by defining a mathematical expression.

✦   ✦   ✦

Using Expressions

Of all the Controllers that are available, the Expression Controller has limitless possibilities that could fill a book of its own. In this short chapter, the basics of building expressions are covered along with several examples.

Understanding Expressions

Expressions refer to mathematical expressions or simple formulas that compute one value based on other values. These expressions can be simple, as with moving a doll object a distance equal to the height of a monster; or complex as with computing the sinusoidal translation of a boat on the sea as a function of the waves beneath it.

Almost any value can be used as a variable in an expression, from object coordinates and Modifier and Controller parameters, to light and material settings. The results of the expression are computed for every frame and used to affect various parameters in the scene. The number of frames and time variables can be included in the expression to cause the animation results to repeat for the entire sequence.

Variables, Operators, and Functions

Each expression can produce either a number, called a scalar, or a vector. *Scalars* are used to control parameter values, and *vectors* define actual coordinates in space. Expressions are composed of variables, operators, and functions.

Variables

Variables are placeholders for different values. For example, creating a variable for a sphere's radius called "r" would simplify an expression for doubling its size from "take the sphere's radius and multiply it by two," to a simple "r times 2."

MAX includes several pre-defined variables that have constant values or meanings. These pre-defined variables are defined in Table 33-1. They are case-sensitive and must be typed exactly as they appear in the Syntax column.

Table 33-1 Constant Variables		
Variable	**Syntax**	**Value**
PI	pi	3.14159
Natural Logarithm	e	2.71828
Ticks per Second	TPS	4800
Frame Number	F	Current frame number
Normalized Time	NT	The entire time of the active number of frames
Seconds	S	The number of seconds based on the frame rate
Ticks	T	The number of ticks based on the frame rate, where 4800 ticks equals 1 second

In addition to these predefined variables, you can choose your own variables to use. These variables cannot contain spaces, and each variable must begin with a letter. Once a variable is defined, you need to assign a Controller in order to fill the variable with its value. This is covered in the "Defining Variables" section that appears later in the chapter.

Operators

An *Operator* is the part of an expression that tells how to deal with the variables. One example of an Operator is addition — it tells you to add a value to another value. These operators can be grouped as basic operators, which are the standard math functions such as addition and multiplication; logical operators, which compare two values and return a true or false result; and vector operators, which enable mathematical functions between vectors. Tables 33-2 through 33-4 identify the operators that are in each of these groups.

Table 33-2
Basic Operators

Operator	Syntax	Example
Addition	+	i+j
Subtraction	-	i-j
Negation	-	-i
Multiplication	*	i*j
Division	/	i/j
Raise to the power	^ *or* **	i^j *or* i**j

Table 33-3
Logical Operators

Operator	Syntax	Example
Equal to	=	i=j
Less than	<	i<j
Greater than	>	i>j
Less than or equal to	<=	i<=j
Greater than or equal to	>=	i>=j
Logical Or (Returns a 1 if either value is 1)	|	i|j
Logical And (Returns a 1 if both values are 1)	&	i&j

Table 33-4
Vector Operators

Operator	Syntax	Example
Component (Refers to the x component of vector V)	.	V.x
Vector Addition	+	V+W
Vector Subtraction	-	V-W

Continued

Table 33-4 *(continued)*		
Operator	**Syntax**	**Example**
Scalar Multiplication	*	i*V
Scalar Division	/	V/i
Dot Product	*	V*W
Cross Product	x	VxW

The order in which the operators are applied is called *Operator Precedence*. The first things to be calculated are the operators contained inside of parentheses. If you're in doubt about which expression gets evaluated first, place each expression in separate parentheses. For example, the expression (2 + 3) * 4 would equal 20 and 2 + (3 * 4) would equal 14.

Functions

Functions are like mini-expressions that are given a parameter and return a value. For example, the trigonometric function for Sine takes an angle and returns a Sine value. Table 33-5 lists the functions that are used to create expressions.

Tip   You can see a full list of all the possible functions with explanations by clicking the Function List button in the Expression Controller dialog box.

Table 33-5 **Expression Functions**		
Function	**Syntax**	**Description**
Sine	sin(i)	Computes the sine function for an angle
Cosine	cos(i)	Computes the cosine function for an angle
Tangent	tan(i)	Computes the tangent function for an angle
Arc Sine	asin(i)	Computes the arc sine function for an angle
Arc Cosine	acos(i)	Computes the arc cosine function for an angle

Function	Syntax	Description
Arc Tangent	atan(i)	Computes the arc tangent function for an angle
Hyperbolic Sine	hsin(i)	Computes the hyperbolic sine function for an angle
Hyperbolic Cosine	hcos(i)	Computes the hyperbolic cosine function for an angle
Hyperbolic Tangent	htan(i)	Computes the hyperbolic tangent function for an angle
Convert Radians to Degrees	radToDeg(i)	Converts an angle value from radians to degrees
Convert Degrees to Radians	degToRad(i)	Converts an angle value from degrees to radians
Ceiling	ceil(i)	Rounds floating values up to the next integer
Floor	floor(i)	Rounds floating values down to the next integer
Natural Logarithm (base e)	ln(i)	Computes the natural logarithm for a value
Common Logarithm (base 10)	log(i)	Computes the common logarithm for a value
Exponential Function	exp(i)	Computes the exponential for a value
Power	pow(i,j)	Raises i to the power of j
Square Root	sqrt(i)	Computes the square root for a value
Absolute Value	abs(i)	Changes negative numbers to positive
Minimum Value	min(i,j)	Returns the smaller of the two numbers
Maximum Value	max(i,j)	Returns the larger of the two numbers
Modulus Value	mod(i,j)	Returns the remainder of i divided by j
If	if(i,j,k)	Tests the value of i, and if it's not zero then j is returned, or if it is zero then k is returned
Vector if	vif(i,V,W)	Same as the if function, but works with vectors
Vector Length	length(V)	Computes the vector length
Vector Component	comp(V,i)	Returns the i component of vector V
Unit Vector	unit(V)	Returns a vector of length 1 that points in the same direction as V
Random Noise Position	noise(i,j,k)	Returns a random position

Building Expressions

Now that all the variables, operators, and functions have been covered, you need to understand the return types before we start building expressions. *Return types* are the values that you start with that are assigned to the Controller.

Scalar return type

A *scalar value* is a single value typically used for an object parameter, such as a sphere's radius. A scalar value appears in the Expression pane of the Expression Controller dialog box. This is the return value that you can use to build into the expression. Any resulting value from the expression is passed back to the assigned parameter.

For example, if the sphere's radius is equal to 1, then a simple expression for increasing the radius as the frame number increases would look like this:

```
1 * F
```

Caution   The frame number typically starts at 0, so, if you use the variable F in your expression, beware of calculations, such as dividing by 0, which produces an undefined value and makes your object disappear.

The trigonometric functions can be used to produce a smooth curve from 0 to 360. Using the Sine function, you can cause the sphere's radius to increase to a maximum value of 50 and then decrease to its original radius. The expression would look like this:

```
50 * sin(360*NT)
```

Vector return type

If a transform such as position is assigned, the Expression pane shows three values separated by commas and surrounded by brackets. These three values represent a vector, and each value is a different positional axis.

To make our sphere example move in a zigzag path, we can use the mod function. This causes the position to increase slowly to a value and then reset. The expression looks like this:

```
[0, 10*mod(F,20), 10*F]
```

The square root function can be used to simulate ease in and ease curves causing the object to accelerate into or from a point. The expression would look like this:

```
[100*sqrt(NT*200), 10, 10]
```

RGB return type

Materials work with yet another return type called a *Point3*. This type includes three numbers separated by commas and surrounded by brackets. Each of these values, which can range between 0 and 255, represents the amount of red, green, or blue in a color.

Note   Any value that is out of range is automatically set to its nearest acceptable value. For example, if your expression returns a value of 500 for the green component, the color is shown as if green were simply 255.

Understanding the Expression Controller Interface

The Expression Controller is just one of the many Controllers that are available for automating animations. This Controller enables you to define how the object is transformed by means of a mathematical formula or expression, which can be applied to an object's Position, Rotation, or Scale tracks.

Before the Expression Controller can be used on a track, it must be assigned to a track. Controllers can be assigned using the Motion panel or the Track View. Once it is assigned, you can open the Expression Controller dialog box by right-clicking the track and selecting Properties from the pop-up menu. This dialog box can be used to define expressions and their results. The dialog box, shown in Figure 33-1, includes four separate panes, which are used to display a list of Scalar and Vector variables, build an expression, and enter a description of the expression.

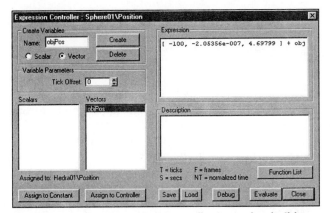

Figure 33-1: The Expression Controller is used to build expressions and define their results.

Defining variables

To add Variables to the list panes in the Expression Controller dialog box, type a name in the Name field, select the Scalar or Vector option type, and click the Create button — the new variable appears in the Scalars or Vectors list. To delete a variable, select it from the list and click the Delete button. The Tick Offset value is the time added to the current time and can be used to delay variables.

Variables used in an expression need to match the return type. For example, if you have a Vector return type describing an object's position, it can use a scalar or vector variable, but a scalar return type (such as a sphere's Radius) cannot be multiplied by a vector or an error appears.

Any new variable can either be assigned to a Constant or assigned to a Controller. Assigning a variable to a constant does the same thing as typing the constant's value in the expression. Constant variables are simply for convenience in writing expressions. The Assign to Controller button opens the Track View Pick dialog box, shown in Figure 33-2, where you can select the specific Controller track for the variable.

Figure 33-2: The Track View Pick dialog box displays all the tracks for the scene. Tracks that can be selected are displayed in black.

Assigning a variable to a Controller enables you to animate the selected object based on other objects in the scene. To do this, assign an Expression Controller to a track of an object. In the Expression Controller dialog box, create a variable and assign it to an animated track of another object. Then add a plus sign and the variable name to the end of the return type in the Expression pane — this causes the first object to move with the Hedra object.

Building expressions

Expressions can be typed directly into the Expression pane of the Expression Controller dialog box. To use a named variable from one of the variable lists

(Scalars or Vectors), type its name in the Expression pane. Predefined variables such as F and NT do not need to be defined in the variable panes. The Function List button opens a list of functions, shown in Figure 33-3, where you can view the functions that can be included in the expression.

Figure 33-3: The Function List dialog box lets you view all the available functions that can be used in an expression.

Note The Expression pane ignores any white space, so you can use line returns and spaces to make the expression easier to see and read.

Debugging expressions

After typing an expression in the Expression pane, you can check the values of all variables at any frame by clicking the Debug button. This opens the Expression Debug window, shown in Figure 33-4. This window displays the values for all variables as well as the return value. The values are automatically updated as the Time Slider is moved.

Figure 33-4: The Expression Debug window offers a way to test the expression before applying it.

Evaluating expressions

The Evaluate button in the Expression Controller dialog box commits the results of the expression to the current frame segment. If there is an error in the expression, an alert dialog box warns you of the error, and the completed part of the expression is displayed in the Expression pane. Replacing the Controller with a different one can erase the animation resulting from an Expression Controller.

Managing expressions

The Save and Load button can be used to save and recall expressions. Saved expressions are saved as files with an .XPR extension. Expression files do not save variable definitions.

Controlling Object Transformations

Expressions can be used to control the transforms of objects. The transforms can be accessed from the Track View or from the Motion panel.

Animating transforms with the Expression Controller

To assign the Expression Controller, select an object and open the Motion panel. Then click the Parameters button and open the Assign Controller rollout. This presents all the transform tracks for the object. Select a Position or Scale track, click the Assign Controller button, and select the Expression option.

Note   To use expressions for Rotation transforms, you must first select either the Euler XYZ or Local Euler XYZ Controller. You must then select the Expression Controller for the individual X, Y, or Z-axis.

Once the Expression Controller is assigned, right-click the track and select Properties from the pop-up menu to open the Expression Controller dialog box. Within this dialog box, the Expression pane includes the current values of the selected object. Position transforms display the X, Y, and Z coordinates of the object; Rotation transforms display the rotation value in Radians, and Scale transforms display values describing the relative scaling values for each axis.

Note   Radians are another way to measure angles. A full revolution equals 360 degrees, which equates to 2 times pi Radians. The Expression dialog box includes the degToRad and radToDeg functions to convert back and forth between these two systems.

Tutorial: Controlling a model plane

There are a lot of flight simulators used to train pilots, but there aren't too many designed to train pilots of model airplanes. In this tutorial, we control an airplane's motion by maneuvering a simple joystick.

To control an airplane with a joystick using the Expression Controller, follow these steps:

1. Import the airplane model created by Viewpoint Datalabs. Select all the parts and group them using the Group ➪ Group command. Give the airplane the group name of **Cessna**. Next, create a simple joystick using cone, cylinder, and sphere objects. Group the joystick parts and call it **joystick**.

2. Position the airplane at the 200, 0, 50 position. To do this, select the airplane and the Select and Move button, and then right-click the same button to open the Transform Type-In. Enter the values **200**, **0**, and **50** respectively for the Absolute World coordinates. Position the joystick anywhere in the scene where it can be seen.

3. With the airplane selected, open the Motion panel, click the Parameters button, and open the Assign Controllers rollout. Select the Position track and click the Assign Controller button. Select the Position Expression Controller option and click OK. Select the joystick object and, in the Motion panel, select the Rotation track, click the Assign Controller button, and select the Local Euler XYZ Controller. Click OK.

4. With the joystick object still selected, open the Hierarchy panel. Click the Affect Pivot Only button, move the Pivot to the base of the joystick, and click the Affect Pivot Only button again to exit this mode. Now, enable the Animate button and, using the Select and Rotate tool, rotate the joystick approximately 30 degrees in the counterclockwise direction about the X-axis. Disable the Animate button.

5. Open the Track View and select the Position track for the airplane. Right-click the track and, from the pop-up menu, select Properties to open the Expression Controller dialog box. In the Variables Name field, type the name **joyRot**, and then select the Scalar type and click the Create button. Click the Assign to Controller button and, from the Track View Pick dialog box, select the Local X Rotation track (which is under the joystick object track) and click OK.

6. In the Expression pane, you should see the value [200, 0, 50]. Modify the expression to read like this:

```
[200-(NT+200), 0, 50+(2*degToRad(joyRot))]
```

Figure 33-5 shows the Expression Controller dialog box holding the expression.

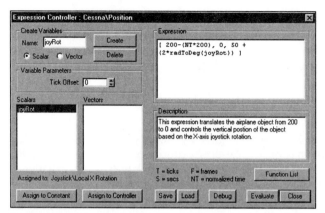

Figure 33-5: The Expression Controller dialog box includes all the variables and the expression for this motion.

7. Now click the Debug button to see the value results. With the Expression Debug window open, drag the Time Slider and notice whether the expression value for X drops to 0. If the expression looks fine, click the Close button for the Debug window and again for the Expression Controller dialog box.

Note   Clicking the Debug button applies the expression to the objects.

If you apply any X-axis rotations to the joystick, the airplane automatically rises or dives. Figure 33-6 shows the airplane as it dives.

Controlling Parameters

Expressions can also be used to control object parameters such as a box's length or the Angle of the Bend modifiers. All these parameters can be accessed from the Track View.

Animating parameters with the Expression Controller

To assign the Expression Controller, select an object with a parameter or a Modifier applied and open the Track View. Find the track for the parameter you want to change and click the Assign Controller button. Select the Float Controller from the list and click OK.

Note   The actual Controller type depends on the parameter selected. Many parameters use Float Expressions, but some use Transform Controllers.

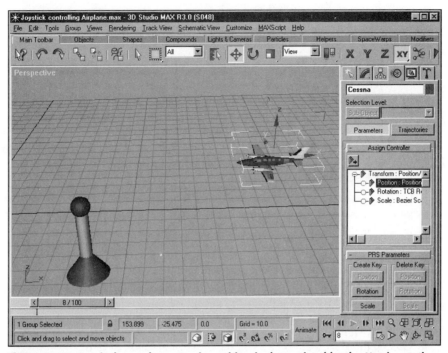

Figure 33-6: An airplane whose Z-axis position is determined by the X-axis rotation of the joystick

Once the Expression Controller is assigned, right-click the track and select Properties from the pop-up menu. This loads the Expression Controller dialog box. Within this dialog box, the Expression pane includes the current value of the select parameter.

Tutorial: Inflating a balloon

The Push Modifier (new to Release 3) mimics filling a balloon with air by pushing all its vertices outward. In this tutorial, we use a balloon model created by Zygote Media to demonstrate how the Expression Controller can be used to control the parameters of a Modifier.

To inflate a balloon using the Expression Controller, follow these steps:

1. Import a balloon model. Use several cylinders and a Loft object to create a pump. Link the handle of the pump to its center rod. Next, enable the Animate button, move the Time Slider to 100, and move the center rod object down along its Z-axis. Then disable the Animate button.

2. Position the balloon at the end of the pump. Open the Hierarchy panel, click the Affect Pivot Only button, and move the balloon's pivot to the base of the balloon. Disable the Affect Pivot Only button when finished.

3. With the balloon still selected, open the Modify panel, click the More button, and, from the additional modifiers list dialog box, select the Push Modifier and click OK.

4. Next, open the Track View by selecting Track View ⇨ Open Track View. Navigate the balloon object's tracks until you find the Push Value track located under the Modified Object track. Select the Push Value track and click the Assign Controller button. From the list of Controllers, select Float Expression and click OK.

5. Select and right-click the Push Value track and select Properties from the pop-up menu to open the Expression Controller dialog box. In the Expression pane, you should see a single scalar value of 0. Modify the expression to read like this:

```
2 * NT
```

Click the Debug button to see the value results. With the Expression Debug window open, drag the Time Slider and notice whether the balloon inflates.

6. The final step is to create another key so the base of the balloon stays connected to the pump tube. Enable the Animate button, drag the Time Slider to frame 100, and then select and move the balloon so that it touches the base at frame 100.

Figure 33-7 shows the balloon as it's being inflated.

Animating materials with the Expression Controller

Locating the material's parameter in the Track View and assigning the Expression Controller to it can control materials, such as parameters. Some of these parameters are scalar values, but any material parameter set with a color swatch has a Point3 return type.

When using material parameters and color values, be sure to not combine them in expressions with vector values.

Tutorial: Controlling a stoplight

In this example, we use the if function to turn the colors of a sphere on and off to simulate a traffic light. We accomplish this by applying the Expression Controller to the Diffuse color track. The goal is to show the color green for the first third of the animation, yellow for the second third, and red for the last third of the time.

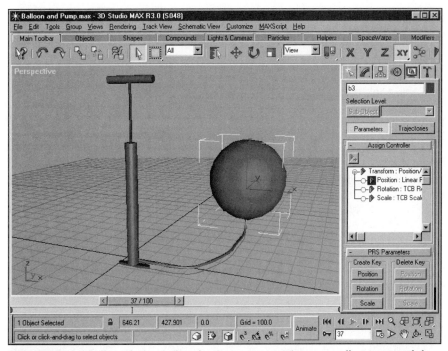

Figure 33-7: A balloon being inflated using an Expression Controller to control the Push Modifier

To change the colors of spotlight sphere using the Expression Controller, follow these steps:

1. Open the Create panel, click the Sphere button, and drag in the Top view to create a simple sphere.

2. Open the Material Editor and select the first sample slot. Click the Diffuse color swatch and select a bright green color. Drag this material onto the sphere to apply it.

3. Open the Track View and locate and select the Diffuse Color track, which can be found under the Objects ➪ Sphere01 ➪ Object (Sphere) ➪ Material #1 tracks. Click the Assign Controller button and double-click the Point3 Expression selection. This assigns the Expression Controller to the Diffuse Color track.

4. Open the Expression Controller dialog box by right-clicking the Diffuse Color track and selecting Properties from the pop-up menu.

5. In the Expression pane, enter the following:

```
[if(NT>=.33,255,0), if(NT<.66,255,0), 0]
```

Then click the Evaluate button and close the Expression Controller dialog box.

6. Click the Play Animation button to see the results.

Figure 33-8 shows the function curves for this stoplight. Notice how the blue values are constant at zero and the red and green values change at frames 33 and 66.

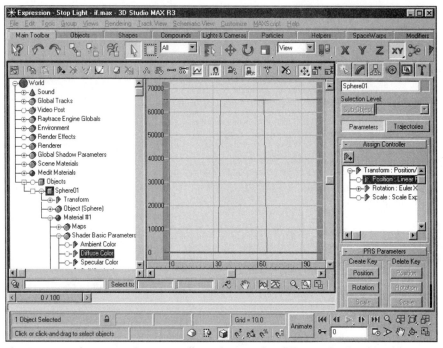

Figure 33-8: The Expression Controller animates the diffuse color for this object.

Before leaving this example, let's examine the expression. The expression works with a Point3 number that includes the values of red, green, and blue. The first Point3 value represents red. Because yellow, in the RGB color system, is composed of equal parts of red and green, we want red to be visible for the last two thirds of the time. To do this, we make the expression include the following statement:

```
if (NT >= .33, 255, 0)
```

This basically says that if the Normalized Time falls in the last two-thirds of the time, then set the red value to 255; and if it does not, then set red to 0.

The second Point3 value is green, which appears for the first third of the animation and along with red for the second third to make yellow. So the following expression needs to go where the green value would be located:

```
if (NT < .66, 255, 0)
```

This expression says that if the Normalized Time is less than two thirds of the time, then set the green value to its maximum, and, if it isn't, then set its value to 0.

The third Point3 value is for blue. Blue doesn't appear at all in green, yellow, or red, so its value is set to 0 for the entire animation.

The completed expression for the entire animation (which you entered in Step 5 of the tutorial) looks like this:

```
[if (NT >= .33, 255, 0), if (NT < .66, 255, 0), 0]
```

Summary

This chapter covered the basics of using the Expression Controller. Using mathematical formulas to control the animation of an object's transformation and parameters offers a lot of power. You can also use the values of one object to control another object.

In this chapter, you've:

✦ Learned about expressions and what they can do

✦ Reviewed the available operators, variables, and functions

✦ Practiced building expressions in the Expression dialog box

✦ Tried out examples of controlling object transformations and parameters

In the next chapter, we explore the ability to animate dynamic simulations

✦   ✦   ✦

Creating a Dynamic Simulation

If something is dynamic, it moves. Dynamic simulations in MAX can animate an object automatically by setting object properties such as bounce and friction. Any forces used in the simulation are added to the system with Space Warps.

Understanding Dynamics

Dynamics is a branch of physics that deals with forces and the motions they cause, and regardless of your experience in school, physics is your friend — especially in the world of 3D. Dynamics in MAX can automate the creation of animation keys by calculating the position, rotation, and collisions between objects based on physics equations.

Consider the motion of a simple yo-yo. To animate this motion with keys is fairly simple: set rotation and position keys halfway through the animation and again at the end, and you're done.

Now think of the forces controlling the yo-yo. Gravity causes the yo-yo to accelerate toward the ground, causing the string to unwind, which makes the yo-yo spin about its axis. When it reaches the end of the string, the rotation reverses and the yo-yo rises. Now, using Gravity and Motor Space Warps, you can simulate this motion, but setting the keys manually is probably easier for these few objects.

But before you write off dynamics, think of the motion of popcorn popping. With all the pieces involved, setting all the position and rotation keys would take a long time. For this system, using dynamics makes sense.

The Dynamics utility lets you specify objects to include in a simulation, the forces they interact with, and the objects to be involved in collisions. After the system is defined, the Dynamics utility automatically calculates the movement and collisions of these objects according to the forces involved and sets the keys for you.

Object properties determine the physical characteristics of the objects. These properties are set in the Dynamics utility and in the Material Editor and include properties such as bounce, friction, density, and volume. Using these properties you can make objects act like ice, rubber, steel, or Styrofoam.

Forces in a dynamic simulation are created using Space Warps, but not every Space Warp can be used in a dynamic simulation. Additional forces can be produced using dynamic objects such as springs and dampers. In the next section, we look at these dynamic objects. (Dynamic Space Warps are covered later in this chapter.)

Using Dynamic Objects

In the Create panel under the Geometry category is a subcategory for creating two dynamic objects: spring and damper. These primitive objects are the same as other objects except they can be used in dynamic simulations.

 New Feature The spring and damper objects are both new with Release 3.

Spring

The spring object not only looks like a simple spring but also acts with all the forces of an actual spring. In the Spring Parameters rollout, shown in Figure 34-1, are settings that determine the spring diameter, the number of turns, and whether it winds in a clockwise or counterclockwise direction. Segments can be created automatically based on the number of turns using the Automatic Segments option, or manually using the Manual Segments option. Smoothing options include All, None, Sides, and Segments. You can specify whether the spring is renderable and whether or not to automatically generate mapping coordinates.

The Wire Shape section lets you specify which type of cross section the spring will use. Parameters for the Round Wire option include Diameter and Sides. Parameters for the Rectangular Wire option include Width, Depth, Fillet, Fillet Segs (Segments), and Rotation. D-Section Wire is the same as Rectangular Wire type except that its

Figure 34-1: The Spring Parameters rollout includes a variety of parameters.

edge corners are smoothed to form a cross section that looks like the letter D. For this type of wire, you can define the number of round sides. Figure 34-2 shows each of these spring types. On the left is the Round Wire spring type, in the middle is the Rectangular Wire spring type, and on the right is the D-Section Wire spring type.

The Dynamics Parameters section, not shown in either of the previous figures, includes properties for controlling the forces that the spring applies. The Relaxed Height value is the height of the spring when no forces are applied to it. The Constant k value determines the stiffness of the spring and is a measurement of the force produced by stretching the spring. This is an actual physical constant that relates to real-world springs. The measurement unit can be pounds per inch or newtons per meter. You can also specify whether the spring works in compression only, extension only, or both. Compressing a spring means pushing the ends together, and extension means pulling the ends apart from one another.

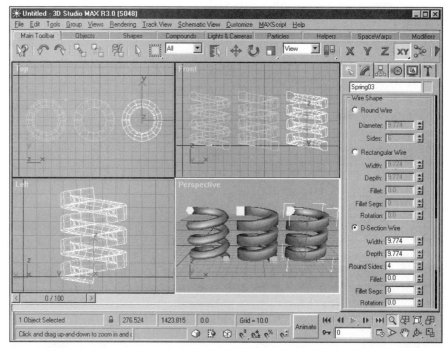

Figure 34-2: Spring objects can have three different cross sections: Round, Rectangular, or D-Section.

Springs typically move in a linear fashion: when you pull on them, they return to the same location if released. Stretching a spring beyond its limits causes nonlinear motion. By selecting the Enable Nonlinearity option, the spring is allowed to move in a nonlinear fashion if it is pulled too far from its relaxed state.

Damper

A *damper* is like a shock absorber — it is an object that absorbs force and transmits it at a lower level. A damper can also act as an actuator that causes regular forces. A damper object includes a base and a piston with a boot inside of a housing. These damper parts can be seen in Figure 34-3. Damper objects in MAX are essentially massless and cannot be used in collisions.

The Damper Parameters rollout, shown in Figure 34-4, includes two End Point Method options. The first, Free Damper/Actuator, produces the forces but isn't bound to any objects. The second, Bound to Object Pivots, actually transmits forces to the bound objects. The Pick Piston Object and Pick Base Object buttons let you select the objects to bind to either end of the damper.

Piston   Boot

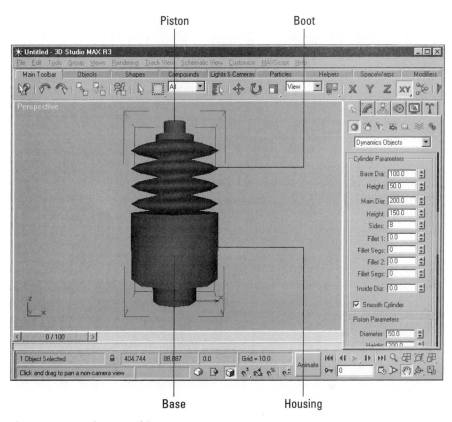

Base   Housing

Figure 34-3: A damper object

Figure 34-4: The Damper Parameters rollout includes many defining parameters.

When Free Damper/Actuator is selected, the Pin-to-Pin Height spinner becomes active. This spinner lets you specify the height of the free damper. Dampers can be made renderable and can be set to automatically generate mapping coordinates.

In the Cylinder Parameters and Piston Parameters sections, you can set the diameters of the base, main, inside, and piston parts of the damper. You can also specify the heights of the base, main, and piston cylinders. For the main cylinder, you can fillet the top and bottom. There is also a Smooth Cylinder option for smoothing the base, main, and piston cylinders.

The Boot Parameters section enables you to create a boot within the main cylinder. The boot adds more dampening effect to the damper. In shock absorbers, it consists of a rubber cylinder with several folds, and a similarly shaped part is found in the dynamic damper object. The Boot Parameters section holds values for defining this part, including Minimum and Maximum Diameter, the number of Folds, and Stop Diameter and Thickness. There is also an option for a Smooth Boot.

In the Dynamics Parameters section, shown in Figure 34-5, you can specify whether the object is a damper or an actuator. These are the opposite from one another. A damper absorbs force, and an actuator produces force. The Drag value is the measure of how much force the damper absorbs. It can be measured in pounds per in/sec or newtons per m/sec. Dampers can also be set to work in compression only (when end objects are pushed toward each other), extension only (when the end objects are pulled apart), or both. For an actuator, you can specify the force that it applies in pounds or newtons.

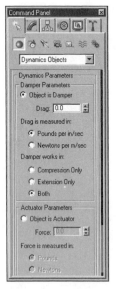

Figure 34-5: The Dynamics Parameters section of the Damper Parameters rollout defines the physical characteristics of the damper object.

Defining Dynamic Material Properties

Any objects can be used in a dynamic simulation. The Material Editor can endow these objects with materials that include dynamic surface properties. These properties define how the object is animated during collisions in a dynamic simulation and can be accessed in the Material Editor by selecting the Dynamics Properties rollout, shown in Figure 34-6. The default material settings on this rollout are similar to properties for steel.

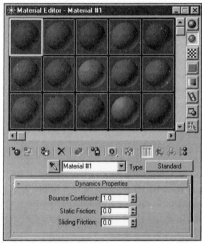

Figure 34-6: The Dynamics Properties rollout in the Material Editor lets you define physical properties.

Cross-Reference   The Material Editor is covered in Chapter 17, "Exploring the Material Editor."

The Bounce Coefficient value on the Dynamics Properties rollout determines how high an object will bounce after a collision. The default of 1.0 is equal to a normally elastic collision. A ball with a value higher than 1 will continue to bounce higher with each impact.

The Static Friction value determines how difficult it is to start an object moving when it's pushed across a surface. Objects with high Static Friction values require a lot of force to move them.

The Sliding Friction value determines how difficult it is to keep an object in motion across a surface. Ice would have a low Sliding Friction value because once it starts moving, it continues easily.

Using Dynamic Space Warps

Several Space Warps are designed to work specifically with dynamic simulations. These can be used to define global effects — such as gravity — that apply to all objects in the simulation.

Space Warps that can be used in a dynamic simulation include all Space Warps in the Particles and Dynamics and the Dynamics Interface subcategories, including Gravity, Wind, Push, Motor, Pin, Bomb, PDynaFlect, SDynaFlect, and UDynaFlect.

 Cross-Reference   For details on these Space Warps, see Chapter 25, "Using Space Warps."

Once these Space Warps are added to a scene, you can specify their binding using the dialog boxes in the Dynamics utility rollouts shown in the next section. You don't need to bind them with the Bind to Space Warp button.

Using the Dynamics Utility

Dynamic simulations are set up and run using the Dynamics utility, which can be found in the Utilities panel. To access the Dynamics utility, open the Utilities panel and click the Dynamics button. This opens two rollouts in the Utilities panel. These rollouts are covered in the following sections.

Using the Dynamics rollout

The Dynamics rollout, shown in Figure 34-7, lets you create a new simulation. To do this, click the New button and enter a name in the Dynamics rollout. TheRemove button can be used to delete an existing simulation from the list, and the Copy button creates a new version of the current simulation settings.

The Edit Object List button is used to add new objects to be included in the simulation. It opens the Edit Object List dialog box, shown in Figure 34-8. This dialog box includes two panes: the one on the left holds all the objects in the scene, and the one on the right holds the objects to include or exclude in the simulation. To include an object in the simulation, select it and click the arrow pointing to the right. This moves the object name to the right pane. Similar versions of this dialog box are used to specify the objects to include in collisions and which effects to include. The Edit Object List dialog box also supports Selection Sets and the Display Subtree, Select Subtree, and Case Sensitive options. When you've selected all the objects to include, click the OK button to close the dialog box.

Figure 34-7: The Dynamics rollout includes buttons for defining which objects to include in a simulation.

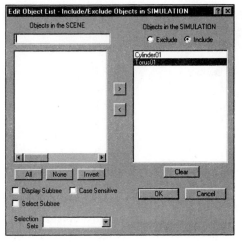

Figure 34-8: The Edit Object List dialog box lets you add objects to the simulation.

Object properties can be set for each object included in the simulation. To edit these properties, click the Edit Object button in the Dynamics rollout to open the Edit Object dialog box. This dialog box is explained later in this chapter.

The Select Objects in Sim button in the Dynamics rollout selects the objects in the viewports that are included as part of the simulation, as defined by the Edit Object List dialog box.

Simulation effects can be assigned in the Edit Object dialog box individually for each object, or you can select the Global Effects option in the Dynamics rollout to make all objects subject to the same effects. The Assign Global Effects button in this rollout opens the Assign Global Effects dialog box, shown in Figure 34-9. This dialog box lists all the Space Warps included in the scene. Selecting a Space Warp and clicking the right-pointing arrow includes the selected Space Warp as a global effect. Clicking the OK button closes this dialog box.

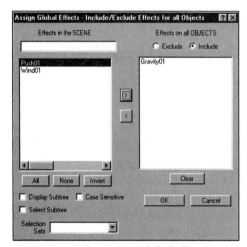

Figure 34-9: The Assign Global Effects dialog box lets you select which Space Warps to include in the simulation.

Collisions are handled in the same way as effects — they can be assigned to react either with specific objects or globally. The Assign Global Collisions button in the Dynamics rollout opens the Assign Global Collisions dialog box, shown in Figure 34-10, where you can select from all the objects included in the simulation. Objects not selected are subject to the other simulation effects but pass right through other objects rather than colliding.

At the bottom of the Dynamics rollout is the Solve button, which creates the actual keys. You can also select the Update Display w/ Solve option to update the viewports as the simulation is solved.

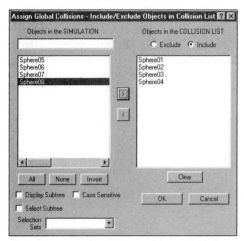

Figure 34-10: The Assign Global Collisions dialog box lets you select which objects to include in collisions.

Using the Timing & Simulation rollout

The Timing & Simulation rollout, shown in Figure 34-11, specifies the frame range for the dynamic simulation. The Calc Intervals Per Frame value determines how many calculations are made at each frame. This value can range from 1 to 160 — the higher the value, the more time it takes to compute the solution.

Figure 34-11: The Timing & Simulation rollout includes additional parameters for defining a simulation.

The Keys Every N Frames setting determines how often keys are created. For example a value of 2 would create a key for every other frame. The Time Scale can be used to speed or slow a simulation. A setting of 1 is normal speed, values from 0.1 up to 1 slow the animation, and values greater than 1 and up to 100 speed up the animation. This setting can be used to create a slow-motion animation of the simulation.

Inverse Kinematics systems can constrain motion through the specification of IK Joint Limits and IK Joint Damping. The Simulation Controls section includes options to enable or disable these settings.

Air resistance is a force that resists motion and is caused by an object crashing into air molecules. Air is denser the closer you are to sea level, which equates to a value of 100. In space, the air density is negligible and is represented by a value of 0.

The Close button at the bottom of the rollout closes the utility.

Editing simulation objects

In the Edit Object dialog box, shown in Figure 34-12, you can select which object to edit from the drop-down list in the upper left. This list includes all the objects in the simulation.

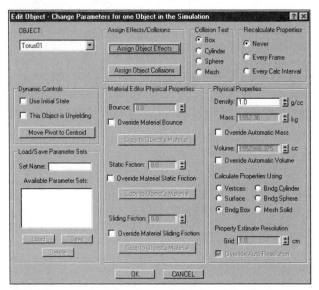

Figure 34-12: The Edit Object dialog box lets you assign simulation properties to an object.

In the Dynamic Controls section are two options: Use Initial State and This Object is Unyielding. The Use Initial State option computes the object's motion and momentum at the start time. If this option is disabled, the object is considered to be motionless at the start time and all existing keys are overwritten during the solution. The This Object is Unyielding option makes it so that the object isn't moved by collisions during the solution and is the setting to use to simulate a ground plane.

The Move Pivot to Centroid button repositions the object's pivot to the object's center of mass. Moving the pivot to the center of mass speeds the simulation calculations, but it alters the positions of any linked objects that are built based on the pivot.

In the Load/Save Parameter Sets section, you can save all the parameters in the Edit Object dialog box set by giving the set a name in the Set Name field and clicking the Save button. This parameter set can then be easily loaded and applied to another object. This feature saves you from having to set all the parameters for each object individually. To load a set, select the set from the list and click the Load button.

In the Assign Effects/Collisions section, each object can be assigned different effects using the Assign Object Effects button. You can also use the Assign Object Collisions button to assign which objects to collide with. These buttons open dialog boxes that are very similar to the Assign Global Effects and Assign Global Collisions dialog boxes shown previously in Figures 34-9 and 34-10.

In the Material Editor Physical Properties section, you can set the same properties for Bounce, Static Friction, and Sliding Friction that can be set for materials in the Material Editor. For each of these, you also have options that enable you to override the setting in the Material Editor as well as copy the property value to the object's material.

The Collision Test section offers Box, Cylinder, Sphere, and Mesh options for use in computing the collisions between objects. The Box option calculates more quickly than the other options because it uses the object's bounding box to compute collisions, but these collisions will not be as accurate. The Mesh option determines collisions by looking at the actual object surface, but this takes the longest to calculate.

The Recalculate Properties section lets you specify how often properties are recalculated. For example, material properties (such as mass) are animatable and can change over the course of an animation — with the volume of an object, for example, increasing as the object is scaled. Recalculation options include Never, Every Frame, and Every Calc Interval. The more often these properties need to be calculated, the longer the calculation will take.

The Physical Properties section enables you to set values for density, mass, and volume. *Density* is the material thickness of an object, measured in grams per cubic centimeter; *mass* is the base weight of an object, measured in kilograms; and *volume* is the space that the object takes up, measured in cubic centimeters. Because these values are interrelated, the Override options enable you to modify them independent of the other values.

The Calculate Properties Using subsection enables you to compute the property values using different volumes, depending on the accuracy you need. Options include Vertices, Surface, Bndg (Bounding) Box, Bndg Cylinder, Bndg Sphere, and Mesh Solid. The bounding options enclose the objects in an easy-to-compute bounding form. The Mesh Solid option increases the computation time significantly. Selecting the Mesh Solid option enables automatic resolution, but you can override this with the Override Auto Resolution option, in which case you can set the Grid value to determine how large each cell in the mesh grid is. These cells are measured in centimeters.

Optimizing a simulation

Solving a dynamic simulation once per frame can generate an enormous number of keys. This can significantly increase the file size. Using the Track View, you can reduce the number of keys while preserving the main keys used in the simulation.

To learn more about the Track View, check out Chapter 31, "Working with the Track View."

After solving a simulation, open the Track View and select the object tracks with keys in them. Then click the Edit Keys button, select all the keys, and click the Reduce Keys button. This opens a simple dialog box where you can specify the threshold value.

Tutorial: Bowling a strike

When I go bowling, I get a strike every once in a while, but in MAX I can get a strike every time. (I can also secure the pins so that no one can get a strike.)

To run a dynamic simulation of a bowling lane, follow these steps:

1. Start by creating a simple bowling pin from a lathed spline. Duplicate this pin and place ten of them like you see in a bowling lane. The bowling ball can be a simple sphere, and the lane is a thin box.

I could have used the plane object for the bowling lane, but the simulation works with the actual plane size visible in the viewport. When the simulation is solved, a warning would appear stating that the plane object has unshared edges, and the results could be unpredictable.

2. Open the Create panel, click the Space Warps category, select the Particles and Dynamics subcategory, and create a Gravity Space Warp. Position this Space Warp behind the bowling ball and point it at the bowling ball. In the Parameters rollout, set the Strength to **10**.

3. Open the Utilities panel and click the Dynamics button. This opens the Dynamics rollout. Click the New button and give the simulation the name **Bowling**. Then click the Edit Object List button, select all the objects in the left pane, move them to the right pane by clicking the arrow pointing to the right, and click OK.

4. Select the Effects by Object option in the Effects section of the rollout. Click the Edit Object button and select the sphere object in the Object drop-down list in the upper left corner. Then click the Assign Object Effects button, double-click the Gravity Space Warp to move it to the right pane, and click OK. Next select the box object used for the lane, enable the This Object is Unyielding option, and click OK.

Note

Because Space Warps are assigned using the Dynamics rollout, you don't need to use the Bind to Space Warp button.

5. For collisions, select the Global Collisions option and click the Assign Global Collisions button. Select all the objects in the left pane, and move them to the right pane by clicking the arrow pointing to the right. Then click OK.

6. In the Timing & Simulation rollout, set End Time to **40**. Then select Update Display w/ Solve and click the Solve button. This displays the simulation frames in the viewport. When the solution is finished, click the Play Animation button to see the entire simulation

Summary

This chapter covered the basics of animating a dynamic simulation using the Dynamics utility. In this chapter you:

✦ Created and used spring and damper dynamic objects

✦ Defined dynamic material properties for different objects using the Material Editor

✦ Used Space Warps to add forces to dynamic simulations

✦ Learned how the Dynamics utility is used to set up dynamic simulations

✦ Optimized simulation keys using the Track View Reduce Keys button

This concludes the part of the book on animation. In the next part, we look at rendering and post-production. The first chapter in that part discusses backgrounds, environments, and atmospheric effects.

✦   ✦   ✦

Rendering and Post-Production

Working with Backgrounds, Environments, and Atmospheric Effects

◆ ◆ ◆ ◆

In This Chapter

Creating an environment using background colors, images, and global lighting

Viewing the background image in a viewport

Using Atmospheric Apparatus gizmos to position atmospheric effects

Creating atmospheric effects, including Combustion, Fog, and Volume Fog

◆ ◆ ◆ ◆

In the real world, an environment of some kind surrounds all objects. The chapters thus far have focused on working with single-scene objects, but MAX has several tools that help create environments for these objects. Generally, this is one of the last steps you need to complete before you're ready to render the scene.

Creating an Environment

Whether it's a beautiful landscape or just clouds drifting by, the environment behind the scenes can do a lot to make the scene more believable. In this section, you learn about displaying a viewport background and using the Environment dialog box to create an environment.

Environment maps are used as background for the scene and can also be used as images reflected off shiny objects. Environment maps are displayed only in the final rendering and not in the viewports, but you can add a background to any viewport and even set the environment map to be displayed as the viewport backdrop.

But there is more to an environment than just a background. It also involves altering the global lighting and introducing atmosphere effects.

Defining the rendered environment

The dialog box where environments are created is the Environment dialog box, shown in Figure 35-1, which can be opened using the Rendering ⇨ Environment command. There are several settings that make up an environment, including a background color or image, global lighting, and atmospheric effects. All of these elements are available in the Environment dialog box.

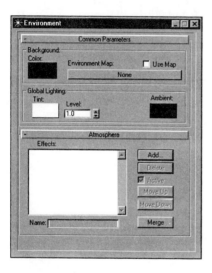

Figure 35-1: The Environment dialog box lets you select a background color or image, define global lighting, and work with atmospheric effects.

Setting a background color

The first color swatch in the Environment dialog box lets you specify a background color. This color appears by default if there is no environment map specified or if the Use Map option is disabled (and is black by default). The background color is animatable.

Using a background image

To select a background image to be used as an environment map, click the Environment Map button in the Environment dialog box — this opens the Material/Map browser. If you wish to load a bitmap image as the background image, double-click the Bitmap selection. The Select Bitmap Image dialog box opens. Locate the bitmap to use and click OK. The bitmap name appears on the Environment Map button.

Tip   If the environment map you wish to use is already displayed in one of the Material Editor sample slots, you can drag it directly from the Material Editor and drop it on the Map button in the Environment dialog box.

To change any of the environment map parameters (such as the mapping coordinates), you need to load the environment map into the Material Editor. This can be done by dragging the map button from the Environment dialog box onto one of the sample slots in the Material Editor. After releasing the material, the Instance (Copy) Map dialog box asks whether you want to create an Instance or a Copy. If you select Instance, any parameter changes you make to the material automatically update the map in the Environment dialog box.

Cross-Reference   For more information about the types of parameters that are available, see Chapter 18, "Using Material Maps."

The background image doesn't need to be an image — you can also load animations. Supported formats include AVI, FLC, and IFL files.

Figure 35-2 shows a scene with an image of the Golden Gate Bridge loaded as the environment map. Viewpoint Datalabs created the airplane model.

Figure 35-2: The results of a background image loaded into the Environment dialog box

Setting global lighting

The Tint color swatch in the Global Lighting section of the Environment dialog box specifies a color used to tint all lights. The Level value increases or decreases the overall lighting level for all lights in the scene. The Ambient color swatch sets the color for the ambient light in the scene, which is the darkest color that any shadows in the scene can be. All of these settings can be animated.

Adding atmospheric effects

At the bottom of the Environment dialog box is the Atmosphere rollout where you can add and set the parameters for several Atmospheric Effects. These Atmospheric Effects are discussed in the "Creating Atmospheric Effects" section that follows.

Tutorial: Creating a mystery with an environment map

The inspector has been called to investigate a robbery threat, but he happens to have a bad case of the flu and can't get out of bed, so he sends his apprentice to cover for him. The apprentice decides to set up a camera with a trip wire to catch the thief in the act.

The next day, after retrieving the camera, the inspector's apprentice is excited to see that a picture has been taken. It looks as if his plan has worked, but, after developing the film, the apprentice is shocked to see that someone bumped the camera and the thief got away — or did he?

To reflect an environment map, follow these steps:

1. We start by importing an image to use for the environment map. Select Rendering ➪ Environment to open the Environment dialog box and then click the Environment Map button to open the Material/Map Browser. Double-click the Bitmap selection and open the interior.jpg image. (This image was taken from a Corel Photo CD.) Before closing the Environment dialog box, make sure the Use Map option is selected.

2. Import and position the thief model at the foot of the stairs. (This thief is a model imported from Poser.) Then render the image and save it as a file named **mystery.jpg**.

3. Now you need to create another scene. Select the File ➪ New command and, in the New Scene dialog box, select the New All option and click OK.

4. Using several cylinder objects, create an umbrella holder and position it in the center of the scene. Open the Material Editor and click the first sample slot. Name the material **Gold** and then click the Type button to open the

Material/Map Browser. Select the Raytrace material and click OK. Back in the Material Editor, change the Diffuse color to a yellowish brown and change the Reflect color to a medium gray. Apply the material to the two bands around the container. Next create another material named **Silver** with similar settings. Change the Diffuse color to light gray and apply it to the rest of the container.

5. Select Rendering ➪ Environment to open the Environment dialog box. Click the Environment Map button to open the Material/Map Browser. Double-click the Bitmap selection to open the Select Bitmap Image File dialog box and locate and load the mystery.jpg file you created earlier.

6. Open the Material Editor and drag the environment map to the third sample slot. Select the Instance option from the Instance (Copy) Map dialog box that appears and click OK. Under the Coordinates rollout, select Cylindrical Environment from the Mapping drop-down list. Set the U Tiling value to **0.5** and the V Tiling value to **2.0**. This positions the thief where you can see his reflection on the umbrella holder. Because the material for the Environment Map is an Instance, it is automatically updated when these changes are made.

Figure 35-3 shows the resulting image with the thief reflected.

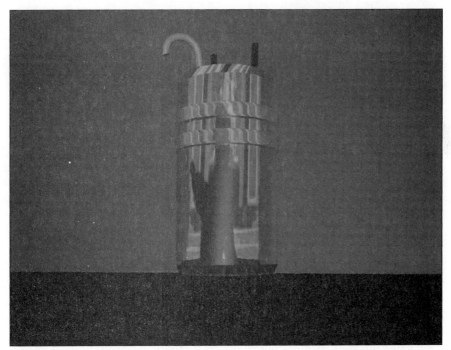

Figure 35-3: This rendered image shows an environment map being reflected.

Loading a viewport background

Even if the environment map is enabled, it is only visible in rendered images unless you make it visible in the viewport. Each viewport can have a different background image and the images can be animations.

To make the background image visible in the viewport, use the Views ⇨ Viewport Background command. This opens the Viewport Background dialog box, shown in Figure 35-4.

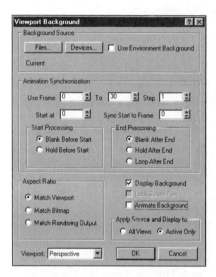

Figure 35-4: The Viewport Background dialog box lets you select a background source image or animation.

The Files button opens the Select Background Image dialog box where you can select the image to load. The Devices button lets you obtain a background from a device such as a Video Recorder. If an environment map is already loaded into the Environment dialog box, you can simply click the Use Environment Background option. Figure 35-5 shows the Environment map from the previous example displayed as a viewport background.

Note   The background is not actually visible unless the Display Background option is selected.

The Animation Synchronization section lets you set which frames of a background animation sequence are displayed. The Use Frame and To values determine which frames of the loaded animation are used. The Step value trims the number of frames that are to be used by selecting every Nth frame. For example, a Step value of 4 would use every fourth frame.

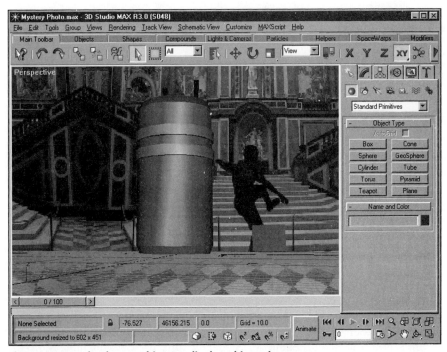

Figure 35-5: A background image displayed in a viewport

The Start At value is the frame in the current scene where this background animation would first appear. The Sync Start to Frame value is the frame of the background animation that should appear first. The Start and End Processing options let you determine what appears before the Start and End frames. Options include displaying a blank, holding the current frame, and looping.

Note   If an animation is selected as the background, make sure the Animate Background option is selected.

The Aspect Ratio section offers options for setting the size of the background image. You can select to Match Viewport, Match Bitmap, or Match Rendering Output.

The Apply Source and Display to option can be set to display the background in All Views or in the Active Only.

The Lock Zoom/Pan option locks the background image to the geometry so that when the objects in the scene are zoomed or panned, the background image follows. If the background gets out of line, you can reset its position with the Views ➪ Reset Background Transform command.

Caution   Zooming in too far on a background image can exceed your virtual memory and cause problems.

The background image can be updated at any time with the Views ⇨ Update Background Image command.

Obtaining background images

There are many different ways to obtain images to use as backdrops. Most of the background images I've used in my examples are taken from a library of CD-ROM photos such as Corel's Photo CD library. Similar photo CD-ROMs are available from many different publishers, including the following:

✦ **FotoSearch**—www.fotosearch.com

✦ **PhotoDisc**—www.photodisc.com

✦ **MetaCreation's MetaPhotos**—www.metacreations.com

✦ **PhotoAlto**—www.photoalto.com

✦ **Corel Galleria**—www.corel.com

For more customized images you could take your camera out and take your own pictures, and then scan them in. MAX doesn't support scanning images directly, but most image-editing packages enable you to scan images.

MAX can also be used to create background images. This is typically accomplished using the Video Post interface, but you could also render an image and load it back into the Environment dialog box, similar to what we did in the Mystery tutorial earlier in the chapter.

Cross-Reference   For more information on the Video Post interface, see Chapter 39, "Using the Video Post Interface."

Using Atmospheric Apparatus Gizmos

Before an atmospheric effect can be applied, you need to select an Atmospheric Apparatus gizmo, which tells the effect where it should be located. However, only the Combustion and the Volume Fog effects need Atmospheric Apparatus gizmos. To create an Atmospheric Apparatus gizmo, open the Create panel, click the Helper category, and from the subcategory drop-down, select Atmospheric Apparatus.

There are three different Atmospheric Apparatus gizmos: BoxGizmo, SphereGizmo, and CylGizmo. Each of these has a different shape, as shown in Figure 35-6.

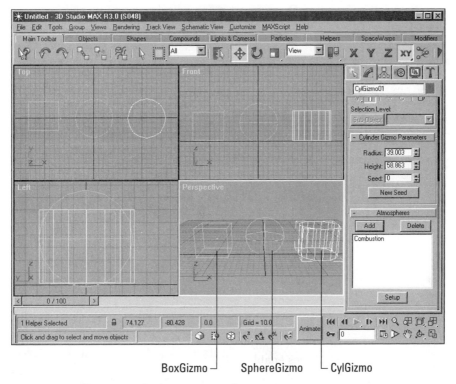

BoxGizmo ⌐   SphereGizmo   ⌐ CylGizmo

Figure 35-6: The Atmospheric Apparatus gizmos

Selecting a gizmo and opening the Modify panel reveals two different rollouts — one for defining the basic parameters such as the gizmo dimensions, and the other labeled Atmospheres that can be used to Add an Environment Effect to the gizmo. These rollouts can be seen in the previous figure. Each gizmo parameters rollout also includes a Seed value and a New Seed button. The Seed value sets a random number used to compute the atmospheric effect, and the New Seed button automatically generates a random seed. Two gizmos with the same seed values have nearly identical results.

If you select an Atmospheric Apparatus gizmo and open the Modify panel, an Atmospheres rollout appears. This rollout includes an Add button that opens the Add Atmosphere or Effect dialog box where you can select an effect. The selected effect is then included in a list in the Atmospheres rollout. You can delete these atmospheres by selecting them from the list and clicking the Delete button. The Setup button is active if an effect is selected in the list. It opens the Environment dialog box where the parameters for the effect are located. Adding Atmospheric Effects in the Modify panel is purely for convenience. They can also be added using the Environment dialog box, which is discussed next.

Creating Atmospheric Effects

In the Atmosphere section of the Environments dialog box (shown previously in Figure 35-1) is the Effects pane where the current effects for the scene are listed. To add a new effect, click the Add button. This opens the Add Atmospheric Effect dialog box, shown in Figure 35-7, where you can select from one of four default effects: Combustion, Fog, Volume Fog, and Volume Light. With plug-ins, you can increase the number of effects in this list.

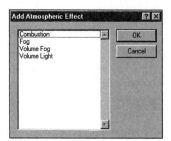

Figure 35-7: The Add Atmospheric Effect dialog box lets you select atmospheric effects.

You can delete an effect from the current Effects list in the Environment dialog box by selecting the effect and clicking the Delete button. The effects are applied in the order in which they are listed, so the effects at the bottom of the list are layered on top of all other effects.

Underneath the Effects pane is a Name field where you can type a new name for any effect in this field—this enables you to use the same effect multiple times. The effects are applied in the order in which they are listed in the Effects pane. To the right of the Effects pane, the Move Up and Move Down buttons are used to position the effects in the list.

The Merge button opens the Merge Atmospheric Effects dialog box where you can select a separate MAX file. You can then select and load any Render Effects from the other file.

Using the Combustion effect

To add the Combustion effect to the scene, click the Add button and select the Combustion selection. This opens the Combustion Parameters rollout, shown in Figure 35-8. At the top of the Combustion Parameters rollout is the Pick Gizmo button—clicking this button lets you select a gizmo in the scene. The selected gizmo appears in the drop-down list to the right. Multiple gizmos can be selected. To remove a gizmo from the list, select it and click the Remove Gizmo button.

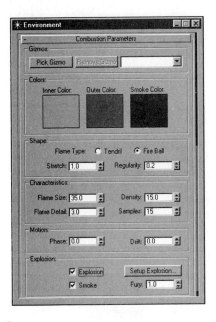

Figure 35-8: The Combustion Parameters rollout lets you define the look of the effect.

Note The Combustion effect only renders in nonorthographic views such as Perspective or a camera view.

The three color swatches define the color of the combustion effect and include an Inner Color, an Outer Color, and a Smoke Color. The Smoke Color is used only when the Explosion option is set.

The Shape section includes two Flame Type options: Tendril and Fireball. The Tendril shape produces veins of flames, and the Fireball shape is rounder and puffier. Figure 35-9 shows two spherical gizmos with the Combustion effect applied. The one on the left has a Tendril shape, and the one on the right is set to Fireball.

The Stretch value elongates the individual flames along the gizmo's Z-axis. Figure 35-10 shows the results of using the Stretch value. Both these gizmos are set to the Tendril shape, but the one on the left has a Stretch value of 1, and the one on the right has a Stretch value of 10.

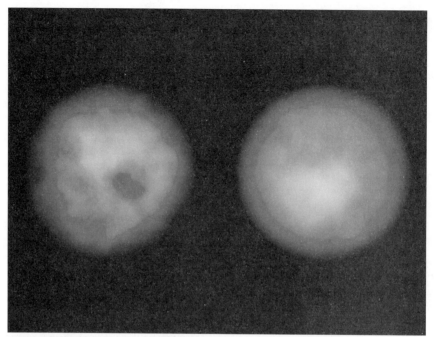

Figure 35-9: The Combustion atmospheric effect can be either Tendril or Fireball shape.

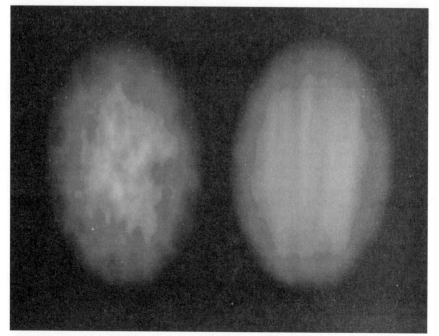

Figure 35-10: The Stretch value can elongate flames.

The Regularity value determines how much of the Atmospheric Apparatus is filled. The spherical gizmos in the previous figures were all set to 1. This adds a spherical look to the Combustion effect, because the entire gizmo is filled. For a more random shape, use a small Regularity value.

The Flame Size value affects the overall size of each individual flame (though this is dependent on the gizmo size as well). The Flame Detail value controls the edge sharpness of each flame and can range from 0 to 10. Lower values produce fuzzy, smooth flames, but higher values result in sharper, more distinct flames.

The Density value determines the thickness of each flame in its center — higher Density values result in flames that are brighter at the center, while lower values produce thinner, wispy flames. Figure 35-11 shows the difference caused by the Density values. The left effect has a Density of 10, and the right effect has a Density of 25.

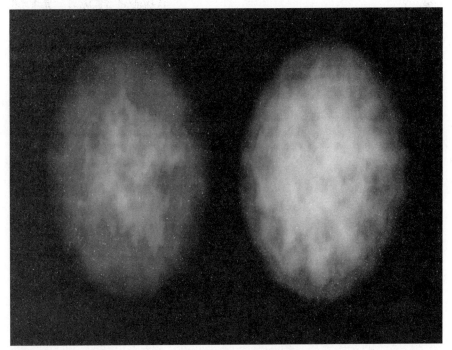

Figure 35-11: The Combustion effect brightness is tied closely to the flame Density value.

The Samples value sets the rate at which the effect is sampled. Higher sample values are required for more detail, but increase the render time.

Tutorial: Creating the sun

The Combustion effect can be used to create a realistic sun. The modeling part is easy — all it requires is a simple sphere — but the real effects come from the materials and the Combustion effect.

To create a sun, follow these steps:

1. Open the Create panel, click the Sphere button, and drag a simple sphere in the viewport.

2. Select Tools ⇨ Material Editor to open the Material Editor. Select the first sample slot and name the material **Sun**. Select an orange-yellow color for the Diffuse color swatch and a light brown color for the Self-Illumination color. Set the Opacity value to **90** and keep the Specular Highlights minimal.

3. In the Maps rollout, enable the Bump map, set the Amount value to **30,** and click the Map button. From the Material/Map Browser, double-click the Noise map. Under the Noise Parameters rollout, select the Turbulence Noise Type option and set the Size to **50**. Then drag the material onto the sphere object.

4. Back in the Create panel, select the Helpers category. Select the Atmospheric Apparatus subcategory. Click the SphereGizmo button and drag a sphere in the viewport that encompasses the "sun" sphere.

5. With the SphereGizmo still selected, open the Modify panel and click the Add button in the Atmospheres & Effects rollout. Select Combustion from the Add Atmospheres dialog box and click OK. Then select the Combustion effect and click the Setup button.

6. In the Combustion Parameters rollout, set the Inner Color to yellow, the Outer Color to red, and the Smoke color to black. For the Flame Type, select Tendril with Stretch and Regularity values of **1**. Set the Flame Size to **30**, the Density to **15**, the Flame Detail to **10**, and the Samples to **15**.

Figure 35-12 shows the resulting sun after it's been rendered.

Tutorial: Creating clouds

Sky images are fairly easy to find, or you could just take your camera outside and capture your own. The trick comes when you are trying to weave an object in and out of clouds. Although this can be done with a Shadow/Matte mask, it would be easier if the clouds were actual 3D objects. In this tutorial, we create some simple clouds using the Combustion effect.

Figure 35-12: A sun image created with a simple sphere, a material with a Noise Bump map, and the Combustion effect.

To create some clouds for a sky backdrop, follow these steps:

1. Select Rendering ⇨ Environment to open the Environment dialog box. Click the Background Color swatch and select a light blue color. In the Atmosphere section, click the Add button, select Combustion from the Add Atmospheric Effect list, and click OK.

2. Name the effect **Clouds**, and click each of the color swatches. Change the Inner Color to a dark gray, the Outer Color to a light gray, and the Smoke Color to white. Set the Shape to Fireball with a Stretch of **1** and a Regularity of **0.2**. Set the Flame Size to **35**, the Flame Detail to **3**, the Density to **15**, and the Samples to **15**.

3. If you want to add some motion to the clouds, click the Animate button, drag the Time Slider to the last frame, and change the Phase value to **45** and the Drift value to **30**. This causes the clouds to slowly drift through the sky. Disable the Animate button when you're finished. Close the Environment dialog box.

4. Open the Create panel, click the Helpers category, and select the Atmospheric Apparatus subcategory. Click the SphereGizmo and drag a sphere in the viewport. In the Sphere Gizmo Parameters rollout, select the Hemisphere option. Orient the hemisphere so that the dome is on the top.

5. Hold down the Shift key while moving the SphereGizmo about the scene to create several copies of the gizmo. Position these new gizmos around the scene at regular intervals.

6. Select a gizmo and open the Modify panel. In the Atmospheres & Effects rollout, click the Add button. In the Add Atmosphere or Effect dialog box, click the Atmosphere and Existing options, and then select Clouds from the list and click OK. Repeat this for each gizmo.

Figure 35-13 shows the resulting sky backdrop. By altering the Combustion parameters, you can create different types of clouds.

Figure 35-13: The Combustion atmospheric effect can be used to create clouds.

Using the Fog effect

Fog is an atmospheric effect that obscures objects or backgrounds by introducing a hazy layer—objects farther from the view are less visible. The normal Fog effect is used without an Atmospheric Apparatus and appears between the camera's environment range values. The camera's Near and Far Range settings set these values.

In the Environment dialog box, the Fog Parameters rollout appears when the Fog effect is added to the Effects list. This rollout, shown in Figure 35-14, includes a color swatch for setting the fog color. There is also an Environment Color Map button for loading a map. If a map is selected, the Use Map option turns it on or off. You can also select a map for the Environment Opacity, which affects the fog density.

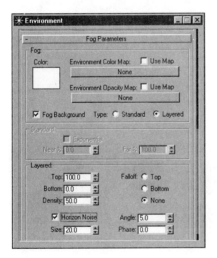

Figure 35-14: The Fog Parameters rollout lets you use either Standard fog or Layered fog.

The Fog Background option applies fog to the background image. The Type options include Standard and Layered fog. Selecting one of these fog background options enables its corresponding parameters.

The Standard parameters include an Exponential option for increasing density as a function of distance. If this option is disabled, the density is linear with distance. The Near and Far values are used to set the range densities.

Layered fog simulates layers of fog that move from dense areas to light areas. The Top and Bottom values set the limits of the fog, and the Density value sets its thickness. The Falloff option lets you set where the fog density goes to 0. The Horizon Noise option adds noise to the layer of fog at the horizon as determined by the Size, Angle, and Phase values.

Figure 35-15 shows several different fog options. The upper left image uses the Standard option, and the upper right image uses the Layered option with a Density of 50. The lower left image also uses the Layered option and has a Density value of 20. The lower right image has the Horizon Noise option enabled.

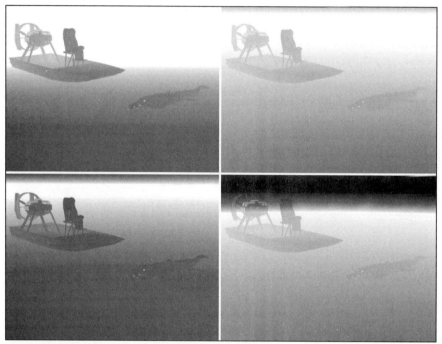

Figure 35-15: A rendered image with several different Fog effect options applied

Using the Volume Fog effect

The Volume Fog effect can be added to a scene by clicking the Add button and selecting the Volume Fog selection. This effect is different from the Fog effect in that it gives you more control over the exact position of the fog. This position is set by an Atmospheric Apparatus gizmo. The Volume Fog Parameters rollout, shown in Figure 35-16, lets you select a gizmo to use with the Pick Gizmo button. The selected gizmo is included in the drop-down list to the right of the buttons. Multiple gizmos can be selected. The Remove Gizmo button removes the selected gizmo from the list.

Note   The Atmospheric Apparatus gizmo contains only a portion of the total Volume Fog effect. If the gizmo is moved or scaled, it displays a different cropped portion of fog.

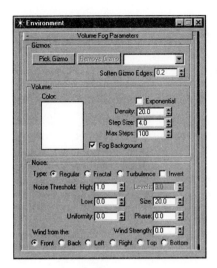

Figure 35-16: The Volume Fog Parameters rollout includes parameters for controlling the fog.

The Soften Gizmo Edges value feathers the fog effect at each edge. This value can range from 0 to 1.

Many of the settings for Volume Fog are the same as those for the Fog effect, but Volume Fog has several settings that are unique to it. These settings help set the patchy nature of Volume Fog. Step Size determines how small the patches of fog are. The Max Steps value limits the sampling of these small steps to keep the render time in check.

The Noise section settings also help determine the randomness of Volume Fog. Noise types include Regular, Fractal, Turbulence, and Invert. The Noise Threshold limits the effect of noise. Wind settings include direction and Wind Strength. The Phase value determines how the fog moves.

Tutorial: Creating a swamp scene

When I think of fog, I think of swamps. In this tutorial, we model a swamp scene.

To use the Volume Fog effect to create a swamp scene, follow these steps:

1. Start by creating a cattail plant. This can be done easily using the Capsule primitive (found under the Extended Primitives subcategory), some cylinders, and leaves made from a patch object. Clone and randomly position the cattails around the scene.

2. Import the dragonfly model created by Zygote Media and position it on top of one of the cattails.

3. Open the Create panel and select the Helpers category. Select the Atmospheric Apparatus subcategory and click the BoxGizmo button. Drag a box that covers the lower half of the cattails.

4. Select Rendering ⇨ Environment to open the Environment dialog box. Click the Add button to open the Add Atmospheric Effect dialog box and select Volume Fog. Click OK. In the Volume Fog Parameters rollout, click the Pick Gizmo button and select the BoxGizmo in a viewport.

5. Set the Density to **0.5** and the Noise Type to Turbulence. Then set the Wind Strength to **10** from the Left.

Figure 35-17 shows the finished image. Using Atmospheric Apparatus gizmos, you can position the fog in the exact place where you want it.

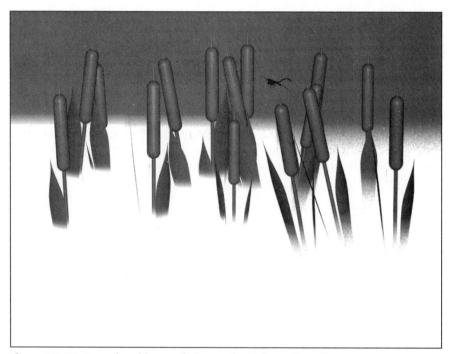

Figure 35-17: A rendered image that uses the Volume Fog effect

Using the Volume Light effect

The final choice in the effects dialog box is the Volume Light effect. This effect shares many of the same parameters as the other atmospheric effects. Although this is one of the atmospheric effects, it deals with lights and fits better in that section.

Cross-Reference The Volume Light effect is covered in Chapter 21, "Lighting Special Effects."

Summary

Creating the right environment can add a lot of realism to any rendered scene. Using the Environment dialog box, you can alter the background color, load an environment map, set global lighting, and work with atmospheric effects. Atmospheric Effects include Combustion, Fog, Volume Fog, and Volume Light.

In this chapter, you've:

✦ Learned to use the Environment dialog box to change the background color and image

✦ Loaded a viewport background image

✦ Created Atmospheric Apparatus gizmos for positioning atmospheric effects

✦ Worked with atmospheric effects, including Combustion, Fog, and Volume Fog

With an environment applied, your scene is finally ready to render. The next chapter looks at the details of rendering a scene.

✦   ✦   ✦

Setting Rendering Parameters

✦ ✦ ✦ ✦

In This Chapter

Understanding the MAX renderers

Working with previews

Render parameters

Rendering preferences

Creating VUE files

Using the Virtual Frame Buffer

Using the RAM Player

Render types

Rendering problems

✦ ✦ ✦ ✦

After modeling, applying materials, positioning lights and cameras, and animating your scene, you're finally ready to render the final output. MAX R3 includes a new Scanline Renderer that is optimized to speed up this process, and there are several settings that can be used to make this process even faster. Understanding the Render Scene dialog box and its functions can save you many headaches and computer cycles.

Understanding the MAX Renderers

Rendering deals with viewing the objects that make up a scene at various levels of detail. MAX uses several different rendering engines: one to view objects in the viewport, another to view material previews, and another to produce the final output. Each of these represents a trade-off between speed and quality. For example, the renderer used to display objects in the viewports is optimized for speed, but the renderer used to output final images leans toward quality.

Each renderer includes many different settings that can be used to speed the rendering process or improve the quality of the results. For example, the objects in a viewport can be set to different shading types such as Smooth, Faceted, or Wireframe. These settings can be found in the Viewport Configuration dialog box and in the pop-up menu that appears when you right-click the viewport title.

The plug-in nature of MAX enables you to select the renderer to use to output images. To change the default renderer, select the Customize ⇨ Preferences command to open the Preference Settings dialog box, and select the Rendering panel. You can select different renderers for the Production and Draft renderers.

The Material Editor Options dialog box also lets you specify which renderer is used to render material previews as seen in the sample slots. The options are the default Scanline renderer or the renderer currently selected in the Preferences dialog box.

The selected output renderer is used when you click the Render button in the Render Scene dialog box or from the Video Post dialog box. The Scanline renderer generates images one horizontal line at a time, with its progress shown in the Virtual Frame Buffer and the line currently being rendered shown as a white line.

Note   Although the viewports use a renderer to display objects, this chapter focuses mainly on producing output using the Render dialog box.

Working with Previews

Because output normally must be of high quality, rendering a completed scene can take a long time. Waiting for the final output in order to identify problems is an inefficient way to work. Even viewing animation sequences in the viewports with the Play Animation button cannot catch all problems.

One way to catch potential problems is to create a sample preview animation. *Previews* are test animation sequences that render quickly to give you an idea of the final output. The Rendering menu includes several commands for creating, renaming, and viewing previews. The rendering options available for previews are the same as the shading options that are available in the viewports.

Creating previews

Previews are created using the Rendering ⇨ Make Preview command. This opens the Make Preview dialog box, shown in Figure 36-1.

In the Make Preview dialog box, you can specify what frames to include using the Active Time Segment or Custom Range option. You can also choose Every Nth Frame or select a specific frame rate in the Playback FPS field. The image size is determined by the Percent of Output value, which is a percentage of the final output size. The resolution is also displayed.

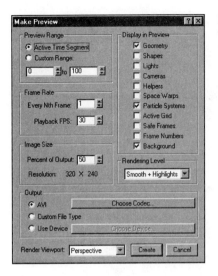

Figure 36-1: The Make Preview dialog box lets you specify the range, size, and output of a preview file.

The Display in Preview section offers a variety of options to include in the preview. These options include Geometry, Shapes, Lights, Cameras, Helpers, Space Warps, Particle Systems, Active Grid, Safe Frames, Frame Numbers, and Background. Because the preview output is rendered like the viewports, certain selected objects such as Lights and Cameras will actually display their icons as part of the file. The Frame Numbers option prints the frame number in the upper left corner of each frame.

The Rendering Level drop-down list includes the same shading options that are used to display objects in the viewports, including Smooth, Smooth + Highlights, Facets, Facets + Highlights, Lit Wireframes, Wireframe, and Bounding Box.

Output options include the default AVI option; a Custom File Type option, which enables you to choose your own format; and the Use Device option, which you can use to render the preview to a different device. For the AVI option, you can select a Codec, which is used to compress the resulting file. Options include Cinepak Code by Radius, Microsoft Video 1, and Full Frames (uncompressed), depending on the Codecs that are installed on your system. When the Use Device option is selected, the Choose Device button becomes active. Clicking this button opens the Select Output Image Device dialog box, where you can select and configure output devices such as a Digital Recorder.

At the bottom of the dialog box is a Render Viewport drop-down list where you can select which viewport to use to create your preview file. The Create button starts the rendering process. When a preview is being rendered, the viewports are replaced with a single image of the current render frame, and the Status Bar is replaced by a Progress Bar and a Cancel button. Figure 36-2 shows a preview file being created.

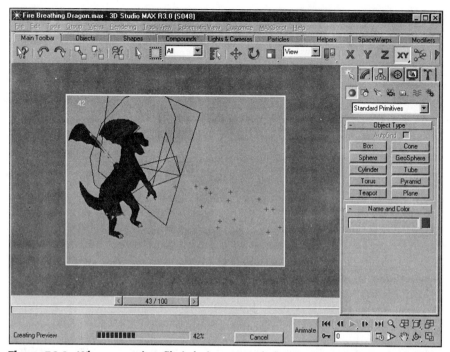

Figure 36-2: When a preview file is being created, the viewports are replaced with a single view of the current frame.

Tip   The Esc key on your keyboard can also be used to cancel a rendering job.

If you cancel the rendering, the Make Preview alert box offers the options Stop and Play, Stop and Don't Play, and Don't Stop.

Viewing previews

When a preview file is finished rendering, the default Media Player for your system loads and displays the preview file. This autoplay feature can be disabled using the Autoplay Preview File option in the General panel of the Preference Settings dialog box.

At any time, you can replay the preview file using the Rendering ➪ View Preview command. This loads the latest preview file and displays it in the Media Player.

Renaming previews

The preview file is actually saved as a file named scene.avi and is saved by default in the previews subdirectory. Be aware that this file is automatically overwritten when a new preview is created. You can save a preview file by renaming it using the Rendering ➪ Rename Preview File command. This opens the Save Preview As dialog box, where you can give the preview file a name.

Render Parameters

Once you're comfortable with the preview file and you're ready to render a file, you need to open the Render Scene dialog box, shown in Figure 36-3, by means of the Rendering ➪ Render command or by clicking the Render Scene button in the main toolbar. This dialog box has two rollouts: the Common Parameters rollout and a rollout for the selected renderer. The default renderer is the Scanline A-Buffer renderer. The parameters in these rollouts are covered later in this chapter.

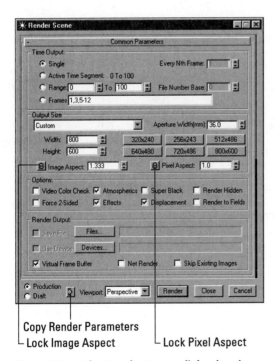

Copy Render Parameters
└ Lock Image Aspect   └ Lock Pixel Aspect

Figure 36-3: The Render Scene dialog box is used to render the final output.

Tip   The keyboard shortcut for opening the Render Scene dialog box is Shift+R.

Initiating a render job

At the bottom of the Render Scene dialog box are several controls that are always visible; these controls let you initiate a render job. There are two render modes: Production and Draft. Each of these modes can use a different renderer with different render settings. The Copy Render Parameters button to the right of the render mode buttons lets you duplicate the settings from the current mode to the other mode.

The Viewport drop-down list includes all of the available viewports. The one selected is the one that gets rendered when the Render button is clicked. The Render button starts the rendering process, and the Close and Cancel buttons are both used to exit the dialog box. You can click the Render button without changing any settings, and the default parameters will be used.

Note   When the Render Scene dialog box is opened, the currently active viewport appears in the Viewport drop-down list.

When the Render button is clicked, the Rendering dialog box is displayed. This dialog box, shown in Figure 36-4, displays all the settings for the current render job and tracks its progress. The Rendering dialog box also includes Pause and Cancel buttons for halting the rendering process. If the rendering is stopped, the Rendering dialog box disappears, but the Virtual Frame Buffer stays open.

Caution   If you close the Virtual Frame Buffer window, the render job will still continue. To cancel the rendering, click the Pause or Cancel button, or press the Esc key on your keyboard.

Tip   Once you've set up the render settings for an image, you can re-render an image without opening the Render Scene dialog box by clicking the Render Last button or by using the Shift+E keyboard shortcut.

Common parameters

The Common Parameters rollout in the Render Scene dialog box (shown previously in Figure 36-3) includes the same controls regardless of the renderer being used.

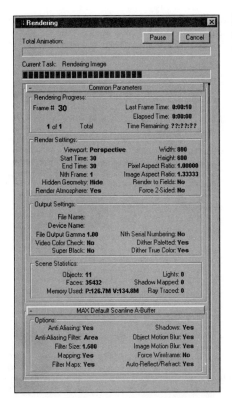

Figure 36-4: The Rendering dialog box displays the current render settings and progress of the render job.

The Time Output section defines which animation frames to include in the output. The Single option renders the current frame specified by the Time Slider. The Active Time Segment option renders the complete range specified by the Time Slider. The Range option lets you set a unique range of frames to render by entering the beginning and ending frame numbers. The last option is Frames, where you can enter individual frames and ranges using commas and hyphens. For example, entering **1, 6, 8-12** will render frames 1, 6, and 8 through 12. There is also an Every Nth Frame value, which is active for the Active Time Segment and Range options. It renders every nth frame in the active segment. For example, entering **3** would cause every third frame to be rendered. This is useful for sped-up animations. The File Number Base is the number to add or subtract from the current frame number for the reference numbers attached to the end of each image file. For example, a File Number Base value of 10 for a Range value of 1–10 would label the files as image0011, image0012, and so on.

The Output Size section defines the resolution of the rendered images or animation. The drop-down list includes a list of standard film and video resolutions, including the following:

✦ Custom

✦ 35mm 1.33:1 Full Aperture (cine)

✦ 35mm 1.37:1 Full Academy (cine)

✦ 35mm 1.66:1 (cine)

✦ 35mm 1.75:1 (cine)

✦ 35mm 1.85:1 (cine)

✦ 35mm Anamorphic (2.35:1)

✦ 35mm Anamorphic (2.35:1) (squeezed)

✦ 70mm Panavision (cine)

✦ 70mm IMAX (cine)

✦ VistaVision

✦ 35mm (24mm × 36mm) (slide)

✦ 6cm × 6cm (2¼" × 2¼") (slide)

✦ 4" × 5" or 8" × 10" (slide)

✦ NTSC (video)

✦ PAL (video)

✦ HDTV (video)

Aperture Width is a property of cameras that defines the relationship between the lens and the field of view. The resolutions listed in the Aperture Width drop-down list alter this value without changing the view by modifying the Lens value in the scene.

For each resolution, you can change the Width and Height values. Each resolution also has six preset buttons for setting these values.

Tip   You can set the resolutions of any of the preset buttons by right-clicking the button you want to change. This opens the Configure Preset dialog box, where you can set the button's Width, Height, and Pixel Aspect values.

The Image Aspect is the ratio of the image width to its height. You can also set the Pixel Aspect ratio to correct rendering on different devices. Both of these values have lock icons to their left that lock the aspect ratio for the set resolution. This automatically changes the Width dimension whenever the Height value is changed and vice versa. The Aperture Width, Image Aspect, and Pixel Aspect values can be set only when Custom is selected in the drop-down list.

The Options section includes the following options:

✦ **Video Color Check** — Enables a check for nonsafe NTSC or PAL colors. Nonsafe colors are displayed incorrectly when these formats are used.

✦ **Force 2-Sided** — Renders both sides of every face. This essentially doubles the render time and should be used only if singular faces or the inside of an object are visible.

✦ **Atmospherics** — Renders any atmospheric effects that are set up in the Environment dialog box.

✦ **Effects** — Enables any Render Effects that have been set up.

✦ **Super Black** — Enables Super Black, which is used for video compositing. Rendered images with black backgrounds have trouble in some video formats. The Super Black option prevents these problems.

✦ **Displacement** — Enables any surface displacement caused by an applied displacement map.

✦ **Render Hidden** — Renders all objects in the scene, including hidden objects. Using this option, you can hide objects for quick viewport updates and include them in the final rendering.

✦ **Render to Fields** — Enables animations to be rendered as fields. Fields are used by video formats. Video animations include a field with every odd scan line and one field with every even scan line. These fields are composited when displayed.

The Render Output section enables you to output the image or animations to a file, a device, or the Virtual Frame Buffer. To save the output to a file, click the Files button and select a location in the Render Output File dialog box. Supported formats include AVI, BMP, Postscript (EPS), JPEG, Kodak Cineon (CIN), FLC, Quicktime (MOV), PNG, RLA, RPF, SGI's Format (RGB), Targa (TGA), and TIF. The Device button can output to a device such as a video recorder. If the Virtual Frame Buffer option is selected, then both the Files and Devices buttons are disabled. (The Virtual Frame Buffer is discussed later in this chapter.)

The Net Render option enables network rendering. The Skip Existing Images option doesn't replace any images with the same file name, a feature that can be used to continue a rendering job that has been canceled.

For more information on network rendering, see Chapter 38, "Using Network Rendering."

Scanline A-Buffer renderer

The MAX Default Scanline A-Buffer rollout, shown in Figure 36-5, is the default renderer rollout that appears in the Render Scene dialog box. If a different renderer is loaded, then a different rollout for that renderer is displayed in the dialog box.

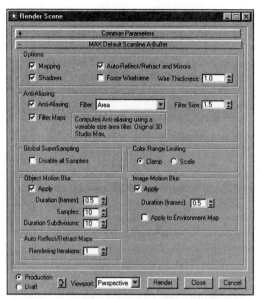

Figure 36-5: The Scanline A-Buffer rollout includes settings unique to this renderer.

You can use the Options section at the top of the Scanline A-Buffer rollout to quickly disable various render options for quicker results. These options include Mapping, Shadows, Auto Reflect/Refract and Mirrors, and Force Wireframe. For the Force Wireframe option, you can define a Wire Thickness value in pixels.

Another way to speed up rendering is to disable the Anti-Aliasing and Filter Maps features. Anti-Aliasing smoothes jagged edges that appear where colors change. The Filter Maps option enables you to disable the computationally expensive process of filtering material maps. The Filter drop-down list lets you select image filters that are applied at the pixel level during rendering. Below the drop-down list is a description of the current filter. The Filter Size value applies only to the Soften filter. Available filters include the following.

✦ **Area**—Does an anti-aliasing sweep using the designated area specified by the Filter Size value.

✦ **Blackman**—Sharpens the image with a 25-pixel area. It provides no edge enhancement.

✦ **Blend**—Somewhere between a sharp and a coarse Soften filter. It includes Filter Size and Blend values.

✦ **Catmull-Rom**—Sharpens with a 25-pixel filter and includes edge enhancement.

✦ **Cook Variable** — Can produce sharp results for small Filter Size values and blurred images for larger values.

✦ **Cubic** — Based on cubic-spline curves and produces a blurring effect.

✦ **Mitchell-Netravali** — Includes Blur and Ringing parameters.

✦ **Quadratic** — Based on a quadratic spline and produces blurring with a 9-pixel area.

✦ **Sharp Quadratic** — Produces sharp effects from a 9-pixel area.

✦ **Soften** — Causes mild blurring and includes a Filter Size value.

✦ **Video** — Blurs the image using a 25-pixel filter optimized for NTSC and PAL video.

Global SuperSampling is an additional anti-aliasing process that can be applied to materials. This process can take a long time to render and can be disabled using the Disable all Samplers option.

Color Range Limiting offers two methods for correcting overbrightness caused by applying filters. The Clamp method lowers any value above a relative ceiling of 1 to 1 and raises any values below 0 to 0. The Scale method scales all colors between the maximum and minimum values.

The Scanline A-Buffer rollout also offers two different types of motion blur: Object Motion Blur and Image Motion Blur. Either of these can be enabled using the Apply options.

Object Motion Blur is set in the Properties dialog box for each object. The renderer completes this blur by rendering the object over several frames. The movement of the camera doesn't affect this type of blur. The Duration value determines how long the object is blurred between frames. The Samples value specifies how many Duration units are sampled. The Duration Subdivision value is the number of copies rendered within each Duration segment. All these values can have a maximum setting of 16. The smoothest blurs occur when the Duration and Samples values are equal.

Image Motion Blur is also set in the Properties dialog box for each object. This type of blur is affected by the movement of the camera and is applied after the image has been rendered. It is done by smearing the image in proportion to the movement of the various objects. The Duration value determines the time length of the blur between frames. The Apply to Environment Map option lets you apply the blurring effect to the background as well as the objects.

Note   Two additional blur effects can be added to a scene: the Blur Render Effect, found in the Rendering Effects dialog box (covered in Chapter 37, "Using Render Effects"), and the Scene Motion Blur effect, available through the Video Post dialog box (covered in Chapter 39, "Using the Video Post Interface").

The Auto Reflect/Refract Maps section lets you specify a Rendering Iterations value for reflection maps within the scene. The higher the value, the more objects are included in the reflection computations and the longer the rendering time.

Rendering Preferences

In addition to the settings available in the Render Scene dialog box, the Rendering panel in the Preference Settings dialog box includes many global rendering settings. Figure 36-6 shows this panel.

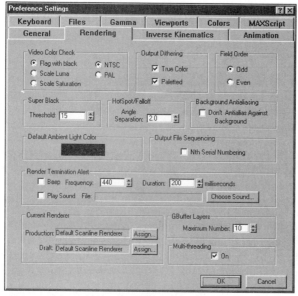

Figure 36-6: The Rendering panel in the Preference Settings dialog box lets you set global rendering settings.

The Video Color Check options specify how unsafe video colors are flagged or corrected. The Flag with black option shows the unsafe colors, and the Scale options correct them by scaling either the luminance or the saturation. You can also choose to check NTSC or PAL formats.

Caution   Be aware that the Scale options can actually discolor some objects.

Output Dithering options can enable or disable dithering of colors. The options include True Color for 24-bit images and Paletted for 8-bit images.

The Field Order options let you select which field is rendered first. Some video devices use even first, and others use odd first. Check your specific device to see which setting is correct.

The Super Black Threshold setting is the level below which black is displayed as Super Black.

The Angle Separation value sets the angle between the Hotspot and Falloff cones of a light. If the Hotspot angle equals the Falloff angle, then alias artifacts will appear.

The option Don't Anti-alias Against Background should be enabled if you plan on using a rendered object as part of a composite image.

The Default Ambient Light Color is the darkest color for rendered shadows in the scene. Selecting a color other than black brightens the shadows.

You can set the Output File Sequencing option to list the frames in order if the Nth Serial Numbering option is enabled. If the Nth Serial Numbering option is disabled, the sequence uses the actual frame numbers.

In the Render Termination Alert section, you can elect to have a beep triggered when a rendering job is finished. The Frequency value changes the pitch of the sound and the Duration value changes its length. You can also choose to load and play a different sound. The Choose Sound button opens a File dialog box where you can select the sound file to play.

The Current Renderer section lets you assign the renderer to use for Production and Draft render modes. Click the Assign button to select a new renderer for each mode. In the default setup, the two renderer options are the Default Scanline Renderer (which was covered earlier in the chapter) and the VUE File Renderer (which is described in the next section).

The GBuffer Layers value is the maximum number of graphics buffers to allow during rendering. This value can range between 1 and 1000. The value you can use depends on the memory of your system.

The Multi-threading option enables the renderer to complete different rendering tasks as separate threads. Threads use the available processor cycles more efficiently by subdividing tasks. This should be enabled, especially if you're rendering on a multiprocessor computer.

Creating VUE Files

One of the default Current Renderer options available in the Preference Settings dialog box is the VUE File Renderer. This renderer creates VUE files. A *VUE file* is a text-based script for rendering a scene and can be edited using a text editor.

The contents of a VUE file include keywords followed by a list of parameters. These keywords include objects such as "light" and "camera," and commands such as "transform" and "top." Parameters can include the part name and values separated by commas. Figure 36-7 shows a sample VUE file.

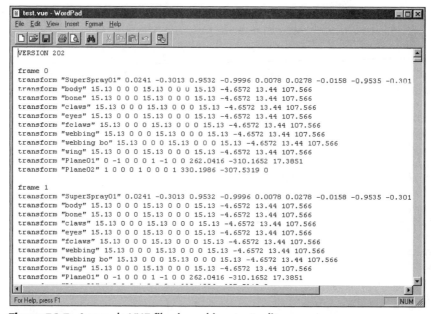

Figure 36-7: A sample VUE file viewed in a text editor

When the VUE File Renderer is selected, the rollout in the Render Scene dialog box includes only a single Files button for giving the VUE file a name.

Caution   Be sure to use the Files button in the VUE File Renderer rollout and not the Files button in the Common Parameters rollout. When a VUE file is rendered, the Virtual Frame Buffer opens, but no image is created.

Using the Virtual Frame Buffer

The Virtual Frame Buffer is a temporary window that holds any rendered images. Often when developing a scene, you want to test-render an image to view the shadows or transparency not visible in the viewports. The Virtual Frame Buffer, shown in Figure 36-8, enables you to view these test renderings without saving any data to the network or hard drive.

Note   The scene in the figure uses a background image from Corel's Photo CD and a crocodile model created by Viewpoint Datalabs.

This buffer is opened when the Virtual Frame Buffer option is selected and the Render button is clicked in the Render Scene dialog box.

To zoom in on the buffer, hold the Ctrl key down and click the buffer. Click with the right mouse button while holding down the Ctrl key to zoom out. The Shift key enables you to pan the buffer image. You can also use the mouse wheel (if you have a scrolling mouse) to zoom and pan within the frame buffer.

Tip   You can zoom and pan the image while it is rendering.

At the top of the frame buffer dialog box are several icon buttons. The first is the Save Bitmap button, which enables you to save the current frame buffer image. The Clone Virtual Frame Buffer button creates another frame buffer dialog box. Any new rendering is rendered to this new dialog box, which is useful for comparing two images.

The next four buttons enable the red, green, blue, and alpha channels. The alpha channel holds any transparency information for the image. The alpha channel is a grayscale map, with black showing the transparent areas and white showing the opaque areas. Next to the Display Alpha Channel button is the Monochrome button, which displays the image as a grayscale image. The Clear button erases the image from the window.

Save Bitmap

Clone Virtual Frame Buffer

Enable Red Channel

Enable Green Channel

Enable Blue Channel

Display Alpha Channel

Monochrome

Clear   Channel Display list

Last selected pixel
color swatch

Figure 36-8: The Virtual Frame Buffer displays rendered images
without saving them to a file.

The Channel Display drop-down list lets you select the channel to display. The
color swatch at the right shows the color of the currently selected pixel. You can
select new pixels by right-clicking and holding on the image. This temporarily
displays a small dialog box with the image dimensions and the RGB value of the
pixel directly under the cursor. The color in the color swatch can then be dragged
and dropped in other dialog boxes such as the Material Editor.

Using the RAM Player

Just as the Virtual Frame Buffer can be used to view and compare rendered images, the RAM Player enables you to view rendered animations in memory. With animations loaded in memory, you can selectively change the frame rates. Figure 36-9 shows the RAM Player interface, which is opened by selecting Rendering ➪ RAM Player.

Figure 36-9: The RAM Player interface lets you load two different images or animations for comparison.

New Feature   The RAM Player is new to Release 3.

The button icons at the top of the RAM Player interface window enable you to load an image to two different channels named A and B. The two Open Channel buttons open a file dialog box where you can select the file to load. When a file is selected, the RAMPlayer Configuration dialog box opens, as shown in Figure 36-10. In this dialog box you can select the dimensions, frames, and memory to use.

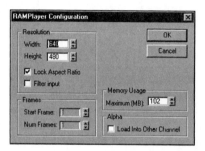

Figure 36-10: The RAMPlayer Configuration dialog box lets you specify the resolution of the loaded image.

The Open Last Rendered Image button in the RAM Player interface window provides quick access to the last rendered image. The Close channel button clears the channel. The Save Channel button opens a file dialog box for saving the current file.

Caution   All files that are loaded into the RAM Player are converted to 24-bit images.

The Channel A and Channel B (toggle) buttons enable either channel or both. The Horizontal/Vertical Screen Split button switches the dividing line between the two channels to a horizontal or vertical line. When the images are aligned one on top of the other, two small triangles mark where one channel leaves off and the other begins. You can drag these triangles to alter the space for each channel.

The frame controls let you move between the frames. You can move to the first, previous, next, or last frame and play the animation forward or in reverse. The drop-down list to the right of the frame controls displays the current frame rate setting.

You can capture the color of any pixel in the image by holding down the Ctrl key while clicking the image with the right mouse button. This puts the selected color in the color swatch. The RGB value for this pixel is displayed in the blue title bar.

The Double Buffer button synchronizes the frames of the two channels.

Tip   You can use the arrow keys and Page Up and Page Down keys to move through the frames of the animation. The A and B keys are used to enable the two channels.

Render Types

From the main toolbar, the Render Type drop-down list enables you to render subsections of the scene. The default setting is View. This renders the entire view as seen in the active viewport. Once a selection is picked from the list, click the Quick Render button or the Render button in the Render Scene dialog box to begin the rendering.

The Selected setting renders only the selected objects in the active viewport. The Region setting puts a frame of dotted lines with handles in the active viewport. This frame lets you define a region to render. You can resize the frame by dragging the handles. When you have defined the region, click the OK button that appears in the lower right corner of the active viewport. Figure 36-11 shows a region being defined.

Figure 36-11: To render a region, drag the frame over the region and click the OK button.

The Crop setting is similar to Region in that it uses a frame to define a region, but the Crop setting doesn't include the areas outside the defined frame. The Blowup setting takes the defined region and increases its size to fill the render window. The frame for Blowup is constrained to the aspect ratio of the final resolution.

The Box Selected setting renders the selected objects, but it presents a dialog box where you can specify the dimensions for rendering the bounding box of the selected objects. Constrain the Aspect Ratio is an additional option.

Rendering Problems

The single greatest problem with rendering is that it takes too long. Changing the render settings can alleviate this; however, there are other problems that can hamper the rendering process.

If an object has an applied material with a map that can't be located, the renderer will open a warning dialog box listing the maps that can't be found. The dialog box gives you the option to Continue, Cancel, or Browse for the missing file. The Browse button opens the Configure Bitmap Paths dialog box, where you can add a path to include in the search.

Summary

This chapter covered the basics of producing output using the Render Scene dialog box. Although rendering a scene can take a long time to complete, MAX includes many settings that can speed up the process, as well as helpful tools such as the Virtual Frame Buffer and the RAM Player.

In this chapter, you've:

- ✦ Learned to work with previews
- ✦ Discovered how to control the various render parameters
- ✦ Configured the global rendering preferences
- ✦ Created VUE files
- ✦ Learned to use the Virtual Frame Buffer and the RAM Player
- ✦ Seen the different render types

In the next chapter, we cover effects that you can add to a scene after it has been rendered without using the Video Post dialog box. These effects are called Render Effects.

✦   ✦   ✦

Using Render Effects

MAX Release 3 has added a new class of effects that can be interactively rendered to the Virtual Frame Buffer without using any post-production features such as the Video Post dialog box. These new effects are called Render Effects. This chapter presents the various Render Effects and shows you how to use them.

Adding Render Effects

All Render Effects can be set up from the Rendering Effects dialog box, which is opened by selecting Rendering ⇨ Effects. Figure 37-1 shows this dialog box.

Figure 37-1: The Rendering Effects dialog box lets you apply interactive post-production effects to an image.

New Feature   Render Effects are new to Release 3.

The Effects pane displays all the effects that are included in the current scene. To add a new effect, click the Add button — this opens the Add Effect dialog box where you can select from a default list of seven effects. Each of these effects is covered in more detail later in the chapter. You can delete an effect from the current list by selecting that effect and clicking the Delete button.

Below the Effects pane is a Name field. You can type a new name for any effect in this field — doing so enables you to use the same effect multiple times. The effects are applied in the order in which they are listed in the Effects pane. To the right of the Effects pane, the Move Up and Move Down buttons are used to reposition the effects in the list. The effects are added to the scene in the order that they are listed.

Caution   It is possible for one effect to cover another effect. Rearranging the order can help resolve this problem.

The Merge button opens the Merge Effect dialog box where you can select a separate MAX file. If you select a MAX file and click Open, the Merge Rendering Effects dialog box presents you with a list of Render Effects used in the opened MAX file. You can then select and load any of these Render Effects into the current scene.

The Preview section holds the controls for interactively viewing the various effects. Previews are displayed in the Virtual Frame Buffer and can be set to view All the effects or only the Current one. The Show Original button displays the scene before any effects are applied, and the Update Scene button updates the rendered image if any changes have been made to the scene.

Note   If the Virtual Frame Buffer isn't open, any of these buttons opens it and renders the scene with the current settings in the Render Scene dialog box.

The Interactive option automatically updates the image whenever an effect parameter or scene object is changed. If this option is disabled, the Update Effect button can be used to manually update the image.

Caution   If the Interactive option is enabled and the Rendering Effects dialog box is open, the image is re-rendered in the Virtual Frame Buffer every time a change is made to the scene. This can slow down the system dramatically.

The Currently Updating bar shows the progress of the rendering update.

The remainder of the Rendering Effects dialog box contains rollouts for the selected Render Effect. These rollouts are covered in this chapter along with their corresponding effects.

Render Effect Types

The Add Effect dialog box includes seven different Render Effects that you can select, which are described in this section. MAX also enables you to add even more options to this list via plug-ins.

Cross-Reference

Plug-ins are covered in Chapter 40, "Extending MAX with Plug-Ins."

Lens Effects

Lens Effects simulate the types of lighting effects that are possible with actual camera lenses and filters. When the Lens Effects selection is added to the Effects list, several different effects become available, including Glow, Ring, Ray, Auto Secondary, Manual Secondary, Star, and Streak. These effects are listed in the Lens Effects Parameters rollout in the Rendering Effects dialog box, and, when an effect is included in a scene, rollouts and parameters for that effect are added to the dialog box as well.

Several of these Lens Effects can be used simultaneously. To include an effect, go to the Lens Effects Parameters rollout, shown in Figure 37-2, select the desired effect from the list on the left, and click the arrow button pointing to the right. The included effects are listed in the pane on the right.

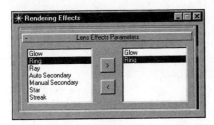

Figure 37-2: The Lens Effects Parameters rollout lets you select one of seven different effects.

Basic Parameters

Under the Lens Effects Parameters rollout in the Rendering Effects dialog box is the Lens Effects Globals rollout. All effects available in Lens Effects use two common panels in this rollout: Parameters and Scene.

The Parameters panel

The Parameters panel of the Lens Effects Globals rollout, shown in Figure 37-3, includes Load and Save buttons for loading and saving parameter settings specified in the various rollouts. These settings are saved as LZV files.

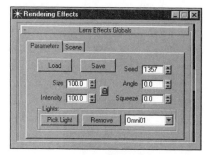

Figure 37-3: The Parameters panel of the Lens Effects Globals rollout lets you load and save parameter settings.

The Size value determines the overall size of the effect as a percentage of the rendered image. The Intensity value controls the brightness and opacity of the effect. Large values are brighter and more opaque, and small values are dimmer and more transparent. The Size and Intensity values can be locked together. Figure 37-4 shows three Star Lens Effects. The one on the left has a Size of 20 and an Intensity of 200, the middle one has a Size of 40 and an Intensity of 100, and the one on the right has a Size of 60 and an Intensity of 50.

Figure 37-4: These three Star Lens Effects vary in size and intensity.

The Seed value provides the randomness of the effect. Changing the Seed value changes the effect's look. The Angle value spins the effect about the camera's axis. The Squeeze value lengthens the horizontal axis for positive values and lengthens the vertical axis for negative values. Squeeze values can range from -100 to 100. Figure 37-5 shows the affect of the Squeeze value—the left glow effect has a Squeeze value of –50, the middle one's value is 0, and the right glow's Squeeze value is 50.

Figure 37-5: The Glow Render Effect can be squeezed either horizontally or vertically.

All effects are applied to light sources, and the Pick Light button lets you select a light to apply the effect to. Each selected light is displayed in a drop-down list. You can remove any of these lights with the Remove Light button.

The Scene panel

The second Lens Effects Globals panel common to all effects is the Scene panel, shown in Figure 37-6. This rollout includes an Affect Alpha option that lets the effect work with the image's alpha channel. The alpha channel holds the transparency information for the image. If you plan on using the effect in a composite image, then enable this option.

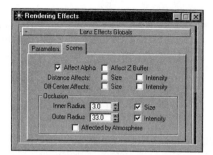

Figure 37-6: The Scene panel of the Lens Effects Globals rollout includes additional lens effects settings.

 Tip   Click the Display Alpha Channel button in the Virtual Frame Buffer to view the alpha channel.

The Affect Z-Buffer option stores the effect information in the Z-buffer, which is used to determine the depth of objects from the camera's viewpoint.

The Distance Effects option alters the effect's Size and/or Intensity based on its distance from the camera. The Off-Center Effects option is similar, except it affects the effect's Size and Intensity based on its Off-Center distance.

The Occlusion settings can be used to cause an effect to be hidden by an object that lies between the effect and the camera. The Inner Radius value defines the area that an object must block in order to hide the effect. The Outer Radius value defines where the effect begins to be occluded. You can also set the Size and Intensity options for the effect. The Affected by Atmospheres option allows effects to be occluded by atmospheric effects.

Glow

The Glow Element rollout, shown in Figure 37-7, includes parameters for controlling the look of the Glow Lens Effect. This rollout has two panels: Parameters and Options.

Parameters panel

In the Parameters panel, there is a Name field. Several glow effects can be added to a scene, and each one can have a different name. The On option can turn each glow on and off.

The Parameters panel also includes Size and Intensity values. These work with the Global settings to determine the size of the glow and can be set to any positive value. The Occlusion and Use Source Color values are percentages. The Occlusion value determines how much of the occlusion set in the Scene panel of the Lens Effects Globals rollout is to be used. If the Use Source Color is at 100 percent, then the glow color is determined by the light color; if it is set to any value below 100, then the colors specified in the Source and Circular Color sections are combined with the light's color.

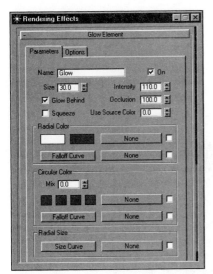

Figure 37-7: The Glow Element rollout lets you set the parameters for the Glow effect.

There are also options for Glow Behind and Squeeze. Glow Behind makes the glow effect visible behind objects. The Squeeze option enables any squeeze settings specified in the Parameters panel.

If the Use Source Color value is set to 0 percent, only the Radial Color swatches determine the glow colors. Radial colors proceed from the center of the glow circle to the outer edge. The first swatch is the inner color and the second is the outer color. The Falloff Curve button opens the Radial Falloff function curve dialog box, shown in Figure 37-8, where you can use a curve to set how quickly or slowly the colors change.

The Circular Color swatches specify the glow color around the glow circle starting from the top point and proceeding clockwise. The Mix value is the percentage to mix the Circular colors with the Radial Colors. Although it is difficult to see in this grayscale image, Figure 37-9 shows three glows. The left glow uses the source color, the middle glow uses Radial Color, and the right glow uses Circular Colors.

You can also access the Falloff Curve dialog box for the Circular Falloff and the Radial Size. Clicking the Size Curve button accesses the Radial Size dialog box. Figure 37-10 shows a glow where the Radial Size function curve moves linearly from 1 to 0.

All of these colors and function curves have map buttons (initially labeled None) that enable you to load maps. A map can be enabled by using the check box to its immediate right.

Move
Scale
Add Point
Delete Point

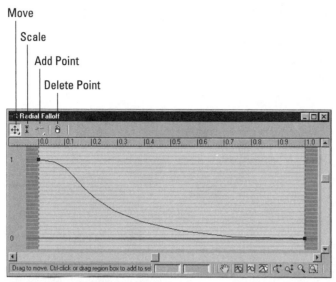

Figure 37-8: The Radial Falloff dialog box lets you control how the inner radial color changes to the outer radial color.

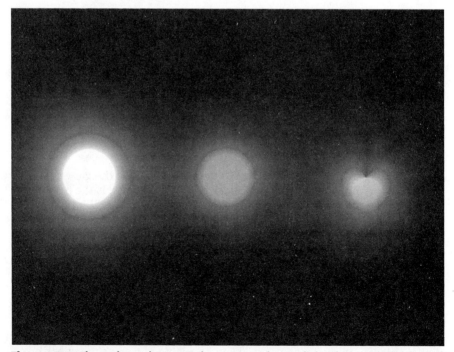

Figure 37-9: These three glows use the source color, Radial Colors, and Circular Colors.

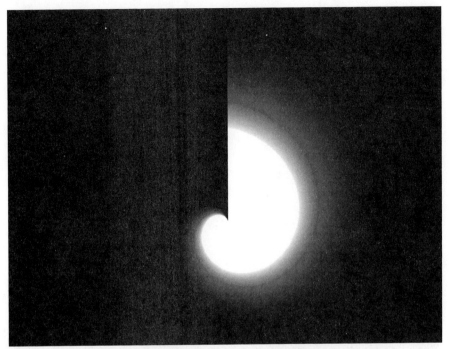

Figure 37-10: The Radial Size function curve for this glow moves from 1 to 0.

Options panel

The Options panel of the Glow Element rollout, shown in Figure 37-11, defines where to apply the glow effect. In the Apply Element To section, the first option is to apply a glow to the Lights. These lights are selected in the Parameters panel of the Lens Effects Globals rollout using the Pick Light button. The other two options — Image and Image Centers — apply glows using settings contained in the Options panel.

In the Image Sources section, glows can be applied to specific objects using the Object ID option and settings. Object IDs are set for objects in the Object Properties dialog box. If the corresponding Object ID is selected and enabled in the Options panel, the object is endowed with the Glow Lens Effect.

The Effects ID option and settings work in a manner similar to Object IDs, except that they are assigned to materials in the Material Editor. Effects IDs can be used to make only a subobject selection glow.

The Unclamp option and settings enable colors to be brighter than pure white. Pure White is a value of 1. The Unclamp value is the lowest value that glows. The Surf Norm (Surface Normal) option and value let you set object areas to glow based on the angle between the surface normal and the camera. The "I" button to the right inverts the value.

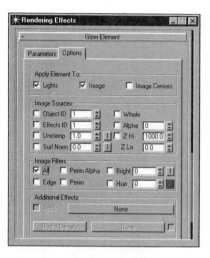

Figure 37-11: The Options panel of the Glow Element rollout lets you apply the glow effect to an object and/or materials.

Figure 37-12 shows an array of spheres with the Surf Norm glow enabled. Because the glows multiply, a value of only 2 was applied. Notice how the spheres in the center have a stronger glow.

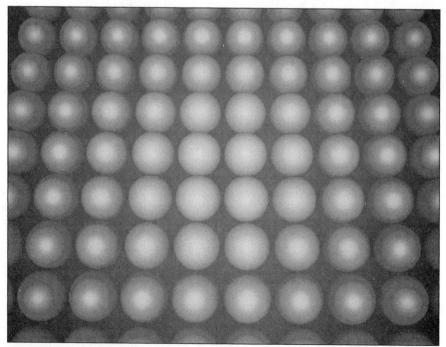

Figure 37-12: The Surf Norm option causes objects to glow, based on the angle between their surface normals and the camera.

In the Image Sources section, options enable these glows to be applied to the Whole scene, the Alpha channel, or the Z-buffer with specified Hi and Lo values.

The Image Filters section can further refine which objects to apply the glow effect to. Options include All, Edge, Perim (Perimeter) Alpha, Perim, Brightness, and Hue. The All option applies the effect to all pixels that are part of the source. The Edge, Perim Alpha, and Perim options only apply the effect to the edges, perimeter of the alpha channel, or perimeter of the source. The Brightness option includes a value and an "I" invert button. This applies the effect only to areas with a brightness greater than the specified value. The Hue option also includes a value and a color swatch for setting the hue, which receives the effect.

The Additional Effects section lets you apply a map to the Glow Lens Effect with an Apply option and a map button. You can also control the Radial Density function curve or add a map for the Radial Density.

Ring

The Ring Lens Effect is also circular and includes all the same controls and settings as the Glow Lens Effect. The only additional values are the Plane and Thickness values. The Plane value positions the Ring center relative to the center of the screen, and the Thickness value determines the width of the Ring's band.

Figure 37-13 shows three Ring effects with various thicknesses. The one on the left has a thickness of 10, the middle one has a thickness of 40, and the right one has a thickness of 75.

Ray

The Ray Lens Effect emits bright, semitransparent rays in all directions from the source. They also use the same settings as the Glow effect, except for the Num (Number) and Sharp values. The Numb value is the number of rays, and the Sharp value can range from 0 to 10 and determines how blurry the rays are.

Figure 37-14 shows the Ray effect applied to three lights. The left one has 10 rays with a Sharp value of 5, the middle one has 50 rays with a Sharp value of 7, and the right one has 100 rays with a Sharp value of 10.

Star

The Star Lens Effect radiates semitransparent bands of light at regular intervals from the center of the effect. It uses the same controls as the Glow effect, with the addition of Width, Taper, Qty (Quantity), and Sharp values. The Width sets the width of each band. The Taper value determines how quickly the width angles to a point. The Qty value is the number of bands, and the Sharp value determines how blurry the bands are.

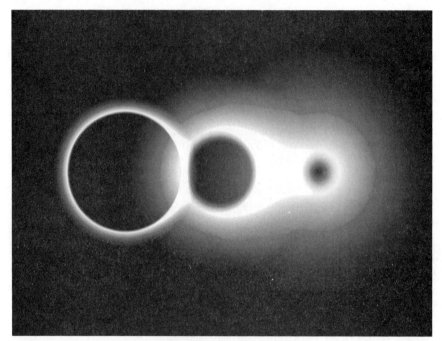

Figure 37-13: Ring effects can vary in thickness.

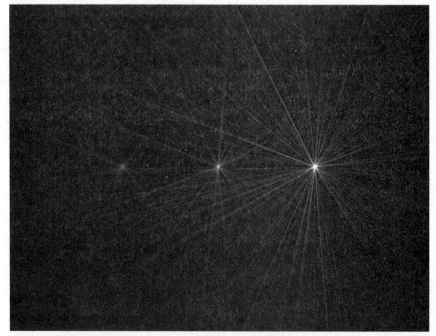

Figure 37-14: The Ray effect extends a given number of rays out from the effect center.

Figure 37-15 shows three Star effects with 3, 5, and 6 bands.

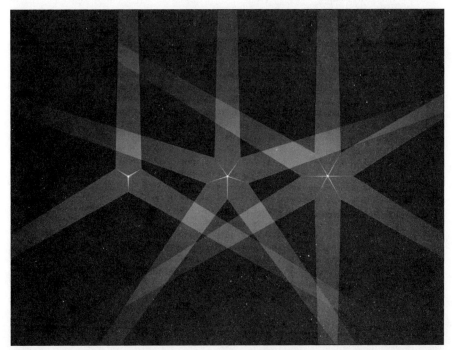

Figure 37-15: The Star effect lets you set the number of bands emitting from the center.

Streak

The Streak Lens Effect adds a horizontal band through the center of the selected object. It is similar to the Star effect, except it only has two bands that extend in opposite directions.

Figure 37-16 shows three Streak effects angled at 45 degrees with Width values of 2, 5, and 10.

Auto Secondary

When a camera is moved past a bright light, several small circles appear lined up in a row proceeding from the center of the light. These are secondary lens flares caused by light refracting off the lens. This effect can be simulated using the Auto Secondary Lens Effect.

Many of the settings in the Auto Secondary Element rollout are the same as in the Glow effect rollout described previously, but there are several unique values. Figure 37-17 shows this rollout.

Figure 37-16: The Streak effect enables you to create horizontal bands.

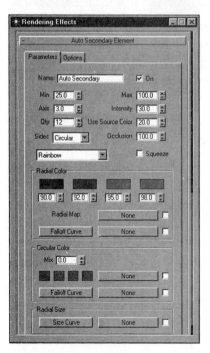

Figure 37-17: The Auto Secondary Element rollout sets the parameters for this effect.

The Min and Max values define the minimum and maximum size of the flares. The Axis is the length of the axis along which the flares are positioned. Larger values spread the flares out more than smaller values. The actual angle of the flares depends on the angle between the camera and the effect object.

The Quantity value is the number of flares to include. The Sides drop-down list lets you select a Circular flare or flares with Three to Eight sides. Below the Sides drop-down list are several preset options in another drop-down list. These include options such as Brown Ring, Blue Circle, and Green Rainbow, among others.

There are also four Radial Colors that you can use to define the flares. The color swatches from left to right define the colors from the inside out. The spinners below each color swatch indicate where the color should end.

Figure 37-18 shows the Auto Secondary effect with the Rainbow preset and the Intensity increased to 50.

Figure 37-18: The Auto Secondary effect displays several flares extending at an angle from the center of the effect.

Manual Secondary

In addition to the Auto Secondary Lens Effect, you can add a Manual Secondary Lens Effect to add some more flares with a different size and look. This effect includes a Plane value that places the flare in front of (positive value) or behind (negative value) the flare source.

Figure 37-19 shows the same flares from the previous figure with an additional Manual Secondary effect added.

Figure 37-19: The Manual Secondary effect can add some randomness to a flare lineup.

Blur

The Blur Render Effect displays three different blurring methods in the Blur Type panel: Uniform, Directional, and Radial. These can be found in the Blur Parameters rollout, shown in Figure 37-20.

The Uniform blur method applies the blur evenly across the whole image. The Pixel Radius value defines the amount of the blur. The Directional blur method can be used to blur the image along a certain direction. The U Pixel Radius and U Trail values define the blur in the horizontal direction, and the V Pixel Radius and V Trail values blur in a vertical direction. The Rotation value rotates the axis of the blur.

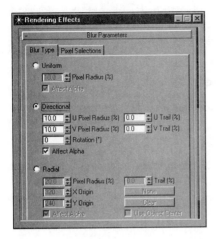

Figure 37-20: The Blur Parameters rollout lets you select a Uniform, Directional, or Radial blur type.

The Radial blur method creates concentric blurred rings determined by the Radius and Trail values. When the Use Object Center option is selected, the None and Clear buttons become active. Clicking the None button lets you select an object about which you want to center the radial blur. The Clear button clears this selection.

Figure 37-21 shows a teddy bear model created by Viewpoint Datalabs. The actual rendered image shows the sharp edges of the polygons, which don't look so soft and cuddly. The Blur effect can help this by softening all the hard edges. This image uses the Uniform blur type set to 3 percent.

Figure 37-21: The Blur effect can soften an otherwise hard model.

The Blur Parameters rollout also includes a Pixel Selection panel, shown in Figure 37-22, that contains parameters for specifying which parts of the image get blurred. Options include the Whole Image, Non-Background, Luminance, and Map Mask.

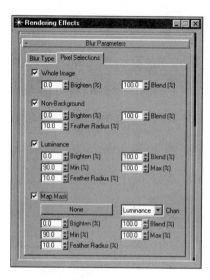

Figure 37-22: The Pixel Selections panel of the Blur Parameters rollout lets you select the parts of the image that get the blur effect.

Brightness and Contrast

The Brightness and Contrast effect can alter these amounts in the image. The Brightness and Contrast Parameters rollout, shown in Figure 37-23, includes values for both the Brightness and Contrast, which can range from 0 to 1. It also contains an Ignore Background option.

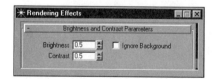

Figure 37-23: The Brightness and Contrast Parameters rollout lets you alter the amount of brightness and contrast in the image.

Color Balance

The Color Balance effect enables you to tint the image using separate Cyan/Red, Magenta/Green, and Yellow/Blue channels. To change the color balance, drag the sliders in the Color Balance Parameters rollout, shown in Figure 37-24. Other options include Preserve Luminosity and Ignore Background. The Preserve Luminosity option tints the image while maintaining the luminosity of the image, and the Ignore Background option tints the rendered objects but not the background image.

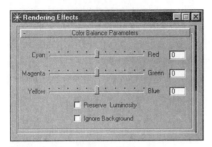

Figure 37-24: The Color Balance Parameters rollout lets you change the color tinting of an image.

Depth of Field

The Depth of Field effect enhances the sense of depth by blurring objects close to or far from the camera. The Pick Cam button in the Depth of Field Parameters rollout, shown in Figure 37-25, lets you select a camera in the viewport to use for this effect. Multiple cameras can be selected, and all selected cameras are displayed in the drop-down list. There is also a Remove button for removing cameras.

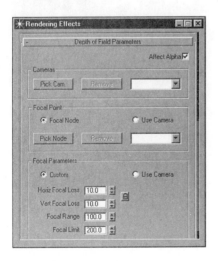

Figure 37-25: The Depth of Field Parameters rollout lets you select a camera or a Focal Point to apply the effect to.

In the Focal Point section, the Pick Node button lets you select an object to use as the focal point. This object is where the camera focuses. Objects far from this object are blurred. These nodes are also listed in a drop-down list. You can remove objects from the list by selecting them and clicking the Remove button. The Use Camera option uses the camera's own settings to determine the focal point.

In the Focal Parameters section, if the Custom option is selected, then you can specify values for the Horizontal and Vertical Focal Loss, the Focal Range, and the Focal Limit. The Loss values indicate how much blur occurs. The Focal Range is where the image starts to blur, and the Focal Limit is where the image stops blurring.

Figure 37-26 shows a line of magnolia flowers created by Viewpoint Datalabs. For this figure, the Depth of Field effect has been applied using the Pick Node button and selecting the flower in the middle of the line. Then I set the Focal Range to 300 and the Focal Limit to 0 and locked the Focal Loss values for Horizontal and Vertical to 5.

Figure 37-26: The Depth of Field effect focuses a camera on an object in the middle and blurs objects closer or farther away.

File Output

The File Output Render Effect enables you to save the rendered file to a File or to a Device at any point during the render effect's post-processing. Figure 37-27 shows the File Output Parameters rollout.

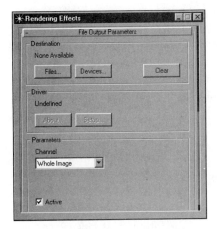

Figure 37-27: The File Output Parameters rollout lets you save a rendered image before a render effect is applied.

Using the Channel drop-down list in the Parameters section, you can save out Whole Images, as well as grayscale Luminance, Depth, and Alpha images.

Film Grain effect

The Film Grain effect gives an image a grained look, which softens the overall look of the image. You can also use this effect to match rendered objects to the grain of the background image. This helps the objects blend into the scene better. Figure 37-28 shows the Film Grain Parameters rollout.

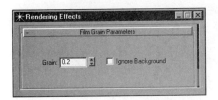

Figure 37-28: The Film Grain Parameters rollout lets you specify a Grain value.

The Grain value can range from 0 to 1. The Ignore Background option applies the grain effect to only the objects in the scene and not to the background.

Tutorial: Shining genie's lamp

We all know what happens when you rub the genie's lamp, so I wonder what happens if we just make it appear to be shiny? Adding some Lens Effects to the lamp should do the trick.

To make an object bright and shiny using Lens Effects, follow these steps:

1. Import the genie lamp model created by Viewpoint Datalabs. Position the object in the scene.

2. Open the Create panel and click the Lights category button. Create several Omni lights and position them around the scene to provide adequate lighting. Position a single light close to the lamp's surface where you want the highlight to be located—make it near the surface and set the Multiplier value to **0.5**.

3. Open the Rendering Effects dialog box by selecting Rendering ➪ Effects. Click the Add button and select Lens Effects. Then, in the Lens Effects Parameters rollout, select the Glow effect in the left pane and click the button pointing to the right pane.

4. In the Parameters panel, click the Pick Light button and select the light close to the surface. Set the Size around 30 and the Intensity at **100**. Go to the Glow Element rollout, and in the Parameters panel set the Use Source Color to **0**. Then, in the Radial Color section, click the second Radial Color swatch, and, in the Color Selector dialog box, select a color that is close to the color of the lamp and click the Close button.

5. Back up to the Lens Effects Parameters rollout, select Star, and add it to the list of effects. It automatically uses the same light specified for the Glow effect. In the Star Element rollout, set the Quantity value to 6, the Size to 200, and the Intensity to 20. Click the Quick Render (Production) button to see the results.

Figure 37-29 shows the resulting lamp with a nice shine.

Figure 37-29: The genie's lamp has had a sparkle added to it using the Glow and Star Lens Effects.

Summary

MAX's new Render Effects are useful, because they enable you to create effects and update them interactively. This gives a level of control that was previously unavailable. This chapter explained how to use Render Effects and described the various types.

In this chapter, you've:

✦ Learned how to use the various Render Effects

✦ Discovered all the available Render Effects and their parameters, including Lens Effects, Blur, Brightness and Contrast, Color Balance, Depth of Field, File Output, and Film Grain

✦ Practiced using several Render Effects

The next chapter offers a way to speed the rendering process using a network. Network rendering enables several machines connected to a network to work together to render a scene.

✦   ✦   ✦

Using Network Rendering

CHAPTER

38

MAX can help you create some incredible images and animations, but that power comes at a significant price—time. Modeling scenes and animation sequences take enough time on their own, but once you're done you still have to wait for the rendering to take place, which for a final rendering at the highest detail settings can literally take days or weeks. Because the time it takes to render is directly proportional to the amount of processing power you have access to, MAX lets you use network rendering to add more hardware to the equation and speed up those painfully slow jobs.

This chapter shows you how to set up MAX to distribute the rendering workload across an entire network of computers, helping you finish big rendering jobs in record time.

When you use network rendering to render your animation, MAX divides up the work between several machines connected via a network, with each machine rendering some of the frames. The increase in speed depends on how many machines you can devote to rendering frames—add just one computer and you double the rate at which you can render. Add seven or eight machines and instead of missing that important deadline by a week, you can get done early and take an extra day off.

The price of all this (besides the extra machines) is a time investment on your part. It does take a little work to get things set up properly, but it's an investment that you have to make only once. If you take the time now to make sure you do things right, you should be up and running fairly quickly and have far fewer headaches down the road.

Machines connected to handle network rendering are often referred to collectively as a *rendering farm*. The basic process during a network rendering goes like this: one machine manages the entire process and distributes the work between all the computers in the farm. Each machine signals the managing computer when it is ready to work on another frame. The manager then sends or "farms out" a new frame, it gets drawn by a computer in the rendering farm, and the finished frame gets saved in whatever format you've chosen.

MAX has several additional features to make the network rendering process easier. If one of the computers in your rendering farm crashes or loses its connection with the manager, the manager reclaims the frame that was assigned to the down computer and farms it out to a different machine. You can monitor the status of any rendering job you have running, and you can even have MAX e-mail you when a job is complete.

In this chapter we step through the process of setting up network rendering on a small network I use at home. You'll find out first-hand what's involved so that setting up your own network can go smoothly.

Note   There is one additional caveat to using network rendering: you have no guarantee that the frames of your animation will be rendered in order. Each participating computer renders frames as quickly as possible and saves them as bitmap files, so you cannot use network rendering to create AVI or FLC files, for example. Instead you have to render the scene with each frame saved as a separate bitmap file, and then use Video Post or a third-party program (such as Adobe Premiere) to combine them into an animation file format such as AVI.

Network Requirements

Now that you're anxious to get things under way, let's look at what you need to set up a rendering farm:

> ✦ **Computers**—First and foremost, of course, you need computers. The more the merrier, but all of them need to be connected via some sort of network and need to be running TCP/IP, a very common communications protocol (we'll talk more about TCP/IP and setting it up later). As with most things related to computers, the more powerful the hardware you can get your hands on, the faster things go. All computers in your farm should meet at least the basic requirements for MAX, but if they have more memory, more disk space, and faster processors, you're better off. Also, it's preferable to have nothing else running on the machines. Rendering is a CPU-intensive process, so any other programs you have running compete for the processor and increase the time it takes to finish your rendering job.

✦ **Networking hardware**—Each computer needs some way to connect to the network. The most common way is to use a network adapter card in the computer and a cable that connects it to the rest of the network. If a computer is connected via a dial-up connection, then its networking hardware is a modem. It is also possible to use network rendering on a single computer to do batch rendering, in which case only one computer is used instead of a real network. In this case the network "hardware" isn't hardware at all—it's a piece of software that simulates a network adapter and tricks MAX into thinking that it's connected to a network.

✦ **Windows NT**—According to the MAX documentation, each computer in your rendering farm must be running under Windows NT because MAX isn't stable enough when running under Windows 95 or 98. I personally have some machines that run Windows NT and others that run Windows 98, and I haven't had any problems to date, but it's up to you (you've been warned). The screenshots in this chapter are based on Windows NT. Things may look slightly different in Windows 98.

Note

If your network has not been set up yet, you will probably need Windows NT administrative privileges on each machine.

✦ **3D Studio MAX**—Obviously you need MAX to do all this, but the good news is that only one machine in your farm needs to have an *authorized* copy of MAX installed. In order to start a network rendering job you have to be running an authorized copy of MAX; the other machines will, in effect, get their authorization via the authorized copy. (We look into this further in the next section.)

New Feature

As of 3D Studio MAX R3, no authorization whatsoever is needed on machines that are used for network rendering only. Simply install MAX, and each network rendering machine gets its authorization from the computer that launched the render job.

Basically that's all you need to network render with MAX. But before we move on, there are two important things you should remember.

First, the display capabilities of the machines in your rendering farm are irrelevant. MAX uses its own rendering engine, so in network rendering, a top-of-the-line graphics adapter won't give you any better performance or quality than the cheap, factory-installed adapters that often come built into the motherboard. In fact, you can even omit the monitor on each rendering farm computer, which can really cut down on how much you have to invest to set up a good network rendering farm.

Second, if you don't have access to a bunch of computers that can be exclusively dedicated to network rendering, don't give up. MAX has some great scheduling features that enable you to configure each computer so that it's available to render at certain times of the day. If you have administrative access to additional computers at work or a university lab, you can use those computers at night or on weekends, when they are generally free.

Setting up a Network Rendering System

Before we get into the details of setting up MAX and the network itself, it's important to understand the different parts of the network rendering system. Here is a list of the major players involved:

✦ **Manager**—The *manager* is a program (manager.exe) that acts as the network manager. It's the network manager's job to coordinate the efforts of all the other computers in your rendering farm. Only one machine on your network needs to be running the manager, and that same machine can also be used to render.

✦ **Server**—A *rendering server* is any computer on your network that is used to render frames of your animation. When you run the server program (server.exe), it contacts the network manager and informs it that this particular computer is available to render. The server starts up MAX when the manager sends a frame to be rendered.

✦ **3D Studio MAX**—Some computer in your rendering farm must have an authorized copy of MAX running, although it does not need to be the same computer that is running the manager. It is from this machine that you initiate a rendering job.

✦ **Queue Manager**—The *Queue Manager* (queueman.exe) is a special program that lets you monitor your rendering farm. You can use it to check the current state of jobs that are running or that have been queued. You can also use it to schedule network rendering times. The Queue Manager is completely independent from the actual rendering process, so you can use it on one of the machines in your rendering farm, or you can use it to remotely check the status of things by connecting over the network.

We address the task of setting up the network rendering system in three stages. The first thing you need is a functioning network, so we first go through the steps of how to get it working. Next, we look at setting up the MAX software on each computer, and finally we describe how to tell MAX where to find scene data it needs and where to put the finished scenes.

Setting up the network

To communicate with the different machines on the network, MAX uses *TCP/IP* (Transmission Control Protocol / Internet Protocol), a very common network protocol. It's so common, in fact, that if your computers are already set up with some sort of network, you might already have TCP/IP installed and configured properly. If so, you are saved from several hours of work. Each machine on a network is identified by an IP address, which is a series of four numbers, each between 0 and 255, separated by periods, such as:

```
192.1.17.5
```

Each computer on a network has a unique IP address as well as a unique, human-readable name. In order to use MAX to do network rendering, you need to find the IP address and name of each computer used on the network.

The precise details of what constitutes a "correct" IP address are too long and boring to go into here, but for a nonpublic network all the addresses start with 192 or 10. The second and third numbers can be anything between 0 and 255 inclusive, and the last number can be between 1 and 254 inclusive (0 and 255 have special meanings). As an example, I've chosen to set up my home network as follows:

Machine Name	IP Address
Wookie	10.0.0.1
Jawa	10.0.0.2
Endor	10.0.0.3
Dagobah	10.0.0.4

Notice that each address is unique and that because it's a private network, the first number in each address is 10.

Tutorial: Locating TCP/IP and gathering IP addresses

To get the computers to talk to one another, you need to make sure that each computer has the TCP/IP protocol installed and you need to gather the IP addresses for all the machines on the network.

To see if you already have TCP/IP installed and to find out the IP address and name of each computer, follow these steps:

1. Open the Windows Control Panel by going to the Windows taskbar and choosing Start ⇨ Settings ⇨ Control Panel.

2. Double-click the Network icon to open the Network dialog box.

3. In the Identification panel is a field for Computer Name. Write the name in this field down in a list of all the computers you are using to network-render. Each computer on your network needs a unique name, so if the field is blank, enter a unique name and add this computer to your list.

4. Under the Protocols panel is a list of installed network protocols, similar to the list in Figure 38-1. Look through the list until you find a line that starts with "TCP/IP." If you find one, double-click it to bring up the TCP/IP Properties. If you don't see the TCP/IP protocol anywhere, then you have to add it yourself in order to do network rendering (see the next section for instructions).

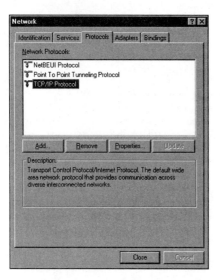

Figure 38-1: A list of network the protocols installed on this computer

Note   In Windows 98, the protocols and network adapters are all listed together on the Configuration panel in the Network dialog box.

5. The most interesting thing in the TCP/IP Properties dialog box is on the very first panel, called IP Address, shown in Figure 38-2. Midway down the dialog box you should see your network adapter (such as the brand and model of your Ethernet card). If it is not listed, you need to get it set up before proceeding. (Refer to the Windows NT help files for more on this.) Double-click this field.

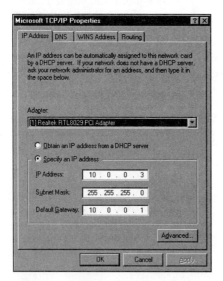

Figure 38-2: The IP Address panel of the TCP/IP Properties dialog box

6. Do one of the following:

- If "Obtain an IP address from a DHCP server" is selected ("Obtain an IP address automatically" on Windows 98), you don't have to worry about the exact IP address of this computer, because each time the computer connects to the network it gets an IP address from a server, and the address it gets may be different every time.

- If "Specify an IP address" is selected, add the IP address to your written list of computers on the network. In the IP Address panel shown in the figure, the IP address has been statically assigned, which means that this computer will always have the same IP address.

Repeat this procedure for each computer that will participate in your rendering farm. If you're lucky and all your machines have TCP/IP installed and ready to go, you can skip the next section and move on to setting up MAX on your network. If not, then follow the steps for configuring TCP/IP in the next section.

Tutorial: Installing and configuring TCP/IP

If your computer doesn't already have TCP/IP installed, you have to install it in order to network-render in MAX.

Be careful about changing the TCP/IP settings of computers that are on a public network or are part of a large corporate network. Incorrect settings can not only keep your computers from communicating properly but can also cause problems in many other computers on the network.

If the computers you plan on using for your rendering farm are part of a public or corporate network, seek the assistance of the network administrator. If you're in charge of the computers yourself, dig out your Windows NT installation CD-ROM, because you're going to need it.

To install and configure TCP/IP, follow these steps:

1. Go to the Protocols panel on the Network dialog box if you're not still there from the previous section. To get there click Start on the task bar, and then select Settings ➪ Control Panel ➪ Network ➪ Protocols.

2. Click Add. This opens the Select Network Protocol dialog box. Scroll down until you see TCP/IP, select it, and click OK.

3. At this point Windows asks you if you want to use DHCP. If you know for sure that there is a DHCP server running, go ahead and choose Yes. If you're setting up the network yourself or you have no idea what DHCP is, choose No. If DHCP is already set up and working, it can save you a lot of time, but if not and if you're setting up the network yourself, I recommend steering away from it. You can change the settings to use DHCP at a later time if you're feeling ambitious.

4. Now Windows starts looking for the files that it needs to install, and it pops up a dialog box asking for their location. The default path it lists is probably the right one, so you can just click OK and continue. If Windows guessed wrong, or if you have the CD-ROM in a different drive, correct the path and then click OK.

5. After Windows finishes copying the files, click Close on the Network dialog box. TCP/IP is now installed but not configured, and Windows should detect this and bring up the Microsoft TCP/IP Properties dialog box. If for some reason it doesn't, just double-click Network again in the Control Panel, go to the Protocol panel, select TCP/IP, and then click Properties.

6. The first panel in the TCP/IP Properties is called IP Address (refer back to Figure 38-2). You should see your network adapter listed in the Adapter section.

7. Below the Adapter section is a section where you choose whether you want to have the DHCP server assign an IP address or if you want to choose one. If you're not using DHCP, choose "'Specify an IP address" and enter an IP address for this machine. Refer back to the beginning of this section if you need help choosing a valid IP address. (If you're a little confused about what numbers to use, you should be safe using the same numbers that I did.)

Caution It's extremely important that you choose an IP address that is unique on the network. (Duplicate IP addresses are a great way to guarantee a nonfunctional rendering farm.)

8. Underneath the IP address section, you have to enter a subnet mask. Enter

   `255.255.255.0`

   The subnet mask is used in conjunction with the IP address to identify different networks within the entire domain of every network in the world. If for any reason you do have to change this, be sure to change it in the 3dsnet.ini files that each rendering server creates (see "Using the Network Rendering Manager" later in this chapter).

9. Now click the DNS panel. Make sure that the Host Name field shows the same name for your computer as you have listed in the Identification panel of the Network dialog box. If the field is blank, go ahead and enter the computer name.

10. Click OK on the TCP/IP Properties dialog box to close it, and then click OK on the Network dialog box to close it. Windows needs to shut down and restart in order for the changes to take effect. This computer now has the proper network setup for your rendering farm.

Remember to repeat these instructions for every computer that you want to use in your rendering farm. Each computer must be properly connected to the network and have TCP/IP installed and configured. This may seem like a lot of work, but fortunately it's a one-time investment.

Tutorial: Setting up MAX on the networked computers

If you've made it this far, then you'll be happy to know that the worst is behind you. We've covered the most difficult parts of setting up a network rendering system; by comparison, everything else is relatively simple.

At this point, you should have a complete list of all the computers used in your network rendering system. Each computer should have a unique name and a unique IP address, and all should have TCP/IP installed and configured. You are now ready to move on to the actual MAX installation for your rendering servers.

You have to set up MAX on each computer in your rendering farm. Fortunately, this is as simple as a normal installation. To set up MAX on each computer, follow these steps:

1. Run the setup.exe program on the MAX installation CD-ROM.

Note　You don't have to have a CD-ROM drive in every computer in your rendering farm. Once your computers are networked, you can map a drive from your current machine to a computer that has the MAX CD-ROM in its CD-ROM drive. In Windows Explorer, select Tools ⇨ Map Network Drive and enter the path to the computer and drive with the CD-ROM. For more information on mapping drives, see the next section.

2. Move past the first few introduction screens until you get to the Setup Type screen. Choose the Compact option so that MAX installs only the minimum number of files it needs to be able to render. You also need to choose a destination directory where you want MAX to be installed. If possible, just accept the displayed default destination and click Next.

Tip　Installing 3D Studio MAX in the same directory on every computer can save you some maintenance headaches later on. It is much easier to manage bitmap and plug-in directories if each machine has the same directory layout.

3. Continue with the rest of the installation as you would do for a normal installation of MAX (although you can skip installing the online reference manuals if you want to save some disk space).

Once the installation files get copied over, you'll probably have to reboot your computer for the changes to take effect.

Configuring shared directories

The last step in building your rendering farm is to tell MAX where it can find the information it needs to render a scene. MAX must be able to find textures and other information, and it must know where to put each frame that it renders.

Tutorial: Sharing directories

Instead of copying needed files to every machine in your rendering farm, you can share your directories across the network, which means that other computers on the network will be able to use the files in that directory.

To make a directory shared, follow these steps:

1. Open Windows Explorer by selecting Start on the Windows taskbar and then selecting Programs ➪ Windows NT Explorer.

2. Find the directory that you want to share, right-click it, and choose Properties. This opens the Properties dialog box for that directory.

3. Click the Sharing panel. Choose Shared As, and type a name for this directory in the Share Name field if it is blank. Figure 38-3 shows the "maps" directory being set up to be shared.

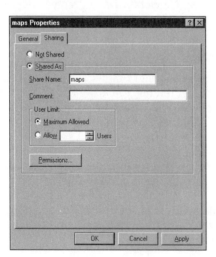

Figure 38-3: Sharing a directory so that other computers on the network can use it

Tip

Other computers will refer to the shared directory by its shared name instead of its actual name, so to keep things simple, accept the default of using the actual name for the shared name.

4. Click Permissions to open the Access Through Share Permissions dialog box. This dialog box lets you control who has access to this directory and how much access each person or group has (access could be restricted to read-only, for example). For now, make sure that the Everyone user group is listed and that this group has Full Control, as shown in Figure 38-4. If the Everyone user group is not listed, click Add, scroll down to Everyone, and double-click it. Then choose Full Control in the Type of Access pull-down menu and click OK.

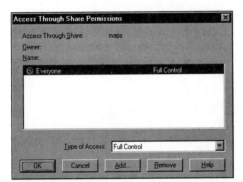

Figure 38-4: Setting share permissions for a directory. These permissions let anyone read or write to this directory.

Caution

Giving "Everyone" the Full Control access type does just what it says it does: everyone on the entire network can read *and write or erase* the files in your shared directory. For now it's best to leave it this way until you're sure everything is configured properly. Later, however, it would be a good idea to restrict access to only those accounts that should have access.

5. Click OK on each dialog box to close them all until you're back at the Windows Explorer. If you press F5, Windows refreshes the display and your directory now has a little blue hand holding the folder. Figure 38-5 shows the "maps" directory denoted as a shared directory.

Other computers can access your shared directory by specifying the full name of the directory's location. In the example we've been using, the "maps" directory is on a computer named "Endor," so the full path to that directory is as follows:

```
\\endor\maps
```

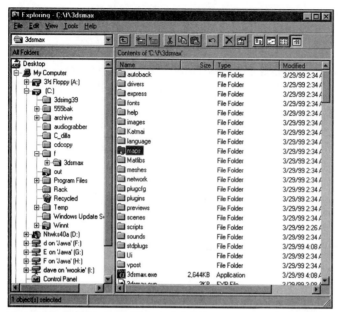

Figure 38-5: The shared "maps" directory can now be accessed by other computers

You can test this by opening a Windows Explorer (like we just did in the procedure) on a different computer, selecting Tools ➪ Map Network Drive, and entering the full path to that directory. Once you've mapped a drive to a directory, Windows treats that directory as if it were an actual drive on your machine. In Figure 38-6 the M drive is mapped to point to the "maps" directory on Endor.

Figure 38-6: Mapping the M drive to point to \\endor\maps\

After you've mapped to a new drive, go back to the Windows Explorer and press F5 to refresh the display again. You now have a new drive for that network directory, as shown in Figure 38-7.

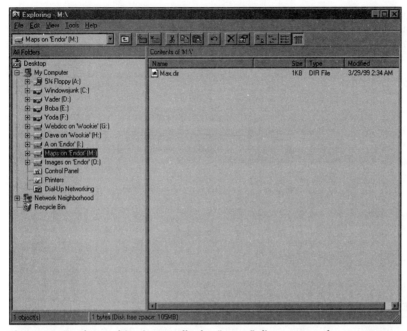

Figure 38-7: The M drive is actually the "maps" directory on the computer named Endor.

Tutorial: Choosing shared directories

Now you need to decide where to put the maps and the output files. These directories are the place from which all machines in your rendering farm read maps and images and to which they all write finished frames of your animation. The following procedure takes you through the steps for doing this using the directories I've set up on my own rendering farm.

To set up your shared directories, follow these steps:

1. First, decide which drives to use and then share them. On my network, Endor has plenty of disk space, so I used the maps and images directories that were already there from when I installed MAX.

Tip

Use the maps and images directories for all the scenes that you network-render. In each directory you can create other directories to organize files for your different scenes, but putting all maps and output in the same place facilitates maintenance.

2. On each computer in your rendering farm, map a drive to your shared maps and images directories as described in the previous section. If possible, choose the same drive letters on all machines. I used the letter *M* for the maps directory on each computer, and *O* for the images (output) directory. (Refer back to Figure 38-7 where, on Jawa, I've mapped drives M and O to point to my shared directories on Endor.)

Congratulations — you've made it through the installation and setup of your network rendering system. And no matter how long it took you, it was time well spent. The ability to network-render will easily save you more time than you invested in setting up your network.

Starting the Network Rendering System

You can finally put all your hard work into action. We're ready to start up your network rendering system.

Tutorial: Initializing the network rendering system

The very first time you start your rendering farm, you need to help MAX do a little initialization.

To initialize the network rendering system, follow these steps:

1. Start the network manager on one machine in your rendering farm. This program, manager.exe, is in the same directory as the rest of the 3D Studio MAX files. You can start the manager by selecting it and pressing Enter in Windows Explorer. After it starts up, you see the Network Manager window, shown in Figure 38-8. You need only one active network manager for your entire network, so leave this one running.

Figure 38-8: Starting the network manager

2. Now start a network server on each computer that you plan to use for rendering. To do this, find and start the server.exe program just like you did with manager.exe. When you start this program, the Network Server window will appear, as shown in Figure 38-9.

Figure 38-9: Starting a network server. Notice that the server found the manager successfully.

Notice that the server printed the message that it successfully registered itself with the manager. Whenever a server starts, it automatically searches for the manager and tries to connect. You can also see in the Network Manager window shown in Figure 38-10 that the manager successfully connected to the server.

Figure 38-10: The network manager's screen also shows the successful connection with the network server.

If the server had trouble connecting to the manager, you need to follow these two additional steps:

1. If automatic detection of the manager fails, the server keeps trying until it times out. If it times out, or if you just get tired of waiting, click Properties. In the TCP/IP section, uncheck the Automatic box and type in the name or IP address of the computer that is running the network manager, as shown in Figure 38-11. In this case, the server tried but couldn't quite find the manager, so it had to be told that the manager was running on the computer named Dagobah, whose IP address is 10.0.0.4.

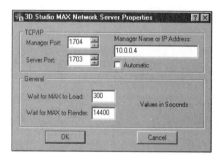

Figure 38-11: Manually choosing the manager's IP address

2. Click OK to close the Network Server Properties dialog box, and then click Close to shut down the server (doing this forces the server to save the changes you've made). Restart the server the same way you did before, and now the server and manager are able to find each other.

Note   The network manager does not need to have a computer all to itself, so you can also run a network server on the same computer and use it to participate in the rendering.

Tutorial: Completing your first network rendering job

Your rendering farm is up and running and just dying to render something, so let's put those machines to work.

To start a network rendering job, follow these steps:

1. Load 3D Studio MAX and create a simple animation scene. This should be as simple as possible because all we're doing here is verifying that the rendering farm is functional

2. In MAX, select Rendering ⇨ Render to bring up the Render Scene dialog box. In the Time Output section of this dialog box, be sure that Range is selected so that you really do render multiple frames instead of the default single frame. Figure 38-12 shows the Time Output Range set to render 100 frames.

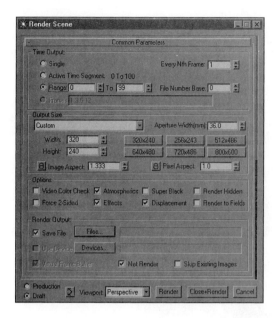

Figure 38-12: Preparing to network-render

3. In the Render Output section of the Render Scene dialog box, click Files to open the Render Output File dialog box, shown in Figure 38-13. In the Save In section, choose the output drive and directory that you created in the "Configuring Shared Directories" section.

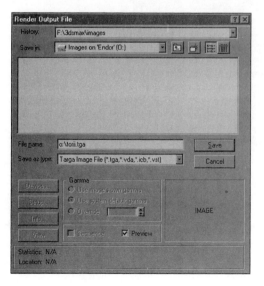

Figure 38-13: Specifying an output location. MAX numbers the frames for you, so you just have to give it the filename of the first frame.

4. In the File name section of the Render Output File dialog box, type in the name of the first frame. MAX automatically numbers each frame for you. Choose a bitmap format from the Save as type list (remember, an animation format will not work).

5. Click Save to close the Render Output File dialog box. (Some file formats might ask you for additional information for your files; if so, just click OK to accept the default options.) Back in the Render Scene dialog box, MAX displays the full path to the output directory, including the computer name, as you can see in Figure 38-14.

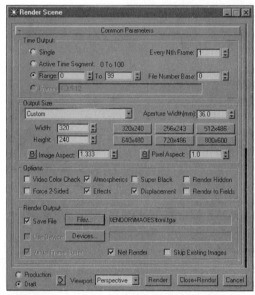

Figure 38-14: MAX shows the full output directory path.

6. In the Render Output section of the Render Scene dialog box, check the Net Render box. Change any other settings you want, such as selecting a viewport, and then click Render. This opens a Network Job Assignment dialog box like the one shown in Figure 38-15.

7. In the Network Manager section of the Network Job Assignment dialog box, click Connect if the Automatic Search box is checked. If it isn't checked, or if your servers had trouble finding the manager in the "Initializing the Network Rendering System" section earlier in this chapter, type in the IP address of the machine that's running the manager and then click Connect.

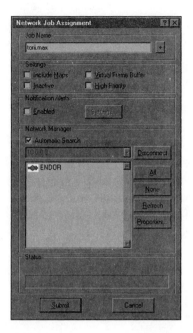

Figure 38-15: Using the Network Job Assignment dialog box to locate the manager to handle the rendering job

8. MAX then searches for the rendering manager and connects with it, and it adds its name to the list of available managers. Click the manager name once — the icon appears as a ball with an arrow through it. Now click Submit.

Tip

If you try to submit the same job again (after either a failed or a successful attempt at rendering), MAX complains because that job already exists in the job queue. You can either remove the job using the Queue Manager (which is discussed later) or you can click the + button on the Network Job Assignment dialog box, and MAX will add a number to the job name to make it unique.

Once you've submitted your job, notices appear on the manager and the servers (like the ones shown in Figures 38-16 and 38-17) that the job has been received. Soon MAX will start up on each server and you'll see a Rendering dialog box like Figure 38-18. As you can see, this displays useful information such as what frame is being rendered and how long the job is taking. When the entire animation has been rendered, you can go to your output directory to get the bitmap files that MAX generated. The render servers and the render manager keep running, ready for the next job request to come in.

Figure 38-16: The network manager detects the new job.

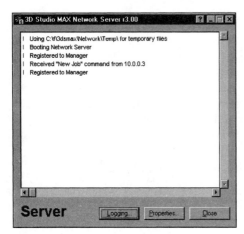

Figure 38-17: One of the network servers receives the command to start a new job.

Job assignment options

The Network Job Assignment dialog box, shown in Figure 38-15, has two important sections that we didn't use for our first simple render job: Settings and Notification Alerts.

The Settings section has the following options:

✦ **Include Maps**—Checking this box makes MAX compress everything that it needs to render the scene (including the maps) into a single file and send it to each server. This option is useful if you're setting up a rendering farm over the Internet, although it does take more time and network bandwidth to send all that extra information.

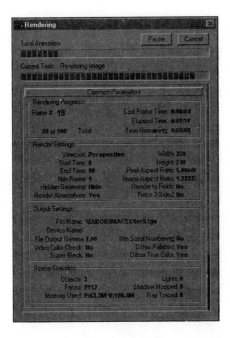

Figure 38-18: Status of the current frame being rendered

✦ **Virtual Frame Buffer**—Use this option if you want to be able to see the image on the server as it gets rendered.

✦ **Inactive**—If you check this option, your job will be added to the job queue when you click Submit, but it will not be rendered until you manually activate it using the Queue Manager (as described later in this chapter).

✦ **High Priority**—When this box is checked and you submit a rendering job, the new job goes to the start of the rendering queue, even if another job is currently under way. A server that gets a command to render a high-priority frame stops working on whatever frame it currently has, renders the high-priority frame, and then picks up where it left off.

The Notification Alerts section lets you tell MAX when to notify you that certain events have occurred. If you check the Enabled box and click Settings, you can use the Alert Notification Settings dialog box (shown in Figure 38-19) to tell MAX what events you want to be alerted to:

✦ **Notify Failures**—MAX sends you a notification on any type of failure.

✦ **Notify Progress**—MAX notifies you every time it completes a certain number of frames.

✦ **Notify Completion**—MAX sends you a notification when a job is complete.

Figure 38-19: Letting MAX know if you want to be notified of certain events

Using the Network Rendering Manager

The rendering manager has some options that let you modify how it behaves. You specify these options in the Network Manager Properties dialog box, shown in Figure 38-20. To open this dialog box, click Properties in the Manager window.

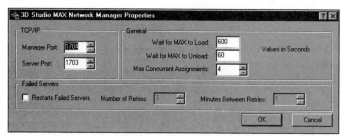

Figure 38-20: The Network Manager Properties dialog box

This dialog box includes the following sections:

✦ **TCP/IP** — Here you can change the communications ports used by the manager and the servers. In general, it's a good idea to leave these alone. If some other program is using one of these ports, however, MAX won't be able to network-render, so you need to change them. If you change the Server Port number, be sure to change it to the same number on all your rendering servers. If you change the Manager Port number, you'll also need to change two files on your hard drive to match: queueman.ini (in your 3dsmax directory) and client.ini (in your 3dsmax\network directory) — both have lines for the Manager Port, and you can edit these files with any text editor or word processor.

✦ **General** — The first two settings here govern how long the manager waits to get a response from a server. When the manager sends a frame to a server, it expects to get a message from the server that the frame has been received and is being rendered. If the time in the Wait for MAX to Load field passes before MAX loads and starts rendering, the manager assigns the frame to a different server. Similarly, Wait for MAX to Unload tells how long the manager should wait for the server to say that it is ready for a new frame once it completes the previous frame and shuts down MAX.

The MAX Concurrent Assignments field is used to specify how many jobs the rendering manager sends out at a time. If you make this number too high, the manager might send out jobs faster than the servers can handle them. The default value here is fine for most cases.

In MAX R3, the network manager can automatically attempt to restart servers that failed, giving your rendering farm much more stability.

✦ **Failed Servers** — Usually MAX doesn't send more frames to a server that previously failed. If you check the Restarts Failed Servers box, MAX tries to give the server another chance. The Number of Retries field tells MAX how many times it should try to restart a server before giving up on the particular server for good, and the Minutes Between Retries field tells MAX the number of minutes it should wait before trying to give the failing server another job.

The rendering manager writes the configuration settings to a file on the disk that gets read when the manager loads. If you make changes to any of the settings, it's best to shut down the manager and start it up again to guarantee that the changes take effect.

Using Network Rendering Servers

As you may have guessed, the Properties button on the Network Server window serves a similar purpose as the one on the Network Manager window — it enables you to specify the behavior of the network server. Clicking this button displays the Network Server Properties dialog box, shown in Figure 38-21.

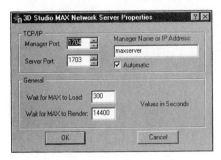

Figure 38-21: The Network Server Properties dialog box

This dialog box has the following sections:

✦ **TCP/IP** — The port numbers serve the same function as they do for the rendering manager, described in the previous section. If you change them in the manager properties, change them here. If you change them here, change them in the manager properties.

The Manager Name or IP Address setting lets you override automatic detection of the rendering manager and specify its exact location on the network. Generally it's best to let MAX attempt to find the manager itself and then, if it fails, override the automatic detection by clearing the Automatic check box. If you happen to be running multiple managers on the same network, the servers connect to the first one they find. In this case, you have to manually choose the correct server.

✦ **General** — The Wait for MAX to Load field is similar to the one in the Network Manager Properties dialog box, except that if the specified time passes before MAX loads, the server won't even bother trying to render the frame because it knows that the manager has already given the frame to a different server. The Wait for MAX to Render setting tells the server how long to wait for MAX to render a frame before it tells the manager that the rendering failed. The default value is to wait several hours, but if you have an extremely complex scene and slow computers, it is possible that you might need more time.

Keep in mind that the server properties aren't shared among your servers, so if you want something to change on all your servers, you have to make that change on each machine.

Note   As with the rendering manager settings, if you change anything in the Network Servers Properties dialog box, be sure to shut down the server and restart it.

Logging Errors

Both the Network Manager and Network Server windows have a Logging button that you can click to access the Logging Properties dialog box, where you can configure how log information gets handled. This dialog box, shown in Figure 38-22, looks the same for managers and servers.

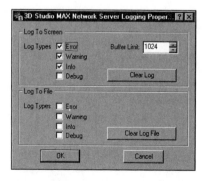

Figure 38-22: The logging options for managers and servers let you tell MAX where to report what.

MAX generates the following types of messages:

✦ **Error** — Anything that goes wrong and is serious enough to halt the rendering of a frame

✦ **Warning**—A problem that MAX can still work around. If a server fails, for example, a warning is generated, but MAX continues the rendering job by using other servers

✦ **Info**—A general information message, such as notification that a job has arrived or that a frame is complete

✦ **Debug**—A lower-level message that provides information to help debug problems with the rendering farm

MAX displays the type of message and the message itself in two locations: in the list window and in a log file (in your 3dsmax\network directory). The Logging Properties dialog box lets you choose whether each type of message gets reported to the screen, the log file, both places, or neither place. You can also use the Clear buttons to get rid of old messages.

Using the Queue Manager

The Queue Manager is a powerful utility that helps you manage your rendering farm and all the jobs in it. If you use network rendering frequently, then the Queue Manager will quickly become your best friend. You start it the same way you start a rendering server or manager: go to the 3dsmax directory, find queueman.exe, and double-click it. Every computer that has MAX installed on it also has a copy of the Queue Manager, so you can use it from any machine on your network. The main screen is shown in Figure 38-23.

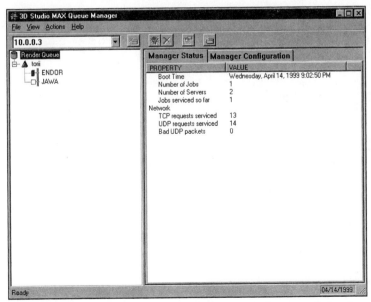

Figure 38-23: The Queue Manager makes managing a rendering farm quick and easy.

When the Queue Manager starts up, it automatically searches for the rendering manager and connects to it. (If you have more than one manager running, you have to choose which one to connect to.)

The main screen is divided into two panes. The left pane shows the job queue, all the jobs in it, and the servers working on each job; and the right pane shows information about whatever you have selected in the left pane. Next to each job or server in the left pane is an icon that reflects its current status. Green icons mean that the job or server is active and hard at work. Red means that something has gone wrong, and gray means that a job has been inactivated or that a server is assigned to a job but is absent. A pale blue circle next to a job means that the job is complete, was successful, and can now be deleted from the queue.

If you click Render Queue in the left pane, the Queue Manager displays information about your rendering farm, as shown in Figure 38-24.

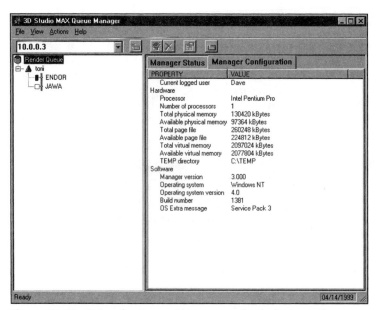

Figure 38-24: Using the Queue Manager to check the overall status of the rendering farm

The right pane has two panels:

> ✦ **Manager Status**—Shows general statistics about the rendering farm, such as how many servers are running and how many jobs have been serviced. It also gives information about the state of the network.

✦ **Manager Configuration** — Provides specific information about the computer that the manager is running on, such as the type of operating system and the amount of total and available memory.

Jobs

If you choose a job in the left pane, the right pane displays information about the selected job, as shown in Figure 38-25.

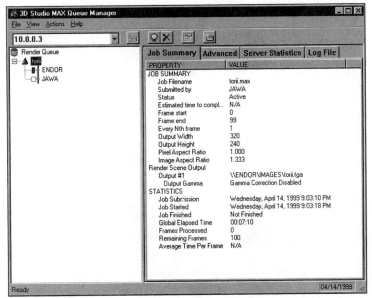

Figure 38-25: Using the Queue Manager to check the current job queue

The panels in the right pane are as follows:

✦ **Job Summary** — Lists some of the rendering options you chose before you submitted the job. Among other things, the example in the figure shows that the job was rendered to 320 × 240 pixels and was submitted by Jawa.

✦ **Advanced** — Lists advanced settings from the Render Scene dialog box and gives limited information about the scene itself.

✦ **Server Statistics** — Provides statistics that offer some insight into which servers did what in rendering your animation. This panel shows which servers participated and how long each server spent working on this job. It also rates the servers overall to see which ones were the fastest.

✦ **Log File** — Displays important messages from the job log. Whereas the log file on each server lists events for a particular server, this pane lets you see all the messages relating to a particular job.

When you point at a job in the left pane and right-click, a small pop-up menu appears. On this menu, you can delete a job from the queue or you can choose to activate or deactivate it. If you deactivate a job, all the servers working on that job save their work in progress to disk and then move on to the next job in the queue. This feature is very useful when you have a lower-priority job that you run when no other jobs are waiting; when something more important comes along, you deactivate the job so that you can later activate it when the servers are free again.

One last useful feature for jobs is that you can reorder them by dragging a job above or below other jobs. Jobs higher on the screen will be rendered before lower ones, which enables you to "bump up" the priority of a particular job without having to deactivate other ones.

Servers

If you choose a server in the left pane, the right pane displays information about the selected server, as shown in Figure 38-26.

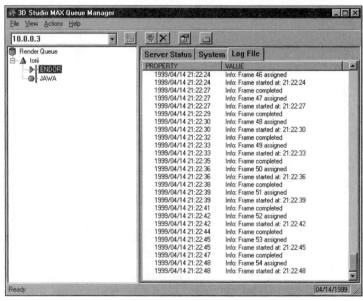

Figure 38-26: Checking the status of the rendering server

The panels in the right pane are as follows:

✦ **Server Status**—Lets you know if a server is active and ready to work, if it's currently working, or if it's inactive and not ready to accept a rendering job.

✦ **System**—Provides information about the computer that the server is running on.

✦ **Log File**—Displays the logged messages from this server. The Log File panel for jobs lists all messages related to a particular job, whereas this one lists only the messages that originated from this server.

You can get more detailed information about any server by right-clicking the server in the left pane and choosing Properties from the pop-up menu. This opens the Server Properties dialog box, shown in Figure 38-27.

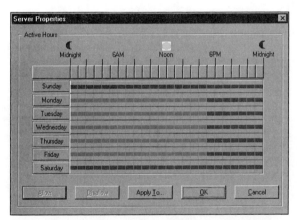

Figure 38-27: Using Queue Manager to schedule the hours that a computer is available for rendering

The Server Properties dialog box lets you decide when a particular machine is available for rendering. (For example, you could have your coworker's computer automatically become available for rendering once he or she goes home for the night.)

Click and drag with your mouse over different hours to select a group of times. Alternatively, you can click a day of the week to select the entire day or click a time to select that time for every day. In the example shown in Figure 38-27, the server is scheduled to render every weekday from midnight to 5 P.M., but not in evenings or on weekends.

Once you've selected a group of times, click Allow to make the server available for rendering during that time or click Disallow to prevent rendering. When you're done, click OK to close the Server Properties dialog box and return to the Queue Manager dialog box.

If you have several jobs going at once but suddenly need to get one done quickly, you can take servers off one job and put them on another. To remove a server, right-click its name in the left pane of the Queue Manager dialog box and choose Delete from the pop-up menu. The icon next to the server turns black, indicating that it has been unassigned. To assign this server to another job, right-click the server name in the list of servers for the job you want to assign it to, and choose Activate.

Event Notification

In the Network Job Assignment dialog box (shown in Figure 38-15) you have the option to turn Notification Alerts on or off. When a notification event occurs, MAX sends that message to a program in your 3dsmax directory called Notify.

The Notify program that comes with MAX plays a different sound when each type of notification alert occurs. (You can run notify.exe in your 3dsmax directory and configure it to use whatever sounds you want.) Although this is only moderately useful, the interesting thing is that you can replace this program with any other program or batch file that you want MAX to launch when a notification event occurs.

MAX calls Notify like this:

```
Notify file alert
```

The *file* argument is the name of a text file that contains more information about the alert. The *alert* argument indicates the type of alert that occurred (Failure, Progress, or Completion).

You can replace the Notify program with any program named Notify that has a .BAT, .CMD, or .EXE extension. MAX calls the program, and your program can do whatever it wants with the information. For example, you can have a program that e-mails you when something goes wrong so that you don't have to continually monitor the progress with the Queue Manager. Or you can have it page you on the golf course each time it successfully renders another 100 frames. Or when a big job completes, you can have it fax an order to your favorite pizza joint so you can celebrate.

Tutorial: Setting up Batch Rendering

Network rendering provides several features that make managing many different rendering jobs easy. If you don't have a network card installed but still want to use these features (such as the Queue Manager), there's still hope — MAX supports what is known as a loopback adapter so that you can set up a "network" on a single computer.

A *loopback adapter* is a piece of software that simulates a real network adapter. Data that is sent out to the adapter gets "looped back" to your own computer. And because Windows treats it as a normal network adapter, any networking programs (such as MAX) don't know any better.

If you're sure you don't have a network card installed, you can add the loopback adapter by following these steps (you'll probably need your Windows NT CD-ROM):

1. Open the Control Panel in Windows by clicking the Windows Start button and selecting Settings ⇨ Control Panel.

2. Double-click Network to open the Network dialog box. Click the Adapters panel, and then click Add.

3. Scroll through the list of adapters until you see the MS Loopback Adapter, as shown in Figure 38-28. Select it and click OK.

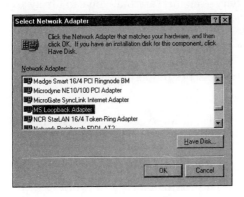

Figure 38-28: Installing the loopback adapter to enable batch rendering on a single computer

4. When Windows prompts you for a frame type, click OK to accept the default.

5. Once the installation files have been copied over from the CD-ROM, you need to reboot your computer for the new adapter to finish installation.

Now that you've installed the loopback adapter, you need to set up TCP/IP. Just follow the directions for setting up TCP/IP as if you were configuring it to be used as part of a real network. You have to reboot your computer one more time before you can actually use your new "network."

To use batch rendering, start a rendering manager and a rendering server on your computer and then load up MAX. Again, follow the same steps to submit the job as if you were rendering to a real network rendering system: choose Net Render in the Render Scene dialog box and submit the job.

You can use the loopback adapter to submit several jobs to the rendering queue and then use the Queue Manager to manipulate them. That way you can still have flexible job control even if you don't have a true network rendering system.

Summary

If your goal is to spend more time modeling and less time waiting for rendering jobs to complete, then the network rendering services provided by 3D Studio MAX can help you take a step in the right direction. Once the initial complexities of setting up a rendering farm are out of the way, network rendering can be a great asset in helping you reach important deadlines, and it lets you enjoy your finished work sooner. Even if you can afford to add only one or two computers to your current setup, you'll see a tremendous increase in productivity—an increase that you can't truly appreciate until you've completed a job in a fraction of the time it used to take!

In this chapter you learned how to:

✦ Set up a network suitable for network rendering with MAX

✦ Set up a 3D Studio MAX rendering farm

✦ Use the rendering manager and servers to carry out rendering jobs

✦ Use the Queue Manager to control job priority

✦ Make MAX notify you when problems occur or when jobs finish

✦ Perform batch rendering even if you don't have a network

In the next chapter, we look into how to add post-production effects using the Video Post interface.

✦   ✦   ✦

Using the Video Post Interface

◆   ◆   ◆   ◆

In This Chapter

Learning about
post-production
and the Video
Post dialog box

Working with
sequences

Adding events
to the queue

Exploring the
various filter types

Adding and
editing events

Specifying
event ranges

Using Lens
Effects filters

◆   ◆   ◆   ◆

The Video Post window can be used to composite the final rendered image with several other images and filters. It provides a post-processing environment within the MAX interface. This chapter describes the Video Post interface and lets you practice using it.

Many of the post-processing effects such as glows and blurs are also available as Render Effects, but the Video Post window is capable of much more.

Understanding Post-Production

Post-production is the work that comes after the scene is ready to render. It can be used to add effects, such as glows and highlights, as well as add transitional effects to the animation, for example, including a logo on the front of your animation. Post-production also lets you composite several images into one.

The Video Post dialog box is a compositing interface within MAX that can be used to combine the current scene with different images, effects, and image processing filters. *Compositing* is the process of combining several different images into a single image. Each element of the composite is included as a separate event. These events are all lined up in a queue and processed in the order in which they appear in the queue. The queue can also include looping events.

The Video Post dialog box, like the Render Scene dialog box (covered in an earlier chapter), provides another way to produce final output. You can think of the Video Post process as an artistic assembly line. As the image moves down the line, each item in the queue adds an image, drops a rendered image on the stack, or apples a filter effect. This process continues until the final output event is reached.

Using the Video Post dialog box

The Video Post dialog box, shown in Figure 39-1, includes a toolbar, a pane of events and ranges, and a status bar. The dialog box can be opened by selecting Rendering ⇨ Video Post or by clicking the Video Post button on the main toolbar.

Toolbar   Queue Window

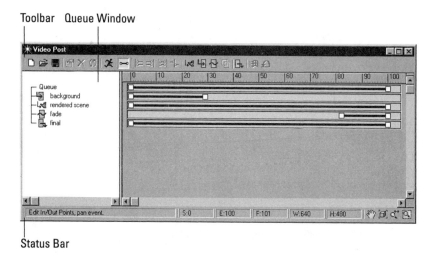

Status Bar

Figure 39-1: The Video Post dialog box lets you composite images with your final rendering.

In many ways, the Video Post dialog box is similar to the Track View dialog box. Each event is displayed in a track along with a range. These ranges can be edited by dragging the squares on either end.

The Video Post toolbar

At the top of the Video Post dialog box is a toolbar with several buttons for managing the Video Post features. These buttons are displayed and explained in Table 39-1.

Table 39-1 Video Post Toolbar Buttons		
Toolbar Button	**Name**	**Description**
☐	New Sequence	Creates a new sequence.

Toolbar Button	*Name*	*Description*
	Open Sequence	Opens an existing sequence.
	Save Sequence	Saves the current sequence.
	Edit Current Event	Opens the Edit Current Event dialog box where you can edit events.
	Delete Current Event	Removes the current event from the sequence.
	Swap Events	Changes the position in the queue of two selected events.
	Execute Sequence	Runs the current sequence.
	Edit Range Bar	Enables you to edit the event ranges.
	Align Selected Left	Aligns the left ranges of the selected events.
	Align Selected Right	Aligns the right ranges of the selected events.
	Make Selected Same Size	Makes the ranges for the selected events the same size.
	Abut Selected	Places event ranges end-to-end.
	Add Scene Event	Adds a rendered scene to the queue.
	Add Image Input Event	Adds an image to the queue.
	Add Image Filter Event	Adds an image filter to the queue.
	Add Image Layer Event	Adds a compositing plug-in to the queue.
	Add Image Output Event	Sends the final composited image to a file or device.
	Add External Event	Adds an external image processing event to the queue.
	Add Loop Event	Causes other events to loop.

The Video Post queue

Below the toolbar are the Video Post queue panes. The left pane lists all the events to be included in the post-processing sequence in the order that they are processed. You can rearrange the order of the events by dragging an event in the queue to its new location.

You can select multiple events by holding down the Ctrl key and clicking the event names, or you can select one event, hold down the Shift key, and click another event to select all events between the two.

Each event has a corresponding range that appears in the pane to its right. Each range is shown as a line with a square on each end. The left square marks the first frame of the event, and the right square marks the last frame of the event. These ranges can be expanded or contracted by dragging the square on either end of the range line.

If you click the line between two squares, you can drag the entire range. If you drag a range beyond the given number of frames, then additional frames are added. Ranges are covered in more detail in the "Working with Ranges" section later in the chapter.

The time bar (shown earlier in Figure 39-1) is at the top of the right pane. This shows the number of total frames included in the animation. You can also slide the time bar up or down to move it closer to a specific track by dragging it.

The Video Post status bar

The status bar (shown in Figure 39-1) includes a prompt line, several value fields, and some navigation buttons. The fields to the right of the prompt line include Start, End, Current Frames, and the Width and Height of the image. The navigation buttons include (in order from left to right) Pan, Zoom Extents, Zoom Time, and Zoom Region.

Working with Sequences

All the events that are added to the queue window make up a *sequence*. These sequences can be saved and opened at a later time. The Execute Sequence button, found on the toolbar, starts the compositing process.

To save a sequence, click the Save button on the toolbar. This opens the Save Sequence dialog box where the queue sequence can be saved. Sequences are saved along with the MAX file when the scene is saved, but they can also be saved independently of the scene. By default, these files are saved with the .VPX extension in the vpost directory.

Caution   Saving a sequence as a VPX file maintains the elements of the queue, but it resets all parameter settings. Saving the file as a MAX file maintains the queue order along with the parameter settings.

Saved sequences can be opened using the Open Sequence button on the toolbar. When a saved sequence is opened, all the current events are deleted. Clicking the New Sequence button also deletes any current events.

The Execute Sequence toolbar button opens the Execute Video Post dialog box, shown in Figure 39-2. The controls in this dialog box work exactly the way those in the Render Scene dialog box work. They are explained in Chapter 36, "Setting Rendering Parameters."

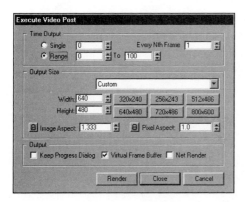

Figure 39-2: The Execute Video Post dialog box includes the controls for producing the queue output.

The Time Output section enables you to specify which frames to render, and the Output Size section lets you specify the size of the output. The Custom selection lets you enter Width and Height values, or you can use one of the pre-sets in the drop-down list or one of the preset resolution buttons. This dialog box also includes controls for entering the Image and Pixel Aspect ratios.

The Output options let you select to keep the Progress dialog box open, to render to the Virtual Frame Buffer, and/or to use network rendering. When you're ready to render the queue, click the Render button.

Cross-Reference   For more information on network rendering, see Chapter 38, "Using Network Rendering."

Adding and Editing Events

There are seven different event types that can be added to the queue including Image Input, Scene, Image Filter, Image Layer, Loop, External, and Image Output. Each of these types is covered in the following sections.

If no events are selected, then adding an event positions the event at the bottom of the list. If an event is selected, the added event becomes a subevent under the selected event.

Every event dialog box, such as the Add Input Image Event dialog box shown in Figure 39-3, includes a Label field where you can name the event. This name shows up in the queue window and is used to identify the event.

Figure 39-3: The Add Image Input Event dialog box lets you load an image to add to the queue.

Each event dialog box includes a Video Post Parameters section, also shown in Figure 39-3. This section contains VP Start Time and VP End Time values for defining the length of the Video Post range. It also includes an Enabled option for enabling or disabling an event. Disabled events are grayed out in the queue.

To edit an event, you simply need to double-click its name in the queue. This opens an Edit Event dialog box.

Adding an image input event

The Add Image Input Event dialog box, previously shown in Figure 39-3, lets you add a simple image to the queue. For example, a background image can be added using this dialog box rather than the Environment dialog box. To open the Add Image Input Event dialog box, click the Add Image Input Event button on the toolbar.

The Files button on this dialog box opens the Select Image File for Video Post Input dialog box where you can locate an image file to load from the hard disk or network. Supported image types include AVI, BMP, Kodak Cineon, FLC, GIF, IFL, IPP, JPEG, PNG, PSD, MOV, SGI Image, RLA, RPF, TGA, TIF, and YUV. The Devices button lets you access an external device such as a video recorder. The Options button becomes enabled when an image is loaded. It opens the Image Input Options dialog box, discussed below. The Cache option causes the image to be loaded into memory, which can speed up the Video Post process by not requiring the image to be loaded for every frame.

The Image Driver section of the Add Image Input Event dialog box lets you specify the settings for the image driver, such as the compression settings for an AVI file. This is different, depending on the image format.

This dialog box also includes the Video Post Parameters section described earlier.

The Image Input Options dialog box, shown in Figure 39-4, lets you set the alignment, size, and frames where the image appears. The Alignment section of the Image Input Options dialog box includes nine different presets for aligning the image. Preset options include top left corner, top centered, top right corner, left centered, centered, right centered, bottom left corner, bottom centered, and bottom right corner. You can also use the Coordinates option to specify in pixels the image's upper left corner.

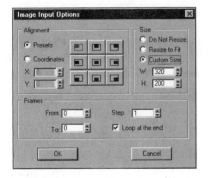

Figure 39-4: The Image Input Options dialog box lets you align and set the size of the image.

In the Size section of this dialog box, you can control the size of the image, using the Do Not Resize, Resize to Fit, or Custom Size options. The Custom Size option lets you enter Width and Height values.

The Frames section only applies to animation files. The From and To values define which frames of the animation to play. The Step value lets you play every nth frame as specified. The Loop at the End value causes the animation to loop back to the beginning when finished.

Adding scene events

A scene event is the rendered scene that you've built in MAX. By clicking the Add Scene Event button on the toolbar, the Add Scene Event dialog box shown in Figure 39-5 opens. This dialog box lets you specify the scene ranges and define the render options.

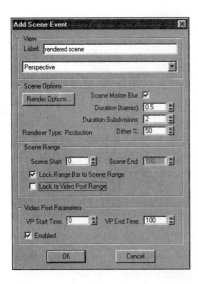

Figure 39-5: The Add Scene Event dialog box lets you specify which viewport to use to render your scene.

Below the Label field where you can name the event is a drop-down list that lets you select which viewport to use to render your scene. The active viewport is selected by default.

The Scene Options section includes a Render Options button. This button opens the Render Options dialog box, shown in Figure 39-6. This dialog box includes two rollouts: the Common Parameters rollout and a rollout for the designated rendering engine. The default rollout is the MAX Scanline A-Buffer rollout. The Common Parameters rollout includes the same rendering Options found in the Render Scene dialog box covered in Chapter 36, "Setting Rendering Parameters," and the MAX Scanline A-Buffer rollout includes the same controls also explained in Chapter 36.

Back in the Add Scene Event dialog box, the Scene Options section also includes an option for enabling Scene Motion Blur. This motion blur type is different from the object motion blur that is set in the Object Properties dialog box. Scene motion blur is applied to the entire image and is useful for blurring objects that are moving fast. The Duration (frames) value sets how long the blur effect is computed per frame. The Duration Subdivisions value is how many computations are done for each duration. The Dither % value sets the amount of dithering to use for blurred sections.

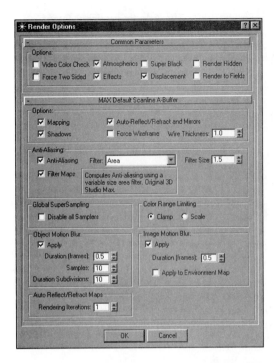

Figure 39-6: The Render Options dialog box lets you specify how the scene is to be rendered.

In the Scene Range section, the Scene Start and Scene End values let you define the range for the rendered scene. The Lock Range Bar to Scene Range option maintains the range length as defined in the Time Slider, though you can still reposition the start of the rendered scene. The Lock to Video Post Range option sets the range equal to the Video Post range.

This dialog box also includes the Video Post Parameters section as described earlier.

Adding image filter events

The Add Image Filter Event button on the toolbar opens the Add Image Filter Event dialog box, shown in Figure 39-7, where you can select from many different filter types. The available filters are included in a drop-down list under the Label field.

Below the filter drop-down list are two buttons: About and Setup. The About button gives some details about the creator of the filter. The Setup button opens a separate dialog box that controls the filter. The dialog box that appears depends on the type of filter that you selected in the drop-down list. The filter types and their dialog boxes are described in the proceeding sections.

Figure 39-7: The Add Image Filter Event dialog box lets you select from many different filter types.

Several filters require a mask such as the Image Alpha filter. To open a bitmap image to use as the mask, click the Files button in the Mask section and select the file in the Select Mask Image dialog box that opens. The Options button opens the Image Input Options dialog box (shown earlier in Figure 39-4) for aligning and sizing the mask. There is also a drop-down list for selecting the channel to use. Possible channels include Red, Green, Blue, Alpha, Luminance, Z Buffer, Material Effects, and Object. The mask can be Enabled or Inverted.

Note   Several Lens Effects filters are also included in the drop-down list. These filters use an advanced dialog box with many options, which are covered in a later section.

This dialog box also includes the Video Post Parameters section as described earlier.

Adobe Photoshop filter

When it comes to image filters, Adobe Photoshop probably has more available than any other product. These filters extend the usefulness of the product far beyond its standard features. MAX can use any Adobe Photoshop plug-ins installed on your system. Selecting this filter type in the drop-down list and clicking the Setup button opens the Adobe Photoshop Plug-In Setup dialog box, shown in Figure 39-8. This dialog box enables you to access and set up the Adobe Photoshop filters.

The Browse Filter button opens the Select plug-in directory dialog box and lets you specify the path where MAX should look for plug-ins. The current filter Category and Filters are displayed in drop-down lists. Many plug-ins use the Foreground and Background colors and the Alpha Plane in their processing, which can also be specified in this dialog box. To look at the filter results in the plug-in interface, you can select the Use Stand-in Image option to display a checkerboard image, or you can click the Browse Image button to load an image to display. For the Plug-in Preview, you can set the Width, Height, and Pixel Aspect Ratio values.

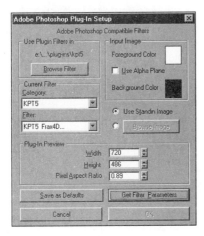

Figure 39-8: The Adobe Photoshop Plug-In Setup dialog box lets you access Adobe Photoshop filters for use in the Video Post dialog box.

The Get Filter Parameters button opens the plug-in interface where you can set the various parameters for the plug-in. The settings found in the plug-in interface can be saved with the Save as Defaults button.

Adobe Premiere video filter

Adobe Premiere does for animation and video segments what Photoshop does for images, and, just as Photoshop does, Premiere supports a variety of plug-ins that enable new editing features. You can access these filters in MAX by selecting the Adobe Premiere Video Filter option from the drop-down list in the Add Image Filter Event dialog box and clicking Setup. This opens the Adobe Premiere Video Filter Setup dialog box, shown in Figure 39-9.

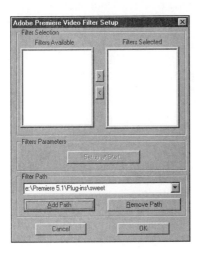

Figure 39-9: The Adobe Premiere Video Filter Setup dialog box lets you work with Adobe Premiere Video filters.

This dialog box includes two panes that list the Filters Available on the left and the Filters Selected on the right. Filters can be moved between the two panes using the arrow buttons in the middle. Once a filter is selected, the Setup at Start button becomes active. This button enables you to display the filters interface.

The Add Path button opens a Choose Directory dialog box that lets you specify a path where MAX should look for available filters. Each filter path that points to a specific directory where a filter is located is maintained in a drop-down list for easy selection. You can remove these paths with the Remove Path button.

Contrast filter

The Contrast filter is used to adjust the brightness and contrast. Selecting this filter and clicking the Setup button opens the Image Contrast Control dialog box, shown in Figure 39-10. This dialog box includes values for Contrast and Brightness. Both values can be set from 0 to 1. The Absolute option computes the center gray value based on the highest color value. The Derived option uses an average value of the components of all three colors (red, green, and blue).

Figure 39-10: The Image Contrast Control dialog box lets you alter the brightness and contrast of an image.

Fade filter

The Fade filter can be used to fade the image out over time. It can be selected from the drop-down list. The Fade Image Control dialog box, shown in Figure 39-11, lets you select to fade In or Out. The fade takes place over the length of the range set in the queue window.

Figure 39-11: The Fade Image Control dialog box includes options to fade In or Out.

Image Alpha filter

The Image Alpha filter sets the alpha channel as specified by the mask. This filter doesn't have a setup dialog box.

Negative filter

The Negative filter inverts all the colors, as in the negative of a photograph. The Negative Filter dialog box, shown in Figure 39-12, includes a simple Blend value.

Figure 39-12: The Negative Filter dialog box lets you set the amount of Blend for the negative image.

Pseudo Alpha filter

The Pseudo Alpha filter sets the alpha channel based on the pixel located in the upper left corner of the image. This filter can make an unrendered background transparent. When this filter is selected, the Setup button is disabled, because it doesn't have a setup dialog box.

Simple wipe filter

The Simple Wipe filter removes the image by replacing it with a black background. The length of the wipe is determined by the event's time range. The Simple Wipe Control dialog box, shown in Figure 39-13, lets you wipe from the left to the right or from the right to the left. You can also set the mode to Push, which displays the image, or to Pop, which erases it.

Figure 39-13: The Simple Wipe Control dialog box lets you select which direction to wipe the image.

Starfield filters

The Starfield filter creates a starfield image. By using a camera, you can motion blur the stars. The Stars Control dialog box, shown in Figure 39-14, includes a Source Camera drop-down list that you can use to select a camera.

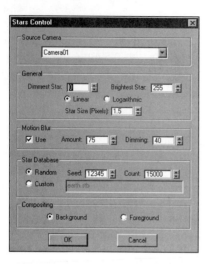

Figure 39-14: The Stars Control dialog box lets you load a custom database of stars.

The General section sets the brightness and size of the stars. You can specify brightness values for the Dimmest Star and the Brightest Star. The Linear and Logarithmic options use two different algorithms to compute the brightness values of the stars as a function of distance. The Star Size value sets the size of the stars in pixels. Size values can range from 0.001 to 100.

The Motion Blur settings let you enable motion blurring, set the blur Amount, and specify a Dimming value.

The Star Database section includes settings for defining how the stars are to appear. The Random option displays stars based on the Count value and the random Seed that determines the randomness of the star's positions. The Custom option reads a star database specified in the Database field.

Tip MAX includes a starfield database named earth.stb that includes the stars as seen from Earth.

You can also specify whether the stars are composited in the background or foreground.

Adding image layer events

In addition to the standard filters that can be applied to a single image, there are several more filters, called *layer events,* that can be applied to several images. The Add Layer Event button is only available on the toolbar when two images are selected. The first image (which is the selected image highest in the queue) becomes the source image, and the second image is the compositor. Both image events become subevents under the layer event.

Tip   If the layer event is deleted, the two subevent images remain.

The dialog box for the Add Image Layer Event, shown in Figure 39-15, is the same as the Add Image Filter Event dialog box shown earlier in Figure 39-7, except that the drop-down list includes filters that work with two images.

Figure 39-15: The Add Image Layer Event dialog box lets you apply filters to two images.

Selecting the filter in the drop-down list and clicking the Setup button can open the Setup dialog boxes for all the filters in the Add Image Layer Event dialog box.

Adobe Premiere transition filter

The same filters that are available in the Add Image Filter Event dialog box can also be used to transition between two filters. These filters can be accessed through the Adobe Premiere Transition Filter Setup dialog box, shown in Figure 39-16.

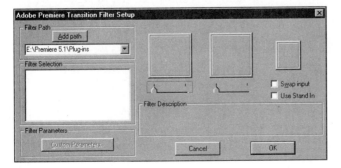

Figure 39-16: The Adobe Premiere Transition Filter Setup dialog box lets you use Premiere filters to transition between two images.

This dialog box includes an Add path button to tell MAX where to look for filters. All available filters are displayed in the Filter Selection list. You can access the filter interface with the Custom Parameters button. The two preview windows to the right display the filter effects. You also have options to Swap Input (which switches the two images) and Use Stand-In (which lets you specify a sample image to preview the effect).

Alpha compositor

The Alpha Compositor can be used to composite two images, using the alpha channel of the foreground image. When this filter is selected, the Setup button is disabled because it doesn't have a setup dialog box.

Cross Fade transition compositor

The Cross Fade Transition Compositor fades one image out as it fades another image in. It also doesn't have a setup dialog box.

Pseudo Alpha compositor

The Pseudo Alpha Compositor can be used to combine two images if one doesn't have an alpha channel. This Compositor uses the upper-left pixel to designate the transparent color for the image. It also doesn't have a setup dialog box.

Simple additive compositor

The Simple Additive Compositor combines two images based on the intensity of the second image. As is the case with the other filters, it doesn't have a setup dialog box, so the Setup button is disabled.

Simple wipe compositor

The Simple Wipe Compositor is similar to the Simple Wipe filter, except that it slides the image in or out instead of erasing it. Its setup dialog box looks just like that of the Simple Wipe Control dialog box shown earlier in Figure 39-13.

Adding external events

The Add External Event button on the toolbar lets you use an external image-processing program to edit the image. This button is only available when an image event is selected and the image event becomes a subevent under the external event. The Add External Event dialog box, shown in Figure 39-17, includes a Browse button for locating the external program. There is also a Command Line Options field for entering text commands for the external program. Many external programs use the clipboard to do their processing, so the Write image to clipboard and Read image from clipboard options make this possible.

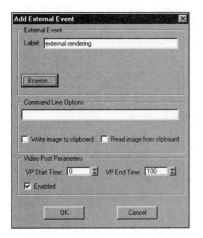

Figure 39-17: The Add External Event dialog box lets you access an external program to edit images.

Using loop events

The Add Loop Event button is enabled when any single event is selected. This button enables an event to be repeated a specified number of times or throughout the Video Post range. The Add Loop Event dialog box, shown in Figure 39-18, includes a value field for the Number of Times to repeat the event, along with Loop and Ping Pong options. The Loop option repeats from beginning to end until the Number of Times value is reached. The Ping Pong option alternates playing the event forward and in reverse. Loop events can be named using the Label field.

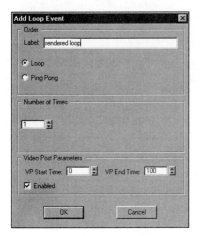

Figure 39-18: The Add Loop Event dialog box lets you play an event numerous times.

Adding an image output event

If you've added all the events you need and configured them correctly, and you click the Execute Sequence button and nothing happens, then chances are you've forgotten to add an Image Output event. This event adds the surface that all the events use to output to and should appear last in the queue.

The Add Image Output Event dialog box looks the same as the Add Image Input Event dialog box shown earlier in Figure 39-3. The output can be saved to a file or to a device, using any of the standard file types.

Tip   If you don't give the output event a name, the file name automatically becomes the event name.

Working with Ranges

The pane to the right of the queue displays the ranges for each event. These turn red when selected. The beginning and end points of the range are marked with squares. You can move these points by dragging the squares. This moves the beginning and end points for all selected events.

When two or more events are selected, several additional buttons on the toolbar become enabled including Swap Events, Align Selected Left, Align Selected Right, Make Selected Same Size, and Abut Selected. (Each of these buttons was shown earlier in Table 39-1.)

The Swap Events button is enabled only if two events are selected. When clicked, it will change the position of the two events. Because the order of the events is important, this can alter the final output.

The Align Selected Left and Align Selected Right buttons move the beginning and end points of every selected track until they line up with the first and last points of the top selected event.

The Make Selected Same Size button resizes any bottom events to be the same size as the top selected event. The Abut Selected button moves each selected event under the top event until its first point lines up with the last point of the selected event above it.

Figure 39-19 shows four image events that have been placed end-to-end using the Abut Selected button. Notice how the queue range spans the entire distance.

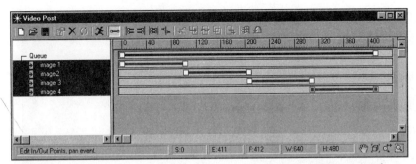

Figure 39-19: The Abut Selected button can be used to position several events end-to-end.

Working with Lens Effects Filters

The Add Image Filter Event dialog box's drop-down list has several Lens Effects filters. These filters include Lens Effects Flare, Focus, Glow, and Highlight. Each of these filters is displayed and discussed in the sections that follow, but there are several parameters that are common to all of them.

Many lens effects parameters in the various Lens Effects setup dialog boxes can be animated. These include Size, Hue, Angle, and Intensity. These are identified in the dialog boxes by green arrow buttons to the right of the parameter fields. These buttons work the way the Animate button in the main interface works. To animate a parameter, just click the corresponding arrow button, move the Time Slider to a new frame, and change the parameter. Figure 39-20 shows how these buttons look in the Lens Effects Flare dialog box.

Each Lens Effects dialog box also includes a preview pane in the upper left corner with three buttons underneath. Clicking the Preview button renders all enabled lens effects in the preview pane. The VP Queue button renders the current Video Post queue. Using the preview pane, you can get an idea of how the final output should look. With the Preview button enabled, any parameter changes in the dialog box are automatically updated in the preview pane. The Update button enables you to manually update the preview.

You can save the settings in each Lens Effect dialog box as a separate file that can be recalled at any time. These saved files have a .LZF extension and can be saved and loaded with the Save and Load buttons at the bottom left of the dialog box.

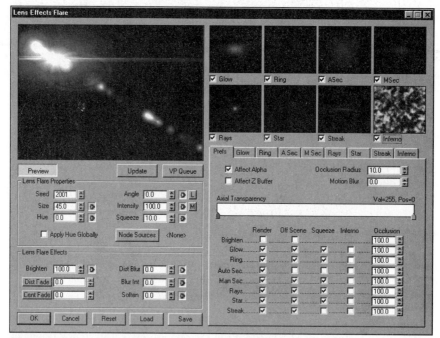

Figure 39-20: Green arrow buttons in the Lens Effects Flare dialog box identify the parameters that can be animated for this effect.

Adding flares

The Lens Effects Flare dialog box includes controls for adding flares of various types to the image. This dialog box, shown earlier in Figure 39-20, includes a main preview pane and several smaller preview panes for each individual effect. The check boxes underneath these smaller preview panes let you enable or disable these smaller panes.

Under the main preview pane are several global commands, and to their right is a series of panels that contain the settings for each individual effect type. The various flare types include Glow, Ring, A Sec, M Sec, Rays, Star, Streak, and Inferno. Each of these types has a corresponding preview pane.

Adding focus

The Lens Effects Focus dialog box, shown in Figure 39-21, includes options for adding Scene Blur, Radial Blur, and Focal Node effects. If the Focal Node option is selected, you can click the Select button to open the Select Focal Object dialog box in order to choose the object that sets the focal point for the scene.

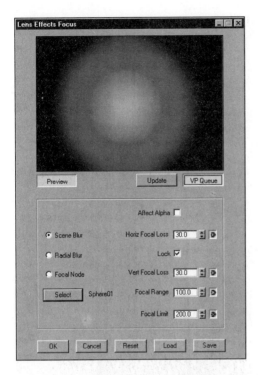

Figure 39-21: The Lens Effects Focus dialog box can be used to blur an image.

You can also set values for the Horizontal and Vertical Focal Loss or enable the Lock button to lock these two parameters together. The Focal Range and Focal Limit values determine the distance from the focal point where the blurring begins or reaches full strength. You can also set the blurring to affect the Alpha channel.

Adding glow

The Lens Effects Glow dialog box, shown in Figure 39-22, enables you to apply glows to the entire scene or to specific objects based on the Object ID or Effects ID. Other Source options include Unclamped, Surface Norm (Normals), Mask, Alpha, Z High, and Z Lo. This dialog box also enables you to Filter the glow, using options such as Edge, Perimeter Alpha, Perimeter, Bright, and Hue.

Additional panels under the preview pane let you control the Preferences, Gradients, and Inferno settings.

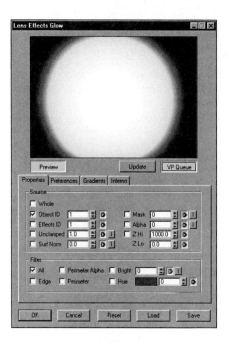

Figure 39-22: The Lens Effects Glow dialog box can make objects and scenes glow.

Adding highlights

The Lens Effects Highlight dialog box, shown in Figure 39-23, is very similar to the Glow dialog box, except that the effects it produces are highlights instead of glows.

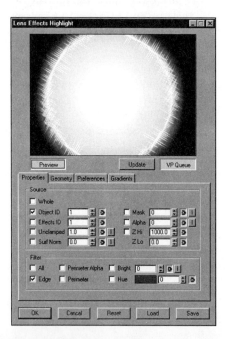

Figure 39-23: The Lens Effects Highlight dialog box can add highlights to scene objects.

Tutorial: Adding backgrounds and filters using Video Post

As an example of the Video Post dialog box in action, we composite a background image, a rendered scene, and some filter effects to produce a final output image.

To composite an image with the Video Post dialog box, follow these steps:

1. Import and position the Cessna airplane model created by Viewpoint Datalabs.

2. Open the Environment dialog box by selecting Rendering ⇨ Environment, and change the background color to bright green.

3. Open the Video Post dialog box by selecting Rendering ⇨ Video Post.

4. Add a background image to the queue by clicking the Add Image Input Event button. Name the event **background** and click the Files button. Locate the waterfall image and click OK. Then click OK again to exit the Add Image Input Event dialog box.

5. Next add the rendered image by clicking the Add Scene Event button and selecting the Perspective view. Name the event **rendered airplane**. Click the Render Options dialog box, disable the Anti-Aliasing option, and click OK. Click OK again to exit the Edit Scene Event dialog box.

6. Select both the background and rendered airplane events and click the Add Image Layer Event button. Select the Pseudo Alpha option and click OK. This composites the background image and the rendered image together by removing all the green background from the rendered scene.

7. Add an output event by clicking the Add Image Output Event button. Name the event **final** and click the Files button. This opens the Select Image File for Video Post Output dialog box where you can select a name and location to use for the saved output file. Click OK when finished, and then click OK again to exit the Add Image Output Event dialog box. The final queue looks like the one shown in Figure 39-24.

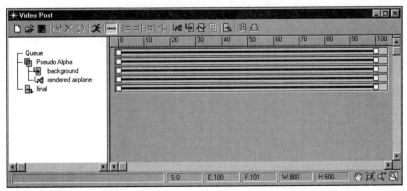

Figure 39-24: This Video Post queue is defined and ready to execute.

8. To run the processing, click the Execute Sequence button to open the Execute Video Post dialog box, select the Single output range option, click the 640×480 size button, and click Render.

Figure 39-25 shows the final composited image.

Figure 39-25: The airplane in this image is rendered and the background is composited.

Tutorial: Creating space backdrops

Space backgrounds are popular backdrops, and MAX includes a special Video Post filter for creating Starfield backgrounds. You would typically want to use the Video Post dialog box to render the starfield along with any animation that you've created, but, in this tutorial, we just render a starfield that can be saved as an image and used as an environment map.

To create a starfield background, follow these steps:

1. The starfield filter requires a camera, so open the Create panel, select the Cameras category, and click the Free button. Then click in the Front view to create the camera.

2. Select Rendering ⇨ Video Post to open the Video Post dialog box. A Scene Event must be added to the queue in order for the render job to be executed. Click the Add Scene Event button, type **empty** in the Label field, and click OK.

3. Click the Add Image Filter Event button to open the Add Image Filter Event dialog box and, in the Label field, type the name **Starfield**. Select Starfield from the drop-down list and click the Setup button to open the Stars Control dialog box. Select Camera01 as the Source Camera and click OK to accept the defaults. Click OK again to exit the Add Image Filter Event dialog box.

4. Click the Add Image Output Event button to open the Add Image Output Event dialog box and, in the Label field, type the name **Starfield Background**. If you want to save the image directly, click the Files button and select a name and location in the File dialog box. Click OK when finished.

5. Click the Execute Sequence button, select the Single output time option and an Output Size, and click the Render button.

I didn't include a figure of the resulting background here because it would not show up well as a figure, but the image can now be used as an environment map.

Summary

Using the Video Post dialog box, you can composite several different images, filters, and effects together. All these different compositing elements are listed as events in a queue. The Video Post dialog box provides, along with the Render Scene dialog box, another way to create output.

In this chapter, you've:

✦ Learned about the post-production process

✦ Explored the Video Post dialog box

✦ Worked with sequences

✦ Explored all the various filter types

✦ Learned to add and edit events and manipulate their ranges

✦ Discovered the Lens Effects filters

This concludes the Rendering and Post-Production part of the book. The next part presents ways to extend MAX, starting with plug-ins.

✦　　✦　　✦

Extending MAX

Extending MAX with Plug-Ins

A *plug-in* is an external program that integrates seamlessly with the MAX interface to provide additional functionality. Kinetix has adopted an architecture for MAX that is open and enables all aspects of the program to be enhanced. MAX ships with a Software Developer's Kit (SDK) that enables users to generate their own plug-ins. Many different companies currently produce plug-ins, and other users create and distribute freeware and shareware plug-ins.

This chapter covers many of the existing plug-ins. From this random sampling, you can gain an idea of the types of plug-ins that are available and their capabilities.

A Plug-In Overview

The entire architecture of MAX is built around plug-ins, and many of the core components of MAX are implemented as plug-ins. This is evident by the occasional About credit screen located throughout the product.

To see all the currently installed plug-ins, select File ⇨ Summary Info to open the Summary Info dialog box and click the Plug-In Info button. This will open the Plug-In Info dialog box that lists all installed plug-ins with their details, as shown in Figure 40-1. As you can see, there are many plug-ins installed with just the default installation.

In This Chapter

Understanding plug-ins

Freeware and shareware plug-ins

Installing plug-ins

Plug-in examples

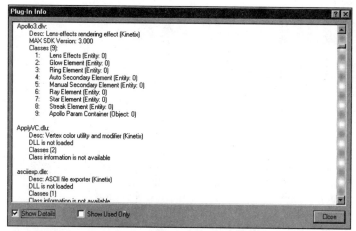

Figure 40-1: The Plug-In Info dialog box includes a list of all the currently loaded plug-ins, both internal and external.

Freeware and Shareware Plug-Ins

In addition to the commercially developed plug-ins, many plug-ins are available as freeware or shareware. Many of these plug-ins can be found and downloaded via the Web.

Here are some Web sites that offer freeware or shareware plug-ins for download:

- ✦ **MAX3D** — www.max3d.com/plugins/
- ✦ **3Dstudio.net** — www.3dstudio.net/
- ✦ **BoboLand** — gfxcentral.com/bobo
- ✦ **MAX World Wide** — www.maxww.com/
- ✦ **3D Café** — www.3dcafe.com/
- ✦ **HABWare** — www.habware.at/

As a special bonus to this book, programming master and contributing author Dave Brueck has created eight exclusive plug-ins that are included on the CD-ROM. For detailed information on these plug-ins, check out Appendix B, "Exclusive Bible Plug-Ins." The CD-ROM also includes a collection of plug-ins compiled for R3 by Harald Blab and found on his HABWare site.

Installing Plug-Ins

Most commercial plug-ins include an installation program. During the installation process, these programs ask where the MAX root directory is located. From this root directory, the plug-in program files are installed in the "plugins" directory, help files are installed in the help directory, and example scenes are installed in the "scenes" directory.

Plug-in program files typically have a .DLR, .DLO, or .DLM extension, depending on the type of plug-in. When MAX loads, it searches the plugins directory for these files and loads them along with the program files. Freeware plug-ins can be installed simply by copying the plug-in file into the plugins directory and restarting MAX.

You can also place plug-ins in a different directory and load them from this directory. The Path Configuration dialog box is where additional plug-in paths can be specified.

The Path Configuration dialog box is discussed in Chapter 3, "Customizing the MAX Interface."

Most commercial plug-ins require that the plug-in be authorized after installation. This must be done before the plug-in can be used, and it can usually be done via telephone, fax, or e-mail.

To remove a plug-in, use the uninstall feature that is part of the setup process, or delete the associated program files from the plugins directory.

Plug-In Types and Examples

There are many different types of plug-ins used to add many different kinds of features. This section lists several of the different types that are available along with tutorials that you can use to sample some of the commercial plug-ins.

At the time of this writing, many of the plug-ins had not been updated to work with Release 3. Therefore, the tutorials were created using MAX R2. However, you can assume that the new updates will work in a similar manner with R3.

Environment plug-ins

Many plug-ins are added to the scene by means of the Environment dialog box. These plug-ins can include new atmospheric effects, such as the Afterburn plug-in, or specialized effects, such as the Shag:Fur plug-in.

Tutorial: Creating a fuzzy spider with Shag:Fur

Modeling hair is one of the trickiest 3D modeling tasks, but Digimation has produced two plug-ins that make this process a lot easier. In this tutorial, we'll use the Shag:Fur plug-in to give a spider model a furry look.

To create a fuzzy spider using the Shag:Fur plug-in, follow these steps:

1. Import the spider model created by Zygote Media using the File ⇨ Import command.

2. With the Shag:Fur plug-in installed and authorized, you first need to add a specialized type of light. Open the Create menu, click the Lights category button, and from the subcategory drop-down, select Hair Enabled Lights. Then click the HTargetSpot button and drag in the Front view to create a light. Position the light and target so that the spider is lighted.

3. Select Rendering ⇨ Environment to open the Environment dialog box. Click the Add button, select the Shag:Render option, and click OK. Then click the Add button again and select the Shag:Fur option to open the Shag:Fur rollout, where the parameters for the fur are set.

4. Click the Pick button and then select each of the spider parts that you want to apply fur to. Set the Maximum Length value to **5.0** with a Random Factor of **0.3**. Select the Absolute Density option with a value of **3.0**.

Figure 40-2 shows our spider model covered in fur.

Tutorial: Creating a fireball with Afterburn

Afterburn is a great plug-in for creating amazing atmospheric effects such as clouds, nebulae, and fireballs, as this tutorial will show. The Afterburn plug-in is also implemented through the Environment dialog box and includes a custom rendering engine.

To create a fireball using the Afterburn plug-in, follow these steps:

1. Open the Create panel and click the Helper category button. From the subcategory drop-down, select Atmospheric Apparatus and then click the SphereGizmo button. Create a sphere gizmo in the center of the Front viewport.

2. Select Rendering ⇨ Environment to open the Environment dialog box. In the Atmospheric Effects rollout, click the Add button. Select the Afterburn Renderer and click OK.

Figure 40-2: The Shag:Fur plug-in can add fur to models like this spider.

3. Click the Add button again and select Afterburn Combustion to open the Combustion Parameters rollout. Click the Pick button and select the sphere gizmo in the viewport.

4. Set the Density to **15** and select Fireball as the Flame Type.

Figure 40-3 shows the resulting fireball.

Rendering plug-ins

In the previous Shag:Fur and Afterburn tutorials, you saw that these plug-ins load and use their own rendering engines. This gives them control over the final rendering that isn't possible with the default rendering engine.

Tutorial: Producing a cartoon rendering with Incredible Comicshop

Using the Incredible Comicshop plug-in, you can change the way objects and scenes are rendered. Figure 40-4 shows the laser truck model created by Viewpoint Datalabs before it is rendered as a cartoon.

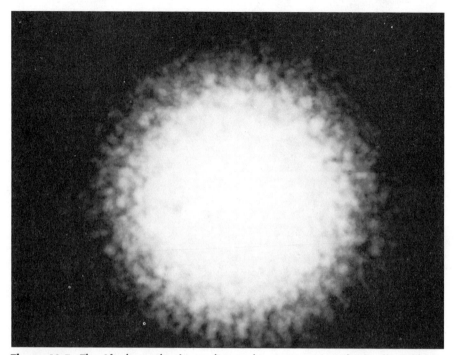

Figure 40-3: The Afterburn plug-in can be used to create atmospheric effects like this fireball.

To render a 3D scene as a cartoon using the Incredible Comicshop plug-in, follow these steps:

1. First, you need to change the default renderer. To do this, select Customize ⇨ Preferences to open the Preferences dialog box. Then select the Rendering panel and click the Assign button to the right of the Production renderer. Select Comicshop from the Choose Renderer dialog box and click OK.

2. Select Tools ⇨ Material Editor to open the Material Editor. Select the first sample slot and click the Pick Material from Object button. Then click the body of the laser truck to load its current material into the first sample slot. Then click the Type button. From the Material/Map Browser, double-click the Comicshop: Ink and Paint option.

3. Click the color swatch next to the Cel Paint button and select a light green color. Keep the Ink color set to black. Repeat this for each material in the laser truck model.

Figure 40-5 shows the completed rendering in the cartoon style. Compare this image to the one in Figure 40-4.

Figure 40-4: The laser truck model as it normally would render

Material plug-ins

Material plug-ins can add new material or new map types to the Material/Map Browser. These materials have their own set of parameters for added functionality. Other material plug-ins are included in the Utilities panel, such as the plug-in for Painter 3D.

Cross-Reference

The Painter 3D plug-in is covered in Chapter 19, "Working with Materials and Maps."

Tutorial: Weathering a model with DirtyReyes

As an example of a material plug-in, we'll take a look at DirtyReyes by REM Infografica. This product is called a "weathering tool" because it can add a layer of grime and dirt to a product to remove the "new" look common with most rendered models. Once again, we'll use the laser truck model created by Viewpoint Datalabs for this tutorial.

Figure 40-5: The Incredible Comicshop plug-in can render a model to look like a cartoon.

To weather the laser truck model using the DirtyReyes plug-in, follow these steps.

1. Import the laser truck model and position it in the scene.

2. Select the body of the truck and open the Modify panel. Click the More button and in the additional Modifiers dialog box, locate and double-click the DirtyReyes Modifier. In the DirtyReyes Parameters rollout, click the Start Calculations button and the map for the truck will be computed. When the calculations finish, click the Apply Material button.

3. Repeat Step 2 for each part of the model that you wish to weather.

Figure 40-6 shows the completed rendering of the model using the DirtyReyes plug-in. Compare this image to the one shown in Figure 40-4.

Animation plug-ins

An animation plug-in can be either a new Controller or an entire interface added through the Utilities panel. The HyperMatter plug-in is implemented in the form of specialized objects with dynamic properties built-in. These dynamic properties control the way the objects are animated when dropped in the scene.

Figure 40-6: The DirtyReyes plug-in can weather a model to make it look more realistic.

Tutorial: Dropping a teddy bear with the HyperMatter plug-in

The HyperMatter plug-in was created by Second Nature Industries. It can model what are known as *soft-body dynamics*. A *soft body* is one that gives to an applied force, such as a pillow or a balloon. When moved quickly, the entire object doesn't move uniformly as a solid object would; rather, it bends and flexes with the applied force.

MAX Release 3 includes the new Flex Modifier to simulate this type of motion, but the HyperMatter plug-in goes much further. In this simple tutorial, we use the HyperMatter plug-in to drop a teddy bear model created by Viewpoint Datalabs.

To use the HyperMatter plug-in to drop a teddy bear model, follow these steps:

1. Import and group the teddy bear model and position it in the center of the viewport. Select one part of the heart and open the Modify panel. Click the Attach Multiple button to open the Select Object dialog box. Select the remainder of the teddy bear parts and click Select to group the entire teddy bear as one mesh object.

2. Open the Create panel, select the Second Nature subcategory, and click the Hypermatter button. In the Automatic Solids rollout, click the Solidify Object button. This causes an orange box to surround the teddy bear.

3. Next click the Walls button and drag in the Top view to create a wall that encompasses the teddy bear. Open the Modify panel and select the Make Walls Global option. This automatically sets the walls to collide with solid objects like the teddy bear.

4. Click the Select and Move button, and move the teddy bear up above the floor of the Wall object.

5. Click the Play Animation button, and the teddy bear will descend and squish realistically against the floor.

Figure 40-7 shows four frames as the teddy impacts and rebounds from the floor.

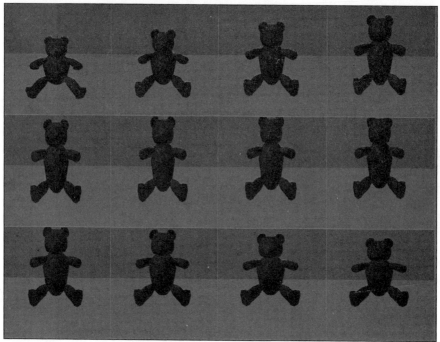

Figure 40-7: The HyperMatter plug-in can create realistic soft-body dynamics.

Particle Systems plug-ins

Particle Systems plug-ins can add new features to existing particle system types or add completely new particle systems. For example, the SandBlaster plug-in has the capability to create a model out of particles, and then dissolve those particles and reorganize them as a different model.

Tutorial: Converting a dolphin to a shark with the SandBlaster plug-in

In the briny blue, you can find fun-loving dolphins and mean-spirited sharks, and in the MAX world you can find a vicious beast that can morph from a dolphin to a shark. This tutorial uses a dolphin model created by Zygote Media and a hammerhead shark model created by Viewpoint Datalabs.

To dissolve a dolphin into a shark with the SandBlaster plug-in, follow these steps:

1. Import and group the dolphin and shark models. Position them one on top of the other.

2. Open the Create panel, select the Digimation Particles subcategory, and click the SandBlaster button. Then drag in the Top view to create the particle system icon.

3. In the Setup rollout, click the Set Emitter button and select the dolphin model. Then click the Set Target button and select the shark model. Select the Particle Activation and Render Activation options. In the Particle Parameters rollout, set the Render Particle Count to **4000** and select the Spheres option. Set the Particle Scale to **3**.

4. Select both models and then select Tools ➪ Display Floater to open the Display Floater. Click the Selected button and close the Display Floater. This hides the objects so that only the particle is visible.

Figure 40-8 shows four frames as the dolphin composed of particles changes into a shark.

Figure 40-8: The SandBlaster plug-in can explode an object into particles and reorganize them to form another object.

Summary

By adding plug-ins, you can increase the functionality of MAX far beyond its default setup. In this chapter, you've:

✦ Learned what plug-ins are and how they can extend MAX

✦ Learned where to find freeware and shareware plug-ins

✦ Discovered how to install plug-ins

✦ Tried out the capabilities of plug-ins through several tutorials

The next chapter demonstrates another way to extend MAX — using MAXScript.

✦　　✦　　✦

Using MAXScript

The designers of 3D Studio MAX went to great lengths to make sure that you are limited only by your imagination in terms of what you can do in MAX. They've packed in so many different features and so many different ways to use those features that you could use MAX for years and still be learning new ways of doing things. Despite MAX's wide range of capabilities, there may still come a time when you wish for a new MAX feature. With MAXScript you can actually extend MAX to meet your needs, customize it to work the way you want, and even have it do some of the more monotonous tasks for you.

What Is MAXScript?

In this chapter we look at MAXScript — what it's for and why in the world you would ever want to use it. But before we get into the nitty-gritty details, let's start with a brief overview.

Simply put, MAXScript is a tool that you can use to expand the functionality of 3D Studio MAX. You can use it to add new features or to customize how MAX behaves, so that it's tailored to your needs and style. You can also use MAXScript as a sort of VCR — it can record your actions so you can play them back later, eliminating repetitive tasks.

You can use MAXScript to "talk" to MAX about a scene and tell it what you want to happen, either by having MAX watch what you do or by typing in a list of instructions that you want MAX to execute.

The beauty of MAXScript lies in its flexibility and simplicity: it is easy to use and was designed from the ground up to be an integral part of MAX. But don't let its simplicity fool you — MAXScript as a language is rich enough to let you control just about anything.

In fact, you have already used MAXScript without even knowing it. Some of the buttons and rollouts use bits of MAXScript to carry out your commands. And once you've created a new feature with MAXScript, it can be integrated into MAX transparently and be used just as easily as any other MAX feature.

MAXScript is a fully functional and very powerful computer language, but you don't have to be a computer programmer or even need any previous programming experience to benefit from MAXScript. In the next few sections, we look at some simple ways to use MAXScript. For now, just think of a script in MAX as you would a script in a movie or play — it tells what's going to happen, who's going to do what, and when it's going to happen. With your scene acting as the stage, a script directs MAX to put on a performance for you.

One final note before we dive in: MAXScript is so powerful that an entire book could be written about it and every last feature it supports, but that is not the purpose here. This chapter is organized to give you an introduction to the world of MAXScript and to teach you the basic skills you need to get some mileage out of it. What is given here is a foundation that you can build upon according to your own interests and needs. The chapter shows you how to do some pretty neat things and, if you want to learn more, how to go about doing just that.

The MAXScript Architecture

This section looks at some of the basic MAX features you use when working with MAXScript and how different scripts are used.

MAXScript tools

Let's take a look at some of the tools used in working with MAXScript. MAX has several tools that make creating and using scripts as simple as possible.

The MAXScript Utility rollout

You access the MaxScript Utility rollout, shown in Figure 41-1, by opening the Utilities panel and clicking MAXScript.

From this rollout, you can choose the following:

✦ **Open Listener** — Opens the MAXScript Listener window (which is covered in the next section). You can also open this window by pressing F11.

✦ **New Script** — Opens a MAXScript editor window, a simple text editor in which you write your MAXScript.

Figure 41-1: The MAXScript rollout on the Utilities panel is a great place to start working with MAXScript.

✦ **Open Script** — Opens a Windows file dialog box that you can use to locate a MAXScript file. Once you find a script file you want to open, MAX loads it and opens a MAXScript editor window for you. MAXScript files have an .MS extension.

✦ **Run Script** — Use this button to search for a script file to load. This is similar to Open Script, except that once you find the file you want, MAX loads it and performs whatever action the script is supposed to do. When you use Run Script, some scripts will do something right away, while others will install themselves as new tools.

✦ **Utilities** — This pull-down menu shows a list of installed scripted utilities. Each scripted utility acts as a new feature for you to use (as described later in this chapter).

✦ **Close** — Use this button to close the MAXScript Utility rollout, as well as any scripted utilities you've loaded.

Note

You can also access most of the items on the MAXScript Utility rollout from the MAXScript menu.

Tutorial: Using the SphereArray script

Here's a chance for you to play around a little and get some experience with MAXScript in the process. On the CD-ROM is a simple script called SphereArray. It's similar to the Array command found in the Tools menu, except that SphereArray creates copies of an object and randomly positions them in a spherical pattern.

To load and use the SphereArray script, follow these steps:

1. Reset MAX by selecting File ⇨ Reset.

2. In the Top view, create a small box near the origin, as shown in Figure 41-2. In the Parameters rollout, set the Length, Width, and Height values to **10** and the Segs (Segment) value to **1**.

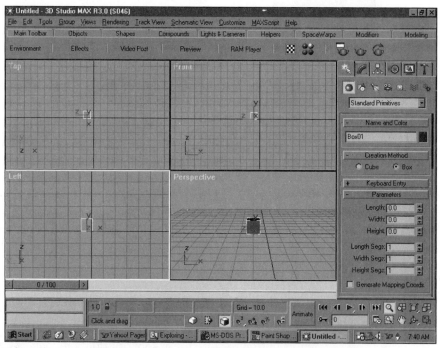

Figure 41-2: Start the SphereArray tutorial by creating one simple object.

3. Open the Utilities panel and click the MAXScript button.

4. Click the Run Script button to open the Choose Editor file dialog box, locate the SphereArray.ms file on the CD-ROM, and click Open. The SphereArray utility is installed. (Because SphereArray is a scripted utility, running it only installs it.)

5. Choose SphereArray from the Utilities drop-down list. The SphereArray rollout is displayed, as shown in Figure 41-3.

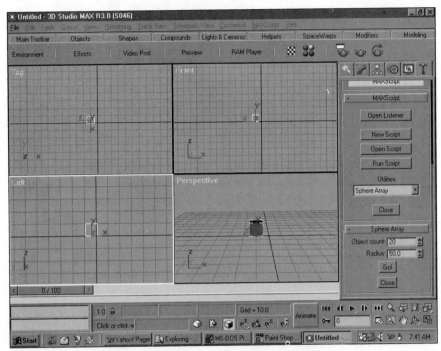

Figure 41-3: The custom rollout for the SphereArray MAXScript

6. Enter **50** in the Object Count field. (Leave Radius at 50.0.) Now click the Go! button to run the script. The script adds 50 copies of your box to the scene and randomly positions them 50 units away from the box's position.

7. Each time you click the Go! button, MAX adds that many more boxes to the screen. You can play around with different selections, object counts, and radii.

In this example, notice how the SphereArray script looks a lot like any other function or tool in MAX.

The MAXScript Listener window

Figure 41-4 shows the MAXScript Listener window, which lets you work interactively with the part of MAX that interprets MAXScript commands. The bottom pane of the Listener window displays any output from MAX when a MAXScript executes. You can type MAXScript commands in the bottom pane, and MAX will display the results in the same pane.

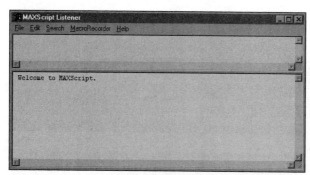

Figure 41-4: The MAXScript Listener window interprets your commands.

The top pane works in almost exactly the same way except that when you enter commands into it, the output is still displayed in the bottom pane. Why bother having two panes so similar in functionality? The top pane is great for creating small pieces of MAXScript code: as you are testing out an idea or refining a small script, you can enter it all in the top pane and see the results displayed in the bottom pane. Then, when you are ready to save your work or paste it into a larger script, you don't have to sift through a bunch of output to find your MAXScript commands — they're all in one place.

The Listener window has these menus:

✦ **File** — You can use this menu to close the window, save your work, run scripts, open a script for editing, or create a new script from scratch.

✦ **Edit** — This menu is where to access all the common editing functions you'll need, such as cutting, pasting, and undoing.

✦ **Search** — This menu is used for searching through the window to find specific text.

✦ **MacroRecorder** — This menu lets you set various options for the MAXScript Macro Recorder (which is covered later in this chapter).

Tutorial: Talking to the MAXScript interpreter

This tutorial gives you a little experience in working with the MAXScript Listener window and a chance to try some basic MAXScript commands.

To start using MAXScript, follow these steps:

1. Select File ➪ Reset to reset MAX.

2. Press F11 to open the MAXScript Listener window.

3. Click anywhere in the bottom pane of the Listener window and type the following:

```
2+2
```

As you can see in Figure 41-5, the MAXScript interpreter calculates this and writes back the answer: 4. (MAX sees whatever you type and tries to evaluate it.)

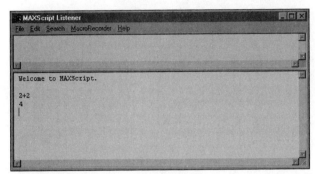

Figure 41-5: Using the MAXScript interpreter to do rocket science–type math

4. Let's try something more complex: using MAXScript to create a torus. First, click anywhere in the upper frame and type the following:

```
Torus radius1:50 radius2:5
```

MAX creates a torus and adds it to your scene, as shown in Figure 43-6. As you specified in your MAXScript, the outer radius (radius1) is 50, and the radius of the torus itself (radius2) is 5. MAX also displays the output in the bottom pane. (You could have entered the Torus command in the bottom pane too.) The output tells you that MAX created a new torus at the origin of the coordinate system. I gave that torus a name: Torus01.

Note   MAXScript is *case-insensitive*, which means that upper- and lowercase letters are the same as far as MAX is concerned. Thus you can type **Torus**, **torus**, or **TORUS** and MAX sees no difference.

5. Now use MAXScript to move the torus. In the Listener window, type the following:

```
$Torus01.position.x = 20
```

Once you press Enter you see the torus move along the positiveX-axis. Each object in MAX has certain properties or attributes that describe it, and what you've done is access one of these properties programmatically instead of by using the rollout or the mouse. In this case, you're telling MAX, "Torus01 has a position property. Set the X-coordinate of that position to 20."

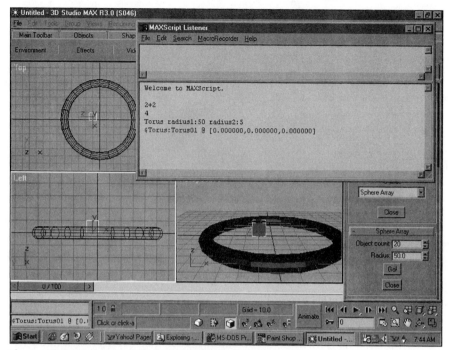

Figure 41-6: Using MAXScript to add objects to a scene

Note

The $ symbol identifies a named object. You can use it to refer to any named object.

6. To see a list of some of the properties specific to a torus, type the following:

```
Showproperties $Torus01
```

A list of the Torus01 properties is displayed in the window, as shown in Figure 41-7.

7. Notice that one of the properties listed is called radius1. Let's see what the current value of this property is. Type the following:

```
$Torus01.radius1
```

MAX displays the value for radius1 — 50.0 — as shown in Figure 41-8.

8. Now make the radius1 value bigger by typing the following:

```
$Torus01.radius1 = 70
```

9. Finally, use MAXScript to delete the torus. Type the following:

```
delete $Torus01
```

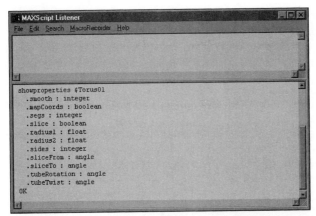

Figure 41-7: Listing the properties of a Torus object

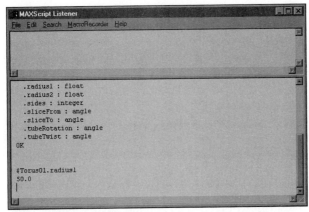

Figure 41-8: Using MAXScript to query MAX about an object's properties

An important thing to understand from this tutorial is that you can do almost anything with MAXScript. Any property of any object that you can access via a rollout is also available via MAXScript. You could go so far as to create entire scenes using just MAXScript, although the real power comes from using MAXScript to do things for you automatically. Feel free to play around some more by investigating other properties of different types of objects. Before moving on, you should be comfortable with using MAXScript to create, modify, and delete objects.

Tip   MAX remembers the value of the last MAXScript command that it executed, and you can access that value through a special variable: ? (a question mark). For example, if you type **5 + 5** in the Listener window, MAX displays the result, 10. You can then use that result in your next MAXScript command by using the question mark variable. For example, you could type **$Torus01.radius2 = ?,** and MAX would internally substitute the question mark with the number 10.

MAXScript editor windows

The MAXScript editor window enables you to open and edit any type of text file, although its most common use is for editing MAXScript files. Although you can have only one Listener window open, you can open as many editor windows as you want.

To open a new MaxScript editor window (like the one shown in Figure 41-9), you can choose File ⇨ New from the MAXScript Listener window, or you can click the New Script button in the MAXScript rollout. You can also use MaxScript editor windows to edit existing scripts. In general, it's best to use the MAXScript editor windows for working on larger scripts, and the MAXScript Listener window for small scripts or portions of a script.

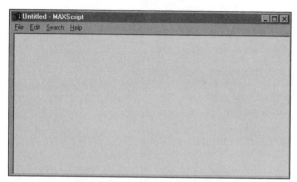

Figure 41-9: The MAXScript editor window is used to edit larger scripts.

For creating a new script, it's usually best to open both an editor window and the Listener window. Then you can try things out in the Listener window, and when the pieces of the MAXScript work, you can cut and paste them into the main editor window. Then you can return to the Listener window, work on the next new thing, and continue creating, cutting, and pasting until the script is done.

Tip   You can also send text back to the Listener window for MAX to evaluate. Just select some text with the cursor or mouse, and press Shift+Enter (or just Enter on the numeric keypad). MAX copies the selected text to the Listener window and evaluates it for you.

The File menu in the MAXScript editor window is very similar to the one for the Listener window, with the exception of the Evaluate All command. This command (choose File ⇨ Evaluate All to access it) is a fast way of having MAX evaluate your entire script. The result is the same as if you had manually selected the entire text, copied it to the Listener window, and pressed Enter.

Tip

The *bracket balancer* helps you quickly select blocks of text between pairs of parentheses, brackets, or curly braces. Click anywhere in an editor window to position the cursor, and press Ctrl+B. MAX searches forward and backward from the cursor to find a (), [], or {} pair. Each time you press Ctrl+B again, MAX searches for the next largest block of text enclosed in brackets.

Figure 41-10 shows two additional features that the MAXScript editor window provides to help you work with scripts. The first is a pop-up script navigation menu that you access by holding down the Ctrl key and right-clicking the mouse. MAX opens a small pop-up menu that lists various parts of the script you're working on. When you choose one of them, MAX moves the cursor to that part of the script.

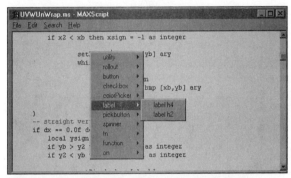

Figure 41-10: MAXScript editor window features

The other useful feature (which you may have difficulty seeing in the black-and-white figure) is called *syntax highlighting*. If you press Ctrl+D, MAX redraws the editor window using different colors for different types of script commands. This handy tool makes it easier to focus on different parts of the script.

These features won't be really useful until you start working with real scripts, so it might be worthwhile to review this section later.

The Macro Recorder

The MAXScript Macro Recorder is a tool that records your actions and creates a MAXScript that can be recalled to duplicate those actions. Using the Macro Recorder is a quick and easy way to write entire scripts, but it is also a great way to make a working version of a script that you can then refine. Once the Macro Recorder has created a MAXScript from your recorded actions, you can edit the script using a MAXScript editor window to make any changes you want.

You can turn the Macro Recorder on and off either by selecting MAXScript ⇨ Macro Recorder in the main toolbar or by choosing Macro Recorder ⇨ Enable in the MAXScript Listener window. In Figure 41-11, you can see a check mark next to Macro Recorder on the MAXScript menu, which means that the Macro Recorder is turned on.

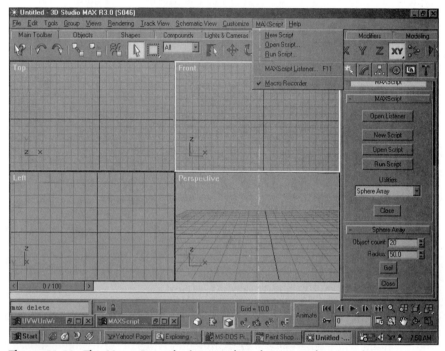

Figure 41-11: The Macro Recorder is on and ready to record your actions

When the Macro Recorder is on, every action is converted to MAXScript and sent to the MAXScript Listener window's top pane. You can then take the MAXScript output and save it to a file or copy it to a MAXScript editor window for additional editing. The Macro Recorder continues to monitor your actions until you turn it off, which is done in the same way as turning it on.

Caution   In general, the Macro Recorder keeps track of buttons you press, changes you make to objects in your scene, and so on; however, it doesn't capture every single thing you do in MAX. Some dialog boxes may not produce MAXScript output for the Macro Recorder, so occasionally you have to experiment to see what works.

Figure 41-12 shows the MacroRecorder menu in the MAXScript Listener window.

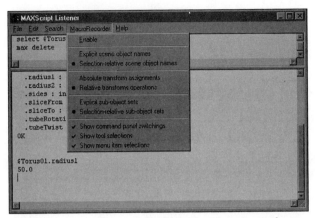

Figure 41-12: Options available in the MacroRecorder menu

The MacroRecorder menu has these options:

✦ **Enable**—This option turns the Macro Recorder on or off.

✦ **Explicit scene object names**—With this option the Macro Recorder writes the MAXScript using the names of the objects you modify so that the script always modifies those exact same objects, regardless of what object you have selected when you run the script again. For example, if the Macro Recorder watches you move a pyramid named $Pyramid01 in your scene, then the resulting MAXScript will always and only operate on the scene object named $Pyramid01.

✦ **Selection-relative scene object names**—With this option the Macro Recorder writes MAXScript that will operate on whatever object is currently selected. So if (when you recorded your script) you moved the pyramid named $Pyramid01, you could later select a different object and run your script, and the new object would move instead.

Tip

To decide which of these options to use, ask yourself, "Do I want the script to always manipulate this particular object, or do I want the script to manipulate whatever I have selected?"

✦ **Absolute transform assignments**—This tells the Macro Recorder that any transformations you make are not relative to an object's current position or orientation. For example, if you move a sphere from (0,0,0) to (10,0,0), the Macro Recorder writes MAXScript that says, "Move the object to (10,0,0)."

✦ **Relative transforms operations**—Use this option to have the Macro Recorder apply transformations relative to an object's current state. For example, if you move a sphere from (0,0,0) to (10,0,0), the Macro Recorder says, "Move the object +10 units in the X-direction from its current location."

✦ **Explicit subobject sets** — If you choose this option and then record a script that manipulates a set of subobjects, running the script again will always manipulate those same subobjects, even if you have other subobjects selected when you run the script again.

✦ **Selection-relative subobject sets** — This tells the Macro Recorder that you want the script to operate on whatever subobjects are selected when you run the script.

✦ **Show command panel switchings** — This option tells the Macro Recorder whether or not to write MAXScript for actions that take place on the command panel. Most of the time you don't really need to have this on because MAXScripts usually run independent of whatever mode the user interface is in; unless you really care, though, it's best to just leave it selected.

✦ **Show tool selections** — If this option is selected, the Macro Recorder records MAXScript to change to different tools. Again, this option usually isn't needed because which tool is currently selected is a user interface issue that is irrelevant to the MAXScript.

✦ **Show menu item selections** — This option tells the Macro Recorder whether or not you want it to generate MAXScript for menu items you select while recording your script.

Tutorial: Recording a simple script

In this tutorial, we'll create a simple script that squashes whatever object you have selected and turns it purple.

To create a script using the Macro Recorder, follow these steps:

1. Select File ➪ Reset to reset MAX.

2. Create a pyramid near the center of the Top viewport, like the one shown in Figure 41-13. Make sure it's some color besides purple (the script is going to change the color to purple, so we want to be able to see that it's working).

3. Select the pyramid but don't do anything with it. (We want to make our script work on whatever object is currently selected, so we need to start recording with something already selected.)

4. Select MAXScript ➪ MAXScript Listener to open the MAXScript Listener window.

5. In the Listener window, open the MacroRecorder menu and make sure that all the options are set to the relative and not the absolute object settings, as shown in Figure 41-14. This way, the script will work on any object that is selected instead of always modifying the same object.

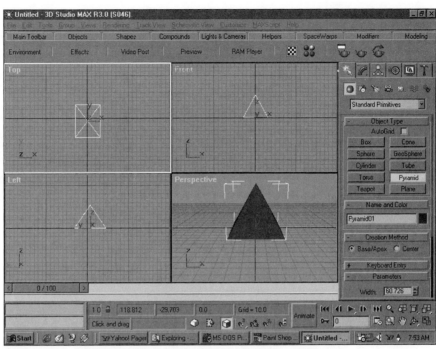

Figure 41-13: A simple object to use while recording a script

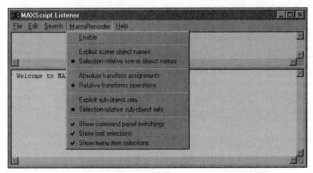

Figure 41-14: Using the relative object settings while
recording a new script

6. Returning to the MacroRecorder menu, select Enable. The Macro Recorder is
now on and ready to start writing MAXScript. Minimize the Macro Recorder
window (or at least move it out of the way so you can see the other viewports).

Tip You can dock the MAXScript Listener window in one of the viewports by right-clicking the viewport name and selecting Views ➪ Extended ➪ MAXScript Listener. This makes it easy to keep things out of the way while you work.

7. Open the Modify panel and click the XForm button to add an XForm Modifier to the object stack. As you can see in Figure 41-15, the MacroRecorder writes MAXScript that basically tells MAX, "Add an XForm Modifier."

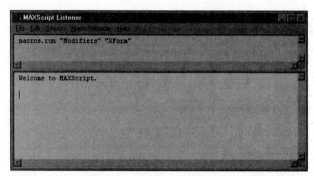

Figure 41-15: The Macro Recorder tracks your moves and writes MAXScript for you.

8. Select the nonuniform scale tool and restrict it to the Y-axis. In the MAXScript Listener window, you'll see that the Macro Recorder has added these lines of MAXScript:

```
max scale
max tool y
```

9. Right-click anywhere in the Front viewport to make it active (if it's not already), and then drag the Y-axis gizmo downward to squash the pyramid.

10. In the Modify panel, click the color swatch next to the object name field to open the Object Color dialog box. Pick one of the purple colors and click OK.

11. The script is done, so in the MAXScript Listener window, select MacroRecorder ➪ Enable to turn off the Macro Recorder.

12. Now it's time to try out your first MAXScript effort. Add a sphere to your scene. Make sure it's selected before moving to the next step.

13. In the top pane of the MAXScript Listener window, select all the text (an easy way to do this is by pressing Ctrl+A), and then press Shift+Enter to tell MAX to execute the MAXScript. As you can see in Figure 41-16, the script squashed the sphere and changed its color.

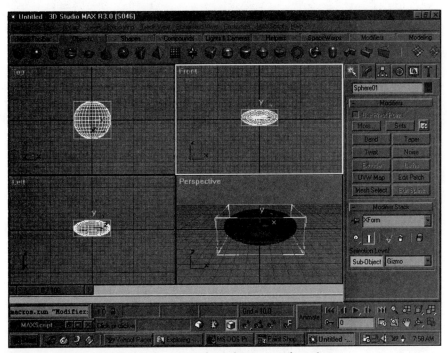

Figure 41-16: Running the new squash-and-turn-purple script

14. For the grand finale, we try out one of the most useful MAXScript tricks
around. Click the Objects toolbar at the top of the MAX interface, and then go
to the MAXScript Listener window and select all the text again. Now press and
hold the left mouse button over the text, drag it up to the Object toolbar, and
release the mouse button.

You should now see a new icon on the Object toolbar where you dropped the
text, as shown in Figure 41-17. (You might have to grab the toolbar and scroll
it if the toolbar is longer than your screen.) This icon is the result of the
Macro Script you just created — a special type of MAXScript that gets
executed anytime you press the script's button.

Figure 41-17: By dragging the new script onto the toolbar, you instantly create new
buttons.

15. To try out your new MaxScript, create a new object in your scene, select it, and click the script's button. You'll see that your squash-and-turn-purple script gets executed.

Tip If you right-click the script's button on the toolbar, you'll open a pop-up where you can customize the button to give it a more meaningful look than the generic Macro Script icon. You can also move it to a different toolbar or create a new toolbar that holds just the scripts you've made and want to make easily accessible.

With this new scripting skill, you now have the power to add new tools to MAX that look and behave like any other feature.

Executing scripts

A script is basically a list of commands or actions that you want MAX to perform. The process of performing these instructions is called *executing* or *running* the script. Here are some of the ways that scripts can be executed:

✦ **Startup**—When you launch 3D Studio MAX, it searches for a script named startup.ms in the Scripts directory. If it can't find one there, it looks in the Startup Scripts directory, the main MAX directory, the Windows system directories (system32 and system), and finally in any other directories listed in your environment path. If and when MAX finds a file named startup.ms, it executes the script and then quits searching.

Tip You can configure your Scripts, Startup Scripts, and Plug-In directories by using the Configure Paths dialog box. To get to it, select the Customize ⇨ Configure Paths command. This dialog box is covered in Chapter 3, "Customizing the MAX Interface."

After MAX has attempted to run startup.ms, it searches through your Startup Scripts and Plug-In directories for any MAXScript files and loads them. This is very useful if you want MAX to always run certain scripts at startup, and it's one of many ways that you can use MAXScript to customize MAX to your tastes. For example, if you use a particular animation script all the time, you could put it in your Startup Scripts directory so that it is loaded for you automatically when you load MAX.

Note You can prevent MAX from loading the startup scripts by selecting Customize ⇨ Preferences to open the Preference Settings dialog box, and selecting the MAXScript panel. In the Startup section, uncheck the box next to Load Startup Scripts.

✦ **Command line**—MAX has a command line option that lets you load MAX and run a specific MAXScript. One use for this would be to have a script that loads a scene, renders it, and saves the output, so that you could make your own batch rendering jobs.

If you open an MS-DOS shell and go to the 3D Studio MAX directory, you can run a script from the command line like this:

```
3dsmax -U MAXScript myscript.ms
```

✦ **Buttons and user interface controls**—As we saw in the SphereArray tutorial, some scripts get executed through a rollout. Or, as we saw in the Macro Recorder script tutorial, you can attach a script to a button on a toolbar. Using user interface controls such as buttons and rollouts makes your scripts look like an integrated part of MAX.

✦ **Menus**—You can also run scripts from the main menu by selecting the MAXScript ➪ Run Script command or from the Utilities panel in the MAXScript rollout.

✦ **MAXScript Listener and editor windows**—Each line you enter in the Listener window is executed as soon as you press the Enter key. In a MAXScript editor window, however, the script isn't executed unless you press Ctrl+E (which works the same as choosing File ➪ Evaluate All from the editor window's menu). This tells MAX to execute all the text in the editor window.

✦ **Other scripts**—One last way to run scripts is from other scripts. MAXScript provides techniques that let any script call any other script, so that you don't need to have everything in a single, monstrous script.

Writing Your Own MAXScripts

The next level of MAXScript proficiency is the ability to write scripts yourself. In the previous section, you learned how to get the Macro Recorder to write them for you, and that might be enough for a lot of what you want to do. If, on the other hand, you're anxious to make more powerful scripts, you need to know how to dream up the things that the Macro Recorder figured out for you. With those skills you can not only create a script from scratch, but you can also take a script that the Macro Recorder generated and customize it to do even more.

This section presents the basics of the MAXScript language and shows you how to use the various parts of MAXScript in your own scripts. Go ahead and open the MAXScript Listener window so that you can try things out as we progress.

Variables and data types

A *variable* in MAXScript is sort of like a variable in algebra. It represents some other value, and when you mention a variable in an equation you're actually talking about the value that the variable holds. You can think of variables in MAXScript as containers that you can put stuff into and take it out of later. Unlike variables in algebra, however, variables in MAXScript can "hold" other things besides numbers, as we'll soon see.

To put a value into a variable, you use the equals sign. For example, if you type

```
X = 5 * 3
```

in the MAXScript Listener window, MAX evaluates the expression on the right side of the equals sign and stores the result in the variable named X. In this case, MAX would multiply 5 by 3 and store the result (15) into X. You can then see what is in X by just typing **X** in the Listener window and pressing Enter. MAX then displays the value stored in X, or 15.

You can name your variables whatever you want, and it's a good idea to name them something that helps you remember what the variable is for. For example, if you want a variable that keeps track of how many objects you're going to manipulate, the name "objCount" would be better than something like "Z."

Note   Variable names can be just about anything you want, but you must start a variable name with a letter. Also, the variable name can't have any special characters in it, like spaces, commas, or quote marks. You can, however, use the underscore character and any normal alphabetic characters.

Variables can also hold *strings,* which are groups of characters. For example:

```
badDay = "Monday"
```

stores the word "Monday" in the variable badDay. You can attach two strings together using the plus sign, like this:

```
grouchy = "My least favorite day is" + badDay
```

Now the variable grouchy holds the value "My least favorite day is Monday."

Try this:

```
wontWork = 5 + "cheeze"
```

MAX prints out an error because it's confused—you're asking it to add a number to a string. The problem is that 5 and "cheeze" are two different data types. *Data types* are different classes of values that you can store in variables. You can almost always mix values of the same data type, but values of different types usually don't make sense together.

Tip   To see the data type of a variable, use the classof command. Using the previous example, you could type **classof grouchy** and MAX would in turn print out String.

Another very common data type is Point3, which represents a three-dimensional point. Following are a few examples of using points, with explanatory comments:

```
Pos = [5,3,2]         -- Create a new point at (5,3,2)
Pos.x = 7             -- Change the x-coordinate to 7
                      -- Now the point is at (7,3,2)
Pos = Pos + (1,2,5)   -- Take the old value for Pos,
                      -- move it by (1,2,5) to (8,5,7)
                      -- and store the new value in Pos
```

In addition to these basic data types, each object in your scene has its own data type. For example, if you use `classof` on a sphere object, MAX prints out `Sphere`. Data types for scene objects are actually *complex data types* or *structures*, which means that they are groups of other data types in a single unit. The pieces of data inside a larger object are called *members* or *properties*. Most scene objects have a member called Name, which is of type String. The Name member tells the specific name of that object. Another common property is Position, a Point3 variable that tells the object's position.

MAX has a special built-in variable that represents whatever object is currently selected. This variable is $ (the dollar sign), which is used in the following tutorial.

Tutorial: Using variables

In this tutorial you learn more about variables in MAXScript by using them to manipulate an object in your scene.

To use variables to manipulate scene objects, follow these steps:

1. Reset MAX by choosing File ➪ Reset from the main menu.

2. Draw a teapot near the center of the Top viewport, as shown in Figure 41-18. Make sure you have the teapot selected before moving to the next step.

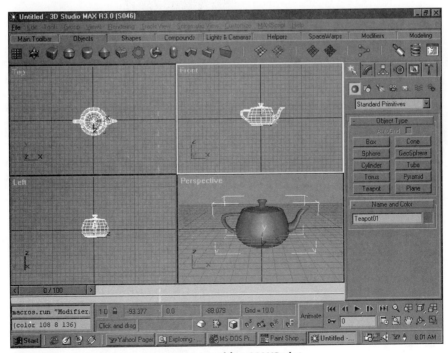

Figure 41-18: Creating a teapot to use with a MAXScript

3. Select MAXScript ➪ MAXScript to open the MAXScript Listener window.

4. Type **$** and press Enter. MAX displays information about the teapot, as shown in Figure 41-19. (Your numbers will probably be different depending on where you placed your teapot.)

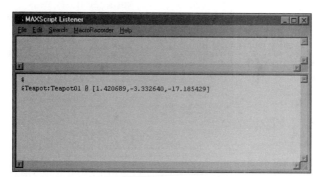

Figure 41-19: Querying MAX about the current selection

5. Type in the following lines one at a time to see the values stored in the different members of the teapot object:

```
$.position
$.wirecolor
$.radius
$.name
$.lid
```

After the last line, $.lid, MAX printed out true. Why? The Lid member of a teapot object is of type *Boolean*, which is a simple type that has only two possible values: true or false. When MAX draws the teapot, it looks at the Lid member to find out if it should display the lid or not. If Lid is true, MAX draws the lid. If Lid is false, it doesn't. (Think of it like the check box on the Teapot creation rollout: if you check the box next to Lid, the teapot has a lid; if you uncheck it, no lid.)

6. Now type in these lines, one at a time, to set some of the values of variables in the teapot object:

```
$.lid = false
$.position = [0,0,0]
$.position.x = -20
$.wirecolor = (color 0 255 0)
$.name = "UglyTeapot"
$.spout = false
$.radius = 50
$.segs = 20
```

When you're done, you'll have a teapot like the one shown in Figure 41-20. Notice that in the Command panel, the various parameters have been updated to reflect the effects of the MAXScript. (You might have to deselect the teapot and select it again before MAX reprints the parameters, but they really have been changed.)

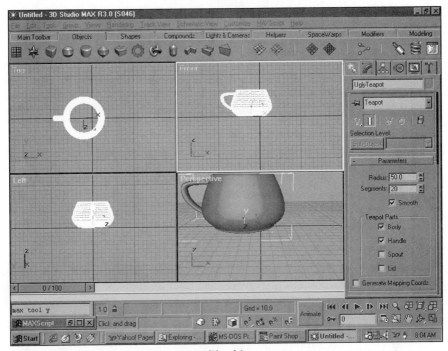

Figure 41-20: Using MAXScript to modify objects

One more thing: you can use the dollar sign together with an object's name as a variable. So from the tutorial, you could now type

```
$UglyTeapot.spout = true
```

to tell MAX to turn on the spout of the teapot object that you named "UglyTeapot."

Program flow and comments

In general, when MAX begins executing a script it starts with the first line of the script, processes it, and then moves on to the next line. Execution of the script continues until there are no more lines in the script file. (Later we look at some MAXScript keywords that let you change the flow of script execution.)

MAX lets you embed comments or notes in your script file to help explain what is happening. To insert a comment, precede it with two hyphens (--). When MAX encounters the double hyphen, it skips the comment and everything else on that line and moves to the next line of the script. For example, in this line of MAXScript

```
$Torus01.pos = [0,0,0]    -- Move it back to the origin
```

MAX processes the first part of the line (and moves the object to the origin) and then moves on to the next line once it reaches the comment.

It's very important that you use comments in your MAXScript files because once your scripts start to become complex, it can get difficult to figure out what is happening. Also, when you come back a few months later to improve your script, comments will refresh your memory and help keep you from repeating the same mistakes you made the first time around.

Tip   Because MAX ignores anything after the double hyphen, you can use comments to temporarily remove MAXScript lines from your script. If something isn't working right, you can *comment out* the lines you want MAX to skip. Later, when you want to add them back in, you don't have to retype them. You can just remove the comment marks and your script is back to normal.

Expressions

An expression is what MAX uses to make decisions. An *expression* compares two things and draws a simple conclusion based on that comparison.

Simple expressions

The expression

```
1 < 2
```

is a simple expression that asks the question, "Is 1 less than 2?" Expressions always ask yes/no type questions. When you type an expression in the MAXScript Listener window (or inside of a script), MAX evaluates the expression and prints true if the expression is valid (like the example above) and false if it isn't. Try the following expressions in the Listener window, and MAX will print the results as shown in Figure 41-21 (you don't have to type in the comments):

```
1 < 2             -- 1 IS less than 2, so expression is true
1 > 2             -- 1 is NOT greater than 2, so false
2 + 2 == 4        -- '==' means "is equal to". 2 + 2 is
                  -- equal to 4, so true
2 + 2 == 5        -- 4 is NOT equal to 5, so false
3 * 3 == 5 + 4    -- 9 IS equal to 9, so true
```

```
3 * 3 != 5 + 4     -- '!=' means 'not equal to'. '9 is not
                   -- equal to 9' is a false statement, so
                   -- the expression is false

a = 23             -- store 23 in variable a
b = 14 + 9         -- store 23 in variable b
a == b             -- 23 IS equal to 23, so true
```

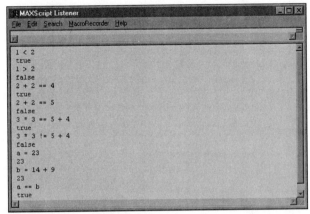

Figure 41-21: Using the MAXScript Listener to evaluate expressions

Play around with simple expressions until you're familiar with what they mean and have an intuitive feel for whether or not an expression is going to evaluate to true or false.

Complex expressions

Sometimes you need an expression to decide on more than just two pieces of data. MAXScript has the and, or, and not operators to help you do this.

The and operator combines two expressions and asks the question, "Are both expressions true?" If both are true, then the entire expression evaluates to true. But if either is false, or if they are both false, then the entire expression is false. You can use parentheses to group expressions, so an expression with the and operator might look something like this:

```
(1 < 2) and (1 < 3)     -- true because (1 < 2) is true AND
                        -- (1 < 3) is true
```

The or operator is similar to and, except that an expression with or is true if either of the expressions is true or if both are true. Here are some examples:

```
(2 > 3) or (2 > 1)     -- even though (2 > 3) is false, the
                       -- entire expression is true because
```

```
                              -- (2 > 1) is true
(2 > 3) and (2 > 1)           -- false because both expressions are
                              -- not true
```

Try some of these complex expressions to make sure you understand how they work:

```
a = 3
b = 2
(a == b) or (a > b)       -- true because a IS greater than b
(a == b) and (b == 2)     -- false because both expressions are
                          -- not true
(a > b) or (a < b)        -- true because at least one IS true
(a != b) and (b == 3)     -- false because b is NOT equal to 3
```

The not operator negates or flips the value of an expression from true to false or vice versa. For example

```
(1 == 2)                  -- false because 1 is NOT equal to 2
not (1 == 2)              -- true. 'not' flips the false to true
```

Conditions

Conditions are one way in which you can control program flow in a script. Normally, MAX processes each line, no matter what, and then quits; but with *conditions*, MAX executes certain lines only if an expression is true.

For example, suppose you have a script with the following lines:

```
a = 4
If (a == 5) then
(
  b = 2
)
```

MAX would not execute the line b = 2 because the expression (a == 5) evaluates to false. Conditional statements, or "if" statements, basically say, "If this expression evaluates to true, then do the stuff inside the block of parentheses. If the expression evaluates to false, skip those lines of script."

Conditional statements follow this form:

```
If <expr> then <stuff>
```

where <expr> is an expression to evaluate and <stuff> is some MAXScript to execute if the expression evaluates to true. You can also use the keyword else to specify what happens if the expression evaluates to false, as shown in the following example:

```
a = 4
if (a == 5) then
(
  b = 2
)
else
(
  b = 3
)
```

After this block of MAXScript, the variable b would have the value of 3 because the expression (a == 5) evaluated to false. Consequently, MAX executed the MAXScript in the else section of the statement.

Collections and arrays

MAXScript has some very useful features to help you manipulate groups of objects. A group of objects is called a *collection*. You can think of a collection as a bag that holds a bunch of objects or variables. The things in the bag are in no particular order; they're just grouped together.

You can use collections to work with groups of a particular type of object. For example, the MAXScript

```
a = $pokey*
a.wirecolor = red
```

creates a collection that contains every object in your scene whose name starts with "Pokey" and makes every object in that collection turn red.

MAXScript has several built-in collections that you might find useful, such as cameras and lights, containing all the cameras and lights in your scene. So

```
delete lights
```

removes all the light objects from your scene (which may or may not be a good idea).

An *array* is a type of collection in which all the objects are in a fixed order, and you can access each member of the array by an index. For example

```
a = #()       -- creates an empty array to use
a[1] = 5
a[2] = 10
a[5] = 12
a
```

After the last line, MAX prints out the current value for the array:

```
#(5, 10, undefined, undefined, 12)
```

Notice that MAX makes the array big enough to hold however many elements we want to put in it, and that if we don't put anything in one of the positions, MAX automatically puts in undefined; this simply means that array location has no value at all.

One last useful trick is that MAX lets you use the as keyword to convert from a collection to an array:

```
LightArray = (lights as array)
```

MAX takes the built-in collection of lights, converts it to an array, and names the array LightArray.

The members of an array or a collection don't all have to have the same data type, so it's completely valid to have an array with numbers, strings, and objects, like this:

```
A = #(5,"Mr. Nutty",box radius:5)
```

Tip

You can use the as MAXScript keyword to convert between data types. For example, (5 as string) would convert the number 5 to the string "5," and (5 as float) would convert the whole number 5 to the floating-point number 5.0.

Loops

A *loop* is a MAXScript construct that lets you override the normal flow of execution. Instead of processing each line in your script once and then quitting, MAX can use loops to do something several times.

For example:

```
j = 0
for i = 1 to 5 do
(
  j = j + i
)
```

This MAXScript uses two variables — i and j — but you can use any variables you want in your loops. The script sets the variable j to 0 and then uses the variable i to count from 1 to 5. MAX repeats the code between the parentheses 5 times, and each time the variable i is incremented by 1. Inside the loop, MAX adds the current value of i to j. Can you figure out what the value of j is at the end of the script? If you guessed 15, you're right. To see why, look at the value of each variable as the script is running:

```
When                    j    i
--------------------------------
First line              0    0
Start of loop           0    1
After first loop        1    1
Start of second loop    1    2
After second loop       3    2
Start of third loop     3    3
After third loop        6    3
Start of fourth loop    6    4
After fourth loop       10   4
Start of fifth loop     10   5
After fifth loop        15   5
```

A loop is also useful for processing each member of an array or collection. The following MAXScript shows one way to turn every teapot in a scene blue:

```
teapots = $teapot*              -- get the collection of teapots
for singleTeapot in teapots do
(
  singleTeapot.wirecolor = blue
)
```

You can use a for loop to create a bunch of objects for you. Try this MAXScript:

```
for I = 1 to 10 collect
  (
  sphere radius:15
  )
```

The collect keyword tells MAX to create a collection with the results of the MAXScript in the block of code inside the parentheses. The line

```
sphere radius:15
```

tells MAX to create a sphere with radius of 15, so the entire script created 10 spheres and added them to your scene. Unfortunately, MAX puts them all in the same spot, so let's move them around a bit so we can see them:

```
i = -50
For s in spheres do
(
  s.position = [i,i,i]
  i = i + 10
)
```

Study this script to make sure you understand what's going on. We use a for loop to process each sphere in our collection of spheres. For each one we set its position to [i,i,i], and then we change the value of i so that the next sphere will be at a different location.

Functions

The last feature of basic MAXScript that we look at is the function. *Functions* are small chunks of MAXScript that act like program building blocks. For example, say you need to compute the average of a collection of numbers many times during a script you're writing. The MAXScript to do this might be

```
Total = 0
Count = 0
For n in numbers do
(
 total = total + n
 count = count + 1
)
average = total / (count as float)
```

Given a collection of numbers called numbers, this MAXScript will compute the average. Unfortunately, every time you need to compute the average, you have to type all that MAXScript in again. Or you might be smart and just cut and paste it in each time you need it. Still, your script is quickly becoming large and ugly, and you always have to change the script to match the name of your collection you're averaging.

A function will solve your problem. At the beginning of your script, you can define an average function like this:

```
Function average numbers =
( -- Function to average the numbers in a collection
 local Total = 0
 local Count = 0
 For n in numbers do
 (
 total = total + n
 count = count + 1
 )
 total / (count as float)
)
```

Now anytime you need to average any collection of numbers in your script, you could just use this to take all the numbers in the collection called num and store their average in a variable called Ave:

```
Ave = average num        -- assuming num is a collection
```

Not only will this make your script much shorter if you need to average numbers a lot, but it makes it a lot more readable too. It's very clear to the casual reader that you're going to average some numbers. Also, if you later realize that you wrote the average function incorrectly, you can just fix it at the top of the script. If you weren't using functions, you'd have to go through your script and find every case where you averaged numbers and then fix the problem. (What a headache!)

Let's take another look at the function definition. The first line

```
Function average numbers =
```

tells MAX that you're creating a new function called `average`. It also tells MAX that to use this function, you have to pass in one piece of data, and that inside the function you'll refer to that data using a variable called `numbers`. It doesn't matter what the name of the actual variable was when the function was called; inside the function you can simply refer to it as `numbers`.

Tip It's also easy to create functions that use multiple pieces of data. For example

```
Function multEm a b c = (a * b * c)
```

creates a function that multiplies three numbers together. To use this function to multiply three numbers and store the result in a variable called B, you'd simply enter

```
B = multEm 2 3 4
```

The next two lines

```
local Total = 0
local Count = 0
```

create two variables and set them both to 0. The `local` keyword tells MAX that the variable belongs to this function. No part of the script outside of the function can see this variable, and if there is a variable outside the function with the same name, changing the variable inside this function won't affect that variable outside the function. That way you never have to worry about what other variables are in use when someone calls `average`; even if there are variables in use that are named `Total` or `Count`, they won't be affected.

The last line

```
total / (count as float)
```

uses the `Total` and `Count` values to compute the average. How does that value get sent back to whoever called the function? MAX evaluates all the MAXScript inside the function and returns the result. Because the last line is the last thing to be evaluated, MAX uses the result of that calculation as the result of the entire function.

Tutorial: Creating a school of fish

Let's look at an example that puts into practice some of the things you've been learning in this chapter. In this multipart tutorial, we use MAXScript to create a simple behavior for a character in a scene — animating a fish that follows a path.

Part 1: Making the fish follow a path

In this part of the tutorial, you use MAXScript to move one of the fish along a path in the scene. To do this, follow these steps:

1. Reset MAX by choosing File ➪ Reset.

2. Load FishScene.max from the CD-ROM. This scene consists of two fish and a dummy object that follows a path, as shown in Figure 41-22. What we need to do is use MAXScript to create a small school of fish that follows the dummy object around the path.

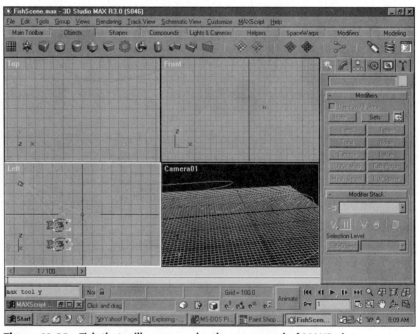

Figure 41-22: Fish that will move under the command of MAXScript

3. Open the MAXScript Listener window, choose File ➪ New Script, and in the MAXScript editor window, type in the following script (you could have snagged the finished FishPath.ms from the CD-ROM, but you'll appreciate the work more if you type it in yourself):

```
pathObj = $Dummy01
fishObj = $Fish1/FishBody
```

```
relPos = [0,-150,-50]    -- How close the fish is to the path

animate on
(
  for t = 1 to 100 do at time t
  (
  fishObj.position = pathObj.position + relPos
  )
)
```

4. Press Ctrl+E to evaluate all the MAXScript in the editor window, right-click the Camera01 viewport to activate it, and press the Play Animation button. You'll see the fish rigidly follow the dummy object's path. Figure 41-23 shows one frame of this animation.

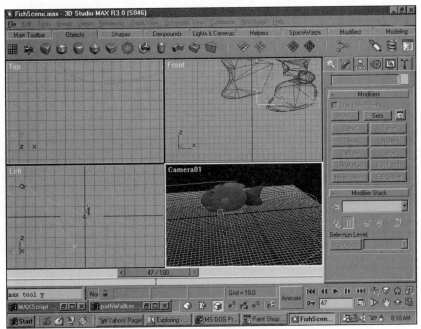

Figure 41-23: First attempt at making the fish follow a path

Now let's explain the MAXScript entered in the previous tutorial. The first few lines create some variables that the rest of the script uses. pathObj tells the name of the object that the fish will follow, and fishObj is the name of the fish's body. (Notice that we can reference parts of the group hierarchy by using the object name, a forward slash, and then a child part.) Why bother creating a variable for the fish object? Once we get this first fish working, we want to apply the same script to another fish. All we'll have to do is rename Fish1 as Fish2, re-execute the script, and we're done!

The script also creates a variable called relPos, which we use to refer to the relative position of the fish with respect to the dummy object. If we have several fish in the scene, we don't want them all in the exact same spot, so this is an easy way to position each one.

The next block of MAXScript is new: we're using the animate on construct. This tells MAX to generate key frames for our animation. It's the same as if we had pressed MAX's Animation button, run our script, and then shut Animation off. So, any MAXScript inside the animate on parentheses will create animation key frames. These parentheses define a section of the script we call a *block*.

Inside the animation block, we have a loop that counts from 1 to 100 (corresponding to each frame of our animation). On the end of the loop line we have at time t, which tells MAX that for each time through the loop, we want all the variables to have whatever values they'll have at that time. For example, if we want the fish to follow the dummy object, we have to know the position of the object at each point in time instead of just at the beginning, so each time through the loop MAX figures out where the dummy object will be for us.

Inside the loop we set the fish's object to be that of the dummy object (at that point in time) and then adjust the fish's position by relPos.

Part 2: Adding body rotation and tail animation

Let's make that fish look a little more lifelike by animating its tail and having it rotate its body to actually follow the path. Also, we'll add a little unpredictability to its motion so that when we add other fish they won't be exact copies of each other.

To improve the fish's animation, follow these steps:

1. Type in the revised version of the script (the lines that are new are in bold):

```
pathObj = $Dummy01
fishObj = $Fish1/FishBody
fishTail = $Fish1/FishBody/FishTail
relPos = [0,-150,-50]  -- How close the fish is to the path

fishTail.bend.axis = 0 -- 0 is the x-axis
zadd = 4                     -- vertical movement at each step
tailFlapOffset = (random 0 100)
tailFlapRate = 25 + (random 0 25)
animate on
(
  for t = 0 to 100 do at time t
  (
    fishObj.position = pathObj.position + relPos
    fishObj.position.z = relPos.z
    relPos.z += zadd

    -- let's say that there's a 10% chance that the fish will
    -- change directions vertically
```

```
if ((random 1 100) > 90) then
(
 zadd = -zadd
)

fishTail.bend.angle = 50 * sin (t * tailFlapRate +
tailFlapOffset)

oldRt = fishObj.rotation.z_rotation
newRt = (in coordsys pathObj pathObj.rotation.z_rotation)

if ((random 1 100) > 85) then
(
 fishObj.rotation.z_rotation += (newRt - oldRt) *
 (random 0.5 1.5)
)
)
)
```

2. Save your script (File ⇨ Save) and then press Ctrl+E to evaluate the script again. Make the Camera01 viewport active and press Play Animation. Figure 41-24 shows another frame of the animation. As you can see, the fish is heading in the right direction this time, and the tail is flapping wildly.

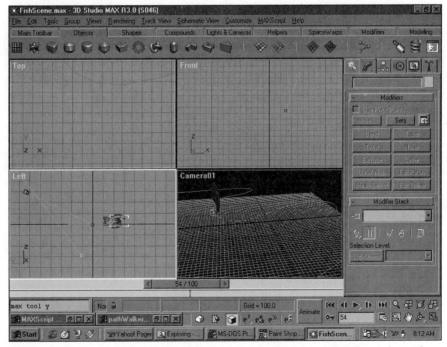

Figure 41-24: Tail-flapping fish that faces the right direction as it follows the path

Okay, let's look at what changed. First, we added a variable to refer to the fish's tail, so that it will be easy to change when we add another fish. Also, we accessed the bend Modifier of the tail and set its axis to 0, which corresponds to the X-axis. (You can try other values to see that it really does change the axis parameter in the rollout.)

Next we created some more variables. We use zadd to tell MAX how much to move the fish in the Z direction at each step (we don't want our fish to always swim at the same level). tailFlapOffset and tailFlapRate are two variables used to control the tail flapping (this is explained when we get to the part of the script that uses them).

Inside the for loop notice that we've overridden the fish's Z-position and replaced it with just the relative Z-position, so that each fish will swim at its own depth and not the dummy object's depth. Then, at each step we add zadd to the Z-position so that the fish changes depth slowly. We have to be careful or our fish will continue to climb out of the scene or run into the ground, so at each step we also choose a random number between 1 and 100 with the function (random 1 100). If the random number that MAX picks is greater than 90, we flip the sign of zadd so that the fish starts moving in the other direction. This is a fancy way of saying, "There's a 90% chance that the fish will continue moving in the same direction and a 10% chance that it will switch directions."

In the next part we again access the tail's bend Modifier, this time to set the bend angle. To get a nice back-and-forth motion for the tail, we use the sin function. In case you've forgotten all that math from when you were in school, a sine wave oscillates from 1 to –1 to 1 over and over again. By multiplying the function by 50 we get values that oscillate between 50 and –50 (pretty good values to use for our bend angle). We use tailFlapOffset to shift the sine wave so that the tail flapping of additional fish is out of synch slightly with this one (remember, we're trying to get at least a little realism here) and tailFlapRate to make each fish flap its tail at a slightly different speed.

The only thing left for us to do is to make the fish "follow" the path, that is, rotate its body so that it's facing the direction it's moving. The simplest way to do this is to use the following MAXScript (split into two lines to make it easier to read):

```
newRt = (in coordsys pathObj pathObj.rotation.z_rotation)
fishObj.rotation.z_rotation = newRt
```

The in coordsys construct tells MAX to give us a value from the point of view of a particular coordinate system. Instead of pathObj we could have asked for the Z-rotation in the world, local, screen, or parent coordinate system, too. In this case we want to rotate the fish in the same coordinate system as the dummy object. In order to randomize the direction of the fish a little, we've made the rotation a little more complex:

```
oldRt = fishObj.rotation.z_rotation
newRt = (in coordsys pathObj pathObj.rotation.z_rotation)

if ((random 1 100) > 85) then
(
  fishObj.rotation.z_rotation += (newRt - oldRt) *
                                  (random 0.5 1.5)
)
```

First we save the old Z-rotation in `oldRt`, and then we put the new rotation in `newRt`. Once again we pick a random number to decide if we'll do something; in this case we're saying, "There's an 85% chance we won't change directions at all." If our random number does fall in that other 15%, however, we adjust the fish's rotation a little. We take the difference between the new rotation and the old rotation and multiply it by a random number between 0.5 and 1.5, which means we'll adjust the rotation by anywhere from 50% to 150% of the difference between the two rotations. So any fish will basically follow the same path, but with a little variation here and there.

Tip   MAX lets you use shorthand when adjusting the values of variables. Instead of saying a = a + b, you can just say a += b. Both have the same effect.

Part 3: Animating the second fish

This scene actually has two fish in it (the other one has been sitting patiently off to the side), so for the final part of this tutorial we'll get both fish involved in the animation. To animate the second fish alongside the first one, follow these steps:

1. At the top of the script, change these three lines (what changed is in bold):

```
pathObj = $Dummy01
fishObj = $Fish2/FishBody
fishTail = $Fish2/FishBody/FishTail
relPos = [50,75,0]    -- How close the fish is to the path
```

2. Press Ctrl+E to run the script again, and then animate it. Figure 41-25 shows both fish swimming merrily.

This script generates key frames for the second fish because we changed the `fishObj` and `fishTail` variables to refer to the second fish. We've also moved the second fish's relative position so that the two don't run into each other.

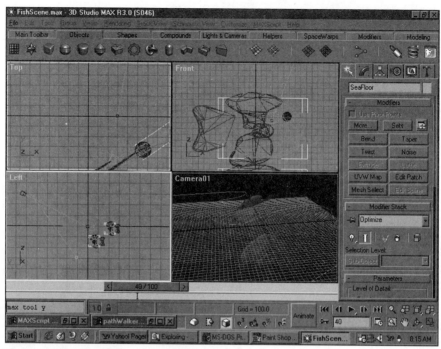

Figure 41-25: Both fish swimming together

Tip   If you're cloning object groups and plan to use them in MAXScript, it helps to name the child objects the same in each clone. After creating a clone of the first group, change the names of the parts to match those of the original group. That way you have to change only the name of the group in your script, and all references to the parts of the groups can remain unchanged.

Is your head spinning yet? Go through this entire tutorial several times and play around with the different variables, comment things out, or change the random number parameters until it's all clear in your mind. We did a lot in this particular script but they're all tasks that, with a little practice, will seem fairly simple to you.

If you don't want to wait for the whole thing to render, or if you're skimming this chapter and trying to decide if it's worth the work to go through the tutorial, the CD-ROM contains an AVI file called FishScene.avi that shows the final rendering. The animation looks pretty good (see Figure 41-26), and we got a lot of mileage out of our MAXScript. The really great thing is that if you want to tinker with the settings, you can do it easily without having to worry about doing everything over again by hand. Or, if you want to add a few more fish to the school, you can do so very quickly.

Figure 41-26: The final animation of the fish

Types of Scripts

All scripts are not created equal, and MAX categorizes different scripts based on how they work. For more information, the MAXScript online help provides exhaustive information on their various options.

The main thing to consider when deciding what type of script to create is the user interface. Ask yourself what the most logical user interface would be for the type of tool you're creating, and this will give you a hint as to which type of script is well suited for the task.

Macro scripts

Macro scripts are the type of scripts you used earlier in the "Recording a Simple Script" tutorial. Any script that is associated with a toolbar button is considered a Macro script. MAX organizes Macro scripts by their category, which you can change by editing the script file. To call a Macro script from another script, you can use the macros command. For example

```
macros.run "objects" "sphere"
runs the sphere" script in the "objects" category.
```

Macro scripts are generally scripts that require no other user input; you just click a button and the script works its magic.

Scripted utilities

A *scripted utility* is a MAXScript that has its own custom rollout in the Utilities panel, like the SphereArray MAXScript you used earlier. This type of script is particularly useful when your script has parameters that the user needs to enter, such as the radius in the SphereArray script.

Scripted right-click menus

When you right-click an object in your scene, MAX opens a pop-up menu of options for you to choose from. Scripted right-click menus let you append your own menu items to the right-click menu. If you create a script that modifies some property of an object, making the script available through the right-click menu makes it easily accessible. Use wisdom in adding things to the right-click menus, though, as a list of too many options becomes annoying.

Scripted mouse tools

You can use scripted mouse tools to create scripts that handle mouse input in the viewports. These scripts listen for commands from the mouse, such as clicking the mouse buttons and clicking and dragging the cursor. For example, you would use this type of MAXScript if you were making a new primitive object type so that users could create the new objects just like they would a sphere or a box.

Scripted plug-ins

Scripted plug-ins are by far the most complex type of MAXScript available. They mirror the functionality of non-MAXScript plug-ins (which are written in other programming languages such as C++). You can create scripted plug-ins that make new geometry, create new shapes, control lights, act as Modifiers on the Modifier Stack, control texture maps and materials, and even produce special rendering effects.

Advanced Uses of MAXScript

You've mastered the basics of MAXScript, so what's next? As you become more proficient in using MaxScript, look for ways in which you can effectively use it to improve your productivity or expand the functionality of MAX. Although MAXScript is not the ultimate tool for every situation, its power and flexibility make it something that you'll definitely benefit from. The following sections describe a few additional ways in which you might use MAXScript.

Tutorial: Setting up batch rendering

As you saw earlier in this chapter, you can execute MAXScript from the command line. You can take advantage of this feature to set up batch rendering jobs to run at night.

To set up batch rendering, follow these steps:

1. The first thing you need is a MAXScript that will render a scene for you. A script to do this can be as simple as this:

```
loadMaxFile "myScene.max"
render camera:$myCam fromframe:1 toframe:100 \
   outputwidth:320 outputheight:240 \
   outputfile:("c:\3dsmax\images\myScene.avi")
quitMax #noPrompt
```

Note

The `render` command has a ton of different options, and the most useful ones are listed here. You can have MAX save the file somewhere else if you want (and obviously, you should change this to a scene that you really want to render).

2. To use this script, you first need to save it using File ➪ Save. (Name it whatever you want.)

3. Next, you need to create an MS-DOS batch file to run MAX and your script. An MS-DOS batch file is similar to a MAXScript except that it contains a list of commands for Windows to run. You can use a MAXScript Editor window to create the batch file. Select File ➪ New and enter the following line:

```
C:\3dsmax\3dsmax -U MAXScript myScript.ms
```

Note

Batch files can be much more powerful than this, but this simple one will suffice for now.

4. Save the batch file by choosing File ➪ Save. You must end a filename with a .bat extension so that Windows will know it's a batch file. For example, name the file render.bat. Make a note of which directory you save the batch file in (by default it is saved in your scripts directory).

5. To try out this script, you must first close down MAX completely. (You can have only one copy of MAX running at a time.)

6. Now click Start on the Windows taskbar and choose Run. Enter the command to run the script as follows (be sure to use the correct directory name and filename if they are different on your computer):

```
C:\3dsmax\scripts\render.bat
```

7. Press Enter, and MAX will load up, render your scene, and then shut down. You can then go check your images directory (or wherever your MAXScript saved the file) to see that it really did work.

Encrypting MAXScript

MAXScript has built-in features that let you encrypt and decrypt files so that other people can't look at the contents of the file. Although it will work on any file, there is a special MAXScript command that will work on MAXScript files so MAX can still use them. For example, to encrypt your script that is in the file called myscrypt.ms, type in the following command in the MAXScript Listener window:

```
encryptScript "myscript.ms"
```

After you've done this, a file called myscript.mse is created in your scripts directory. You can run it just like any other script, but no one can see the actual MAXScript commands contained in the file.

 Tip You can use encrypted script files with the MAXScript variable hardwareLockID to create encrypted scripts that can be run on only one computer. If you ever sell a script and don't want people to make illegal copies, you can use this technique to make sure that only the right person can use your script. For more information, search for "hardwareLockID" in the MAXScript online documentation.

MAXScript as a prototyping tool

In addition to using MAXScript, you can also create custom plug-ins to extend the functionality of 3D Studio MAX. Plug-ins generally execute more quickly than MAXScript does, but they require a lot more work to create. If you do decide to create a custom plug-in, you can use MAXScript as a prototyping tool to help you decide exactly what you want your plug-in to do. Because it's so easy to modify scripts, you can use MAXScript to help you develop your idea for your plug-in, and then once you have the design you want, you can rewrite it as an actual plug-in. This helps you make important design decisions when it's easy to change things around, and it makes creating the final plug-in much more straightforward.

Summary

This chapter gave you a brief introduction to MAXScript, 3D Studio MAX's powerful, built-in scripting language. Besides describing the different types of scripts you can create, the chapter covered:

✦ Using the Macro Recorder to create scripts

✦ Writing your own scripts

✦ Integrating scripts with MAX

✦ Using MAXScript to create simple character behavior in your scenes

This concludes the "Extending MAX" part of the book. The appendixes that follow provide information on configuring a MAX system and the contents of the book's CD-ROM, including plug-ins that were developed exclusively for this book.

✦   ✦   ✦

Configuring a System for 3D Studio MAX

◆ ◆ ◆ ◆

In This Appendix

Choosing an operating system

Hardware requirements

Installing 3D Studio MAX

Using the hardware lock

Authorizing the software

Setting the display driver

◆ ◆ ◆ ◆

Before you can enjoy all the great features in 3D Studio MAX, you have to get your system configured properly, and this appendix will help you do just that. Once you're done here, you're ready to go.

Choosing an Operating System

If you're starting from scratch and have the luxury of customizing your system so that it works best with 3D Studio MAX, there are several things you can do that will make life easier for you. One of the big decisions you have to make is what operating system to use to run MAX.

If you have the option, run 3D Studio MAX on Windows NT, version 4.0 or later. Make sure that you have also installed Service Pack 3 or higher (which you can download for free from Microsoft's Web page at www.microsoft.com). Windows NT 4.0 is more stable than other versions of Windows, and it does a better job of managing your computer's resources (such as memory). It also enables you to run multiple copies of 3D Studio MAX at the same time on a single machine.

If Windows NT is not an option, you can also run MAX on Windows 98. Windows 98 is not as robust as Windows NT, so you might encounter more program crashes in MAX. On a Windows 98 machine, you can run only one copy of MAX at a time, and network rendering is not officially supported.

Hardware Requirements

To get good performance from 3D Studio MAX, you need a pretty meaty machine. A good default system to use would be a Pentium-II or Pentium-III based computer (MAX would prefer the Xeon processor over the Celeron) with 256MB or more of RAM, and a decent-sized hard drive and monitor. If need be, you can get by with a Pentium packing as little as 64MB of RAM, but you may spend a lot of time watching your computer churn furiously to keep up.

Tip   MAX under NT can take advantage of dual-processor machines.

There is one element of your system that will probably have the greatest impact on the performance of 3D Studio MAX and that is the graphics card. Any good graphics card has specialized hardware that will take a lot of the workload off your computer's CPU, freeing it up to do other tasks. All of MAX is pretty graphics-intensive, and a little extra money in the graphics card department will go a long way toward boosting your performance.

The good news is that hardware accelerated graphics cards are becoming cheaper — you can get great cards for $200–$300. When searching for a graphics card, make sure it comes with drivers for OpenGL 1.1 or later (and/or DirectX if you're using Windows 98). You can use some of the graphics boards built to run computer games — however, be aware that some boards claim to support OpenGL but actually support only a subset of it. Before going out to make your purchase, visit the Kinetix Web site (www.ktx.com) to see performance metrics for different popular graphics cards.

Installing 3D Studio MAX

Installing MAX is pretty straightforward. Here's what you need to do:

1. Insert the MAX CD-ROM into the CD-ROM drive, and the setup program will start up automatically. If you don't have Windows Autorun enabled, or if the setup program doesn't start, run the Setup.exe program on the CD-ROM.

2. Once the setup program starts, the Choose Setup Program dialog box is displayed, as shown in Figure A-1. As you can see, you can also install Microsoft Internet Explorer (so that you can use the online help system), Apple's Quicktime software (which lets you view Quicktime animations), or Character Studio (if you own a previous version). Click the 3D Studio MAX button to start the MAX installation.

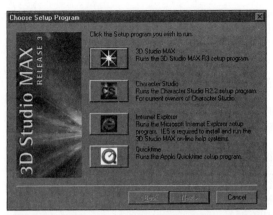

Figure A-1: The installation program lets you install more than just MAX.

3. A Welcome screen appears, advising you to shut down other applications before proceeding. Click the Next button to move on.

4. The next screen is the Software License Agreement. Choose your country, and read the corresponding License Agreement. You can't proceed until you've read the entire thing (or until you've scrolled to the bottom). Once you've read the agreement, click the now-enabled "I accept" button (shown in Figure A-2).

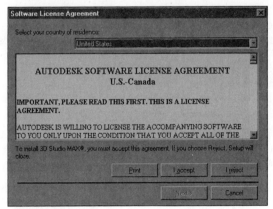

Figure A-2: You must accept the license agreement to install MAX.

5. Click the now-enabled Next button to move on.

6. MAX now asks you if you want to view the Readme file. It's a good idea to read this, as it has last-minute information that they couldn't put in the manual. If you choose Yes, you can read the Readme file while MAX continues with the installation.

7. On the Serial Number screen (shown in Figure A-3), enter the serial number and the CD-ROM key, both of which you can find on the CD-ROM's case. Then click the Next button.

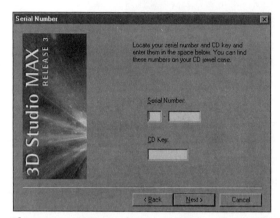

Figure A-3: MAX requires two separate pieces of information, both of which are on the CD-ROM case.

8. From the Setup Type screen (shown in Figure A-4), choose the type of installation you want. Which of the three choices you select depends on how you plan to use MAX. If you're installing MAX on a computer that you plan to use exclusively as a network-rendering computer, choose Compact. If you want to control exactly which parts of MAX get installed (especially if you want to install the SDK so you can write your own plug-ins), choose Custom. In most cases, however, you can just choose Typical.

9. By default, MAX will be installed in c:\3dsmax3, but you can choose a different destination by clicking the Browse button and navigating to a different directory. Once you're happy with the installation location, click the Next button to continue.

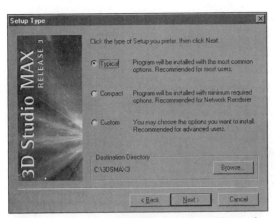

Figure A-4: The installation you choose depends on how you plan to use MAX.

10. Next is the Select Program Folder screen (shown in Figure A-5), which lets you choose the program folder where you want the MAX shortcuts to reside. By default, they're in the Kinetix folder, which means you can get to them by clicking the Start button on the Windows taskbar and then choosing Programs ➪ Kinetix. Click the Next button to continue.

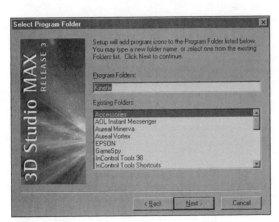

Figure A-5: Choose which program group to place MAX in.

11. Figure A-6 shows the last screen, the point-of-no-return Start Copying Files screen. Review the summary of what it says is going to happen and then click the Next button.

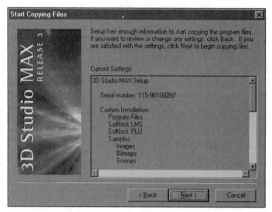

Figure A-6: Click Next to start installing MAX.

It takes a few minutes for MAX to install completely (a great time to read through the Readme file). Once the installation program is done, it's a good idea to shut down your computer and restart, just to be safe.

Using the Hardware Lock

After the software is installed, you need to attach the hardware lock to the parallel port before you can run MAX. The hardware lock is a small software protection device that you must have in order to run MAX. Whenever you start MAX, the software will look for the hardware lock. If it is missing, then a message box will appear asking you to connect the hardware lock before continuing.

If the hardware lock is removed during the session, MAX will detect its absence and quit working.

Caution Do not remove the hardware lock from the computer or install it onto the computer while the power is on. Doing so could damage your system.

Authorizing the Software

Once MAX is installed and the hardware lock is in place, you need to authorize the software through Kinetix. The software will continue to run for 30 days without authorization, but after 30 days will quit working. The Authorization Wizard automatically appears the first time you run MAX and takes you through the authorization process.

Figure A-7 shows the first step of the Authorization Wizard. You can authorize the software using e-mail, fax, phone, or regular mail.

Figure A-7: The first step of the Authorization Wizard lets you select how you want to obtain an authorization code.

Figure A-8 shows the second step of the Authorization Wizard where you can enter the serial number of a previous version of MAX. If you're upgrading your MAX version, you need to include this number. The Serial Number and Application Key will be automatically filled in using the numbers entered during the installation.

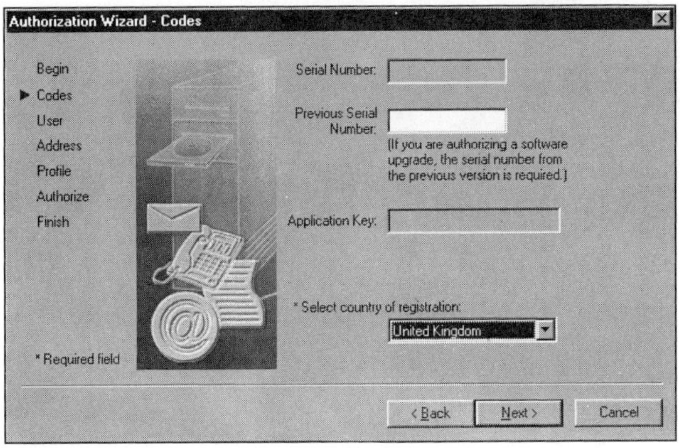

Figure A-8: The second step of the Authorization Wizard

Figures A-9 through A-12 show the next several steps of the Authorization Wizard where you enter profile information such as name, address, type of system you're using, and the intended use for MAX. The required information is marked with an asterisk.

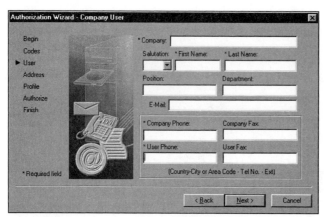

Figure A-9: Step for entering user information

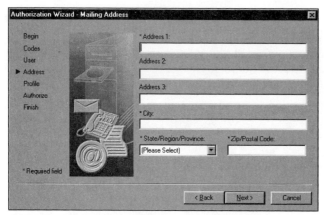

Figure A-10: Step for entering the mailing address

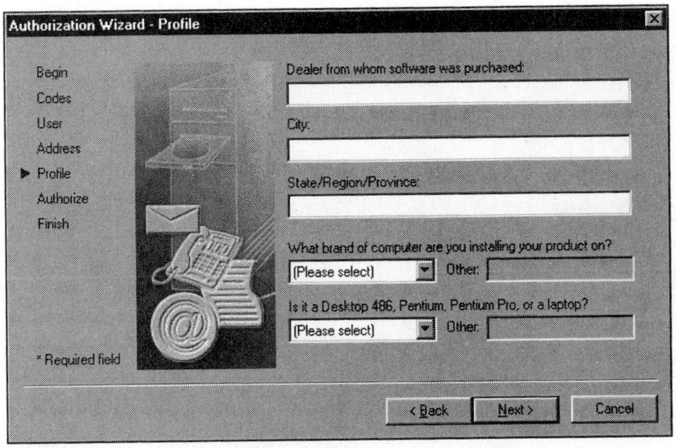

Figure A-11: Step for entering the user profile

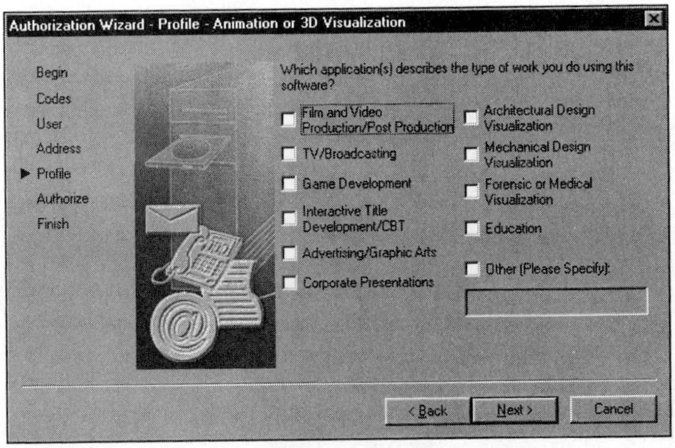

Figure A-12: Step for selecting the type of industry

Figure A-13 shows all the information that you've entered and gives you a chance to verify this information before sending it.

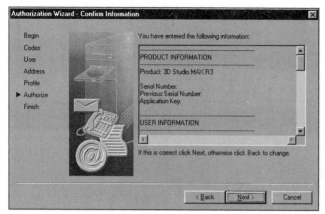

Figure A-13: Verifying the information

Figure A-14 includes a button for sending an e-mail message. In the coming days a valid authorization code should be returned to the e-mail address that you listed.

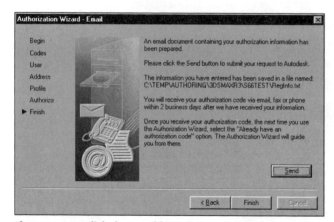

Figure A-14: Click the Send button to send the information.

Once you receive the authorization code, you can select the "Already have an authorization code" option on the first Authorization Wizard screen (previously shown in Figure A-7) and click Next. This will open the screen shown in Figure A-15. Here you can enter the authorization code, and the wizard will register this number with MAX. This will complete the registration process.

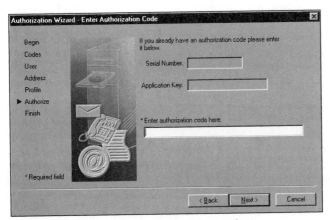

Figure A-15: Entering the authorization code

Setting the Display Driver

Choosing the correct display driver is important for getting the best performance out of your computer. You can choose a display driver in MAX by selecting Customize ➪ Preferences ➪ Viewports ➪ Choose Driver. This opens the 3D Studio MAX Driver Setup dialog box, as shown in Figure A-16. (This dialog box also appears the very first time you start up MAX.)

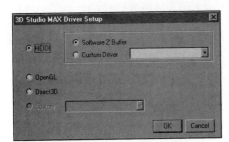

Figure A-16: Choosing the display driver to use

Available Drivers

You can choose one of three different drivers to use in MAX: HEIDI, Direct3D, or OpenGL.

HEIDI

HEIDI is 3D Studio MAX's own built-in software graphics driver. Because it is a software driver, it does not take advantage of any special graphics hardware that your graphics card supports, so your computer's CPU will do all the work. The nice thing about HEIDI is that it works on any computer, even if you don't have a very good graphics card.

Direct3D

MAX can currently use Microsoft's Direct3D only on Windows 98 version 6 or later. Direct3D uses the hardware capabilities of the graphics cards that are present and simulates anything else it needs in software. Simulating different features makes Direct3D run on a wide range of computers, but it can also be much slower. If your graphics card's drivers support all of Direct3D in hardware, then using this driver might give you good performance. If it switches to software mode, however, it will be much slower than HEIDI.

OpenGL

If your graphics card supports OpenGL in hardware, then this is definitely the driver to use. OpenGL works under both Windows NT and Windows 98 and is always present on high-end graphics cards. In order for MAX to use OpenGL, the drivers must support OpenGL 1.1 or later. (Windows NT ships with OpenGL 1.1.)

Initial Configuration

Once you've installed MAX, start it up using HEIDI to make sure that everything installed correctly. From there try out the different graphics drivers to see if you can move up to something faster.

Tip

If you ever choose a display driver that doesn't work on your system, MAX probably won't load up properly. However, there's an easy way to correct the problem. Click Start on the Windows taskbar and choose Run. Type **c:\3dsmax3\3dsmax -h** in the Run dialog box and press Enter. (Type in a different directory if you installed MAX somewhere else.) This forces MAX to present the Driver Setup dialog box again so you can choose a different drive.

✦   ✦   ✦

APPENDIX

◆ ◆ ◆ ◆

In This Appendix

Installing the
CD-ROM plug-ins

About the plug-ins

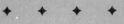

◆ ◆ ◆ ◆

Exclusive Bible Plug-Ins

T his book's CD-ROM comes with several free plug-ins for 3D Studio MAX that you can use free of charge. They are included in the Plugins directory.

This appendix describes how to install the plug-ins and gives a brief description of how to use each one.

Tutorial: Installing the Plug-Ins

Before the plug-ins can be used, you need to install them. The installation procedure is fairly straightforward.

To install the plug-ins from the CD-ROM, follow these steps.

1. Insert the disc into the CD-ROM drive. Locate and run the install.exe file in the /Plugins/Furious Research Plugins directory.

2. Or you can locate the setup program by clicking Start on the Windows taskbar and then click Run to open the Windows Run Program dialog box.

3. Type *X:\plugins\Furious Research Plugins\install.exe* (where *X* is the drive letter of your CD-ROM drive) in the installation program shown in Figure B-1, and press Enter.

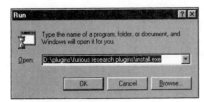

Figure B-1: Launching the plug-in installation program

4. Once the installation program loads, you need to tell it where to put the plug-ins. Unless you've used Configure Paths in MAX to choose a different location for your MAX files, you can just install the plug-ins in the plug-ins directory in your 3dsmax directory. (I have MAX installed in c:\apps\3dsmax3.) Figure B-2 shows the path for a system where MAX is installed on the C: drive.

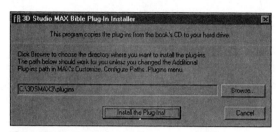

Figure B-2: Enter the path to your plug-ins directory if needed.

5. Click Install the Plugins! to copy the plug-ins to your computer. You need to shut down and restart MAX in order to use the new plug-ins.

About the Plug-Ins

This section provides a brief overview of each plug-in and gives you an idea of what you can do with it. These plug-ins work like any other feature in MAX, so it's worthwhile to review the related chapters elsewhere in the book. For example, if you need help using one of the following render effect plug-ins, be sure to review Chapter 37, "Using Render Effects," which discusses render effects in detail.

3D Image render effect

You can use this plug-in to create 3D stereographic images, such as the one shown in Figure B-3. (If you stare at it for a while and let your eyes relax somewhat, you begin to see an actual three-dimensional image come out of the page.)

As shown in Figure B-4, when you add this render effect to your scene you can choose whether to use random dots for the background color or whether to use a tiled image. It may take some experimentation to get the best effect if you use a bitmap to tile the background, but in general the best bitmaps to use are small ones (so that they get tiled 8 to 10 times across the page) with a fair amount of detail that isn't too distracting. If you choose to use random dots, you can configure the plug-in to use any three colors of your choice.

Figure B-3: Image generated by the 3D Image render effect

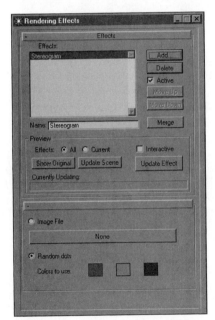

Figure B-4: 3D Image render effect
rollout

TV Image render effect

The TV Image render effect plug-in simulates television-quality images, as shown
in Figure B-5.

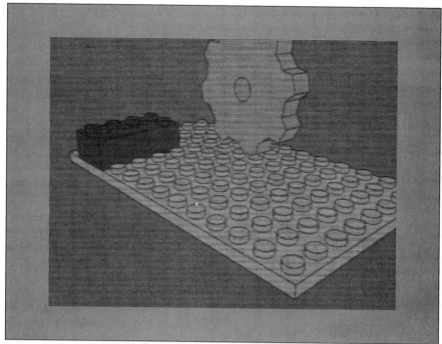

Figure B-5: Sample output from the TV Image render effect

Television images are not very sharp, and this plug-in simulates this effect as well as the interlaced lines (light and dark lines) found especially in older TVs. You can control how blurred the image is, the intensity of the interlacing, and the quantity and intensity of static using the plug-ins rollout, shown in Figure B-6.

Sketch render effect

You may have noticed that the objects in Figure B-5 were outline drawings instead of normal objects. You can accomplish this effect using the Sketch render effect plug-in. Instead of making your scene look more realistic, it reduces detail and color depth and outlines everything in the black lines typical of cartoons or sketches.

The rollout for this render effect, shown in Figure B-7, includes three options for controlling the colors of your scene. By default the plug-in won't adjust the colors at all, though you can have it render in black and white "coloring book" style or a flat shading so it looks more like a cartoon.

The Crease Angle option specifies how sharply two faces of an object can meet before the plug-in draws an actual line on their connection edge. The Roughness option lets you control how the plug-in treats irregular surfaces: a lower value means that the plug-in is less likely to sketch a line showing how the surface changes.

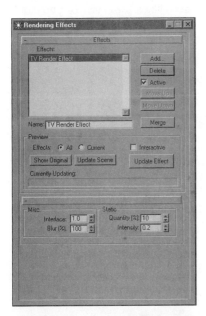

Figure B-6: TV Image render effect rollout

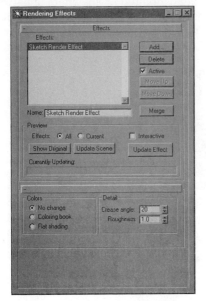

Figure B-7: Sketch render effect rollout

Gear primitive

The rollout for this gear plug-in is shown in Figure B-8. You can choose to lock the number of gear teeth so that resizing the gear also resizes the teeth, or you can lock the tooth width so that, as the gear is resized, the plug-in adds or removes teeth as needed but always makes them have the same width. This feature is useful if you need to create several gears that fit together—just choose a tooth width and create as many gears as you need. Because they all share a common tooth width, they all fit together nicely.

Figure B-8: More features in the new Gear plug-in

This version of the plug-in also has a parameter that lets you adjust the taper on the gear teeth from extremely blocky to extremely pointed or anywhere in between. This gives you much more realistic-looking gears and makes two gears interlock better as well. See Figure B-9 for an example of this plug-in in action.

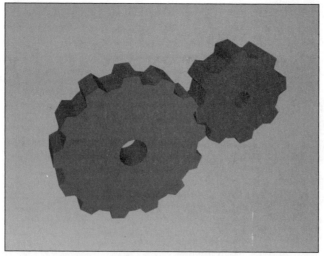

Figure B-9: The new Gear plug-in creates more realistic gears.

Brick primitive

This plug-in adds a new brick primitive to MAX's set of primitives. As shown in Figure B-10, this plug-in creates interlocking building bricks (similar to Lego blocks and their various imitations).

Figure B-10: The Brick primitive

Each brick is accurately proportioned, although you can change the scale to whatever you want in this plug-in's rollout, shown in Figure B-11. The Flat checkbox lets you create thin bricks, and you can use the Detail radio boxes to choose between high and normal detail. In most cases normal detail is sufficient, but, if you plan to be doing close-up renderings, you might want to use high detail for smoother curves.

Figure B-11: The Brick rollout

Brick Snap

The Brick Snap plug-in is a helper plug-in that assists you in creating large objects made up of building block primitives. The plug-in provides you with snapping points on bricks that enable you to easily position two bricks so that they accurately "lock" together.

Choose Customize ⇨ Grid and Snap Settings to open the Grid and Snap Settings dialog box and then choose Construction on the Snaps tab to bring up the Brick Snap panel shown in Figure B-12. From here, you can choose what parts of a building block you want to be considered snap points. After you choose which parts of the brick are to generate snap points, you need to turn snapping on before MAX can actually use the snap points.

Figure B-12: Customizing how the brick snaps work for you

Balls and Sticks utility

The Balls and Sticks utility plug-in takes an object and converts it to a balls-and-sticks representation as shown in Figure B-13. It's an easy way to create models of molecules, although there are far more interesting applications as well.

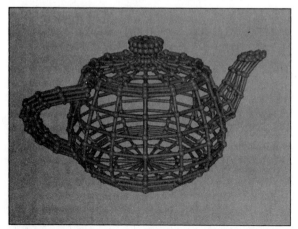

Figure B-13: Balls and Sticks utility plug-in

The rollout for this plug-in, shown in Figure B-14, lets you decide whether to create just balls, just sticks, or both. You also have the option to generate a stick for every edge or for visible edges only, and you can choose to have the plug-in remove the original object from the scene after converting it to balls and sticks. The other options in the rollout let you adjust the size of the balls and sticks and the level of detail for each ball or stick.

Figure B-14: Balls and Sticks rollout

Tip   This plug-in adds a sphere object for each ball and a cylinder object for each stick, which could mean adding thousands of polygons to your scene. Unless you want very high detail, it's best to use low numbers for the Ball segments and Stick sides fields in the rollout to reduce scene complexity.

✦   ✦   ✦

What's On the CD-ROM?

◆   ◆   ◆   ◆

In This Appendix

Chapter example files and tutorials

Plug-ins

3D models

The 3D Studio MAX R3 demo CD-ROM

◆   ◆   ◆   ◆

Throughout the book you'll find many tutorials that help you to understand the principles being discussed. All of the example files used to create these tutorials are included on the CD-ROM that came with this book. In addition to these files you'll find sample 3D models, exclusive MAX plug-ins, and the 3D Studio MAX R3 demo CD-ROM developed by Kinetix.

Example Files and Tutorials

The example files used in the tutorials throughout the book are included in the /Chapter Example Files directory. Within this directory are separate subdirectories for each chapter. Supplemental files such as models and images are also included in these directories. Animated scenes include a rendered AVI file of the animation.

Several subdirectories include bonus tutorials and example files not mentioned in the text.

Note   Several bonus tutorials are included in various chapters.

Plug-Ins

To extend the functionality of MAX, the \Plug-Ins directory on the CD-ROM includes many full-function plug-ins. All of these plug-ins have been compiled for Release 3.

Caution   These plug-ins only work on the Release 3 version of MAX and are not compatible with any previous versions.

The \Furious Research Plug-Ins directory contains plug-ins developed exclusively for this book. This directory also includes an installation program to install these plug-ins. To install the plug-ins, run the Setup.exe file.

Cross-Reference For more information on these plug-ins, see Appendix B, "Exclusive Bible Plug-Ins."

The \Habware Plug-Ins directory includes plug-ins created by Harald Blab. These plug-ins are freeware. More information on these plug-ins can be found at the HABWare Web site located at `www.habware.at/duck3.htm`.

3D Models

Several companies have provided sample 3D models. Many of these models were used in the tutorials, and the respective models can be located in the tutorial directories as well as in the \3D Models directory.

Table C-1 lists the model companies and the models that are included on this book's CD-ROM.

Table C-1 3D Models	
Model Company	*3D Models*
3D Paralex	Artillery Gun, Bell Tower, Canon, Darkstar Spaceship, Destroyer Spaceship, Grinder, Handrill, Machine Gun, Minigun, Musket Pistol, Musket Rifle, Ratchet, Sam Missiles, Socket Adapter, Submarine
3D Toons Shop	Ant, Deer, Fish, Moon
Dedicated Digital	Cartoon Face, Dalmatian, Heart, Parathion, Tiger
Viewpoint Datalabs	'32 Dodge Truck, '57 Chevy, Airboat, Al Character, Baby Doll, Building, Cessna, Chess Set, Cow, Crocodile, Dragon, F14A Tomcat Jet, Flamingo, General, Genie Lamp, Heart, Lamp, Laser Truck, Magnolia, Paddle Boat, Pelican, Pool Table, Porsche, Power Lines, Sandal, Hammerhead Shark, Shuttle, Skyscraper, Slot Machine, Submarine, Surfboard, Teddy Bear, Tommy Gun, Trumpet, Violin Case
Zygote Media	Basketball, Basketball Hoop, Balloons, Butterfly, Ceiling Fan, Dart, Dartboard, Dolphin, Dragonfly, Firecracker, Lamp, Fireplace, Hammer, Houseplant, Ice Cream Cone, Old Tree, Park Bench, Place Setting, Post Box, Rake, Rocket, Roses in Vase, Soda Can, Spider, Step Ladder, Sword, Table and Chairs, Turtle, TV, Umbrella

3D Studio MAX R3 Demo CD-ROM

The \3D Studio MAX R3 demo directory on the CD-ROM holds all the content created by Kinetix for their R3 demo CD-ROM. This content can be accessed by running the MAX3Demo.exe file or installed by running the Setup.exe file.

The demo content includes advanced tutorials, a gallery of images, and detailed information on 3D Studio MAX R3 and Character Studio.

✦   ✦   ✦

Index

Continued

Continued

Continued

Continued

Continued

Continued

Continued

Continued

IDG Books Worldwide, Inc.
End-User License Agreement

READ THIS. You should carefully read these terms and conditions before opening the software packet(s) included with this book ("Book"). This is a license agreement ("Agreement") between you and IDG Books Worldwide, Inc. ("IDGB"). By opening the accompanying software packet(s), you acknowledge that you have read and accept the following terms and conditions. If you do not agree and do not want to be bound by such terms and conditions, promptly return the Book and the unopened software packet(s) to the place you obtained them for a full refund.

1. **License Grant.** IDGB grants to you (either an individual or entity) a nonexclusive license to use one copy of the enclosed software program(s) (collectively, the "Software") solely for your own personal or business purposes on a single computer (whether a standard computer or a workstation component of a multiuser network). The Software is in use on a computer when it is loaded into temporary memory (RAM) or installed into permanent memory (hard disk, CD-ROM, or other storage device). IDGB reserves all rights not expressly granted herein.

2. **Ownership.** IDGB is the owner of all right, title, and interest, including copyright, in and to the compilation of the Software recorded on the disk(s) or CD-ROM ("Software Media"). Copyright to the individual programs recorded on the Software Media is owned by the author or other authorized copyright owner of each program. Ownership of the Software and all proprietary rights relating thereto remain with IDGB and its licensers.

3. **Restrictions On Use and Transfer.**

   (a) You may only (i) make one copy of the Software for backup or archival purposes, or (ii) transfer the Software to a single hard disk, provided that you keep the original for backup or archival purposes. You may not (i) rent or lease the Software, (ii) copy or reproduce the Software through a LAN or other network system or through any computer subscriber system or bulletin-hyboard system, or (iii) modify, adapt, or create derivative works based on the Software.

   (b) You may not reverse engineer, decompile, or disassemble the Software. You may transfer the Software and user documentation on a permanent basis, provided that the transferee agrees to accept the terms and conditions of this Agreement and you retain no copies. If the Software is an update or has been updated, any transfer must include the most recent update and all prior versions.

4. Restrictions on Use of Individual Programs. You must follow the individual requirements and restrictions detailed for each individual program in Appendix C of this Book. These limitations are also contained in the individual license agreements recorded on the Software Media. These limitations may include a requirement that after using the program for a specified period of time, the user must pay a registration fee or discontinue use. By opening the Software packet(s), you will be agreeing to abide by the licenses and restrictions for these individual programs that are detailed in Appendix C and on the Software Media. None of the material on this Software Media or listed in this Book may ever be redistributed, in original or modified form, for commercial purposes.

5. Limited Warranty.

(a) IDGB warrants that the Software and Software Media are free from defects in materials and workmanship under normal use for a period of sixty (60) days from the date of purchase of this Book. If IDGB receives notification within the warranty period of defects in materials or workmanship, IDGB will replace the defective Software Media.

(b) **IDGB AND THE AUTHOR OF THE BOOK DISCLAIM ALL OTHER WARRANTIES, EXPRESS OR IMPLIED, INCLUDING WITHOUT LIMITATION IMPLIED WARRANTIES OF MERCHANTABILITY AND FITNESS FOR A PARTICULAR PURPOSE, WITH RESPECT TO THE SOFTWARE, THE PROGRAMS, THE SOURCE CODE CONTAINED THEREIN, AND/OR THE TECHNIQUES DESCRIBED IN THIS BOOK. IDGB DOES NOT WARRANT THAT THE FUNCTIONS CONTAINED IN THE SOFTWARE WILL MEET YOUR REQUIREMENTS OR THAT THE OPERATION OF THE SOFTWARE WILL BE ERROR FREE.**

(c) This limited warranty gives you specific legal rights, and you may have other rights that vary from jurisdiction to jurisdiction.

6. Remedies.

(a) IDGB's entire liability and your exclusive remedy for defects in materials and workmanship shall be limited to replacement of the Software Media, which may be returned to IDGB with a copy of your receipt at the following address: Software Media Fulfillment Department, Attn.: *3D Studio MAX R3 Bible*, IDG Books Worldwide, Inc., 10475 Crosspoint Blvd., Indianapolis, IN 46256, or call 1-800-762-2974. Please allow three to four weeks for delivery. This Limited Warranty is void if failure of the Software Media has resulted from accident, abuse, or misapplication. Any replacement Software Media will be warranted for the remainder of the original warranty period or thirty (30) days, whichever is longer.

(b) In no event shall IDGB or the author be liable for any damages whatsoever (including without limitation damages for loss of business profits, business interruption, loss of business information, or any other pecuniary loss) arising from the use of or inability to use the Book or the Software, even if IDGB has been advised of the possibility of such damages.

(c) Because some jurisdictions do not allow the exclusion or limitation of liability for consequential or incidental damages, the above limitation or exclusion may not apply to you.

7. U.S. Government Restricted Rights. Use, duplication, or disclosure of the Software by the U.S. Government is subject to restrictions stated in paragraph (c)(1)(ii) of the Rights in Technical Data and Computer Software clause of DFARS 252.227-7013, and in subparagraphs (a) through (d) of the Commercial Computer — Restricted Rights clause at FAR 52.227-19, and in similar clauses in the NASA FAR supplement, when applicable.

8. General. This Agreement constitutes the entire understanding of the parties and revokes and supersedes all prior agreements, oral or written, between them and may not be modified or amended except in a writing signed by both parties hereto that specifically refers to this Agreement. This Agreement shall take precedence over any other documents that may be in conflict herewith. If any one or more provisions contained in this Agreement are held by any court or tribunal to be invalid, illegal, or otherwise unenforceable, each and every other provision shall remain in full force and effect.

my2cents.idgbooks.com

Register This Book — And Win!

Visit **http://my2cents.idgbooks.com** to register this book and we'll automatically enter you in our fantastic monthly prize giveaway. It's also your opportunity to give us feedback: let us know what you thought of this book and how you would like to see other topics covered.

Discover IDG Books Online!

The IDG Books Online Web site is your online resource for tackling technology — at home and at the office. Frequently updated, the IDG Books Online Web site features exclusive software, insider information, online books, and live events!

10 Productive & Career-Enhancing Things You Can Do at www.idgbooks.com

- Nab source code for your own programming projects.

- Download software.

- Read Web exclusives: special articles and book excerpts by IDG Books Worldwide authors.

- Take advantage of resources to help you advance your career as a Novell or Microsoft professional.

- Buy IDG Books Worldwide titles or find a convenient bookstore that carries them.

- Register your book and win a prize.

- Chat live online with authors.

- Sign up for regular e-mail updates about our latest books.

- Suggest a book you'd like to read or write.

- Give us your 2¢ about our books and about our Web site.

You say you're not on the Web yet? It's easy to get started with IDG Books' *Discover the Internet,* available at local retailers everywhere.

CD-ROM Installation Instructions

Many tutorials throughout this book help you understand the principles being discussed. All of the example files used to create these tutorials are included on the CD-ROM that comes with this book. In addition to these files are sample 3D models, exclusive MAX plug-ins, and the 3D Studio MAX R3 demo program developed by Kinetix.

Please take a look at the ReadMe file and Appendix C for more information about using and installing the contents of the CD-ROM.